Host Societies and the Reception of Immigrants

CCIS Anthologies, 2
Center for Comparative Immigration Studies
University of California, San Diego

Contributors

Richard D. Alba
Heather Antecol
Irene Bloemraad
George J. Borjas
Monica Boyd
Stephen Castles
Deborah A. Cobb-Clark
Wayne A. Cornelius
Don J. DeVoretz
Nancy Foner
Philip Kasinitz
Ivan Light
Lang Lin
John R. Logan
John Ma
Philip Martin
Suzanne Model
John Mollenkopf
Victor Nee
Jan Rath
Jeffrey G. Reitz
Brian J. Stults
Stephen J. Trejo
Harold Troper
Takeyuki Tsuda
Zulema Valdez
Roger Waldinger
Mary C. Waters
Kenny Zhang

Host Societies and the Reception of Immigrants

Edited by

Jeffrey G. Reitz

La Jolla, California

Center for Comparative Immigration Studies
University of California, San Diego

Printed in the United States of America

Library of Congress Cataloging-in-Publication Data

Host societies and the reception of immigrants / edited by Jeffrey G. Reitz.
p. cm. – (CCIS anthologies)
Includes bibliographical references and index.
ISBN 0-9702838-3-0 (paper)
1. Immigrants—Cultural assimilation. 2. Immigrants—Government policy. 3. Emigration and immigration—Government policy. I. Reitz, Jeffrey G. II. Series.

JV6342.H68 2003
305.8—dc21

2003046198

CONTENTS

Part II. Labor Markets and Related Institutions

Part III. Governments and Immigrant Incorporation

ACKNOWLEDGMENTS

Scholarly contributions to this volume were assembled through the organization of a conference held at the Harvard University Weatherhead Center for International Affairs, May 10–12, 2001, and sponsored by the Center's Canada Program, for which I was responsible as the Visiting William Lyon Mackenzie King Professor of Canadian Studies. Special thanks are due to Helen Clayton, staff assistant to the Canada Program, who handled the conference logistics brilliantly, and to Elizabeth Thompson, program administrator for the R.F. Harney Program in Ethnic, Immigration and Pluralism Studies at the University of Toronto, who provided expert administrative and editorial assistance in the preparation of the manuscripts. Six chapters included here (portions of Reitz's introductory chapter and the chapters by Kasinitz, Mollenkopf, and Waters; Boyd; Model and Lin; Borjas; and Martin) appeared as part of a special issue of the *International Migration Review* (36, no. 4: Winter 2002).

About the Contributors

Richard D. Alba is Distinguished Professor of Sociology and Public Policy at the University at Albany, State University of New York. His most recent book is *Remaking the American Mainstream: Assimilation and Contemporary Immigration* (2003), written with Victor Nee. Dr. Alba is currently investigating the second-generation situation in the different immigration societies of Europe and North America.

Heather Antecol is Assistant Professor at Claremont McKenna College. She is a labor economist whose research focuses on the labor market outcomes of immigrants and minorities. Antecol recently coauthored a related article entitled "Immigration Policy and the Skills of Immigrants to Australia, Canada, and the United States," *Journal of Human Resources*, vol. 38.

Irene Bloemraad is Assistant Professor of Sociology at the University of California, Berkeley. Her research focuses on the political incorporation of immigrants in the United States and Canada. Her recent publications include: "Who Claims Dual Citizenship? The Limits of Postnationalism, the Possibilities of Transnationalism, and the Persistence of Traditionalism," *International Migration Review* (2003), and "The North American Naturalization Gap: An Institutional Approach to Citizenship Acquisition in the United States and Canada," *International Migration Review* (2002).

George J. Borjas is the Robert W. Scrivner Professor of Economics and Social Policy at the John F. Kennedy School of Government, Harvard University. He is also a Research Associate at the National Bureau of Economic Research. Borjas has written extensively on labor market issues; his titles include *Friends or Strangers: The Impact of Immigrants on the U.S. Economy* (1990); *Labor Economics* (2nd ed., 2000); and *Heaven's Door: Immigration Policy and the American Economy* (1999). Professor Borjas's research on the economic impact of immigration is widely perceived as playing a central role in the debate over immigration policy in the United States and abroad.

Monica Boyd is the Canada Research Chair in Sociology at the University of Toronto and a Visiting Senior Scholar at Statistics Canada. She is the author of numerous articles, books, and monographs on social inequality, with an emphasis on gender, international migration (with foci on policy, immigrant integration, and immigrant women), and ethnic stratification. Her work on the second generation is a continuation of past projects, including "Triumphant Transitions: Socio-economic Achievements of the Second Generation in Canada," *International Migration Review*, vol. 32 (coauthored with Elizabeth Grieco). Dr. Boyd is currently investigating the intermarriage patterns, ethnic affiliations, and economic performance of the second generation using data from the 2001 Canadian census. She also is continuing her research on the jobs, earnings, and re-accreditation problems of immigrant professionals.

Stephen Castles is Professor of Migration and Refugee Studies, and Director of the Refugee Studies Centre at the University of Oxford. Until January 2001 he was Director of the Centre for Asia Pacific Social Transformation Studies at the Universities of Wollongong and Newcastle, Australia. He has carried out research on migration and multicultural societies in Europe, Australia, and Asia for many years. From 1994 to 2001, Dr. Castles helped establish and coordinate the UNESCO-MOST Asia Pacific Migration Research Network. His books include: *The Age of Migration: International Population Movements in the Modern World* (with Mark Miller, 1998); *Citizenship and Migration: Globalization and the Politics of Belonging* (with Alastair Davidson, 2000); and *Ethnicity and Globalization: From Migrant Worker to Transnational Citizen* (2000).

Deborah A. Cobb-Clark is Director of the Social Policy Evaluation, Analysis and Research (SPEAR) Centre and Fellow in the Economics Program, Research School of Social Sciences at the Australian National University. Her research interests include immigration, social policy evaluation, gender differences in promotions, old-age support in developing countries, and sexual and racial harassment in the U.S. military.

Wayne A. Cornelius is Gildred Professor of Political Science and International Relations, and Director of the Center for Comparative Immigration Studies at the University of California, San Diego. His current research includes a comparative study of the political economy of immigration in the United States and Japan, an analysis of the efficacy and consequences of U.S. border enforcement strategy, and a study of voting in home-country elections among Mexican immigrants in the United States. His recent books include *The International Migration of the Highly Skilled* (coeditor/coauthor, 2001) and *Controlling Immigration: A Global Perspective* (coeditor/coauthor, 2nd ed. 2003).

Don J. DeVoretz is Co-Director of the Centre of Excellence on Immigration Studies and Professor of Economics at Simon Fraser University. He is a scholar with the Institute for Research on Public Policy, a Senior Research Fellow with IZA, and a Governor of the Council for Canadian Unity. Dr. DeVoretz was named a British Columbia Scholar to China in 2000. In addition, Dr. DeVoretz sat on the Academic Advisory Board of Employment and Immigration (Canada) from 1987 until 1991, and in 1994 chaired the economic section of Canada's Ten Year Strategic Immigration Review. His main research interests include the economics of immigration with special emphasis on the employment, income, and savings effects of Canadian immigration flows. His research findings have been reported in both professional journals and major print media.

Nancy Foner is Lillie and Nathan Ackerman Visiting Professor of Equality and Justice in America at the School of Public Affairs, Baruch College, City University of New York. She has written extensively on immigration to New York and West Indian migration. She is the author or editor of many books, including: *From Ellis Island to JFK: New York's Two Great Waves of Immigration* (2000), winner of the 2000 Theodore Saloutos Book Award of the Immigration and Ethnic History Society; *New Immigrants in New York* (rev. ed. 2001); and *Islands in the City: West Indian Migration to New York* (2001).

Philip Kasinitz is Executive Officer of the Ph.D. Program in Sociology and Associate Director of the Center for Urban Research at the City University of New York. He studies urban issues, race and ethnicity, and international migration. His book *Caribbean New York: Black Immigrants and the Politics of Race* (1992) won the Thomas and Znaniecki Award from the International Migration Section of the American Sociological Association. Among his other publications are the *Handbook on International Migration* (coeditor, 1999) and *Metropolis: Center and Symbol of Our Time* (coeditor, 1995).

Ivan Light is Professor of Sociology at the University of California, Los Angeles. He is the author of many books, including *Ethnic Economies* (with Steven Gold, 2000); *Immigrant Entrepreneurs and Immigrant Absorption in the United States and Israel* (with Richard E. Isralowitz, 1997); *Race, Ethnicity, and Entrepreneurship in Urban America* (with Carolyn Rosenstein, 1995); and *Immigration and Entrepreneurship* (with Parminder Bhachu, 1993). His immigration research has directly treated African American internal migrants, as well as Chinese, Iranian, Japanese, and Korean international migrants to the United States. Recent research has dealt with immigration to France, Germany, Israel, and the Netherlands. His research on immigrant credit schemes still stands as the *locus classicus* of social capital theory. His research career pioneered, promoted, and expanded the concept of "ethnic economy."

Lang Lin is a doctoral student in sociology at the University of Massachusetts, Amherst. Her research interests include comparative analysis of socioeconomic outcomes for immigrants in different receiving countries, the labor force participation of immigrant women from various sending countries, and gender in the immigrant family. She is currently working on her dissertation, which focuses on whether helping family relatives to immigrate is an incentive for immigrants to obtain U.S. citizenship and the effect of gender in deciding whose relatives are sponsored first.

John R. Logan is Distinguished Professor of Sociology and Public Policy at the University at Albany and Director of the Lewis Mumford Center for Comparative Urban and Regional Research. His current projects include studies of urban change in China, the historical incorporation of immigrants and minorities in U.S. cities in the nineteenth century, and contemporary research on ethnic neighborhoods and employment niches. His most recent edited book, *The New Chinese City: Globalization and Market Reform*, was published in 2002.

Zhongdong (John) Ma is Associate Professor in the Division of Social Science at the Hong Kong University of Science and Technology. Previously he was a Research Associate at the University of Quebec. His research interests focus on internal migration, regional development, and immigration and human capital transfer in the Asia-Pacific region. His recent publications include "Social Capital Mobilization and Income Returns to Entrepreneurship: The Case of Return Migration in

Rural China," *Environment and Planning A*, vol. 34, and "Urban Labor Force Experience as a Determinant of Rural Occupation Change: Evidence from Recent Urban-Rural Return Migration in China," *Environment and Planning A*, vol. 33.

Philip Martin is Professor of Agricultural and Resource Economics at the University of California, Davis, Chair of the University of California's Comparative Immigration and Integration Program, and editor of the monthly *Migration News* and the quarterly *Rural Migration News*. Dr. Martin assessed the prospects for Turkish migration to the European Union between 1987 and 1990, evaluated the effects of immigration on Malaysia's economy and labor markets in 1994–95, and was a member of the Binational Study of Migration between 1995 and 1997. In 2001–2002 he assessed the options for dealing with unauthorized migration into Thailand.

Suzanne Model is Professor of Sociology at the University of Massachusetts. Dr. Model's research focuses on immigration, with a special emphasis on cross-national differences in immigrants' economic success. She is especially interested in African-origin immigrants from the Caribbean and Chinese immigrants from Asia. A recent publication is "Unions between Blacks and Whites: England and the US Compared" (with Gene Fisher), *Ethnic and Racial Studies*, vol. 25.

John Mollenkopf is Distinguished Professor of Political Science and Sociology at the City University Graduate Center and Director of its Center for Urban Research. He has authored or edited many books on urban politics, urban policy, the politics of urban development, and New York City, including *E Pluribus Unum? Historical and Contemporary Perspectives on Immigrant Political Incorporation* (coedited with Gary Gerstle, 2001). With Philip Kasinitz and Mary Waters, he is currently writing a book about educational attainment, labor market outcomes, and political and civic involvement among second-generation immigrant and native minority young adults in the New York metropolitan area.

Victor Nee is Director of the Center for the Study of Economy and Society, and the Goldwin Smith Professor of Sociology at Cornell University. His research interests are in economic sociology and immigrant labor markets, about which he has published extensively. His most recent publications include: *Remaking the American Mainstream* (with

Richard Alba, 2003) and the *New Institutionalism in Sociology* (coedited with Mary Brinton, 1998).

Jan Rath is Associate Professor and Co-Director of the Institute for Migration and Ethnic Studies at the University of Amsterdam. An anthropologist, he is also active in economic and urban sociology and is co-founder of an international network of experts on immigrant entrepreneurship. He is the author or editor of numerous articles, chapters, and reports on the sociology, politics, and economics of postmigratory processes. These publications include *Immigrant Businesses: The Economic, Political and Social Environment* (2000), *Unravelling the Rag Trade: Immigrant Entrepreneurship in Seven World Cities* (2002), and *Immigrant Entrepreneurs: Venturing Abroad in the Age of Globalization* (2003).

Jeffrey G. Reitz is R.F. Harney Professor of Ethnic, Immigration and Pluralism Studies and Professor of Sociology at the University of Toronto. His research examines immigration, race, and ethnic relations, focusing from a comparative perspective on Canada, the United States, Britain, Australia, and Germany. His books include *Warmth of the Welcome: The Social Causes of Economic Success for Immigrants in Different Nations and Cities* (1988) and *The Illusion of Difference: Realities of Ethnicity in Canada and the United States* (1994). Other recent publications include "Immigrant Success in the Knowledge Economy: Institutional Change and Immigrant Experience in Canada, 1970–1995," *Journal of Social Issues* (2001), and "Immigration and Canadian Nation-Building in the Transition to the Knowledge Economy," in *Controlling Immigration: A Global Perspective* (2nd ed., 2003).

Brian J. Stults is Assistant Professor of Sociology at the University of Florida. His primary areas of interest are urban sociology and criminology. His urban research involves analyzing racial residential segregation in metropolitan America over several decades. His criminological research examines racial variation in arrest rates and the effect of social threat on racial disparities in the criminal justice system.

Stephen J. Trejo is Associate Professor of Economics at the University of Texas at Austin. His research focuses on public policy issues involving labor markets, including overtime pay regulation, the experiences of immigrants, and obstacles to the economic progress of minority groups. He is the author of "Intergenerational Progress of Mexican-

Origin Workers in the U.S. Labor Market," *Journal of Human Resources* (Summer 2003).

Harold Troper is Professor in the Department of Theory and Policy Studies at the University of Toronto, where he teaches on the history of immigration and on ethnicity and intergroup relations. Professor Troper has been honored with a John Simon Guggenheim Memorial Fellowship, the American Jewish Book Award, and the Sir John A. Macdonald Prize for the best book published on Canadian history. His books include *Immigrants: A Portrait of the Urban Experience* (1975), *None Is Too Many* (1982), *Old Wounds* (1985), *Friend or Foe?* (1997), *Ethnicity, Politics and Public Policy in Canada* (1999), and *The Ransomed of God* (1999). He is currently conducting research into issues of ethnic identity in Canada during the late 1960s and early 1970s.

Takeyuki Tsuda is Associate Director of the Center for Comparative Immigration Studies at the University of California, San Diego. He previously taught at the University of Chicago as a Collegiate Assistant Professor. Dr. Tsuda has published numerous articles in anthropological and interdisciplinary journals, as well as *Strangers in the Ethnic Homeland: Japanese Brazilian Return Migration in Transnational Perspective* (2003). He is also coeditor of the second edition of *Controlling Immigration: A Global Perspective* (2003).

Zulema Valdez is a joint Visiting Research Fellow of the Center for U.S.-Mexican Studies and the Center for Comparative Immigration Studies at the University of California, San Diego, where she is completing a book manuscript entitled *Economic Strategies of Survival and Mobility: Ethnic Entrepreneurship in the United States*. Dr. Valdez has recently accepted a fellowship at the Ford School of Public Policy and Social Welfare at the University of Michigan. Her upcoming project will explore how ethnic entrepreneurship under capitalism constitutes a strategy of upward mobility for some, a strategy of economic survival for others.

Roger Waldinger is Professor and Chair, Department of Sociology at the University of California, Los Angeles. He is the author of numerous books, most recently: *How The Other Half Works: Immigration and the Social Organization of Labor* (with Michael Lichter, 2003) and *Strangers at the Gates: New Immigrants in Urban America* (2001).

Mary C. Waters is Harvard College Professor and Chair of the Department of Sociology at Harvard University. She is the author of numerous books and articles on immigrant assimilation and racial and ethnic identity, including the prize-winning *Black Identities: West Indian Immigrant Dreams and American Realities* (1999). Her current research focuses on patterns of assimilation among the second generation in New York City, patterns of racial intermarriage and identity formation in the United States, and the ethnic variations in the transition to adulthood in America today.

Kenny Zhang is a Research Analyst at the Asia Pacific Foundation of Canada. His major academic interests include China-Canada immigration issues, bilateral trade and investment relations, and internal labor migration in China. He previously was Associate Research Professor at the Shanghai Academy of Social Science and a Senior Researcher at the Vancouver Centre for Excellence: Immigration (RIIM/SFU).

1

Host Societies and the Reception of Immigrants: Research Themes, Emerging Theories, and Methodological Issues

JEFFREY G. REITZ

Immigration's impact on the economy and on society is shaped not only by characteristics of the immigrants themselves but also by basic features of the society that those immigrants have joined. The importance of characteristics of host societies has been attracting increased scholarly attention and scrutiny, and the chapters in this volume—reflecting a range of disciplines and comparative perspectives—illustrate, examine, and contribute to this development.

Interest in the impact of host societies on immigrants reflects recognition that international migration is an ongoing and increasingly global process. As societies change and as immigrant destinations include an ever increasing number of nations, it seems clear that the social processes by which immigrants are received and incorporated into their destination societies also change. Today's immigrants in the so-called second great migration enter host societies very different from those that received earlier "first wave" immigrants. Immigrants settling in California, Florida, and Texas encounter conditions unlike those found in New York and other eastern U.S. cities that played host to so many previous immigrants. The immigrants' experiences also seem to vary among destination countries, such as the traditional immigration societies of the United States, Canada, and Australia; the variation is even greater across newer immigrant destinations in Europe and Asia. And with the rapid economic and social transformations under way in the contemporary world, the reception of immigrants may also change. Immigrants in the 1990s and the new millennium face conditions that differ in many ways from those encountered by immigrants only a few years earlier.

Current research among immigration scholars has begun to explore the implications of this theme theoretically and empirically. The following eighteen chapters represent the efforts of scholars whose ongoing work reflects an interest in the impact on immigrants of some particular host-society features. They illustrate a variety of approaches.

The distinctive focus of all the chapters is on *features of host societies*—and not only on the characteristics of immigrants themselves—as determinants of the successful incorporation of immigrants. There are, I suggest, four major dimensions of society that emerge as significant in this new research thrust. These are:

- preexisting ethnic or race relations within the host population;
- differences in labor markets and related institutions;
- the impact of government policies and programs, including immigration policy, policies for immigrant integration, and policies for the regulation of social institutions; and
- the changing nature of international boundaries, part of the process of globalization.

These four dimensions intersect one another in significant ways. In the analyses of these intersections, the additional concept of culture often plays a role. For example, preexisting ethnic or race relations affect labor market processes because they shape cultural orientations and intergroup attitudes. Government policy is affected by labor market structures and the ethnic composition of the host society population, as well as by broader cultural trends. In this brief introductory essay, I will describe each of the four themes and illustrate how they become manifest in the various chapters that follow. I also suggest, as a context for considering each specific analysis, that it is useful to think of an emerging model or framework for studying the impact of host societies.

Developing a theory of immigrant reception that takes proper account of the impact of host societies is greatly aided by comparative perspectives. Accordingly, many of the chapters in this collection are comparative, across cities or regions within a single national society, across societies, or across different time periods. And yet, often the impact of a particular host-society characteristic is inferred from evidence available within a single setting. Of the following eighteen chapters, only about half can be considered to include cross-national or interregional comparative analysis. A few others include comparative observations or points of reference. Cross-national differences often raise significant issues not identified as prominent in debate within any given country. The latter often mirror conflicts and values prevailing in a particular context, which deflect attention from issues of comparative significance across countries. On the other hand, it may be difficult to inject comparative perspectives into existing national discourses.

Even though the collection was designed with an emphasis on the American and Canadian cases[1] and comparisons between and within these two countries, there are comparisons also involving Australia, Britain, various European cities, Japan, and China. Clearly there are enormous possibilities for comparative analysis with other countries as well. Such comparative work will be important in clarifying what is actually distinctive about the experience of each country, in addition to raising new issues based on the diversity of immigrant experiences. A reading of these chapters will suggest that prospects for greater and more effective comparative analysis also hinge in part on methodological advances—specifically, strategies to isolate the impact of each of the four intersecting dimensions of host societies.

PREEXISTING ETHNIC AND RACE RELATIONS IN HOST SOCIETIES

Preexisting relations among ethnic and racial groups in a host society affect the reception of new immigrants because such reception is a matter of intergroup adjustment and accommodation. Preexisting ethnic attitudes, as well as intergroup boundaries and hierarchies, provide the social framework within which integration processes occur. They may give rise to formal and informal institutional arrangements, including laws, organizational policies and practices, interest groups, and popular culture, all of which may affect the opportunities available to newcomers and the constraints they face.

---

[1] The source of this collection was a conference sponsored by the Canada Program at Harvard University's Weatherhead Center for International Affairs, which emphasizes issues of joint concern to Canada and the United States.

In recent years, the most basic concepts required for analysis of immigrant reception—such as "assimilation" and "retention"—have been reconsidered in light of circumstances created by preexisting ethnic and race relations within the host society. The question is whether—or the extent to which—multicultural societies with histories of immigration and ethnic diversity can be thought of as settings for assimilation at all. A prior history of open immigration and great ethnic diversity may create a situation in which there is no clearly identifiable "majority" or "dominant group," either in numerical terms or in any other socially meaningful way. Assimilation loses its meaning, and instead it may be preferable to speak of various forms of diversity that arise from the reception of new immigrants. This is a long-standing issue in Canada, where both the French-English duality and the 1970 declaration of official status for "multiculturalism" raised the matter quite forcefully. Alba and Nee (1997) have affirmed their view that a version of assimilation still occurs at least in the United States. Roger Waldinger, in his chapter on "The Sociology of Immigration: Second Thoughts and Reconsiderations," reasserts his own doubts by examining various meanings that may be attached to concepts including not only assimilation but also "ethnic retention," "acculturation," and even "ethnic group" in any ethnically and racially diverse host society. From the standpoint of immigrant reception, the preexisting pattern of ethnic and racial relations is the most critical starting point for defining the "host society." As Waldinger puts it: "we would do better if we conceptualized immigration as a characteristic of our society and its insiders, who interact with the newcomers in ways that enhance, rather than diminish, difference."

In the empirical chapters here, a number of subthemes appear. These include not only the distinctiveness of the traditional countries of immigration as compared to newer European and Asian destinations for immigrants, but also two others: the impact of established ethnic minority communities and the impact of the United States' history of racial polarization and segregation. Examinations of these situations reveal that preexisting ethnic or race relations vary not only in terms of the extent of preexisting diversity but also in two more specific ways: the extent to which one or more of the existing groups share characteristics with newly arriving groups, and the status or resources of such existing groups within the host society.

Nancy Foner's chapter, "Immigrants and African Americans: Comparative Perspectives on the New York Experience across Time and

Space," is a wide-ranging examination of the impact of American race relations on new immigrants, and it illuminates many of these themes. Foner presents two comparative frames of reference: differences over time in New York City and differences in the experiences of one group of immigrants—West Indian blacks—in New York versus London. Both comparisons demonstrate a great many ways in which the growing presence of native-born African Americans in New York has complicated reception processes for most immigrant groups. The comparison over time shows clearly that a competitive relation between African Americans and many immigrant groups can produce diverse outcomes on all sides. The impact on West Indians is additionally influenced by the racial commonality, of course; and the contrasts with London show differences in virtually every institutional sphere: in private- and public-sector employment, in ethnic enclave employment, in politics, in education, in housing, and in family, neighborhoods, and community life. Totaling an overall "bottom line" for the impact will require the fulfillment of a very substantial research agenda.

The next two chapters—those by Philip Kasinitz, John Mollenkopf, and Mary Waters, and by Monica Boyd—focus on what some call "segmented assimilation." This concerns processes arising in the context of the United States' history of racial polarization that impact mainly on the second generation within the racial minority immigrant groups. In the context of racial barriers restricting integration into the dominant social groups in society, segmented assimilation refers to the potential options for affiliation with different host-society subgroups based on race or ethnic background (Portes and Zhou 1993; Portes and Rumbaut 2001). Toward which groups do these young people become oriented, and what are the consequences? Pressures may prevail toward integration into established racial minority groups; and for an impressionable second generation, this integration may promote exposure to an "oppositional" subculture, potentially directing energies away from mobility-oriented efforts. On the other hand, aversion to assuming the status of a stigmatized minority reinforces the natural tendency to form communities based on specific foreign origins. Black Americans do not necessarily all belong to the same group—at least from the viewpoint of newcomers such as black West Indians. The importance of similar racial status is a construction imposed by the dominant white group. The two chapters approach this whole matter in very different ways. They both challenge segmented assimilation scenarios, but both also suggest that the United States' racial polarization has definite effects.

In "Becoming Americans/Becoming New Yorkers: Immigrant Incorporation in a Majority Minority City," Kasinitz, Mollenkopf, and Waters use field data to illustrate that reality, at least in New York City, is more complex and not constrained by such hard choices. The children of foreign-born racial minorities may benefit from racial minority institutions within the native-born society while also retaining distinctive identities and cultural orientations based on foreign origins. Particularly in New York, the historical gateway for millions of America's immigrants and abounding in complex possibilities, an environment exists in which a sense of creative adventure resists stereotyped patterns. The data suggest that the children of racial minority immigrants are by no means a "high-problem" group. They do experience the real downside of exposure to the racial categories themselves, as structured by the wider society, but they also find useful resources for coping with that experience, within both native-born minority and immigrant community institutions. The authors' emphasis on New York as a quite distinct "host society" within the United States—and the fact that immigrants seem to become "New Yorkers" more clearly than they become "Americans"—underscore Waldinger's second thoughts, that immigration becomes a characteristic of the preexisting society.

Boyd's chapter, "Educational Attainments of Immigrant Offspring: Success or Segmented Assimilation?," focuses on Canada and provides a quantitative analysis. Canada provides an example of a host society lacking a history of racial polarization parallel to the American experience. Several differences would be possible: the lack of native-born minority institutions or resources (presumed effect: negative), the lack of related cultural models (presumed effect: positive), and possible differences in basic majority group racial attitudes (presumed effect: also positive). In this context, the positive educational attainments Boyd finds among these children constitute crucial data. If this confirms that segmented assimilation does not exist in a setting like Canada, it may also suggest a comparative reference point for its existence in the United States. It may be—as Foner also suggests—that the most appropriate benchmark against which to assess the experiences of young people represented in the Kasinitz-Mollenkopf-Waters study is not that of whites after all, but rather racial minorities in settings lacking an indigenous racial polarization.

The final chapter in this group opens this topic up still further by showing how segmented assimilation would be affected by the status of particular minority communities within a host society. In the research literature, the most prevalent and long-standing interest has been the impact of established immigrant ethnic communities on newcomers. The traditional presumption that immigrant communities may assist new arrivals with short-term support but may retard integration over the longer term or for the second generation has been challenged by studies that suggest minority communities may provide positive resources for social integration in the larger society, and that affluent minority communities may be viable. Richard Alba, John Logan, and Brian Stults present comparative analysis of immigrant residential concentrations within U.S. urban areas in "Residential Inequality and Segregation in an Immigration Era: An Analysis of Major U.S. Metropolitan Regions in 1990." They show the extent to which these patterns of the traditional immigration destinations in New York are being repeated in the newer immigrant destinations across the country. In particular, the presence of affluent Asian immigrant communities makes possible the retention of ethnic community residential ties even after significant upward occupational or income mobility has occurred. These established Asian communities clearly affect the orientations and experiences of newcomers. Large cities such as New York and Los Angeles provide for the greatest community differentiation. The authors speculate that as ethnic and racial diversity increases across the United States, including in smaller urban areas, intergroup contacts in affluent neighborhoods will increase correspondingly.

LABOR MARKETS AND RELATED INSTITUTIONS

Labor markets are a second theme—one of the most traditional in the study of immigrant integration but also one that is being expanded in important ways by cross-setting comparative study. The human capital model often has been the starting point for analysis within a single society, with its premise that individual immigrant characteristics determine labor market outcomes. A focus on labor market structure, and the concentration of immigrants in particular labor market segments and niches, shifted the emphasis to a host-society characteristic. But most research still focused on a single setting. Rather than comparing the impact of different structures, the tendency has been to compare immigrants located differently within the same structure, as well as to compare labor market segments within a given setting. In this context it was commonly observed that the vulnerabilities of certain immigrants in marginal work settings were exploited, often to the immigrants' extreme disadvantage. However, the research served primarily descriptive purposes because of the uncertain explanatory power of labor market structure, beyond the simpler concepts of "discrimination" and "human capital."

In a comparative context the analytic opportunities increase, but so does the complexity. It is very meaningful to ask whether different labor market structures might lead to different outcomes and, if so, what those differences might be. The answer, however, must take account of two major issues. First, labor markets vary along several dimensions, including not only the size of immigrant segments and niches but also overall employment regimes and industrial relations processes, earnings dispersions, gender inequalities, career structures, and unemployment rates. Because these dimensions are frequently interrelated, the comparative perspective requires that they be considered together and in terms of their joint impact.

Second, labor markets also are interrelated with other institutions of society, including education, the welfare state, and even immigration policy. Again, comparative analysis must expand to consider the impact of these related institutions. As an illustration, a comparison of the United States with Canada and Australia shows the joint impact of labor market structures and related institutions (Reitz 1998). The results were something of a surprise: the impact of educational differences was the most pronounced, more than labor market structure itself. This suggests that educational change may be important in determining trends in immigrant earnings, a subject I pursue in my own chapter here, "Educational Expansion and the Employment Success of Immigrants in the United States and Canada, 1970–1990." The rapid rise in native-born educational levels in Canada, converging toward the already higher levels in the United States, tended to reduce the advantage previously enjoyed by immigrants to Canada compared to their American counterparts. Shifts in immigrant educational levels have a relatively modest effect, partly because immigrant educational qualifications are discounted in labor markets. Immigrant educational levels rose in Canada while they fell in the United States, and yet immigrant earnings fell in both countries. The increased role of education in labor markets reflects a broader institutional transformation captured by the terms "postindustrialism" and "knowledge economy." Understanding the impact of this institutional change on immigrant reception may be as important as understanding the impact of trends in the skills of immigrants themselves.

The addition of newer countries of immigration further increases the potential complexity, revealing more substantial differences related to the institutional and cultural contexts of labor markets. The chapter by Suzanne Model and Lang Lin, "The Cost of Not Being Christian: Hindus, Sikhs, and Muslims in Britain and Canada," begins with a careful search for discriminatory differences related to observed cross-national differences in attitudes toward religious groups already resident in a society. This illustrates an intersection with our first theme, the impact of preexisting ethnic and racial relations. These authors then consider the impact of a series of labor market dimensions, including labor demand (measured by the unemployment rate, a standard "host society" characteristic for economists), earnings dispersion, and occupational polarization. This chapter illustrates clearly how understanding the impact of specific host-society characteristics on labor market discrimination can be greatly enhanced in a comparative context.

Much more dramatic cultural differences in how labor markets affect the integration of new immigrants emerge in "Human versus Social Capital: Immigrant Wages and Labor Market Incorporation in Japan and the United States," by Takeyuki Tsuda, Zulema Valdez, and Wayne A. Cornelius. Their analysis is based on an interurban comparison—specifically, between the Japanese industrial city of Hamamatsu and San Diego, California. Because of specific labor market locations assigned to migrants in Japan, education and other forms of human capital count far less for migrants there than they do for migrants in the United States. Social capital counts more. If immigrants in Western countries encounter barriers to full participation in the economy, in Japan it would appear to be a case of greater exclusion. To fully accommodate such findings in a theory of immigrant labor market participation would require not only an extension of cultural variability but also a meaningful elaboration of the viability of social boundaries within a modern industrial economy.

Another "traditional topic" for labor market analysis of immigration is self-employment, usually linked to preexisting ethnic community resources. A large group of community studies suggests that immigrant self-employment significantly affects integration, but as yet only a few studies examine its comparative significance across host societies (one example is Light and Rosenstein 1995). In his "Undressing the Garment Industry: Immigrant Entrepreneurship in Seven Cities," Jan Rath asks what features of host societies affect the success of immigrant entrepreneurs in a specific industry such as the garment industry. Based on analyses of seven major immigration receiving cities—Amsterdam, Birmingham, London, Los Angeles, Miami, New York, and Paris—Rath clearly underscores the importance of basic labor market conditions that are not related specifically to ethnic variables. These include conditions such as competition, the role of large buyers (in this case, retail chains), competition, labor market regulation, and the strength of the welfare state. Immigrant entrepreneurs thrive in an environment of institutional individualism—open immigration, an unregulated market economy, and a weak welfare state—with Amsterdam and Los Angeles representing opposite extremes on these dimensions. Exploitation of immigrant workers appears to be the flip side. Other cases show various patterns for which the role of offshore competition is a kind of wild-card variable. New York, for example, is an intermediate case in which unions play a larger role, with local political authorities responding to this reality. Rath's analysis points to labor markets' interdependence with their institutional context and with related government policies.

GOVERNMENT POLICIES AND PROGRAMS

There are many types of government policies and programs potentially affecting immigrant reception and incorporation. The most obvious, of course, is immigration policy itself. Research in many countries shows that immigrant selection is an important determinant of the character of immigrant populations and communities. However, such research also shows that this impact has very serious limitations; in fact, in a comparative context it is the *impotence* of immigration policy that may be most apparent (Cornelius, Martin, and Hollifield 1994; Cornelius, Tsuda, Martin, and Hollifield 2003). As an example, U.S. immigration policy is less skill selective than its Canadian and Australian counterparts, and yet for most origins groups, immigrants to the United States are more highly skilled (the primary exception being Mexicans, for obvious reasons; see Duleep and Regets 1992; Reitz 1998: 88–97).

Immigrant reception also is at least potentially affected by various other government policies, which of course may be formulated partly in relation to immigration policy. These include programs to assist immigrant settlement and integration—such as language training and counseling—and also policies for the regulation of intergroup relations—such as equal rights provisions in employment, housing, and other areas of society, and policies regarding "multiculturalism." More broadly, immigrant incorporation actually may be affected by any government policy or program regulating important institutional sectors of society, such as labor markets, economic development, education, urban development, and the welfare state. This is true particularly when those policies may have specific provisions affecting immigrants or minority groups, but it also may be true when there are no such provisions.

In the United States, welfare reform initiatives in the 1990s were in part directed at immigrants, and the chapter here by George Borjas, "Welfare Reform and Immigrant Participation in Welfare Programs," presents an extremely valuable assessment of how the Personal Responsibility and Work Opportunity Reconciliation Act of 1996 (PRWORA) has affected immigrants. There is an institutional "fit" between a weak welfare state and an unselective immigration policy, as Borjas notes in his opening quote from Milton Friedman. Given the perception of ineffective immigration control in the United States, PRWORA sought to create a better "institutional fit" with its welfare state by limiting access to welfare for noncitizen immigrants. Borjas shows essentially that the policy itself has not worked. Although there has been a faster reduction in welfare use by immigrants than by the native-born, PRWORA itself played little role in producing the outcome. Interestingly, an interstate comparative analysis is key to the findings. Borjas's data show that the reduction in the relative use of welfare by immigrants occurred almost entirely in California and that no real basis exists either in the legislation itself, in the responses of states to offset the impact on immigrants by substituting their own benefits, or in the responses of immigrants themselves to become naturalized that could explain this "California effect." He suggests that the debate over Proposition 187 in California (which sought to cut off some health and social services, including public education, to illegal immigrants and their children, and was passed by voters in 1994) may have had a chilling effect that, in turn, deterred immigrants from welfare use. In other words, in the U.S. context, government action may have little impact without strong and visibly expressed support from public opinion directed at immigrants in local communities.

Three other chapters in this section also underscore the point that the impact of government policy on immigrants may be indirect and conditional upon more subtle social forces. Regarding immigration policy, skill selectivity is more often applied to immigrant men than to women, so one might have expected to see gender differences in its impact. Yet Heather Antecol, Deborah Cobb-Clark, and Stephen Trejo, in "Human Capital and Earnings of Female Immigrants to Australia, Canada, and the United States," show that the cross-national skill differences are virtually identical for men and women. Most likely, selection on the basis of family ties has definite skill implications, more than most immigration policymakers are inclined to believe. The authors conclude with considerable skepticism about the potential for immigrant selection policies to determine the human capital of immigrants.

In the broader area of immigrant settlement policies, the effect of the rather laissez-faire U.S. policy may be contrasted with the more interventionist and managerial Canadian and Australian policies. There is little direct information on the impact of the Canadian and Australian policies, perhaps because, although responsibility for immigrant settlement exists at the federal level, specific programs are designed by local groups with activities tailored to specific needs, and hence they vary widely. Many have assumed that such programs probably have little impact from a comparative perspective—as has also been suggested in the case of Canadian and Australian "multiculturalism" policy (Reitz and Breton 1994). Yet when Irene Bloemraad examined political participation among immigrants in Canada, she found it substantially higher than comparative rates in the United States. Her analysis, in "Institutions, Ethnic Leaders, and the Political Incorporation of Immigrants: A Comparison of Canada and the United States," suggests that the reasons lie in what she calls the Canadian "immigrant settlement industry." This is defined as a sector composed of government agencies, nonprofit organizations, and private businesses that cater to immigrants' settlement needs, such as English as a second language (ESL), employment assistance, and interpretation services. Bloemraad suggests that an immigrant settlement industry in Canada exerts important effects on community leadership, mobilizing structures, and legitimate political discourses. The effect is to draw more immigrants into the political process than is typical in the United States, where the settlement industry, if it exists, is far less developed.

Government policies more generally also may affect immigrants in ways not readily visible. One example is local housing codes, which affect the availability of different types of housing, with potential implications for the settlement of immigrants. An innovative analysis by

Ivan Light, in "Immigration and Housing Shortage in Los Angeles, 1970–2000," shows that Los Angeles County housing codes imposed two generations ago now restrict the availability of low-cost multi-family apartment buildings needed by many Mexican and Central American immigrants. Light argues that today there is a conflict between these immigrants and the native-born population, one that has remained largely "concealed" in the sense that the relevant interests of these two groups are not openly declared. The consequence is that many immigrants destined for Los Angeles are forced to look elsewhere for housing, disrupting the powerful impact of social networks on settlement processes. This may be one of the factors in the recent growth of Mexican communities in areas of the United States where their populations have been relatively small in the past.

INTERNATIONAL BOUNDARIES AND GLOBALIZATION

The place of each host society within the international system—in terms including geographic, economic, political, and social aspects—has an important impact on immigration and immigrant settlement. At least since Sassen (1988) elaborated in detail how U.S. investments abroad might have affected the flow of immigrants, there has been a recognition that changing international boundaries, and forces lumped together under the heading of "globalization," may be changing the character of immigration in important ways. The boundary that each host society maintains with other societies is the set of opportunities and constraints operating to regulate the flow of persons, goods, and information between them. Although maintenance of national borders to regulate flows between societies is a government responsibility, transborder activity is subject to influence by so many other circumstances that it has come to be considered a distinct institutional sector.

In this collection, each of the two most important themes related to international boundaries is represented by a chapter. One theme is the impact of "globalization" on immigrant communities. The focus here is on the erosion of national boundaries caused by the increase in transborder networks and commitments of all kinds. Stephen Castles's chapter, "Transnational Communities: A New Form of Social Relations under Conditions of Globalization?," puts forward seven propositions about transnational activities of immigrants and a range of potential impacts on processes related to immigrant incorporation, such as assimilation, multiculturalism, multiple identity formation, and citizenship. The decline of the "territorial principle" introduces further considerations into the reformulation of these concepts, as suggested in Waldinger's chapter. Castles cautions that the evidence suggests the impact of transnationalism today remains limited and that, under certain circumstances, transnational communities may promote rather than retard assimilation.

A second theme is that of illegal immigration. The seminal research by Massey et al. (1987) on cross-border networks in northern Mexican communities clearly showed how extensive opportunity structures within the United States overwhelmed border enforcement as a determinant of migration patterns. This opportunity structure regulates access to employment in the first instance, but what next comes into play are longer-term involvements that affect access to the means for more general social participation, including education and other social services. Philip Martin's analysis, "Mexican Workers and U.S. Agriculture: The Revolving Door," shows the interrelation of employment and other opportunities with government efforts to regulate cross-border activity. Cross-border opportunity structures explain why the Immigration Control and Reform Act of 1986 (IRCA) was so ineffective in reducing illegal immigration. By attempting to legalize various activities in which illegal Mexican migrants were involved while simultaneously maintaining agricultural employers' access to Mexican workers, IRCA actually created a range of new employment opportunities for illegal migrants. Hence the flow of workers across the border continued. Law enforcement at the border itself in some ways also increases the incentives for migrant workers to establish permanent residence in the United States because of the reduced opportunity for cross-border commuting. Moreover, the existence of undocumented workers in significant numbers creates pressures to supply additional opportunities for illegal migration from other sources—further weakening border controls.

Changing international boundaries also may promote the phenomenon of secondary or serial migration. Many immigrants are sojourners, moving from one country to another seeking continuing improvements in economic opportunity. Workers who experience a series of jobs or employment relocations may find that these more often involve movement across national borders, with no particular move necessarily perceived as a "final destination." The chapter by Don DeVoretz, John Ma, and Kenny Zhang, "Triangular Human Capital Flows: Empirical Evidence from Hong Kong and Canada," suggests that these movements may, however, have distinct observable patterns in relation to characteristics of host societies. Some nations may be more likely to serve as stopover locations. These include Canada or individual European Union (EU) countries where generous social programs can be useful to migrants but where potentially more attractive migration destinations are close at hand. Migrants from Hong Kong, as an instance, might first relocate to Canada and take advantage of its relatively generously subsidized postsecondary education system to acquire training needed to obtain employment in the United States, or to return to Hong Kong. DeVoretz, Ma, and Zhang provide an innovative use of census data from Hong Kong and Canada. Their conclusions raise important practical questions for any country serving as an entrepôt nation.

HOST SOCIETIES AND IMMIGRATION: TOWARD THEORY AND COMPARATIVE METHODS

Collectively, the chapters presented here suggest that elaboration of the impact of each of the four dimensions outlined above may be useful in developing an emerging theory about how host societies affect immigrant integration. A key theoretical challenge is the articulation of the relations among the various dimensions and subdimensions. The most ambitious attempts to examine migration in a global context—for example, the overviews by Castles and Miller (1998) and Massey et al. (1998), or the monograph by Hatton and Williamson (1998)—all grapple with this challenge, as do most of the chapters in the present collection.

All comparative studies are complex, but perhaps most difficult is the attempt to compare the "new" immigration of the current era with the old immigration, the "great migration" of a century ago. Not only are the immigrants themselves very different, virtually all aspects of host societies also are now dramatically different. Attempting to sort out effects of particular host-society changes is a daunting task indeed. The comparison of immigration over time would have to take account of:

- preexisting ethnic and race relations: the background of the "old" immigration itself affects "new" immigration, and the migration of blacks from the rural south in the United States has changed the urban north as destinations for immigration;

- labor markets and related institutions: the transformation from agricultural to industrial to postindustrial, with accompanying alterations in relations among social groups based on class, region, gender, and age;
- government policy and programs: the creation of a welfare state, massively expanded and subsidized postsecondary education, with immigration policies adjusted to fit new circumstances; and
- changing international boundaries and globalization: the modernization of Europe, the emergence of new developing nations, and the dramatic reduction in effective distances between nations.

Underlying each dimension—and implicitly a feature of each of them—is the question of cultural change in the direction of evolution toward greater tolerance of ethnic and racial diversity. Cultural and institutional changes work together and are part of each of the interrelated themes.

Despite such complexity, two chapters approach this topic in a direct and meaningful way. First, Victor Nee ("Institutional Change and Immigrant Assimilation in the United States") suggests that in the American case, government institutions embody cultural advances that clearly inject equity concerns into intergroup relations to a far greater extent than in the past. In his view, the civil rights movement was a pivotal force and changed the rules of the game in the United States so that "informal racism" has far less impact today. This important hypothesis is part of the context considered in Nancy Foner's earlier chapter on the impact of African Americans on differences between "old" and "new" immigration in New York, as well as in her impressively comprehensive treatment of change over time, *From Ellis Island to JFK: New York's Two Great Waves of Immigration* (2000), upon which her chapter draws.

The same theme of evolution toward greater tolerance also pervades the discussion of "old" and "new" immigration to Canada, by Harold Troper ("To Farms or Cities: A Historical Tension between Canada and Its Immigrants"). This is true despite significant differences in institutional and historical experience: for example, the importance of agricultural development in the earlier phase in Canada and the quite different issues of intergroup relations emerging over time within the host society. Perhaps conditions affecting the changing reception of immigrants in the two neighboring countries are not as different as might first appear.

Beneath all these analyses of change is the basic question of "progress" in the matter of immigration. Has the accommodation of society's new members improved over the past century? If so, to what extent, in what ways, and for what reasons? Extracting these basic lessons from such complex changes over time may be one of the most compelling and yet difficult tasks regarding the study of "host societies."

References

Alba, Richard, and Victor Nee. 1997. "Rethinking Assimilation Theory for a New Era of Immigration," *International Migration Review* 31, no. 4: 826–74.

Castles, Stephen, and Mark J. Miller. 1998. *The Age of Migration: International Population Movements in the Modern World*. 2d ed. New York: Guilford Press.

Cornelius, Wayne A., Philip L. Martin, and James F. Hollifield, eds. 1994. *Controlling Immigration: A Global Perspective*. Stanford, Calif.: Stanford University Press.

Cornelius, Wayne A., Takeyuki Tsuda, Philip L. Martin, and James F. Hollifield, eds. 2003. *Controlling Immigration: A Global Perspective*. 2d ed. Stanford, Calif.: Stanford University Press, in collaboration with the Center for Comparative Immigration Studies, University of California, San Diego.

Duleep, Harriet Orcutt, and Mark C. Regets. 1992. "Some Evidence on the Effects of Admissions Criteria on Immigrant Assimilation." In *Immigration, Language and Ethnicity: Canada and the United States*, edited by Barry Chiswick. Washington, D.C.: AEI Press.

Foner, Nancy. 2000. *From Ellis Island to JFK: New York's Two Great Waves of Immigration*. New York: Russell Sage Foundation.

Hatton, Timothy J., and Jeffrey G. Williamson. 1998. *The Age of Mass Migration: Causes and Economic Impact*. New York: Oxford University Press.

Light, Ivan, and Carolyn Rosenstein. 1995. *Race, Ethnicity and Entrepreneurship in Urban America*. New York: Aldine de Gruyter.

Massey, Douglas S., Rafael Alarcón, Jorge Durand, and Humberto González. 1987. *Return to Aztlan: The Social Process of International Migration from Western Mexico*. Berkeley: University of California Press.

Massey, Douglas S., Joaquin Arango, Graeme Hugo, Ali Kouaouci, Adela Pellegrino, and J. Edward Taylor. 1998. *Worlds in Motion: Understanding International Migration at the End of the Millennium*. Oxford: Clarendon Press.

Portes, Alejandro, and Rubén Rumbaut. 2001. *Legacies: The Story of the Immigrant Second Generation*. New York: Russell Sage Foundation.

Portes, Alejandro, and Min Zhou. 1993. "The New Second Generation: Segmented Assimilation and Its Variants," *Annals of the American Academy of Political and Social Sciences* 530: 74–96.

Reitz, Jeffrey G. 1998. *Warmth of the Welcome: The Social Causes of Economic Success for Immigrants in Different Nations and Cities*. Boulder, Colo.: Westview.

Reitz, Jeffrey G., and Raymond Breton. 1994. *The Illusion of Difference: Realities of Ethnicity in Canada and the United States*. Toronto: C.D. Howe Institute.

Sassen, Saskia. 1988. *The Mobility of Labor and Capital: A Study in International Investment and Labor Flow*. Cambridge: Cambridge University Press.

Part I

Preexisting Ethnic and Race Relations in Host Societies

2

The Sociology of Immigration: Second Thoughts and Reconsiderations

ROGER WALDINGER

The contemporary study of immigration has come a long way. The domain three decades ago of historians and ethnopietists, it has now transfixed the attention of a legion of social scientists, who approach the subject with theories and methodological tools of an ever more sophisticated kind. But if the intellectual record is one of steady progress, the students of this defining American feature have too often succumbed to the perils that inevitably attend their way.

The root problem involves the potential overlap between native and social science understandings of the question at hand. Common sense tells us that the United States comprises a bounded entity, in which the entry of immigrants represents a foreign phenomenon, the immigrants' difference somehow anomalous, an imported feature that is neither expected nor desired to last. Unfortunately, much of the social scientific literature frames the matter in much the same way.

After all, no sooner do the immigrant outsiders arrive than they turn out to be ethnics, a term we now take for granted but whose etymological roots should make room for concern. *Ethnos* was the Greek word used for the Hebrew term "goy" when the Bible was translated more than two millennia ago, later to be applied as a synonym for "heathens." And this was more or less how the word "ethnicity" was intended when Lloyd Warner first brought it into the American social science lexicon. In his classic, depression-era studies, Warner labeled all of "Yankee City's" groups as ethnic, but not the "Yankees or Natives"—implicitly accepting the Yankee point of view that this rubric applied to others but not to them (Warner and Lunt 1941; Warner and Srole 1945). While much has changed since Warner, the scholarly taken-for-granted may be much the same. As astute a student of the American ethnic scene as Herbert Gans (1998) recently thought it appropriate to distinguish immigration researchers as either insiders or outsiders, classifying insiders as those who shared either an ancestry with the group they studied or a commitment to its persistence, as opposed to all others, whom he called "outsiders." But if immigration is a distinguishing American trait that is at once persistent and defines everyday understandings of what it means to be an American, then Gans's so-called outsiders are no less implicated than his insiders in the phenomenon they both study. Too much of our literature amounts to a sociology of the "goy," of the other, written from the standpoint of the insider posing as outsider, always remaining external to the analysis itself, indeed entirely invisible.

Moreover, the assumption of boundedness is no less common to self-proclaimed critical perspectives than it is to conventional ones, the former underscoring the twin force of in-group exclusion and newcomer solidarity, the latter emphasizing the absorptive power of American society. In revolt against assimilation, today's scholars often highlight the salience of immigrants' ethnic identities and attachments; theirs is a differentialist view, portraying an America in which ethnic boundaries are hard and fast. But in so doing, contemporary scholarship simply echoes the established account. Both assume that immigrants comprise a *group* right from the start, a view that presumes stability and homogeneity in the structure of immigrants' affiliations, when in fact migration destabilizes and diversifies those relationships.

Taking issue with both established and critical approaches, this essay is organized in contrapuntal form. I first discuss the concept of "assimilation," contending that it assumes a normally integrated society and is therefore vitiated by its inherent assimilationism. I then turn to assimilation's opposite, the notion of ethnic retention, arguing that retentionism involves a projection of a past that never was. Next I return to the critique of the conventional wisdom, tackling the concept of "acculturation" and arguing that it misconstrues culture as a list of traits, as opposed to an understanding of the world. Consequently, the conventional approach neglects the most decisive moments in cultural change: first, the process by which immigrants take on a native theory of American society, and second, the changes that occur as they encounter the negative images that insiders have of them. I end by returning to the discussion of differentialism, arguing that the necessary critique of assimilation has produced a positive program that wrongly insists on the existence of groups of different kinds. Instead, we would do better to think of the relationship between "them" and "us" in terms of a continuum, where the relationship between ethnic category and pattern of association varies from one dimension of social life to another.

ASSIMILATION

Let me begin with assimilation, our most enduring, most influential concept. Long in disgrace, assimilation is now back in style. For the most eloquent and justifiably influential of the recent defenses, we can turn to the work of Richard Alba and Victor Nee (1998, 2003). Although their effort at rehabilitation is a major achievement, one does not detract from their accomplishment to note that they jumped on a horse that was already in full stride. Whether we take as indicators works designed to engage a broader literate public or those directed purely at an academic audience, it is clear that numerous writers have found appeal in an idea so often rejected. What they observe is an America too porous and too mutable to be captured by the differentialist vision, in which ethnic boundaries are depicted as hard and fast, just as we understand them to have been one hundred years ago. Searching for a vocabulary to describe the reality they discern, many of our colleagues have inevitably returned to the concept of assimilation (Kazal 1995; Brubaker 2001; Hollinger 1995).

While I sympathize, I cannot agree. As Alba and Nee argued, assimilation entails a reduction in ethnic difference, a definition that seems accurately to describe the way in which social scientists have generally understood assimilation. However, it does seem to beg the question of how the intellectual problematic should be defined and why.

The issues at hand clearly fall into the general concerns raised by the study of stratification, in that our interests involve the relationship between some birth-ascribed characteristic and outcomes later on in life or in subsequent generations. In principle, the same framework that is applied when considering the influence of one trait, let us say foreign birth or ancestry, should hold when the interest turns to the impact of another, let us say parents' social class. But imagine that I were to propose a concept that entailed "the decline, and at its endpoint the disappearance of a *class* distinction and the cultural and social differences that express it," thus exactly rephrasing the definition provided by Alba and Nee but substituting the word "class" for "ethnic" (Alba and Nee 1998: 159). While a formulation of this sort might appeal to the more egalitarian readers of this essay, it also reflects my own, lamentably outdated social democratic views, as opposed to the specification of an analytic concept around which a field of study can be organized. More charitably, one could suppose that "assimilation" could be usefully invoked to identify an outcome of a stratificational process of uncertain outcome, very possibly eventuating in diminished difference but no less likely to lead to difference of an increased or persistent sort, or very possibly a shift in the nature of the relevant differences. To pose the question in stratificational terms, however, implies that difference is a normal and *not* a deviant outcome and, therefore, that the production and reproduction of difference, and *not just its reduction*, belongs at the heart of the inquiry.

In its very formulation, the sociology of assimilation thus reveals its assimilationist cast. It begins with the presence of outsiders, whose appearance on the scene requires no explanation and whose distinctiveness can be assumed without making reference to those parties that perceive difference and make it socially significant. Moreover, it has never seriously asked how difference might decline—or conversely, how similarity might come to be. An obvious answer involves one of the other, usually forgotten meanings of assimilation, namely, treating similarly. If, as I have argued above, the intellectual problem involves the relationship between ethnic origins and ethnic destinies, then we need to enlarge the analytical frame to include those others—whether located at subordinate, lateral, or superior levels—that play a crucial role in affecting both "who gets what" and "who is what." Understood this way, assimilation is a process whose subjects are not simply outsiders but insiders as well, and who make "assimilation" through an interactional process that both redefines the lines between insiders and outsiders and determines who is "in" and who is "out."

And just why one should be concerned with the disappearance of difference—or its converse, similarity—has never been adequately explained. After all, similarity is a very specific distributional attribute, in which persons with an origin in a particular source population need to have a wide spread, so that there is extensive overlap between them and the reference population. Why could we not define assimilation as the process whereby members of a source population *converge* around the mean for the reference population? Convergence could still entail very great difference if the source population turns out to be much more tightly clustered around the mean than the reference population. But clustering around the mean would be closely correlated, though not perfectly, with *similar treatment*. From a normative standpoint, I do not see why we should care about anything else. Now there may be an intellectual or scientific reason to be interested in similarity rather than convergence with the mean, but such an argument is one that I have yet to encounter. As assimilation necessarily involves the dissolution of ethnic groups—it is hard to imagine ethnic persistence without dissimilarity—the expectation of similarity seems uncomfortably close to the ideological preoccupations that have shaped this field right from the start.

Moreover, difference is only meaningful within a relational framework, which means that we cannot talk about "them" without also referring to "us." The literature on assimilation, however, cannot quite manage to identify those actors who make difference important, nor why or how they do so. If we cannot answer such questions as "different from whom?" can we have anything to say about difference at all?

To be fair, the literature does make some effort to identify the target population to which outsiders are supposed to assimilate, but at the expense of muddying things further. Our leading analysts—Alba and Nee, Portes and Rumbaut (1996)—tell us that assimilation involves absorption into a majority or a mainstream. However, it takes but a few seconds of reflection to realize that there is no such thing there. Detach the "majority" from its inherent opposition to the minoritarian outsiders and it collapses along the class, regional, religious, and ideological cleavages that keep members of the "majority" regularly at odds with one another. In effect, the concept of assimilation presumes a society that would be normally integrated, were it not for the unfortunate appearance of the outsiders from abroad.

Moreover, majority necessarily implies minority: to assert that the former is somehow less ethnic than the latter is simply to adopt the dominant group's own self-concept. As used by Alba and Nee, moreover, "majority" means "white majority," a term that is certainly part of the everyday discourse of race and ethnicity but is otherwise lacking in intellectual content. Simply put, "white majority" are just two words for continued exclusion on the basis of descent; thus assimilation into the "white majority" simultaneously means disassimilation, since the former necessarily links the conditions of one group's acceptance to another's rejection. Were our literature truly interested in the nature of the U.S. system of ethnic stratification, it would ask just how the entry of immigrant outsiders might eventuate in an outcome of this sort. But too many of our colleagues have concluded that this is a question that we can blithely ignore.

Our older commentators did better, in part because they could talk more freely, avoiding the circumlocutions favored by the right-thinking academics of today, ever on guard against offending thoughts. Good old Milton Gordon (1964)—where would we be without him?—had no compunctions about naming the group to whose acceptance outsiders were supposed to aspire. In the early 1960s, one could not only write about a "core cultural group" but also name it—white Protestants of vaguely British descent. Of course, identifying the target population in terms such as these simply described the world from the standpoint of the particular communal group standing at the top of the system, and whose centrality and dominance therefore required no further discussion. Although the perspective of one's betters certainly warrants attention, it would be good to label it as such. The ability of any group to assert itself as "core" is bound to affect the mechanisms by which outsiders seek and gain acceptance, not to speak of their motivations for doing so. And in any case, that was then, this is now, everything solid—yesterday's cultural core included—having since melted into thin air.

My own guess is that our literature struggles with stating the target group because it cannot quite get itself around to stating the obvious: namely, that as the process transforming outsiders into insiders, assimilation takes foreigners and turns them into "Americans." Of course, to put it that way makes it clear that we can no longer describe assimilation as a shift from particularism to universality, as was the wont of the earlier literature and as some contemporary scholars continue to pretend. Rather, we need to confront assimilation for what it is—a substitution of just one particularism for another. I do not mean to impugn particularism as such: after all, the importance of belonging is one of the few sociological maxims that we possess. And why not cultivate a sense of membership in a national collectivity? In theory, if not in practice, the American people is surely wider and more inclusive than other forms of ethnic affiliation. But still the point stands: assimilation is a very peculiar scholarly concept, resonating with that normative vision of national life that envisions a direct relationship between the individual and the nation, unmediated by ties of an ethnic type. As such, the ideological echo sounds all too clear: too much of our social scientific literature amounts to little more than a mildly intellectualized version of the folk understanding of what it means to become American, obscuring our ability to approach the phenomenon with the critical distance it requires.

ETHNIC RETENTION

Our literature typically opposes assimilationist with retentionist points of view (Gans 1998). Retentionism is an anachronism, mirroring many of the assumptions of the view that it contests, and subject, therefore, to many of the same liabilities. Retentionism needs to posit some stable, fixed entity; after all, what would there be to retain, were there not a coherent, self-conscious collectivity enacting and reenacting the life of its group? There would be nothing wrong with such a description, if only it specified the time and place. The problem is that retentionism freezes a single point in time, projecting it backwards as if patterns of self-awareness and interaction had not always been changing, which, in turn, makes the American ethnic group moment but a stage in the broader sweep of time.

Like assimilationism, retentionism begins with the assumption of a bounded, undifferentiated group. But the reality is almost always otherwise, and all the more so if we move out of the group-ist assumptions common to the literature and think of the subjects of our inquiry as actors in a relational field, whose self-awareness shifts as the pattern of interaction changes. From this standpoint, migration necessarily yields greater diversity in the structure of interpersonal relations, though the significance of that change varies depending on how one situates oneself relative to the actors at hand.

Let us begin by considering the peasant migrant. This prototypical newcomer begins from a small-scale society, where alliances are either knitted together among locals or through connections that extend to neighboring villages; self-sufficiency, isolation, and customary patterns of local social control reduce exposure to unknown outsiders. While existing contacts to friends and kin lubricate the movement to a new society, they cannot possibly reproduce the same level of encapsulation. The hometowners are a small element in a new context, whose size, heterogeneity, and complexity almost surely increase the probability of exposure to outsiders. The most relevant group of outsiders may turn out to consist of members of related categories, removed in terms of dialect, customs, and habit, and yet not so distant as to preclude effective contact. Notwithstanding the preference for familiarity, similarity will often suffice. Moreover, the prohibitions or suspicions that might have constrained relations back home no longer have the same force; the elders are not around and the power of loneliness is frequently sufficient to overcome all other restraints. Some migrants will end up venturing still further afield, if for no other reason than a taste for adventure and the chance encounters made more probable by the fluidity of life in a less structured context. As always, necessity is the mother of invention, the gender imbalance characteristic of so many migrations providing ample reason to effect alliances of a totally innovative kind. Thus, while the balance of relationships may shift toward connections with elements that were known, if unfamiliar, in the home context, others will extend to categories and groups entirely absent from the original interactional field.

For observers working from the standpoint of the host society, the only relevant shifts are those that can be mapped on to the categories it recognizes, regardless of how these correspond to the self-understandings of the persons whom one purports to describe. Thus what I might describe as the growth of an ethnic niche, using official census data that obscure differentiations below the national-origin level (for example, Waldinger 1996), may simply be a case of misplaced concreteness. From the standpoint of the home society, the environment that appears so homogeneous to the outsiders is more likely to represent unparalleled diversity. After all, relatively small shifts in the number of persons having out-group contacts quickly diminish the proportion of relationships that are entirely encapsulated within the group; before too long everyone has a contact that extends beyond the original circle.

While the new society offers opportunities for exposure far wider than those ever imagined back home, a variety of factors keeps the options circumscribed. At the bottom of the labor market, like meets like—which is to say, workers differing in ethnic and national origins but otherwise quite similar in social traits and related dispositions. To the extent that ethnicity and class bear little relationship, persons who qualify as outsiders by virtue of national origin will run into those who also lack acceptance, but by virtue of social class position. On the other hand, the forces that create the demand for immigrant workers tend to be the same as those that put native-born labor in short supply (Waldinger 1996). Past and present, there have been relatively few members of the American working class in those sectors of the economy where peasant migrants have made a living. Rephrased in somewhat more abstract terms, the potential for immigrant exposure to dominant group outsiders is limited by the degree of overlap in the distribution of other, relevant social characteristics. Where the occupational, educational, and geographic distributions barely overlap—as, for example, in the case of native-born Euro-Americans and Mexican immigrants in early twenty-first-century Los Angeles—these sets of strangers will frequently encounter one another as subordinates and superiors, but far more rarely as potential neighbors, friends, or intimates (Waldinger and Lichter 2003).

Moreover, exposure does not guarantee acceptance. Peasant migrants are preferred precisely because they are despised, a quality that makes them all the more desirable in performing a society's least desired tasks. As it happens, those tasks are dishonoring, which is why the stigma associated with dirty jobs rubs onto their incumbents. And all the worse if the children of immigrants retain their parents' stigma while acquiring American aspirations—in which case we can expect that they will be neither liked nor preferred (Waldinger and Lichter 2003). So migration may induce far-reaching changes in the ethnic social structure of any source population without in any way yielding the diminished differences between source and reference populations that are predicted by the sociology of assimilation.

To each, his—or her—own ethnic myth. Assimilation is the myth of the dissolution of ethnic boundaries as told from the standpoint of the nation-state society, which imagines itself to be a bounded, sharply demarcated entity. But the economic networks of goods, services, information, and people cut across any single nation-state society and other like units of the world, propelling migrants across those interactional cleavages—to borrow a concept from Michael Mann (1986)—that states try so hard to create. Even while noting states' remarkable effectiveness at bounding the unit they seek to enclose, it is our misfortune that this intellectual field crystallized just when the interactional cleavage at the national boundary was at its height—leading us to mistake a contingent event for an inevitability.

By contrast, retention is the myth of persistence, projected backward from a moment of relatively stable association and affiliation to an interactional field of a totally different type. In a sense, one myth is at the service of the other, the assumption of entitivity (Handler 1988) no less applicable, in the sociology of assimilation, to the immigrants than it is to the host society. Not for nothing do we have a concept with a digestive meaning, the very notion of assimilation implying the existence of foreign groups who are absorbed as their boundaries are dissolved.

But the idea of retention is no less fallacious, since the networks that breach the nation-state society simultaneously pull the migrants out of their home environment, progressively diffusing them across a broader interactional field. Consequently, the diversity of contacts, especially as measured against the interaction networks known back home, vastly expands. Since only a modest proportion of the home community ever leaves, one cannot ever recapture the same homogeneity of contact. No matter where one settles, the new environment is sure to be a place of high exposure probabilities to persons whose traits would have surely marked them as outsiders back home. On the other hand, members of the host population are incapable of making the same discriminations as insiders, leading to fundamental attribution errors, which provide the bases for new identities. If, back home, sensitivities to regional or linguistic differences rank high, they diminish or even collapse in the new context, thanks to the lumping efforts of the unknowing members of the native group. The ethnic moment is the time when an interactional field, whose internal ethnic differentiations are either slight or forgotten, takes hold; but the same forces that bring it into being will almost surely produce its demise. In the end, ethnic retention and ethnic assimilation emerge, not just as simplistic, but also as false polarities, two complementary ways of obscuring the reality we wish to understand.

ACCULTURATION

Like its twin, assimilation, the concept of acculturation has shown the capacity for absorbing innumerable intellectual beatings and yet endure. By acculturation our literature refers to the process by which an outsider group adopts the culture of the society into which it has moved. The standard complaints lodged against this particular conceptualization are too well known to merit extensive review (but see Alba and Nee 1998: 141–42). That there may be *a* host society onto which could be mapped a single, uniform culture is pure illusion; at best one can identify an amalgam of subcultures, varying by region or class, all of which are changing over time. Moreover, the notion that the transmission of tastes, styles, and beliefs between ethnic outsiders and insiders follows a single direction is just simplistic. Not only do the immigrants import a set of influences that diffuse far beyond the initial, bounded category. They and their descendants also engage in a new set of cultural activities—partially in an attempt to respond to or make sense of their new environment—that turn out to have broader, innovative effects. Case in point: the Jewish immigrant tycoons and the Hollywood they invented and sustained.

But complaints of this sort, which can be accommodated without much trouble, only begin to scratch the surface of the problem. As it is conceptualized in our literature, culture turns out to be nothing more than an inventory of traits. However, a trait inventory, as Michael Moerman (1974) has pointed out, is merely a list, and lists lack closure, which means that they cannot provide an adequate summary of the parts, let alone the cultural "whole" that they purport to represent. The difficulties get more serious when one asks how to identify the group (or category) to which the traits supposedly belong. Since ethnicity is a relational concept (Eriksen 1993), identifying some set of traits as characteristic of one group implies something about the features that typify some other—each of which is equally "ethnic," albeit in its own peculiar way. But then it turns out that "groupness" is precisely in question, proving too variable to support any fixed set of traits. As the boundary between groups is not given—but rather constructed, negotiated, and contested—it too needs to be understood as a cultural product. Of course, the same holds true for the categories—native and foreign, American and ethnic, "white" and "colored"—around which the boundaries are maintained.

If categories and boundaries are both cultural, then the bedrock distinction between acculturation and assimilation collapses. That opposition, as Herbert Gans (1998: 162) has written, rests on the contrast between culture and society, a difference that remains alive and well in our specialized literature but fares less well outside our native land. At the very least, we need to avoid assuming that the relevant actors are cultural dopes, to paraphrase Harold Garfinkel (1967), lacking a finely elaborated understanding of the social structures in which they may be encased. On the contrary, we would do better to ask about the everyday theories of the world with which ethnics on both sides of the native/immigrant divide work—that is to say, the intellectual and emotional toolkits that allow them to both make distinctions between "us" and "them" and also make sense of the consequences that ensue.

From this perspective, examining shifts in immigrant traits becomes secondary to understanding the evolution of immigrants' view of the world and their place in it. To ask that question, however, demonstrates a greater connectedness between culture and society than our usual approaches allow. Immigration, after all, is a transitional phenomenon, in which immigrants slowly give up the attachments that rooted them to their earlier lives. At the outset, immigrants begin with a "dual frame of reference" (Ogbu 1991), judging conditions "here" in light of the standards that prevail back "home," which means that they understand their condition relative to a benchmark that the native population does not share.

But meanings change as the frame of reference—and related social attachments—shift: "here" replaces "there" as the benchmark by which immigrants and their descendants judge their condition. While the foreign-born may consent to circumstances that natives cannot accept, the children almost always want more, having been exposed to different wage and consumption standards from the start (Waldinger and Perlmann 1998). However, the causes of second-generation revolt go beyond the strictly material—as economic disparities would not be a source of grievance among immigrants and the offspring were it not for the fact that the latter saw these differences as unjust.

Justice—and related political—frames change because acculturation transmits a native theory of American society, as well as the associated ways of acting and feeling. In "becoming American," immigrants come to understand themselves as candidate insiders in a loosely structured, democratic society where a special premium is placed on the expression and development of the individual self. But the gratified American self is likely to be more than a materially satiated self; an American self also derives a sense of worth from a situation of presumed equality with ethnic insiders. Therefore, the explosive potential is greater still, given that fully Americanized immigrants and their descendants will be unlikely to accept the subordination that the new arrivals take as a given.

Of course, the way in which one understands the world is related to the tools employed for comprehending it. For that reason, the diffusion of cultural patterns from insiders to outsiders yields an effect at considerable variance from what our standard accounts suggest. Contrary to the conventional wisdom, as epitomized by the so-called straight-line theory, one would do better to forecast a pattern of nonlinear change. Reducing cultural difference is probably the best means for increasing sensitivity to any disparities that persist. The better one reads, talks, and speaks the native code, the easier it is to see which of its promises have not been delivered; the more one has bought into the national creed, the more bitter the disappointment if one's expectations go unfulfilled.

Moreover, culture as theory of the world or worldview necessarily implicates insiders in ways that our conventional literature manages to elide. The distinction between native and foreign traits only holds if we assume that the latter are truly alien. Since the presence of social outsiders imported from beyond the boundaries of the state is a recurrent, and therefore native, phenomenon to the United States, the culture of its natives also encompasses their everyday, working theories of immigrants and immigration. Consequently, the culture shared by Americans includes a set of understandings about the boundaries that separate native-born insiders from immigrant outsiders, as well as interpretations of the conditions for membership in the American people and the meanings entailed by that status.

Thus the very recruitment of immigrant labor needs to be understood as a culturally informed, if not cultural, activity itself. Marxist or Marxist-inspired theories have it largely right: the dynamic, unequal nature of capitalist economies yields perpetual recourse to cheaper, more tractable sources of labor from beyond the society's bounds (for example, Piore 1979). Nonetheless, they assume what needs to be explained: namely, the existence of the categories distinguishing immigrant from native labor, and the understandings entailed in that discrimination. Let me put it crudely if not in the least bit unfairly: immigrants compose a group of workers whom their employers at once prefer but also despise. The employers' contempt is the stuff of the social psychological literature, a body of work that points to some universal cognitive mechanisms but which cannot explain the specific discriminations between particular groups of them and us in other than cultural terms. But the employers' preference for immigrants can be best understood as an everyday theory of immigrant labor, in which immigrants are perceived as that class of worker that evaluates conditions "here" in light of how bad they are "there." That quality makes immigrants preferable to the native-born alternatives, comprising people who set their sights on rewards a good deal higher than those available at the bottom of the totem pole. And thus we can see why immigration needs to be thought of as a property of the national culture, as native employers value foreigners, doing so precisely because they understand the immigrants to be different.[1]

If understandings about immigrants and immigration form part of the national culture, then those processes conventionally denoted as "acculturation" also entail the mechanisms whereby immigrants and their descendants become oriented toward insiders' views of ethnic outsiders. Those views need not always imply derision or rejection, and one can trace a shift, over the course of the last century, from more exclusive to more accepting understandings. On the other hand, our own literature reveals a continuing perception of immigrants as different, a preoccupation that can only suggest that such difference is a source of discomfort and trouble. Certainly, our older commentators took rejection of ethnic difference for granted; recall that Milton Gordon identified a decline of the prejudices held by insiders as one of the very *last* stages in his assimilation typology (Gordon 1964: 70–71). And the large majorities that continue to voice opposition to large-scale immigration, if only when asked (not to speak of the smaller, though more vocal group of nativists and restrictionists), do leave grounds for thinking that acceptance remains problematic.

Thus, in construing immigration as an occurrence of a foreign, and not native, type, both public and social scientific understandings construct the familiar as strange. From the standpoint of the self-proclaimed normals—that is to say, our literature's so-called majority group—difference appears undesirable. Moreover, the views of these particular normals count, not simply because they possess the key to acceptance and the goodies it unlocks; acculturation itself at once orients outsiders toward the standards of insiders and leads them to accept insiders' standards of judgment. From this point on, the analysis proceeds straightforwardly: as Goffman (1963) explained, the stigma associated with an ethnic or any other sort of difference at once confirms the usualness of the stigmatizer while discrediting the stigmatized. Since one is stigmatized by association, with the stigma spreading from the stigmatized person to his or her intimates, disaffiliation from the more stigmatized elements provides one route of obtaining acceptance. To quote Goffman, "the very notion of *shameful* differences assumes a similarity in regard to crucial beliefs" (1963: 131). Therefore, acculturation and stigmatization can turn out to be one and the same, as immigrants and their descendants display their growing attachment

---

1 For an elaboration, with empirical evidence, see Waldinger and Lichter 2003: chaps. 8 and 9.

to the host society by adopting the ways of the insider group and seeking their approval.

One can easily go further. In orienting themselves toward insiders' views, outsiders also accept the view that the reference group holds of the outsiders themselves. The outsiders wish to do more than simply erase the difference that separates them from insiders. They feel compelled to reject the very qualities of their own group to which insiders object, which not only belong to others of their originating kind but regrettably are to be found within the self. At its best, the result is the phenomenon of "double consciousness" described by Du Bois: "this sense of always looking at one's self through the eyes of others, of measuring oneself by the tape of a world that looks on in amused contempt and pity" (1999: 11). At its worst, the stigmatized outsiders find their way to self-hatred (Lewin 1948).

These are the terms that we do not usually find in our lexicon. After all, can we doubt that ours is an unself-consciously assimilationist sociology of assimilation when the author of our canonical text is none other than a Goldberg turned Gordon, the name change the symbolic equivalent of the nose job? Yes, one can concede that name changes and nose jobs are possibly motivated by a quintessentially American desire to start afresh. Still, we have to admit that some distaste for one's prior self almost surely plays a significant role. And is it an innocent—or revealing—slip that in the fifteen-page, double-column index to the recent 500-page *Handbook of International Migration* (Hirschman, DeWind, and Kasinitz 1998), there is not a single entry to stigma or self-hatred?

On the other hand, the stigmatizers of immigrant America—that is to say, the assimilation literature's "core cultural group"—do not always have the good fortune of encountering a human material equally susceptible to stigmatization. The peasant migrants of the turn of the twentieth century did not need a sociology professor to tell them that they were expected to act as inferiors, as that was the lesson they had absorbed in the old world, where the peasant's stigmatized status, relative to townsmen or aristocrats, was beyond question. And was there any reason to doubt the claims of the insiders who sought to Americanize them? After all, the United States was then the very acme of modernity, its material abundance and growing national power the demonstration of its superiority, as against the immigrants and the old worlds from which they came.

But today's immigrants have entered a different world, one where stigmatized outsiders have learned a new trick. Inversion was always one of the weapons of the weak: it is better to be "bad," as even squares like us know. But inversion is now utilized in self-conscious ways, with stigma at once revalued as the positive pole of one's identity, as Christian Joppke (1999) has pointed out, but also turned around, forcing the stigmatizers to confront their own shameful deeds. "Black is beautiful" was a revolutionary slogan, and all the more powerful because it worked. The ethnic revival of the late 1960s and early 1970s, so scorned by our literature, illustrates a glimmer of belated recognition: the young ethnic intellectuals of the time realized that their parents had swallowed the American dream hook, line, and sinker, when in fact they need not have gone so far. And while that particular ethnic revival had no hope—history had moved too fast—the new immigrants arrived just in time to take up the cultural toolkit that the civil rights revolution had invented and legitimated.

Moreover, today's immigrants are especially well suited to use this particular tool. Relative to the past, contemporary immigrants are distinguished by their considerable symbolic capital and competence; as for the less skilled immigrants, they tend to find a proximal host, equipped with the necessary intellectual arsenal. So even if Frederik Barth's (1969) crucial insight holds—the influence of America's democratic, consumerist culture quickly rendering ethnicity an empty vessel, absent of most content—the collectivities in which the immigrants participate have the capacity to both create and consume a symbolic content for the vessel that they inhabit. That symbolic capacity is fateful since the stakes involve the relationship between "who is what" *and* "who gets what." In that contest, today's immigrants fare relatively well, since the ability to tap into desired resources largely rests on the ability to legitimize some particular who.

ETHNIC GROUP—OR GROUPNESS?

If the sociology of assimilation prefers to ignore the identity of the insiders to whom the (at best, ambivalently welcomed) outsiders are to be oriented, it shows no similar shyness regarding the "them-ness" of the outsiders whose behavior it is so intent on describing. The literature makes that "them-ness" crystal clear: we are talking about the assimilation of "immigrant *groups*."

But it is groupness precisely that is at question. At the very least, the degree of groupness is likely to vary, a good deal lower among those categories of persons for whom groupness is embedded in a highly particular, place-specific way of life, as opposed to the self-conscious sense of belonging engendered by a process of nation-building. The peasant migrants of the past came from a set of folk societies, not yet nationalized and therefore not possessing the common traits and corporate sense that the nation-building project imparts. By contrast, today's newcomers typically arrive with a prior experience of nationalization, which means that they show up fully equipped with the resources for understanding themselves as self-conscious entities of an ethnic sort. Moreover, the capacity for groupness also hinges on the symbolic and cultural resources required to articulate an explicit understanding of groupness, that is to say, how I fit in with those "like me" and those who are different. From this standpoint, almost all of yesterday's migrations were lacking the human resources needed for the articulation of ethnic differences. In comparison, the extraordinarily high level of education characteristic of many of today's flows implies far greater symbolic competence, crucial for both elaborating and legitimating ethnic identities.

While I am suggesting that we think in terms of "groupness" rather than "group," much of our literature has moved in a different direction, largely out of an understandable reaction to the problems bequeathed by our intellectual legacy. The standard critique of the older literature starts with the point I predictably offered in *Ethnic Los Angeles*, namely, that the assimilation model seems to fit the trajectory of European-origin groups, but that "the historical experience of immigrants of non-European origin requires a different approach" (Waldinger and Bozorgmehr 1996: 18).

Rereading this sentence with some years' distance, I now realize that I failed to make an adequate case for a different approach; indeed, I am not certain that I made a case at all. But behind the confusion lay a common enough thought: that these two immigrations contained groupings of a fundamentally different sort. However impoverished or stigmatized, I thought, the European immigrants shared a common cultural and racial background with the majority whose acceptance they sought; by contrast, the non-European newcomers were far more distinctive, and on both counts. In effect, race mattered, to paraphrase the title of Cornel West's (1993) well-known book, facilitating inclusion in one case while hindering it in the other.

Unfortunately, this formulation mistakes cause and effect: acceptance did not occur because the European immigrants were white when they stepped off the boat; their children *became* white *in America*, which is what then allowed for inclusion. Not to make excuses, but my own failings reflect the shortcomings of our literature. The older scholarly formulations imagined the process by which immigrants became Americans as if it could be abstracted from the system of ethnic stratification into which the immigrants entered. Oscar Handlin wrought an earlier revolution in immigration historiography when he realized that the "history of immigration was the history of the American people"; in the process, he also excised a large portion of the people he purported to describe (Handlin 1951: 3). Thinkers of a slightly later vintage did not commit the same slip: they understood that the American ethnic order was made up of the descendants of those who had become Americans, not just by consent but by force as well. But in extending the field of vision, they also saw an identity among these outsiders of different sorts, as announced by Irving Kristol in his famous article entitled "The Negro of Today Is Like the Immigrant of Yesterday" (1966). Kristol was hardly alone. As Nathan Glazer noted in his introduction to the second edition of *Beyond the Melting Pot,* he and Daniel Moynihan had assumed that "Negroes and Puerto Ricans could be seen as the latest of the series of major ethnic groups that had … come as *immigrants*" (1970: xiii, emphasis added). As all groups had begun on the bottom, it followed that the blacks, like the European immigrants, would gradually move ahead. Similarly, Milton Gordon applied the same assimilation scheme to Italians, Jews, Negroes, and Mexicans, providing further indication that the scholarly authorities of the time understood these as minorities of a similar, if not necessarily the same, type.

Not only did the analysis proceed as if all groups of outsiders moved in at the bottom, confronting barriers of similar sorts. The underlying framework neglected the contrastive nature of the social identities that the immigrants and their descendants gradually absorbed, assuming instead that ethnicity is a property of the individual, like age or sex.

However, social identities are different: we know who we are only by reference to who we are not. Though acceptance came slowly for the descendants of the immigrants from southern and eastern Europe, it affected them in two quite different ways, transforming foreigners into Americans but also making them members of a majority that defined itself through exclusion. While the making of Americans was there for all to see, few scholars noted that majority necessarily implied minority. And so when the descendants of the European immigrants made an unexpected appearance in the late 1960s, they did so in a completely new guise, with the Poles, Italians, and others of the sort that were described as plain "ethnics" in Warner's Yankee City studies transformed into a new entity called the "white ethnics" (Novak 1972). Though it was never transparent just why and how "white" should modify "ethnic," rather than the other way around, few seemed to care, which is why this folk concept came to define an entire field of academic study.

Of course, today we know better, though it is depressing to note that historians, not sociologists, have been chiefly responsible for changing our views. A rapidly expanding corpus (see, for example, Roediger 1991; Ignatiev 1995) tells us that the once swarthy immigrants from southern, eastern, and even northern Europe eventually became white, which is another way of saying that "race" is an achieved, not an ascribed, status. One can try to reconcile this observation with the older assimilation story, contending that racial perceptions changed as the Irish, Poles, Italians, and Jews moved ahead, and were then able to move among the same people who had previously held them in contempt (see Alba and Nee 1998: 148–49). However, this formulation leaves out the essential, contrastive element: in becoming white, the immigrants and their descendants also became party to strategies of social closure that maintained others' exclusion (Nelson 2001).

But the whiteness literature only gets us so far. After all, the man and woman in the street will tell us that Jews, Italians, Irish, Poles, you name the group, are whites. We then still need reference to some other set of concepts to explain what the everyday categorization as "white" entails. The new literature's contribution is to remind us that the European immigrants were once not-quite-white, and that reminder underscores the fluidity that the everyday notions obscure. Yet having said this, we run the risk of circularity, describing this "not-quite-white" status in ways that make recourse to the concept of race itself. And once we have underscored the mutability of racial status, our customary option of contrasting groups of different kinds no longer holds. Though we say that a group has changed its colors, we really mean something else: it has now acquired eligibility for participation among established groups, all the while engaging in efforts to maintain boundaries against some other, more stigmatized entity.

Thus our newer scholarship too often maintains the vices of the old. It is one thing to argue that the struggle for place in a contested, ethnic order has historically provided ample motivations for newcomers to resolve the ambiguities over how their racial identities are to be defined (Orsi 1992). But it is another thing altogether to insist that these racialized categories represent real, substantial groupings of a fundamentally different sort. Though everyday language portrays insiders and outsiders as mutually exclusive, bounded entities, the reality is often otherwise, with the nexus between ethnic category and pattern of association varying from one dimension of social life to another. True, our unfortunate history has produced far too many situations in which excluded outsiders were never eligible for acceptance—whether as coworkers, neighbors, friends, or intimates. But it is also the case that rejection has often been replaced by acceptance, though only in some spheres and rarely without pushing and fuss. Furthermore, it is precisely the nonlinear nature of the shifts from rejection to acceptance—with interethnic contacts proceeding smoothly at work, for example, but ending the minute everyone leaves the job for home—that provides impetus for continued contestation.

Yet in phrasing the matter this way, we abandon the absolute distinctions implied by the concept of "race," adopting an analytic language that emphasizes the contrasts between outsiders of differing degrees of unacceptability, and those for whom membership in the national community can be taken for granted. We thereby convert the relationship between "them" and "us" into a multidimensional continuum: at one end of the continuum are situations in which acceptability is *never* a possibility; at the other end are situations in which acceptability is *always* a possibility and ethnic difference is of symbolic value only. In between lie many intervening points at which eligibility for acceptance occurs on one or more dimensions, but not all. In the end we gain purchase on the dynamic nature of ethnic life without succumbing to the groupist illusion that has so often clouded our vision in the past.[2]

CONCLUSION

As an ongoing effort to bound social relations at the territory's edge, the nation-state society can boast a record of considerable success. Not least among its triumphs ranks the everyday assumption that the nation comprises an entity apart, its separation from the rest of the world

[2] For further critique of the "groupist illusion," see Brubaker 2002; Brubaker's thinking on these and related matters has been an inspiration for many of the ideas developed here.

representing the normal state of affairs. While we could expect the man and the woman in the street to therefore regard immigration as an unexpected surprise, we run into problems if our own social scientific views similarly present immigration as a foreign, not native phenomenon. We would do better if we conceptualized immigration as a characteristic of our society and its insiders, who interact with the newcomers in ways that enhance, rather than diminish, difference. And we should also take insiders' understandings more seriously since the folk view of immigration as anomalous, immigrants as different, and difference as undesirable helps define the native theory of the world, which immigrants are in turn expected to absorb. The analytic task gets tougher because the response to immigration engenders a reaction among the newcomers themselves, in which new identities and forms of affiliation take hold. But the intensity of these attachments obscures their innovative, mutable character, if for no other reason than the extraordinary utility furnished by the image and idea of the bounded, ethnic group. While appreciating the compelling nature of ethnic identities, we should recall their relational foundation and remember that boundaries rarely enclose the same people at all times and in all places.

In the end, of course, we confront the intellectual difficulties that inevitably impinge on those of us who study a phenomenon of which we are also a part. This is our abiding dilemma and our greatest intellectual challenge.

References

Alba, Richard, and Victor Nee. 1998. "Rethinking Assimilation Theory for a New Era of Immigration." In *The Handbook of International Migration*, edited by Charles Hirschman, Josh DeWind, and Philip Kasinitz. New York: Russell Sage Foundation.

———. 2003. *Remaking the American Mainstream: Assimilation and Contemporary Immigration*. Cambridge, Mass.: Harvard University Press.

Barth, Frederik, ed. 1969. *Ethnic Groups and Boundaries: The Social Organization of Culture Difference*. Boston, Mass.: Little, Brown.

Brubaker, Rogers. 2001. "The Return of Assimilation? Changing Perspectives on Immigration and Its Sequels in France, Germany and the United States," *Ethnic and Racial Studies* 24, no. 4 (July): 531–48.

———. 2002. "Ethnicity without Groups," *Archives Europeenes de Sociologie*, November.

Du Bois, W.E.B. 1999 [1903]. *The Souls of Black Folk: Authoritative Texts, Contexts, Criticism,* edited by Henry Louis Gates, Jr. and Terri Hume Oliver. New York: Norton.

Eriksen, Thomas Hylland. 1993. *Ethnicity and Nationalism: Anthropological Perspectives*. London: Pluto Press.

Gans, Herbert. 1998. "Toward a Reconciliation of 'Assimilation' and 'Pluralism': The Interplay of Acculturation and Ethnic Retention." In *The Handbook of International Migration,* edited by Charles Hirschman, Josh DeWind, and Philip Kasinitz. New York: Russell Sage Foundation.

Garfinkel. Harold. 1967. *Studies in Ethnomethodology*. Englewood Cliffs, N.J.: Prentice-Hall.

Glazer, Nathan, and Daniel P. Moynihan. 1970. *Beyond the Melting Pot*. 2d ed. Cambridge, Mass.: MIT Press.

Goffman, Erving. 1963. *Stigma: Notes on the Management of Spoiled Identity*. Englewood Cliffs, N.J.: Prentice-Hall.

Gordon, Milton Myron. 1964. *Assimilation in American Life: The Role of Race, Religion, and National Origins*. New York: Oxford University Press.

Handler, Richard. 1988. *Nationalism and the Politics of Culture in Quebec*. Madison: University of Wisconsin Press.

Handlin, Oscar. 1951. *The Uprooted*. Boston, Mass.: Little, Brown.

Hirschman, Charles, Josh DeWind, and Philip Kasinitz, eds. 1998. *The Handbook of International Migration*. New York: Russell Sage Foundation.

Hollinger, David A. 1995. *Postethnic America*. New York: Basic Books.

Ignatiev, Noel. 1995. *How the Irish Became White*. New York: Routledge.

Joppke, Christian. 1999. *Immigration and the Nation-State: The United States, Germany, and Great Britain*. Oxford: Oxford University Press.

Kazal, Russell A. 1995. "Revisiting Assimilation: The Rise, Fall, and Reappraisal of a Concept in American Ethnic History," *American Historical Review* 100, no. 2 (April): 437–71.

Kristol, Irving. 1972 [1966]. "The Negro of Today Is Like the Immigrant of Yesterday." In *Nation of Nations: The Ethnic Experience and the Racial Crisis*, edited by Peter I. Rose. New York: Random House.

Lewin, Kurt. 1948. "Self-hatred among Jews." In *Resolving Social Conflicts.* New York: Harper Brothers.

Mann, Michael. 1986. *The Sources of Social Power*. Cambridge: Cambridge University Press.

Moerman, Michael. 1974. "Accomplishing Ethnicity." In *Ethnomethodology,* edited by Roy Turner. Harmondsworth: Penguin.

Nelson, Bruce. 2001. *Divided We Stand: American Workers and the Struggle for Black Equality*. Princeton, N.J.: Princeton University Press.

Novak, Michael. 1972. *The Rise of the Unmeltable Ethnics: Politics and Culture in the Seventies.* New York: Macmillan.

Ogbu, John. 1991. "Immigrant and Involuntary Minorities in Comparative Perspective." In *Minority Status and Schooling: A Comparative Study of Immi-*

grant and Involuntary Minorities, edited by Margaret Gibson and John Ogbu. New York: Garland.

Orsi, Robert. 1992. "The Religious Boundaries of an Inbetween People: Street *Feste* and the Problem of the Dark-Skinned Other in Italian Harlem, 1920–1990," *American Quarterly* 44, no.3.

Piore, Michael. 1979. *Birds of Passage.* Cambridge: Cambridge University Press.

Portes, Alejandro, and Rubén Rumbaut. 1996. *Immigrant America.* Berkeley: University of California Press.

Roediger, David R. 1991. *The Wages of Whiteness: Race and the Making of the American Working Class.* London: Verso.

Waldinger, Roger. 1996. *Still the Promised City? African Americans and New Immigrants in Postindustrial New York.* Cambridge, Mass.: Harvard University Press.

Waldinger, Roger, and Mehdi Bozorgmehr, eds. 1996. *Ethnic Los Angeles.* New York: Russell Sage Foundation.

Waldinger, Roger, and Michael Lichter. 2003. *How the Other Half Works: Immigration and the Social Organization of Labor.* Berkeley: University of California Press.

Waldinger, Roger, and Joel Perlmann. 1998. "Second Generations: Past, Present, Future," *Journal of Ethnic and Migration Studies* 24, no. 1.

Warner, W. Lloyd, and Paul Lunt. 1941. *The Social Life of a Modern Community.* New Haven, Conn.: Yale University Press.

Warner, W. Lloyd, and Leo Srole. 1945. *The Social Systems of American Ethnic Groups.* New Haven, Conn.: Yale University Press.

West, Cornel. 1993. *Race Matters.* Boston: Beacon.

3

Immigrants and African Americans: Comparative Perspectives on the New York Experience across Time and Space

Nancy Foner

At the dawn of a new millennium New York is, once again, an immigrant city. It is also home to a large African American population. New York's immigrants and African Americans are, inevitably, connected—indeed, the African American presence has had a significant impact on the lives of immigrants as well as on the scholarship about them. These influences and interconnections are, I believe, brought into sharper focus through a comparative lens that places present-day immigrant New Yorkers in historical and cross-national perspective. A look back in time to the city a hundred years ago, when African Americans were a small fraction of the population, and across space to London, where African Americans are noticeably absent, illuminates how the African American community shapes the "host city" context of reception and incorporation for today's immigrant New Yorkers. In this way the comparisons contribute to the goal of understanding the distinctive features of host societies as determinants of incorporation of immigrants.

The comparison across time involves the two great waves of immigration to New York City in the last hundred years: the first wave, between 1880 and 1920, brought hundreds of thousands of eastern Europeans and southern Italians to the city; the recent influx of Asians, Latin Americans, and Caribbeans began in the 1960s and is still going strong. In the first wave the African American community was insignificant, and the total black population did not even reach a hundred thousand. By the time of the second wave, the city had been on the receiving end of a massive flow of African Americans from the South that began around World War I and continued until the 1960s.[1] African Americans are now a major component of the city's population; they shape, among other things, debates about immigrants' impact on the economy and outlooks for the second generation, and they play a more important role than they did a hundred years ago in racial/ethnic identity formation among immigrant groups and in intergroup relations.

The comparison across space—between New York and London—is concerned with one group of immigrants—West Indians—in the contemporary era. From the 1950s to the early 1960s, there was an enormous West Indian migration to Britain, such that the West Indian population, which had measured some 15,300 in 1951, increased to around 500,000 by 1991, with over half living in London.[2] In New York City, West Indians from the English-speaking Caribbean, if counted together as one group, are now the largest immigrant group; in the late 1990s, foreign-born West Indians numbered about a half million (Foner 2001). The presence of the African American community has had complex and contradictory implications for West Indian migrants in New York. On the one hand, it has played a key role in insulating—or perhaps more accurately, segregating—West Indian New Yorkers from whites in neighborhoods, schools, and informal contexts in a way that has not happened in Britain. On the other hand, it has created opportunities for political and other alliances with African Americans. The presence of African Americans has also shaped West Indian attempts to maintain ethnic distinctiveness in a way that their cousins in Britain have not experienced.

NEW YORK IMMIGRANTS IN TWO ERAS

New York City has been transformed by two great waves of immigration in the twentieth century. Between 1880 and 1920, close to a million and a

[1] In 1910 the total black population in New York City was 91,709, with 87 percent native-born; in 1960 the total black figure was 1,087,931, with 94 percent native-born and the overwhelming majority of the native-born being either migrants or children of migrants from the South (Kasinitz 1992: 42). In 1930, for example, after several decades of heavy migration from the South, almost half of New York City's black population had been born in southeastern and south-central states (Osofsky 1963: 129).

[2] The figures for England are from Peach 1995. The 1991 figures include Afro-Caribbeans born in Britain. See also Owen 2001.

half immigrants arrived and settled in the city, so that by 1910 fully 41 percent of New York City's 4.8 million residents were foreign-born. Although they were not the only immigrants of the time, it was the enormous wave of eastern European Jews and southern Italians that defined what was then thought of as the new immigration. In 1880, just before the mass migration began, only 12,000 foreign-born Italians and 14,000 Russian Jews lived in the city. By 1910 the number of Italian immigrants had soared to 341,000, and Russian Jewish immigrants numbered 484,000.

The last great wave ended, of course, with immigration restrictions in the 1920s and the back-to-back cataclysms of the Great Depression and World War II. By 1970 only 18 percent of New Yorkers were foreign-born—a century low. This was soon to change. From the late 1960s on, immigrants have been streaming into New York City in another great wave. Altogether, more than two and a half million have arrived since 1965, and in the early 1990s they were entering at a rate of over 100,000 a year. By the late 1990s more than one out of three New York residents was foreign-born. No two groups predominate the way they did in the last great wave, and the newest arrivals are from countries all over the globe. In the late 1990s, according to Current Population Survey estimates, the top nine groups in the city, in descending order, were immigrants from the Dominican Republic, the former Soviet Union, China, Jamaica, Mexico, Guyana, Ecuador, Haiti, and Trinidad and Tobago. This includes over 400,000 foreign-born Dominicans, about 240,000 former Soviets, and almost 200,000 Chinese (Kraly and Miyares 2001).

In *From Ellis Island to JFK* (Foner 2000), I analyze the role of contextual features in New York City, along with the characteristics of the immigrants themselves, in explaining similarities and differences in the immigrant experience in the two eras—from where immigrants live and work to the dynamics of race and homeland ties, the nature of migrant women's lives, and the role of education. Today's immigrants are not only more diverse in that they come from a greater variety of countries and cultures than their predecessors, but they also exhibit much more occupational and class variety as well. Although many now arrive, as in the past, with little education and few skills, substantial numbers of the newest New Yorkers enter with college degrees and professional qualifications. The New York urban landscape has also undergone radical changes in every way, from its residential contours to its very economic foundations. Jews and Italians arrived at a time of industrial expansion, filling a seemingly insatiable demand for labor as the city churned out jobs. In today's postindustrial economy, there is no similar kind of growth, and the enormous outflow of native whites has been an important source of job openings. For immigrant women, a key change is that marriage no longer spells a retreat to the home; now they enter the labor force later and tend to stay, even when they have small children. And immigrant children now need more education to get ahead. Whereas a high school degree was all it took to move into a decent white-collar job in the past—and not even this was required for the many well-paid blue-collar jobs—now the supply of relatively high-paid, low-skill jobs has shrunk and a college degree is essential for the growing number of professional, technical, and managerial positions.

My concern here is with a comparative issue that I touched on only briefly in *From Ellis Island to JFK*: what difference it makes that a hundred years ago few African Americans were living in New York City, while at the end of the twentieth century they were not only a major population component, but they were also key players in the political, cultural, and social life of the city. The main emphasis is on how the size of the city's African American population has affected immigrants' relations and identities, as well as the popular and scholarly perceptions of immigrants. Of importance too is that blacks in early-twentieth-century New York faced more intense discrimination and more rigid racial barriers than they do today, and a much smaller proportion of immigrants themselves had African ancestry.

Immigrants and African Americans in the Last Great Wave

In 1910, New York was a city of European immigrants and their descendants. Only about 80,000 African Americans resided in the city—a little under 2 percent of the population.[3] Most were southern-born, giving New York's black community a southern flavor (Osofsky 1963: 32). Although an appreciable West Indian migration had begun at the start of the twentieth century—and continued until the mid-1920s—the numbers were small: in 1910, 12,000 foreign-born blacks lived in New York; by 1920 the figure was 37,000, representing 24 percent of the city's black population.[4] There were very few Hispanics: only 22,000 in 1916 (Haslip-Viera 1996 : 7).

---

[3] In 1910 only one census tract in the city, in the West 50s, had a black majority. In that year Harlem was more Jewish and Italian than black—home to some 100,000 Russian Jews, 72,000 Italians, and 22,000 blacks, the latter clustering in the newly built northwest sections (Gurock 1979: 49–50). Most blacks lived in the Manhattan neighborhoods then known as the Tenderloin and San Juan Hill, which stretched on the west side from around Twentieth Street to Sixty-fourth Street.

[4] Kasinitz 1992: 41. For full-length studies of West Indians in early-twentieth-century New York, see James 1998 and Watkins-Owens 1996.

What did these small numbers mean for the hundreds of thousands of Jewish and Italian immigrants who were pouring into New York City? For one thing, at the beginning of the twentieth century, questions of race were much more focused on these new immigrants than on African Americans. In 1910, after several decades of heavy immigration, foreign-born Italians and Jews were nearly a fifth of the city's population; ten years later, Italian Americans and Jews (including the American-born children of immigrants) numbered around 2.4 million, or 43 percent of the city's population. Their huge numbers made Italians and Jews a visible presence in the city—and a threat to the existing ethnic/racial order. Indeed, the main race issue in New York a century ago was the influx of what were then seen as inferior white races who were polluting the country's Nordic or Anglo-Saxon stock.

Many old-stock New Yorkers felt that the "deluge" of the newest immigrants was ruining the country, sweeping America, in the words of Madison Grant, toward a racial abyss (Grant 1916). Hostility toward the new arrivals was often put in racial terms: Jews and Italians were viewed as belonging to different races than people with origins in northern and western Europe (see Jacobson 1998). Jews and Italians looked different to most New Yorkers, and they were believed to have distinct biological features and innate character traits. The courts recognized them as white and they were seen as superior to blacks and Asians, yet they were not the equals of northern and western Europeans. Respected scholars, public intellectuals, and opinion leaders wrote about the "mongrel" races of Jews and Italians that were overrunning the country and diminishing the quality of American blood (see Foner 2000: chap. 5). The racial attack on southern and eastern Europeans was, as John Higham (1955) notes, a powerful ideological weapon of the movement to reduce immigration, helping to mobilize sentiment in favor of restriction. Genetic arguments about inferior races gave those wanting to cut immigration from southern and eastern Europe a scientific sanction; restriction against the new immigration seemed like a biological imperative.

If old-stock New Yorkers focused their anxieties about race on Jewish and Italian newcomers, this does not mean that they looked positively on blacks. Far from it. As Frederick Binder and David Reimers (1995: 110) observe, New York blacks confronted a "virulent racism in the late nineteenth and early twentieth centuries." In the racial continuum of the time, blacks were at the very bottom; racial notions underlying the response of whites to blacks were both deeper and more pervasive than toward European immigrants, wherever they came from (Lieberson 1980: 31, 34–35).[5] The second-class status of the city's blacks is illustrated by the August 1900 riot in which white residents in the West 40s Tenderloin District ranged through the streets and beat blacks who crossed their path. "Negroes were set upon wherever they could be found and brutally beaten," one journalist observed, and the *New York Times* noted that "Every car passing up or down Eighth Avenue ... was stopped by the crowd and every negro on board dragged out.... The police made little or no attempt to arrest any of [the] assailants" (in Osofsky 1963: 48). In fact, the police joined the assaults on blacks in the streets and in the jails. While some white newspapers criticized police brutality, there was "little chance ... that the city government controlled by Tammany Hall's Democrats would move against the police department ... and blacks had no influence whatsoever in Democratic party politics. Clearly racial hatreds ran deep, but blacks, constituting less than two percent of the city's population, could find few politicians willing to offer their support" (Binder and Reimers 1995: 113).

Interestingly, two years later, when Irish workers attacked a Jewish funeral procession on the Lower East Side and the police joined in assaulting the mourners—"Kill those Sheenies! Club them right and left!" shouted the police inspector in charge—protest rallies led Mayor Seth Low to appoint a commission that produced a devastating indictment of the police (despite the recommendations of Low's committee, the guilty policemen were exonerated by their peers) (Dinnerstein 1994: 71–72). Because Jews were a much larger proportion of New York's population than blacks—and had large numbers of regular voters in concentrated areas—they were able to win political influence and office not long after arrival.[6]

---

[5] However, it is interesting that in the 1890s landlords often considered African Americans preferable to "the lower grade of white people." In 1890 a New York newspaper reported a landlord who "remarked that he 'would rather have negro tenants' in his 'poorest class of tenements than the lower grades of foreign white people.' Negroes are 'cleaner' and 'do not destroy the property so much,' the proprietor concluded" (in Scheiner 1965: 32).

[6] Also a factor: Irish Tammany bosses gave Jews a number of positions to prevent their defection to the Socialists and Republicans. As early as 1900, Tammany "gave the nod" to a municipal court judge, Henry Goldfogle, who became the first Jew to represent the Lower East Side in Congress (McNickle 1993). Before 1920, Italians, the other large new immigrant group at the time, held fewer political positions and had less political influence than Jews. Italian political organization was slowed by the large number of returnees to Italy and the high illiteracy rate among Italian immigrants. Italians were slower than Jews to adopt citizenship or to register to vote. They were also less concentrated geographically than Jews: they neither dominated a district nor won a Tammany district leadership before World War I (Henderson 1976). Moreover,

Indeed, Jews had helped to elect Mayor Seth Low. As early as 1900 a Jew won a seat in Congress from the Lower East Side; in 1913 the East Side's Aaron Jefferson Levy became the Democrats' majority leader in the state assembly; and in 1914 the Lower East Side elected Meyer London as the first Socialist congressman from New York (McNickle 1993; Rischin 1962).[7] Blacks' access to political power was stymied in part by their lack of demographic strength.[8] It was not until 1945 that New York City sent its first black, Adam Clayton Powell, Jr., to Congress (see Lieberson 1980: 57–65).

What about African Americans' impact on immigrant relations and identities? Unfortunately we know little about relations between African Americans and the new Italian and Jewish arrivals at the time of the last great wave.[9] In the pre-1915 years, before the massive black migration to northern cities, Jews and blacks, as Hasia Diner (1995: 19) observes, did not really have much contact.[10]

This was less true of African Americans and Italians. Italian "pick and shovelmen," one historian writes, often "occupied a disquieting position between their black fellow workers and their 'white' supervisors and un-

---

Tammany was less worried about wooing Italians, who were more likely than Jews to give the Democrats a majority of their vote.

7 A Republican, Isaac Siegel, the son of Russian Jewish immigrants, represented East Harlem in Congress from 1914 to 1922, defeating Jewish rivals supported by Tammany and the Socialist Party (Gurock 1979: 73–85).

8 In 1900 the largest concentration of blacks in an assembly district in Manhattan was the 19th District, the area between 61st and 63rd Streets and between Amsterdam and 11th Avenues commonly called "San Juan Hill," where they were 13.8 percent of the total (Haynes 1968: 49).

9 As Diner (1997: 102) notes, the "actual history of Black-Jewish interaction has not yet been written. No historian has yet tackled such issues as Jewish business relations with Blacks or the way in which Jews and Blacks inhabited and used the same neighborhoods."

10 Generally, in this pre–World War I period, blacks and Jews did not meet in the world of work since they occupied very different niches in the economy (Diner 1997: 98). Nor did they live in the same neighborhoods, although there was some interaction in Harlem as working-class Jews began to move there after the turn of the twentieth century and as a small number of African Americans drifted northward into Harlem as well. Indeed, between 1910 and 1920 one Harlem census tract saw the number of Jews increase (from 600 to 730) as blacks became the overwhelming predominant group there (Gurock 1979: 148, 167). This was unusual. On the whole, blacks and Jews settled in their own well-defined sections of Harlem, and blacks did not make their "major incursion into the predominantly Jewish sections of Lower Central and East Harlem" until after World War I (Gurock 1979: 50). By and large, Diner (1997: 97) argues, Jews did not respond violently to the increasing black presence in Harlem, although reports of friction between Jewish homeowners and the increasingly large pool of black renters in Harlem showed up in the black press as early as 1908.

ion leaders" (Goldstein 1997). In churches, according to Rudolph Vecoli, Italians were often turned away or "seated in the rear with Negroes" (1969: 23). Still, African Americans and Italians in New York City basically moved in separate worlds, and it is unclear whether the interactions that occurred at work or at church led to a willingness to sympathize and fraternize with African Americans and/or to tensions and distancing in this early period (cf. Roediger 1994).

As for immigrants' racial or ethnic identities, in the pre–World War I era, distancing strategies from African Americans were not yet a significant component in Jews' and Italians' self-images. Granted, the word commonly used to describe Italians—"swarthy"—had such strong emotive power (and negative meaning) mainly because it linked Italians with blacks; an epithet for Italians, "guinea," had long referred to African slaves. Yet it was not until later decades—after the immigrant influx came to a halt, after Jews and Italians began to move up the social ladder, after a huge second generation was entering adulthood, and, significantly, after a sizable African American population was present in the city—that an important dynamic in eastern and southern Europeans' claims to membership in the racial/ethnic majority was setting themselves apart from blacks (see, for example, Jacobson 1998; Roediger 1994). Thus historians have noted that as Jews acculturated in the 1920s, 1930s, and 1940s, they marked themselves off as different from African Americans to attain the status of full-fledged whites (Goldstein 1997), although at the same time their history of persecution and exclusion in Europe led them to identify with the plight of African Americans (Diner 1995). A posture of sympathy for blacks, as Eric Goldstein argues, fulfilled Jews' emotional need to distinguish themselves as "whites of another kind" (Goldstein 1997).[11]

Finally, the tiny size of New York's African American population in the early twentieth century—along with intense discrimination against African Americans and their lack of political influence—helps to explain why questions of black-immigrant economic competition were not major public issues then and lacked the urgency that they have today. Not that

[11] With regard to Italians, historians disagree as to when a broad white identity developed among them. Orsi (1992), for example, argues that conflicts with black New Yorkers in Harlem in the 1930s contributed to the development of a white self-image among Italians, a process that was intensified by Puerto Rican migration into East Harlem in the prewar years. Luconi (2001: 125–26), however, argues that it was not until after World War II that Philadelphia's Italian Americans "renegotiated their ethnic identity beyond ancestral boundaries" in the context of an anti-black backlash in the 1960s and 1970s. On the complex question of Jews' and Italians' status as whites in light of recent critiques of the scholarship on whiteness, see Foner 2002.

such competition did not happen. It has been argued that the immigrant influx resulted in African Americans' eviction from trades where they had previously been accepted and their confinement to the most menial, least attractive jobs, such as janitors, elevator operators, and domestic servants (see Model 1993: 182; Waldinger 1996: 62, 141).[12] According to Suzanne Model, black barbers and caterers in nineteenth-century New York were serving a white population, but by 1910 immigrant competitors had captured most of the white market for these services (1993: 181–82). Roger Waldinger writes that blacks in New York City had a well-established role in the domestic production of clothing at the turn of the twentieth century, but the huge immigrant influx crowded them out of the industry (1996: 141).

Yet to the extent that immigrant competition in the labor market was an issue at the time, it was Irish laborers' resentment that took center stage as they were displaced by Italians on the docks and in unskilled construction work. The special hatred that the Irish harbored for Italians, writes one scholarly observer, was displayed in the job market. The "Irish workers struck back by attempting to intimidate the Italians and drive them away from the work site." In one of the more serious incidents, at a worksite in Mamaroneck (Westchester County), about two hundred Irishmen attacked a group of Italian workers who were receiving their monthly pay; the Irish injured several Italians and forced them and their families to abandon their homes and flee south to the Bronx (La Sorte 1985: 151; compare Kessner 1977: 57).

Immigrants and African Americans Today

Today, New York's African American population has a much greater impact on the new immigrants, and the effects of immigrants on African Americans are of much greater public policy concern. A substantial proportion of the latest arrivals are themselves of African ancestry; in the late 1990s more than a half million New Yorkers were born in the West Indies or Africa (Kraly and Miyares 2001). Also, the current immigration takes place in post–civil rights America, in which blacks have made enormous social and political gains. And, as I have stressed, African Americans are a significant segment of New York's population. In 1998, despite the heavy inflow of black immigrants, more than half (53 percent) of New York's

[12] Suzanne Model's (2001) analysis of 1925 census data for Manhattan shows that black men, whether native or foreign-born, were (compared to all New York men) overrepresented in transport and personal service jobs; black women mainly toiled in personal services.

black population was native-born to native-born parents—1.1 million people, or one out of seven New Yorkers. African Americans' numerical strength in contemporary New York—in combination with their residential concentration and the creation of minority legislative districts under the mandate of the Voting Rights Act—has given them political clout. By the 1990s, as John Mollenkopf (1992: 224) notes, blacks, in a nontrivial sense, had become part of New York City's political establishment, with relatively high rates of voter registration and turnout and electing representatives in proportion to their population size. In the 1990s, New York had a black mayor (David Dinkins) as well as numerous elected black officials in Congress and state and city legislative bodies (see also Mollenkopf 1999).

In this context, the issue of whether immigrants are hurting African Americans is of much greater concern to public commentators, scholars, and policymakers than it was a hundred years ago. And the evidence shows that immigrants are hurting segments of the African American population in the labor market. Low-skilled, poorly educated native-born blacks (and Puerto Ricans) have borne the brunt of the negative impact of immigration, and they are lagging behind their foreign-born peers. (Despite gains in the past few decades and the growth of the black middle class, large numbers of native blacks are low skilled and poorly educated.) Census data for 1990 show native blacks trailing immigrants on the bottom rungs of the labor market. Among those without a high school diploma, the foreign-born earned a third more than native blacks; their unemployment rates were half what they were for native blacks (Foner 2000: 101).

Why are native blacks lagging behind in these ways? One reason for lower unemployment among immigrants is that they are more willing to tolerate harsh conditions, low pay, and dead-end jobs because even rock-bottom wages look good compared to what they can earn back home and because many see their stay as temporary. Native-born blacks, particularly those who have come of age in post–civil rights America, have different expectations. To them, menial, minimum wage jobs that offer no possibility for upward movement and require deference to better-off, often white supervisors and customers are decidedly unattractive. They are less likely than immigrants to seek out these kinds of jobs in the first place, and when they do, they have less motivation to stay.

But it is not just a question of attitudes and expectations. The immigrant influx has contributed to making low-level jobs more unattractive to native workers by lowering wage rates. One analysis found that an increasing share of immigrant workers in jobs between 1979 and 1989 had a strong negative effect on native-born blacks' earnings in New York City (Howell and Mueller 1997). Many studies also show that employers prefer to hire immigrants, whatever their race or ethnicity, over native blacks and Puerto Ricans. Employers often see immigrants as willing to work hard and long for low wages, as reliable and pliable, and as likely to stay on the job; they often view native blacks and Puerto Ricans as a bad risk, fearing that native minorities will be less productive, less reliable, and less tractable than immigrants (see Kirschenman and Neckerman 1991; Kasinitz and Rosenberg 1996; Lee 1998; Newman 1999; Waldinger 1997; Wilson 1996).

Once immigrants become a dominant presence in particular firms, network hiring ends up perpetuating their advantage—and excluding native blacks and Hispanics. When private-sector employers rely on referrals from current workers—which saves time and money, is efficient, and reduces the risk in acquiring unknown workers—native minorities are out of the loop. They often do not hear about openings, which are rarely advertised, and when they do, they often lack a sponsor on the job. Moreover, once a particular ethnic group penetrates a workplace, employers are often reluctant to bring in native minorities for fear of interethnic conflict. And if the language on the shop floor is, say, Chinese or Spanish, native English speakers will not be able to communicate or fit in (Foner 2000; Kasinitz and Rosenberg 1996; Waldinger 1997).

Bear in mind that there is a positive side to the balance sheet. Without the addition of immigrants to the city's population base, there would have been less need for workers to supply public services of all kinds, and there is a strong African American representation in the public sector. In this way, immigrants have benefited the more skilled segments of the African American population that have entered government employment in large numbers in the last thirty years. Less happily, a recent analysis shows African Americans experiencing losses in public-sector jobs in the 1990s in the face of retrenchment in public employment—with other groups, particularly certain immigrant groups, gaining public-sector jobs (Wright and Ellis 2001).

Modern-day demographic realities—the size of the African American population as well as the large numbers of immigrants of African ancestry—have also affected racial/ethnic identity formation and intergroup relations in a way that did not happen in the past. Today the presence, and the continued stigmatization, of New York's huge African American community invariably shape the identities of the foreign-born. The city's ethnic-racial hierarchy has undergone a sea change in the last hundred years, and the once salient distinctions among white races are long forgotten. In recent decades, in the wake of the "new" immigration, New Yorkers have increasingly come to think in terms of a four-race framework of white, black, Hispanic, and Asian. Yet blacks remain on the bottom and, despite remarkable progress since the civil rights revolution, continue to suffer discrimination and prejudice. Black New Yorkers—native and foreign-born—continue to be highly residentially segregated from whites and other groups, thereby limiting informal social contacts at the neighborhood level. According to national figures, blacks have much lower rates of intermarriage with whites than Hispanics or Asians (see Foner 2000).

What does this mean for immigrants? For West Indians, it is in many ways a case of déjà vu. I discuss West Indian ethnic and racial identities more fully below, but a few points are worth noting here. Today, as in the first decades of the twentieth century, black West Indian immigrants develop new racial and ethnic identities in the New York racial context, where they confront racial discrimination of a sort unknown in their home countries, are defined as black ("Negro" a hundred years ago) on the basis of their African ancestry, and are lumped with African Americans. Now, as in the past, West Indians' relations with African Americans, whom they often live among and work beside, are a complex combination of conflict and cooperation and of distancing and identification (see Foner 2001; Kasinitz 1992; Watkins-Owens 1996).

Today, however, these processes and dynamics affect a much larger proportion of the city's population: the African American community is more than twelve times the size it was ninety years ago, and the West Indian community is fifty times the size it was then. (The astounding growth of the West Indian population is one factor behind the rise of a distinctly West Indian ethnic politics, something that did not exist in New York in the early twentieth century, when identification with African Americans was the key defining fact of West Indian public activities; see Kasinitz 1992.) Today as well, there are new black immigrants—most notably, a growing number of immigrants from Africa—who are subject to many of the same cross-pressures that West Indians experience in their relations with African Americans.

The impact of the African American community on immigrants' identities and relations is most deeply felt by immigrants who share a common African ancestry with African Americans and who are closest in phenotype to them—particularly West Indians and Africans. But the significant African American presence affects other immigrants as well. Dark-skinned Hispanic immigrants, who find it unsettling to be confused with African Americans, often engage in distancing strategies to avoid prejudice and discrimination; Mexicans, Robert Smith (2001) reports, make clear that they see themselves as "not black" and "not Puerto Rican." Asian Indian immigrants, whose darker skin color puts them at risk of being confused with black Americans, emphasize their ethnic identity and distinctive history, customs, and culture as a way to avoid such mistakes (see Lessinger 1995, 2001). Many South Asians, writes Margaret Abraham (2000: 13), have sought "identification with the dominant group by drawing the color divide between themselves and African Americans ... [and] used avoidance and disassociation strategies toward other minorities whom they perceived as unsuccessful."[13] Quite apart from distancing, some middlemen minority groups, especially Koreans, confront racial hostility from African American (and Afro-Caribbean) customers that occasionally has led to boycotts of Korean stores and even arson (Min 1996; see also Foner 2000: 164–65). This has a familiar ring, not unlike the hostility that Jewish shopkeepers and landlords in Harlem experienced, but black hostility to Jewish entrepreneurs was mainly an issue after the Great Migration from the South rather than in the pre–World War I period under consideration in this chapter (see Diner 1995: 79–81 on the 1930s period).

The presence of an enormous African American community—and large numbers of African Americans who are doing poorly in school—also has shaped debates about the second generation in a different way from the past. In the late 1990s over a third of New York City's public school students were non-Hispanic blacks, and as a group they were not faring well academically.[14] A common concern in the literature is that the children of immigrants will be contaminated by the negative attitudes said to prevail among native minority youth in inner-city schools. This is a contrast from concerns about the children of immigrants in the past. Educators a century ago did worry about the school progress of the second generation, particularly Italians, who had especially high dropout and truancy rates and were stereotyped by teachers as irresponsible and difficult to discipline. In the 1930s and 1940s, when high schools had become mass institutions, an oppositional culture flourished among Italian American working-class boys, involving a cynicism and hostility to school and teachers. There was no concern, however, in those years—or earlier in the

[13] In a similar vein, Vijay Prashad (2000: 94) observes that although South Asians in the United States "realize they are not 'white,'... there is certainly a strong sense among most ... that they are not 'black.' In a racist society, it is hard to expect people to opt for the most despised category."

[14] Unfortunately, Board of Education figures, on which this proportion is based, do not distinguish between native and foreign-born blacks.

century—that the children of the "new" European immigrants were absorbing the values of African Americans. Policymakers and educators in those days were worried about Italian Americans'—not blacks'—attitudes to education. (The Jews, of course, were another story; they were viewed as committed to education as a path to mobility.)

Something different is going on today. Many second-generation immigrants attend schools in inner-city neighborhoods with native black (and Hispanic) minorities with whom they share a bond of race or ethnicity. (The native minority children in New York schools, it should be noted, are themselves the children, grandchildren, and sometimes great-grandchildren of internal migrants from the South and Puerto Rico.) Following the lead of Alejandro Portes and Min Zhou (1993), many scholars worry that segmented assimilation will spell disaster for many second-generation youths as they adopt the peer culture of "downtrodden" native black and Hispanic ghetto schoolmates (see Portes and Rumbaut 2001).

The peer culture in inner-city ghetto neighborhood schools has its roots in the structure of opportunities and constraints facing native minority teenagers, including racial inequality, poverty and crime in their neighborhoods, and overcrowded, unsafe, poorly equipped, and often "out of control" schools with low academic standards. Whatever its origins, the peer culture is described as devaluing educational achievement and encouraging behavior that impedes academic success. In the past the oppositional culture that flourished among Italian American working-class boys was less of a problem; despite not doing well in school, they could enter the unionized blue-collar labor force and earn enough to support a stable and secure middle-class lifestyle.

In the present era the disappearance of industrial job ladders and increasing educational requirements in a technology-driven economy will, it is argued, consign those without much education to unskilled and low-paid service employment. Whether these predictions are correct is an open question (for more optimistic scenarios, see Foner 2000; Perlmann and Waldinger 1997; Waldinger and Perlmann 1998). Also open to question is how extensive an oppositional culture actually is among native minority—and immigrant—youth. What is clear, however, in New York City is that the experiences of many of the children of today's immigrants are deeply colored by their interactions with African Americans. Indeed, the children of immigrants are exposed to, and often adopt, the styles of African American youth culture, including music, dress, and speech patterns. Certainly this was not the case among Jews and Italians a century ago.

WEST INDIAN IMMIGRANTS IN TWO COUNTRIES

The presence of the large African American population and the dynamics of race in America have had enormous implications for the experience of West Indian migrants who come to New York—as an emerging literature attests.[15] A comparison of West Indians in New York with those in London brings this fact out in a particularly dramatic way, highlighting both the benefits and the drawbacks of residing in a city where West Indians live among a much larger population of native-born blacks.[16]

West Indians who arrive in London or New York must cope with living in a radically different racial order, where blacks are not just a minority but a disparaged minority (Foner 1978, 1983, 1985, 1986, 1987, 1998a, 1998b, 2001). In most West Indian societies, people of African ancestry are the overwhelming majority (the exceptions are Trinidad and Guyana, with their enormous East Indian populations), and there are hardly any whites or Europeans. That people with dark skin occupy high status roles (including dominant political positions) is unremarkable. "Blackness," as Milton Vickerman (2001a) puts it, is normal in the West Indies the way that "whiteness" is normal in the United States (see also Vickerman 1999). In the West Indies, moreover, there is a keen consciousness of shade; many people defined as "black" in the United States would not be seen this way in West Indian societies. Those who combine features from several types (African and European, Asian, and Middle Eastern) are traditionally considered "brown" or "colored"; blacks are generally thought of as impoverished individuals with African ancestry, dark skin, and certain facial features and hair type. Moreover, money "whitens." As individuals

15 For a review of this literature, see Foner 2001; Kasinitz 2001; Waters 1999.

16 The presence of the African American population is not the only significant difference between West Indians in Britain and the United States. Compared to the post-1965 West Indian migration to the United States, the post–World War II West Indian migration to Britain included a smaller proportion of professional and highly skilled individuals. The West Indian migration flow to Britain was also smaller in size. Moreover, the movement to Britain covered a much shorter period, beginning in the early 1950s and cut off by 1962 legislation; the mass movement to the United States dates from 1965 legislation and is still going strong. Other contextual features—from cultural features of the United States to the structure of the American (and New York) educational system—also influence West Indians in each country. Geography—that is, closeness to the Caribbean—also enables West Indian New Yorkers to visit and maintain contact with the Caribbean more easily than their counterparts in Britain. For a fuller comparative analysis of West Indian migration in New York and London, see Foner 1998a. For a comparison of the economic achievements of West Indians in Britain and the United States, also see Model 1997; Model and Ladipo 1996; Model, Fisher, and Silberman 1999.

improve their income, education, lifestyle, and wealth, they seem progressively "whiter"; two individuals with the exact same skin coloring can be seen as different degrees of white or black if one is middle class and the other poor (Waters 1999: 30). What matters above all else are education, wealth, manners, and well-placed associates, not race.

In both Britain and the United States, education, income, and culture do not partly "erase" one's blackness. Nor are whites sensitive to shade differences. Whatever their achievements or their shade, West Indians find themselves subject to prejudice and discrimination of a sort they had not encountered back home. They come up against racial barriers in housing and employment. They confront hostility from sections of the white population. And for the first time they become acutely and painfully aware that black skin is a significant status marker. In a real sense West Indians learn to "become black" in America and Britain. "I wasn't aware of my color till I got here," one New York man told me. In nearly identical words, a London migrant said that he had never known he was black until he came to England.

Yet there are crucial differences in the London and New York experience. Being submerged in a wider African American community in New York has affected West Indians there in ways that their London counterparts simply do not encounter. For one thing, West Indians in New York are less visible to the white population than West Indians in London. When they moved to Britain in the 1950s and 1960s, West Indians, along with immigrants from India and Pakistan, entered a society that, in racial terms, was homogeneous and white. In the course of political debate, in media treatment of topics connected with them, and in statements by public officials, black immigrants were stigmatized as inferior. Whereas West Indians in London have a history of being seen in the public eye as a problem or threat to the British way of life, in New York they are often seen as part of a sea of anonymous black faces, undifferentiated from the wider black population. As West Indians have grown in numbers and become a much larger proportion of black New York, they are increasingly visible to white New Yorkers (see Kasinitz 2001; Waters 1999); yet West Indians still often find themselves lumped with black Americans. Even when other New Yorkers recognize them as West Indian, foreign, or, as many whites say, "from the islands," West Indians are perceived as an ethnic group within the larger black population. And this means being identified with African Americans.

One response has been to emphasize their ethnic identity as West Indians as a way to distinguish themselves from, and avoid the stigma associated with, African Americans. Many West Indians assert an ethnic identity in order to make a case that they are culturally different from and superior to black Americans, emphasizing their strong work ethic, their valuing of education, and their lack of antisocial behaviors (see also Waters 1999: 64–76). In my research among Jamaican New Yorkers, I was often told that Jamaicans are more likely than American blacks to buy homes and that they place more value on education and discipline. Many felt that when whites found out they were Jamaican and not African American, they were viewed and treated more favorably. "Once you say something," one man explained, "and they recognize you're not from this country, they treat you a little different" (Foner 1987). To what extent this is actually the case is hard to say (for a discussion of this issue, see Waters 1999). What is clear, however, is that many West Indian New Yorkers believe it to be true, and the belief itself further bolsters their sense of ethnic pride and distinctiveness and their feeling of superiority to African Americans. This is in contrast to London, where "blacks" is generally synonymous with West Indians (or Africans), and stressing West Indianness, as David Lowenthal (1978) has remarked, is "seldom affirmative." When an Afro-Caribbean television producer in London complains, "here we behave like black Americans in northern cities; our experience is the just the same as that of blacks who migrated from the South to Chicago," he is, I think, getting at the notion that in Britain West Indians are the structural equivalents of American blacks. In New York, by contrast, West Indians feel (and are sometimes viewed as) superior to African Americans (Trevor Phillips, quoted in Gates 1997: 200).

Paradoxically, the extraordinary residential segregation that West Indian New Yorkers experience has produced some benefits. West Indians, like African Americans, tend to be confined to areas of New York City that have large black concentrations, where they are residentially isolated from non-Hispanic whites and most other groups. In 1990 the index of dissimilarity between West Indians and non-Hispanic whites in New York City was 82, almost the same as for African Americans (84). West Indians have carved out distinct enclaves within the larger black sections of the city (in Brooklyn, Queens, and the Bronx), yet overall they are not very segregated from African Americans; in 1990 the dissimilarity index comparing West Indians and African Americans (42) was in the mid-moderate range. In fact, West Indians were less segregated from African Americans than from any other group (Crowder and Tedrow 2001). In analyzing black residential patterns in the city between 1970 and 1990, Arun Peter Lobo and Joseph Salvo (2000) describe a process whereby West Indians pioneered the movement into formerly white neighborhoods, to be joined by native blacks looking for housing.

That New York West Indians live out much of their lives apart from whites reduces the opportunities for racial tensions and conflicts to develop. When West Indians walk in the street, shop, talk to neighbors, worship, and send their children to school, it is mostly other blacks whom they see and with whom they deal. Said one black Briton: "I love going to New York because I can walk down the street and the place is full of black people" (in Gates 1997: 201). Although many West Indians distance themselves from African Americans, at the same time strong affinities draw the two groups together, so that West Indians are caught in a welter of contradictory pressures, or cross-pressures, of ethnic separatism and racial identification (Vickerman 2001a). Members of the second generation feel a much closer identification with African Americans than do their immigrant parents because they are American by birth and have assimilated into the African American community (Vickerman 1999, 2001b).

As much as West Indians in London move in West Indian social circles, they are less insulated from contact with whites. Despite the fairly dense concentration of West Indians in particular areas and particular streets of London, there is not the same pattern of residential segregation found in New York. Ceri Peach's (1995) analysis of the 1991 census found that the index of dissimilarity for London's black Caribbean population at the enumeration district level (the smallest census unit, about 700 people) was 49 percent; only 3 percent of the black Caribbean population of London lived in enumeration districts in which they formed 30 percent or more of the population (see also Glazer 1999). According to another analysis of 1991 census data, over three-quarters of London's Afro-Caribbeans lived in areas where whites were the majority population (Johnston, Forrest, and Poulsen 2002). In black sections of New York, as one West Indian activist in London pointed out, you can walk about and not see a white face except in a passing car. "But that's not the case in Britain. We see them every day. We move with them every day" (in Cockburn and Ridgeway 1982). Brixton (in south London) may be a heavily West Indian neighborhood, but as Henry Louis Gates (1997) notes, "Americans who imagine Brixton to be analogous to Harlem are always surprised to see how large its white population is." In the 1970s many incidents that London migrants told me to illustrate their experience with racial prejudice involved contacts with whites in the neighborhood—queuing for buses, buying groceries at the corner, speaking to neighbors, or observing fights between local white and black children (Foner 1978).

The presence of the large native African American population affects the way that West Indians participate in the political process. Even though most West Indians in New York cannot vote because they are not naturalized citizens, from the very start they have tended, unlike their English counterparts, to live in districts where black voters predominated and where they were represented in city, state, and federal legislative bodies by black politicians who spoke for black interests. Gaining political office has taken longer in London, and blacks do not have as much political clout as in New York. In New York City, non-Hispanic blacks are the most reliably Democratic of any voting group and a significant racial/ethnic component of the electorate; in 2000 they were about a quarter of the city's voters and a third of Democratic primary voters (Mollenkopf 1992, 2001).

The shared experience of being black in America and West Indians' identification with African Americans around a "linked racial outlook" provide a basis for coalition building. West Indians often unite with African Americans in a black bloc, especially when black and white interests are seen as being in conflict (Kasinitz 1992; Rogers 2001). By the same token, as Reuel Rogers (2001) argues, a politically unified black community does not exist on all issues and in all political contexts, in part because West Indians have a different frame of reference than African Americans for making sense of the political world (see also Vickerman 2001a). Indeed, West Indian politicians in New York increasingly play the ethnic card to appeal to the growing number of West Indian voters, and some local elections have been fought, quite explicitly, between native-born blacks and Caribbean blacks. A recent example was the fight between Major Owens (African American) and Una Clarke (Jamaican) in a Brooklyn Democratic primary for Congress (which Owens won).

Part of the romance with America among black Britons, Henry Louis Gates (1997: 202) notes, has to do with a sense that America "has, racially speaking, a critical mass." In fact, West Indian New Yorkers have benefited from political initiatives put in place as a result of the gains African Americans won in the civil rights movement. Una Clarke owed her seat on the city council to redistricting in Brooklyn in the wake of the Voting Rights Act. West Indians have also reaped rewards from affirmative action programs and policies designed to assist African Americans in gaining access to government employment as well as entry and scholarships to colleges and universities—programs that do not exist in Britain. In addition to programs promoting black educational achievement, the African American community has provided first- and second-generation West Indian New Yorkers with a market for goods and services (Kasinitz 2001). For aspiring West Indian Americans, incorporation into the growing African American middle-class "minority culture of mobility" has also offered strategies for economic mobility, including black professional and fraternal associations and organizations of black students in racially integrated high schools and universities (see Neckerman, Carter, and Lee 1999).

There is, of course, another side to the story. Being submerged in black America—and living in such highly residentially segregated neighborhoods—brings many disadvantages. Residential segregation in New York may reduce the likelihood for day-to-day conflicts with whites to develop at the neighborhood level, but it also reduces opportunities for friendships with whites in informal settings and for West Indians and whites to become comfortable with each other in noninstitutional and nonwork locations. Listen, again, to Henry Louis Gates, an African American observer of the British scene: "I'm always struck by the social ease between most blacks and whites on London streets. I was recently near the Brixton market ... and two men—tall, coal-black, muscle-bound—came loping toward a small young white woman who was walking by herself in the opposite direction. What happened then was—well nothing. The needle on the anxiety meter didn't so much as quiver. Throughout the area, blacks and whites seemed comfortable with one another in a way that most American urbanites simply aren't and never have been" (1997: 201). Whereas most West Indians in New York attend virtually all-black schools in ghetto neighborhoods, in London their classmates are often white children. Britain also offers a more hospitable environment for black-white interracial unions. An analysis of 1990 U.S. and 1991 U.K. census data shows that Black Caribbeans in Britain are significantly more likely than their U.S. counterparts to have a white partner: in the United States only 3 percent of foreign-born West Indian men and 2 percent of foreign-born West Indian women had a native white partner; the comparable figures for foreign-born West Indian men and women in Britain were 18 percent and 8 percent, respectively. Among the native-born, 12 percent of West Indian men and 9 percent of West Indian women in the United States had a native white partner; in Britain, the figures were 40 percent for native-born West Indian men and 24 percent for native-born West Indian women (Model and Fisher 2002).

The American racial situation has also shaped scholarship on West Indians so that in the United States, unlike in Britain, West Indians are constantly compared with African Americans rather than with other groups. This has led to a situation, Philip Kasinitz (2001) argues, in which scholarship on West Indians has ignored or minimized the significance of certain critical features of their economic incorporation. Although researchers have paid much attention to the fact that West Indians are slightly more entrepreneurial than African Americans, they have largely missed the significance of the lack of an autonomous West Indian economic enclave and of West Indians' low self-employment rates compared with those of other immigrant groups. Also, because African Americans in New York are well represented in public-sector employment, it is not considered particularly noteworthy that West Indians' rates in this sector are also relatively high. Often overlooked is that they have extremely high rates of public-sector employment compared with other immigrant New Yorkers.

CONCLUSION

Whether comparing West Indians in New York and London, or immigrant New Yorkers today and a century ago, an exploration of immigration across time and space illustrates how features of the host society shape the immigrant experience. In this chapter, I have focused on one particular contextual feature in New York: the presence—and demographic weight—of the African American community. Although African Americans have long been central in the dynamics of race in the United States, at the beginning of the twentieth century, before the Great Migration from the South, African Americans were a tiny proportion of the city's population. After decades of heavy internal black migration this was no longer the case, and the huge numbers of African Americans in New York have had a significant impact on the way that contemporary immigrants experience life in New York, as well as on scholarly analysis of these experiences.

Demography is not destiny, and numbers alone are not what makes the African American presence so significant. Attitudes and policies toward people with African ancestry—and the continuation of the color line in American society—are what set African Americans apart and underpin conceptions by others, and by African Americans themselves, that they are a stigmatized racial group. It is wise to recall that African Americans had only just been released from slavery when the last great wave of European immigration began, and not until the civil rights revolution of the 1960s would the structures of segregation in the American South begin to be dismantled.

If immigrants today often try to distance themselves from African Americans, this is owing to the wider society's view of African Americans. Although some immigrants bring negative views of blacks with them from their home countries (see, for example, Abraham 2000 on Asian Indians; Min 1996 on Koreans; Levitt 2001 on Dominicans), many acquire these prejudices in the United States. Whatever immigrants' attitudes on arrival, part of the process of becoming American is learning America's culture of race and learning that identification with African Americans is something they may wish to avoid. This dynamic, of course, is absent in Britain, where post–World War II black immigrants and their descendants are *the* nation's blacks.[17] This has drawbacks for Afro-Caribbeans in London, who cannot profit from alliances with a large native black community or "piggyback" on gains won by African Americans. At the same time, the racial system in London is less rigid than in New York, where West Indians find themselves more segregated residentially and less likely to intermarry with whites.

I have described the contemporary experience for New York immigrants, but continued immigration will bring new changes and new demographic realities. With increased immigration from the West Indies and continued out-migration of native blacks, New York City's black population will become more and more Caribbeanized and, with growing African immigration, probably more Africanized as well. At the same time, a second and third generation of black immigrants are coming of age, and the question is whether they will become part of black America, as happened in the past, or whether, particularly under conditions of immigrant replenishment, significant sectors will retain a strong ethnic identity. One observer has suggested that the large-scale West Indian migration is one factor beginning to "tweak" monolithic notions of "blackness" in New York by enhancing the visibility of ethnic differences within the African ancestry population (Vickerman 2001b). Less optimistic are predictions that continued immigration will lead to a black/nonblack racial order, in which an Asian-Hispanic-white melting pot will be offset by a minority comprising those with African ancestry—African Americans, black Caribbean and African immigrants, and Hispanics of visible African heritage (see Foner 2000; Gans 1999; Waters 1999). If this comes to pass, then the distancing strategies observed among many contemporary immigrant groups are likely to continue as these groups try to ensure their position on the "right" side of the color line. In 1903 W.E.B. Du Bois wrote that the problem of the twentieth century is the problem of the color line; this may also prove, unfortunately, to be true well into the twenty-first century.

---

[17] Whether the notion of "blackness" in Britain encompasses Asians as well as Afro-Caribbeans and Africans has been a subject of debate. Although activists in Britain have been reconstructing black identity to encompass people of Asian, African, and Caribbean descent, "black" commonly refers to those of African ancestry, with Asians viewed as not black, as "ambiguous blacks," or as occupying a space between black and white (Sudbury 2001; Alexander 1996).

References

Abraham, Margaret. 2000. *Speaking the Unspeakable: Marital Violence among South Asian Immigrants in the United States.* New Brunswick, N.J.: Rutgers University Press.

Alexander, Claire. 1996. *The Art of Being Black.* Oxford: Clarendon Press.

Binder, Frederick M., and David M. Reimers. 1995. *All the Nations under Heaven: An Ethnic and Racial History of New York City.* New York: Columbia University Press.

Cockburn, Andrew, and James Ridgeway. 1982. "The Revolt of the Underclass," *Village Voice,* January.

Crowder, Kyle, and Lucky Tedrow. 2001. "West Indians and the Residential Landscape of New York." In *Islands in the City: West Indian Migration to New York,* edited by Nancy Foner. Berkeley: University of California Press.

Diner, Hasia. 1995 [1977]. *In the Almost Promised Land: American Jews and Blacks, 1915–1935.* 2d ed. Baltimore, Md.: Johns Hopkins University Press.

———. 1997. "Between Words and Deeds: Jews and Blacks in America, 1880–1935." In *Struggles in the Promised Land: Toward a History of Black-Jewish Relations in the United States,* edited by Jack Salzman and Cornel West. New York: Oxford University Press.

Dinnerstein, Leonard. 1994. *Anti-Semitism in America.* New York: Oxford University Press.

Du Bois, W.E.B. 1990 [1903]. *The Souls of Black Folk.* New York: Vintage Books.

Foner, Nancy. 1978. *Jamaica Farewell: Jamaican Migrants in London.* Berkeley: University of California Press.

———. 1983. "Jamaican Migrants: A Comparative Analysis of the New York and London Experience." Occasional Paper 36. New York: Center for Latin American and Caribbean Studies, New York University.

———. 1985. "Sex Roles and Sensibilities: Jamaican Women in New York and London." In *International Migration: The Female Experience,* edited by Rita Simon and Caroline Brettell. Totowa, N.J.: Rowman and Allenheld.

———. 1986. "Race and Color: Jamaican Migrants in New York and London," *International Migration Review* 19: 708–27.

———. 1987. "The Jamaicans: Race and Ethnicity among Migrants in New York City." In *New Immigrants in New York,* edited by Nancy Foner. New York: Columbia University Press.

———. 1998a. "Towards a Comparative Perspective on Caribbean Migration." In *Caribbean Migration: Globalised Identities,* edited by Mary Chamberlain. London: Routledge.

———. 1998b. "West Indian Identity in the Diaspora: Comparative and Historical Perspectives," *Latin American Perspectives* 25: 173–88.

———. 2000. *From Ellis Island to JFK: New York's Two Great Waves of Immigration.* New Haven, Conn.: Yale University Press.

———. 2001. "West Indian Migration to New York: An Overview." In *Islands in the City: West Indian Migration to New York*, edited by Nancy Foner. Berkeley: University of California Press.

———. 2002. "Response," *Journal of American Ethnic History* 21: 102–19.

Gans, Herbert. 1999. "The Possibility of a New Racial Hierarchy in the Twenty-First Century United States." In *The Cultural Territories of Race: Black and White Boundaries*, edited by Michele Lamont. Chicago: University of Chicago Press.

Gates, Henry Louis. 1997. "Black London," *The New Yorker*, April 28, pp. 194–205.

Glazer, Nathan. 1999. "Comment on 'London and New York: Contrasts in British and American Models of Segregation' by Ceri Peach," *International Journal of Population Geography* 5: 319–51.

Goldstein, Eric. 1997. "A White Race of Another Kind: Immigrant Jews and Whiteness in the Urban North, 1914–1945." Paper presented at a meeting of the Organization of American Historians, San Francisco.

Grant, Madison. 1916. *The Passing of the Great Race*. New York: Scribners.

Gurock, Jeffrey S. 1979. *When Harlem Was Jewish, 1870–1930*. New York: Columbia University Press.

Haslip-Viera, Gabriel. 1996. "The Evolution of the Latino Community in New York City: Early Twentieth Century to the Present." In *Latinos in New York*, edited by Gabriel Haslip-Viera and Sherrie Baver. Notre Dame, Ind.: University of Notre Dame Press.

Haynes, George E. 1968 [1912]. *The Negro at Work in New York City*. New York: Arno.

Henderson, Thomas M. 1976. *Tammany Hall and the New Immigrants: The Progressive Years*. New York: Arno.

Higham, John. 1955. *Strangers in the Land*. New Brunswick, N.J.: Rutgers University Press.

Howell, David, and Elizabeth Mueller. 1997. "The Effects on African-American Earnings: A Jobs-Level Analysis of the New York City Labor Market, 1979–1989." Working Paper No. 210. Annandale-on-Hudson, N.Y.: The Jerome Levy Economics Institute, Bard College.

Jacobson, Matthew. 1998. *Whiteness of a Different Color: European Immigrants and the Alchemy of Race*. Cambridge, Mass.: Harvard University Press.

James, Winston. 1998. *Holding Aloft the Banner of Ethiopia: Caribbean Radicalism in Early Twentieth Century America*. London: Verso.

Johnston, Ron, James Forrest, and Michael Poulsen. 2002. "Are There Ethnic Enclaves/Ghettos in English Cities?" *Urban Studies* 39: 591–618.

Kasinitz, Philip. 1992. *Caribbean New York*. Ithaca, N.Y.: Cornell University Press.

———. 2001. "Invisible No More? West Indian Americans in the Social Scientific Imagination." In *Islands in the City: West Indian Migration to New York*, edited by Nancy Foner. Berkeley: University of California Press.

Kasinitz, Philip, and Jan Rosenberg. 1996. "Missing the Connection: Social Isolation and Employment on the Brooklyn Waterfront," *Social Problems* 43: 180–96.

Kessner, Thomas. 1977. *The Golden Door: Italian and Jewish Immigrant Mobility in New York City, 1880–1915*. New York: Oxford University Press.

Kirschenman, Joleen, and Kathryn Neckerman. 1991. "We'd Love to Hire Them, But—: The Meaning of Race for Employers." In *The Urban Underclass,* edited by Christopher Jencks and Paul Peterson. Washington, D.C.: The Brookings Institution.

Kraly, Ellen Percy, and Ines Miyares. 2001. "Immigration to New York: Policy, Population and Patterns." In *New Immigrants in New York,* edited by Nancy Foner. 2d ed. New York: Columbia University Press.

La Sorte, Michael. 1985. *La Merica: Images of Italian Greenhorn Experience*. Philadelphia, Penn.: Temple University Press.

Lee, Jennifer. 1998. "Cultural Brokers: Race-based Hiring in Inner City Neighborhoods," *American Behavioral Scientist* 41: 927–37.

Lessinger, Johanna. 1995. *From the Ganges to the Hudson*. Boston: Allyn and Bacon.

———. 2001. "Class, Race, and Success: Two Generations of Indian Americans Confront the American Dream." In *Migration, Transnationalization, and Race in a Changing New York,* edited by Héctor Cordero-Guzmán, Robert Smith, and Ramon Grosfoguel. Philadelphia, Penn.: Temple University Press.

Levitt, Peggy. 2001. *The Transnational Villagers*. Berkeley: University of California Press.

Lieberson, Stanley. 1980. *A Piece of the Pie: Blacks and White Immigrants since 1880*. Berkeley: University of California Press.

Lobo, Arun Peter, and Joseph Salvo. 2000. "The Role of Nativity and Ethnicity in the Residential Settlement Patterns of Blacks in New York City, 1970–1990." In *Immigration Today: Pastoral and Research Challenges,* edited by Lydio Tomasi and Mary Powers. New York: Center for Migration Studies.

Lowenthal, David. 1978. "West Indian Emigrants Overseas." In *Caribbean Social Relations,* edited by Colin Clarke. Monograph No. 8. Liverpool: Center for Latin American Studies, University of Liverpool.

Luconi, Stefano. 2001. *From Paesani to White Ethnics: The Italian Experience in Philadelphia*. Philadelphia, Penn.: Temple University Press.

McNickle, Chris. 1993. *To Be Mayor of New York*. New York: Columbia University Press.

Min, Pyong Gap. 1996. *Caught in the Middle: Korean Communities in New York and Los Angeles*. Berkeley: University of California Press.

Model, Suzanne. 1993. "The Ethnic Niche and the Structure of Opportunity: Immigrants and Minorities in New York City." In *The "Underclass" Debate: Views from History,* edited by Michael Katz. Princeton, N.J.: Princeton University Press.

———. 1997. "An Occupational Tale of Two Cities: Minorities in London and New York," *Demography* 34: 539–50.

———. 2001. "Where West Indians Work." In *Islands in the City: West Indian Migration to New York,* edited by Nancy Foner. Berkeley: University of California Press.

Model, Suzanne, and Gene Fisher. 2002. "Unions between Blacks and Whites: England and the U.S. Compared," *Ethnic and Racial Studies* 25: 728–54.

Model, Suzanne, Gene Fisher, and Roxane Silberman. 1999. "Black Caribbeans in Comparative Perspective," *Journal of Ethnic and Migration Studies* 25: 187–212.

Model, Suzanne, and David Ladipo. 1996. "Context and Opportunity: Minorities in New York and London," *Social Forces* 75: 485–510.

Mollenkopf, John. 1992. *A Phoenix in the Ashes: The Rise and Fall of the Koch Coalition in New York City Politics*. Princeton, N.J.: Princeton University Press.

———. 1999. "Urban Political Conflicts and Alliances: New York and Los Angeles Compared." In *The Handbook of International Migration*, edited by Charles Hirschman, Philip Kasinitz, and Josh DeWind. New York: Russell Sage Foundation.

———. 2001. "The Democratic Vote in Living Color," *New York Times*, March 14.

Neckerman, Kathryn, Prudence Carter, and Jennifer Lee. 1999. "Segmented Assimilation and Minority Cultures of Mobility," *Ethnic and Racial Studies* 22: 945–65.

Newman, Katherine. 1999. *No Shame in My Game: The Working Poor in the Inner City*. New York: Knopf.

Orsi, Robert. 1992. "The Religious Boundaries of an Inbetween People: Street *Feste* and the Problem of the Dark-Skinned Other in Italian Harlem, 1920–1990," *American Quarterly* 44: 313–47.

Osofsky, Gilbert. 1963. *Harlem: The Making of a Ghetto*. New York: Harper and Row.

Owen, David. 2001. "A Profile of Caribbean Households and Families in Great Britain." In *Caribbean Families in Britain and the Transatlantic World*, edited by Harry Goulbourne and Mary Chamberlain. London: Macmillan Education.

Peach, Ceri. 1995. "Profile of the Black Caribbean Population of Great Britain." In *Profile of the Ethnic Minority Populations of Great Britain*, edited by Ceri Peach. London: Office of the Population Censuses and Surveys.

Perlmann, Joel, and Roger Waldinger. 1997. "Second Generation Decline? Children of Immigrants, Past and Present: A Reconsideration," *International Migration Review* 31: 893–923.

Portes, Alejandro, and Rubén Rumbaut. 2001. "The Forging of a New America: Lessons for Theory and Policy." In *Ethnicities*, edited by Rubén Rumbaut and Alejandro Portes. Berkeley: University of California Press.

Portes, Alejandro, and Min Zhou. 1993. "The New Second Generation: Segmented Assimilation and Its Variants among Post-1965 Immigrant Youth," *Annals of the American Academy of Political and Social Science* 530: 74–98.

Prashad, Vijay. 2000. *The Karma of Brown Folk*. Minneapolis: University of Minnesota Press.

Rischin, Moses. 1962. *The Promised City: New York's Jews, 1870–1914*. Cambridge, Mass.: Harvard University Press.

Roediger, David. 1994. *Toward the Abolition of Whiteness*. London: Verso.

Rogers, Reuel. 2001. "'Black Like Who?' Afro-Caribbean Immigrants, African Americans, and the Politics of Group Identity." In *Islands in the City: West Indian Migration to New York,* edited by Nancy Foner. Berkeley: University of California Press.

Scheiner, Seth. 1965. *Negro Mecca: A History of the Negro in New York City, 1865–1920.* New York: New York University Press.

Smith, Robert C. 2001. "Mexicans: Social, Educational, Economic and Political Problems and Prospects in New York." In *New Immigrants in New York,* edited by Nancy Foner. 2d ed. New York: Columbia University Press.

Sudbury, Julia. 2001. "(Re)constructing Multiracial Blackness: Women's Activism, Difference and Collectivity in Britain," *Ethnic and Racial Studies* 24: 29–49.

Vecoli, Rudolph. 1969. "Prelates and Peasants: Italian Immigration and the Catholic Church," *Journal of Social History* 2: 217–68.

Vickerman, Milton. 1999. *Crosscurrents: West Indians and Race in America.* New York: Oxford University Press.

———. 2001a. "Jamaicans: Balancing Race and Ethnicity." In *New Immigrants in New York,* edited by Nancy Foner. 2d ed. New York: Columbia University Press.

———. 2001b. "Tweaking the Monolith: The West Indian Immigrant Encounter with 'Blackness.'" In *Islands in the City: West Indian Migration to New York City,* edited by Nancy Foner. Berkeley: University of California Press.

Waldinger, Roger. 1996. *Still the Promised City? African Americans and New Immigrants in Postindustrial New York.* Cambridge, Mass.: Harvard University Press.

———. 1997. "Black/Immigrant Competition Re-assessed: New Evidence from Los Angeles," *Sociological Perspectives* 40: 365–86.

Waldinger, Roger, and Joel Perlmann. 1998. "Second Generations: Past, Present and Future," *Journal of Ethnic and Migration Studies* 24: 5–24.

Waters, Mary. 1999. *Black Identities: West Indian Immigrant Dreams and Immigrant Realities.* Cambridge, Mass.: Harvard University Press.

Watkins-Owens, Irma. 1996. *Blood Relations: Caribbean Immigrants and the Harlem Community, 1900–1930.* Bloomington: Indiana University Press.

Wilson, William Julius. 1996. *When Work Disappears.* New York: Knopf.

Wright, Richard, and Mark Ellis. 2001. "Immigrants, the Native Born, and the Changing Division of Labor in New York City." In *New Immigrants in New York,* edited by Nancy Foner. 2d ed. New York: Columbia University Press.

4

Becoming Americans/Becoming New Yorkers: Immigrant Incorporation in a Majority Minority City

PHILIP KASINITZ, JOHN MOLLENKOPF, AND MARY C. WATERS

Many observers have noted that immigrants to the United States are highly concentrated in the largest metropolitan areas of a relatively few states. Though immigrants have diffused into many places that had previously seen relatively few immigrants during the 1990s, as of the 2000 census 77 percent of the nation's 31.1 million foreign-born residents still lived in six states—California, New York, Texas, Florida, New Jersey, and Illinois. According to the 2000 census, the two largest metro areas, Los Angeles and New York, accounted for a third of all immigrants.[1] While immigrants moved into many new areas during the 1990s, making the challenge of incorporating their children a national issue, their concentration in our largest cities remained pronounced.

This chapter examines how immigrants are being incorporated into American society in gateway cities by examining second-generation immigrants in New York City. In contrast to the prevailing theoretical

We are grateful to the Russell Sage Foundation, the Andrew W. Mellon Foundation, the Ford Foundation, the Rockefeller Foundation, the UJA-Federation, and the National Institute of Child Health and Human Development for their generous support for collection of the data on which this chapter draws.

1 See http://www.census.gov/Press-Release/www/2002/demoprofiles.html.

approach, which views immigrants as seeking a favorable place along the racial continuum between a native white elite on the top and native nonwhite minorities on the bottom, we argue that second-generation experiences in New York are being shaped by the *history of immigration among whites*, by the *predominance of ethnic minorities* in the city's population and institutions today, and by the *interaction among immigrant and native minority groups*, not the interaction between immigrants and some core group of white Americans. We ask the reader to think not only about the social distances that immigrants must travel from their countries of origin to become integrated into American society, but also about the changing nature of the society that they are joining. Reflecting along these lines, we argue, requires us to challenge and revise certain key aspects of the theory of segmented assimilation.

Our larger project asks how the contexts in which young second-generation immigrants have grown up in New York have affected their experiences in school and on the job, how they feel about their progress, and where they think they fit within American society. Here we focus on the ways in which it matters a great deal that young second-generation people are growing up in a city with a long history of immigration for all groups—including whites and blacks as well as Latinos and Asians. (The implicit contrast, of course, is with Los Angeles, where the non-Hispanic white and black populations are overwhelmingly native stock.) Given that these youths come largely from non-European ethnic origins, we ask what it means to grow up in a "majority minority" city.

We base our conclusions on a large-scale study under way since 1999. It included telephone interviews with random samples of 3,424 men and women aged eighteen to thirty-two living in New York City (except Staten Island) and the inner suburban areas of Nassau and Westchester counties and northeastern New Jersey, followed up with in-depth, in-person interviews with 10 percent of these respondents. We chose them according to whether their parents were from (1) China (including Taiwan, Hong Kong, and the Chinese diaspora); (2) the Dominican Republic; (3) the West Indies (including Jamaica, Trinidad, Barbados, and other English-speaking islands, and Guyana, but excluding Haiti and those of Indian origin); (4) the South American countries of Colombia, Ecuador, and Peru (subsequently designated CEP); and (5) Jewish immigrants from the former Soviet Union. These groups comprised 39 percent of the 1990 second-generation population in the defined sample area.[2] For comparative purposes, we also interviewed samples of native-born people with native-born parents from among (6) whites, (7) blacks, and (8) Puerto Ricans. About two-thirds of the immigrant second-generation respondents were born in the United States, mostly in New York City, while one-third were born abroad but arrived in the United States by age twelve and had lived here for at least ten years.

In 1999–2000 we also fielded six ethnographies targeted on institutions and sites where these second-generation and native young people were likely to encounter each other, including a four-year college of the City University of New York (CUNY), a CUNY community college, a large public service employees union, a retail store, several Protestant churches, and community political organizations. Together, these data sources provide the best picture yet available of the life situations of a representative cross section of the major racial and ethnic groups in metropolitan New York. It is the first study based on a random sample of the adult children of immigrants who arrived in the United States after 1965.[2]

After outlining the main contours of the school and work outcomes of the different second-generation groups, we address the question of what it means for them to come of age in a heavily nonwhite, heavily immigrant context. We take issue with some of the assertions of the theory of segmented assimilation, arguing that it has an unsophisticated model of intergroup contact, conflict, and discrimination. That theory also does not take into account the ways that institutions which promote minority advancement also facilitate the incorporation of the second generation, including mainstream as well as minority institutions. Finally, we argue that the dominance of those who are not non-Hispanic whites among our age group (where non-Hispanic whites make up only about a quarter of the population) means that immigrant and native minority young people are creating a vibrant youth culture that is neither "immigrant" nor "middle American," but rather something new. The previous literature has failed to appreciate the importance of this development. We conclude that simple theories about assimilation, whether of the old-fashioned "straight line" or new "segmented" varieties, fail to capture the complexity of the ways in which

---

[2] To represent the full range of children of immigrants, we included people who were born abroad but arrived in the United States by age twelve and had lived there for ten or more years. To complete the Russian sample, we had to relax this requirement to arrival by age eighteen.

our respondents are becoming "New Yorkers." As New Yorkers, they are forging identities that differ strongly from that of their parents' countries of origin but that also differ from those of mainstream white or black Americans.

IMMIGRATION TO NEW YORK

Immigration has profoundly transformed the population of metropolitan New York, just as it has those of other gateway cities like Los Angeles or Miami. About 10 percent of the 900,000 legal immigrants and refugees who arrive in the country every year settle in New York City proper. The foreign-born now make up 36 percent of the city's population, and the second generation another quarter. Native-born whites with native-born parents make up only 18 percent of the city's population. In short, New York City is overwhelmingly a city of minorities and immigrants. Moreover, its immigrant stock population is far more diverse in racial and ethnic terms than those of other cities. Unlike its main rival, Los Angeles, where Mexicans alone make up 40 percent of the immigrant population (Zhou 2001: 215), New York receives immigrants from all of the world's sending regions, including Europe, the Caribbean, Latin America, and Asia.

Table 4.1. Racial Composition of Second Generation, by City

	Hispanic	Non-Hispanic Asian	Non-Hispanic Black	Non-Hispanic White
New York City	30.0%	13.2%	20.7%	36.1%
Los Angeles County	74.5	13.1	1.1	11.3
Gateway central cities	51.0	23.9	2.6	22.4
U.S. total	43.0	14.3	4.2	38.5

Source: March 2000 Current Population Survey.

As table 4.1 illustrates, the native children born to two immigrant parents living in New York City are less likely to be Hispanic than in Los Angeles County, the other gateway cities (San Francisco, Chicago, Houston, Miami), or the country as a whole, even though New York is still home to many Hispanic second-generation people. The Asian and non-Hispanic white shares of its second generation resemble those of the nation as a whole, while New York also has a large black second generation. Note that table 4.1 shows that New York is home to many *white* children of immigrants, unlike Los Angeles County. For fiscal year 2000, the Immigration and Naturalization Service (INS) reports that the top ten countries sending immigrants to New York City (a total of 85,000) were the Dominican Republic, China, Jamaica, Haiti, the Ukraine, Bangladesh, Pakistan, Ecuador, India, and Russia (INS 2002: table 18).

The large flow of black and Latino immigrants into New York has strongly affected the city's traditional "minority" groups. In 2000 the foreign-born and their children constituted more than half of all blacks and Hispanics and virtually all of the Asian population in the city (Mollenkopf, Olson, and Ross 2001: table 1.5). Of course, this is a tradition in New York. Between 1892 and 1924, thousands of European immigrants arrived at Ellis Island every day. In 1910 two out of five New Yorkers were born abroad, mostly in Europe, but also the West Indies. In 1920 a quarter of the city's black population was West Indian (Kasinitz 1992: 24–25). Thus both the white and black residents of New York have a strong immigrant tradition. We will argue that this crucially shaped the ways in which mainstream and minority institutions have reacted to new immigrants, making the city porous and welcoming even to new immigrants from previously unrepresented groups.

Mollenkopf (1999) has noted that the impact of immigration on the city's population and its self-conscious position as America's quintessential immigrant destination have shaped New York's culture, economy, and political structure. Waldinger (1996) has outlined patterns of ethnic succession in the city's economy that have been paralleled in its politics (Foner 2000; Mollenkopf, Olson, and Ross 2001). Irish and German immigrants began to challenge New York's Anglo Saxon Protestant elite in the 1860s and 1870s, followed by Italian and Central European Jewish immigrants at the turn of the century.

Beginning in the 1960s the rapid growth of the city's black and Puerto Rican populations in the previous decades resulted in growing minority activism, culminating in political alignments. Today, as Mollenkopf (2000: 419) writes, "In New York, white Protestants are practically invisible, if still economically and socially powerful. Instead the city's white population is dominated by first, second and third generation Catholics and Jews. Far from finding intergroup competition threatening, they are masters of the art." In short, when new immigrants and their children encounter white—or black—Americans in New York, they do so along an ethnic continuum, not across a sharp boundary between nonwhite immigrants and native whites, as they do in Southern California, Texas, or Florida.

SCHOOL AND WORK

Among our respondents, as might be expected, the native whites, Russian Jews, and Chinese are significantly more likely to have completed a four-year college or to have postgraduate education than the other groups, and significantly less likely to have dropped out of high school. (Table 4.2 shows these outcomes for the older members of our sample, who have had time to complete their educations.) On this score, Puerto Ricans are faring the worst, with Dominicans, native blacks, and the CEP countries also having relatively high dropout rates and low college graduation rates. The general pattern is that Latinos do worst and blacks only slightly better, while the Chinese, Russians, and whites do best. Within those broad groupings, the second-generation groups are somewhat more successful than their native-born counterparts. This underlying pattern becomes even stronger after controlling for parents' education, gender, and age, in part because the parents of Puerto Ricans have somewhat higher levels of education than those of the Dominican and CEP second generation, while the education levels among parents of the Chinese and Russian second generation are not as high as those among the native white parents (Mollenkopf, Kasinitz, and Waters 2002).

Refining this analysis, it is also apparent that those of our respondents who do attend a four-year college attend institutions that systematically vary in quality, as indicated by *US News and World Report* college rankings.[3] In our sample, 23 percent of the Chinese, 16 percent of Russian Jews, and 38 percent of native whites attended "national tier one" colleges—compared to only 6 percent of native African Americans, 8 percent of Puerto Ricans, 7 percent of Dominicans, and 7 percent of West Indians. By contrast, 22 percent of college-educated Dominicans, 38 percent of native African Americans, 35 percent of Puerto

[3] We use an 8-point scale: national 1, 2, 3, and 4, and regional 1, 2, 3, and 4. National colleges and universities recruit students from across the country, with 1 being the most selective and 4 the least. Regional schools recruit from local areas, again with 1 being the most selective and 4 the least. National 1 schools include Harvard, Yale, Columbia, and New York University, while the regional 4's include the least selective of the CUNY schools, such as York College, Medgar Evers, and Lehman, as well as private institutions like Pace.

Ricans, and 39 percent of West Indians had gone to "regional tier four" schools—as opposed to 4 percent of Chinese and 9 percent of the Russian Jewish respondents. Thus not only the quantity but also the quality of education varies greatly across our groups of respondents.

We also compared the occupation and industry profile of our second-generation respondents with those of their parents and the city as a whole. As one might suspect, the parents of our second-generation respondents were highly concentrated in ethnic "niche" occupations and segmented by gender. Two out of every five fathers of our Chinese respondents worked in restaurants, while more than a third of the mothers of our West Indian respondents are nurses or nurses aides. New York's beleaguered manufacturing sector continues to play an important role for immigrants, particularly for those immigrant women who (unlike West Indians) do not speak English upon arrival. Forty-six percent of the mothers of our Dominicans respondents, 43 percent of the CEP mothers, and a staggering 57 percent of the Chinese mothers worked in manufacturing, primarily in the garment industry.

Our second-generation respondents depart strongly from this pattern. They are markedly less occupationally concentrated than their parents, and their occupational distributions instead resemble each other and those of all New Yorkers their age and gender. For example, only 3 percent of the male Chinese respondents worked in restaurants, and 9 percent of West Indian female respondents worked as nurses or nurses aides. (This last number is a much higher percentage than for any other second-generation group but still far lower than that of their mothers.) While greater economic opportunity has pushed the second generation away from their parents' jobs, these young people also have a distaste for stereotypical "ethnic" occupations. When asked what job he would never take, one of our Chinese in-depth respondents replied, "delivering Chinese food." When the daughter of a Chinatown jewelry shop owner was asked if her father would like her to take over the business, she laughingly replied, "No, he doesn't hate me that much!"

Even less successful groups have exited from parental niches. There is a striking drop-off in manufacturing employment between the generations. While manufacturing is an important employer of fathers, and particularly mothers, for all second-generation groups except West Indians (including Puerto Ricans), second-generation employment in manufacturing drops below that of the general population of the study area. As one Colombian respondent put it when asked if he would consider taking his father's job, "Hey, I don't do that factory thing."

Table 4.2. Educational Attainment by Group (aged 24 to 32)

	CEP	Dominican	Puerto Rican	West Indian	Native Black	Chinese	Russian	Native White
High school dropout	10.1%	12.4%	19.6%	3.5%	12.8%	.5%	1.8%	3.7%
Still in high school	.5	1.1	1.4	.6	.7			.4
GED	3.2	2.3	3.7	2.3	4.4	.5	.9	1.1
High school graduate	14.4	11.9	19.6	12.3	19.0	4.1	6.3	9.2
In two-year college	3.2	4.5	2.7	7.0	2.9	2.3	1.8	1.1
Some college, no degree	26.6	21.5	26.9	22.8	31.0	11.7	10.8	9.9
Two-year college graduate	5.3	9.6	3.2	9.4	4.0	2.3	4.5	5.5
In four-year college	8.5	6.8	6.8	9.4	5.8	9.0	10.8	1.8
Four-year college graduate	19.7	20.9	10.0	22.2	14.6	45.9	36.0	37.1
In graduate/professional school	5.9	4.5	3.7	7.0	2.9	12.6	6.3	11.4
Some grad school, no degree	.5	1.7	1.4		.7	2.3	.9	4.0
Graduate or professional degree	2.1	2.8	.9	3.5	1.1	9.0	19.8	14.7

Source: Second Generation Study.

What do they do? Many have been attracted to New York's large finance, insurance, and real estate (FIRE) sector. Indeed, Chinese and Russian respondents are more likely to work in this sector than are native whites or New York City residents as a whole. The sector also employs many CEP respondents. Interestingly, FIRE employment is higher among the second generation than their parents in every group *except* West Indians. For the most part, however, second-generation respondents report working at the same kinds of jobs that most young people get. Given their age and the era in which they entered the labor market, retailing and clerical work are the first or second most common occupations for every group except native whites, for whom they are the second and third most common.

Some interesting ethnic particularities in the occupational distribution suggest that some new "ethnic niches" may be forming: Chinese work in finance and as computer and design specialists; Russians specialize in work with computers; Dominicans, the CEP, and Puerto Ricans are often financial clerks; West Indians work in health care; and native whites work in media and entertainment. The overwhelming story is nevertheless one of similarity rather than recapitulating the group differences evident among their parents. Our education and occupation data show some evidence of downward mobility for Puerto Ricans, somewhat stronger occupational differentiation for West Indians, and significant upward mobility for the Chinese second generation. But the second generation are going to school and working with each other, and most do not show any signs of the second-generation decline that distressed some analysts at the beginning of the 1990s (Gans 1992; Portes and Zhou 1993).

INTERGROUP CONTACT AND CONFLICT

Because minority and second-generation immigrant young people dominate their age cohort, our respondents have a great deal of contact with each other, but they sometimes have little contact with native white New Yorkers. Recalling their experiences of discrimination in the multiethnic worlds in which they grew up, members of the second generation often found themselves at odds not with whites but with other nearby groups. While the second generation is on average less concentrated in immigrant neighborhoods than are their parents, many still live in such areas. The 2000 census data show that first-generation West Indians are the most highly segregated, living in central Brooklyn, southeast Queens, and the north Bronx in New York, as well as in

Hempstead, Long Island, and Jersey City, New Jersey. Dominicans remain heavily concentrated in Washington Heights, with lesser concentrations on Manhattan's Lower East Side, Sunset Park and Bushwick in Brooklyn, and Elmhurst and Jackson Heights in Queens. Although many Chinese immigrants still live in Manhattan's Chinatown, Chinese residents, especially the second generation, are spreading through South Brooklyn and Corona, Elmhurst and Flushing in Queens. The CEPs mostly live in Queens and in Jersey City. Russian Jews are concentrated in the Brighton Beach section of Brooklyn.

Table 4.3. Experience of Prejudice by Group

	Percent of Individuals Experiencing Prejudice:				
	At Work	In Shops/ Restaurants	From Police	At School	Looking for Work
CEP	20%	41%	22%	17%	17%
Dominican	19	37	25	14	20
Puerto Rican	26	40	22	15	22
West Indian	30	57	35	17	26
Black	35	55	34	15	33
Chinese	14	41	13	25	12
Russian Jew	8	12	8	11	9
White	14	15	6	9	6

Source: Second Generation Study.

The responses that our survey and follow-up interviews gathered to a series of questions about experiences of prejudice and discrimination are summarized in table 4.3. As we might expect, blacks and West Indians reported facing the highest levels of discrimination while shopping, from the police, or while looking for work or at work, with the Hispanic groups not far behind. The Chinese, Russians, and whites experienced the least discrimination in these realms. We were surprised at the high levels of prejudice that the Chinese reported experiencing in school—more than any other group. Our in-depth interviews indicated that this experience did not stem from interactions with whites but with African Americans. The Chinese also report a relatively high level of prejudice experienced in stores.

We also asked whether parents had ever talked with our respondents about discrimination against their group, as reported in table 4.4. Three-quarters of native blacks said that their parents had talked with them about discrimination against their group. But a large proportion of Russian and Chinese respondents (66 percent and 60 percent, respectively) also report talking to their parents about discrimination. Even though the Russians and the Chinese are doing the best in terms of educational attainment and labor market outcomes, they are also the most likely to spontaneously tell our in-depth interviewers that discrimination has been an impediment to their success.

Table 4.4. Discussions about Racism and Discrimination

	Respondents Who Report Having Discussed Racism and Discrimination against [Group] with Parents
Chinese	61%
CEP	44
Dominican	58
Black	77
Puerto Rican	58
Russian Jew	66
West Indian	54

Source: Second Generation Study.

We can understand the variation in "paths of discrimination" as responses to differing group opportunity sets, as outlined in figure 4.1. The in-depth interviews reveal that native blacks and West Indians, as well as Dominicans, Puerto Ricans, and some CEPs, report that whites often discriminate against them or show prejudice in public spaces such as the streets, stores, and the like. These experiences include harassment by the police, "driving while black," whites moving across the street to avoid passing near them, and store clerks following them to make sure they do not shoplift. This treatment often resulted in the kinds of discouragement, anger, and reactive ethnicity that Portes and his colleagues identified in their theory of segmented assimilation.

In contrast to this "minority experience" in public settings, Chinese and the upwardly mobile blacks and Hispanics in our sample often met a more personal form of discrimination from whites while attending school or on the job. This "face to face" prejudice is more common for better-off respondents who leave their neighborhoods, shop in more upscale stores, and work in predominantly white settings. As a result, they are more likely to encounter, and compete with, native whites. These are the situations that parents have warned their children about, situations in which they can expect prejudice and should devise ways to cope with it. But in contrast to the anger and disengagement that often result from experiences of impersonal discrimination, many of these respondents reported that they believed they needed to try harder when encountering what was in effect a "glass ceiling." Instead of disengaging, they reacted with increased effort and a sustained focus on success.

Figure 4.1. Prejudice/Discrimination

▽	▽	▽
From whites in public spaces	From whites at work and school	From blacks and Puerto Ricans in public spaces and school
▽	▽	▽
Blacks and Hispanics	Chinese, upwardly mobile blacks, and Hispanics	Chinese, Russians, West Indians, Dominicans, CEP
▽	▽	▽
Discouragement, anger, reactive ethnicity	Try harder	Distancing, stereotyping

Finally, given that native whites constitute a small minority in New York City, it is not surprising that many members of the second generation report encounters with other immigrant and minority group members that involved conflict, prejudice, and discrimination. They often reacted to this type of conflict with distancing behaviors, as when West Indians try to distance themselves from African Americans, when Dominicans seek to distinguish themselves from Puerto Ricans, or when Chinese and Russians distance themselves from blacks and Latinos from various backgrounds.

REASSESSING SEGMENTED ASSIMILATION

In recent years, thoughtful observers have advanced the disturbing hypothesis that the new second generation will experience downward mobility as they are absorbed into the native black or Latino populations living in concentrated poverty neighborhoods. Gans (1992) outlines several scenarios in which the children of the new immigrants could do worse than their parents or most others their age. He speculates that second-generation immigrants who go to low-performing inner-city schools, get bad jobs, and enter shrinking economic niches will experience downward mobility.

Drawing on ethnographic case studies and the Children of Immigrants Longitudinal Study (CILS) of second-generation schoolchildren in Miami and San Diego, Portes and Zhou (1993) refine this approach by arguing that the differing modes of incorporation in the first generation endow their children with differing amounts of cultural and social capital (ethnic networks and values) and different opportunity structures, resulting in several distinct paths toward incorporation. Those who live among American blacks or Latinos and face racial discrimination will, in their view, adopt a "reactive" native minority ethnicity. But those who come from groups with strong ethnic networks, access to capital, and fewer ties to U.S. minorities will, they postulate, follow one of two other paths: the "linear ethnicity" of assimilation into a native white ethnic category, or "segmented assimilation" into a retained immigrant identity that distinguishes them from American blacks or Puerto Ricans/Chicanos.

As for Gans, the fundamental point for Portes and Zhou is that second-generation young people who cast their lot with America's minority groups, whose peer culture supposedly rejects success at school and work, will experience downward social mobility. This dynamic inverts the normal model of acculturation: when "becoming American" for the children of brown and black immigrants means embracing the values of their native ghetto peers rather than their immigrant parents, they will suffer for it. They will embrace American definitions of status and success, but according to this view they will also be loath to accept the poorly paid jobs held by their immigrant parents. They will disconnect from opportunities within the ethnic economy, but racial discrimination within the mainstream economy will limit their alternatives, fostering an "oppositional" identity, rebelliousness, or a questioning of the value of education.

Our study suggests that this model holds a far too negative stereotype of native minorities and the supposed self-defeating role model they provide for second-generation immigrants. Since much of the research on segmented assimilation fails to include comparisons with native whites, blacks, or Latinos, it fails to appreciate either the full range of experience within these groups—much of which is quite successful—or the fact that whites as well as minorities engage in oppositional behaviors. A case in point involves the arrest rates among males in our study, presented in table 4.5. The arrest rate for native whites surpasses that of every second-generation group except for West Indians. But getting arrested apparently does not have the same lasting negative consequence for whites that it does for those who are branded by negative racial stereotypes or whose families have fewer resources to help them overcome youthful mistakes. In other words, the key factor is not a *group trait* but a *societal response*. White youths often exhibited oppositional behaviors and made mistakes, but they typically were able to recover from the same behaviors that left members of minority groups at a lasting disadvantage. Thus the theory of segmented assimilation needs to pay more attention to the consequences of behaviors and beliefs, and not solely their existence.

Table 4.5. Arrest Rate by Group (males)

	Never Arrested	Arrested
CEP	79.8%	20.2%
Dominican	78.4	21.6
Puerto Rican	70.9	29.1
West Indian	75.5	24.5
Native black	65.8	34.2
Chinese	90.2	9.8
Russian	89.6	10.4
Native white	76.9	23.1

Source: Second Generation Study.

INSTITUTIONS' UNANTICIPATED POSITIVE IMPACT ON MINORITY MOBILITY

While the segmented assimilation model sees assimilation into native minority status as a path toward downward mobility, our study reveals that being classified as a native minority can also provide access to institutional supports that promote success. The civil rights movement, along with the minority advancement in mainstream institutions, has created a legacy of opportunity for new members of old minority groups. The struggle for minority empowerment has established new entry points into mainstream institutions and created many new minority-run institutions. By operating in contexts where "American" means African American or Puerto Rican, our respondents have developed ethnic solidarity with native blacks or Latinos, and received signals that they will be easily accepted into "America." This dynamic also puts native blacks and Puerto Ricans in the strange position of managing the ethnic succession of second-generation individuals in colleges, labor unions, and political groups while continuing to see themselves as outsiders to these power structures. Although community-based social services or affirmative action "second chance" entry points into white institutions were initially set up to aid blacks and Puerto Ricans, new second-generation immigrants are well situated to take advantage of them.

Two accounts from our ethnographies illustrate this point. One involves a Puerto Rican studies class at a community college in Queens. Founded in the late 1960s in the first wave of open admissions to CUNY, this college was designed to be particularly sensitive to New York City's Hispanic population, then overwhelmingly Puerto Rican. This class, which met the college's American studies requirement, was taught by a Cuban American professor to students who were all Colombian, Ecuadorian, Peruvian, or Dominican. In other words, an immigrant professor was using the Puerto Rican experience to teach first- and second-generation Latino immigrants what it means to be American (Trillo n.d.).

Another ethnographer studied a public employee union that had been founded in the 1960s by Jewish radicals for a largely African American membership with origins mostly in the American South. Today its leaders are mostly African Americans who rose through the civil rights movement, but the rank and file has become overwhelmingly first- and second-generation West Indians. At a union meeting celebrating their Caribbean heritage, the union's members shouted out recognition for each of the various islands. Listening to this response, the African American union leader asked plaintively, "Isn't anyone here from Alabama?" (Foerster n.d.).

These stories illustrate the enormous significance of racial and ethnic succession within the city's institutions. Originally designed as agencies of advancement for native minorities, this community college and social service union are now "Americanizing" and "ethnicizing" immigrants and their children. In quite practical material as well as symbolic terms, they are promoting upward mobility—through skills, credentials, and financial support. As they make educational progress, especially compared to native blacks and Puerto Ricans, second-generation West Indians, Dominicans, and CEPs are well situated to inherit leadership positions within minority institutions and to gain greater access to mainstream institutions. We thus posit that becoming identified as a member of a racial minority can have tangible benefits for second-generation New Yorkers. Segmented assimilation theory posits that this heralds downward mobility due to the negative influences of native minority peers. This misses both the fact that native minority young people are not alone in acting out in negative ways—which may be endemic to the age group—and the fact that native minorities also provide positive role models and have paved the way for access to minority and mainstream institutions that promote minority upward mobility.

CREATING HYBRID MINORITY CULTURES

We have noted that members of the second generation interact a lot more with each other and with native minorities than they do with native whites, with important consequences for the patterns of prejudice and intergroup conflict experienced by different groups. But this intergroup contact also has positive dimensions. The second generation is creating a new kind of multiculturalism, not of balkanized groups huddled within their own enclaves but of hybrids and fluid exchanges across group boundaries. For example, the city abounds in clubs where African American hip hop has been fused with East Indian and West Indian influences into new musical forms. The real action is not in the interplay of immigrant cultures with a homogenous dominant American culture, but in the interactions between first- and second-generation immigrant groups and native minorities. African American young people dance to Jamaican dance hall and imitate Jamaican patois, even as West Indian youngsters learn African American slang. Puerto Ricans can meringue, and Dominicans can play Salsa and rap in two languages.

Second-generation youth growing up in an Indian/South American/Irish/Pakistani neighborhood like Jackson Heights, Queens, or in a Puerto Rican/Mexican/Chinese/Arabic neighborhood like Sunset Park (where the aged population of "real Americans" comprises Norwegians) do see themselves as Americans and New Yorkers, but they are not assimilating into the mainstream typical in, say, Iowa. (Indeed, even in Iowa Mexican workers have moved into the meatpacking industry.) Whether one looks at the music in dance clubs, the eclectic menus in restaurants, or the inventive slang on the streets, one cannot help but be impressed by the creative potential that second-generation and minority young people are contributing to New York today.

This is reflected in how our respondents identified themselves. They used the term American in two different ways. One was to describe themselves as American, compared to the culture, values, and behaviors of their parents. (For example, they were not inclined to endorse physical punishment of children.) They definitely thought that the United States had influenced them to approach the world differently than their parents did. But they also used "American" to refer to the native whites they encountered at school, the office, or in public places but whom they knew far better from television and the movies. They saw those "Americans" as a different group that would never include them because of their race/ethnicity.

Many respondents sidestepped this ambivalent understanding of the term "American" by describing themselves as "New Yorkers." This option was open to them even as blacks or Hispanics or Asians, and it embraced them as second-generation immigrants. A "New York" identity embraced the dynamic cultural activities familiar to them, but not necessarily the larger white society. "New Yorkers," for our respondents, could come from immigrant groups, native minority groups, or be Italians, Irish, Jews, or the like. We argue that the individual changes necessary to become a New Yorker are not nearly so large as those required to become American. As immigration continues to transform the nation, New York may serve as a positive model of creative multiculturalism and inclusion. Whether other parts of the United States can replicate that openness remains an unanswered question. Although some skeptics might argue that New York is unique and not likely to be replicated elsewhere, we would counter that by being a quintessentially immigrant city, New York is in fact at its very core American.

References

Foerster, Amy. n.d. "Isn't Anyone Here from Alabama? Solidarity and Struggle in a Mighty Mighty Union." In *Becoming New Yorkers: The Second Generation in a Global City*, edited by Philip Kasinitz, John Mollenkopf, and Mary Waters. Forthcoming.

Foner, Nancy. 2000. *From Ellis Island to JFK: New York's Two Great Waves of Immigration*. New Haven, Conn.: Yale University Press.

Gans, Herbert. 1992. "Second Generation Decline: Scenarios for the Economic and Ethnic Futures of the Post-1965 American Immigrants," *Ethnic and Racial Studies* 15, no. 2: 173–93.

INS (U.S. Immigration and Naturalization Service). 2002. *2001 Statistical Yearbook of the Immigration and Naturalization Service*. Washington, D.C.: U.S. Government Printing Service.

Kasinitz, Philip. 1992. *Caribbean New York: Black Immigrants and the Politics of Race*. Ithaca, N.Y.: Cornell University Press.

Mollenkopf, John Hull. 1999. "Urban Political Conflicts and Alliances: New York and Los Angeles Compared." In *The Handbook of International Immigration: The American Experience*, edited by Charles Hirschman, Philip Kasinitz, and Josh DeWind. New York: Russell Sage Foundation.

———. 2000. "Assimilating Immigrants in Amsterdam: A Perspective from New York," *Netherlands Journal of Social Sciences* 26, no. 2: 126–45.

Mollenkopf, John, Philip Kasinitz, and Mary Waters. 2002. "Chutes and Ladders: Educational Attainment among Young Second-Generation and Native New Yorkers." Center for Urban Research Working Paper. New York: CUNY Graduate Center.

Mollenkopf, John Hull, David Olson, and Timothy Ross. 2001. "Immigrant Political Participation in New York and Los Angeles?" In *Governing American Cities: Inter-Ethnic Coalitions, Competition, and Conflict*, edited by Michael Jones Correa. New York: Russell Sage Foundation.

Portes, Alejandro, and Min Zhou. 1992. "Gaining the Upper Hand: Economic Mobility among Immigrant and Domestic Minorities," *Ethnic and Racial Studies* 15, no. 4: 491–521.

———. 1993. "The New Second Generation: Segmented Assimilation and Its Variants," *Annals of the American Academy of Political and Social Science* 530: 74–97.

Trillo, Alex. n.d. "Pan Ethnicity and Educational Trajectories among Latino Community College Students." In *Becoming New Yorkers: The Second Generation in a Global City*, edited by Philip Kasinitz, John Mollenkopf, and Mary Waters. Forthcoming.

Waldinger, Roger. 1996. *Still the Promised City? African Americans and New Immigrants in Postindustrial New York*. Cambridge, Mass.: Harvard University Press.

Waters, Mary C. 1999. *Black Identities: West Indian Dreams and American Realities*. New York: Russell Sage Foundation.

Zhou, Min. 1997. "Growing Up American: The Challenge Confronting Immigrant Children and Children of Immigrants," *Annual Review of Sociology* 23: 69–95.

———. 2001. "Contemporary Immigration and the Dynamics of Race and Ethnicity." In *America Becoming: Racial Trends and Their Consequences*, edited by Neil Smelser, William Julius Wilson, and Faith Mitchell. Washington, D.C.: National Academy Press.

5

Educational Attainments of Immigrant Offspring: Success or Segmented Assimilation?

MONICA BOYD

Nearly one hundred years ago, North American scholars, policymakers, and the lay public were mindful of the numbers and consequences associated with the great migrations from Europe. Today there is renewed interest, stimulated by both the large volume of current immigration and the changing source countries from which migrants are coming. The result has been an abundance of research on immigration flows, policy, and immigrant integration. Although attention has focused mostly on foreign-born migrants, scholars also have shown renewed interest in the experiences of the offspring of foreign-born parents. This focus acknowledges that the time span of immigrant integration and/or assimilation extends beyond that of the first generation of migrants.

American integration models suggest three possible outcomes for immigrant offspring. The straight line, or "linear assimilation," model implies that after two to three generations in the host society, the descendants of immigrants usually are indistinguishable from the rest of society in their behaviors and socioeconomic characteristics (Gans 1992:

The author thanks Scott Davies and Jeffrey Reitz for their helpful comments on an earlier version of this essay. I also am grateful to Statistics Canada for giving me access to the Survey of Labour and Income Dynamics (SLID) data necessary to undertake the analysis.

174, 1997). According to the second model, some groups will experience intergenerational socioeconomic improvement, but such improvement will be accompanied by deliberate preservation of ethnic membership and values and by continued economic attachment to ethnic communities. Immigrant offspring most likely to display this pattern of "segmented assimilation" are members of immigrant groups that have well-developed ethnic economies, such as Chinese- or Cuban-origin groups (Portes 1995; Portes and Zhou 1993; also see Waters 1994, 1997). The third model implies socioeconomic disadvantages, particularly for groups that are visibly distinct from the (white) majority and in which parental and community-based resources are few. Caribbean youths—whose ethnicity is synonymous with skin color—are examples of this type of segmented, "truncated assimilation" (Portes 1995; Portes and Zhou 1993; Zhou 1997a, 1997b).

Recent investigations associated with these new theoretical visions have three characteristics: they study groups in the United States, they focus primarily on immigrant offspring still living at home, and their research design is an in-depth study of selected ethnic or racial groups (see *International Migration Review* 1994, 1997; Waters 1994, 1997; Zhou and Bankston 1998). Although such studies are exceptionally innovative and have revitalized and redirected research on the second generation, they are not without critics. Boyd (2000) suggests that the third model, which is basically one of marginalization, rests on the unique history of race relations in the United States and may not hold elsewhere (also see Boyd and Grieco 1998; Reitz 1998). Alba and Nee (1997) note that childhood circumstances for young immigrant offspring are not necessarily identical to, or predictive of, experiences in adulthood. Such observations point to the need for additional studies that extend the U.S. focus to other countries and that assess the socioeconomic situations of the second generation in adulthood.

This chapter undertakes these tasks by investigating the educational attainments of the second-generation population aged twenty to sixty-four in Canada. Analysis of a 1996 survey shows that "1.5" and second-generation adults in this age group have more years of schooling and higher percentages completing high school compared with the third-plus generation. Contrary to the "second-generation decline" thesis or the segmented "underclass" assimilation model found in the United States, adult immigrant offspring in Canada who are "people of color" (visible minorities) exceed the educational attainments of "not-visible-minority" groups. Although the analysis is hampered by small sample size, the results are consistent with country differences in historical and contemporary race relations.

INTEGRATING IMMIGRANT OFFSPRING: DOES COUNTRY CONTEXT MATTER?

In the United States, renewed interest in the fortunes of immigrant offspring coincides with revisions to existing theoretical models. The orthodox "linear" scenario, firmly embedded in the "classical" model of acculturation and assimilation, was first articulated by academics headquartered at the University of Chicago during the early 1900s and subsequently embellished by successive generations of American scholars (for reviews, see Alba and Nee 1997; Driedger 1996: 23–37; Gans 1992). According to this approach, with immigrants' increasing length of time spent in the host society or with each generation further removed from foreign-born predecessors, the behaviors and socioeconomic characteristics of "newcomer" groups would become similar to those of the American-born. One variant of this approach suggests that the children of American-born parents (the third-plus generation) would outperform the American-born offspring of foreign-born parents (the second generation), who in turn would outperform the foreign-born (the first generation).

By the 1990s this script had been rewritten, infused with new empirically and theoretically relevant insights. Empirically, the ethnic and racial characteristics of immigrants altered as a consequence of new immigration policies.[1] Starting in the 1960s, barriers to migration from non-European areas were dismantled through new immigration acts and legislative changes in both the United States and Canada. In the United States, the Immigration and Nationality Act of 1965 (effective in 1967) abolished the national origins quota system, which had severely restricted non-European permanent migration. Canada modified immigration regulations in 1962 and in 1967, and formally included the changes in the Immigration Act of 1976, which went into effect in 1978.

1 Other empirically based motivators for new assimilation models derived from the straight-line or linear model's neglect of factors that alter the context within which the assimilation of immigrant offspring occurred. These factors included shifts from an industrial to a service-based economy, economic booms and busts, changing residential patterns in the context of post–World War II metropolitan growth and suburbanization, and the cessation of immigration flows between World Wars I and II (Alba and Nee 1997; Gans 1992; Massey 1995; Zhou 1997a, 1997b).

These regulatory and legislative changes removed national origins as the basis of admissions, substituting family ties, humanitarian concerns, and economic contributions as admissibility criteria (Boyd 1976; Hawkins 1988).

Combined with improved postwar economies in Europe, increasing economic and cultural globalization, and geopolitical events that included the United States' disengagement from Vietnam, these new North American regulations and acts produced a shift in the source countries of immigrants. By the 1980s and 1990s, immigrants to the United States came primarily from Mexico and Latin America, including the Caribbean Basin, as well as Asia (Zlotnik 1996: table 1). Reflecting Canada's lack of a contiguous border with a less developed region and its physical distance from such an area, Canada did not receive large numbers of Mexican migrants, but instead experienced substantial immigration from Asia and, to a lesser extent, Caribbean countries (Boyd and Vickers 2000).

Census data from 1996 clearly demonstrate the imprint of Canada's changing immigration flows (see table 5.1). Among immigrants admitted prior to 1961, 95 percent were born in the United States or in European countries. These percentages declined steadily with each decade, such that after 1990 only one in five persons (21.5 percent) admitted and resident in 1996 came from the United States or Europe. Whereas immigrants born in Asia represented less than 5 percent of those admitted to Canada prior to 1961, they were over half of all those entering Canada after 1990. Altogether, close to 80 percent of immigrants who arrived after 1990 and were enumerated in the May 1996 census were from countries outside Europe and the United States.

The color composition of the immigrant population also changed. Prior to regulation changes in the early 1960s, it was extremely difficult for persons from non-European countries to enter Canada. Preference was given to immigrants from the United States and Europe, and annual quotas ranging from 50 to 300 existed for India, Japan, and China (see Boyd and Vickers 2000; Henry et al. 2000; Kelley and Trebilcock 1998). Not surprisingly, less than 3 percent of the 1996 immigrant stock who entered Canada before 1960 were persons of color (visible minorities). This jumped to over half of those entering Canada during the 1970s, reflecting the regulation changes of the 1960s and the new Immigration Act of 1976 (table 5.1). The pendulum swing continued throughout the remainder of the century. Of those who entered Canada after 1990 and were enumerated in the 1996 census, three-quarters were members of "visible minorities." This term, which denotes groups that are distinctive by virtue of their race, color, or "visibility," includes ten subgroups: black, South Asian, Chinese, Korean, Japanese, Southeast Asian, Filipino, other Pacific Islanders, West Asian/Arab, and Latin American. It is a socially constructed term, developed by the federal government to meet data needs of federal employment equity legislation and program requirements during the 1980s and 1990s.[2]

Country of origin shifts and the altered racial and ethnic composition of immigration flows stimulated a rethinking of the orthodox model of assimilation, which had largely ignored long-term impediments arising from race and ethnicity. American scholars noted the possibility of "second-generation decline" (Gans 1992) or "second-generation revolt" (Perlmann and Waldinger 1997), in which immigrant offspring would have lower achievements than their parents or the third generation. In a separate but related initiative, Portes and others advanced two models of segmented assimilation. These models build on the U.S. experience, highlighting how race and ethnicity intersect with parental and community-based resources to shape the experiences of immigrant offspring (Portes 1995; Portes and Zhou 1993; Zhou and Bankston 1998). One model of segmented assimilation posits economic advancement for the second generation but with deliberate preservation of ethnic membership and values, and with continued economic attachment to ethnic communities. The second model depicts immigrant offspring who are racialized on the basis of their origins and color, as acculturated into a primarily black inner-city underclass. In contradiction to the imagery of attaining the American dream, the assimilation of immigrant youth into an inner-city, largely black underclass, with its implied low school attainments and downward mobility, conveys a highly problematic outcome.

Left relatively unexplored, however, is the applicability of these segmented assimilation models to other countries and the conditions under which immigrant offspring in other societies might follow the models of ethnic incorporation or underclass assimilation. At least three factors appear necessary for the segmented model of socioeconomic

2 Why the term "visible minority" was constructed to depict color differentials invites speculation. Part of the answer may lie in the studied avoidance of the term "race" by Canadian governments since World War II (see Boyd, Goldman, and White 2000; Wargon 2000). In the 1996 census questionnaire, data on the visible-minority groups were collected by a question that asked, "Is this person …" and provided categories of "white" along with the designated visible-minority groups. No mention was made of "race."

Table 5.1. Birthplace and Visible-Minority Status, by Period of Immigration, Canada, 1996

	Total (1)	<1961 (2)	1961–1970 (3)	1971–1980 (4)	1981–1990 (5)	1991–1996 (6)
United States, United Kingdom, Europe	51.7	94.8	75.2	43.0	29.6	21.5
United States	4.9	4.1	6.5	7.3	4.5	2.8
Europe, including United Kingdom	46.8	90.7	68.7	35.8	25.1	18.7
Subtotal	100.0	100.0	100.0	100.0	100.0	100.0
Asia	31.6	3.0	12.3	32.9	47.3	57.5
Africa	4.5	0.6	3.4	5.6	5.6	7.1
Latin America and Caribbean	11.2	1.3	8.1	16.8	16.5	12.7
All other areas	1.0	0.3	1.1	1.6	1.0	1.1
Subtotal	48.3	5.2	24.8	57.0	70.4	78.5
Member of a visible-minority group						
No	56.0	97.1	80.4	48.3	34.6	25.6
Yes	44.0	2.9	19.6	51.7	65.4	74.4
Subtotal	100.0	100.0	100.0	100.0	100.0	100.0

Source: Statistics Canada, Public Use Microdata File, Individual Sample.

success but continued ethnic group attachment: high volume of migration from a given area, sustained flows of large numbers over time, and residential concentration. Even here, two caveats must be noted. First, this model assumes relatively low institutional barriers to participation in core societal institutions such as education and the economy. Second, the strong version of the model assumes the existence of an ethnic economy that is large enough to absorb successive generations of offspring. In their critique of the ethnic enclave concept, Alba and Nee (1997) suggest that ethnic economies have not been large enough to offer much employment for subsequent generations. They note that most immigrants and their offspring work in the "open," or nonethnic, American economy.

The segmented assimilation model that emphasizes downward mobility into an underclass assumes low levels of parental and community resources. It also assumes a highly racialized population (Miles 1989) with structural barriers curbing the life chances of groups differentiated from the majority on the basis of phenotype. In the United States, the history and political economy of colonial and postcolonial settlement fostered a process of racialization in which immigrant arrivals were defined as members of the white, nonwhite, and black groups. These distinctions were integral components of key institutions, ranging from the polity (the right to vote and Jim Crow), to (racially segregated) education and housing, to the economy (no blacks need apply) (Omi and Winant 1994; Small 1994, 1998).

As a result, a large "involuntary minority" population of blacks is a key feature of contemporary American society. Defined as people who were brought into their present society though slavery, conquest, or colonization, involuntary minorities may, after arrival, develop their own oppositional cultural frames of reference and identity, including an anti-academic orientation and peer pressure not to use education as a route to socioeconomic success (Gibson 1991; Ogbu 1991). Clearly this depiction is an oversimplification of the experiences and identities of black Americans. However, along with the existence of structural barriers, the segmented assimilation model of underclass assimilation in the United States also demands the existence of a large involuntary minority population, characterized by an oppositional culture and identity, living in close proximity to recently arrived immigrant minorities.

Given these assumptions for segmented assimilation into the underclass, I argue that the "underclass" scenario for immigrant offspring is less likely to be observed in Canada, for two reasons. First, the historical context that fueled the development of institutional barriers differs in degree from that of the United States. To be sure, racialization and discrimination along color lines existed throughout Canada's history and continue into the present day (Henry et al. 2000; Kelley and Trebilcock 1998; Li 1999; Satzewich 1998). However, slavery was outlawed in Britain and in the dominions in 1834. Canada did not experience a war of succession over slavery. In all, the particular configuration of forces shaping race relations in the United States—reliance on slavery to maintain the plantation economy, a civil war rooted in a pervasive and pernicious system of black exploitation, and subsequent actions by the white majority to maintain power over blacks in the South—was not replicated to the same extent in Canada.[3]

Second, and equally important, Canada's black population was small in contrast to the American black population, and it never dominated a geographical area. Notwithstanding the formation of a black community in Nova Scotia in the aftermath of the American Revolution, numbers were more dispersed across Canada in comparison to the heavy concentration of the American black population in the South. Further, the Canadian black population is internally diverse in history, origins, and arrival dates. In addition to those arriving after the American Revolution, U.S. blacks also came in the 1800s, and other black peoples have immigrated since World War II from the Caribbean, Latin America, and, to a much lesser extent, Africa. The small size and heterogeneity of Canada's black population make it unlikely that it would act as a reference group for segmented assimilation. Other possible groups also are limited in size, suggesting that Canada currently lacks a readily identifiable racial group that acts as a reference group for the segmented assimilation of immigrant offspring (Boyd 2000).

Taken together, the absence in Canada of the major fault line visible in the United States' experience with race and the lack of a clearly discernible underclass reference group imply that that anti-school stance and the downward mobility that are predicted in the second seg-

---

[3] Many studies have documented the existence of prejudicial beliefs and attitudes in Canada (Berry and Kalin 2000; Driedger and Reid 2000). However, very few compare the degree of prejudicial attitudes held by Canadians with those observed in the United States. In a rare study that compares different surveys in both countries, Reitz and Breton (1994) suggest that country differences in prejudicial attitudes, social distance, and acceptance of intermarriage are not large, although these authors concede that on some dimensions Canadians may be more accepting of diversity than are Americans.

mented assimilation model will not be observed in Canada. Alternative scenarios may be more likely. In their analysis of men and women between the ages of twenty-five and sixty-four, Boyd and Grieco (1998) found that educational and socioeconomic attainments of the second generation are equal to or exceed those of the first and third generations. These findings support the "linear" assimilation model as well as a "success orientation" model. This latter model, also labeled "the immigrant optimism hypothesis" (Kao and Tienda 1995), stresses the relative overachievements of the second generation. Such overachievements are attributed to the success orientation of the foreign-born family of origin, which communicates high aspirations and expectations to its offspring.

Informed largely by the U.S. context, models of "second-generation decline" and segmented "underclass" assimilation hold for certain ethnic and racial groups and not for others. The 1994 survey analyzed by Boyd and Grieco (1998) lacked both the sample numbers and the racial and detailed birthplace data needed to study the experiences of specific immigrant offspring groups. As a result, Boyd and Grieco could not determine if the more negative outcomes observed in the United States held in Canada. In the analysis that follows I return to this issue, arguing that the anti-school stance and downward mobility depicted in the second segmented assimilation model will not be observed in Canada. I use data from a 1996 Canadian survey, separating generation groups into visible minorities and the remainder of the population, hereafter referred to as "not-visible-minorities."

DATA AND METHODOLOGICAL ISSUES

In Canada as in the United States, research on the second generation is handicapped by the failure of censuses to include questions on parents' birthplace. The last Canadian census to do so was conducted in 1971. As a result, analysts rely on specific case studies or on smaller surveys. Data analyzed in this chapter are from the second panel of the Survey of Labour and Income Dynamics (SLID), fielded in 1996 by Statistics Canada. This national household survey drew its sample from the Labour Force Survey (LFS), Canada's main source of monthly employment data and comparable to the U.S. Current Population Survey. The analysis reported below uses the master database available at Statistics Canada.

Respondents to SLID were asked to indicate if they belonged to one of the ten visible-minority groups specified in federal government programs. Unlike the first (1993) panel of SLID, the 1996 panel also asked respondents to indicate if their parents were born in or outside of Canada. In comparison to the 1994 General Social Survey of approximately 10,000 respondents (Boyd and Grieco 1998), the second panel of SLID is considerably larger, including approximately 30,000 adults sixteen years of age and older. Even so, sample numbers are not large, particularly when multiple generation groups are considered. Numbers become even more attenuated when generation categories are separated into visible-minority groups or further refined by any other variable of interest, such as sex. Small sample numbers for major categories of interest are problematic in analyses for at least two reasons. First, small sample size raises the possibility that respondents in any given category are not representative of the underlying population. Second, because of such fluctuation, statistical results are often insignificant.

The numbers problem has two research design consequences. First, careful inspection of sample numbers reveals that the analysis would not be supported for subpopulations defined by cross-tabulating specific visible-minority groups with gender and with generation status.[4] The solution was to create eight groups of interest, consisting of four generation groups each for those respondents who indicated visible-minority status and for those who were not members of a visible minority. The four generation groups are: (1) the third-plus generation, comprising respondents who were born in Canada and had Canada-born parents; (2) the second generation, consisting of respondents who were born in Canada and had one or more parent born in Canada; (3) the 1.5 generation, encompassing respondents who were foreign-born but who immigrated to Canada before age fifteen; and (4) the remainder of the foreign-born, consisting of those who were foreign-born but immigrated at age fifteen or later.

Second, the problem of small numbers affects the selection of the outcome variable used to depict the experience of immigrant offspring. Attenuated sample size becomes even more severe when respondents

---

[4] Blacks and Chinese were the two major groups of visible minorities found in panel 2 of the 1996 SLID survey, with the remainder consisting of the eight other designated groups or those with multiple visible-minority members. Although these percentages rest on very small sample numbers, black visible minorities were 32, 16, 20, and 14 percent of the respective third-plus, second, 1.5, and other foreign-born generation groups. Chinese visible minorities were 14, 32, 31, and 28 percent of the respective third-plus, second, 1.5, and other foreign-born generation groups.

fail to give information on variables usually included in multivariate analysis. This is particularly true when the dependent variable is the occupational status or employment earnings of the eight generation groups, partly because not all respondents in SLID are in the labor force and partly because even those in the labor force do not always provide information on relevant labor market characteristics. Selecting educational attainment as an indicator of immigrant offspring success or decline resolves this dilemma. Empirically, educational attainment permits including respondents who were not in the labor force, thereby keeping the subpopulation sample size as large as possible. Conceptually, educational attainment also taps directly into the second-generation decline and segmented assimilation models, both of which emphasize rejection of education-based mobility by racialized immigrant offspring.

Numerous American studies have been done on the educational performance of the 1.5 and second-generation youth, in part because few national surveys contain data on adult immigrant offspring (but see Farley 1999) and in part because the educational needs of immigrant children are highly visible locally and constitute a major policy challenge in the educational field.[5] Mindful of the caveat that education in process may not be equivalent to final educational achievements (Alba and Nee 1997), one advantage of the SLID survey is that it provides data on the educational attainments of adults.

The population aged twenty to sixty-four was selected for analysis because younger respondents may not have completed high school, and selective mortality could affect the educational patterns of elderly respondents. Even here, the underlying sample numbers are not large (table 5.2). The distribution of visible-minority and not-visible-minority groups across the four generation groups mirrors the pattern observed earlier in census data on period of arrival (table 5.2, panel 1). Nearly three-quarters of the not-visible-minority population in the 1996 SLID second panel are third generation, compared to less than 5 percent for the visible-minority population (table 5.2, panel 1).[6] Fewer than seventy

---

5 On this topic, see Board on Children and Families 1995; Dentler and Hafner 1997; Gibson 1991; Glick and White 2000; McDonnell and Hill 1993; Portes and MacLeod 1996, 1999; Kao and Tienda 1995; Rumbaut 1997; Rumbaut and Cornelius 1995; Stewart 1993; Vernez, Abrahamse, and Quigly 1996; White and Glick 2000.

6 The distributions and summary statistics presented in tables 5.2 through 5.4 are based on weighted data. Logistic and ordinary least squares (OLS) regression estimates in tables 5.4 and 5.5 are calculated from data that are first weighted to approximate population estimates and then downweighted so that statistical tests of significance reflect the approximate sample size.

Table 5.2. Demographic and Educational Characteristics of the Canadian Population, Aged 20 to 64, by Visible-Minority Status and Generational Status

		Visible Minority				Not Visible Minority			
				First Generation				First Generation	
	Total (1)	Third Generation (2)	Second Generation (3)	Immigrants < Age 15 (4)	Immigrants Age 15+ (5)	Third Generation (6)	Second Generation (7)	Immigrants < Age 15 (8)	Immigrants Age 15+ (9)
PANEL ONE: Demographic Characteristics									
Total population, 20–64 years	16,550,900	69,700	149,100	212,100	1,270,700	10,758,100	2,320,300	622,700	1,148,200
Sample N	24,189	85	134	151	865	16,644	2,824	687	1,077
Population, 20–64 years in analysis[a]	14,461,000	53,700	131,600	173,600	1,070,400	9,526,500	1,958,300	529,300	1,017,800
Sample N	19,742	65	118	127	722	14,763	2,366	583	943
Total	100.0%	0.4%	0.9%	1.2%	7.4%	65.9%	13.5%	3.7%	7.0%
Visible minority	100.0	3.8	9.2	12.1	74.9	NA	NA	NA	NA
Other	100.0	NA	NA	NA	NA	73.1	15.0	4.1	7.8
Females	50.9	58.7	46.7	42.8	54.9	50.4	51.7	46.8	52.4
Males	49.1	41.3	53.3	57.2	45.1	49.6	48.3	53.2	47.6
Average age	39.7	36.2	29.1	28.4	40.2	39.2	39.4	38.6	48.2

PANEL TWO: Respondents' Education

< Grade 9 education	8.4%	2.4%	0.3%	2.8%	13.0%	8.1%	4.1%	5.0%	19.2%
High school, no degree	11.9	20.3	4.0	1.3	10.6	12.9	10.9	9.7	9.2
High school degree	32.6	39.0	46.9	37.5	31.6	33.0	33.1	33.6	25.5
Postsecondary	28.6	21.9	24.6	33.0	22.6	29.4	29.8	28.3	25.3
University and above	18.5	16.6	24.1	25.5	22.2	16.6	22.2	23.4	20.9
High school diploma, certificate	79.7%	77.4%	95.6%	95.9%	76.4%	79.0%	85.1%	85.3%	71.6%
No H.S. diploma or certificate	20.3	22.6	4.4	4.1	23.6	21.0	14.9	14.7	28.4
Current student	14.3%	18.6%	44.8%	42.5%	15.5%	13.6%	16.8%	14.1%	5.8%
Not current student	85.7	81.4	55.2	57.5	84.5	86.4	83.2	85.9	94.2
Average education (years)	13.3	13.1	14.8	14.9	12.8	13.2	14.0	13.8	12.7
Age standardized	RG	13.0	14.2	15.4	14.8	14.7	15.4	15.7	15.8
Difference		–0.2	–0.7	0.4	2.0	1.4	1.4	1.9	3.0

Source: Statistics Canada, 1996 Survey of Labour and Income Dynamics (SLID).

[a] Listwise population in table 5.4.

NA = not available.

RG = reference group. Age distribution of the entire population used to standardize for age, using the direct age standardization technique (Shryock and Siegel 1971: 289–90).

actual cases exist for the third-generation visible-minority population in the multivariate analyses, and although the results are presented for comparative purposes, the potential for nonrepresentativeness should be kept in mind.

A MAPLE LEAF IS READ ALL OVER

Several different educational measures and a multivariate analysis offer no support for the "second-generation decline" argument that the 1.5 or second generation will have lower educational attainments than the first or third-plus generations. The measures and analysis also are not consistent with the patterns expected from a segmented underclass model. Indeed, the findings are closer to the "success" or "immigrant optimism" model, in which the achievements of the 1.5 and second generations exceed those of their parents and the third-plus generation. Educational attainments of visible-minority immigrant offspring are the highest of all generation groups and exceed those of their not-visible-minority counterparts.

These conclusions rest on the following educational measures: highest educational level attained, receipt or nonreceipt of a high school diploma or certificate, and average years of education (table 5.2). On all three measures, the 1.5 and second generations have higher attainments than do the first and third-plus generations. In contrast to the "downward mobility" motif, visible-minority immigrant offspring display the highest educational attainments (table 5.2, panel 2, columns 3 and 4).

Part of the explanation for the visible minority's "success" may be their propensity to remain in school into the university years. On average, this group is young, and the percentage who have been students during the past twelve months is high.[7] However, the pattern persists even after age differences are taken into account through standardization techniques (the one exception is that there is virtually no difference between the 1.5 generation and the remainder of the foreign-born not-visible-minority population). An equal, if not more plausible, explana-

[7] The question on attending school is a general one and could include short sessions. However, the overall pattern of school attendance reaffirms the need for caution when examining occupational or earnings differentials for generation groups and visible-minority status using the SLID data. If they are in school and employed part-year or part-time, visible-minority immigrant offspring may have lower earnings relative to other generational and not-visible-minority groups.

tion is that visible-minority immigrant offspring are likely to have parents who are themselves well educated, and thus influence the attainments of their offspring (table 5.3). Such influence occurs because parents communicate their academic expectations to offspring and/or have resources that facilitate the higher educational attainments of the 1.5 and second-generation groups. The transmission of educational attainment across generations is well documented in both the general social stratification literature and in specific studies of the educational achievement of school-age children, differentiated by ethnic status and race (see Fejgin 1995; Portes and MacLeod 1996). It also is supported by SLID data which show that by any measure—educational level, percentages having a high school diploma or certificate, or years of schooling—parents of the visible-minority 1.5 or second generations have the highest attainments of all parents (table 5.3, columns 3 and 4).

SUSTAINED ACHIEVEMENTS

To what extent do higher educational attainments of visible-minority offspring in Canada simply reflect the higher education of their parents? This question is answered with two multivariate analyses that include parental education levels along with demographic controls for age and sex composition differences among generation groups. Despite their extensive use in models of occupational status or earnings, province or city of residence are not included as control variables. When using census data or labor force surveys, analysts assume a close temporal correspondence between occupations, earnings, and current residence. However, because geographical movement often occurs after the completion of schooling and throughout the life cycle, there is no necessary correspondence between where education was received and the current place of residence for many older adults included in this analysis. Indeed, controlling for age may be a better indirect measure of where schooling is completed, simply because place of residence and place of schooling are most likely to be the same for those who are young or still in school.

The dependent variable in the first model is attaining a high school degree or higher. This variable was selected for two reasons. First, much of the American research that focuses on immigrant youth emphasizes the importance of high school completion in postindustrial economies. Second, because twenty was the lower age limit of the population under analysis, some respondents were still in the process

Table 5.3. Parental Educational Attainment for the Canadian Population, Aged 20 to 64, by Visible-Minority Status and Generational Status

		Visible Minority				Not Visible Minority			
				First Generation				First Generation	
	Total (1)	Third Generation (2)	Second Generation (3)	Immigrants < Age 15 (4)	Immigrants Age 15+ (5)	Third Generation (6)	Second Generation (7)	Immigrants < Age 15 (8)	Immigrants Age 15+ (9)
FATHER'S EDUCATION									
< Grade 9 education	44.2	38.6	24.6	26.9	53.5	44.1	41.2	43.4	48.0
High school, no degree	19.6	18.9	20.7	12.2	10.0	21.8	18.8	15.2	13.5
High school degree	19.8	24.3	19.7	25.3	19.8	19.9	20.0	16.5	19.3
Postsecondary	7.2	9.1	9.9	8.6	4.6	6.8	9.2	10.8	6.9
University and above	9.2	9.2	25.2	27.0	12.1	7.4	10.8	14.0	12.2
High school diploma, certificate	36.2	42.6	54.7	61.0	36.5	34.1	40.0	41.3	38.4
No H.S. diploma or certificate	63.8	57.4	45.3	39.0	63.5	65.9	60.0	58.7	61.6
Average education (years)	10.1	10.5	12.1	12.1	9.8	9.9	10.4	10.5	10.2
Age standardized	RG	10.9	11.7	12.6	12.3	12.2	12.5	12.8	13.7
Average age									

		Visible Minority				Not Visible Minority			
				First Generation				First Generation	
	Total (1)	Third Generation (2)	Second Generation (3)	Immigrants < Age 15 (4)	Immigrants Age 15+ (5)	Third Generation (6)	Second Generation (7)	Immigrants < Age 15 (8)	Immigrants Age 15+ (9)
MOTHER'S EDUCATION									
< Grade 9 education	41.6	24.6	31.8	28.5	65.8	38.8	39.1	43.8	50.8
High school, no degree	19.9	31.1	8.9	17.3	7.7	22.4	19.0	15.3	14.2
High school degree	24.2	30.8	31.1	22.3	16.4	24.6	26.2	22.6	23.9
Postsecondary	9.4	9.6	18.6	17.0	4.7	10.0	9.8	9.8	5.4
University and above	5.0	3.9	9.6	14.9	5.5	4.1	6.0	8.5	5.6
High school diploma, certificate	38.5	44.3	59.3	54.2	26.5	38.8	41.9	41.0	35.0
No H.S. diploma or certificate	61.5	55.7	40.7	45.8	73.5	61.2	58.1	59.0	65.0
Average education (years)	10.0	10.8	11.2	11.4	8.7	10.1	10.3	10.2	9.6
Age standardized	RG	10.5	10.6	10.8	9.6	9.6	9.8	9.8	10.2

Source: Statistics Canada, 1996 Survey of Labour and Income Dynamics (SLID), panel 2.

RG = reference group. Age distribution of the entire population used to standardize for age, using the direct age standardization technique (Shryock and Siegel 1971: 289–90).

of completing their postsecondary education. This was particularly true for visible-minority 1.5 and second-generation offspring, who were young and more likely to still be attending school (table 5.1, panel 2). This censoring affected multivariate analyses of university degree receipt.

Logistic regression analysis confirms the importance of parental educational achievements for attaining a high school degree and beyond. Three other conclusions can be drawn with respect to the educational attainments of the generation groups. First, the odds of attaining a high school degree or higher are below that of the general population for persons who immigrated at age fifteen or later. This is true for both the visible-minority and not-visible-minority foreign-born. Many possible explanations exist for these lower educational achievements, including a decline in the quality of immigrants as a result of family-based immigration and refugee flows. None can be tested with the data at hand.

Second, and most important for this study, even after the effects of parental education are taken into account, the educational achievements of visible-minority immigrant offspring remain ahead of other groups. The first eight rows of figures in table 5.4 indicate that the odds of attaining at least a high school degree were almost three times higher for the 1.5 and second-generation visible minorities compared to the entire population aged twenty to sixty-four (table 5.4, column 2). In contrast, the log odds of at least a high school degree or certificate are not significantly different from the overall average for the not-visible-minority immigrant youth (table 5.4, column 1), and by implication neither are the odds.

Reflecting Canada's colonization history and eighteenth- and nineteenth-century migration from the British Isles and Ireland, the third-plus not-visible-minority generation primarily comprises Canada's two charter groups: the French and the "British," and it is the largest of all generation groups, accounting for nearly two-thirds of the population under analysis (table 5.1, panel 1). If this generation group is taken as the reference group, a third conclusion is that the odds of attaining a high school degree or more are greater for all 1.5 and second-generation groups, regardless of color. However, the "success" story of those who are visible minorities continues. Compared to the not-visible-minority third-plus generation, the odds of attaining at least a high school certificate or degree are over four times greater for the visible-minority 1.5 and second generations.

Table 5.4. Logits and Odds Ratios for Attaining a High School Degree or Higher, by Generation and Visible-Minority Status, Population Aged 20 to 64, Canada, 1996

	Logits[a] (1)	Odds Ratio Relative to: Overall Population (2)	Third Generation, Not Visible Minority (3)
GENERATION	***		
Member, visible-minority group			
3rd+ generation	−0.809**	0.4	0.7
2nd generation	1.064 **	2.9	4.5
Foreign-born, immigrated age <15	1.023 ***	2.8	4.3
Foreign-born, immigrated age 15+	−0.373 ***	0.7	1.1
Not visible minority			
3rd+ generation	−0.445 ***	0.6	RG
2nd generation	0.071	1.1	1.7
Foreign-born, immigrated age <15	−0.020	1.0	1.5
Foreign-born, immigrated age 15+	−0.512 ***	0.6	0.9
SEX			
Female	0.079 ***	1.1	
Male	−0.079 ***	0.9	
Age group	***		
20–24	0.042	1.0	
25–34	0.334 ***	1.4	
35–44	0.383 ***	1.5	
45–54	0.061	1.1	
55–64	−0.820 ***	0.4	
FATHER'S EDUCATION	***		
< Grade 9	−1.229 ***	0.3	
High school, no degree	−0.534 ***	0.6	
High school, degree	−0.199 *	0.8	
Postsecondary	0.118	1.1	
University	0.446 **	1.6	
Above university degree	1.398 ***	4.0	
MOTHER'S EDUCATION	***		
< Grade 9	−1.311 ***	0.3	
High school, no degree	−0.757 ***	0.5	
High school, degree	−0.165	0.8	
Postsecondary	0.116	1.1	
University	0.213	1.2	
Above university degree	1.903 *	6.7	
Constant	3.339 ***		

Source: Statistics Canada, 1996 Survey of Labour and Income Dynamics, panel 2.
[a] Deviation coding: * $p < .05$, ** $p < .01$, *** $p < .001$.

Table 5.5. Regression Coefficients for Years of Education, for Population Aged 20 to 64, by Generation and Visible-Minority Status, Canada, 1996

	OLS Regression B's		Deviations from Grand Mean of 13	
	Model 1 (1)	Model 2 (2)	Model 1 (3)	Model 2 (4)
GENERATION AND VISIBLE MINORITY				
Visible minority				
3rd+ generation	0.370	−0.430	−0.48	−0.5
2nd generation	1.090 ***	0.883 ***	0.98	0.7
Foreign-born, immigrated age <15	0.998 ***	0.770 ***	0.89	0.6
Foreign-born, immigrated age 15+	−0.141	−0.209 *	−0.25	−0.3
Not visible minority				
3rd generation	RG	RG	−0.11	−0.0
2nd generation	0.692 ***	0.661 ***	0.59	0.5
1.5 generation	0.339 **	0.342 **	0.23	0.2
Other foreign-born	−0.146	−0.123	−0.25	−0.2
AGE GROUP				
20–24	−0.926 ***	−1.641 ***		
25–34	0.116	−0.046		
35–44	0.241 ***	0.201 **		
45–54	RG	RG		
55–64	−1.519 ***	−1.468 ***		
SEX				
Male	RG	RG		
Female	−0.104 *	−0.123 **		
FATHER'S EDUCATION				
< Grade 9	−1.910 ***	−1.794 ***		
High school, no degree	−0.955 ***	−0.878 ***		
High school, degree	−0.479***	−0.397 ***		
Postsecondary	RG	RG		
University	0.555 ***	0.507 ***		
Above university degree	1.281 ***	1.239 ***		
MOTHER'S EDUCATION				
< Grade 9	−1.797 ***	−1.746 ***		
High school, no degree	−1.025 ***	−0.987 ***		
High school, degree	−0.473 ***	−0.430 ***		
Postsecondary	RG	RG		
University	−0.014	−0.107		
Above university degree	0.825 ***	0.675 **		
Not currently a student	RG			
Currently a student	1.656 ***			
Constant	15.551 ***	15.354 ***		
Multiple R	0.44	0.47		
R Square	0.20	0.22		

Source: Statistics Canada, 1996 Survey of Labour and Income Dynamics, panel 2.
* p <. 05, ** p <.01, *** p <.001.

The second multivariate analysis uses ordinary least squares (OLS) regression to assess the effects of visible-minority status and generational status on years of education, net of other factors. The regression model repeats the variables found in the logistic regression analysis, and the second model adds whether respondents attended school, either full time or part time, during the preceding twelve months. In the regressions, the third-plus not-visible-minority population is the reference group. The results for immigrant offspring are remarkably consistent with those observed for receipt of at least a high school degree or certificate. Compared to the years of education for the third-plus not-visible-minority generation, educational attainments are significantly greater for the 1.5 and second generations (table 5.5). Relative to the reference group, immigrant offspring who are members of visible-minority groups have close to a year more of schooling, net of age, sex, and parental education. The gap drops somewhat when being a student is factored in, simply because being a student is associated with higher education and thus more years of education.

Transforming regression coefficients into deviations from the overall average years of schooling for the entire population aged twenty to sixty-four also highlights the higher educational achievements of visible-minority immigrant offspring. Again, the findings are consistent with previous conclusions. When compared to the overall average of 13.3 years of education for persons aged twenty to sixty-four, 1.5 and second-generation visible minorities have more education. Compared to other groups, their average years of education (obtained by adding the deviations to the mean of 13.3) are also higher.

CONCLUSION

Contrary to the "second-generation decline" and segmented "underclass" assimilation models found in the United States, adult visible-minority immigrant offspring in Canada do not have lower educational attainments than their parents or their not-visible-minority counterparts. In fact, the 1.5 and second generations who are visible minorities exceed the educational attainments of other not-visible-minority groups.

How are these results to be understood, and what are the implications for future studies of the second generation in postindustrial economies? There are three possible answers. First, the failure to find evidence consistent with "second-generation decline" or "segmented assimilation" returns us to the earlier argument that the history of race relations in Canada differs from that in the United States, and that a large and racially identifiable underclass is absent in Canada. Although this argument may have contemporary validity, it needs to be reexamined in future research. As discussed in Boyd (2000), the aboriginal population comes closest to the U.S. black population in terms of historically rooted marginalization. Within the recent past, the size of this group in off-reserve areas has not been large enough to influence immigrant youth. However, off-reserve migration to cities is high in some areas of Canada, as are this group's fertility rates. Whether a sizable aboriginal youth population in urban areas will emerge over the next two decades and whether such youths will become an oppositional reference group for immigrant offspring are questions to be answered in future studies.

A second possible explanation rests on country differences in the demographics of immigration. Canada has a population approximately one-tenth that of the United States, but a far higher proportion is foreign-born (17 percent in 1996). In some cities, particularly Montreal, Toronto, and Vancouver, nearly one-half the population is foreign-born, many having arrived after the changes in immigration policies of the 1960s and 1970s. U.S. scholars argue that heavy and unrelenting immigration flows throttle integration into mainstream American institutions (see Massey 1995). However, one possibility is that sustained immigration into postindustrial societies can create and perpetuate a strong advocacy for educational attainment among immigrants and their children. Rather than acting as a damper, large numbers of immigrants may create a critical mass supporting education and the role of the schools in the lives of their children. Since most recent immigrants are visible minorities, this could influence the educational outcomes of visible-minority offspring.

Finally, the findings presented in this chapter rest on aggregations of the educational attainments of diverse groups. It is possible that greater stratification, and even educational decline, would be observed if information on specific racial groups were available. However, other Canadian studies have observed findings that are consistent with those found in this chapter. Most of these investigations focus on a limited number of groups (blacks or Chinese), and at most they employ a Canadian-born versus foreign-born distinction (for a review, see Davies and Guppy 1998; Simmons and Plaza 1998). The most comprehensive analysis to date was conducted by Guppy and Davies. Using 1991 census data, they found that virtually all of the visible-minority groups have high school graduation rates that are superior to other Canadians. Both foreign-born and Canadian-born blacks have graduation rates that exceed those of other Canadians. Similar patterns of high educational achievement are reached with years of schooling. Davies and Guppy suggest there is no evidence of blocked educational mobility for many visible-minority groups in Canada (Davies and Guppy 1998; Guppy and Davies 1998).

Nevertheless, U.S. research, which focuses primarily on adolescents and young adults, offers findings that suggest the desirability of focusing on specific ethnic and racial groups in future studies of immigrant offspring in Canada. For example, among Asian American students, researchers observe differences in the levels of performance by Chinese, Filipinos, Koreans, Japanese, South Asians, and Southeast Asians (Louie 2001). Long and Brown (2001) observe that Caribbean second-generation black youths share similar educational achievement patterns with European white immigrant youths, whereas African youths show declining educational attainment with each generation. Although these studies emphasize the performances of students and/or youths in the school-to-work transition stages, the broad message is one that emphasizes the need for future research to focus on specific groups when examining the educational attainments of adult immigrant offspring.

References

Alba, Richard, and Victor Nee. 1997. "Rethinking Assimilation Theory for a New Era of Immigration," *International Migration Review* 31 (Winter): 826–75.

Berry, John, and Rudolf Kalin. 2000. "Racism: Evidence from National Surveys." In *Race and Racism: Canada's Challenge*, edited by Economic Adaptation of Asian Immigrants. Montreal: McGill-Queen's University Press.

Board on Children and Families. 1995. "Immigrant Children and Their Families: Issues for Policy and Research," *The Future of Children* 5, no. 2 (Summer/Fall): 72–89.

Boyd, Monica. 1976. "International Migration Policies and Trends: A Comparison of Canada and United States," *Demography* 13, no. 10 (February): 73–80.

———. 2000. "Ethnicity and Immigrant Offspring." In *Race and Ethnicity*, edited by Madeline Kalbach and Warren Kalbach. Toronto: Harcourt Brace.

Boyd, Monica, Gustave Goldman, and Pamela White. 2000. "Race in the Canadian Census." In *Visible Minorities in Canada*, edited by Leo Driedger and Shiva Halli. Montreal: McGill-Queen's University Press.

Boyd, Monica, and Elizabeth Grieco. 1998. "Triumphant Transitions: Socio-economic Achievements of the Second Generation in Canada," *International Migration Review* 32 (Winter): 857–76.

Boyd, Monica, and Michael Vickers. 2000. "100 Years of Immigration," *Canadian Social Trends* 58 (Autumn): 2–12.

Davies, Scott, and Neil Guppy. 1998. "Race and Canadian Education." In *Racism and Social Inequality in Canada,* edited by Vic Satzewich. Toronto: Thompson Educational Publishing.

Dentler, Robert A., and Anne L. Hafner. 1997. *Hosting Newcomers: Structuring Educational Opportunities for Immigrant Children*. New York: Teachers College Press, Columbia University.

Driedger, Leo. 1996. *Multi-Ethnic Canada: Identities and Inequalities*. Toronto: Oxford University Press.

Driedger, Leo, and Angus Reid. 2000. "Public Opinion on Visible Minorities." In *Race and Racism: Canada's Challenge,* edited by Leo Driedger and Shiva S. Halli. Montreal: McGill-Queen's University Press.

Farley, Reynolds. 1999. "A New Look at Second Generation Immigrants." Paper presented at the annual meeting of the Population Association of America.

Fejgin, Naomi. 1995. "Factors Contributing to the Academic Excellence of American Jewish and Asian Students," *Sociology of Education* 68 (January): 18–30.

Gans, Herbert. 1992. "Second Generation Decline: Scenarios for the Economic and Ethnic Futures of the Post-1965 American Immigrants," *Ethnic and Racial Studies* 15 (April): 173–91.

———. 1997. "Toward a Reconsideration of 'Assimilation' and 'Pluralism': The Interplay of Acculturation and Ethnic Retention," *International Migration Review* 31 (Winter): 875–92.

Gibson, Margaret A. 1991. "Minorities and Schooling: Some Implications." In *Minority Status and Schooling: A Comparative Study of Immigrant and Involuntary Minorities,* edited by Margaret A. Gibson and John U. Ogbu. New York: Garland.

Glick, Jennifer E., and Michael J. White. 2000. "Immigrant Cohorts and Achievements in High School." Paper presented at the annual meeting of the Population Association of America.

Guppy, Neil, and Scott Davies. 1998. *Education in Canada: Recent Trends and Future Challenges*. Ottawa: Statistics Canada/Ministry of Industry.

Hawkins, Freda. 1988. *Canada and Immigration: Public Policy and Public Concern*. Montreal: McGill-Queen's University Press.

Henry, Frances, Carol Tator, Winston Mattis, and Tim Rees. 2000. *The Color of Democracy: Racism in Canadian Society*. 2d ed. Toronto: Harcourt Brace.

International Migration Review. 1994. "The New Second Generation," edited by Alejandro Portes, vol. 28 (Winter).

———. 1997. "Immigrant Adaptation and Native-Born Responses in the Making of Americans," edited by Josh DeWind, C. Hirschman, and P. Kasinitz, vol. 31 (Winter).

Kao, Grace, and Marta Tienda. 1995. "Optimism and Achievement: The Educational Performance of Immigrant Youth," *Social Science Quarterly* 76 (March): 1–19.

Kelley, Ninette, and Michael Trebilcock. 1998. *The Making of the Mosaic: A History of Canadian Immigration Policy*. Toronto: University of Toronto Press.

Li, Peter. 1999. *Race and Ethnic Relations in Canada*. 2d ed. Toronto: Oxford University Press.

Long, Xue Lan, and Frank Brown. 2001. "The Effects of Immigrant Generation and Ethnicity on Educational Attainment among Young African and Caribbean Blacks in the United States," *Harvard Educational Review* 71, no. 3: 536–65.

Louie, Vivian. 2001. "Parents' Aspirations and Investments: The Role of Social Class in the Educational Experience of 1.5 and Second-Generation Chinese Americans," *Harvard Educational Review* 71, no. 3: 438–74.

Massey, Douglas. 1995. "The New Immigration and Ethnicity in the United States," *Population and Development Review* 21 (September): 631–52.

McDonnell, Lorraine M., and Paul T. Hill. 1993. *Newcomers in American Schools: Meeting the Educational Needs of Immigrant Youth*. Santa Monica: Rand Corporation.

Miles, Robert. 1989. *Racism*. London: Routledge.

Ogbu, John U. 1991. "Immigrant and Involuntary Minorities in Comparative Perspective." In *Minority Status and Schooling: A Comparative Study of Immigrant and Involuntary Minorities*, edited by Margaret A. Gibson and John U. Ogbu. New York: Garland.

Omi, Michael, and Howard Winant. 1994. *Racial Formation in the United States: From the 1960s to the 1980s*. 2d ed. London: Routledge.

Perlmann, Joel, and Roger Waldinger. 1997. "Second Generation Decline? Children of Immigrants, Past and Present—A Reconsideration," *International Migration Review* 31 (Winter): 893–922.

Portes, Alejandro. 1995. "Children of Immigrants: Segmented Assimilation and Its Determinants." In *The Economic Sociology of Immigration: Essays on Networks, Ethnicity and Entrepreneurship*, edited by Alejandro Portes. New York: Russell Sage Foundation.

———. 1997. "Immigration Theory for a New Century: Some Problems and Opportunities," *International Migration Review* 31 (Winter): 799–825.

Portes, Alejandro, and Dag MacLeod. 1996. "Educational Progress of Children of Immigrants: The Roles of Class, Ethnicity and School Context," *Sociology of Education* 69: 255–75.

———. 1999. "Educating the Second Generation: Determinants of Academic Achievement among Children of Immigrants in the United States," *Journal of Ethnic and Migration Studies* 25, no. 3: 373–96.

Portes, Alejandro, and Min Zhou. 1993. "The New Second Generation: Segmented Assimilation and Its Variants," *Annals of the American Academy of Political and Social Science* 530 (November): 74–96.

Reitz, Jeffrey G. 1998. *Warmth of the Welcome: The Social Causes of Economic Success for Immigrants in Different Nations and Cities*. Boulder, Colo.: Westview.

Reitz, Jeffrey G., and Raymond Breton. 1994. *The Illusion of Difference: Realities of Ethnicity in Canada and the United States*. Toronto: C.D. Howe.

Rumbaut, Rubén G. 1997. "Assimilation and Its Discontents: Between Rhetoric and Reality," *International Migration Review* 31 (Winter): 923–60.

Rumbaut, Rubén G., and Wayne A. Cornelius, eds. 1995. *California's Immigrant Children: Theory, Research, and Implications for Educational Policy*. La Jolla: Center for U.S.-Mexican Studies, University of California, San Diego.

Satzewich, Vic, ed. 1998. *Racism and Social Inequality in Canada: Concepts, Controversies and Strategies of Resistance*. Toronto: Thompson Educational Publishing.

Shryock, Henry S., and Jacob S. Siegel. 1971. *The Methods and Materials of Demography*. Vol. 1. Washington, D.C.: U.S. Department of Commerce, Bureau of the Census.

Simmons, Alan B., and Dwaine E. Plaza. 1998. "Breaking through the Glass Ceiling: The Pursuit of University Training among African-Caribbean Migrants and Their Children in Toronto," *Canadian Ethnic Studies* 30, no. 3: 99–120.

Small, Stephen. 1994. *Racialised Barrier: The Black Experience in the United States and England*. New York: Routledge.

———. 1998. "The Contours of Racialization: Structures, Representation and Resistance in the United States." In *Racism and Social Inequality in Canada*, edited by Vic Satzewich. Toronto: Thompson Educational Publishing.

Stewart, David W. 1993. *Immigration and Education: The Crisis and the Opportunity*. New York: Lexington Books.

Vernez, George, Allan Abrahamse, and Denise Quigley. 1996. *How Immigrants Fare in U.S. Education*. Santa Monica, Calif.: Rand Corporation.

Wargon, Sylvia. 2000. "Historical and Political Reflections on Race." In *Visible Minorities in Canada*, edited by Leo Driedger and Shiva Halli. Montreal: McGill-Queen's University Press.

Waters, Mary. 1994. "Ethnic and Racial Identities of Second-Generation Black Immigrants in New York City," *International Migration Review* 28 (Winter): 795–820.

———. 1997. "Immigrant Families at Risk: Factors That Undermine Chances for Success." In *Immigration and the Family: Research and Policy on U.S. Immigrants*, edited by Alan Booth, Ann C. Crouter, and Nancy Landale. Mahwah, N.J.: Lawrence Erlbaum.

White, Michael J., and Jennifer E. Glick. 2000. "Generation Status, Social Capital and the Routes Out of High School," *Sociological Forum* 15, no. 4: 671–91.

Zhou, Min. 1997a. "Growing Up American: The Challenge Confronting Immigrant Children and Children of Immigrants," *Annual Review of Sociology* 23: 63–95.

———. 1997b. "Segmented Assimilation: Issues, Controversies, and Recent Research on the New Second Generation," *International Migration Review* 31 (Winter): 975–1008.

Zhou, Min, and Carl L. Bankston, III. 1998. *Growing Up American: How Vietnamese Children Adapt to Life in the United States.* New York: Russell Sage Foundation.

Zlotnik, Hania. 1996. "Policies and Migration Trends in North American Systems." In *International Migration, Refugee Flows and Human Rights in North America: The Impact of Trade and Restructuring,* edited by A. Simmons. New York: Center for Migration Studies.

6

Residential Inequality and Segregation in an Immigration Era: An Analysis of Major U.S. Metropolitan Regions in 1990

RICHARD D. ALBA, JOHN R. LOGAN, AND BRIAN J. STULTS

Three conceptions of incorporation dominate the contemporary discussion of immigration to the United States. At one vertex of a triangle of possibilities is assimilation, associated with gradual cultural, social, and socioeconomic integration into the mainstream society. While prevalent among the descendants of past immigrants to the United States—and also of those to other societies, such as France—its applicability to present-day immigrations has been called seriously into question (Alba and Nee 1997; cf. Zhou 1997). At another vertex lies the possibility of a vigorous, enduring ethnic pluralism, whose prospects seem enhanced by the advantages to be derived from ethnic affiliations in heterogeneous societies and by the border spannings enabled by enormous advances in transportation and communication (Portes and Bach 1985; cf. Sanders and Nee 1987; Glick Schiller, Basch, and Blanc-Szanton 1995; cf. Foner 1997). Occupying the third vertex is a widely

---

This research was supported by a grant from the National Science Foundation (SBR95-07920) and by a Russell Sage Foundation Visiting Scholar Fellowship to the first author. The Center for Social and Demographic Analysis, University at Albany, provided technical and administrative support through grants from NICHD (P30 HD32041) and NSF (SBR-9512290). We are grateful for the comments we received from conference participants.

discussed possibility that represents a special form of assimilation, but not of the kind generally highlighted in assimilation theory. It foresees the possibility that many in the second and third generations from the new immigrant groups, hindered by their very disadvantaged initial locations in American society and barred from entry to the mainstream by their skin color, are incorporated as racial minorities, either by absorption into domestic minorities, especially African Americans, or possibly by the establishment of other racialized categories (Portes and Zhou 1993; Waters 1999).

We need not choose among these models, as if only one is valid and the others must therefore be false. Each can apply under some range of circumstances, and the task for research ought to be to identify the patchwork of their application. One domain in which this task can be pursued is that of residential situation, for each of these conceptions can be mapped into a residential pattern that can be looked for among the new immigrant minorities. The assimilation conception is represented by the spatial assimilation model, which envisions that immigrants and their descendants are increasingly likely to mix residentially with the majority population as their socioeconomic status improves and as they acculturate (Massey 1985).

Models of ethnic pluralism, such as the enclave model of the labor market, propose by contrast that immigrants and the second and perhaps later generations need not be disadvantaged by remaining within an ethnic social matrix. This would imply that at least some portions of immigrant groups remain tied to ethnic residential communities even though they may have the socioeconomic resources to leave. Presumably, such loyalty would be most likely when those communities offer some of the same amenities to be found in areas where the white majority is the dominant element among residents (Breton 1964; Logan, Alba, and Zhang 2002).

Finally, incorporation as a racial minority implies residential disadvantages that are hard to overcome. At the extreme this may take the form of ghettoization, which entails not simply residence in a racially and ethnically homogeneous area but in one that is substantially disadvantaged by comparison with most other areas (Massey and Denton 1993). But even when members of a racial minority are able to escape the ghetto, they are not able to fully convert their socioeconomic and other resources into residence in advantaged neighborhoods because of dual housing markets and what Logan and Molotch (1987) call "the hierarchy of places." In other words, the "qualities" of their residence remain less than those found where members of the majority who are otherwise similar (for example, in socioeconomic characteristics or family structure) reside.

The predominant tradition in research on racial and ethnic inequality in residence—namely, the segregation tradition—is not adequate to examine the differences among these three conceptions. This is in no way to deny the impressive contributions to knowledge produced by segregation studies, but they suffer from two kinds of limitations that are relevant here. First, they do not allow the analyst in a natural way to bring to bear characteristics of communities other than racial/ethnic composition—the "qualities" of the places where members of different racial/ethnic groups typically reside. Second, they do not make it easy to take into account the variety of individual and household characteristics other than race/ethnicity that may account for residential location. For these reasons we prefer to take a different approach—through what we have elsewhere called "locational-attainment" models. In contrast to the summary-measure approach (for example, citywide index-of-dissimilarity values) associated with segregation research, locational-attainment models take characteristics of the communities where people live as dependent variables and attempt to account for the sorting of individuals and households among these communities in terms not only of race/ethnicity but also of income, family structure, and other variables.

Such models do permit one to study segregation in the sense that the racial/ethnic composition of communities can be used to form the dependent variable or variables, but one is no longer limited to the question of how segregated a group is overall. One can also answer an ancillary question: who in a minority group lives in communities with many members of the majority, and who does not? One can, in addition, examine characteristics of communities, such as their wealth or affluence, either of which is sure to correlate very strongly with many other desired features of communities, from the quality of their schools to the safety of their streets. This latter kind of analysis has no analogue in the segregation tradition, but it is invaluable in detecting whether residence in communities with many co-ethnics is a form of ghettoization or pluralism.

Other important questions concern the ways in which patterns of residential inequality and segregation hinge on the features of the metropolitan contexts in which groups are embedded. While these questions have formed a part of the segregation tradition (see, for example,

Farley and Frey 1994), they have not yet received much attention in the literature on contemporary immigrant groups. Indeed, that literature has focused heavily on immigrant communities in some of the largest metropolitan regions of the United States, such as Los Angeles and New York, where immigrants have also concentrated (Foner 2000; Sassen 1991; Waldinger 1996; Waldinger and Bozorgmehr 1996). But it seems logical to hypothesize that residential patterns are different in these regions than in smaller ones, where there is probably less neighborhood differentiation to start with. Moreover, the concentration of immigrant populations in a limited number of regions implies that others may lack the critical mass necessary for the emergence of ethnic communities. Such hypotheses are naturally incorporated in the locational-attainment approach through the inclusion of contextual—that is, metropolitan-level—variables in a model.

The current chapter applies this approach to the major racial/ethnic populations (non-Hispanic whites, non-Hispanic blacks, Hispanics, and Asians) in the thirty largest U.S. metropolitan regions as of 1990. The list encompasses the regions that have received a disproportionate share of contemporary immigration, such as New York, Los Angeles, Miami, and San Diego (Farley 1996; Portes and Rumbaut 1996). In that year, the top thirty regions accounted for a large share of the nation's nonwhite, nonblack diversity, and included 69 percent of all Asians and 66 percent of all Hispanics. But even though contemporary immigration has so far concentrated on the largest regions, the top-thirty list includes some that have been only lightly touched by it, such as Cleveland and Columbus. Because our analysis goes beyond the high-immigration regions that have so far been prominent in the study of immigration's impact on residential patterns, it is better positioned to assess that impact.

THEORETICAL BACKGROUND AND RESEARCH QUESTIONS

The point of departure for most analyses of the linkage of race and ethnicity to distribution across metropolitan space is the spatial assimilation model (Massey 1985). This model envisions segregation and locational inequality as arising from market-based processes, combined with the residential enclaves that groups form during their migration phase. Thus, in-migrating groups initially settle in inner-city enclaves, typically in disadvantaged areas. As their individual members experience social mobility and acculturation, they usually leave these enclaves in search of more residential amenities. Since amenities are generally concentrated in neighborhoods where the majority group is dominant, this search generally implies entry into majority-group areas. Hence success depends to an important extent on minority acceptability to the majority, and for this reason African Americans and other minorities with a substantial admixture of African ancestry (such as Puerto Ricans) are viewed as exceptions to the model (Massey and Denton 1993). The departure from cities and entry into suburbs represents a particularly significant stage of spatial assimilation because of the greater residential intermixing in suburbia and the greater average affluence of suburban neighborhoods (Massey and Denton 1988). According to the model, locational inequalities should be largely explained by household socioeconomic and assimilation status, as measured for instance by household income and nativity/length of residence in the United States, and also by residence in city versus suburb.

An established alternative model is that of place stratification (Logan and Molotch 1987), which is consistent with the notion of racialized incorporation. It starts from the premise that communities and neighborhoods are ordered hierarchically. This stratification is seen as a means by which more advantaged groups—non-Hispanic whites, say—preserve social distance from less advantaged ones. The model emphasizes the structural impediments to residential assimilation, which include public and private discrimination (Massey and Denton 1993). Discrimination engenders a dual housing market, making it difficult for racial and ethnic minorities to enter some areas and adding to the cost they must pay for housing. As a result, personal assets such as income and cultural adaptation do not have the same locational value for all groups; members of the majority or other advantaged groups are better able to convert them into favorable residential situations. The racial distinctiveness of the large majority of contemporary immigrants, more than 80 percent of whom are of non-European origin, suggests one reason to suspect that the stratification model may apply to their residential patterns. To that can be added Blalock's (1967) well-known linkage of perceived threat and minority size, which indicates that the rapid influx into some metropolitan regions could heighten the social boundary between the majority and the new groups, leading to increased discrimination against the latter. Consequently, the residential patterns of immigrant minorities would begin to resemble those of African Americans, a possibility already anticipated by Wilson (1987:

35–36), who forecast increasing segregation for Asians and Hispanics as their numbers rise.

In previous research examining the locational situations of racial/ethnic groups in five diverse metropolitan regions in 1980 and 1990, we found qualified support for both models, each with its own distinctive sphere of application (see Alba, Logan, and Stults 2000; Logan, Alba, McNulty, and Fisher 1996; Alba and Logan 1993; Logan and Alba 1993). To start with, there were quite substantial racial/ethnic inequalities in terms of the two dependent variables we used to measure neighborhood standing: median household income, an obvious measure of neighborhood affluence; and the percent of non-Hispanic whites among residents, an indicator of residential exposure to the racial/ethnic majority. In general, non-Hispanic whites were the most locationally advantaged (in terms of neighborhood affluence, say), and African Americans the most disadvantaged, with Asians and Latinos in between. The locational disparities were partly a function of the degree of concentration in cities rather than suburbs, and they reflected as well the socioeconomic and other characteristics of group members that determine the kind of neighborhood in which they can reside.

But even when all these factors were controlled, inequality was not fully explained. In the case of African Americans, higher socioeconomic attainment did lead to residence in more affluent neighborhoods and in ones shared with larger numbers of whites, but these "improvements" largely paralleled similar shifts for whites, so that the locational gap between the races remained large. In this respect, the place-stratification model is supported. For Asians and Hispanics, by contrast, residential disparities in comparison to whites were greatest at the lower end of the socioeconomic scale, and for Hispanics, among the linguistically unassimilated and those with darker skins. At the upper end of the socioeconomic scale, white Hispanics fluent in English and Asians, regardless of English ability, resided in neighborhood settings similar to those where socioeconomically comparable whites were found. In this sense, one can conclude that a process of spatial assimilation was at work.

But the rapid growth of new immigrant populations and their distinctive characteristics may require a third model. In contrast to the immigrants of past eras, the new arrivals include a large stratum with high levels of human and financial capital. Their presence has facilitated settlement throughout the metropolis; some immigrant groups are going in large numbers to suburbia, where some middle-class ethnic areas have emerged, epitomized by Monterey Park (Alba, Denton, Leung, and Logan 1995; Alba, Logan, Stults, et al. 1999; Horton 1995). These novel immigrant settlement patterns could forestall spatial assimilation, for the emergence of affluent immigrant neighborhoods in suburbs alters the opportunity structure on which spatial assimilation theory is predicated; they may also represent a break with the segregation envisioned in the place-stratification model, which is accompanied by locational disadvantage. This suggests the possible utility of an "ethnic community" model that has yet to be delineated in the same detail as its predecessors (Logan, Alba, and Zhang 2002). But it would allow for the possibility that new immigrants and their second generation are able to attain desirable qualities in communities, such as good schools and low risks of crime victimization, without sacrificing their proximity to co-ethnics and to the infrastructure (including ethnic stores and organizations) associated with an ethnic community.

This need not imply a great deal of segregation from the majority—indeed, some of the suburban communities where new immigrants are found, such as those in northern New Jersey, also contain many whites. These residential niches are therefore not "enclaves" in the usual sense of the term, but they do encompass greater racial/ethnic diversity than is indicated by spatial assimilation. In terms of the community indicators we will employ here, the model suggests a decoupling of the patterns of prediction for community affluence and racial composition. If the model applies, then immigrant minorities would realize gains in community affluence in accordance with their own personal and household characteristics and, at some point, would reside in communities as affluent as those in which comparable members of the white majority are found. But their residential exposure to the majority would not increase commensurately.

The emergence of ethnic communities arising from immigration could also impact on the residential patterns of African Americans. It appears that African American segregation is lower in more diverse metropolitan regions, especially in the South and West (Farley and Frey 1994). Some evidence suggests that African Americans may find it easier to enter neighborhoods that already have a presence, even a thin one, of other minorities than to enter overwhelmingly white areas (Denton and Massey 1991). In addition, the suburbanization of African Americans has increased substantially in recent decades (Frey 1994). Both trends may have increased African American access to more affluent neighborhoods, but especially where racially and ethnically diverse neighborhoods have been created by immigration.

DATA AND METHOD

At the core of our analysis are locational-attainment models, which take the form:

$$(1) \qquad Y_j = a + b_1 X_{1ij} + b_2 X_{2ij} + \ldots + e_{ij}$$

where Y is a neighborhood (census tract) characteristic and the X's are individual- or household-level characteristics, such as household type, educational attainment, and household income; the subscript j indexes neighborhoods and subscript i, the individuals who reside in them. The coefficients in equations of this type can be interpreted in terms of the ability of the members of a given group to convert some personal or household characteristic into a favorable residential location. While the advantages of this modeling approach are obvious, in the past it has been difficult to employ because of the rarity of data sets at the individual or household level that also contain community characteristics measured for small areas. The advent of census confidential data centers may radically alter this calculus by making it much easier to estimate directly models that contain individual- and household-level variables as well as contextual ones. Until then, the existing cross-level data sets that allow direct estimation, such as the Panel Study of Income Dynamics (PSID) with tract-level data appended (South and Crowder 1999) or special census public-use samples (White, Biddlecom, and Guo 1993), have critical limitations for our purposes.

Hence, for now our approach uses an indirect strategy, achieved by splicing together covariances generated from tract-level data and from public-use microdata (see Alba and Logan 1992). A disadvantage is that our strategy does not allow us the control over the precise definition of micro-level variables that can be attained with existing cross-level data sets such as the PSID; our variables are limited by the tabulations available in census summary tape files. But a countervailing advantage is that a large number of cases is available for relatively small populations, such as Asians, who cannot be studied in the PSID. And a second is that we are able to estimate models by metropolitan region, which allows fullest play to the residential idiosyncrasies of regions. We estimate models specifically in each of the thirty largest metropolitan regions. Where Census Bureau definitions allow, these regions are each defined by their CMSA boundaries, the broadest possible form.[1]

As noted, the current analysis will employ two dependent variables: median household income measures the affluence and amenities of a community; and the percent non-Hispanic white among residents, the prevalence of the majority group in its population. We estimate models separately for four major racial/ethnic populations—namely, Asians, Hispanics, non-Hispanic blacks, and non-Hispanic whites. While we recognize that there is interest also in models for the groups within these broad umbrella categories, our method does not allow us to create them (because the necessary tables are not reported at the tract level by the Census Bureau). In any event, the segregation literature has generally adhered to this level of aggregation (see, for example, Farley and Frey 1994; Massey and Denton 1988), making our results comparable to it. We do take finer group memberships into account by including them among the independent variables (see below).

The individual- and household-level independent variables—which are represented in categorical form, as dummy variables, in the models—are the following:

- Socioeconomic status: annual household income (in thirteen categories, with the highest $100,000 and above; the omitted category contains individuals in households with under $5,000); class of worker (in four categories defined for individuals sixteen years and older, with those employed in private firms constituting the omitted category); education (in five categories defined only for individuals twenty-five and older; the omitted category contains those with only a grammar school education); housing tenure (owner occupied versus rental, with the latter omitted).
- Assimilation status: nativity/year of immigration (in four categories, with the native-born forming the omitted category); English language proficiency (in three categories, with those who speak only English at home as the omitted category).
- Location: suburban versus central city (the latter is omitted).
- Race among Latinos: white, black, and other (the first is omitted).

[1] The top thirty metropolitan regions as we have defined them encompass thirteen Metropolitan Statistical Areas (MSAs) and sixty-two Primary Metropolitan Statistical Areas (PMSAs); the latter are the components of Consolidated Metropolitan Statistical Areas (CMSAs).

In addition, our models include several control variables that play no role in our interpretation. Among them are age and household structure (married-couple households, other family households, non-family households, and institutional and other group-quarters settings). Further, we include national or ethnic origin as a control: among Asians this involves dummy variables for the six most populous groups (Asian Indians, Chinese, Filipinos, Japanese, Koreans, and Vietnamese); among Hispanics, for the four most populous (Cubans, Dominicans, Mexicans, and Puerto Ricans). Among non-Hispanic whites we specify dummy variables for the six most numerous ancestries (English, French, German, Irish, Italian, and Polish). Though ethnic differences also exist within the black population, they overlap extensively with other variables we control, such as foreign birth.

The locational-attainment models estimated with these independent variables yield a superabundance of information: for each dependent variable there are in principle 120 equations (four groups x thirty regions), though we reduce this number slightly by removing from consideration equations where a group has fewer than 20,000 members in a region.[2] In addition, each equation has four socioeconomic variables, two assimilation variables, and one locational variable that are central to our interpretation. To reduce this volume of information to more manageable dimensions, we resort to a standardizing device: namely, we use the models as estimated to predict values of the dependent variables for specified bundles of characteristics that capture the main dimensions of variation at the individual level. For instance, we posit a middle-income, assimilated suburbanite for each group by assigning a common set of values to the independent variables, assuming specifi-

[2] An N less than 20,000 implies that the correlations among the independent variables in the locational-attainment regressions will be based on fewer than 1,000 cases. We adopt this standard because we have observed that the estimation procedure is not well behaved when the N is small.

The R^2's of the equations suggest that the locational-attainment models perform rather well in predicting the characteristics of the neighborhoods where individuals live. Overall, the R^2's are weaker for whites, who are more advantaged on average than others, than for other groups; and they are somewhat stronger in the equations for median household income than in those for the percentage of whites among residents. The lowest R^2 values are found when predicting the racial composition of neighborhoods where whites live; the average across the thirty regions is .17. For the other three groups, the averages for the equations predicting racial composition are in each case greater than .30. In predicting neighborhood affluence, the average R^2 values for Asians and Hispanics are close to .40 (.42 and .37, respectively), while those for whites and blacks are close to .30 (.31 and .28, respectively).

cally in each population an individual who is between the ages of twenty-five and sixty-four, was born in the United States and speaks only English, has graduated from high school but not attended college, and lives in a home-owning household with an annual income between $40,000 and $50,000. Beyond the middle-income assimilated suburbanite, we posit additional types to correspond with the various combinations of socioeconomic status (low, medium, high), assimilation status (native-born English speakers versus recent immigrants who speak English poorly), and location (central city versus suburban)—twelve combinations in all.

In a next step we analyze the predicted values themselves, pooling the predictions for all the groups in all the metropolitan regions (N = 1,344). We formulate the dependent variables for these regressions to reflect the degree of proximity of a given prediction to the residential situation of the average white in a region. The rationale is to take into account basic metropolitan region features such as average affluence of neighborhoods (quite different in Cleveland than in New York, say), which structure the neighborhood values that minority-group members might plausibly attain (and using the white values, rather than overall metropolitan averages, eliminates any influence of minority values on the denominators). Consequently, to analyze the relative affluence of the communities where individuals of various types are predicted to be found, we use as the dependent variable the natural logarithm of the ratio of predicted neighborhood median household income to the average value for whites; for the analysis of racial composition, the dependent variable takes the form of the natural logarithm of the odds ratio between predicted neighborhood percent non-Hispanic white and that observed for the average white. These relative values have meaning for whites themselves and indicate the extent to which whites with particular characteristics can or cannot improve upon the values observed for the average white in a region. We include the white predicted values in the analysis along with those for minority groups in order to examine the residential gains realized by minorities against those of similar whites.

The independent variables include representations of the three dimensions used to construct the predictions. These are represented by dummy variables. Also included are dummy variables to represent the four racial/ethnic populations. Interactions between race/ethnicity and the other variables then are employed to further examine the possible residential gains of the groups.

These equations can be thought of as summaries of the plethora of coefficients to emerge from the metropolitan-specific locational analyses, and they take the following form:

$$\text{(2)} \qquad \text{Ln}\, Y_{ijklm} / \overline{Y_{m.}} = a + b_{1i_i} X_{1i_i} + b_{2j_j} X_{2j_j} + \ldots + b_{12\, i_i j_j} X_{1i_i} X_{2j_j} + \ldots$$

where Y_{ijklm} is the predicted value of Y (census-tract median household income or percent non-Hispanic white) for an individual of group i in metropolitan region m with socioeconomic status j, assimilation status k, and urban/suburban location l. It is normalized by dividing it by the mean of Y for whites in that region. The independent variable X_{1i_i} stands for a series of dummy variables representing the four racial/ethnic groups and is 1 when i_i is the group in question (i) and 0 otherwise. The independent variable X_{2j_j} represents the two dummy variables for socioeconomic status (three categories); similar variables are present for assimilation status and urban/suburban location. The final term exemplifies the interaction terms between race/ethnicity and each of the other variables. A simple way to think of these interactions is that they allow the effects of socioeconomic status and the other variables to vary by racial/ethnic group.

Within this framework, we can scrutinize also the influence of factors that reflect the metropolitan contexts, such as the volume of recent immigration. These factors are investigated by adding them to the equation specified in the preceding paragraph. Since they are posited to have effects that differ by racial/ethnic group, their interactions with the dummy variables representing race/ethnicity are also examined. The metropolitan factors we consider are:

- Metropolitan population size, which is likely to set a limit to the range of variation in neighborhoods and communities. As noted earlier, we expect this to be more constrained in smaller metropolitan regions, causing the residential situations of immigrant minorities to approximate more closely those of whites.
- Regional racial ethnic composition, as represented by the percentages constituted by each of the three minority populations. Diversity in a metropolitan region self-evidently produces diversity in its communities and neighborhoods, increasing the opportunities for minorities to reside with co-ethnics. For Asians and Hispanics, the ethnic community model leads us to predict that this will happen

without detriment to their ability to reside in neighborhoods as affluent as those housing whites. However, larger black populations are likely to be associated with black concentration in poorer neighborhoods, according to the place-stratification model.

- Volume of recent immigration, represented by the percent of the population that immigrated between 1980 and 1990. This variable distinguishes between the regions currently serving as meccas for immigrants and those standing apart from the recent immigrant flow. The ethnic community model envisions the two types as offering qualitatively different residential possibilities for minorities.

FINDINGS

We begin with descriptive data for the thirty regions, presented as table 6.1. The regions are ordered by population size; and for each one, the two characteristics under study—median household income and percent non-Hispanic white—are listed for the communities of residence of the average non-Hispanic white, non-Hispanic black, Hispanic, and Asian. The shaded metropolitan regions are those with above-average percentages of recent immigrants among their residents, and the correlation between population size and above-average immigration is quite visible.

An inspection of the table reveals a fairly clear-cut racial and ethnic ordering in terms of community "quality." It holds not just for the percent non-Hispanic white, which in principle could be affected by the voluntary decisions of minority group members to live in equally good but more diverse communities than those in which comparable whites are found, but also for the affluence of a community. Racial and ethnic differences in the latter are less susceptible to an interpretation that sees segregation as mainly the product of voluntary choices.

In general, whites live in the most affluent communities, though there are some exceptions—for instance, Asians live on average in the most affluent communities in Detroit and a few other regions. Whites also live in the communities that have the largest proportions of white residents, and here their edge over other groups is without exception. Asians are unambiguously in second place in both respects, although the affluence of the communities where they live is closer to that of whites than is true for the prevalence of whites among residents. In a few metropolitan regions, Hispanics, who come next in order, live in areas with more non-Hispanic white residents than do Asians; this is

Table 6.1. Average Residential Situations of Racial/Ethnic Groups in Thirty Largest Metropolitan Regions (1990)

Metropolitan Area	Population (millions)	Average Median Household Income				Average Percent Non-Hispanic White			
		Non-Hispanic Whites	Non-Hispanic Blacks	Hispanics	Asians	Non-Hispanic Whites (%)	Non-Hispanic Blacks (%)	Hispanics (%)	Asians (%)
New York-Northern Jersey-Long Island, NY-NJ-CT CMSA	18.09	47,698	28,397	27,467	39,558	82.2	18.0	33.2	57.4
Los Angeles-Anaheim-Riverside, CA CMSA	14.53	44,995	29,788	31,297	40,990	67.7	23.8	30.4	45.1
Chicago-Gary-Lake County, IL-IN-WI CMSA	8.07	43,610	23,834	28,142	40,201	84.8	14.9	44.7	70.5
San Francisco-Oakland-San Jose, CA CMSA	6.25	47,584	32,166	38,753	43,665	71.5	33.2	48.4	48.6
Philadelphia-Wilmington-Trenton, PA-NJ-DE-MD CMSA	5.90	41,529	25,293	25,788	39,382	88.6	27.9	45.9	75.1
Detroit-Ann Arbor, MI CMSA	4.67	41,082	21,532	30,189	43,870	91.1	17.9	74.6	80.7
Boston-Lawrence-Salem, MA-NH CMSA	4.14	44,482	29,699	28,545	37,397	91.1	40.7	59.5	76.2
Washington, DC-MD-VA MSA	3.92	55,545	37,459	44,874	55,110	76.8	28.9	57.1	68.1
Dallas-Fort Worth, TX CMSA	3.89	38,596	25,209	27,429	37,270	80.3	36.0	52.3	71.2
Houston-Galveston-Brazoria, TX CMSA	3.71	39,025	24,640	27,156	38,599	72.3	27.8	43.7	57.7
Miami-Fort Lauderdale, FL CMSA	3.19	34,833	23,344	28,431	34,518	70.6	22.5	28.3	56.7
Atlanta, GA MSA	2.83	43,140	27,348	36,847	39,750	84.0	30.0	69.6	72.9

Cleveland-Akron-Lorain, OH CMSA	2.76	34,467	20,345	23,456	35,011	92.3	25.1	72.4	85.0
Seattle-Tacoma, WA CMSA	2.56	37,516	27,951	33,519	33,414	87.5	61.5	80.4	71.3
San Diego, CA MSA	2.50	39,980	28,637	30,799	37,223	74.8	41.5	48.3	51.2
Minneapolis-St. Paul, MN-WI MSA	2.46	39,240	25,342	31,588	30,116	93.4	62.2	82.8	74.3
St. Louis, MO-IL MSA	2.44	36,422	21,150	33,479	41,476	91.3	28.0	84.5	85.2
Baltimore, MD MSA	2.38	42,574	26,996	39,307	44,101	86.6	27.8	75.5	77.5
Pittsburgh-Beaver Valley, PA CMSA	2.24	29,152	17,998	*28,208*	*37,131*	94.8	46.9	*87.9*	*89.0*
Phoenix, AZ MSA	2.12	35,328	26,133	25,438	34,774	83.3	54.4	55.3	79.2
Tampa-St. Petersburg-Clearwater, FL MSA	2.07	28,518	19,680	26,940	29,864	88.6	42.0	70.6	83.2
Denver-Boulder, CO CMSA	1.84	38,210	27,316	27,430	34,028	85.0	49.9	62.6	77.0
Cincinnati-Hamilton, OH-KY-IN CMSA	1.74	34,354	20,544	*32,761*	*36,659*	93.5	38.8	*87.1*	*86.8*
Milwaukee-Racine, WI CMSA	1.61	37,219	18,547	23,049	*29,399*	91.3	27.1	62.5	*69.0*
Kansas City, MO-KS MSA	1.57	36,184	21,547	27,881	*35,352*	90.4	34.1	75.0	*82.9*
Sacramento, CA MSA	1.48	35,914	29,162	30,472	32,080	78.4	52.5	63.4	58.3
Portland-Vancouver, OR-WA CMSA	1.48	33,435	23,412	29,909	31,512	90.8	62.1	85.7	87.2
Norfolk-Virginia Beach-Newport News, VA MSA	1.40	34,267	24,660	31,072	35,086	76.8	42.1	70.1	72.3
Columbus, OH MSA	1.38	34,354	21,959	*31,483*	33,072	91.1	44.7	*82.7*	82.7
San Antonio, TX MSA	1.30	28,518	23,839	21,960	*31,774*	88.6	36.3	29.0	*55.6*

Note: Shaded metropolitan areas have above-average proportions of recent immigrants in their populations; italicized numbers indicate populations less than 20,000.

true of Seattle, for instance. In any event, the communities where Hispanics live are in the usual case more affluent than those where non-Hispanic blacks are found, though the margin is often not large, and in a few cases, such as Boston, it is reversed. The margin of difference between Hispanics and African Americans is much larger when it comes to residence in communities with many non-Hispanic whites. With a few exceptions, such as San Antonio, Hispanics reside in communities that are not very different in this respect from those where Asians live.

The differences in table 6.1 include no controls, although the four populations differ in all metropolitan regions in a number of ways that could impact on their locations. Thus Hispanics generally have household incomes well below those of whites, and their locational disadvantages could be overstated in table 6.1—that is, their locations could prove similar to those of whites once income and other factors are accounted for. By contrast, Asians in many regions have higher household incomes on average than do whites (see Alba, Logan, Stults, et al. 1999), and table 6.1 may therefore overstate their proximity to the white residential pattern.

The necessity for additional controls is, of course, the rationale for locational-attainment models, and in table 6.2 we present results that summarize these models for the thirty regions.[3] As explained in the previous section, the dependent variables express predicted neighborhood values in relation to those observed for the average white; and the independent variables represent the categories of socioeconomic position, assimilation status, and location used to construct the predictions, along with dummy variables to represent the racial/ethnic populations. The models reveal that this simple deconstruction does a very good job of summarizing the predictions and thus the detailed results of the original locational-attainment models. Roughly 80 percent of the variation in predicted neighborhood affluence is captured in this way, as is nearly 60 percent of the variance for percent non-Hispanic white.

---

[3] The t-values, normally used to test statistical significance, are not valid as such here; rather, we use them as a rough guide to the selection of effects worth discussing. At the individual level the regressions are based on millions of cases, since the covariances between the dependent and independent variables are derived from STF4, which is based on a roughly one-in-six sample in each metropolitan region, and the correlations between independent variables come from the PUMS data, a one-in-twenty sample. Thus all non-zero coefficients are "significant" in the usual sense of that word.

The regressions in table 6.2 are unweighted.

These simple models demonstrate that the aggregate patterns in table 6.1 are, in fact, somewhat deceptive, that the apparent ethnic order does not hold uniformly across the dimensions that are controlled in the predictions. This finding is signaled immediately in the coefficients of the dummy variables for ethnicity and race in the model summarizing the results for neighborhood affluence. The coefficients for blacks, Hispanics, and Asians are all negative and of approximately the same magnitude, indicating that under some conditions members of the three populations are equally disadvantaged in terms of entry to affluent neighborhoods. Given the construction of the other variables in the model, this is the case for low-socioeconomic-status (SES) recent immigrants in suburbs.

All the groups, whites included, benefit in both models from improvements in socioeconomic status. Relative to the average white in a region, they gain in both the affluence of the neighborhood where they reside and in its percentage non-Hispanic white. These lower-order SES coefficients are among the largest in both models. However, there are racial/ethnic variations in the degree of gain—that is, statistical interactions—and they are especially differentiating when it comes to neighborhood affluence. The negative statistical interaction for high-status blacks in the equation for community affluence indicates that they gain less residentially in this respect than high-status whites (the reference population), while the positive ones for middle- and high-status Asians in both equations indicate that they gain more. In other words, middle- and high-status Asians draw closer in residential situation to whites of similar status, while high-status blacks fall further behind. The interactions for all the minority groups in the equation for neighborhood racial composition indicate that the percent of whites in their neighborhoods rises more sharply with improvements in SES than it does for whites themselves. To be sure, this can be seen as another facet of the fact that even low-SES whites tend to reside in heavily white neighborhoods.

Residing in a suburb versus a central city also has a sizable impact on residential outcomes. This is particularly the case for living in largely white neighborhoods; in the equation for that outcome, the size of the coefficient of the lower-order location variable rivals that of high SES, something that is not true in the equation for neighborhood affluence. In addition, location has an especially great bearing on the residential situations of minority-group members. The relevant interaction terms are, with one exception, sizable, indicating that movement to a

Table 6.2. Regression Analysis of Predicted Community Values from Locational Analyses

	Relative Community Affluence		Relative Racial Composition	
	b	t	b	t
Racial/ethnic groups:				
Non-Hispanic whites	—		—	
Non-Hispanic blacks	-.071	-2.38	-.577	-4.14
White Hispanics	-.093	-3.03	-.675	-4.72
Asians	-.117	-3.75	-.689	-4.71
SES categories:				
Low	—		—	
Medium	.399	17.29	.555	5.15
High	.732	31.69	.788	7.30
Assimilated status	-.023	-1.21	.205	2.33
Central-city residence	-.222	-11.75	-.767	-8.70
SES-race/ethnicity interactions:				
Mid-SES*black	.019	.59	.011	.07
High-SES*black	-.068	-2.09	.604	3.96
Mid-SES*Hispanic	.011	.33	.159	1.01
High-SES*Hispanic	-.028	-.82	.419	2.68
Mid-SES*Asian	.153	4.47	.356	2.23
High-SES*Asian	.112	3.26	.441	2.76
Assimilation-race/ethnicity interactions:				
Assimilation*black	-.039	-1.47	-.867	-6.96
Assimilation*Hispanic	.095	3.47	.510	3.99
Assimilation*Asian	.038	1.37	-.056	-.43
Location-race/ethnicity interactions:				
CC*black	-.131	-4.92	-1.030	-8.27
CC*Hispanic	-.093	-3.39	-.548	-4.28
CC*Asian	-.117	-4.19	-.081	-.62
Intercept	-.409	-19.38	-.401	-4.08
R-squared	.792		.578	

Note: The dependent variables are logged ratios of predicted neighborhood characteristics to metropolitan-wide averages for whites (see text for a more detailed explanation). T-values are not valid for statistical inference but are used as supplementary guides for [illegible] suburb has a larger impact for them than it does for whites. The only exception concerns Asians residing in white neighborhoods; in this case the effect of location is about the same as it is for whites. But in the case of African Americans residing in white neighborhoods, the effect of location is more than double (in the log scale) what it is among whites; for Hispanics it is nearly double. While the minority-specific effects are not so large in terms of community affluence, the interaction terms still augment the locational effect over that among whites by about 50 percent.

The weakest effects are associated with assimilation status. The contrast embodied in the coefficients is between a U.S.-born individual who speaks only English and a recent immigrant who speaks English with difficulty, yet the impact on residential situation is modest. It is most pronounced among Hispanics and is more relevant for the racial/ethnic composition of a community than for its affluence. In the case of the former, more assimilated whites and Asians reside in more heavily white communities, though not by a large margin on average. Among Hispanics the difference made by assimilation status has the same character and is about three times as large. Among blacks, however, it is reversed: recent immigrants are more likely than native-born blacks to reside in largely white communities. For community affluence, assimilation status makes only very small differences.

A critical set of issues concerns whether minorities attain residential parity with whites and, if so, under what circumstances. To address these questions, we use the regression coefficients of table 6.2 to recompose the predictions for the various combinations of the bundled characteristics represented in the three dimensions. We select six sets of predictions for presentation in tables 6.3 (for community affluence) and 6.4 (for community racial composition). They include the combinations for both central cities and suburbs: low-SES recent immigrants; middle-SES native-born English speakers; high-SES native-born English speakers.

In terms of community affluence, Hispanics and Asians catch up to their white counterparts in some of the scenarios; blacks do not under any. Note that a positive value indicates that, under the conditions posited, the predicted residential situation is more favorable than that of the average white (see the left-hand side of equation [2]). Under some circumstances, this happens for all groups, but it does not necessarily indicate residential parity with socially similar whites. This is indicated when the values for similar whites and minority-group members are approximately equal. Such parity is found for middle- and

Table 6.3. Predicted Relative Community Affluence for Six Types, by Race/Ethnicity (logged ratio to metropolitan average for whites)

	Non-Hispanic Whites	Non-Hispanic Blacks	White Hispanics	Asians
In central city:				
Low-SES immigrant	−0.631	−0.833	−0.817	−0.865
Mid-SES native	−0.255	−0.477	−0.335	−0.298
High-SES native	0.078	−0.231	−0.041	−0.006
In suburb:				
Low-SES immigrant	−0.409	−0.480	−0.502	−0.526
Mid-SES native	−0.033	−0.124	−0.020	0.041
High-SES native	0.300	0.122	0.274	0.333

Table 6.4. Predicted Relative Community White Percentage for Six Types, by Race/Ethnicity (logged ratio to metropolitan average for whites)

	Non-Hispanic Whites	Non-Hispanic Blacks	White Hispanics	Asians
In central city:				
Low-SES immigrant	−1.168	−2.775	−2.391	−1.938
Mid-SES native	−0.408	−2.871	−0.962	−0.878
High-SES native	−0.175	−2.045	−0.469	−0.560
In suburb:				
Low-SES immigrant	−0.401	−0.978	−1.076	−1.090
Mid-SES native	0.359	−1.074	0.353	−0.030
High-SES native	0.592	−0.248	0.846	0.288

high-SES assimilated Asians and Hispanics who are located in suburbs (and middle-SES assimilated Asians in cities are close to parity with whites). A proviso for Hispanics must be not be overlooked: namely, in order to avoid confounding issues of Hispanic ethnicity per se and race, these predictions assume that Hispanics are light skinned. Self-described whites represented half of all Hispanics in 1990, but black-skinned Hispanics, who accounted for 3 percent of all Hispanics nationally, are substantially worse off, akin to African Americans. Hispanics who view themselves as neither white nor black fall in between. Finally, although African Americans are behind whites in all the predictions (and behind Asians and Hispanics in most), they do draw close in two scenarios: first, when they are recent immigrants in suburbs, and second, when they are middle-SES assimilated suburbanites.

Racial and ethnic differences are far more pronounced when it comes to the racial composition of communities. The outstanding cleavage is between blacks and everyone else. In general, the predicted percentage of white residents is substantially lower for blacks than for the other groups; the only exception occurs for black immigrants in suburbs. Nevertheless, the only group to attain residential parity with white peers is Hispanics, and this is achieved specifically for assimilated middle- and high-SES Hispanics in suburbs (again, with the implicit proviso that they are light skinned). In this respect, Asians remain distinctive from Hispanics and whites, even though they were closest to whites in table 6.1.

We now turn to the metropolitan-level contextual factors that influence locational attainment, focusing on three sorts of variables: size, racial/ethnic composition, and recent inflows of immigrants. These variables and their interactions with the three group dummy variables are entered sequentially in the columns of tables 6.5 and 6.6.[4]

The rationale for including size can be glimpsed in table 6.1. As populations grow in size, the potential for neighborhood social differentiation rises as well, with the consequence that the disparities in the average residential situations of racial/ethnic groups appear to increase.

---

[4] The findings appear quite robust in the sense that they hold up across different specifications of the model. We have tried, for example, altering the order of introduction of the metropolitan variables (specifically by entering the volume of recent immigration first) and removing the observations for whites so that their residential patterns do not affect the results. The findings remain the same under these different conditions.

Table 6.5. Effects (Regression Coefficients) of Metropolitan Characteristics on Relative Community Affluence of Racial/Ethnic Groups

	b	t	b	t	b	t
Racial/ethnic groups:						
Non-Hispanic whites	—					
Non-Hispanic blacks	–.072	–2.49	–.072	–2.57	–.073	–2.60
White Hispanics	–.089	–3.01	–.092	–3.17	–.092	–3.20
Asians	–.111	–3.65	–.110	–3.71	–.107	–3.65
Logged population size	–.052	–3.75	–.069	–4.79	–.062	–3.54
Population-size interactions:						
With black	–.027	–1.39	–.019	–0.96	.005	0.19
With Hispanic	–.023	–1.15	–.020	–1.01	–.018	–0.70
With Asian	–.012	–0.61	–.012	–0.54	–.009	–0.37
Racial/ethnic composition:						
Percent black			–.001	–1.40	–.001	–0.75
Percent Hispanic			.002	4.01	.004	5.12
Percent Asian			.006	2.81	.010	4.05
Racial/ethnic composition interactions:						
Percent black*black			–.004	–2.79	–.004	–2.99
Percent Hispanic*Hispanic			–.000	–0.10	–.001	–0.66
Percent Asian*Asian			–.003	–0.64	–.003	–0.67
Percent new immigrants						
New immigrant interactions:					–.007	–1.80
With black						
With Hispanic					–.007	–1.55
With Asian					.000	0.07
					–.002	–0.38
R-squared	.806		.816		.819	

Note: The equations also include the variables that appear in table 6.2; as in that table, t-values are presented as guides in assessing the magnitudes of effects.

Table 6.6. Effects (Regression Coefficients of Metropolitan Characteristics on Relative Community [illegible] Racial/Ethnic Groups

	b	t	b	t	b	t
Racial/ethnic groups:						
Non-Hispanic whites	—					
Non-Hispanic blacks	—.598	–4.46	–.602	–4.72	–.600	–4.71
White Hispanics	–.669	–4.86	–.662	–5.04	–.658	–5.02
Asians	–.668	–4.75	–.667	–4.97	–672	–5.02
Logged population size	–.031	–0.48	–.157	–2.40	–.147	1.84
Population-size interactions:						
With black	–.541	–5.93	–.447	–5.07	–.552	–4.94
With Hispanic	–.247	–2.66	–.172	–1.91	–.277	–2.42
With Asian	–.237	–2.48	–.113	–1.17	–.157	–1.40
Racial/ethnic composition:						
Percent black			.003	0.91	.001	0.42
Percent Hispanic			.004	1.70	–.001	–0.32
Percent Asian			.052	5.64	.038	3.56
Racial/ethnic composition interactions:						
Percent black*black			–.044	–6.78	–.043	–6.48
Percent Hispanic*Hispanic			–.023	–5.14	–.026	–4.15
Percent Asian*Asian			–.069	–3.82	–.066	–3.26
Percent new immigrants					.012	0.68
New immigrant interactions:						
With black					.030	1.55
With Hispanic					.033	1.33
With Asian					.015	0.70
R-squared	.610		.648		.650	

Note: The equations also include the variables that appear in table 6.2.

The locational-attainment regressions reveal that these effects persist when individual-level independent variables are controlled, and also that they are more impressive in relation to the racial composition of neighborhoods. For community affluence, the logged ratio of the comparison to the average community affluence of whites is lowered as population size grows. But the effect is modest: an increase in population size by 1 in the logarithmic scale (which corresponds with a near tripling of metropolitan population size) reduces predicted community affluence in relation to the average for whites by between 6 and 7 percent. In relation to neighborhood racial composition, however, there are nontrivial interaction effects of metropolitan population size with each of the racial/ethnic group variables. The effect is especially sizable for African Americans—the coefficient is about as large as that of the lower-order term for non-Hispanic blacks—and indicates that as population size increases, the disparity between the racial composition of black and white neighborhoods does too. The coefficient is about half as large for Asians and Hispanics, though its direction is the same. In sum, then, residential proximity to the majority group is more likely in smaller metropolitan regions, while larger regions allow for the emergence of ethnic areas and segregation.

The racial/ethnic diversity of a metropolitan region also influences the residential situations of groups. The presence of large numbers of a minority population appears to lift the opportunities for its members to live with co-ethnics. For Asians and Hispanics, this enhancement does not generally appear to entail a cost, for the chances to reside in areas as affluent as those of the majority are not reduced; if anything, they increase. For African Americans, by contrast, the presence of a large black population limits their ability to reside in affluent communities, reflecting the consequences of racial segregation.

This set of conclusions rests on a somewhat complex pattern of coefficients. In the equation for neighborhood racial composition, the basic story emerges from the interaction effects, all of which are nontrivial and negative. In general, then, as the presence of a minority group in a region increases, the percentage of whites in the neighborhoods where group members live decreases. This statement requires modification because of one lower-order effect, involving the percentage of Asians in the population (which, like other lower-order terms, applies to the predictions for all groups). As this increases, the percentage of whites in the neighborhoods of most groups does too; in the case of Asians themselves, the lower-order and interaction effects are almost offsetting. In the equation for community affluence, only ting. In the equation for community affluence, only one of the interaction effects appears meaningful. It reveals that as the percentage of blacks in a metropolitan region increases, the relative affluence of the communities where blacks live declines. However, increasing percentages of Asians and Hispanics increase the relative affluence of the communities where all groups are found, according to the lower-order effects.

The contextual variable with the most limited effects is the percentage of the population that immigrated during the 1980s. Neither the lower-order term nor any of the interactions is sizable in either equation, and the full set of terms makes such a small contribution to R^2 in each case that interpretation of these effects appears risky. It might be thought that this negligible effect is a consequence of late entry into the model, but it is not. When the percent of recent immigrants and its interactions are added before the other metropolitan variables, the results are essentially the same.

The negligible impact of the volume of interaction is disappointing in that it is one way of testing for the impact of new immigration on the residential patterns of African Americans. We consequently tried a different approach, adding interactions between the black dummy variable and the percentages of Asians and Hispanics in the population. These tests also failed to yield any apparently meaningful results (by even a generous standard). Thus the only impact of regional diversity on black residential patterns that we are able to detect is the general lift in the relative white percentage provided by the lower-order effects of the Asian and Hispanic population percentages. These are, of course, general effects.

CONCLUSION

The immigration of recent decades, highly focused on a small number of the nation's metropolitan regions, is adding new complexities to residential patterns. Some older ethnic urban neighborhoods that had been in decline are reviving as a consequence of repopulation by fresh inflows, and elsewhere new ethnic neighborhoods are arising, some of them in suburbs such as Monterey Park, California, and Fort Lee, New Jersey (Horton 1995; Sanjek 1998; Winnick 1990). The question is to what extent the impact of new immigrants on metropolitan communities and neighborhoods can be comprehended on the basis of the experiences from past eras of immigration and to what extent they call for new theoretical models. The older experiences have been abstracted in the models of spatial assimilation and place stratification. According to the former, new immigrant communities represent an initial stage of settlement that will gradually weaken with the social mobility and assimilation of the immigrants and, even more, their descendants; according to the latter, new immigrants, who are mainly non-European, will be treated as racial minorities and segregated into communities inferior to those of the majority. Difficulties with both these models have been apparent for some time, and therefore one can glimpse in formulation a third alternative, the model of the "ethnic community," which affords to immigrant ethnics some of the same desirable amenities found in communities of the majority but in a context that retains a significant presence of co-ethnics and of ethnic institutions.

Our analysis of racial and ethnic residential patterns in the thirty largest metropolitan regions suggests that no one of these models is entirely satisfactory, that each has a sphere of applicability. Certainly the model of spatial assimilation seems alive and well, especially when we consider the relationships of micro-level factors to residential situations. Both the percentage of whites in an area and the area's average affluence go up sharply for all groups with rises in individual-level socioeconomic position and changes in location from the city to the suburb. Especially for Hispanics but also for Asians (and whites), these community characteristics further increase in tandem with assimilation status. Equally supportive, Asians and light-skinned Hispanics attain residential parity with white peers under some circumstances, especially when they are assimilated, middle class, and located in suburbs. But African Americans, regardless of their individual-level characteristics, do not reach parity, and in this gap we find support for the model of place stratification. The same holds for nonwhite Latinos, especially for those who have visible African ancestry.

The patterns anticipated by the ethnic-community model can also be found, indicating that the settlement of contemporary immigrant groups is indeed complex and involves elements of all three models. The features of this model seem most discernable in our findings for Asians, who evidently attain parity with whites with respect to community affluence in middle-class suburban settings but without necessarily residing in communities as dominated by the majority group as those in which whites are found. These findings underscore the significance of the Asian-flavored suburbs that are becoming apparent in metropolitan regions with large immigrant inflows and that are made possible by the high levels of human, and sometimes financial, capital associated with some of the major Asian immigration streams. In most cases these suburbs still house populations that have white majorities but with a substantial admixture of Asians. This is true, for instance, of northern Bergen County in New Jersey, a very affluent suburban area that was 15 percent Asian in 1990 (Alba, Logan, Zhang, and Stults 1999).

The significance of such ethnic residential niches is likely to increase in the future as immigration continues to alter the racial and ethnic composition of a select group of metropolitan regions. While we found the direct impact of recent large-scale immigration on residential patterns to be meager, that of racial and ethnic composition was more substantial. More diverse metropolitan regions, as those receiving immigration have inevitably become, afford more latitude to the creation of ethnic communities in places with amenities. In particular, this matters for Latinos: in more diverse regions their parity with whites in terms of neighborhood racial composition lessens but without detriment to the attainment of parity in terms of community affluence. Yet, paradoxically, greater diversity also seems to be associated with improved chances for residential parity for all groups. Thus, in regions with greater percentages of Asians, the relative affluence of and white percentage in the communities of all groups go up (once individual-level characteristics are controlled for).

This differentiation is even greater in the nation's largest metropolitan regions, such as New York City and Los Angeles, where immigration is concentrated for the most part. The largest regions offer the widest range of community differentiation and thus the greatest possibility for ethnics to establish residential niches. At the same time, large population size seems to counteract some of the effects of regional diversity, probably in part by increasing the opportunities for some whites to segregate themselves. Hence large size reduces further minority parity with whites in the racial composition of communities. For African Americans this effect is coupled with an especially strong reduction in the relative affluence of the communities where they reside, an effect that is quite compatible with place stratification. But for Asians and Latinos there is no similar group-specific effect, though for all groups there is a general, quite slight tendency for relative community affluence to be dampened.

Nevertheless, one of the big stories since 1990, when the data analyzed here were collected, is the dispersion of new immigrants throughout the country. The result has been a growth in ethnic and racial diversity in many more parts of the United States, including smaller metropolitan regions that previously had received little of the post-1965 immigration stream (Lee, Matthews, and Zelinksy 2001). If the patterns that have been identified in this chapter hold up—and given their plausibility, there is a high likelihood that this is the case—then we would expect that, in the new areas of immigrant settlement, residential exposure to the majority group and the ability of immigrants to attain residence in communities whose socioeconomic position is commensurate with their own would be relatively high, at least in comparison with the immigrants who have gone to the huge immigrant meccas. This counterpoint between large and small regions, between more and less diverse ones, is one indication that the canvas of intergroup contacts ensuing from contemporary immigration is quite complex and that no single theoretical lens will be adequate to bring all of it into focus. The final conclusion from our research is the need for theoretical pluralism.

References

Alba, Richard, Nancy Denton, Shu-yin Leung, and John Logan. 1995. "Neighborhood Change under Conditions of Mass Immigration: The New York City Region, 1970–1990," *International Migration Review* 29 (Fall): 625–56.

Alba, Richard, and John Logan. 1992. "Analyzing Locational Attainments: Constructing Individual-level Regressions Using Aggregate Data," *Sociological Methods and Research* 20 (February): 367–97.

———. 1993. "Minority Proximity to Whites in Suburbs: An Individual-level Analysis of Segregation," *American Journal of Sociology* 98 (May): 1388–1427.

Alba, Richard, John Logan, and Brian Stults. 2000. "The Changing Neighborhood Contexts of the Immigrant Metropolis," *Social Forces* 79 (December): 587–621.

Alba, Richard, John Logan, Brian Stults, Gilbert Marzan, and Wenquan Zhang. 1999. "Immigrant Groups in the Suburbs: A Reexamination of Suburbanization and Spatial Assimilation," *American Sociological Review* 64 (June): 446–60.

Alba, Richard, John Logan, Wenquan Zhang, and Brian Stults. 1999. "Strangers Next Door: Immigrant Groups and Suburbs in Los Angeles and New York." In *A Nation Divided: Diversity, Inequality, and Community in American Society*, edited by Phyllis Moen, Henry Walker, and Donna Dempster-McClain. Ithaca, N.Y.: Cornell University Press.

Alba, Richard, and Victor Nee. 1997. "Rethinking Assimilation Theory for a New Era of Immigration," *International Migration Review* 31 (Winter): 826–74.

Blalock, Hubert. 1967. *Toward a Theory of Minority-Group Relations.* New York: Wiley.

Breton, Raymond. 1964. "Institutional Completeness of Ethnic Communities and the Personal Relations of Immigrants," *American Journal of Sociology* 70 (September): 193–205.

Denton, Nancy, and Douglas Massey. 1991. "Patterns of Neighborhood Transition in a Multiethnic World: U.S. Metropolitan Areas, 1970–1980," *Demography* 28: 41–63.

Farley, Reynolds. 1996. *The New American Reality: Who We Are, How We Got Here, Where We Are Going.* New York: Russell Sage Foundation.

Farley, Reynolds, and William Frey. 1994. "Changes in the Segregation of Whites from Blacks during the 1980s: Small Steps towards a More Integrated Society," *American Sociological Review* 59 (February): 23–45.

Foner, Nancy. 1997. "What's New about Transnationalism? New York Immigrants Today and at the Turn of the Century," *Disapora* 6, no. 3: 355–75.

———. 2000. *From Ellis Island to JFK: New York's Two Great Waves of Immigration.* New Haven, Conn.: Yale University Press.

Frey, William. 1994. "Minority Suburbanization and Continued 'White Flight' in U.S. Metropolitan Areas: Assessing the Evidence from the 1990 Census," *Research in Community Sociology* 4: 15–42.

Glick Schiller, Nina, Linda Basch, and Cristina Blanc-Szanton. 1995. "From Immigrant to Transmigrant: Theorizing Transnational Migration," *Anthropological Quarterly* 68, no. 1 (January): 48–63.

Horton, John. 1995. *The Politics of Diversity: Immigration, Resistance, and Change in Monterey Park, California.* Philadelphia, Penn.: Temple University Press.

Lee, Barrett, Stephen Matthews, and Wilbur Zelinsky. 2001. "The Spatial Contours of Racial and Ethnic Diversity in the United States, 1980–2000." University Park: Population Research Institute, Pennsylvania State University.

Logan, John, and Richard Alba. 1993. "Locational Returns to Human Capital: Minority Access to Suburban Community Resources," *Demography* 30 (May): 243–68.

Logan, John, Richard Alba, Tom McNulty, and Brian Fisher. 1996. "Making a Place in the Metropolis: Residential Assimilation and Segregation in City and Suburb," *Demography* 33 (November): 443–53.

Logan, John, Richard Alba, and Wenquan Zhang. 2002. "Immigrant Enclaves and Ethnic Communities in New York and Los Angeles," *American Sociological Review* 67 (April): 299–322.

Logan, John, and Harvey Molotch. 1987. *Urban Fortunes.* Berkeley: University of California Press.

Massey, Douglas. 1985. "Ethnic Residential Segregation: A Theoretical Synthesis and Empirical Review," *Sociology and Social Research* 69 (April): 315–50.

Massey, Douglas, and Nancy Denton. 1988. "Suburbanization and Segregation in U.S. Metropolitan Areas," *American Journal of Sociology* 94 (November): 592–626.

———. 1993. *American Apartheid: Segregation and the Making of the Underclass.* Cambridge, Mass.: Harvard University Press.

Portes, Alejandro, and Robert Bach. 1985. *Latin Journey: Cuban and Mexican Immigrants in the United States.* Berkeley: University of California Press.

Portes, Alejandro, and Rubén Rumbaut. 1996. *Immigrant America: A Portrait.* 2d ed. Berkeley: University of California Press.

Portes, Alejandro, and Min Zhou. 1993. "The New Second Generation: Segmented Assimilation and Its Variants," *The Annals* 530 (November): 74–96.

Sanders, Jimy, and Victor Nee. 1987. "Limits of Ethnic Solidarity in the Ethnic Enclave," *American Sociological Review* 52 (December): 745–67.

Sanjek, Roger. 1998. *The Future of Us All: Race and Neighborhood Politics in New York City.* Ithaca, N.Y.: Cornell University Press.

Sassen, Saskia. 1991. *The Global City: New York, London, Tokyo.* Princeton, N.J.: Princeton University Press.

South, Scott, and Kyle Crowder. 1999. "Neighborhood Effects on Family Formation: Concentrated Poverty and Beyond," *American Sociological Review* 64: 113–32.

Waldinger, Roger. 1996. *Still the Promised City? African-Americans and New Immigrants in Postindustrial New York.* Cambridge, Mass.: Harvard University Press.

Waldinger, Roger, and Mehdi Bozorgmehr. 1996. *Ethnic Los Angeles.* New York: Russell Sage Foundation.

Waters, Mary C. 1999. *Black Identities: West Indian Immigrant Dreams and American Realities.* Cambridge, Mass.: Harvard University Press.

White, Michael, Ann Biddlecom, and Shenyang Guo. 1993. "Immigration, Naturalization, and Residential Assimilation among Asian Americans," *Social Forces* 72 (September): 93–118.

Wilson, William J. 1987. *The Truly Disadvantaged: The Inner City, the Underclass, and Public Policy.* Chicago: University of Chicago Press.

Winnick, Louis. 1990. *New People in Old Neighborhoods: The Role of New Immigrants in Rejuvenating New York's Communities.* New York: Russell Sage Foundation.

Zhou, Min. 1997. "Segmented Assimilation: Issues, Controversies, and Recent Research on the New Second Generation," *International Migration Review* 31 (Winter): 975–1008.

Part II

Labor Markets and Related Institutions

7

Educational Expansion and the Employment Success of Immigrants in the United States and Canada, 1970–1990

JEFFREY G. REITZ

The transformation of modern economies from industrialism to post-industrialism, the increased importance of education and education-based skills in labor markets, and the emergence of a "knowledge economy" raise important questions about the economic role of immigrants and immigration. How are the employment prospects of immigrants affected by these changes? As immigration brings increased racial diversity to many advanced industrial societies, can these new immigrants participate meaningfully in the knowledge economy? Do changing labor market processes provide new opportunities for immigrants to overcome prejudicial barriers, creating possibilities for a new interracial dynamic leading to growing pluralism and equality? Or are new obstacles being erected, so that global racial inequalities increasingly are reproduced within such societies?

Available evidence suggests, albeit tentatively, that the emerging knowledge economy may not be entirely immigrant-friendly. Trends over the past three decades in the employment experience of newly arriving immigrants, relative to the native-born, appear to have been generally

---

Michelle Maenck and Breda McCabe provided excellent research assistance in the preparation of this chapter, and it is acknowledged with thanks. An abridged version of this essay is forthcoming in *Globalization and Society: Processes of Differentiation Examined,* edited by Raymond Breton and Jeffrey Reitz.

negative in all three traditional immigration countries: the United States (Borjas 1999), Canada (Reitz 1999), and Australia (Jones 1998). There may be many reasons for this trend; however, mainstream educational expansion and related trends have been linked plausibly to this decline. A recent analysis of trends in immigrant employment by Borjas (1999; see also Borjas 1994) has attempted to explain a decline in the hourly immigrant wage for men in the United States, from parity in 1970 to a 23.0 percent deficiency in 1998, by reference to relative trends in native-born and immigrant education levels. Educational upgrading in the native-born populations outpaced increases in skill levels among immigrants, even though recent cohorts of immigrants have educational levels that are higher than for earlier cohorts. Such a widening skills gap between immigrants from developing countries and native-born populations in the developed world may be related not only to immigrant recruitment patterns but also to an underlying trend toward increasing global inequality in social spending (described, for example, in Korzeniewicz, Moran, and Stach n.d.).

Compounding the impact of an immigrant skills gap is the fact that immigrant skills are heavily discounted in contemporary labor markets (Reitz 2001a). This would magnify the negative impact of rapid educational expansion in advanced countries on immigrants. Moreover, the discounting may be becoming more pronounced, even as the labor market value of education-based skills has risen. In the Canadian case, about half of the overall decline in the relative earnings of newly arriving immigrants over the 1971–1996 period could be attributed to the more rapid increase in native-born educational levels, discounting of immigrant skills, and a relative decline in the value of immigrant skills (Reitz 2001b).

Educational expansion reflects basic processes under way in many or most industrial countries, but not necessarily occurring at the same rates or according to the same patterns. There is variability as a function of rates of economic development, and also according to social, cultural, and political forces that affect the funding and development of educational institutions. Hence, if there is an impact on the integration of immigrants, this too would be expected to vary among the various immigration countries.

The contrast between the United States and Canada is particularly striking in this regard. In the United States, the emergence of secondary school as the minimum educational standard, and the development of mass postsecondary educational opportunities, occurred significantly earlier than in Canada (Wanner 1986). Lack of educational development in Canada appears to be a significant reason why its immigrants in the 1970s experienced substantially greater employment success compared to their counterparts in the United States (Reitz 1998). Given that this 1970s cohort was the first in which non-European origins were prominent, the relatively less developed Canadian educational institutions may have contributed importantly to Canada's fairly successful initiation as a substantially multiracial society.

In more recent years, however, rapid educational expansion in Canada produced a substantial degree of convergence of Canadian with American educational patterns. If educational expansion is important in affecting immigrant employment opportunity, then the expectation would be for a corresponding convergence in immigrant employment and earnings. In Canada these would be expected to decline more rapidly than in the United States, to approach the lower U.S. levels.

Different patterns of educational development in the two countries represent only part of the institutional changes now under way that potentially affect immigrants. Some changes may tend toward convergence, such as the industrial mix and declining proportions of the workforce in manufacturing. Others may reflect divergence, such as labor union strength and earnings inequalities. It is useful to think of these changes in relation to one another and to the backdrop of global change and globalization. Patterns of institutional change may be reinforcing or offsetting. The focus here on educational expansion therefore represents one stream of inquiry within a broader analysis of the impact of globalization and related institutional change.

The following analysis provides a direct U.S.-Canada comparison of the impact of the cross-national difference in patterns of educational expansion on the employment and earnings of successive cohorts of immigrants, based on census data. As a background to this analysis, it is useful to review the existing evidence on immigrant skills utilization, patterns of educational expansion in each country, and various processes by which educational expansion may affect immigrant employment success.

NATIVE-BORN EDUCATION AS CONTEXT FOR IMMIGRANT SKILL UTILIZATION

Appropriate to the age of the knowledge economy, today the analysis of immigrant incorporation usually employs a human capital model and focuses on skills. Unlike a century ago, when immigrants took unskilled jobs to establish themselves in an emerging industrial economy, today's immigrants face the challenge of integration into a postindustrial knowledge economy (Foner 2000: 74 ff). They must bring not only their willingness to work but also a set of skills, increasingly education-based, transferable, and applicable to the economy of the receiving society. This analysis presumes immigrants' economic progress and successful social integration to depend on their skills.

It is perhaps ironic, then, that although the transformation of the host society creates this new context, most contemporary analyses of immigrant adjustment do not examine its impact. Rather, they take for granted the educational profile of the native-born population and the conventional role that education plays in labor market success for the native-born. These are seen simply as part of the established institutional system to which immigrants seek to adjust. In the conventional human capital framework, interest often focuses on equal employment opportunity for immigrants and on the possibility of racial discrimination (Boyd 1992; Baker and Benjamin 1994; Christofides and Swidinsky 1994). Little attention is given to the impact of the changing role of education in the labor market that gave rise to the concern with skills in the first place.

Nevertheless, human capital studies suggest clearly that native-born educational levels are very important determinants of immigrant success, perhaps more so than are the skills of the immigrants themselves. They are more important because in the labor market the value of native-born human capital is so much greater than the value of immigrant human capital, as conventionally measured. This is particularly true for immigrants whose racial backgrounds differ from what is dominant in the host society. Many studies show that immigrant education is valued at half or less the value of formally comparable education among the native-born (Chiswick 1986; Baker and Benjamin 1994; Reitz 2001a). In hiring and promotion, employers give far more attention to educational levels among the native-born than among immigrant workers.

Employers may be acting from a variety of considerations, including a judgment that foreign qualifications have little relevance to domestic work requirements. This judgment might be based on sound considerations or simple ignorance, or out of bias based on either culture or race.

Whether the discounting of immigrant skills is sound management or possibly discriminatory, the consequence is that variations in immigrant educational levels seem to have substantially less impact on their competitive position than do the skills of their native-born competitors. Hence variations in the skills of the native-born across destination societies, or over time, may be expected to have important implications for the employment success of immigrants.

EDUCATIONAL CONTEXTS OF IMMIGRATION IN THE UNITED STATES AND CANADA

The United States and Canada are useful points of comparison because of contrasting patterns of educational expansion over the past three decades, during which immigration has been substantial in both countries. Despite differences in patterns of immigration, the two countries have important similarities that allow for meaningful comparison. The significant differences in their educational institutions provide an important opportunity to assess how native-born education affects the process of immigrant integration into employment.

Canadian and American immigration reform in the 1960s led to large-scale immigration from many of the same non-European sources. These immigrants tended to settle in major urban areas. Canada eliminated formal preferences for European immigration in 1962, three years before the comparable move in the United States. Since then, both countries have become home to large numbers of immigrants from the Caribbean, Asia, Africa, and Latin America. These immigrants have had a major impact, increasing the racial diversity of key cities in both countries.

There are a number of differences in immigration between the two countries (Reitz 2003); however, these do not invalidate labor market comparisons. One such difference is that the numbers of immigrants have been greater for Canada. In fact, Canada has pursued an expansionist "nation-building" approach to immigration throughout most of the post–World War II period, and immigrants now are 18 percent of the total Canadian population, compared to a figure of about 11 percent for the United States (based on the respective censuses for 2001 and 2000). A second difference is in the origins mix of immigrants in the two countries, with immigrants from Mexico and other Latin American countries numerically more prominent in the United States. Hence the impact of host-society characteristics on immigrants is most usefully examined in cross-national comparisons for immigrants from the same origins.

These "new immigrants" to Canada tended on average to perform substantially better in the labor market than did their counterparts from the same origins in the United States, at least in the 1970s (Borjas 1988, 1990). This difference is particularly marked when interurban variation within the United States is taken into account (Reitz 1998: 62–63). Newly arrived black, Chinese, and Asian immigrants earned substantially less in the cities of their largest concentration, such as New York and Los Angeles—and, in the case of the Chinese, San Francisco-Oakland as well—than in Canadian centers such as Toronto. For example, newly arrived black immigrant men earned an average of 49 percent of the average earnings for native-born men in 1980, compared to 70 percent in Toronto. Newly arrived Chinese immigrant men earned an average of 44 percent of the average for native-born men in New York, 51 percent of the average in San Francisco-Oakland, and 60 percent of the average in Los Angeles, compared to 73 percent in Vancouver and 77 percent in Toronto.

Two potential explanations for this cross-national difference turn out to be inadequate. Borjas (1990) pointed toward immigration policy and the supposedly more skill-selective Canadian approach. However, Duleep and Regets (1992) showed that when immigrants from the same origins are compared (setting aside Mexican immigrants to the United States, many of whom have arrived outside normal admission processes), those in the United States are on average *better* educated than those in Canada.[1] A second explanation suggested that the lack of racial tensions in Canadian society might lead to the more rapid incorporation of racial minority immigrants, but empirical indicators show no significant differences (Reitz and Breton 1994; Baker and Benjamin 1997).

Apparently, the single most important reason for greater immigrant success in Canada in the 1970s was simply the lower levels of education in its native-born workforce. Although immigrants to Canada in the 1970s were less skilled than their counterparts from comparable origins in the United States, their skill levels compared more favorably with those of the native-born Canadian population. This native-born educational difference is a consequence of the more rapid expansion of U.S. educational institutions prior to the 1960s (Reitz 1998). Canadian education levels historically were lower, and both high school and university completion rates lagged well behind those in the United States for many years. Possible reasons for this trend include: the more skill-intensive requirements of the U.S. economy at the time, compared to the Canadian emphasis on resources; American values of individualism and the drive for mobility, as Lipset (1989) has argued; and specific government decisions, such as the GI bill which subsidized education for a large number of war veterans.

The significance of higher education in the United States is underscored by comparisons at the urban level. Key immigration cities such as New York, Los Angeles, and San Francisco have among the highest mean educational levels in the country, a product of their dynamic economies and reinforced by patterns of interurban mobility (Barff, Ellis, and Reibel

[1] There may be several reasons: the larger numbers of immigrants to Canada which overwhelms selective admission, differences in the family reunification component of immigration, or differences in self-selection processes.

1995). These high native-born educational levels are a reason for the lower relative earnings of immigrants (see Reitz 1998: 105–48). It happens that these large immigrant concentrations also tend to have *lower* educational levels (see Bartel 1989).[2] The result is a marked pattern of skills polarization. By contrast, there is relatively little variation in the educational profiles of native-born workers among Canada's major cities, creating less difference in the employment position of immigrants.

Since the 1970s, educational expansion in Canada has been rapid, largely eliminating the cross-national difference, at least for the younger generation (Wanner 1986; Freeman and Needels 1993). Today, depending on the indicator, Canadian educational attainments may in some dimensions actually exceed those in the United States. Figure 7.1 shows that university completion rates in Canada rose rapidly (part A) and that the overall university completion rates for the adult population have tended toward convergence with the United States (part B), though more slowly. Canadian educational expansion has emphasized adult vocational training as well, and part C of figure 7.1 shows that if these enrollments are included, then convergence is more marked.

The reasons for the delayed pattern of education in Canada are partly economic, with important social, cultural, and political dimensions. Occupational and industrial shifts clearly were involved. To some extent Canadian economic development has lagged, and educational change reflects this lag. However, rapid change has resulted in increased educational levels within many occupations (Lipset 1989: 158–63). No doubt, technical change and professionalization within occupations are important. At the same time, it appears that political and cultural factors have played a role: all postsecondary education in Canada has been in the public sector, and Canadian governments have sought to compete more aggressively in post-industrial sectors and the knowledge economy. Nor should the impact of the U.S. border be overlooked. An increase in imported American professionals prompted concerns about national independence and required Canada to match U.S. educational levels. Because of the noneconomic factors, then, it should not be assumed that educational levels simply reflect economic values. For example, whether Canadian educational upgrading has produced an anticipated economic payoff is not yet known,

[2] It may be that immigrants with higher levels of education tend to choose areas of settlement based on specific employment opportunities, whereas those with less education prefer to settle in large immigrant communities, which may be helpful in their adjustment and integration.

Figure 7.1

A. Percent Completing University Degree, Young Adults

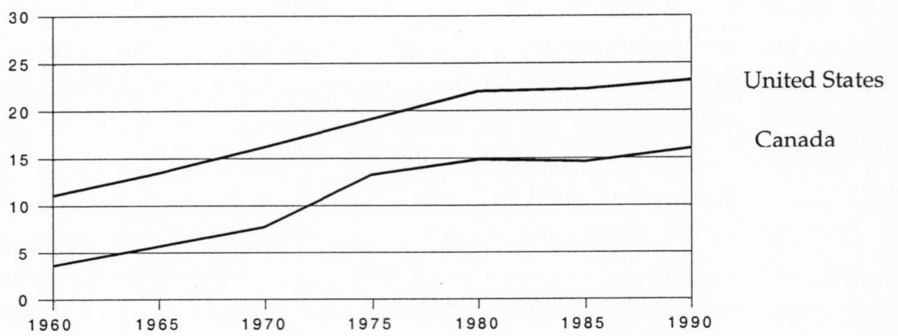

B. Percent Completing University Degree, Adult Population

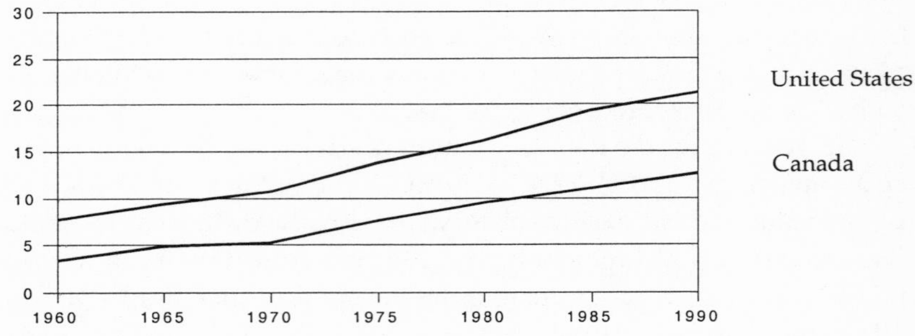

Source: US Bureau of the Census, Statistics Canada; see Reitz 1998: 108.

C. Postsecondary Enrollment Ratios*

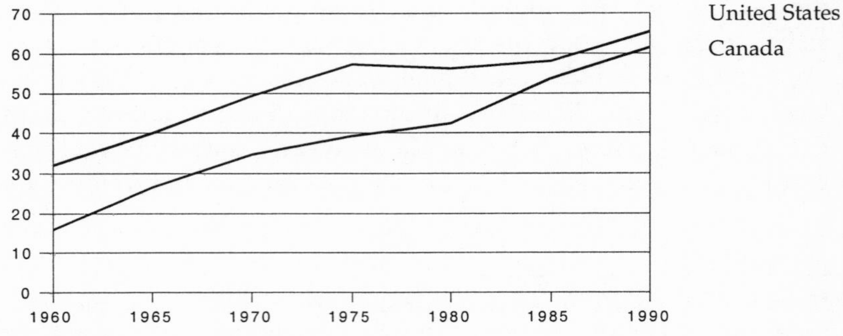

Source: UNESCO; see Reitz 1998: 108.

* Ratio of the number enrolled in all postsecondary schools and universities to the number of persons aged twenty to twenty-four.

and productivity issues in Canada have been debated more intensely in recent years despite the more highly educated workforce.

PROCESSES OF EDUCATIONAL EXPANSION WITH IMPLICATIONS FOR IMMIGRANTS

What are the implications of comparative patterns of educational change for immigrants in the United States and Canada? When native-born educational credentials rise more rapidly than those of immigrants, clearly immigrants suffer a corresponding loss of competitive position. If lower native-born educational levels in Canada accounted for better immigrant performance in the 1970s, then rising relative levels of education in Canada might be expected to eliminate this Canadian advantage and produce a more rapid decline in immigrant earnings in that country.

Analysis of the full impact of educational change also involves a recognition of broader institutional changes under way in the society, in the economy, and in labor markets. Many of the economic changes are technological in origin. In a knowledge economy, specific education-based skill requirements rise more rapidly than others, certain occupations requiring those skills expand, and the way in which skills are perceived and evaluated within many occupations changes (Bell 1973). Employers address technological change in terms of the organization of work, jobs, and careers, with implications for the structure of labor markets. Educational change has a social dimension as well, and the impact of educational change on labor markets may reflect a wide range of forces within society. The implications of these changes for immigrants depend not only on their formal levels of education but also on other individual attributes and on the way immigrants fit into various patterns of ongoing institutional change.

There may be many potentially relevant changes accompanying educational expansion that affect the impact on immigrants. Some of these changes have to do with the uneven distribution of educational expansion across labor market sectors in which various groups of immigrants may be located. For example, educational expansion has occurred at distinct levels such as university degree attainment and high school completion. In the United States, recent changes in the size of the native-born/immigrant education difference is more dramatic for high school completion than for college graduation. According to Borjas's data (1999: 21), college graduate rates for native-born men rose from 15.4 percent in 1970 to 29.8 percent in 1998, an increase of 14.4 percent, while the corresponding immigrant college graduate rate, which was 18.6 percent in 1970, rose only to 28.3 percent as of 1998, an increase of 9.7 percent. Trends in high school completion rates tell a rather more dramatic, albeit similar, story of immigrant lag. The high school completion rate for native-born men rose from 60.3 percent in 1970 to 91.0 percent in 1998, whereas the high school completion rate among immigrants rose from 51.0 percent in 1970 to 66.4 percent in 1998. Hence educational upgrading in the native-born workforce outpaced that of immigrants at both levels, but the emerging gap was far more pronounced at the lower level. Of course, labor market implications depend on trends in the relative value of each type of education.

The development of a knowledge economy also may be specific to certain urban areas, with implications for immigrants depending on their own urban concentrations. As mentioned above, in the United States the pattern of immigrant recruitment to specific urban areas has produced a marked skills polarization in high-immigration cities, primarily because of higher levels of native-born education in those cities. The urban framework for continued expansion of a knowledge economy may shape the evolution of these patterns of polarization over time, at least in the United States and perhaps also in Canada. If immigrant-intensive cities continue to have dynamic economies, then the process of skills polarization seen in the United States may continue and become even more pronounced. On the other hand, if there has been a shift in areas of the most intense economic activity, then skills polarization might shift toward new areas, and the result could be an evening-out of these patterns among cities.

Educational expansion also varies by gender, with implications for the position of immigrants (cf. Reitz et al. 1999). College graduation rates among U.S. native-born women rose more rapidly than for men in the recent period. This rapid change and the associated changes in women's employment may have affected immigrant women. Borjas (1999) suggests that educational patterns help to explain the decline in the relative hourly wage for immigrant women from +3.0 percent in 1970 to −12.1 percent in 1998. On the other hand, the differences in trends in high school completion rates may have been more important, as they were for men, because the change for the native-born in this group was greater than for immigrants.

The impact of educational expansion also may depend on the changing age structure of careers. Often it is assumed that immigrants compete most directly with younger native-born workers as they enter the labor market. These are workers whose educational levels rise most rapidly. However, much may depend on the extent to which the career trajectories of older and less educated workers are protected from direct competition with younger and better-educated workers. If there is significant cross-generational competition, it may be more difficult for native-born workers to maintain traditional advantages, and the impact on immigrants may be less. In effect, the overall educational profile of the population would matter, not just that of the younger workers, and of course the overall educational profile changes more slowly.

Educational expansion is also accompanied by changes in the credential validation process within occupations. In a knowledge economy, occupations requiring specific education-based skills expand, and advancing professionalization increases the emphasis on education within those occupations (Bell 1973). Processes by which employment credentials are evaluated may directly affect immigrants by affecting the transferability of immigrant credentials.

One possibility is that, increasingly, professional standards are more universalistic and "objective," helping immigrants overcome potential bias. This would create increased employment opportunity for immigrants, including those most vulnerable to discrimination, such as racial minorities and, perhaps in particular, racial minority women.

On the other hand, professionalization may lead to changes in credential validation processes that could undermine the position of immigrants. The difficulty that immigrants have in receiving accreditation in licensed occupations is often a source of controversy. Bureaucratization of assessment processes may create barriers that lead to somewhat arbitrary dismissal of foreign qualifications. Credential validation in many professional fields involves personal references, and here too immigrants from distant lands may have difficulty. Professional networks are "weak ties." They are wider than personal networks, but they are limited and may not include those able to validate immigrant qualifications, such as experts in immigrants' countries of origin. Hence an increasing use of networks to assess employment qualifications may place immigrants at greater disadvantage. Lack of skill transferability also may occur in semiprofessional occupations or others that develop professional standards but are not specifically licensed, such as librarians or human resource managers. Any shift toward greater professionalization may increase the difficulty for immigrants, increasing the emphasis on specific credentials and causing employers to look more skeptically at those from unfamiliar sources.

Once native-born/immigrant skill differentials in specific sectors have been assessed, labor markets assign corresponding wage differentials. These differ between Canada and the United States, and they have been changing in different ways (Wolfson and Murphy 2000). All these processes make up a rich agenda for examination of the impact of educational change. The following analysis makes a start by assessing impacts by immigrant origins and gender, focusing specifically on the relative value of education as this changes over time in each country.

DATA AND METHODS

The analysis is based on census microdata samples for the United States in 1980 and 1990 (5 percent samples; Department of Commerce, Bureau of the Census, 1983, 1992) and for Canada in 1981 and 1991 (samples between 2 and 3 percent; Statistics Canada, 1984, 1994). Supplementary information is available from the 1986 and 1996 Canadian censuses (Statistics Canada, 1990, 1999). The respective samples include immigrant and native-born persons aged twenty to sixty-four. Our interest is in newly arrived immigrants in each time period, so analysis focuses on immigrants arriving in the ten-year period prior to each census. The immigrant sample sizes for the United States are 183,790 in 1980 and 296,296 in 1990; in Canada they are 14,947 in 1981 and 25,454 in 1991; native-born samples in both countries are substantially larger.[3]

A description of variables from each census used in the analysis is presented in appendix 7A. In order to assess the impact of immigrant racial origins on employment trends, it is necessary to construct measures of race that are comparable between and across censuses. In the United States, "whites" includes only non-Hispanic whites,[4] and among immigrants, it includes only those born in either Europe or Canada. In Canada, the category of "whites" is based on ethnic origins and includes persons of British, French, other European, and "Canadian" origins. Among immigrants, "whites" include only those born in either Europe or the United States. The validation of the comparison is supported by analysis of the 1996 Canadian census, which includes questions on both ethnic origins and race.[5] The data show that immigrants arriving throughout the entire

---

[3] Further details available from the author on request.

[4] In the United States, the question on race includes a "white" response category. Hispanics such as Mexicans, Cubans, and Puerto Ricans are identified in a separate question.

[5] In Canada the 1981 and 1991 censuses asked only ethnic origins and not race. However, the 1996 Canadian census did include a question asking about each person in the household: "Is this person …," with suggested response options similar to those used in the U.S. census question on race: White, Chinese, South Asian, Black, Arab/West Asian, Filipino, South East Asian, Latin American, Japanese, Korean, and other—specify. The microdata codebook describes the resulting data as a "visible minority indicator," visible minority being an accepted term in Canada for racial minor-

1970–1990 period in the United States and Canada were predominantly nonwhite, and this proportion increased somewhat over time (for details, see appendix 7B). Except for the large number of Hispanic immigrants in the United States, the origins of immigrants to the two countries are quite similar.

The analysis examines the success of immigrants in gaining employment and also their success with regard to the levels of earnings derived from that employment. Both trends are very important, and each should be interpreted in light of the other.[6] Employment here is defined as having any (positive) earnings over the previous year. (The census question on labor force participation refers only to the past week, and would not be appropriate to use in conjunction with an analysis of yearly earnings.)

Earnings for native-born and immigrant groups are regressed on years of education, possession of a university degree, work experience and experience squared (to capture declining returns to experience), urban area of residence, and racial origins. Earnings for immigrants are regressed also on years since immigration, years since immigration squared, and interactions of these variables with origins.

The specific processes by which immigrants may be affected by educational change cannot all be identified in the data. The analysis of institutional change here employs statistical decomposition based on intertemporal substitutions in earnings regression equations (see Reitz 2001b), compared cross-nationally. Previously, such methodology has been employed in the analysis of the changing employment situation of women (Blau and Beller 1988).[7] The impact of changing native-born educational levels (or returns to education) on the earnings of immigrants can be ascertained by substituting native-born educational levels from one time period into earnings equations for a subsequent census year, and noting differences in the estimated trends in immigrant earnings.

---

ity. Analysis confirms the racial status of ethnic origins classified as "white" in these data. Also, in both the United States and Canada, a significant proportion of persons whose "ancestry" or "ethnic origins" were European were born outside Europe or North America, and a significant proportion of these were not identified as "white" on the race indicator. Hence in the analysis they are included in a separate category.

[6] The formal method for examining the relation between employment rates and earnings, developed by Heckman (1979), does not produce stable estimates in these data and is not employed (see also Stolzenberg and Relles 1997).

[7] See Oaxaca 1973 for a discussion of the decomposition method applied in cross-sectional analysis of gender inequality.

COMPARATIVE TRENDS IN EMPLOYMENT AND EARNINGS

From the 1970s to the 1980s there was a downward trend in relative employment rates and earnings of newly arriving immigrants both in the United States and in Canada. A direct comparison of the respective size of these trends shows that, for most specific origins groups, the decline in Canada was steeper and that the Canadian advantage in the 1970s eroded significantly during the 1980s. Put differently, the positive differences for immigrants in Canada in 1980 became less positive by 1990.

The overall pattern of greater decline in Canada applies most clearly to relative immigrant employment rates (see table 7.1). The trend is observed across all origins groups, for both immigrant men and immigrant women, and for whites, blacks, and Chinese. Among immigrant men in 1980, the relative employment rate for recently arrived men was 5.5 percent higher in Canada than in the United States, but by 1990 the Canadian figure was 1 percent lower. Among immigrant women, the relative employment rate for new immigrants was 17.5 percent higher in Canada in 1981, declining to 12.5 percent higher in 1990. For black and Chinese immigrants, the higher Canadian rates for 1980 were greatly reduced or even eliminated by 1990. For white immigrants, the higher Canadian rate in 1980 was greatly reduced for men and slightly reduced for women.

There is also a greater decline in the relative earnings of newly arriving immigrants in Canada for most specific origins groups (see table 7.2). For recently arrived white immigrants, the trend took the form of an improved position in the United States, particularly for men but also for women, coupled with a significant decline in Canada. For recently arrived black immigrants, the relatively low initial earnings declined only slightly between the two periods, while again there was a more significant decline in Canada. For the Chinese, the situation is similar for women, but the case of Chinese men presents a minor exception. In fact, the relative earnings of newly arrived Chinese immigrant men in Canada declined slightly less rapidly than for their counterparts in the United States. A closer analysis of those arriving in the latter part of the 1980s is revealing. Chinese immigrants—both men and women—arriving in Canada in the late 1980s had substantially higher earnings than their U.S. counterparts. This may be an effect of a Hong Kong exodus to Canada in anticipation of the "handover" to China.[8]

---

[8] Many of these immigrants may subsequently have returned to Hong Kong. This possibility is consistent with 1996 census data for Chinese immigrants having arrived in the later 1980s, which show that heightened mean educational levels observed in the 1991 census had returned to their previous pattern.

Table 7.1. Relative Proportion with Earnings,[1] for Immigrants in the Country for 0 to 10 Years, by Census Year, Gender, and Origins, Aged 20 to 64, Canada and the United States

	Men			Women		
Census Year	United States	Canada	Canada Difference	United States	Canada	Canada Difference
Native-born with earnings (%)						
1980/81	89.9	91.0		64.9	63.7	
1990/91	89.4	89.1		74.1	74.4	
All immigrants (ratio to native-born)						
1980/81	0.925	0.980	+0.055	0.880	1.055	+0.175
1990/91	0.920	0.910	-0.010	0.785	0.910	+0.125
White immigrants (ratio to native-born)						
1980/81	0.925	1.005	+0.080	0.860	1.015	+0.155
1990/91	0.935	0.955	+0.020	0.805	0.955	+0.150
Black immigrants (ratio to native-born)						
1980/81	0.855	0.930	+0.075	1.065	1.225	+0.160
1990/91	0.905	0.905	0.000	0.995	0.975	–0.020
Chinese immigrants (ratio to native-born)						
1980/81	0.905	1.005	+0.100	0.960	1.110	+01.50
1990/91	0.865	0.865	0.000	0.825	0.895	+0.070

Source: Statistics Canada, Census of Canada, Public Use Microdata Files for Individuals; U.S. Bureau of the Census, Census of Population and Housing, Public Use Microdata 5% Samples.

[1] The percent having received any earnings during the previous year from wages, salaries, or self-employment. Figures are adjusted for specific year-of-entry composition of immigrant cohorts.

While the primary interest here is in the experiences of particular origins groups, it is important to note that in the cross-national comparison of earnings trends for all origins groups combined, the decline is of approximately the same magnitude in Canada and the United States for men, and it is actually somewhat greater in the United States for women. Trends across groups are affected by shifts in the origins mix of immigrants as well as shifts in the experiences of particular groups of immigrants. In the U.S. case, there was a substantial decline in the relative earnings of new immigrants that arose from shifts toward immigrants by groups with lower average levels of education, as Borjas (1999) has noted.

---

the later 1980s, which show that heightened mean educational levels observed in the 1991 census had returned to their previous pattern.

Table 7.2. Relative Earnings of Immigrants in the Country for 0 to 10 Years (for those with earnings),[1] by Census Year, Gender, and Origins, Aged 20 to 64, Canada and United States

	Census Year	Men			Women, Relative to Women		
		United States	Canada	Canada Difference	United States	Canada	Canada Difference
All immigrants							
	1980/81	0.705	0.890	+0.185	0.880	0.865	-0.015
	1990/91	0.610	0.790	+0.180	0.770	0.805	+0.035
White immigrants							
	1980/81	0.915	1.045	+0.130	0.935	0.870	–0.065
	1990/91	1.020	0.960	-0.060	0.960	0.855	–0.105
Black immigrants							
	1980/81	0.545	0.710	+0.165	0.885	0.840	–0.045
	1990/91	0.540	0.640	0.100	0.845	0.755	–0.090
Chinese immigrants							
	1980/81	0.675	0.785	+0.110	0.880	0.950	+0.070
	1990/91	0.635	0.760	+0.125	0.860	0.820	+0.040
					Women, Relative to Men		
All immigrants							
	1980/81				0.404	0.455	+0.051
	1990/91				0.400	0.484	+0.084
White immigrants							
	1980/81				0.429	0.458	+0.029
	1990/91				0.499	0.514	+0.015
Black immigrants							
	1980/81				0.406	0.442	+0.036
	1990/91				0.439	0.454	+0.015
Chinese immigrants							
	1980/81				0.404	0.500	+0.096
	1990/91				0.447	0.493	+0.046

Source: Statistics Canada, Census of Canada, Public Use Microdata Files for Individuals; U.S. Bureau of the Census, Census of Population and Housing, Public Use Microdata 5% Samples.

[1] Relative earnings is the ratio of mean earnings for an immigrant group to mean earnings for the native-born workforce of the same gender, for persons aged 20 to 64 who had any (positive) earnings. Figures are adjusted for specific year-of-entry composition of immigrant cohorts.

However, for specific groups of immigrants, the decline in earnings was in most cases less than for immigrants overall. Among men, the overall decline in relative earnings of over 9 percent (from 70.5 percent of native-born earnings to 61.0 percent) was only 0.5 percent among blacks and 4.0 percent among Chinese. Among white immigrants, relative earnings actually increased by 10.5 percent (from 91.5 percent of native-born earnings to 102 percent). A similar pattern existed for women. The decline in relative immigrant earnings among women was 11 percent across all groups, but it was only 4 percent for blacks and 2 percent for Chinese, and there was an increase among whites of 2.5 percent.

In general, these comparative trends fit with expectations based on the more rapid rise in native-born education for Canada between the 1970s and 1980s.[9] But more detailed analysis will be required to explore the cross-national differences in labor market change for immigrants.

THE IMPACT OF EDUCATION AND ITS ROLE IN LABOR MARKETS

Statistical decomposition methodology provides a means to assess the impact of educational change on these cross-national trends in quantitative terms. The analysis focuses on earnings among those with any earnings during the previous year. Earnings regressions are estimated, including education and other human capital variables (the variables list includes years of education, years of education squared, years since arrival, work experience, work experience squared, language knowledge, and urban residence; see appendix 7A). Then inter-temporal (forward) substitution (using data from different census periods) will reveal how changing educational levels for native-born and immigrant workers, as well as the changing value of education in labor markets, affect trends in the relative position of immigrants.

The logic of the substitution is as follows. Forward substitution (of 1990 parameters into 1980 equations) is performed separately for the native-born and for immigrants. For the native-born, substitution examines first the impact of increased educational levels (substituting 1990 educational

[9] Antecol, Cobb-Clark, and Trejo (2000) provided a comparison of the earnings of U.S. and Canadian immigrant men based on census data for 1990 and 1991, and inferred change since the 1970s simply by comparing year-of-arrival cohorts. The results, however, were consistent in showing that the Canadian advantage for the most recently arrived immigrants was significantly less than for immigrants who had arrived earlier and in suggesting the relevance of trends in educational attainment. Also see the chapter in this volume by Antecol, Cobb-Clark, and Trejo for an analysis of trends for immigrant women.

levels into 1980 equations), and then the impact of increased value of education (substituting also the 1990 value of education into 1980 equations). For immigrants, substitution is similar, but with two parts. The first substitutions assume no discounting of immigrant education. In this part, substitution examines the impact of changing immigrant educational levels (substituting 1990 educational levels into 1980 equations as for the native-born), assuming that value of education for immigrants is the same as for the native-born (using native-born education coefficients, first for 1980 and then as these changed to 1990). The second substitutions consider the impact of the discounting of immigrant education. In this part, substitution examines how immigrant earnings are affected by lower values of education (substituting immigration education coefficients, first for 1980 and then for 1990). Results for the native-born and immigrants are then compared.

In a previous paper (Reitz 2001b), an inter-temporal substitution analysis was provided for Canada, using data from four census periods (1981, 1986, 1991, and 1996). For native-born workers, both men and women, increases in years of education and in university degrees raised earnings levels by between about 3 and 4.5 percent in each period. Increases in the value of education boosted earnings by an additional 0.5 percent during each period. Against this backdrop, the position of immigrants can be examined. Increases in educational levels among native-born men outpaced increases among immigrants between 1981 and 1991, to an extent that would have produced a 3.2 percent decline in immigrant earnings relative to the native-born, assuming that education was valued equally in the two groups. In the early 1990s, education levels among immigrants rose more rapidly, and if valued at the native-born rates, the resulting earnings increase for immigrants would have exceeded the corresponding increase for native-born men over the same period by 0.5 percent. Still, over the entire 1981–1996 period, the expansion of education increased affected earnings for the native-born by 10.4 percent, compared to only 7.9 percent for immigrants, based on an assumed equal valuation of immigrant education.

When the discounted value of immigrant education is taken into account, the impact of educational change is substantially more negative, even in the early 1990s. Because of the discounting of immigrant education, increases in immigrant earnings over the period were projected as 3.8 percent rather than 7.9 percent. Hence the projected decline in immigrant earnings due to educational change ballooned from 2.5 percent (10.4 minus 7.9) to 6.6 percent (10.4 minus 3.8).

And finally, as the value of education for the native-born increased over the 1981–1996 period, boosting native-born earnings by an additional 1.3 percent, the value of education for newly arriving immigrant men fell by 0.6 percent. This produced a further 1.5 percent reduction in immigrant earnings relative to what would have been the case had the value of their education kept pace.

For the present Canada-U.S. comparison, the focus is on the period 1980–1990. The more rapid expansion of education in Canada during the 1980s definitely created greater downward pressures on the earnings of its newly arriving immigrants (see table 7.3). Although the slower expansion of education in the United States during the 1980s (the increase for men was 0.192 years on average, compared to 0.902 years in Canada; the increase for women was 0.413 years on average, compared to 0.828 years in Canada) was accompanied by a more rapid increase in the labor market value of education (for men by an additional 4.1 percent per year of education, compared to only 1.1 percent in Canada; for women by 4.3 percent per year, compared to only 0.9 percent in Canada), the net effect was to raise native-born earnings by only 3.8 percent for men and 6.2 percent for women, compared to 7.8 percent in Canada for men and 8.8 percent for women (see the panels for native-born whites in table 7.3, the bottom line for "net change in earnings due to education, sum"). These differences translate into 4.0 percent lower earnings for immigrant men in Canada and 2.6 percent lower earnings for immigrant women—large enough in itself to produce significant cross-national differences in immigrant earnings trends.

Immigrant education is discounted in American as well as Canadian labor markets, of course. In 1980 this discounting was somewhat more pronounced in Canada, but by 1990 the cross-national difference was reversed because the very rapid increase in the value of education in the United States did not apply substantially to immigrants (see panels for immigrants in table 7.3, "gap with native-born"). In neither country did immigrants experience any significant change in the value of education.

The discounting of immigrant education is a key element in the overall trends. The substitution analysis in table 7.3 shows that educational trends among immigrants actually have relatively little effect in the context of native-born educational trends because immigrant education is so heavily discounted in the labor market. This point is underscored by the comparisons of the United States and Canada because trends in immigrant education were so different. Whereas in Canada the educational levels of immigrants increased as a result of immigration selection, in the United States the overall educational levels of recent immigrants declined between 1980

Table 7.3. Analysis of Earnings Trends for Native-born and Recent Immigrant Men, United States and Canada[1]

	United States			Canada		
	1980	1990	Change	1981	1991	Change
A. MEN						
Native-born white						
Years of education, mean	12.881	13.073	0.192	11.949	12.851	0.902
Earnings, mean	17531	30819		18056	31649	
Earnings value of education - metric	1425	3771		1397	2799	
Earnings value of education - proportion of NB mean[2]	0.081	0.122	0.041	0.077	0.088	0.011
Forward substitution: earnings change due to education						
1980 value assumed for 1990			0.016			0.070
Adjusted for change to 1990 value			0.022			0.008
Net change in earnings due to education (sum)			0.038			0.078
N	223,717	242,794		102,895	172,889	
Immigrants arriving in last 10 years						
Years of education	11.820	11.204	-0.616	13.331	13.765	0.434
Gap with native-born (difference in means)	1.061	1.869	0.807	-1.382	-0.914	0.468
Earnings value of education - metric	1177	2174		959	1474	
Earnings value of education - proportion of NB mean[2]	0.067	0.071	0.003	0.053	0.047	-0.007
Gap with native-born (difference in coefficient)	0.014	0.052	0.038	0.024	0.042	0.018
Forward substitution: earnings change due to education						
1980 native-born value assumed			-0.050			0.034
Change to 1990 native-born value assumed			-0.062			0.019
Adjusted for lower 1980 immigrant value			0.009			-0.041
Adjusted for change to 1990 relative value			0.030			-0.021
Net change in earnings due to education (sum)			-0.073			-0.009
N	74,524	128,099		6,602	9,569	
Net change, relative earnings of immigrants due to education			-0.110			-0.088

B. WOMEN						
Native-born white						
Years of education	12.504	12.918	0.413	12.279	13.107	0.828
Earnings, mean	8038	16010		9497	19006	
Earnings value of education - metric	689	2056		908	1983	
Earnings value of education - proportion of NB mean[2]	0.086	0.128	0.043	0.096	0.104	0.009
Forward substitution: earnings change due to education						
1980 value assumed for 1990			0.035			0.079
Adjusted for change to 1990 value			0.026			0.009
Net change in earnings due to education (sum)			0.062			0.088
N	165,568	205,827		72,973	147,322	
Immigrants arriving in Last 10 Years						
Years of education	11.161	11.011	-0.149	12.581	13.558	0.977
Gap with native-born (difference in means)	1.343	1.906	0.563	-0.302	-0.451	-0.149
Earnings value of education - metric	627	1277		545	871	
Earnings value of education - proportion of NB mean[2]	0.078	0.080	0.002	0.057	0.046	-0.012
Gap with native-born (difference in coefficient)	0.008	0.049	0.041	0.038	0.058	0.020
Forward substitution: earnings change due to education						
1980 native-born value assumed			-0.013			0.093
Change to 1990 native-born value assumed			-0.053			0.013
Adjusted for lower 1980 immigrant value			0.001			-0.056
Adjusted for change to 1990 relative value			0.014			-0.023
Net change in earnings due to education (sum)			-0.051			0.027
N	50,558	82,230		5,224	8,557	
Net change, relative earnings of immigrants due to education			-0.113			-0.061

[1] Metric coefficients based on regression equations for earnings including variables listed in text. Education is valued at the native-born mean. The coefficient of the education-square term is ignored.

[2] Metric coefficient, expressed as a proportion of mean native-born white earnings.

and 1990. These differences would have mattered greatly if immigrant education was equal in value to native-born education and increased to the same extent. In that case, increased education for immigrants in Canada would have increased their earnings by 5.3 percent for men (3.4 percent based on the 1980 value of education, and an additional 1.9 percent due to the increase to 1990) and 10.6 percent for women—helping greatly to offset the native-born increases. As it was, as a result of educational change the earnings for immigrant men in Canada declined by 0.9 percent, and for women they increased by only 2.7 percent. In the United States the lower immigrant educational levels would have produced an 11.2 percent decline in immigrant earnings for men, and a 6.6 percent decline for women, if the value of that education were equal to native-born education. However, discounting works both ways—whether education increases or decreases. The bottom line is that changes related to education reduced relative immigrant earnings for men and women in both countries. For immigrant men, changes in immigrant education reduced relative immigrant earnings by 8.8 percent in Canada, nearly as great as the 11.0 percent decline in the United States. For immigrant women, changes in education reduced relative earnings by 6.1 percent in Canada, not as much as the 11.3 percent decline in the United States but still quite significant.

SUMMARY AND IMPLICATIONS

Educational expansion has lowered the entry position of newly arriving immigrants both in the United States and in Canada. However, earlier expansion of education in the United States produced an earlier impact on immigrants, so that in the 1970s immigrants to Canada fared somewhat better. But more recently, educational expansion in Canada has narrowed the gap. Educational expansion affects immigrants both because their own credentials have not kept pace and because immigrant skills are so heavily and increasingly discounted. These processes are key to the impact of educational change for both countries, whether the education of immigrants themselves increases (as in Canada) or decreases (as in the United States). As the mainstream workforce has participated in the move toward postindustrialism and the knowledge economy, and the value of its educational skills has increased, the relative impact of immigrant skills has declined.

Most of the processes underlying these trends remain to be examined. An increased emphasis on credentials in the labor market may have changed the process by which skills are perceived and evaluated, with implications for immigrants. The importance of credentials might be expected to enhance objectivity, bringing benefits for minority groups. However, employers may be uncomfortable relying upon diplomas and degrees earned in far-off lands, and immigrant credentials may not be understood or recognized. Informal references may be unavailable for the assessment of individual employment records, and the absence of domestic labor market experience may become more of a handicap. Evaluation may be tinged with racial or ethnic stereotyping, and racial discrimination may acquire a new and somewhat more complex set of rationalizations.

The substitution analysis carries assumptions about segmentation processes within labor markets, such as by gender. Perhaps even more important is the question of whether immigrants compete with all age groups in the native-born workforce, or only with new labor force entrants. If immigrants compete mainly with younger workers, whose educational levels have risen more rapidly, then it is possible that the impact of education may be substantially greater than appears in our analysis.

Differences in educational expansion between the United States and Canada account for part—but only part—of the cross-national differences in immigrant earnings trends. Other institutional forces also impinge on immigrants and may help explain the downward earnings and employment trends. In the United States, immigrant earnings are lower than in Canada partly because of wider earnings disparities in the labor market (Reitz 1998: chap. 5). Not only do earnings inequalities remain greater in the United States, but the trend toward increased earnings inequality has been more pronounced (Gottschalk and Smeeding 1997; Wolfson and Murphy 2000). The salience of the earnings polarization issue has been greater in the United States (Harrison and Bluestone 1988), and the impact of immigration in threatening the already precarious position of the least well paid individuals, blacks in particular, is the subject of considerable discussion and research (Hamermesh and Bean 1998). U.S. experience suggests that as immigrant earnings decline in Canada, the possible impact of immigrants on earnings polarization may receive greater attention.

Regarding immigration policy, it seems clear that efforts to solve the problem of declining immigrant earnings by improved selection alone are doomed to ineffectiveness. Given the discounting of their skills, for immigrants to keep pace with native-born workers requires that their educational levels may have to rise twice as fast. The experience of Canada is instructive. Canada has upgraded its selection criteria several times, with diminishing effects. Skills hurdles were raised, new economic categories for entrepreneurs and investors were introduced, and "family-class" eligibility was reduced. These measures increased educational levels in most immigrant groups, but the decline in immigrant earnings has continued. Even the significant changes made to Canadian immigration selection in the early 1990s appear so far to have yielded little benefit. Evidence on recent trends is being watched closely.

Among the other policy options, the issue of recognition and evaluation of immigrant qualifications is receiving increased attention. Both U.S. and Canadian employers have difficulty evaluating foreign educational credentials, experience, and work histories. It may be possible to provide a better mutual orientation for immigrants and their potential employers. In the contemporary workplace, employers already invest heavily in the recruitment and orientation of new employees. When the prospective new employees are immigrants, the necessary orientation is likely to be more complex because immigrants bring more diverse backgrounds and experiences. There is a role here not only for human resource managers but also for remedial educational institutions, professional and employee associations, and immigration policies themselves. The goal would be to ensure that when immigrants present their background and qualifications, employers can understand them and readily relate them to the requirements of the job at hand.

The emergence of postindustrialism and the knowledge economy, and increased international migration, may both be seen as encouraged by the broader process of globalization. The analysis here also reveals an underlying tension between the two and suggests that global economic change may create increased difficulties related to migration in the future. Successful incorporation of immigrants from developing countries into the economies and societies of the developed world is likely to become a matter of increasing priority.

References

Antecol, H.D., D.A. Cobb-Clark, and S.J. Trejo. 2000. "Immigration Policy and the Skills of Immigrants to Australia, Canada, and the United States." Manuscript.

Baker, M., and D. Benjamin. 1994. "The Performance of Immigrants in the Canadian Labor Market," *Journal of Labor Economics* 12: 369–405.

———. 1997. "Ethnicity, Foreign Birth and Earnings: A Canada/U.S. Comparison." In *Transition and Structural Change in the North American Labor Market*, edited by M.G. Abbott, C.M. Beach, and R.P. Chaykowski. Kingston: John Deutsch Institute and Industrial Relations Centre, Queen's University.

Barff, Richard, Mark Ellis, and Michael Reibel. 1995. "The Links between Immigration and Internal Migration in the United States: A Comparison of the

1970s and 1980s." Working Paper Series, no. 1. Hanover, N.H.: Nelson A. Rockefeller Center for the Social Sciences, Dartmouth College.

Bartel, Ann P. 1989. "Where Do the New U.S. Immigrants Live?" *Journal of Labor Economics* 7, no. 4: 371–91.

Bell, D. 1973. *The Coming of Post-Industrial Society*. New York: Basic Books.

Blau, F.D., and A.H. Beller. 1988. "Trends in Earnings Differentials by Gender, 1971–1981," *Industrial Labor Relations Review* 41: 513–29.

Borjas, George J. 1988. *International Differences in the Labor Market Performance of Immigrants*. Kalamazoo, Mich.: W.E. Upjohn Institute for Employment Research.

———. 1990. *Friends or Strangers: The Impact of Immigrants on the U.S. Economy*. New York: Basic Books.

———. 1994. "Assimilation and Changes in Cohort Quality Revisited: What Happened to Immigrant Earnings in the 1980s?" Working Paper No. 4866. Cambridge, Mass.: National Bureau of Economic Research.

———. 1999. *Heaven's Door: Immigration Policy and the American Economy*. Princeton, N.J.: Princeton University Press.

Boyd, M. 1992. "Gender, Visible Minority and Immigrant Earnings Inequality: Reassessing an Employment Equity Premise." In *Deconstructing a Nation: Immigration, Multiculturalism and Racism in '90s Canada*, edited by V. Satzewich. Toronto: Garamond.

Chiswick, Barry R. 1986. "Is the New Immigration Less Skilled than the Old?" *Journal of Labor Economics* 4: 168–92.

Christofides, L.N., and R. Swidinsky. 1994. "Wage Determination by Gender and Visible Minority Status: Evidence from the 1989 LMAS," *Canadian Public Policy* 22: 34–51.

Department of Commerce, Bureau of the Census. 1983. *Census of Population and Housing, 1980: Public Use Microdata Samples Technical Documentation*. Ann Arbor, Mich.: Inter-university Consortium for Political and Social Research.

———. 1992. *Census of Population and Housing, 1990: Public Use Microdata Samples Technical Documentation*. Washington, D.C.: U.S. Department of Commerce.

Duleep, H.O., and M.C. Regets. 1992. "Some Evidence on the Effects of Admissions Criteria on Immigrant Assimilation." In *Immigration, Language and Ethnicity: Canada and the U.S.*, edited by Barry Chiswick. Washington, D.C.: AEI Press.

Foner, Nancy. 2000. *From Ellis Island to JFK: New York's Two Great Waves of Immigration*. New York: Russell Sage Foundation.

Freeman, Richard B., and Karen Needels. 1993. "Skill Differentials in Canada in an Era of Rising Labor Market Inequality." In *Small Differences That Matter: Labor Markets and Income Maintenance in Canada and the United States*, edited by David Card and Richard B. Freeman. Chicago: University of Chicago Press.

Gottschalk, P., and T.M. Smeeding. 1997. "Cross-National Comparisons of Earnings and Income Inequality," *Journal of Economic Literature* 35: 633–87.

Harrison, B., and B. Bluestone. 1988. *The Great U-Turn: Corporate Restructuring and the Polarizing of America.* New York: Basic Books.

Heckman, J.J. 1979. "Sample Selection Bias as a Specification Error," *Econometrica* 47: 153–61.

Jones, F.L. 1998. "Recent Trends in Labour Market Disadvantage among Immigrants in Australia," *Journal of Ethnic and Migration* Studies 24: 73–85.

Korzeniewicz, R.P., T.P. Moran, and A. Stach. n.d. "Trends in Inequality: Towards a World-Systems Analysis." In *Globalization and Society: Processes of Differentiation Examined,* edited by Raymond Breton and Jeffrey G. Reitz. Westport, Conn.: Greenwood Press. Forthcoming 2003.

Lipset, Seymour M. 1989. *The Continental Divide.* Toronto: C.D. Howe Institute.

Oaxaca, R. 1973. "Sex Discrimination in Wages." In *Discrimination in the Labor Market,* edited by O. Ashenfelter and A. Rees. Princeton, N.J.: Princeton University Press.

Reitz, Jeffrey G. 1998. *Warmth of the Welcome: The Social Causes of Economic Success for Immigrants in Different Nations and Cities.* Boulder, Colo.: Westview.

———. 1999. "Trends in Immigrant Success in the Knowledge Economy: 1970–1995." Paper presented at Fourth International Metropolis Conference, Washington, D.C., December 7–11.

———. 2001a. "Immigrant Skill Utilization in the Canadian Labor Market: Implications of Human Capital Research," *Journal of International Migration and Integration* 2, no. 3: 347–78.

———. 2001b. "Immigrant Success in the Knowledge Economy: Institutional Change and the Immigrant Experience in Canada, 1970–1995," *Journal of Social Issues* 57, no. 3: 579–613.

———. 2003. "Immigration and Canadian Nation-Building in the Transition to a Knowledge Economy." In *Controlling Immigration: A Global Perspective,* edited by Wayne A. Cornelius, Takeyuki Tsuda, Philip Martin, and James Hollifield. 2d ed. Palo Alto, Calif.: Stanford University Press.

Reitz, Jeffrey G., and R. Breton. 1994. *The Illusion of Difference: Realities of Ethnicity in Canada and the United States.* Toronto: C.D. Howe Institute.

Reitz, Jeffrey G., J.R. Frick, T. Calabrese, and G.G. Wagner. 1999. "The Institutional Framework of Ethnic Employment Disadvantage: A Comparison of Germany and Canada," *Journal of Ethnic and Migration Studies* 25, no. 3: 397–443.

Statistics Canada. 1984. *1981 Census of Canada Public Use Sample Tapes User Documentation.* 8-1200-69. Ottawa: Statistics Canada.

———. 1990. *1986 Census of Canada Public Use Microdata File on Individuals.* Documentation and user's guide. 3d preliminary ed. Ottawa: Statistics Canada, March 3.

———. 1994. *1991 Individual Public Use Microdata File Codebook.* DDMS edition. Ottawa: Statistics Canada.

———. 1999. *1996 Public Use Microdata File on Individuals. User Documentation.* Ottawa: Statistics Canada.

Stolzenberg, R.M., and D.A. Relles. 1997. "Tools for Intuition about Sample Selection Bias and Its Correction," *American Sociological Review* 62: 494–507.
Wanner, R.A. 1986. "Educational Inequality: Trends in Twentieth-Century Canada and the United States," *Comparative Social Research* 9: 47–66.
Wolfson, M., and B. Murphy. 2000. "Income Inequality in North America: Does the 49th Parallel Still Matter?" Catalogue no. 11-010-XPB. Ottawa: Statistics Canada.

Appendix 7A. Description of Variables, United States and Canada Census Microdata Files

Census	United States	Canada
Year	1980, 1990	1981, 1991 (also 1986, 1996)
Gender	Men, women	Men, women
Birthplace	Native-born = born in U.S. reporting no "year of arrival" Immigrants = born outside U.S. reporting "year of arrival"	Native-born = born in Canada reporting no "year of arrival" Immigrants = born outside Canada reporting "year of arrival"
Ethnic origins	Race: "Whites" (= white excluding Hispanic, and for immigrants distinguishing those born in Europe or Canada vs. others), Black, Chinese, South Asian, Filipino, Other Asian, "Hispanics" (= white and Hispanic, distinguished by specific Spanish origins)	Ethnic origin: "Whites" (= European origin, and for immigrants, distinguishing those born in Europe or the U.S. versus others), Black, Chinese, and (1991) also South Asian, Filipino, Other Asian
Years since arrival	For immigrants, categories varying across censuses	For immigrants, categories varying across censuses
Employment	Respondents reporting any earnings (positive earnings from wages, salaries, or self-employment) over preceding year (dummy variable)	Respondents reporting any earnings (positive earnings from wages, salaries, or self-employment) over preceding year (dummy variable)
Earnings, in local currency	Dollars (unadjusted) reported as wages, salaries, or self-employment earnings over preceding year	Dollars (unadjusted) reported as wages, salaries, or self-employment earnings over the preceding year
Education	Total number of years of education	Total number of years of education, sum of elementary, secondary, and vocational or other nonuniversity education
Education squared	Square of education (with mean set to zero)	Square of education (with mean set to zero)
Work experience (potential)	Age minus years of education minus 5	Age minus years of education minus 5
Urban residence	Dummy variables Cities over 1,000,000 population Cities 500,000–999,999 population	Dummy variables Cities over 1,000,000 population Cities 500,000–999,999 population
Language knowledge	Knowledge of English = good or fair	Speaking knowledge of English or French

Appendix 7B. Percent of Immigrants in Each Origins Group, by Census Year, Years since Arrival, and Gender, Aged 20 to 64

		United States				Canada			
		Men		Women		Men		Women	
Origins	Years since Arrival	1980	1990	1980	1990	1981	1991	1981	1991
White (non-Hispanic)	0–5	13.0	11.8	14.3	12.9	35.5	24.6	34.7	25.4
	6–10	15.9	8.6	17.2	9.7	41.1	32.1	41.9	32.6
Black	0–5	7.3	6.4	6.9	6.6	4.8	6.3	5.4	6.2
	6–10	9.6	8.3	9.1	9.0	7.1	5.9	6.4	7.6
Chinese	0–5	6.0	6.6	6.9	7.9	14.8	18.4	15.8	20.1
	6–10	5.4	6.5	5.6	7.6	10.7	16.8	10.9	17.6
South Asian	0–5	4.5	4.3	4.3	4.0	NA	12.7	NA	11.4
	6–10	5.1	4.1	4.0	3.7	NA	12.2	NA	10.7
Filipino	0–5	4.4	3.9	7.5	6.6	NA	4.2	NA	6.8
	6–10	5.5	4.3	8.0	6.8	NA	3.3	NA	5.4
Korean	0–5	3.4	3.0	5.6	4.2	NA	NA	NA	NA
	6–10	3.1	3.1	4.8	4.2	NA	NA	NA	NA
Japanese	0–5	2.4	2.5	2.6	2.8	NA	NA	NA	NA
	6–10	1.0	0.6	1.9	0.9	NA	NA	NA	NA
Vietnamese	0–5	5.5	2.1	5.1	2.3	NA	NA	NA	NA
	6–10	0.2	4.5	1.0	3.6	NA	NA	NA	NA

Appendix 7B continued

Other Asian[1]	0–5	3.0	3.5	3.1	3.5	NA	16.5	NA	14.1
	6–10	1.6	4.7	1.7	5.1	NA	15.1	NA	11.4
Mexican	0–5	21.3	12.6	16.9	9.9	NA	NA	NA	NA
	6–10	25.4	11.3	20.2	9.4	NA	NA	NA	NA
Cuban	0–5	1.1	0.8	1.0	0.9	NA	NA	NA	NA
	6–10	4.5	3.2	5.1	2.6	NA	NA	NA	NA
Puerto Rican and other	0–5	10.0	9.1	11.6	10.4	NA	3.4	NA	3.0
Hispanic[2]	6–10	11.8	8.2	12.8	9.6	NA	2.4	NA	2.5
Other European	0–5	14.6	7.3	11.5	6.4	10.0	10.7	9.1	10.4
	6–10	7.8	6.3	5.9	5.1	10.2	10.4	11.5	10.8
Other	0–5	3.6	26.0	2.8	21.6	34.8	2.8	35	2.4
	6–10	3.1	26.3	2.7	22.6	30.9	1.2	29.7	1.1
N, All Immigrants	0–5	53,173	80,554	50,510	75,920	2,972	8,065	3,262	8,497
	6–10	38,840	73,705	41,267	66,117	4,346	4,243	4,367	4,649
	Total	92,013	154,259	91,777	142,037	7,318	12,308	7,629	13,146

[1] Includes Hawaiian; in Canada includes all other Asians.

[2] In Canada, includes all Latin Americans.

NA = Not available.

8

The Cost of Not Being Christian: Hindus, Sikhs, and Muslims in Britain and Canada

SUZANNE MODEL AND LANG LIN

In recent years, students of the economic attainment of immigrants have become increasingly interested in cross-national comparisons (Model, Fisher, and Silberman 1999; Reitz et al. 1999). Rather than examining different groups within a single host society, they contrast similar groups in two or more societies. This new emphasis reflects both an increase in the number of immigrant destinations and an increase in the data available on immigrants within those destinations. To date, the most popular research strategy has been the U.S.-Canada comparison, with the occasional addition of Australia (Borjas 1988; Baker and Benjamin 1997; Card and Freeman 1993; Chiswick 1992; Reitz 1998). The present inquiry takes cross-national comparison in a new direction. We ask: what is the "cost" of being a non-Christian immigrant in a Christian nation (Siegel 1965)? More specifically, is the "cost" or penalty of being Hindu, Sikh, or Muslim greater in Canada or in England?

A comparison of non-Christian trajectories in the Old World versus the New World is certainly timely. For many years, Islamophobia—or as Halliday (1999) puts it, "anti-Muslimism"—was known to be strong in Europe. But scholars are now uncovering the phenomenon in North America as well (Eck 2001). The events of September 11, 2001, doubtless exacerbated this response. Sikhs too have occasionally been in the limelight, especially in the 1980s when Sikh terrorists mounted an unsuccessful attempt to create an independent Punjab state.

Research on the economic consequences of membership in a non-Christian religion has been hampered by the dearth of data about religion. As a result, many scholars use birthplace as a proxy, a strategy that renders impossible a decision as to whether religion makes an independent contribution to ethnic attainment. The present study utilizes the 1991 Canadian census and the 1994 Fourth National Survey of Ethnic Minorities in Britain, both of which contain a religion question. Limiting our inquiry to males, we compare foreign-born Hindus, Sikhs, and Muslims to native-born Christian whites on labor force participation, unemployment status, occupational status, and earnings in Canada and Britain. A later section of this chapter takes a look at the effects of religion separately within each country. Our main conclusion is that cross-national differences are few, but most groups experience at least one shortfall in each country.

THEORETICAL GROUNDING

To develop our hypotheses regarding which nation, Canada or Britain, offers foreign-born non-Christians the more favorable environment, we draw upon a typology that Alejandro Portes and his colleagues developed with a cross-national perspective in mind, though it has not yet been used to inform comparative research (Portes and Manning 1986; Portes and Borocz 1989; Portes and Rumbaut 1996, 2001). The typology identifies three "contexts of reception" as critical for the economic incorporation of immigrants: government policy, labor market conditions, and ethnic community characteristics. However, our focus motivates us to draw selectively from the typology as well as to add to it. For instance, under the rubric of government policy we emphasize official responses to discrimination, in contrast to Portes and Rumbaut (1996), who stress immigration law. Another difference is that we consider several variables under the rubric of labor market policy, whereas Portes and Rumbaut consider only one. Our extension includes indicators relevant to immigrant labor markets and indicators relevant to general labor markets. Finally, our evaluation of the effects of ethnic community characteristics follows Portes and Rumbaut quite closely.

We begin, like Portes and Rumbaut (1996), with government policy. But, as noted above, the policy we consider central in deciding whether Canada or Britain offers non-Christian immigrants the more cordial reception is not immigration law but discrimination law. Both the United Kingdom and Canada offer comprehensive civil legislation that includes mechanisms of redress. Yet we hypothesize that the Canadian system is the more effective, for four reasons. First, Canadian law has a less stringent standard of evidence than British law. Second, Canadian law permits similar complaints filed by more than one individual to be dealt with together, while under British law each case is considered on its own merits. Third, the Canadian government underwrites the cost of pursuing a complaint; in Britain, financial aid is means tested and not always available even then. Fourth, the Canadian code explicitly forbids discrimination on the grounds of religion; the British code does not. For present purposes, this provision is central. To be sure, there are shortcomings in both nations' regulations. A common complaint is inadequate resources for pursuing complaints. Still, compared to Britain, Canada has the stronger policy (de Beijl 1995).

The second context of reception that Portes and Rumbaut identify is labor market conditions. Under this rubric their key variable is labor market discrimination, a factor we consider along with demographic and economic indicators. Portes and Rumbaut start by observing that "widespread discrimination may hold that certain groups should be confined to low-wage menial labor ... or it can hold that they are simply too incompetent to be employable at all" (1996: 85). In other words, gatekeepers do not devalue all outsiders equally; they construct a hierarchy of preference, ranking applicants from some backgrounds more favorably than others.

In the present instance, we are less interested in ethnic than religious discrimination. One of the few Canadian studies to take up this question is a survey of attitudes toward immigrant groups, some of which were described wholly in religious terms. In their 1991 survey, the Angus Reid group asked a sample of over three thousand Canadians, "How comfortable would you feel being around...," filling the blank with members of various immigrant groups. On a scale where 100 would be perfectly comfortable, here are some of the more intriguing scores: British, 90.7; Italians, 88.1; French, 86.5; Jews, 86; Chinese, 84; West Indian Blacks, 79.7; Arabs, 74.9; Muslims, 73.6; Indo Pakistanis, 72; and Sikhs, 68.8. Most relevant for present purposes, the disparity between Muslim and Sikh is statistically significant ($t = 6.7444$, $p <. 0000$).[1] Unfortunately, the researchers neglected to inquire about Hindus.

---

[1] Calculations by the authors, who thank Richard Wanner for furnishing these data.

British data on this topic are also sparse; the data used in the present study, the Fourth National Study of Ethnic Minorities, offer some insights. Members of its white subsample were asked, successively, whether or not they were prejudiced against Asians, Muslims, Caribbeans, and Chinese. Twenty-six percent of whites acknowledged being prejudiced against Asians, 25 percent against Muslims, 20 percent against Caribbeans, and 8 percent against Chinese. This survey also asked all participants, minority or not, the open-ended question: "Of all the racial, ethnic, and religious groups in Britain, against which do you think there is the most prejudice?" The answers varied with the ethnicity/religion of respondents. Among whites, 32.6 percent said "Asians"; 10.6 percent, "Muslims"; 11.7 percent, "Pakistanis"; and 10.4 percent, "Caribbeans." Less than 1 percent of whites selected "Sikhs" as experiencing the most prejudice, an assessment echoed by Sikhs. Taken together, these results suggest that, to the extent that the British take account of religion, Muslims are the group most likely to encounter stigma. Evidently the distinction between Muslims and Sikhs is of less significance in Britain than in Canada.

One reason for the difference may be that Britain was the setting for the infamous "Rushdie affair," in which the Ayatollah Khomeini issued a death threat against India-born British Muslim writer Salman Rushdie. To be sure, Sikhs have also been the recipients of unfavorable publicity, especially in the 1980s, when Sikh separatism on the subcontinent turned violent (Tatla 1993). Yet perhaps it was not this publicity that triggered the strong anti-Sikh sentiment recorded in the Canadian survey, but rather a struggle over the right of male Sikh adolescents to carry kirpahs (a dagger that holds ritual significance) in school. This was a debate that polarized the Peel School Board in suburban Toronto around the time of the survey described above (Hudson 1991; Lakey 1991).

In sum, these surveys suggest that the hierarchy of religious discrimination may be different in the two countries. Yet to understand the implications of this hierarchy, it is also useful to consider the demographic composition of the labor force, especially group size. Calculations based on the 1991 Canadian census show that in Toronto, for instance, the male labor force is 1.0 percent Sikh, 2.7 percent Hindu, and 2.7 percent Muslim. Analogous data for London are not available, but our tabulations based on the ethnic question in the 1991 UK census show that Indians make up about 5 percent of London's male labor force; Pakistanis and Bangladeshis together constitute another 1.5 percent. These figures create queues consonant with the expectation that Sikhs fare better in Britain than in Canada, and Muslims better in Canada than in Britain. But because both minorities are small, it is unlikely that the economic effect of the cross-national differences in their standing is large.

We turn now to a labor market condition that affects all workers but which, we believe, has special potential to produce cross-national differences in the well-being of non-Christian immigrants: unemployment rates. Over the period we examine, Canadians faced an unemployment rate of 9.4 percent; the British rate was 11.3 percent. These values imply that Canadian employers had less discretion in hiring or promotion than did their British counterparts. This difference is potentially important because, when labor markets are tight, employers are freer to indulge in discriminatory behavior than when labor markets are slack (Hodge 1973). High unemployment rates, in turn, depress labor market participation. This phenomenon, called the "discouraged worker effect," occurs because job searches are costly. When individuals believe their chances of success are small, their propensity to search declines. Thus the cross-national difference in unemployment rates suggests that minorities in Canada will have both higher labor force participation and lower unemployment than their British counterparts.

A similar structural effect impacts occupational and earnings attainment: the more unequal the occupational structure or the earnings distribution, the greater the potential disadvantage for subordinate groups; the less unequal the structure, the smaller the gap between subordinate and superordinate (Reitz 1998; Blau and Kahn 2000). Unfortunately, comparable data on the occupational structures of Canada and Britain are hard to come by because the two countries' respective official statistics define occupations differently. We draw on Esping-Andersen, Assimakopoulou, and van Kersbergen's (1993) cross-national comparison of occupational polarization under Fordist and post-Fordist regimes in 1981. They define occupational polarization as the ratio of unskilled to upper white-collar workers within each regime. Using their figures and collapsing Fordist and post-Fordist regimes, we conclude that Canada has the more equitable occupational structure. The ratio there is 2.09; in the United Kingdom it is 2.30.

Turning finally to cross-national differences in earnings inequality, we draw on Katz's (1998) measure: the log of the ratio of wages earned by men in the lowest decile to wages earned by men in the highest decile. In both 1989 and 1994, these ratios were higher in Canada than in Britain; in other words, Britain has the more equitable earnings distribution.

To recapitulate, the effect of labor market structure is not identical across outcomes. The earnings distribution is more favorable in Britain than in Canada; the occupational structure and the unemployment rate are more favorable in Canada than in Britain. Since the latter also affects labor force participation, on three of the four job outcomes the structural variables favor Canada.

The third and final "context of reception" that Portes and Rumbaut identify is ethnic communities—in particular, whether they exist and, if so, whether "they are composed primarily of manual workers or contain a significant professional or business element" (1996: 87). The occupational standing of group members is important both because immigrants encounter discrimination and because they tend to rely on one another to find employment. Thus Portes and Rumbaut expect that newcomers with no compatriots to help them find work will be disadvantaged. Similarly, those joining compatriots who are mostly manual workers are likely to be incorporated into the labor market as manual workers, irrespective of their job qualifications. Newcomers joining communities with a significant professional component are likely to be introduced to jobs in professional services, though which occupations they access will also depend on their credentials. Finally, newcomers entering ethnic communities containing a significant business element are likely to be incorporated as ethnic economy employees. Since the job outcomes of self-employed ethnics and their co-ethnic employees do not depend on the practices of native white employers, ethnic economies are particularly valuable when the dominant economy is weak and/or discrimination is strong.

Attention to the history of the South Asian religious communities in Canada and Britain indeed uncovers some differences. Historically, the first to arrive in Canada in perceptible numbers were Sikhs, recruited at the turn of the last century to replace the newly outlawed Chinese and Japanese. Settling primarily in British Columbia, the overwhelmingly male Sikh population worked primarily in the lumber industry. Between 1908 and 1967, a variety of penalties and quotas restricted immigration from Asia, but the introduction of the point system in 1967 nominally ended discrimination on the basis of national origin. Gupta explains, "With this new emphasis, the immigration of professional South Asians to Canada increased, changing the size and character of the entire community" (1994: 62). Yet once under way, this "new" wave of immigrants doubtless stimulated the relocation of relatives, given that the Canadian immigration system allocates at least some points on the basis of kinship (Reitz 1998). Moreover, in the mid-1970s, Canada accepted modest numbers of South Asian refugees from Africa, who doubtless derived some benefit from the presence of their compatriots from the subcontinent. In short, in Canada connections between the pioneering generation and late-twentieth-century migrants are relatively weak, but those arriving in the last twenty years have joined a well-established community.

In England, too, Sikhs were the first settlers from the subcontinent. Initiating settlement in the post–World War I era, these pioneers were mainly craftsmen, most of whom became peddlers. However, England's post–World War II labor shortage eventually drew most of them into durable manufacturing. According to Hiro, "This wage-earning community was later to prove to be the nucleus around which Indian immigration to Britain grew" because, as economic and political conditions in India worsened, those with relatives or close friends in England were the most likely to emigrate (1971: 121). At first the new states of India and Pakistan limited passport holders to the more educated and affluent. In 1960, however, the Supreme Court of India struck down this law. In response, the Indian government moved from a de jure to a de facto means of emigration control. It restricted access to foreign currency, a policy that reinforced the advantage of those with contacts in Britain. Yet as some of the barriers to exit declined, new barriers to entry appeared. Britain passed its first immigration control act in 1962. To be sure, in the 1970s the door opened briefly to admit African refugees of Indian descent, but with this exception the only applicants able to emigrate from the subcontinent in recent years have been those with close relatives in Britain.

To evaluate the impact of these disparate migration histories on immigrant incorporation requires attending to the interaction between the job locations of earlier waves and the skills of later waves. In the British case, earlier waves held manual jobs; this meant that later arrivals, even if skilled, were likely to follow their compatriots into the factory. Indeed, empirical research suggests this was so. More recently, recession has closed many Midlands factories, and Britain's South Asian population has turned increasingly to self-employment (Ballard 1994). As in most countries, ethnic small business relies heavily on the labor power of kin. In the Canadian case, earlier waves held nonmanual jobs; this meant well-qualified later arrivals could expect to work as professionals, and the less qualified could expect to secure support jobs. Taken together, these considerations suggest that later arrivals to Canada have had channels to slightly better jobs than later arrivals to England.

This concludes our discussion of the many variables we associate with Portes and Rumbaut's three "contexts of reception." Now we use this material to predict which country will offer non-Christian immigrants the more salutary environment. With respect to the policy context, the discussion indicates that the Canadian government is more strongly committed to the protection of non-Christian immigrants than is the British. Similarly, newcomers settling in Canada, most of whom arrived after the mid-1960s, probably entered more resourceful religious communities than newcomers settling in Britain more than a decade earlier. However, the labor market context contains a few variables that work to the British advantage. Probably the most significant of these is the lower earnings inequality in the United Kingdom. Other things equal, stigmatized groups earn more in host societies where earnings inequality is low than where it is high. Because we believe that structural factors are among the more powerful determinants of economic attainment, we expect that the British advantage on this variable will overpower the more numerous variables on which Canada holds the edge. Thus on earnings we associate a better outcome with Britain.

A second variable on which Britain emerges as the more attractive is tolerance for Sikhs. However, we choose to underemphasize this finding for two reasons. The first is the difficulty an outsider has in distinguishing a Sikh from a Hindu, or from a Jain for that matter. To be sure, some Sikhs wear turbans and carry daggers, but in the West such persons are rare. Thus those Canadian employers with a "taste" for discrimination against Sikhs will have difficulty indulging it. Second, in the absence of longitudinal data on Canadian attitudes, we cannot rule out the possibility that the low ranking of Sikhs was simply a reflection of intergroup tensions in suburban Toronto in 1991. Labor market disadvantage is rarely the outcome of brief antagonisms.

These considerations translate into the following hypotheses: all else equal, on labor force participation, unemployment, and occupational status, the "cost" of being Sikh, Hindu, or Muslim will be lower in Canada than in Britain; on earnings, however, the "cost" will be lower in Britain.

Unfortunately, meeting the "ceteris paribus" condition is difficult because of a multitude of confounding factors. Below we identify and discuss the most salient of these, all of which originate in sending countries. Like their counterparts operating in receiving countries, these sending-country traits can be classified under three causal rubrics: ethno-religious traditions (culture), family resources, and the selectivity of migration.

We define ethno-religious tradition as similar values, attitudes, and behaviors of individuals of a given ethno-religious heritage, regardless of socioeconomic status (Light 1984; DiMaggio 1994). As a first approximation at controlling for ethno-religious heritage, we compare groups that are religiously similar but have settled in different destinations (Reitz 1998). To take into account the potential effects of national origin, we control for birthplace.

Unfortunately for our present purposes, most non-Christians in Britain are South Asian, while non-Christians in Canada come from a wide range of countries. This is an especially nettlesome problem in the case of Muslims because South Asia is one of many regions where Islam holds sway. Yet another problem is that culture interacts with context. For example, discrimination tends to exacerbate religious zeal. Thus at least one analysis of Muslims in Britain argues that fundamentalism has gained adherents in response to British intolerance of Islam (Gardner and Shukur 1994). This insight implies that if prejudice is greater in the United Kingdom than in Canada, controlling for a Muslim affiliation in Britain has a different meaning than controlling for a Muslim affiliation in Canada.

Yet the religious effects that we seek to control are those that affect economic behavior. Only if some intra-religious differences in religious practices produce variations in people's motivation to work or to maximize earnings are they relevant to the present undertaking. The first scholar to raise these issues was Max Weber. His analysis of the religions of India showed that some Hindu castes were more successful capitalist competitors than others (Weber 1958). Today some scholars challenge the accuracy of Weber's sources, others the logic of his argument (Huff and Schluchter 1999). Nevertheless, caste is associated with occupation. Some castes are entrepreneurial; others specialize in a craft or a profession. Islam, too, incorporates a variety of economic adaptations. Ismaili Muslims are known for their exceptional ability to raise capital for business enterprise; other Muslim denominations are handicapped in this regard (Nanji 1983; Rafig 1992). These considerations imply that we should control for self-employment and occupation whenever possible. Still, statistical controls are only partial remedies; moreover, self-employment and occupation are inappropriate in models of labor force participation and unemployment. To be sure, omitted variables always plague statistical analysis; the best we can do is remain mindful of them.

The same problem arises with respect to "family resources." Our definition of "family resources" parallels Nee and Sanders' (2001) description of immigrant families as purveyors of "social, financial and cultural-human capital" with one exception: we classify cultural capital as a cultural rather than a family resource. Family resources include social capital (links to the resources of others), human capital (knowledge and skills), and financial capital (wealth). Since our data include no measures of family background, our main control for these resources is education. But the educational advantage of Canadian South Asians relative to British South Asians, as well as the greater skill barriers associated with admission to Canada, suggests that non-Christian Canadians have the relatively more prosperous family origins. Again, this would be a cross-national difference that we cannot adequately control.

The final origin-based source of variation in immigrant attainment is the selectivity of migration. By this term we mean the unobserved traits that distinguish migrants from nonmigrants. Selectivity can be positive or negative; that is, movers may be more or less talented, more or less diligent than stayers. Debates regarding the determinants of selectivity have been shrill. Traditional demographic theory holds that economically motivated movers are positively selected; on the other hand, persons fleeing natural disaster or persecution "may not be selected at all" (Lee 1966: 56). Recent scholarship suggests that sojourners, tied migrants (those who move to join family members), and undocumented migrants are also less positively selected than economic migrants (Chiswick 1999; Duleep and Regets 1999). According to economist George Borjas (1994), the positively selected also include people persecuted because they are members of a professional or entrepreneurial class and people settling in nations where earnings inequality is high relative to the countries from which they emigrated.

These considerations are complex, but we conjecture that they are unlikely to translate into large differences between Canada and England. In the main, non-Christian immigrants, especially the males, are economic migrants. Both countries house some African Indian refugees, most of whom, before migration, were entrepreneurs. The proportion of undocumented non-Christians is likely to be small, but perhaps larger in Canada—where large-scale immigration has been under way for nearly four decades—than in England, where entry for non–European Union nationals is difficult. At the same time, the proportion of sojourners—persons expecting to return home—is likely somewhat greater in England, where many South Asians settled "temporarily." Pakistanis and Bangladeshis especially have clung to this "myth of return," but few do so before retirement; others arrange for their bodies to be shipped home for burial (Anwar 1979; Gardner and Shukur 1994). In sum, countercurrents run in both directions, but we believe that the great majority of both countries' immigrants are positively selected, economically motivated movers.

Assessing these considerations together, we suspect that the factor most likely to contaminate our cross-national comparison is variation in social class background. The bulk of migrants from South Asia to Canada probably have more advantageous social origins than their British counterparts. Controlling for education diminishes but does not eliminate the problem, as scholarship on status attainment has long shown. We know of no way to redress this imbalance save to attend to it when interpreting our results.

DATA AND METHODS

For Canada, the data come from the 1991 Public Use Microdata File of Individuals (PUMFI), a 3 percent sample drawn from the Canadian census of that year, and, for Britain, from the Fourth National Survey of Ethnic Minorities (NSEM). The NSEM, which covers England and Wales, was undertaken by the Policy Studies Institute in 1994. It is less representative than a census-based sample because it does not cover the entire population and because it has a lower response rate than censuses do. Of those successfully contacted, 79 percent of minority households and 71 percent of households headed by British whites participated in the NSEM (Smith and Prior 1996). Moreover, since the absolute size of the NSEM sample (7,949 individuals) is much smaller than the PUMFI sample (809,654 individuals), many ethnic minorities are simply too few in the NSEM to support reliable estimates.

For this reason, the non-Christians that receive primary attention on the British side of the analysis are Hindus, Sikhs, and Muslims born either on the Indian subcontinent or in Africa. Moreover, nearly all the

Africa-born in the NSEM are ethnically South Asian. In Canada, on the other hand, the Africa-born include substantial numbers of Maghrebis (North Africans) and sub-Saharan blacks, along with persons whose origins lie on the subcontinent. The Canadian data include a number of other categories that contain enough persons to support analysis, though the codes used to identify these groups are disappointingly broad. In terms of religion, there are sufficient Jews and Buddhists; in terms of birthplace, in addition to European countries the data distinguish the Middle East, South Asia, Hong Kong, the People's Republic of China, the Philippines, Vietnam, Other Asia, Africa, Latin America, and a residual Other category. Finally, the Canadian data contain an ethnicity question. Although it is coded very crudely and some of its categories overlap with birthplace, it permits the analyst to distinguish "Arabs" from "South Asians" and "West Asians," a distinction relevant to our analysis of the Africa-born. Unfortunately, the ethnicity question assigns some sub-Saharan blacks to a "Black/Caribbean" ethnic code and others to a residual "Other single origins" code; hence we cannot unambiguously identify sub-Saharan blacks among the Africa-born.

In order to render the two data sets as comparable as possible, we deal with these many discrepancies by creating five religious categories (Hindus, Sikhs, Muslims, Christians, and "Others") and four birthplace categories (South Asia, Africa, Britain/Canada, and "Other"). In our multivariate analyses, we omit Christians and Britain/Canada, a strategy that allows us to measure the difference between being a member of a minority religion or nationality relative to being a native-born Christian. In order to assure that this contrast is limited to white people, we delete from our analysis all native-born Christians of non-European origin.

There are a few other limitations and changes in the Canadian data that deserve mention. First, with respect to the PUMFI, in order to keep the analysis of manageable size, native-born European-origin whites were sampled at 2 percent. All other groups were retained in their entirety. Second, for reasons of confidentiality, the codes for cases coming from the Atlantic Provinces and the Territories do not distinguish among non-Christian religions. Residents of these regions were therefore excluded from the study.

Having described our sample, we turn next to our dependent and independent variables, some of which are also problematic. Four dependent variables are used in this research: labor force participation, unemployment, occupational status, and the log of weekly earnings.

Labor force participation is coded 1 if the individual is in the labor force (employed or unemployed), and 0 otherwise; unemployment is coded 1 if the individual is unemployed, 0 if employed. Non–labor force participants are missing on this variable. For occupational status, we rely on Treiman's International Socio-Economic Index (ISEI). Although a translation scheme is available for assigning an occupational status to each of the 333 occupational categories in the NSEM, no such scheme is available for the PUMFI. Equally problematic, the PUMFI divides occupation into only fourteen categories. Thus we had to devise a method for assigning each of these fourteen categories a status score. Following Ganzeboom, De Graaf, and Treiman's (1992) observation that "the costs of being crude" are severe only when the number of occupations falls below six, we computed weighted average ISEIs for each of the fourteen Canadian occupations. Calculating these averages required three pieces of information: the detailed occupational codes associated with each of the categories (Statistics Canada 1994), the title and number of persons in each detailed occupational code (Statistics Canada 1995), and the ISEI score for each occupational title (Ganzeboom and Treiman 1996). To facilitate the mapping process, we used Ganzeboom and Treiman's "numerical dominance rule." That is, when a detailed Canadian occupational code contained titles associated with more than one ISEI, the Canadian occupation was assigned the ISEI of its largest title. After each of the fourteen occupations had been assigned all its component ISEIs, we weighted the ISEIs by the number of their incumbents. Each individual was then assigned an ISEI equal to the weighted average associated with his PUMFI occupation.

Finally, with respect to earnings, there is a paucity of cases in the NSEM. Only 79 percent of employed sample members reported their earnings. As a result, only ninety-four Sikhs, the smallest religious group, appear in the earnings analysis. Nothing can be done about this shortfall save to acknowledge it when interpreting the results. A similar, less worrisome difficulty plagues the cross-national strategy; namely, that the number of cases missing on the dependent variables is not the same in Canada and Britain. Consider, for instance, unemployment; 13.3 percent of the British sample and 11.4 percent of the Canadian sample are missing on this outcome; that is, they are not in the labor force. Neoclassical economists believe that jobless individuals are disproportionately the less qualified and the less diligent. If this is so, then the men appearing on the British side of a British-Canadian comparison involving labor force participants will constitute a more positively selected sample than those appearing on the Canadian side. This disparity, in turn, might lead to an overestimate of the attainment of British workers relative to Canadian workers. Economists have developed several techniques to correct for this "sample selection bias." When estimating unemployment, occupational status, and earnings, we estimate a preliminary equation that distinguishes missing from nonmissing cases on these three dependent variables. This equation allows us to calculate the inverse Mills ratio, a variable that "controls" for the effects of selection bias. Interestingly, the Mills ratio is significant in the unemployment and earnings models but not in the occupational status models. This is probably because we ignore labor force status when analyzing occupational status; that is, any worker who reports an occupation is included in our efforts to predict occupational status, whether or not he is currently working.

The independent variables include human capital measures, indicators of family responsibilities, descriptions of regional characteristics, dummies for birthplace, and dummies for religion. Details about their construction appear in appendix 8A. Information regarding which independent variables predict which dependent variables, as well as regarding which independent variables produce which inverse Mills ratios, appears in appendix 8B.

Both in order to simplify the analysis and because female labor force participation is relatively low among foreign-born Muslims, the analysis is limited to males. Those Muslim immigrant women who report employment are a highly select group—an issue that deserves detailed analysis in its own right. Because of the shortage of cases in the NSEM, all men aged twenty-one to sixty-four (rather than the more customary twenty-five to sixty-four) are included. The analytic strategy is simple. For each dependent variable, a regression for Canada and a regression for England are estimated. The coefficients of the dummies for the religion variables in the two nations are then compared.

Because labor force participation and unemployment are dichotomous, we use logistic regression to estimate these models. This means that cross-national comparisons must be done cautiously; the coefficients generated by separate logistic regression models may be confounded by residual variation. Thus we use Allison's (1999) method for testing whether an adjustment for residual variation is appropriate, and when it is, we test for coefficient differences using his interactive approach rather than the standard Wald chi-square test. On the other hand, we use ordinary least squares regression in our occupational status and earnings models; thus a simple t-test can be used to test for cross-national differences between coefficients.

RESULTS

Table 8.1 conveys all the information available in our microdata about the ascriptive characteristics of the three religious minorities. Looking at the total cases within countries, Muslims are the most numerous, followed by Hindus and Sikhs. But Canada and Britain do not draw their Muslims from the same places. In Canada, about a third come from the Middle East, a third from Africa, and only a fifth from South Asia. In England, nearly 95 percent come from South Asia. Moreover, South Asian birthplace does not have the same meaning in England and Canada. Consulting publications based on the 1991 Canada census, we found that 75.9 percent of Canada's South Asians are born in India (versus 41.0 percent in our British data); 11.0 percent are born in Pakistan (versus 38.2 percent in our British data); and 1.9 percent are born in Bangladesh (versus 20.8 percent in our British data) (Statistics Canada 1992). Similarly, substantial proportions of Canadian Muslims speak Arabic or identify as Arabs; essentially no British Muslims do. These disparities mean that controlling for region of birth will attenuate but not eliminate the effects of place of birth on labor market outcomes.

The cross-national differences among Hindus and Sikhs are less striking though observable. The main one is that England houses a higher proportion of both groups from Africa and that Canada houses a higher proportion of Hindus from the Caribbean. Sikhs do not report Caribbean origins in either destination. Finally, the response to the admittedly limited language choices shows four out of five Canadian Sikhs speaking Punjabi, but only half of their counterparts in Britain select this as their primary language. The differences in nation of previous residence are not great enough to account fully for this difference; perhaps variations in the language questions contribute.[2]

Table 8.2 presents descriptive information by religion on the four dependent variables in the two countries. A good way to see how the structures of the British and Canadian labor markets differ is to compare

---

[2] For this datum we relied on the NSEM question: "Apart from English, what language do you regularly speak in, or do others speak to you in, in Britain?" In the PUMFI we used the mother tongue variable, which "refers to the first language learned at home in childhood and still understood by the individual at the time of the census" (Statistics Canada 1994).

Table 8.1. Characteristics of Foreign-born Hindu, Sikh, and Muslim Men Aged 21–64, Residing in Canada and Great Britain

Characteristic and Country of Residence	Hindu (%)	Sikh (%)	Muslim (%)
BIRTHPLACE			
Canada			
Middle East/West Asia	0.3	0.0	32.9
South Asia	57.7	95.1	20.3
Africa	6.8	1.4	36.3
Caribbean/Latin America	25.4	0.0	7.1
Total cases	1,290	1,182	2,063
England			
India	48.9	83.3	9.7
Pakistan	0.0	1.8	54.6
Bangladesh	0.6	0.0	29.6
Africa	46.5	13.2	5.4
West Indies	0.6	0.0	0.3
Total cases	327	227	766
LANGUAGE			
Canada			
Arabic	0.0	0.0	14.6
Punjabi	6.4	81.7	1.4
England			
Punjabi	11.3	54.2	23.9
Gujarati	39.8	3.5	5.0
Hindi	33.0	22.9	8.1
Urdu	7.0	12.8	31.6
Bengali	1.2	0.0	10.2
Syllethi	0.6	0.0	12.0
ETHNICITY			
Canada			
Arab	0.0	0.0	24.4
West Asian	0.2	0.0	17.2
South Asian	79.2	94.8	38.2
Black or Caribbean	8.6	0.1	6.2
England			
Indian	98.5	99.6	10.4
Pakistani	0.0	0.0	57.6
Bangladeshi	0.3	0.0	29.6
Black Caribbean	0.3	0.0	0.1

Table 8.2. Means and Standard Deviations on Dependent Variables, Men Aged 21 to 64, Residing in Canada and England, by Nativity and Religion[1]

	Foreign-born Hindus	Foreign-born Sikhs	Foreign-born Muslims	Native-born White Christians
Percent in labor force				
Canada	91.5	91.5	86.6	88.3
England	88.9	84.5	86.1	87.8
Percent unemployed				
Canada	13.0	15.2	15.0	7.98
England	8.94	19.4	38.3	8.63
Mean ISEI				
Canada	43.9 (13.7)	36.3 (11.7)	44.7 (12.9)	43.0 (12.9)
England	45.9 (16.0)	40.3 (13.8)	38.2 (12.8)	43.3 (14.9)
Mean weekly earnings[2]				
Canada	677.34 (572)	652.50 (783)	661.89 (872)	755.92 (825)
England	747.43 (488)	558.03 (318)	514.85 (372)	765.78 (408)

[1] Data for Britain are weighted.
[2] Earnings for Britain are adjusted to 1991 Canadian dollars.

the experiences of native-born white Christians, the overwhelming majority in the two countries. The best structural indicators available in the data are the rate of unemployment and the dispersion in occupational status and in earnings. All three operate as expected. Unemployment is lower in Canada than in England (7.96 percent versus 8.63 percent); the standard deviation of ISEI is lower in Canada (12.9) than in England (14.9); and the standard deviation in weekly earnings is greater in Canada (825) than in England (408). To be sure, a portion of these differences reflects coding decisions; for instance, the Canadian census offers only fourteen occupations, and the NESM top codes earnings at 789 pounds a week. Nevertheless, these indicators mesh so well with theoretical expectations that it is unlikely that they reflect only the idiosyncrasies of measurement.

With respect to the dependent variables themselves, the cross-national differences are small. Hence, even though our multivariate analysis compares the gap between minority and whites in Canada with the gap between minority and whites in Britain, our descriptive analysis simply compares minority well-being in Canada with minority well-being in Britain. This undertaking indicates that on most labor market outcomes, Hindus in Britain fare better than Hindus in Canada, while Muslims in Britain fare worse than Muslims in Canada. The most striking disparity concerns Muslim unemployment rates; these are 15.0 percent in Canada and 38.3 percent in Britain. The Sikh comparison yields mixed results: labor force participation, unemployment, and earnings are more favorable in Canada; occupational status is more favorable in Britain. This last finding surprised us. Given Canada's immigration policy, we assumed a goodly proportion of its South Asians would be upper white-collar workers. Returning to the data, we found that slightly over a third of Sikhs in both countries work in manufacturing. In Canada, however, Sikhs are also overrepresented in agriculture and in transport, while in England their largest concentration, after manufacturing, is retail trade. Doubtless, historical differences in the characteristics of the sending communities lie behind these variations.

Table 8.3, which describes the major independent variables, offers some explanation for the cross-national differences on the dependent variables in the previous table. As might be expected given their respective immigration histories, those in Canada are younger, have fewer post-migration years, poorer English, and smaller percents married. In other words, the religious minorities in England incur a smaller deficit, relative to native-born Christians, on all the human capital variables except education, on which immigrants in Canada have a decided edge. Looking within religious communities, education again deserves attention. In England, only 3.8 percent of Muslims have any higher education; the comparable figure for Canada's Muslims is 28.5 percent. Indeed, Canada's least educated religious minority is Sikhs, not Muslims. Sikhs also have the poorest English ability in Canada, while Muslims fit that description in England. These facts are consonant with our observation that Canada's Sikhs have relatively poor labor market outcomes. Another way the groups differ cross-nationally is in their propensity for self-employment. Though all groups report higher self-employment in England than in Canada, within England the religious group with the highest rate is Sikhs (29.1 percent); within Canada it is Muslims (17.2 percent). This pattern suggests that both the characteristics of the migrating group and policies in the host society affect rates of entrepreneurship. The final variable in the table, percent metropolitan residence, shows that England's religious minorities are all less urbanized than Canada's, though in both societies immigrants are far more urbanized than natives.

Table 8.3. Means and Standard Deviations on Independent Variables, Men Aged 21 to 64, Residing in Canada and England, by Nativity and Religion

Variable/ Nation	Foreign-born Hindus	Foreign-born Sikhs	Foreign-born Muslims	Native-born Christians
Age				
Canada	38.4 (11.0)	37.0 (11.4)	37.5 (10.7)	39.1 (12.1)
England	40.0 (8.5)	41.2 (9.3)	39.1 (10.7)	41.3 (10.9)
Years since migration				
Canada	10.8 (8.0)	11.8 (7.7)	10.0 (7.8)	NA
England	20.6 (7.5)	23.3 (8.2)	20.8 (9.3)	NA
Percent higher education				
Canada	28.8	19.3	28.5	12.9
England	13.8	9.3	3.8	11.3
English ability				
Canada	2.7 (1.0)	2.1 (0.6)	2.5 (0.9)	NA
England	3.6 (0.7)	3.3 (0.8)	3.0 (0.9)	NA
Percent married, spouse present				
Canada	74.0	79.2	67.2	58.6
England	91.4	91.7	88.4	69.5
Percent self-employed				
Canada	9.9	12.3	17.2	12.6
England	27.7	29.1	22.0	21.5
Percent reside in metropolitan area				
Canada	95.6	85.2	96.1	57.1
England	70.6	75.1	76.0	28.5

NA = Not available.

The results of our multivariate cross-national comparison of the "cost" of being non-Christian appear in table 8.4. Shaded rows indicate statistically significant cross-national differences. They are relatively few. On labor force participation, Muslims in Canada have a lower rate than their British counterparts; on unemployment, both Hindus and Sikhs have a higher rate in Canada, while Muslims have a lower rate.[3]

[3] Tests for residual variation indicated that an adjustment was appropriate in the unemployment regression. In order to enhance comparability across models, table 8.4 contains the coefficients generated by standard techniques; however, Allison's (1999) interactive method was used to test for cross-national differences in the effects of religion on unemployment (results available on request).

Table 8.4. Net Effects of Birthplace and Religion on Three Labor Market Outcomes in Canada and England

Dependent Variable/ Nation/Religion	Canadian Coefficient	English Coefficient	Δ Parameter[1]
Labor force participation			
South Asia	–0.8532***	–1.0153	0.215
Africa	–1.0435***	–1.2654	0.304
Hindu	0.0498	0.5209	–0.925
Sikh	0.1357	–0.1185	0.442
Muslim	–0.3829***	0.8318	–2.291*
Unemployment			
South Asia	1.5903***	–0.3015	0.34
Africa	1.4629***	–0.7473	1.00
Hindu	0.1691	0.1403	8.60**
Sikh	0.3311*	0.1782	5.10*
Muslim	0.4457***	1.7401***	–7.56**
Occupational status			
South Asia	–0.5048	0.2993	–0.341
Africa	–0.8953	3.1338	–0.923
Hindu	0.0581	–1.6361	1.030
Sikh	–4.8869***	–4.3425**	–0.313
Muslim	–0.6228	–2.6629	1.158
Log of weekly earnings			
South Asia	–0.5466***	–0.8054***	1.671
Africa	–0.5235***	–0.7468***	1.542
Hindu	–0.0403	0.0779	–1.402
Sikh	0.0842*	–0.0446	1.242
Muslim	–0.0741**	–0.0455	–0.316

[1] In models of unemployment, the Δ parameter is chi-square; in all other models, it is the t statistic.

Note: * p < .05, ** p <.01, *** p < .001.

On occupational status and earnings attainment, the effects of membership in a non-Christian religion do not differ cross-nationally. Although not shown in the table, we also compared the effects of region of birth (for example, South Asia and Africa) on attainment in the two countries. No significant differences emerged on any of the four outcomes.

The labor force participation results are surprising. After all, our models control for the structural factor most likely to depress labor force participation: the regional employment rate. In addition, Muslims

(1999) interactive method was used to test for cross-national differences in the effects of religion on unemployment (results available on request).

than among Canadian Muslims. Yet table 8.4 conveys precisely the opposite trend.

Of course, labor market variables are not the only determinants of labor force participation. Supply-side factors represent another source of variation. One potentially relevant supply-side factor is denomination; as pointed out earlier, there are significant variations in beliefs and practices within faiths. Yet we know of no theory that posits differences in Muslims' propensity to work by denomination. A more plausible supply-side factor is the selectivity of migration. We anticipated that most migrants in both countries were economically motivated settlers. However, this assumption might require amendment, especially if a higher proportion of Canada's than England's Muslims are refugees. Not only do theorists consider refugees less positively selected than economically motivated movers, but refugees are eligible for benefits that most other migrants cannot receive. Although detailed figures of refugees by religion, ethnicity, or nationality are rare, Canada appears to accept more refugees than does Britain (Employment and Immigration Canada 1991; NIDI 1994). To be consonant with our results, a refugee-based explanation must show that the key cross-national difference is religion, not national origin.

To test these ideas, we constructed interaction terms in the Canadian data between being Muslim and reporting Arab, South Asian, West Asian, or black/Caribbean "ethnicity." When added to the regression, two of these were significant: West Asian Muslims were less likely, and black/Caribbean Muslims more likely, to be in the labor force. According to the PUMFI documentation, West Asian ethnicity includes Afghanis, Armenians, Iranians, Israelis, Kurds, and Turks; black/Caribbean includes Caribbean backgrounds as well as Ghanians, African blacks, and blacks, but not Ethiopians or Somalis—the two major sources of African refugees. While these regional categories seem arbitrary, they do suggest that West Asian Muslims are an important source of the difference in labor force participation in the two countries, an interpretation we verified by reestimating the cross-national comparison without West Asians. Still, we cannot be sure that a disproportion of refugees is the reason for the low labor force participation of Canada's West Asian Muslims. At this point we can only say that this group is less likely to participate.

Turning next to unemployment, keep in mind that the estimates exclude non–labor force participants but include a selection bias term. Therefore, the possibility that Muslim labor force participants are more favorably selected in Canada than in Britain cannot explain the lower unemployment rate of Muslims in Canada. More compatible with our methodology is the interpretation that Canada's lower unemployment rate is a determinant of the Canadian Muslim advantage. At the same time, Canada's lower unemployment rate does not seem to have helped Canada's Hindus and Sikhs; they fare better in Britain.

How can we understand this apparently contradictory pattern? At least two other variables help resolve the paradox: each group's position in the labor queue and its self-employment rate. Because the self-employed create their own jobs, self-employed members of stigmatized groups can mitigate the potentially deadly combination of high regional unemployment rates and a low position in the labor queue. And, indeed, table 8.3 reported cross-national differences in self-employment rates among religious minorities consonant with this interpretation. The Canadian-British difference is smallest among Muslims (4.8 percent) and substantially greater among Sikhs (16.8 percent) and Hindus (17.8 percent). This means that regional unemployment rates and discriminatory employers are less consequential for Sikhs and Hindus in Britain—where nearly 30 percent are self-employed—than in Canada, where around 10 percent are self-employed.

Furthermore, the survey research described earlier suggests that white employers rank Sikhs at the bottom of the labor queue in Canada but not in Britain. We initially dismissed this finding, perhaps prematurely. One reason for our hesitation was the suspicion that Canadian employers cannot distinguish Sikhs from Hindus or Jains. An admittedly flawed way of examining this assumption is to compare the magnitude of the Canadian religion coefficients. This exercise reveals that the Sikh and Hindu unemployment coefficients are not statistically different from one another (chi-square = 1.46, p = .226), nor are the Sikh and Muslim unemployment coefficients statistically different from one another (chi-square = 0.64; p = 0.424). Thus to the extent that the religion coefficients convey employer attitudes—an admitted simplification—the position of Sikhs in the Canadian labor queue is about the same as the position of other non-Christians. To sum up, Hindus and Sikhs suffer more unemployment in Canada than in Britain because they are less often self-employed and more often discriminated against in the former country.

The causal nexus in the Muslim case is somewhat different. Because the cross-national variations in self-employment rates are small, cross-national variations in regional unemployment rates are more important. In addition, studies suggest that "anti-Muslimism" is stronger in Britain than in Canada. Taken together, these considerations translate into a Muslim unemployment rate that is four times higher in Britain than in Canada.

Finally, the absence of significant cross-national differences on occupational status and earnings implies that neither cross-national differences in labor market structure nor in-group standing are strong enough to translate into cross-national disparities by religion. Additional analysis (not shown) suggests these differences generate variations in human capital returns, but the net effects of religion do not vary between the two countries.[4] That is, from the standpoint of religion, the consequences of settling in Canada or England operate primarily in terms of securing employment; for those with jobs, the effects of living in one country versus the other are statistically indistinguishable.

Before closing, it is appropriate to devote some attention to the "cost" of being non-Christian *within* each country. Table 8.4 offers some information on this point, but the models described there are restricted to variables that appear in both data sets. Moving away from cross-national comparison allows us to include all theoretically relevant variables. Of course, we remain constrained by the available measures; thus in the Canadian data we cannot disaggregate South Asia or Africa into its components. Our main refinement is to add four dummies for ethnic group membership, again highly aggregated. They are black/Caribbean, Arab, South Asian, and West Asian. Though some of these ethnicities are highly correlated with birthplace, they are only moderately correlated with religion.[5]

Table 8.5 conveys the resulting coefficients. In terms of significance, the pattern is nearly the same as in table 8.4. Only one of the religion coefficients has changed: Muslims have significantly lower occupational status than native-born Christians in the more elaborate model (b = −0.8724*) but not in the simpler model (b = 0.6228). Table 8.5 also contains some non-Christian groups too few to support study in the British data; namely Buddhists, Jews, and persons checking "No Religion."[6]

---

[4] For example, equivalent English language skills yield higher earnings in Canada than in England.

[5] The highest religion-ethnicity correlation for Canada is $r = .263$ ($p < .001$) for Muslims and Arabs.

[6] The "no religion" category contains respondents who indicated they had "no religion" but excludes those who wrote in responses like "agnostic," "free thinker,"

Table 8.5. Net Effects of Religion on Four Labor Market Outcomes of Canadian Men, 1991

Religion	Labor Force	Unemploy-ment	Occupational Status	Ln Week Earnings
Hindu	−0.0638	0.1792	0.4613	−0.0255
Sikh	0.0786	0.2811*	−5.3057***	0.1024*
Muslim	−0.3300**	0.3168**	−0.8724*	−0.0658*
Buddhist	−0.1678	0.2554	−0.4551	−0.0155
Jewish	−0.0341	−0.1666	1.6763*	0.1696**
Other	0.0085	0.0070	−1.2762	−0.0197
No religion	−0.1932**	0.2270**	0.2233	−0.0359
R^2 (adj. or pseudo)	0.1325	0.0640	0.3779	0.1704
N of cases	22,820	20,282	19,572	18,058

Using the figures in table 8.5 as indicators of the relative economic well-being of Canada's religious minorities suggests that Muslims are the most handicapped, with Sikhs not far behind. The two groups experience about the same level of unemployment; Sikhs incur the higher occupational status penalty, and Muslims, the higher earnings penalty. Indeed, Sikhs earn significantly more than native white Christians with similar characteristics. To further explore the reason for this result, we reestimated the earnings equation without controlling for occupational status. With this variable deleted, Sikhs no longer register a net earnings advantage; the effects of membership in the other religious groups, however, remain the same. In other words, Sikhs take up occupations for which they are overqualified, but within those occupations they earn somewhat more than similarly qualified native white Christians.

Turning to the remaining minority religions, we find that all four labor market outcomes of Hindus and Buddhists are the same as native white Christians; Jews have slightly higher occupational status and earnings (a finding reported before); and men with "no religion" appear both less likely to work and more likely to be unemployed. This last result suggests that the irreligious have greater employment problems than the religious, but because the category excludes "atheists," "agnostics," and so on, further research is needed before this interpretation should be accepted.

---

and so on. These, along with "Jain" and other minor religious groups, were coded as "Other" (Statistics Canada 1994).

Our last step is to estimate elaborated models for Britain. The data permit an extension of geography; hence, instead of five regions, we use seven, and we disaggregate South Asia into India, Pakistan, and Bangladesh. In addition, we created five ethnic dummies: black, Indian, Pakistani, Bangladeshi, and Other. Again, these are highly correlated with birthplace but only moderately with religion.[7] We aggregated the smaller religious groups into an "other" category; those not supplying a religion are among the "missing" on this variable, and we exclude them from the analysis.

Table 8.6. Net Effects of Religion on Four Labor Market Outcomes of British Men, 1994

Religion	Labor Force	Unemploy-ment	Occupational Status	Ln Week Earnings
Hindu	0.2541	0.5154	–4.4251*	0.0140
Sikh	–0.4151	0.6985	–7.5250***	–0.2220
Muslim	1.1293*	1.6234**	–1.9809	–0.0184
Other	0.1718	0.7293**	–0.3558	–0.0578
R^2 (adj. or pseudo)	0.2627	0.2430	0.3612	0.4051
N of cases	1,740	1,504	2,121	1,240

Table 8.6 conveys the resulting coefficients for religious group membership. Significant findings differ from those generated by the simpler model in two ways: relative to native-born Christians, Muslims are more likely to be in the labor force (1.1293*) and Hindus suffer an occupational status deficit (–4.4251*). Additional analysis did not reveal the reason for the latter change. The stronger Hindu penalty is not due to the addition of the Indian ethnicity variable; if it is excluded from the equation, the Hindu coefficient is only slightly smaller (–3.9100*). This finding means that, were better data available, Hindus might hold higher occupations in Canada than in Britain; but this interpretation is speculative.

Using the figures in table 8.6 as indicators of the relative economic well-being of Britain's religious minorities suggests that the differences among them are small. Relative to native white Christians, Muslims are

[7] The highest religion-ethnicity correlation for Britain is r = .278 (p < .001) for Hindus and Indians.

more often unemployed; Hindus and Sikhs hold lower status occupations. Because access to jobs is a basic human need in industrial societies, some observers may feel unemployment vulnerability is the more pernicious handicap. From this perspective, Britain's Muslims are more disadvantaged than other non-Christians. Another study based on these same data concluded that Muslims were highly vulnerable to unemployment but detected a lower rate for Indian than Pakistani and Bangladeshi Muslims (Brown 2000). This analysis also differed from ours in finding that Sikhs were significantly more likely than Hindus to be jobless. Differences in sample and method probably explain the discrepancies; Brown's sample was restricted to nonwhites but included both sexes and both foreign and native-born South Asians.

DISCUSSION

One way to summarize our cross-national results is to weigh each labor market outcome equally and ask: which nation extracts the lowest "cost" for being non-Christian? Of the four statistically significant outcomes, three favor England; one favors Canada. Substantively, one of the more interesting effects favoring England is the lower labor force participation of Muslims in Canada; this is probably a correlate of Canada's more tolerant refugee policy. Equally intriguing is the higher joblessness of Sikhs in Canada, probably a result of Sikhs' political visibility around the time of the 1991 Canadian census. The higher joblessness of Hindus in Canada is less consequential because in neither nation is the coefficient significantly different from zero. Finally, Muslim unemployment is higher in England.

To us, the most appropriate interpretation of these findings is that, for non-Christian immigrants in general, neither nation extracts a substantially greater "cost" than the other. This is a surprise. We had hypothesized that, with the exception of earnings, Canada would prove the more rewarding host society. Several political, economic, and historical conditions prompted this conclusion—for instance, Canada's more stringent antidiscrimination law, lower unemployment rate, more modest occupational disparities, and the higher proportion of professionals among its South Asians. Indeed, we worried that our inability to control for the potentially more affluent family backgrounds of Canada's South Asians would bias the results in Canada's favor.

As already pointed out, one mechanism that seems to have undercut these Canadian advantages is discrimination against Sikhs. We too quickly discounted the intolerance toward Sikhs that Canadians reported to Angus Reid. This would not have surprised experts on the Bogardus Social Distance Scale, which has long detected a relationship between political events and public perceptions of immigrants and minorities (Schaefer 1998). Were Angus Reid to survey Canadians in the immediate post–September 11 era, Muslims would doubtless emerge the most stigmatized non-Christian religious minority.

Still, Sikh disadvantage represents but one departure from our expectations. The overall pattern of our results—no significant differences by religion for occupation and earnings, and no significant differences by region of birth on any of the four outcomes—implies that our theory was misspecified. In explaining these disparities we turn to the work of Jeffrey Reitz (1988a, 1988b).

In his comparisons of Canada and Britain as immigrant-receiving societies, Reitz argues that Canada appears the more welcoming but that appearances are deceiving. By appearances he means that, in Canada, racist discourse is muted and overt racial conflict is rare, whereas in Britain, public figures are willing to assail foreigners and race riots appear endemic. Yet when comparing levels of racial discrimination rather than levels of rhetoric or conflict, Reitz finds little difference between the two countries. For instance, field studies show that about the same proportion of nonwhites experience hiring discrimination in Britain as in Canada. Indices of segregation in housing are likewise quite similar. Reitz maintains that one reason the differences between the two countries are more apparent than real is that the goal of immigration has been very different in the two societies: "For Britain, nonwhite immigration occurred in the context of the obligations of a declining imperial power to former colonial territories. For Canada, nonwhite immigration was a trend within the context of a long-term program of national development" (1988a: 117). Another cross-national difference that attenuates intergroup conflict in Canada is that its newcomers are relatively skilled. Perceptible inflows of unskilled workers tend to trigger discontent in most societies.

Reitz's perspective suggests we reevaluate some of the variables we found supportive of Canadian advantage. For instance, although Canada has the more effective antidiscrimination law, Reitz believes that the practical effects of the difference are modest. In both countries, complaints must be initiated by individuals, not governments; in both countries, the goal of the legislation is conciliation, not coercion. Other assessments suggest that the crucial legislative distinction is whether discrimination is a civil offense, as it is in both Canada and Britain, or a criminal offense, as it is in France. Civil offenses are considered more congenial to the filing of suits and the securing of redress (Banton 1994).

A second variable deserving of scrutiny is the ethnic community context. Following Portes and Rumbaut (1996), we concluded that recent arrivals to Canada would benefit from the high proportion of their co-religionists in the professions, whereas in Britain most later arrivals were handicapped in finding good jobs because most of their compatriots were factory workers. Recall, however, that by the late 1970s, political and economic events in Britain brought the closing of many factories. Moreover, by the 1980s the Thatcher government launched several initiatives to support small businesses. These structural changes, combined with cultural traditions of entrepreneurship, enhanced the ability of British ethnic and religious communities to absorb labor. Canada, too, has seen its manufacturing decline and its services increase. But its South Asians have been less entrepreneurial than Britain's. This may reflect differences in the two host countries' approach to small business or differences in the castes and denominations of the South Asians settling in the two countries. An additional factor is that Canada's South Asian small business sector faces more competition from other entrepreneurial groups, such as Chinese and Vietnamese, than do Britain's South Asians. This reevaluation suggests that substantial resources inhere in both nations' ethno-religious communities.

Nevertheless, we are unwilling to abandon the idea that general labor market indicators—such as unemployment rates, occupational structure, and earnings distributions—are relevant to cross-national comparisons of minority attainment. Regional unemployment rates did contribute substantively to our understanding of cross-national differences in unemployment; occupational and earnings differences did not operate as predicted. At least in part, the failure was due to our methodology, which was limited to a comparison of dummy variables for religion. Since the effects of occupational and earnings distributions are mediated through human capital, a better way to measure these effects is to compare returns to human capital within groups between countries (see note 4). This could be done by estimating separate equations by country and group, or by adding interactions between human capital and group membership in each country. Either way, these represent potential next steps in cross-national research on immigrant incorporation, whether that research focuses on the "cost" of national origin or the "cost" of religion.

In closing, a comment is advised on the value of Portes and Rumbaut's typology of immigrant incorporation as a tool for cross-national comparison. The typology directs attention to three contexts: governments, labor markets, and ethnic communities. We concur that these are the appropriate contexts to highlight; yet the typology emphasizes only one variable within each. Although this formulation may be adequate for explaining between-group variance within one nation, it is not adequate for explaining within-group variance in two or more nations. In this study, the labor market context proved the rubric of expansion. However, depending on the research question, the government context and/or the ethnic community context might also profit from expansion. For instance, citizenship rules might prove a useful addition to the government context; sex ratios might prove a useful addition to the ethnic community context. Clearly, cross-national research on immigrant attainment is on the rise; scholars are increasingly in need of theoretical guidance. The Portes and Rumbaut typology has much to offer in this regard; with additional refinement it may offer even more.

References

Allison, Paul D. 1999. "Comparing Logit and Probit Coefficients across Groups," *Sociological Methods and Research* 28: 186–208.

Anwar, Muhammad. 1979. *The Myth of Return: Pakistanis in Britain*. London: Heinemann.

Baker, Michael, and Dwayne Benjamin. 1997. "Ethnicity, Foreign Birth and Earnings: A Canada/U.S. Comparison." In *Transition and Structural Change in the North American Labour Market*, edited by M.G. Abbott, C.M. Beach, and R.P. Chaykowski. Kingston, Ont.: John Deutsch Institute and Industrial Relations Centre, Queen's University.

Ballard, Roger. 1994. "Differentiation and Disjunction among the Sikhs." In *Desh Pardesh: The South Asian Presence in Britain*, edited by Roger Ballard. London: Hurst and Co.

Banton, Michael. 1994. *Discrimination*. Buckingham: Open University Press.

Blau, Francine D., and Lawrence M. Kahn. 2000. "Gender Differences in Pay," *Journal of Economic Perspectives* 14, no. 4: 75–99.

Borjas, George J. 1988. *International Differences in the Labor Market Performance of Immigrants*. Kalamazoo, Mich.: W.E. Upjohn Institute.

———. 1994. "The Economics of Immigration," *Journal of Economic Literature* 32: 1667–717.

Brown, Mark S. 2000. "Religion and Economic Activity in the South Asian Population," *Ethnic and Racial Studies* 23, no. 6: 1035–61.

Card, David, and Richard Freeman, eds. 1993. *Small Differences That Matter: Labor Markets and Income Maintenance in Canada and the United States*. Chicago: University of Chicago Press.

Chiswick, Barry R., ed. 1992. *Immigration, Language and Ethnicity: Canada and the United States*. Washington, D.C.: AEI Press.

———. 1999. "Are Immigrants Favorably Self-Selected?" *American Economic Review* 89, no. 2: 181–85.

de Beijl, R.Z. 1995. "Labour Market Integration and Legislative Measures to Combat Discrimination against Migrant Workers." In *The Integration of Migrant Workers in the Labour Market: Policies and Their Impact*. International Migration Papers, no. 8. Geneva: International Labour Office.

DiMaggio, Paul. 1994. "Culture and Economy." In *The Handbook of Economic Sociology*, edited by Neil Smelser and Richard Swedberg. Princeton, N.J.: Princeton University Press.

Duleep, Harriet O., and Mark C. Regets. 1999. "Immigrants and Human Capital Investment," *American Economic Review* 89, no. 2: 186–91.

Eck, Diana L. 2001. *A New Religious America: How a "Christian Country" Has Now Become the World's Most Religiously Diverse Nation*. San Francisco: Harper San Francisco.

Employment and Immigration Canada. 1991. *Immigration Statistics 1990*. Minister of Supply and Services Canada.

Esping-Andersen, G., Zina Assimakopoulou, and Kees van Kersbergen. 1993. "Trends in Contemporary Class Structuration: A Six Nation Comparison." In *Changing Classes*, edited by G. Esping-Andersen. London: Sage.

Ganzeboom, Harry B.G., Paul M. De Graaf, and Donald J. Treiman. 1992. "A Standard Socio-Economic Index of Occupational Status," *Social Science Research* 21: 1–56.

Ganzeboom, Harry B.G., and Donald J. Treiman. 1996. "Internationally Comparable Measures of Occupational Status for the 1988 International Standard of Classification of Occupations," *Social Science Research* 25: 201–36.

Gardner, Katy, and Abdus Shukur. 1994. "I'm Bengali, I'm Asian, and I'm Living Here." In *Desh Pardesh: The South Asian Presence in Britain*, edited by Roger Ballard. London: Hurst and Co.

Gupta, Tania D. 1994. "Political Economy of Gender, Race, and Class: Looking at South Asian Immigrant Women in Canada," *Canadian Ethnic Studies* 26, no. 1: 59–73.

Halliday, Fred. 1999. "'Islamophobia' Reconsidered," *Ethnic and Racial Studies* 22, no. 5: 892–902.

Hiro, Dilip. 1971. *Black British, White British*. London: Eyre and Spottiswoode.

Hodge, Robert W. 1973. "Toward a Theory of Racial Differences in Employment," *Social Forces* 52: 16–31.

Hudson, Kellie. 1991. "Parents Seek Compromise on School Kirpan Ruling," *Toronto Star*, April 11.

Huff, Toby E., and Wolfgang Schluchter, eds. 1999. *Max Weber and Islam*. New Brunswick, N.J.: Transaction.

Katz, Lawrence F. 1998. "Commentary: The Distribution of Income in Industrialized Countries." In *Income Inequality: Issues and Policy Options*. Kansas City: Federal Reserve Bank of Kansas City.

Lakey, Jack. 1991. "Five Arrested as Two Rival Factions Battle for Control at Sikh Temple," *Toronto Star*, April 8.

Lee, Everett S. 1966. "A Theory of Migration," *Demography* 3, no. 1: 47–57.

Light, Ivan. 1984. "Immigrant and Ethnic Enterprise in North America," *Ethnic and Racial Studies* 7, no. 2: 195–216.

Model, Suzanne, Gene Fisher, and Roxane Silberman. 1999. "Black Caribbeans in Comparative Perspective," *Journal of Ethnic and Migration Studies* 25, no. 2: 187–212.

Nanji, Azim. 1983. "The Nizari Ismaili Muslim Community in North America: Background and Development." In *The Muslim Community in America*, edited by Earle H. Waugh, Baha Abu-Laban, and Regula B. Qureshi. Calgary: University of Alberta Press.

Nee, Victor, and Jimy Sanders. 2001. "Understanding the Diversity of Immigrant Incorporation," *Ethnic and Racial Studies* 24, no. 3: 386–411.

NIDI (Netherlands Interdisciplinary Demographic Institute). 1994. *Asylum-Seekers and Refugees: A Statistical Report*. Luxembourg: Office for Official Publications of the European Communities.

Portes, Alejandro, and Jozsef Borocz. 1989. "Contemporary Immigration: Theoretical Perspectives on Its Determinants and Modes of Incorporation," *International Migration Review* 23, no. 3: 606–27.

Portes, Alejandro, and Robert D. Manning. 1986. "The Immigrant Enclave: Theory and Empirical Examples." In *Competitive Ethnic Relations*, edited by Susan Olzak and Joane Nagel. Orlando, Fl.: Academic Press.

Portes, Alejandro, and Rubén G. Rumbaut. 1996. *Immigrant America: A Portrait*. 2d ed. Berkeley: University of California Press.

———. 2001. *Legacies*. Berkeley: University of California Press.

Rafig, Mohammed. 1992. "Ethnicity and Enterprise: A Comparison of Muslim and Non-Muslim Owned Asian Businesses in Britain," *New Community* 19, no. 1: 43–60.

Reitz, Jeffrey G. 1988a. "The Institutional Structure of Immigration as a Determinant of Inter-Racial Competition: A Comparison of Britain and Canada," *International Migration Review* 22, no. 1: 117–46.

———. 1988b. "Less Racial Discrimination in Canada, or Simply Less Racial Conflict? Implications of Comparisons with Britain," *Canadian Public Policy* 14, no. 4: 424–41.

———. 1998. *Warmth of the Welcome*. Boulder, Colo.: Westview.

Reitz, Jeffrey G., Joachim Frich, Tony Calabrese, and Gert Wagner. 1999. "The Institutional Framework of Ethnic Employment Disadvantage: A Comparison of Germany and Canada," *Journal of Ethnic and Migration Studies* 25, no. 3: 397–443.

Schaefer, Richard T. 1998. *Racial and Ethnic Groups.* 7th ed. New York: Longman.

Siegel, Paul. 1965. "On the Cost of Being a Negro," *Sociological Inquiry* 35: 41–57.

Smith, Patten, and Gillian Prior. 1996. *The Fourth National Survey of Ethnic Minorities.* London: Social and Community Planning Research.

Statistics Canada. 1992. *Immigration and Citizenship, 1991 Census of Canada.* Ottawa: Supply and Services Canada.

———. 1994. *User Documentation for Public Use Microdata File on Individuals. 1991 Census of Canada.* Ottawa: Statistics Canada.

———. 1995. *Occupation according to the 1991 Standard Occupational Classification. 1991 Census Technical Reports; Reference Products Series.* Ottawa: Minister of Industry, Science and Technology.

Tatla, Darshan S. 1993. "The Punjab Crisis and Sikh Mobilisation in Britain." In *Religion and Ethnicity: Social Change in the Metropolis,* edited by Rohit Barot. Kampen, The Netherlands: Kok Pharos.

Weber, Max. 1958. *The Religion of India,* edited and translated by Hans Gerth and Don Martindale. Glencoe, Ill.: Free Press.

Appendix 8A. Independent Variables

Variable	Description	Range
Age	Raw value	21–64
Age squared	Square of age	441–4,096
Education	Less than high school	omitted category
	High school diploma	0–1
	Some college	0–1
	Baccalaureate	0–1
	Advanced degree	0–1
Post-migration education	School in Canada or Britain	0–1
Years since migration	Years since arrived or mid-point of interval	0–55
Years squared	Square of years	0–3,025
English skills	No English–English only	1–4
Marital status	Married, spouse present	1–0
Cohabiting	Partner present	1–0
Resides in metro-politan area	Yes/No	1–0
Region of residence	Canada, 5 provinces Britain, 9 regions	1–0
Unemployment rate	Percent unemployed in region	6.8–12. 4
Net weekly household income (Canadian dollars)	Total weekly household income minus individual's weekly earnings	–$1,934–$4,327
Number of persons in household	Total persons in household	1–13
Self-employed	Yes/No	1–0
Occupational status	ISEI	16–85
Full-time worker	Yes / No	1–0
Place of birth	Canada, 11 regions Britain, 6 regions	1–0
Ethnicity	Canada, 5 groups Britain, 7 groups	1–0
Religion	Canada, 8 faiths Britain, 5 faiths	1–0

Appendix 8B. Independent Variables by Dependent Variable[1]

In Labor Force or Not[2]

Age, age squared, education, post-migration schooling, years since arrival, square of years, English skills, marital status, cohabits, resides in metropolitan area, unemployment rate, net household income, household size, place of birth, religion.

Unemployed or Not

Age, age squared, education, post-migration schooling, years since arrival, square of years, English skills, marital status, cohabits, resides in metropolitan area, region of residence, place of birth, religion, inverse Mills ratio.

ISEI (International Socio-Economic Index of Occupation)

Age, age squared, education, post-migration schooling, years since arrival, square of years, English skills, self-employed, marital status, cohabits, resides in metropolitan area, region of residence, place of birth, religion, inverse Mills ratio.

Ln Weekly Earnings

Age, age squared, education, post-migration schooling, years since arrival, square of years, English skills, self-employed, ISEI, full-time, marital status, cohabits, resides in metropolitan area, region of residence, place of birth, religion, inverse Mills ratio.

---

[1] Cross-national models contain five regions, four birthplaces, and four religions. Within-nation models contain the maximum number of regions, birthplaces, religions, and ethnicities for each nation.

[2] This specification was also used to predict "missing or not" on unemployment, occupational status, and earnings. The results of these models provide the basis for calculating the inverse Mills ratios for the associated dependent variable.

9

Human versus Social Capital: Immigrant Wages and Labor Market Incorporation in Japan and the United States

TAKEYUKI TSUDA, ZULEMA VALDEZ, AND
WAYNE A. CORNELIUS

HUMAN CAPITAL AND SOCIAL CAPITAL IN THE IMMIGRANT LABOR MARKET

A common model of wage determination analyzes earnings based on human capital variables such as education and work experience (Becker 1964; Ben-Porath 1967; Mincer 1974). According to this model, the accumulation of such individual skills and knowledge facilitates productivity that is rewarded in the market economy with an increase in real wages (Coleman 1988: S10). More recent work that focuses specifically on immigrant wages includes language proficiency and work experience in the host society as additional human capital measures (Borjas 1995; Portes and Rumbaut 2001; Sanders and Nee 1987; Zhou and Logan 1989). Such research provides compelling evidence that human capital characteristics are important in any explanation of immigrants' wages in the United States.

Yet such factors may not explain immigrants' earnings in other countries, where foreign workers encounter different economic and social conditions. As Portes and Rumbaut (1990, 2001) have observed, it is the combination of what immigrants "bring with them" (that is, human capital) *and* the "context of reception" in the host society that affects labor market incorporation (Portes and Rumbaut 1990: 83–85, 2001: 46–48). When differing contexts of reception are considered, *social* capital can become an important variable that influences economic outcomes among immigrants (cf. Portes and Rumbaut 2001: 46–48).

In contrast to human capital, which is based on individual-level skills and attributes like age, education, language proficiency, and employment experience, social capital is defined simply as "the ability to gain access to resources by virtue of membership [in a social group]" (Granovetter 1985; Massey et al. 1987; Portes and Rumbaut 2001: 353; Portes and Sensenbrenner 1993).[1] Social capital based on gender, ethnic, and other group affiliations supplies key resources, information, and opportunities that can significantly affect wage levels and the economic incorporation of immigrants (Light and Bonacich 1988: 18–19; Portes and Sensenbrenner 1993; Sanders and Nee 1996; Zhou and Logan 1989).

Drawing on data from a comparative study of immigrant labor in the United States and Japan, this chapter illustrates the important variations in the explanatory power of each of these two types of variables from one country to another depending on their different contexts of immigrant reception. In the United States, human capital variables have a much greater positive effect than social capital on foreign workers' wages. In contrast, social capital significantly increases workers' wages in Japan, whereas human capital does not.

The divergent impact of these two variables on foreign workers' earnings is a result of the different socioeconomic conditions that prevail in the two countries in terms of immigrant labor markets as well as gender and ethnic attitudes. Japan is a recent country of immigration, with a less developed and less diversified immigrant labor market compared to the United States. Because most foreign workers are employed as temporary, unskilled workers with limited job mobility, human capital variables based on individual qualifications and experience do not necessarily lead to better job prospects and higher wage levels. Instead, because of the still temporary nature of many foreign workers in Japan, the social capital provided by immigrant social networks is

---

[1] Social capital emerges from group affiliation and consists of "some aspect of social structures" that "facilitate actions within the structure" (Coleman 1988: S98). It can include solidarity, trust, and reciprocal obligations and may be economic or noneconomic in character (Portes and Sensenbrenner 1993: 1322).

used more often as a means of obtaining better-paying jobs. In addition, gender and ethnic affiliation are also important social capital determinants of immigrant wages because of significantly higher levels of gender and ethnic discrimination in Japan compared to the United States. This creates a discriminatory labor market where Japanese employers strongly prefer male foreign workers and Japanese-descent *nikkeijin* immigrants, both of whom earn much higher wages than female and non-*nikkeijin* foreigners.

Because the United States has a longer history of immigration with a much larger number of foreign-born workers, its immigrant labor market is much more developed, extensive, and entrenched, with a variety of long-term jobs at different levels. Therefore, the human capital that immigrants acquire over time in the United States is much more likely to lead to higher wages and job mobility. On the other hand, social capital based on immigrant social networks does not increase wage levels. Because a higher proportion of immigrants in the United States are long-term settlers, they use their social networks not only to obtain higher-paying jobs but also to find ethnically satisfying work conditions. In addition, gender and ethnic discrimination are lower in the United States than in Japan, also reducing the impact of these social capital variables on immigrant wages. In this manner, a comparative framework clearly illustrates how varying contexts of reception in host societies cause different variables to influence the level of economic incorporation of immigrant workers.

DATA AND METHODS

This study analyzes data from a comparative study of the role of immigrant labor in the U.S. and Japanese economies (Cornelius and Kuwahara 1998). Survey interviews were conducted during the first half of 1996 with a randomly selected sample of 110 employers and 478 foreign workers in San Diego, and 104 employers and 244 foreign workers in Hamamatsu, Japan. All employers were known, through telephone screening interviews and other methods, to be employing at least some foreign-born workers. For each firm, the person having primary responsibility for hiring decisions (in most cases, the firm owner) was interviewed. For the immigrant workers in each country, information was collected about their labor market experiences as well as individual-level characteristics such as age, gender, and work experience. All interviews were conducted in person, using standardized questionnaires, and averaged one hour in duration for employers and about forty-five minutes for workers. In the San Diego sample, the immigrant workers were employees of the same firms in which employers were interviewed (5 or 6 immigrant employees were chosen randomly from each firm), except for 116 irregularly employed "street-corner" day laborers. In the Hamamatsu sample, the immigrant workers did not come from the same firms in which employers were interviewed.

Our analysis examines the effect of various human capital and social capital variables on the natural log of monthly earnings for foreign workers (a continuous dependent variable) (see table 9.1 for definitions of the independent, dependent, and control variables). Human capital variables include age, education, years with current employer, and language. Social capital is measured with five variables: the use of a labor broker to find jobs, the use of a friend/relative/previous employer to find jobs, marital status, gender, and ethnicity (nikkeijin versus non-nikkeijin in Japan, Mexican versus non-Mexican in the United States). Since other variables besides human and social capital may influence earnings (such as the immigrant's length of stay in the host society, legal status, number of hours worked per week, and the industry sector of employment), these are held constant as control variables.

CHARACTERISTICS OF FOREIGN WORKER SAMPLES

There are some significant differences between our immigrant samples from San Diego and Hamamatsu (see table 9.2). In Hamamatsu, the mean monthly wage is $1,790.[2] In San Diego, the mean monthly wage is $1,002, significantly less than the wage earned by immigrants in Hamamatsu. Hamamatsu's foreign workers are older than foreign workers in San Diego by an average of 4.5 years. The former are also better educated; they have 4 more years of education than their San Diego counterparts, who average 8.8 years of education. Because immigration to Japan is relatively new, foreign workers in Hamamatsu have lived in Japan for just under four years, whereas their counterparts in San Diego have lived an average of twelve years in the United States. Nonetheless, many more immigrants in our Hamamatsu sample are legal (91 percent compared to 43 percent in San Diego).

---

[2] Earnings are in 1997 U.S. dollars (¥130.6 = $1.00). For present purposes, foreign workers' earnings are compared within each country, rather than across countries.

The ethnic composition of the foreign-born population in each country is also very different, although each country has a large population from one ethnic group. In Japan, the total number of foreign workers is probably close to 950,000, which is less than 1 percent of the country's population of 127 million (Tsuda and Cornelius 2003). The largest immigrant group is the nikkeijin (second- and third-generation Japanese descendants, mainly from Brazil), who number over 350,000, or 37 percent of the total immigrant population. Roughly 60 percent of all registered foreigners in Hamamatsu in 2001 were Brazilian nikkeijin, equivalent to 2 percent of the city's population.[3] According to the most recent census figures (2000), the United States' foreign-born population is 28.4 million, or 10.4 percent of the total population (Schmidley 2001). Mexican immigrants are a relatively large proportion (28 percent) of this foreign-born population, and this is especially true in San Diego, the second largest area of Mexican settlement (Rumbaut 1994: 602; Schmidley and Gibson 1999). And according to census figures, 80 percent of the Latino population in San Diego County in 1990 was Mexican, which was equivalent to 30 percent of the county's entire population at that time. Therefore, although both countries have a single dominant immigrant group, the United States has a much larger foreign-born population. Moreover, there is a much higher concentration of Mexicans in San Diego than of nikkeijin in Hamamatsu.

The sample for our study is not random since it consists of a disproportionate number of nikkeijin in Hamamatsu and Mexicans in San Diego (72 and 82.5 percent, respectively). Although the study may not precisely represent the ethnic proportion of the foreign worker population in each country, it successfully represents the labor market experiences of the majority immigrant group. In terms of gender, the majority of the foreign-born in our sample is male (57 percent in Hamamatsu, 68 percent in San Diego).[4]

---

[3] On the evolution of the return migration of Brazilian nikkeijin to Japan, see Tsuda 1999a, 1999b.

[4] Male and female workers are combined in the multivariate analysis of earnings, with gender included as an explanatory variable. The additional consideration of gender in our discussion and analysis of wages is important since gender is used as an indicator of social capital and therefore contributes to the substantive argument presented here.

Table 9.1. Variable Definitions

Variables by Type	Variable Definitions
DEPENDENT VARIABLE	
l_mwage	natural log of monthly earnings
INDEPENDENT VARIABLES	
Human Capital	
Age	Age, continuous variable ranging from 16 to 75 years
Education	years of school; continuous variable ranging from 0 to 20
Years employed	years with current employer; continuous variable ranging from 1 to 32 years
Japanese/English	dummy variable coded 1 if understand and speak fairly well or very well, 0 if understand and speak little or none
Social Capital	
Job_broker (Japan)	dummy variable coded 1 if used broker to find a job, 0 if did not
Job_friend	dummy variable coded 1 if used friend, relative, or previous employer to find a job, 0 if did not
Male	dummy variable coded 1 if male, 0 if female
Married	dummy variable coded 1 if married, 0 if other
Nikkei (Japan)	dummy variable coded 1 if nikkeijin; 0 if non-nikkeijin (Japan)
Mexican (United States)	dummy variable coded 1 if Mexican-origin, 0 if non-Mexican origin

CONTROLS	
Time (in Japan/United States)	continuous variable ranging from 1 to 600+ months
Legal status	dummy variable coded 1 if working legally, 0 if not
Hours worked per week	hours worked per week; continuous variable ranging from 1 to 80 hours
Sector	
Japan	
Manufacturing[1]	dummy variable coded 1 if work in manufacturing sector, 0 if other
Services	dummy variable coded 1 if work in services sector, 0 if other
Construction	dummy variable coded 1 if work in construction sector, 0 if other
United States	
Agriculture	dummy variable coded 1 if working in agricultural sector, 0 if other
High-tech	dummy variable coded 1 if working in high-tech sector, 0 if other
Construction	dummy variable coded 1 if working in construction sector, 0 if other
Hotel	dummy variable coded 1 if working in hotel sector, 0 if other
Restaurant[2]	dummy variable coded 1 if working in restaurant sector, 0 if other
Landscape	dummy variable coded 1 if working in landscape sector, 0 if other
Apparel	dummy variable coded 1 if working in apparel sector, 0 if other
Food service	dummy variable coded 1 if working in food service sector, 0 if other
Low-tech	dummy variable coded 1 if working in low-tech sector, 0 if other
Miscellaneous	dummy variable coded 1 if working in miscellaneous service sector, 0 if other

[1] The manufacturing sector, which has the lowest average wage, is the reference sector for the Japanese case.

[2] The restaurant sector, which has the lowest entry-level wage, is the reference sector for the U.S. case.

Table 9.2. Distribution of Variables (N = 722)

Variables by Type	Hamamatsu	San Diego
DEPENDENT VARIABLE		
Mean monthly wage	$1,790	$1,002
Log mean monthly wage (l_mwage)	7.49	5.19
INDEPENDENT VARIABLES		
Human Capital		
Mean age (years)	30.15	34.47
Mean years of education	12.76	8.83
Mean years with current employer	5.73	5.69
Japanese/English proficiency	40.57%	35.98%
Social Capital		
Male	57.38%	68.20%
Found job through broker	31.97	—
Found job through friend, relative, previous employer	40.98	71.55
Married	53.28	64.64
Nikkei/Mexican	72.13	82.64
CONTROL VARIABLES		
Mean time in Japan/United States (months)	44.58	144.99
Percent working legally	91.39	42.68
Mean hours worked per week	38.28	36.11
Industrial sector		
Japan		
Manufacturing	77.46%	—
Construction	2.05	—
Service sector	19.26	—
United States		
Agriculture	—	9.83%
High-tech	—	8.37
Low-tech	—	10.67
Construction	—	11.09
Hotel	—	9.83
Restaurant	—	9.83
Landscape	—	9.62
Apparel	—	10.04
Food service	—	11.30
Miscellaneous	—	9.41
N	244	478

RESULTS OF THE MULTIVARIATE ANALYSIS

Two multivariate regression models are presented for the Hamamatsu and San Diego cases (table 9.3). The first measures the effect of human capital and control variables on the natural log of monthly wages, and the second does the same for the social capital variables. None of the human capital variables (age, education, years with current employer, Japanese proficiency) has a significant impact on foreign worker wages in Hamamatsu (table 9.3, model 1). Instead, social capital variables are the important determinants that increase immigrant wages in Hamamatsu (table 9.3, model 2). Foreign workers who find jobs through social networks (friends or relatives) improve their earnings by 11 percent, and those who use labor brokers increase their wages by 13 percent. In addition, male immigrant workers earn 38 percent more than their female counterparts, and ethnic Japanese nikkeijin earn 49 percent more than other foreign workers.

In contrast and consistent with the standard model of immigrant wage determination, findings from San Diego indicate that the human capital variables of employment experience and English proficiency have a statistically significant and positive effect on the wages of foreign workers (table 9.3, model 3). For each year spent with the current employer (cumulative work experience), immigrant wages in San Diego increased by 13 percent. Moreover, foreign workers who understand and speak English received earnings that were 76 percent higher than the wages of those who understand and speak English poorly or not at all. However, age and education do not significantly improve wages among foreign workers in San Diego, despite their importance as human capital. In contrast to human capital, social capital has very little influence on immigrant wages in San Diego (table 9.3, model 4). The use of social networks (friends/relatives or previous employers) to obtain jobs does not improve earnings. In addition, being male or a member of the dominant Mexican ethnic group does not influence economic outcomes.

Yet there are also some similarities in the results from the two countries when we examine the impact of the control variables. Legal status (working legally or illegally) is not a significant predictor of wages in either Hamamatsu or San Diego. Apparently, immigration control policies do not have much impact on the wages of foreign workers and are therefore not a major determinant of immigrant labor market incorporation (cf. Reitz 1998: 69, 238). Not surprisingly, as hours worked per week increase, wages improve among foreign workers in

Table 9.3. Human Capital and Social Capital Effects on Foreign Workers' Log Monthly Wage, Hamamatsu and San Diego

	Hamamatsu				San Diego			
	Model 1		Model 2		Model 3		Model 4	
INDEPENDENT VARIABLES								
<u>Human capital</u>								
Age	.00	(.00)	–.00	(.00)	–.03	(.02)	–.03	(.02)
Education	.01	(.01)	–.00	(.01)	.03	(.03)	07	(.03)
Years with current employer	02	(.02)	.01	(.01)	.13***	(.03)	.13***	(.03)
Japanese/English proficiency	.07	(.06)	.05	(.05)	.79**	(.30)	.76*	(.30)
<u>Social capital</u>								
Found job through broker	—		.13*	(.06)	—		—	
Found job through friend, relative, previous employer	—		.11*	(.05)	—		.29	(.28)
Male	—		.38***	(.05)	—		.24	(.29)
Married	—		–.08	(.05)	—		.21	(.27)
Nikkei/Mexican	—		.49***	(.06)	—		–.27	(.36)
CONTROL VARIABLES								
Time in Japan/United States	.00	(.00)	.00	(.00)	.00**	(.00)	.00*	(.00)
Legal status	24*	(.10)	–.05	(09)	.06	(.27)	.03	(.27)
Hours worked per week	.02***	(.00)	.01***	(.00)	.09***	(.02)	.08***	(.02)

Industrial sector								
Japan[1]								
Construction	.08	(.19)	.15	(.15)				
Services	.04	(.08)	.16**	(.06)				
United States[1]								
Agriculture					.96*	(.58)	.98*	.58
High-tech					2.50***	(.60)	2.43***	(.62)
Construction					3.05***	(.54)	2.99***	(.55)
Hotel					2.57***	(.55)	2.69***	(.57)
Landscape					2.20***	(.56)	2.13***	(.57)
Apparel					1.71**	(.55)	1.76**	(.56)
Food service					.45	(.54)	.51	(.54)
Low-tech					1.99***	(.56)	1.97***	(.57)
Miscellaneous					.45	(.58)	.44	(.58)
Constant	6.14***	(.20)	6.31***	(.16)	–.47	(.77)	–.65	(.93)
N (unweighted)		244		244		478		478

[1] The manufacturing sector, which has the lowest average wage, is the reference sector for the Japanese case.

[2] The restaurant sector, which has the lowest entry-level wage, is the reference sector for the U.S. case.

*** $p < .001$, ** $p < .01$, * $p < .05$.

both Japan and the United States. Finally, the industrial sectors in which foreign workers are employed contribute to earnings outcomes. While it was not possible to measure sectors consistently across countries, foreign workers in Japan in the service sector earn significantly more than those employed in manufacturing and construction. In the United States, most industrial sectors offer better wages than the low-paying restaurant business.

JAPAN: WHEN HUMAN CAPITAL DOES NOT MATTER

Why do human capital variables have little effect in increasing wages in Japan despite their importance in San Diego? Why does Japan deviate strikingly from the standard immigrant wage determination model, which works so well in the United States? What are the differences in the context of reception in these two countries that would account for such divergent results? We argue that the fundamental reason lies in the underdeveloped nature of immigrant labor markets in recent countries of immigration like Japan, where foreign workers are employed almost exclusively in low-level, unskilled jobs with very little upward mobility. As a result, human capital based on individual qualifications and experience does not necessarily lead to better jobs at higher wages.

Japan was for decades the only advanced industrial country in the world that did not rely on immigrant labor. Driven by the country's insistence on ethnic homogeneity and refusal to accept unskilled foreign workers, Japan opted to meet its labor requirements by mechanizing and rationalizing production and by making greater use of "untapped" sources of labor (female and elderly workers). By the mid-1980s, however, the native-born workforce became inadequate to meet the rising demand for unskilled labor because of a sharp decline in the birthrate, the rapid aging of the population, the depletion of rural labor sources, and the refusal of increasingly affluent and well-educated Japanese youth to perform "3K" jobs (the Japanese acronym for dirty, dangerous, and difficult). In addition to this acute labor shortage, growing economic disparities between Japan and underdeveloped countries brought large numbers of foreign workers to Japan, causing the country to succumb to the pressures of global migration. Japan now has an ethnically diverse immigrant population, with significant numbers drawn from various countries in Latin America, East and Southeast Asia, and the Middle East, including over 350,000 immigrant workers from Brazil, Peru, Argentina, Bolivia, and Paraguay who are predominantly Japanese-descent nikkeijin. There is also a substantial population of illegal visa overstayers in Japan (251,697 in 2000). About 100,000 visas were issued to skilled and professional workers in 2000.

The Insignificance of Human Capital in Underdeveloped Immigrant Labor Markets

Ethnographic and survey interviews conducted with employers help explain why educational background and Japanese language competence as human capital do not significantly improve the wages of foreign workers in Hamamatsu. Because Japan is a recent country of immigration, its labor market for foreign workers is still relatively undeveloped and does not provide access to a wide range of jobs at various skill levels. Therefore, a vast majority of foreign workers are hired only for unskilled, manual jobs for which previous education has no impact on performance (Sellek 2001: 100–101). For instance, 91 percent of nikkeijin (who are overwhelmingly from Brazil) are performing unskilled or semiskilled jobs involving simple, repetitive tasks that require no training or can be learned within a week. Therefore, although the nikkeijin were often well-educated, white-collar workers in Brazil,[5] almost none of their employers seriously inquired about their educational background and past occupation. A labor broker explained it as follows:

> We generally ask about the person's educational background and the type of work he did back in Brazil, but we don't care about such issues. We are looking for simple manual laborers, and for such work previous occupational and educational differences simply don't matter. Anyone can do this kind of work, and ability differences don't show up between people of different social backgrounds.

As a result, a higher educational level among immigrants does not correspond with higher wages and better labor market incorporation, as would normally be expected. When hiring Brazilian nikkeijin workers, the most important criteria that all employers used to screen applicants were visa status (whether the person is a legal immigrant), Japanese language ability, and ethnicity (whether the applicant is a pure

---

[5] Thirty-seven percent of the nikkeijin have at least some college education.

Japanese-descent nikkeijin or of mixed heritage). Other factors considered included age (younger workers are preferred), personality and attitude (whether the person seems diligent), and past employment history (some employers avoid workers who have switched jobs too often in the past).

In fact, some Japanese employers even claim that the better-educated nikkeijin perform less well as unskilled workers because they have been spoiled by white-collar working conditions in Brazil and are less prepared to cope with the physical demands and fast pace of factory work. A labor broker who specializes in hiring Brazilian nikkeijin expressed such a view:

> Lots of the nikkeijin are well educated and some are quite intelligent, but they can't do the work as well as a typical unskilled Japanese worker with only a high school education because they have no experience with manual labor. They may have been extremely brilliant in Brazil, but they come to Japan and realize they can't compete with uneducated Japanese factory workers.

As a result, a few employers explicitly stated that they prefer to hire (less educated) nikkeijin from rural farming areas in Brazil because they are more accustomed to physical labor.

Only 9 percent of the nikkeijin in our sample were employed in higher-paid skilled or technical jobs in which educational background and learning ability would be relevant. Previous education seems to have an effect on wages only for those bilingual nikkeijin who are hired as translators and liaisons (either in the factory or in company offices) and serve as intermediaries between Japanese managers and nikkeijin workers. College-educated nikkeijin are usually preferred for these "culturally skilled" higher-level positions, which pay better than jobs on the assembly line.

The same general conditions apply for the employment of non-nikkeijin foreign workers in Japan. Although they are relatively well educated,[6] 89 percent of them are doing unskilled or semiskilled jobs in Japan for which an advanced degree earned abroad has no impact on

---

[6] Educational levels for non-nikkeijin immigrants are even higher than the nikkeijin, with 57 percent having at least some college education.

work performance. As a result, educational background does not improve their employability or their ability to obtain higher-level jobs and wages.

Moreover, as our regression analysis reveals, Japanese language competence as another source of human capital also does not have a positive influence on wages. Since language ability is the most important criterion used by Japanese employers when hiring foreign workers, those who speak some Japanese have a considerably easier time finding employment. However, they are not necessarily given higher-paying jobs because, again, they are employed as low-level, unskilled manual laborers. For instance, Japanese employers who hire nikkeijin workers generally do not pay Japanese speakers better salaries given that they do the same type of unskilled work as the nikkeijin who do not speak good Japanese. In some factories, nikkeijin who speak Japanese are given slightly more technical jobs than the purely physical tasks assigned to most others, but these are not skilled jobs that would command higher wages. Again, the only nikkeijin who are rewarded by higher salaries for their Japanese proficiency are the very few who become cultural intermediaries and translators in company or labor broker offices or are promoted to lower-level supervisory jobs on the factory floor (although the latter do not always receive better pay). In this manner, the structure of the immigrant labor market in Japan as a newer country of immigration helps to explain why human capital does not contribute to wage levels among foreign workers in Japan.

Employment on the Margins and the Marginality of Employment Experience

Education and language ability are not the only human capital attributes that fail to produce significant earnings differentials among immigrants in Hamamatsu. The data also defy the commonsense expectation that the more years a foreign worker remains with a certain employer, the higher would be his/her wages.

The Japanese employment system for foreign workers is the most important reason why immigrant workers remain confined to the informal and unskilled sector of the labor market and do not advance to more skilled and higher-paying jobs even over an extended period. Although both foreign and Japanese workers are employed in factories of subsidiary firms where virtually all of the work is low-skilled[7] and the prospects for long-term job mobility are quite restricted, foreign workers—unlike regular Japanese workers (*seishain*)—are hired strictly as *hi-seishain* (informal, casual workers) and are not put on the promotion track to receive gradual salary increases over time.

This is especially true for foreign workers who are recruited and employed by labor broker firms. Japan has always had a system of labor brokers (*assen gaisha*) who have traditionally supplied companies with an informal, native-born workforce of part-time, seasonal, and day laborers (Sellek 1996: 254). As the supply of temporary and part-time domestic workers became insufficient during Japan's severe labor shortage in the late 1980s, migrant workers increasingly took over as a casual labor force for Japanese companies (see Stevens 1997). In fact, most Japanese employers prefer nikkeijin migrant workers to part-time or temporary Japanese workers because the nikkeijin work harder and more diligently, put in longer hours, and are more willing to work overtime.

As Japan's new informal labor force, migrant workers (including 74 percent of the nikkeijin in our sample) are now employed by Japanese labor broker firms. These firms have extensive contacts with various Japanese companies, which "borrow" foreign workers for limited periods when production increases. When the workers are no longer needed, they are conveniently "returned" to the broker firm, which then shifts the workers to other companies where their labor is needed. The labor broker employment system enables Japanese companies to use foreign workers as a flexible labor force in order to adjust to production fluctuations in a cost-effective manner. Seventy-one percent of employers in our sample preferred to hire nikkeijin through labor brokers precisely for this reason. Sixty-six percent of Japanese employers favor the broker system because it is much more convenient than hiring nikkeijin workers directly (since labor brokers take care of recruitment, housing, transportation, insurance, and other social services).

Because nikkeijin migrants function as a temporary and disposable workforce, Japanese firms rarely hire them as permanent, regular workers who are promoted over time to higher positions with better salaries. Instead, Japanese employers simply pay a fee to an outside

---

[7] As a result, 75 percent of the employers surveyed claim that there is no difference in the jobs that foreign and native workers perform. Only 14 percent indicate that foreigners do less skilled work.

labor broker for the temporary use of foreign laborers. This also means that, for nikkeijin who remain employees of broker firms, a longer stay in Japan does not translate into regular salary increases, since these workers are transferred from company to company at a relatively fixed wage rate. Although the proportion of non-nikkeijin foreign workers who are employed by labor brokers is substantially smaller,[8] the involvement of brokers in the recruitment of foreign workers in general in Japan is increasing (Iguchi 1998).

Foreign workers who are employed directly by Japanese companies, without the mediation of labor brokers, are in a somewhat different situation, since they usually have short-term contracts (for the nikkeijin, a contract usually lasts from six months to a year, with the possibility of renewal).[9] As a result, they generally stay at a single firm for a longer period, and their turnover rate is considerably lower than for brokered foreign workers.[10] However, despite their more stable employment situation, they remain part of the disposable, peripheral workforce of short-term, casual laborers, with little hope for regular promotion and wage increases.

The perception among Japanese employers that foreign migrants are casual workers who fill temporary jobs is undoubtedly reinforced by these workers' tendency to switch jobs frequently. For instance, since most nikkeijin workers are target-earners who wish to earn as much money as possible during a short sojourn,[11] they change companies quite often in search of higher hourly wages, better working conditions, and more overtime. In fact, the nikkeijin in our sample changed jobs almost once a year on average. Non-nikkeijin foreign workers in Japan also switch jobs frequently (during their average stay in Japan of 3.25 years, they changed jobs an average of 2.7 times).

The perpetual marginalization of foreign workers in the Japanese labor market stigmatizes even those who have been hired directly by

---

[8] Among non-nikkeijin foreign workers, only 4 percent found their current jobs through labor brokers. Among Japanese employers who hire only non-nikkeijin workers, only 17 percent use brokers and 61 percent hire them directly.

[9] Forty-one percent of all foreign workers in our sample were employed directly by Japanese companies.

[10] In one survey of nikkeijin workers, conducted by the Japan Statistics Research Institute, 48.5 percent of those employed by brokers had changed jobs, while the comparable percentage was only 21.2 percent for those employed directly (Yamamoto 1994).

[11] The nikkeijin initially intend to stay in Japan only 2.6 years on average.

Japanese companies and have apparently made a long-term commitment to the firm. Since employers assume that the nikkeijin will eventually leave for another job or return to Brazil, they are reluctant to make them permanent *seishain* employees. At best, some companies (and even broker firms) provide foreign workers with a modest salary increase after a certain period of time. The inability of most foreign workers to speak Japanese proficiently may also prevent them from being treated equally with regular Japanese employees. Thus employment as an indicator of human capital does not correlate with higher wages and better economic incorporation in a recent country of immigration such as Japan, where foreign workers are still restricted to the peripheral sectors of the labor market as casual workers and very few are ever incorporated into the mainstream Japanese labor force, regardless of how long they stay with a company.[12]

THE UNITED STATES: THE IMPORTANCE OF HUMAN CAPITAL

In contrast to Hamamatsu, human capital variables have a strong impact on immigrant wages in San Diego because the United States, a much older country of immigration, has a more highly developed and extensive foreign labor market which has accommodated the permanent presence of large numbers of immigrant workers. By the beginning of the twentieth century, most immigration to the United States was from Southern and Eastern Europe, in contrast to earlier waves of predominantly Western European immigrants. This shift resulted in nativist backlashes and restrictionist immigration policies in the 1920s (Rumbaut 1994: 584). The abolition of national origins quotas with the Hart-Cellar Act of 1965 (Zhou 1998) resulted in a third wave of immigration—from Asia and Latin America. California became the leading destination for many immigrants, especially Mexican migrants, both legal and undocumented. Since San Diego is the second largest area of

---

[12] The inability of human capital to influence immigrant wages in Japan also explains why increased age does not result in higher wages (again in contrast to the San Diego case). Since an immigrant's background is not considered when hiring, older workers (with more educational and occupational experience) are not given better jobs with higher wages. Instead, both older and younger immigrants are employed in similar unskilled, entry-level jobs with comparable wages. In San Diego, age is correlated with higher earnings. However, for older immigrants, time spent in the United States has a less positive impact on wages compared to younger immigrants.

Mexican immigrant settlement (Rumbaut 1994: 602), 80 percent of our sample of foreign workers is of Mexican origin (table 9.4).

In the immediate aftermath of World War II, massive growth in durable manufacturing (including the automobile and aerospace industries) opened up unprecedented opportunities for economic mobility among immigrant groups that had previously faced discrimination and limited options in the labor market. However, changing economic conditions since the 1960s, along with rapidly increasing immigration levels, have had a profound effect on the U.S. immigrant labor market generally. As the U.S. economy shifted from manufacturing to services, the Mexican immigrant population was especially hard hit. With low-paid and temporary service jobs replacing manufacturing jobs over the 1960s and 1970s, the earnings of Mexican workers declined (Morales and Bonilla 1993).

The immigrant labor market in the United States is somewhat similar to Japan's since foreign workers in the United States are also disproportionately found in low-paid, unskilled work that requires little or no education (Waters and Eschbach 1995). Our foreign worker sample in San Diego is largely unskilled, uneducated, and not English proficient (see tables 9.2 and 9.4). However, because the United States is a more advanced country of immigration, with a more developed and ethnically integrated immigrant labor market, foreign workers are employed in a more diverse range of jobs at various skill levels. Although a good number work in unskilled jobs (like their counterparts in Japan), some also work in more skilled jobs for which human capital is relevant for employment and therefore results in higher wages.[13]

Unlike Japan, employers in the United States acknowledge that work experience and English language proficiency are desired, despite the largely unskilled nature of the work that immigrants perform. According to the employers we surveyed, 12 percent rank education, language, and work experience among the most important characteristics of their immigrant workers, and over 50 percent consider "work ethic" to be the most important (table 9.5). However, employers often correlate "work ethic" characteristics with human capital so that the two

---

[13] Forty-one percent of foreign workers in Hamamatsu are doing unskilled jobs that require virtually no training; only 26 percent of foreign workers in San Diego are doing such work (see table 9.5). Thirty-seven percent of the jobs in San Diego require two to ten days of training, whereas only 26 percent of Hamamatsu jobs require such training.

Table 9.4. Descriptive Statistics of Foreign Workers

	Hamamatsu		San Diego	
Nationality (country)				
Brazil/Mexico	57.8%		80.5%	
Other	42.2		19.5	
Hours worked per week	Male	Female	Male	Female
0–39	12.9%	22.1%	13.8%	30.9%
40 or more	82.7	77.9	85.4	69.1
Ethnicity				
Nikkeijin/Mexican	69.3%	76.0%	85.1%	77.6%
Other	30.7	24.0	15.0	22.4
Education				
Some high school or less	24.3%	27.9%	67.8%	73.7%
High school graduate	29.3	32.7	16.3	15.8
Some college	13.6	15.4	10.4	6.6
College graduate (or more in San Diego)	32.9	24.0	5.5	3.9
Married				
Yes	47.1%	61.5%	69.9%	53.3%
No	52.9	38.5	30.1	46.7
Years with current employer				
1–4	15.0%	17.3%	51.5%	56.5%
5–9	79.3	81.7	32.2	28.3
10 or more	5.7	1.0	16.3	15.1
Time in Japan/United States				
5 years or less	57.7%	80.7%	22.7%	14.5%
6 years or more (Japan)	24.3	19.2	28.8	32.9
10 years or more (San Diego)	—	—	48.8	52.6
Log monthly wage by gender				
0.1–6.4	4.3%	5.8%	23.3%	32.2%
6.5–6.9	7.1	6.7	36.8	48.0
7.0–7.4	11.4	69.2	29.8	15.8
7.5–8.5	77.1	18.3	10.1	3.9
N	244		[illegible]	

terms become synonymous. In fact, 58 percent of employers claim that English is necessary for the immigrant jobs they offer. Undoubtedly, because of the more varied skill levels of the jobs available for foreign workers, immigrants who speak English are favored over non-English speakers, and the latter cannot be hired for higher-paying jobs. In this manner, employers in the United States continue to rely on human capital to indicate the potential skill of their immigrant employees, and this, in turn, determines their wages.

In addition, although some immigrant workers in San Diego remain casual and temporary laborers, a much higher proportion of jobs available to immigrants are permanent or at least long-term (Cornelius 1998). In addition, there is no entrenched system of labor brokers facilitating employers' use of immigrant workers as an informal and temporary labor force to meet fluctuations in production. According to our survey, over 31 percent of foreign workers in San Diego have worked for the same employer for between five and nine years, and 16 percent have worked for their current employer for ten years or longer. In contrast, only 4 percent of foreign workers in Japan have worked for their current employer for ten years or more. As immigrant workers remain for extended periods at the same company, they move up the job ladder, which has a significant influence on wages and labor market incorporation over time. As a result, work experience (years with current employer) becomes a form of human capital that correlates positively with higher earnings.

Age and education are positively correlated with earnings among most workers in the United States. However, they do not contribute to the earnings of the foreign workers considered here. Education acquired in the country of origin may be less important for some foreign workers, especially those relegated to low-wage, low-skilled occupations (Massey and Espinosa 1997: 948). Further, since age is correlated with length of residence (Archer 1991), its effects may be muted by two other variables: years with current employer (another human capital variable) or time in the United States (a control variable), sometimes called *migration-specific* human capital (Chiswick 1988; Massey and Espinosa 1997).

While it may be surprising from a neoclassical economic perspective that education does not always increase immigrant earnings, recent studies suggest that immigrants "confined to the same menial jobs in the United States" do not benefit from increased education (Massey and Espinosa 1997; Portes and Bach 1985; Zhou and Logan 1989). And

Table 9.5. Descriptive Statistics of Employers

Descriptor	Hamamatsu	San Diego
Percent of workforce that is foreign-born	78.9%	19.1%
0–24	7.7	17.3
25–49	4.8	31.8
50–74	8.7	31.8
75–100		
How employer hires foreign workers		
Employee referral	14.4%	62.7%
Supervisor/manager referral	4.8	9.1
Application	25.0	18.2
Labor contractor/broker	43.3	8.2
Family/friends	8.7	1.8
Other	3.9	—
Documents requested when hiring		
None	32.7%	5.5%
Passport	46.2	—
Social security number	—	68.2
Green card	—	26.4
Other	21.1	—
Training time (days) for foreign workers		
0–1	41.4%	26.4%
2–10	26.0	37.3
10.5–20	8.7	12.7
21 or more	24.0	23.6
Job differences, foreign vs. native employees		
No difference	75.0%	47.3%
Foreign work is more skilled	2.9	15.5
Foreign work is "dirty work"	1.0	12.7
Foreign work is less skilled	14.4	14.6
Foreign work is more insecure	2.0	—
Other	4.8	10.0
Employ nikkeijin	77.9%	
Feel that foreign workers need English		58.2%
Most important worker characteristic		
Human capital	—	11.8%
Work ethic	—	53.6
Social skills	—	29.1
Nationality	—	0.9
Other		4.6
Employer ethnicity		
Anglo		59.1%
Latino		20.0
Asian		5.5
Other		15.5
N	104	110

with respect to Mexican immigrants (80.5 percent of our sample), Massey and Espinosa (1997: 948) claim, "In general, human capital acquired in Mexico is not well remunerated in the United States, especially if a migrant lacks documents." Similarly, Sanders and Nee claim that "foreign-earned human capital of most immigrants is not highly valued by U.S. employers" and does not increase wages (1996: 232). Moreover, because of the low educational levels among foreign workers in our sample (an average of only nine years), education's marginal impact on immigrant wages is to be expected. Thus, although not all of the human capital variables are significant determinants of immigrant wage levels in the United States, those that have been acquired in the host country (English proficiency and work experience) do contribute positively to earnings.

SOCIAL CAPITAL AND IMMIGRANT WAGES

Japan: The Importance of Social Networks, Gender, and Ethnicity

The differential effect of social capital on immigrant wages in Japan and the United States is even more striking than our results for human capital. In Hamamatsu, all of our social capital variables (except marital status) have a positive effect on immigrant wages, whereas none is significant in the San Diego case. Although immigrant workers in Japan are exclusively restricted to unskilled, temporary jobs where human capital makes little difference, some are able to find higher-paying jobs within this peripheral labor market through the social capital they possess based on membership in various social groups.

Although over 70 percent of immigrants in both countries use their social networks to find jobs (table 9.2), such social capital has a positive effect on immigrant earnings only in Hamamatsu (table 9.3). Again, we argue that the differential effect of social networks on immigrant wages in the two countries results from the very different conditions that prevail in recent versus advanced countries of immigration. Since most foreign workers in Japan still consider themselves temporary migrant workers and wish to earn as much as possible during a brief sojourn, they primarily use their social networks of relatives, friends, and labor brokers to find higher-paying jobs with more overtime.

For instance, nikkeijin workers constantly exchange information with acquaintances to compare wages and overtime opportunities at other firms, and they quickly switch to firms where compensation is higher. Nikkeijin who move to other areas of Japan are frequently asked by acquaintances whether that region offers better-paying jobs. In other words, the social networks of the nikkeijin primarily serve an instrumental, economic function.

Two other social capital variables significantly increase immigrant wages in Japan: gender (being male) and ethnicity (being a Japanese-descent nikkeijin). These two attributes are key determinants of wages because Japan is a country with strong gender and ethnic discrimination, resulting in a labor market that significantly disadvantages women and ethnic groups of non-Japanese descent.

Women in Japanese society face considerable wage and labor market discrimination because of persisting traditional gender attitudes, according to which they are expected to dedicate themselves to the family and household at the expense of a personal career, and to stop working once they marry and have children.[14] Because their career aspirations are not taken as seriously as men's, women are frequently confined to part-time[15] or subordinate occupational positions, and even those who work full-time are not placed on the same promotional track. In addition, women are paid less for doing the same type of job. As a result, a significant gender gap in wages continues to persist despite Japanese antidiscrimination laws[16] and litigation by Japanese women (see Brinton 1993 and Ogasawara 1998 for further details).

Although both male and female foreign workers in Japan are employed in predominantly unskilled jobs, men earn 38 percent more than women. For some groups of immigrants, women are in a different line of work than men. For example, among foreign workers from certain Southeast Asian countries (especially the Philippines), a substantial proportion of women work as bar hostesses and "entertainers," while men work in factories or in construction. However, for groups

---

[14] Japanese female labor participation rates continue to exhibit an "M" pattern, where women mainly work before marriage, quit their jobs once they marry, and then reenter the labor force after they are finished raising their children.

[15] Although most women work full-time before marriage, over half of married women are in part-time jobs (Ogawa and Retherford 1993: 727).

[16] Japan has ratified the 1985 United Nations Convention on the Elimination of all Forms of Discrimination against Women (CEDAW) and has a domestic law that forbids workplace gender discrimination.

like the nikkeijin, women frequently do the same types of jobs as men in the same factories, but men earn substantially higher wages.[17]

In addition, in countries like Japan which perceive themselves as ethnically homogenous, immigrant groups that are of the same racial descent as the native-born population can be highly favored over other foreigners and enjoy significantly better employment and wage conditions, producing a discriminatory immigrant labor market. In Japan, the ethnic Japanese nikkeijin from South America are, by far, the most preferred among all foreign workers.

Both employers and labor brokers give first priority to nikkeijin when hiring foreign workers. Since the nikkeijin are in the greatest demand, Japanese employers have to pay high wages in order to attract them and then to prevent them from moving to firms offering better wages.[18] In fact, hourly wages for some nikkeijin equal or exceed those of Japan-born workers (Mori 1994: 627),[19] and only the larger and more reputable companies are generally able to afford them. In our Hamamatsu sample, nikkeijin wages were 49 percent higher than those of other foreign workers.

One primary reason why the nikkeijin are preferred over other foreign workers is their legal status; they are by far the largest group of legal immigrants in Japan. However, this preference also has an important ethnic component based on a certain amount of cultural affinity that Japanese employers feel with the Japanese-descent nikkeijin, who are assumed to be the most culturally Japanese.[20] As one employer put it:

> We have both nikkeijin and non-nikkeijin workers at our firm, but we notice that the nikkeijin have a better work ethic. Those with Japanese blood are more diligent. They think more like the Japanese and are easier to relate to. The

---

[17] Certain manufacturing industries that require more physically demanding labor tend to rely more on male nikkeijin workers. As expected, most nikkeijin workers in construction are men.

[18] During the height of the Japanese labor shortage in the late 1980s, companies sometimes offered such amenities as furnished apartments, free utilities, free plane tickets to Brazil (for visits), and other perks to retain their nikkeijin workers.

[19] However, because nikkeijin workers are not regular employees and do not receive bonuses and benefits, overall they are significantly cheaper to employ than Japanese workers.

[20] See Tsuda 2003 for an in-depth discussion of the ethnic reception of the Brazilian nikkeijin in Japan.

> *nisei* [second generation] are the most orderly and punctual because their parents are Japanese. As you get further away in terms of generation, they become more Brazilian and don't work as seriously. They quit their jobs if the salary is better elsewhere because they care more about economic benefit than human relations. But they are still better than complete foreigners, who have no *ninjo* [Japanese human feeling].

Such attitudes are based on a common assumption that those who are "racially" Japanese will also be somewhat "culturally" Japanese as well. Because they have been raised by Japanese parents (see Kondo 1986; Tsuda 1998), they are much more desirable as workers than are racially and culturally different foreigners.

In fact, a substantial number of employers interviewed in Hamamatsu and elsewhere even preferred nikkeijin workers with little Japanese over non-nikkeijin foreigners with some Japanese language ability. One labor broker claimed that about 50 percent of his corporate clients preferred nikkeijin workers even if they did not speak any Japanese. In others words, the social capital of ethnicity is so valued by some employers that it completely overrides human capital attributes—such as Japanese proficiency—even if the latter is technically more relevant to job performance. Consider the comments of one Japanese employer, who expressed an extreme version of a view not uncommon among his colleagues:

> I always hire nikkeijin workers before I look at other foreigners. Because the nikkeijin are of the same blood, they share some Japanese values. We feel a sense of affinity to them even if they don't speak the language. We may be able to more easily explain work instructions to foreigners (of non-Japanese descent) who speak Japanese, but in general they are no good. The nikkeijin are more *majime* (honest, serious) and reliable because they were raised by Japanese parents.

The ethnic desirability of Japanese descendants is so strong that Japanese employers generally prefer pure Japanese-descent nikkeijin over nikkeijin of mixed descent, although both are allowed to enter Japan legally. Employers and labor brokers often emphasize that they look at the "face" when interviewing nikkeijin for a job. Although a few employers denied that they discriminated on such a basis, many expressed such ethnic preferences. Some claimed that those of mixed blood (*mestiços*) are less culturally Japanese and less easy to relate to, and that they have more undesirable attributes. Among nikkeijin workers, it was general knowledge that mestiços have a harder time finding jobs in Japan. In fact, some mestiços that look sufficiently Japanese "pass" as pure Japanese descendants in order to improve their employment prospects. Even among pure Japanese-descent nikkeijin, there is some preference for *nisei* (second generation) over *sansei* (third generation), who have supposedly become more culturally foreign. Likewise, employers generally favored Brazilian nikkeijin over Peruvian nikkeijin because the latter do not speak Japanese as well and a higher proportion are of mixed descent.[21] As a result, Peruvian nikkeijin earn lower wages than their Brazilian counterparts and are three times more likely to be fired (Kitagawa 1993: 78).

The nikkeijin are by far the largest group of foreigners in Japan (they compose 37 percent of the total population of foreign workers in Japan and 60 percent of the registered foreigners in Hamamatsu). Although such an abundant supply of nikkeijin workers would normally depress their wages, a number of Japanese employers at smaller, subsidiary firms claim they cannot attract a sufficient number of nikkeijin, who are in high demand and therefore command high wages. As a result, these companies generally must settle for less ethnically desirable foreigners, such as workers from East or Southeast Asia and the Middle East, who earn progressively lower salaries (Kajita 1994: 73). The comments of one small employer illustrate this quite well:

> We're always being pressured by our parent company, which keeps telling us, "lower your costs, lower your costs." So we small companies, unlike medium-sized businesses, can't afford nikkeijin wages. We have to hire Asians [foreigners from Asia] or even Iranians. If it's Iranians, they are cheap and work hard. We can't do without them.

The existence of this hierarchy of ethnic preference (basically correlated with wage levels) was acknowledged by another employer (cf. Mori 1994):

> When it comes to hiring foreigners, there are clearly several levels based on like and dislike. We feel [ethnically] the clos-

---

[21] In fact, a substantial percentage of the Peruvians are not of Japanese descent at all, but enter Japan as "fake" nikkeijin with false documents.

> est to the nikkeijin, so they work at the best firms with the best wages. Then come Chinese and Koreans, whom we find less preferable, and therefore they work in less desirable jobs. At the bottom are Bangladeshis and Iranians, who work in the smallest companies that pay the lowest wages. We avoid interacting with Middle Easterners the most, so they get the worst jobs. It really shouldn't be this way, but it is.

In this manner, Japanese employers' strong preference for male and nikkeijin immigrant workers has created a foreign labor market where social capital, rather than human capital, is the primary determinant of immigrant wages and better economic incorporation.

The United States: The Unimportance of Social Capital

While social capital contributes to higher wages among foreign workers in Hamamatsu, it does not influence foreign workers' wages in San Diego because of the different context of reception in the United States as a much older country of immigration. For example, in the United States, the use of immigrant social networks no longer functions as a significant form of social capital that increases wages. Because permanent immigrant settlement is more common in the United States, migrants with a strict sojourner mentality are rare (63.9 percent of foreign workers in San Diego are self-reported permanent settlers, compared to only 9 percent in Hamamatsu). As long as foreign workers consider themselves to be temporary migrants driven by pure economic gain, they tend to shift from one job to another in search of the highest wage. However, once they decide to remain long-term or permanently in the host country, such purely instrumental motives begin to subside. Instead of dedicating their lives exclusively to work and maximization of earnings, long-term immigrant settlers become more concerned with quality-of-life issues and general social well-being (Tsuda 1999a). They no longer focus exclusively on wage levels as they come to place more value on the working and social conditions that prevail at a particular firm.

Therefore, immigrant social networks in San Diego are used for more diverse social purposes than merely facilitating access to better-paying jobs. For instance, through their extensive social networks, Mexican immigrants in San Diego locate jobs with socially satisfying conditions at companies where Spanish is the predominant language and where the workforce includes clusters of Mexican relatives and friends. The firm owners are more likely to be Mexican immigrants as well. Although immigrant-owned businesses in San Diego almost exclusively have immigrant (often co-ethnic) labor forces and tend to pay lower wages (Cornelius 1998: 122–25), labor turnover rates at these firms are *lower* than in U.S. native-owned businesses, which suggests that the incentives of working at a firm with ethnic peers where one can communicate in the native language offsets any economic disadvantages.

In addition, gender and ethnic affiliation as forms of social capital do not affect foreign workers' wages in San Diego as they do in Hamamatsu because of the lower levels of gender and ethnic discrimination in the immigrant labor markets of the United States. Because the United States has a larger number of immigrants (10.4 percent of the population is foreign-born, compared to 0.75 percent in Japan), it is not surprising that there is a much higher concentration of both male and female foreign workers of various ethnicities in a wider range of industries. In addition, the firms in our San Diego sample have a much higher percentage of foreign-born employees than those in Japan. While almost 80 percent of employers in Japan have workforces that are less than 25 percent foreign, over 60 percent of employers in San Diego have workforces that consist of 50 percent immigrants. In other words, foreign workers are the rule rather than the exception in the San Diego labor market. Because immigrants are so entrenched in a diverse labor market, male and female foreign workers of various nationalities have become commonplace, making ethnicity and gender less of a factor in hiring and wage determination. As a result, employers are more likely to use individual-level human capital attributes (work experience, language proficiency) in order to differentiate between prospective employees when making hiring decisions.

This is supported by survey interviews conducted with San Diego employers, who indicated that the social characteristics of immigrants—including ethnicity, gender, and foreign-born status—are not a significant consideration when hiring. For instance, less than 1 percent of employers acknowledge that workers' nationality is important in hiring decisions (table 9.5). Factors such as the immigrant's work ethic and work experience (cited by 53.6 and 12 percent of employers, respectively) are considered much more important than ethnicity, personality, and comfort with the prospective employee. Hence, because employers do not seem to strongly discriminate against immigrants based on ethnic and gender affiliation, these considerations do not appear to affect wages in San Diego, especially when compared to Japan.

Not surprisingly, therefore, there is no strong ethnic preference hierarchy among San Diego employers in which a single ethnic group commands notably higher wages, as was found with the nikkeijin in Japan. Although we did not run a wage regression analysis using foreign workers' national origin as a independent social capital variable, the dominant Mexican ethnic group in San Diego does not receive significantly higher wages than other immigrant workers. This seems to be the case even for Mexican or Mexican American employers who might prefer to hire co-ethnics (in fact, 20 percent of employers in our survey self-identify as Latino, predominantly Mexican). However, even if certain Mexican employers are willing to pay extra to hire Mexican co-ethnics (analogous to Japanese employers preferring to hire ethnic Japanese nikkeijin at higher wages), such ethnic preferences do not put upward pressure on wage levels because of the abundant supply and concentration of Mexican immigrant labor in cities like San Diego where a majority of foreign workers are of Mexican origin.[22] In fact, the oversupply of Mexican workers in San Diego, Los Angeles, Chicago, and other urban centers has caused a number of them to move to rural cities and towns in the United States where job competition is less fierce (Hernández-León and Zúñiga n.d.).

CONCLUSION: MARGINALITY, HUMAN CAPITAL, AND SOCIAL MOBILITY

Our comparative analysis suggests that the relative effect of human capital versus social capital on immigrant wages depends on the specific socioeconomic conditions of the host country in which immigrants are embedded (the context of immigrant reception). Although it seems self-evident that immigrant wages and economic incorporation are determined by human capital, this generalization seems to apply only to foreign labor markets in advanced countries of immigration like the United States that have reached a certain level of internal diversity and differentiation—and not to those in recent countries of immigration that are still relatively undeveloped.

---

[22] In San Diego County, 30 percent of the total population is Mexican. In contrast, only 2 percent of the total population in Hamamatsu consists of Brazilian nikkeijin.

In recent countries of immigration like Japan, foreign workers are concentrated in the peripheral labor market because they are newer immigrants who still have a sojourner mentality and are employed strictly as informal and casual workers. In addition to their high turnover rate, foreign workers in Japan are hired temporarily through labor brokers or employed only on short-term contracts. Even those immigrants who have settled in Japan and have remained with the same employer for a considerable period are still regarded as temporary workers and are not incorporated into the regular labor market and placed on the promotion track. Therefore, because foreign workers are still predominantly confined to unskilled, marginal jobs with few opportunities for advancement, the human capital that they have acquired over time is not reflected in better jobs at higher earnings.

This does not mean that foreign workers in Japan earn low incomes. As noted earlier, the hourly wages of nikkeijin sometimes equal and even exceed those for native Japanese workers. Undoubtedly, certain types of foreign workers in Japan are paid higher wages than others within the limited confines of the peripheral labor market. Although immigrants do not benefit from the human capital they have acquired, those with access to social capital in the form of immigrant networks, gender, and ethnicity are able to obtain jobs with higher wages. Because many foreign workers are still sojourners attempting to maximize their short-term economic returns, social networks are used to gain access to better-paying jobs. In addition, in a country with significant gender and ethnic discrimination that continues to discourage career aspirations among women and cherish ethnic homogeneity, Japanese employers strongly value and prefer men over women and ethnically similar nikkeijin over non-Japanese-descent foreigners, and they are willing to pay significantly higher wages to acquire such workers.

In classic countries of immigration such as the United States, with more developed and differentiated immigrant labor markets, a much greater diversity of jobs at various skill and income levels is available for immigrant workers. In addition, San Diego has many more long-term immigrants and permanent settlers, who are not as prone to change jobs constantly or to be hired as short-term workers. Because immigrants are not confined to temporary employment on the periphery of the labor market, human capital is rewarded, enabling at least some immigrants to escape unskilled, entry-level jobs and advance to higher-status, more stable, and better-paying positions through the acquisition of personal experience and ability. When compared to human capital, the social capital of immigrant workers (based on their ethnic and gender affiliations) seems to have much less effect on wages in San Diego. Because of the much higher proportion of settled immigrants in the United States, these individuals do not utilize their immigrant social networks exclusively for economic purposes (higher wages), as do their counterparts in Japan, but for social purposes (to find jobs with more satisfying social conditions). Because the United States has a stronger tradition of gender equality and multi-ethnicity, it has a less discriminatory labor market with no powerful bias against female workers or overwhelming preference for a certain immigrant ethnic group.

Undoubtedly, the labor markets and institutions of the host societies matter in the determination of immigrant wages. The varying socioeconomic conditions that prevail in different countries account for the differential economic reception and incorporation of immigrants. As a result, the individual characteristics and attributes of immigrants alone do not explain why certain immigrants earn more than others (Reitz 1998). This chapter has shown that differences in the complexity of immigrant labor markets in recent and more advanced countries of immigration, as well as the amount of gender and ethnic discrimination, help explain why human capital determines immigrant economic incorporation in the United States while social capital is the decisive factor in Japan. Different immigrant attributes become salient in the determination of wages only because they are embedded in certain host-country institutional contexts that make them important.

Since immigration to Japan is still in its early stages, it remains to be seen whether immigrant labor markets in Japanese cities like Hamamatsu will eventually evolve toward the more developed San Diego model. As Japan becomes a more advanced country of immigration, will foreign workers escape the peripheral sectors of the economy and enter the mainstream labor market? Does an initially restrictive immigrant labor market always become more diversified and varied over time, enabling immigrants to use their human capital to improve their occupational level and income? Or can foreign workers in certain countries be perpetually marginalized as an unskilled, temporary, and causal labor force?

For the near term, it is likely that foreign workers in Japan will continue to be confined to the peripheral job market. It is unlikely that a "jobs ladder" for foreign workers will begin to emerge as long as

Japanese firms regard them as a temporary and disposable reserve labor force accessible through the labor brokerage system. In addition, there has been a long-term casualization of the Japanese labor market because of an increasing need for an informal labor force of temporary workers.[23] As the globalization of capitalist production has intensified, advanced industrialized economies like Japan have come to rely increasingly on migrant workers in order to cut production costs in the face of intense competition from developing countries with cheaper labor forces. Although many Japanese companies have moved their production to the Third World, those that remain in Japan have been forced to restructure. Because Japanese firms have been unwilling to streamline production by downsizing and dismissing their regular workers (Dore 1986: 93),[24] they have become increasingly dependent on an expanding informal labor force of temporary and disposable migrant workers.[25] Also, as Japanese manufacturers continue to shift production abroad, Japan's domestic economy, like that of the United States, will continue to shift from industrial manufacturing to the service sector, which also relies heavily on casual and unskilled workers (Sassen 1991). As long as this increasing demand for casual labor persists, it appears that foreign workers in Japan will continue to be channeled exclusively into the peripheral labor market of temporary, low-level jobs for which human capital does not translate into occupational advancement and higher wages.

At the same time, there are already indications that Japan's foreign labor market may come to resemble that of the United States. As the permanent settlement of immigrants in Japan becomes more advanced

---

[23] According to Japanese Ministry of Labor surveys, the proportion of part-time workers increased steadily from 7 percent of all workers in 1970 to close to 20 percent in 1999. The increase has been especially notable among women. For instance, in 1980 there were only 5,403,000 part-time female workers, whereas by 1992 the number had jumped almost threefold to 14,456,000.

[24] Japanese companies (especially the larger ones) generally do not lay off excess workers but instead rely on natural attrition (waiting for workers to retire or quit). Other means include encouraging early retirement and moving unnecessary workers to subsidiary firms. This inability of companies to sufficiently downsize and streamline their workforces has been one major reason why the Japanese economy has been unable to recover from a decade-long recession.

[25] In contrast to regular Japanese workers, foreign workers hired on short-term contracts or temporarily borrowed from labor brokers are more cost-effective because they generally command lower hourly wages, are not paid bonuses or other benefits, and can be quickly dismissed during a decline in production.

and their temporary sojourner mentality continues to decline (see Tsuda 1999a),[26] immigrants will make longer-term commitments to their jobs and many may leave the labor broker system to look for more permanent jobs. With increased numbers of permanent immigrants, the immigrant enclave community will continue to develop in Japan and the number of ethnic business owners will increase. Meanwhile, Japan's demographic profile continues to change in ways that may benefit immigrants in the labor market of the future. Because of the country's low fertility and population aging, a recent United Nations report estimates that Japan will have to import over 640,000 immigrants per year just to maintain its present workforce or face a 6.7 annual drop in GDP (United Nations 2000). As a result, the Japanese government will be forced to adopt more open immigration policies and to develop measures to integrate immigrants into Japanese society. This will both increase the number of immigrants in Japan and also promote their eventual labor market incorporation. And there is always the possibility that gender and ethnic discrimination in Japan will decline in the future, improving job opportunities for female and non-nikkeijin migrants. However, it will be some time before these changes take place and Japan's immigrant workers are able to overcome their current marginalization in the labor market. Only then will human capital become effective as a means to attain better jobs and salaries, allowing immigrants to become gradually incorporated into mainstream Japanese society through social mobility.

References

Archer, M. 1991. "Self-Employment and Occupational Structure in an Industrializing City: Detroit 1880," *Social Science History* 15: 67–95.

Becker, Gary S. 1964. *Human Capital*. New York: National Bureau of Economic Research.

Ben-Porath, Yoram. 1967. "The Production of Human Capital and the Life Cycle of Earnings," *Journal of Political Economy* 75: 352–65.

Borjas, George J. 1995. "Assimilation and Changes in Cohort Quality Revisited: What Happened to Immigrant Earnings in the 1980s?" *Journal of Labor Economics* 13, no. 2: 201–45.

---

[26] Sixty-three percent of all immigrant workers in our sample reported that they had already remained in Japan longer than they initially intended.

Brinton, Mary C. 1993. *Women and the Economic Miracle: Gender and Work in Postwar Japan*. Berkeley: University of California Press.

Chiswick, Barry R. 1988. *Illegal Aliens: Their Employment and Employers*. Kalamazoo, Mich.: Upjohn Institute for Employment Research.

Coleman, James S. 1988. "Social Capital in the Creation of Human Capital," *American Journal of Sociology* 94: S95–121.

Cornelius, Wayne A. 1998. "The Structural Embeddedness of Demand for Mexican Immigrant Labor: New Evidence from California." In *Crossings: Mexican Immigration in Interdisciplinary Perspective*, edited by Marcelo Suárez-Orozco. Cambridge, Mass.: Harvard University Press.

Cornelius, Wayne A., and Yasuo Kuwahara. 1998. "The Role of Immigrant Labor in the U.S. and Japanese Economies: A Comparative Study of San Diego and Hamamatsu, Japan." La Jolla: Center for U.S.-Mexican Studies, University of California, San Diego.

Dore, Ronald P. 1986. *Flexible Rigidities: Industrial Policy and Structural Adjustment in the Japanese Economy 1970–80*. Stanford, Calif.: Stanford University Press.

Granovetter, Mark. 1985. "Economic Action and Social Structure: The Problem of Embeddedness," *American Journal of Sociology* 91: 481–510.

Hernández-León, Rubén, and Víctor Zúñiga. n.d. "Mexican Immigrant Communities in the South and Social Capital: The Case of Dalton, Georgia." CCIS Working Paper. At http://www.ccis-ucsd.org/PUBLICATIONS/working_papers.htm.

Iguchi, Yasushi. 1998. "International Migration in East Asia: A Growing Challenge for Japan." Presented at the workshop of the University of California Comparative Immigration and Integration Program, University of California, Davis, October 9–10.

Kajita, Takamichi. 1994. *Gaikokujin Rodosha to Nihon* (Foreign laborers and Japan). Tokyo: NHK Books.

Kitagawa, Toyoie. 1993. "Hamamatsu-shi ni Okeru Gaikokujin no Seikatsu Jittai/Ishiki Chosa: Nikkei Burajiru/Perujin o Chushin ni" (Survey of living conditions and consciousness of foreigners in Hamamatsu City: focusing on Nikkei-Brazilians and Peruvians). Hamamatsu: Hamamatsu Planning Section/International Exchange Office.

Kondo, Dorinne K. 1986. "Dissolution and Reconstitution of Self: Implications for Anthropological Epistemology," *Cultural Anthropology* 1, no. 1: 74–88.

Light, Ivan, and Edna Bonacich. 1988. *Immigrant Entrepreneurs: Koreans in Los Angeles*. Los Angeles: University of California Press.

Massey, Douglas S., Rafael Alarcón, Jorge Durand, and Humberto González. 1987. *Return to Aztlan: The Social Process of International Migration from Western Mexico*. Berkeley: University of California Press.

Massey, Douglas S., and Kristin Espinosa. 1997. "What's Driving Mexico-U.S. Migration? A Theoretical, Empirical, and Policy Analysis," *American Journal of Sociology* 102, no. 4: 939–99.

Mincer, Jacob. 1974. *Schooling, Experience, and Earnings*. New York: Columbia University Press.

Morales, Rebecca, and Frank Bonilla, eds. 1993. *Latinos in a Changing U.S. Economy: Comparative Perspectives on Growing Inequality*. Newbury Park, Calif.: Sage.

Mori, Hiromi. 1994. "Migrant Workers and Labor Market Segmentation in Japan," *Asian and Pacific Migration Journal* 3, no. 4: 619–38.

Ogasawara, Yuko. 1998. *Office Ladies and Salaried Men: Power, Gender, and Work in Japanese Companies*. Berkeley: University of California Press.

Ogawa, Naohiro, and Robert D. Retherford. 1993. "The Resumption of Fertility Decline in Japan: 1973–1992," *Population and Development Review* 19, no. 4: 703–41.

Portes, Alejandro, and Robert Bach. 1985. *Latin Journey: Cuban and Mexican Immigrants in the United States*. Berkeley: University of California Press.

Portes, Alejandro, and Rubén G. Rumbaut. 1990. *Immigrant America: A Portrait*. Berkeley: University of California Press.

———. 2001. *Legacies: The Story of the Immigrant Second Generation*. Berkeley: University of California Press.

Portes, Alejandro, and Julia Sensenbrenner. 1993. "Embeddedness and Immigration: Notes on the Social Determinants of Economic Action," *American Journal of Sociology* 93: 1320–50.

Reitz, Jeffrey G. 1998. *Warmth of the Welcome: The Social Causes of Economic Success for Immigrants in Different Nations and Cities*. Boulder, Colo.: Westview.

Rumbaut, Rubén G. 1994. "Origins and Destinies: Immigration to the United States since World War II," *Sociological Forum* 9, no. 4 (December): 583–621.

Sanders, Jimy M., and Victor Nee. 1987. "Limits of Ethnic Solidarity in the Enclave Economy," *American Sociological Review* 52: 745–73.

———. 1996. "Social Capital, Human Capital, and Immigrant Self-Employment: The Family as Social Capital and the Value of Human Capital," *American Sociological Review* 61: 231–49.

Sassen, Saskia. 1991. *The Global City: New York, London, Tokyo*. Princeton, N.J.: Princeton University Press.

Schmidley, A. Dianne. 2001. "Profile of the Foreign-Born Population in the United States: 2000." U.S. Census Bureau, Current Population Reports, Series P23-P206. Washington, D.C.: U.S. Government Printing Office.

Schmidley, A. Dianne, and Campbell Gibson. 1999. "Profile of the Foreign-Born Population in the United States: 1997." U.S. Census Bureau, Current Population Reports, Series P23-P195. Washington, D.C.: U.S. Government Printing Office.

Sellek, Yoko. 1996. "The U-Turn Phenomenon among South American-Japanese Descendants: From Emigrants to Migrants," *Immigrants and Minorities* 15, no. 3: 246–69.

———. 2001. *Migrant Labour in Japan*. Hampshire, U.K.: Palgrave.

Stevens, Carolyn S. 1997. *On the Margins of Japanese Society: Volunteers and the Welfare of the Urban Underclass*. London: Routledge.

Tsuda, Takeyuki. 1998. "The Stigma of Ethnic Difference: The Structure of Prejudice and 'Discrimination' towards Japan's New Immigrant Minority," *Journal of Japanese Studies* 24, no. 2: 317–59.

———. 1999a. "The Permanence of 'Temporary' Migration: The Structural Embeddedness of Japanese-Brazilian Immigrant Workers in Japan," *Journal of Asian Studies* 58, no. 3: 687–722.

———. 1999b. "The Motivation to Migrate: The Ethnic and Sociocultural Constitution of the Japanese-Brazilian Return Migration System," *Economic Development and Cultural Change* 48, no. 1: 1–31.

———. 2003. *Strangers in the Ethnic Homeland: Japanese Brazilian Return Migration in Transnational Perspective*. New York: Columbia University Press.

Tsuda, Takeyuki, and Wayne A. Cornelius. 2003. "Japan: Government Policy, Immigrant Reality." In *Controlling Immigration: A Global Perspective*, 2d ed., edited by Wayne A. Cornelius, Takeyuki Tsuda, Philip L. Martin, and James F. Hollifield. Stanford, Calif.: Stanford University Press.

United Nations. 2000. *Replacement Migration: Is It a Solution to Declining and Aging Populations?* New York: Population Division, Department of Economic and Social Affairs, United Nations Secretariat.

Waters, Mary C., and Karl Eschbach. 1995. "Immigration and Ethnic and Racial Inequality in the United States," *Annual Review of Sociology* 21: 419–46.

Yamamoto, Kenji. 1994. "Nikkei Burajirujin no Rodo Ido" (The labor migration of Brazilian nikkeijin), *Kenkyu Hokoku* (Bulletin of the Japan Statistics Research Institute).

Zhou, Min. 1998. *Growing Up American: How Vietnamese Children Adapt to Life in the United States*. New York: Russell Sage Foundation.

Zhou, Min, and John R. Logan. 1989. "Returns on Human Capital in Ethnic Enclaves: New York City's Chinatown," *American Sociological Review* 54: 809–20.

10

Undressing the Garment Industry: Immigrant Entrepreneurship in Seven Cities

JAN RATH

Capital, goods, and people move around the globe, linking distant social, political, and economic configurations and generating vast changes at an unprecedented speed and scale. The process of globalization entails the shrinking of the world, but this does not necessarily mean the end of geography. Local differentiations still matter (Raes 2000a). The garment industry is a case in point.

In the late nineteenth century, when the sewing machine and new work floor arrangements were introduced, there was the expectation that productivity would skyrocket and that large factories would become the dominant garment production sites. In the postwar period, the design of "smarter" machines that could work with different garment sizes, materials, styles, and so forth represented another attempt to rationalize garment production. However, the large factories' adoption of advanced technology such as CAD-CAM systems did not prevent manufacturers

---

This chapter is based on research conducted by the Institute for Migration and Ethnic Studies at the University of Amsterdam, in collaboration with a group of international scholars. I would like to thank Marja Dreef, Nancy Green, Guillermo J. Grenier, Joy Husband, Robert Jerrard, Adem Kumcu, Ivan Light, Victoria Ojeda, Prodromos Panayiotopoulos, Stephan Raes, Monder Ram, Flavia Reil, Alex Stepick, Yu Zhou, and Aslan Zorlu for contributing to this project. For more details, see Rath 2002.

from continuing to rely on cheap labor for the assembly of garments, and many outsourced this part of the production process offshore. The exodus of garment manufacturing to low-wage countries, it was argued, was part of a larger process of globalization and only served to strengthen the emergence of a New International Division of Labor (Fröbel, Heinrichs, and Kreye 1980). In various cosmopolitan cities, such as Amsterdam, London, New York, and Miami, the decline of garment manufacturing was dramatic, and the sector began to be viewed as a "sunset industry." However, contrary to such gloomy expectations, small garment factories in advanced economies demonstrated considerable resilience, partly due to the salient role played by immigrants. Today it is hard to imagine the garment sector of these cosmopolitan cities without immigrants.

Each city has a conglomerate garment industry,[1] a proliferation of small enterprises closely connected in chains of dependency, and a strong immigrant presence in the ranks of entrepreneurs and workers. They exhibit profit making and success, but also exploitation, substandard labor conditions, and an abundance of other informal practices that at times provoke public outrage. Any casual observer would rightly conclude that the similarities across cities are telling: what else could be expected in an era when the uniformizing forces of globalization shape economic, social, and political transformations?

However, there are also differences across cities (Rath 2002a). For all the similarities in the industry, each city occupies a different international market position, and the garment sector in each one shows specific features in terms of size, structure, and development. Furthermore, the immigrant presence follows different historical tracks, resulting in differences in the ethnic division of labor, in immigrants' capacity to gain political influence, and in opportunities for economic integration and upward social mobility. In Amsterdam, immigrant entrepreneurs, especially Turks, carved out a niche in the local rag trade, but most of their businesses were wiped out in the early 1990s when the city government embarked on a large-scale crackdown campaign. Entrepreneurs and their spokesmen campaigned for more leniency, to no avail. In Los Angeles, the immigrant rag trade is still thriving, despite ham-handed anti-sweatshop campaigns. Here it is the workers and their organizations that are calling on government to en-

---

[1] I use the terms rag trade and garment, apparel, and clothing industries interchangeably.

force the law, but the authorities seem more inclined toward the interests of the entrepreneurs. In London, immigrant enterprises remain numerous, partly due to business support schemes developed by local government. Cypriot entrepreneurs successfully linked up with the local Labour Party, and this alliance has favored them in their business ventures. Rightly concluding that the differences across garment sectors are telling, a casual observer might now ask: what else could be expected in an era when general processes are largely contingent on local forces?

This combination of general and specific processes and outcomes is intriguing and should have consequences for the framing of social science research. The quest for the interrelationship, or dialectic, of general and specific factors and processes is not new. Karl Marx referred to this problematic in his introduction to *Grundrisse,* conceived in 1857–1858 (1973: 85). He argued that these same kinds of social relations and processes are found in every mode of production and concomitant social formation, but they manifest themselves in ever changing, historically specific shapes (cf. Bovenkerk, Miles, and Verbunt 1990: 477; Miles 1989). It is this specificity that is the most telling.

This chapter deals with the development and structure of the immigrant garment industry in Amsterdam, London, New York City, Miami, Los Angeles, Paris, and the British West Midlands (Birmingham)[2]—seven world cities in four advanced economies. Each of these cities is a major international center of garment production, some since the early nineteenth century or even earlier. Without immigrants, the industry would not have become established in these particular places or have survived so long. But how do immigrant entrepreneurs perform in these metropolitan centers of garment production? What are their roles in the rag trade, the dynamics of their entrepreneurship, and the factors underlying these processes?

The immigrant garment industry has been the subject of numerous academic studies. In addition to the cities mentioned above, studies have been conducted of the garment sector in Johannesburg (Rogerson 1999, 2000), Manchester (Werbner 1980, 1984), Milan and Prato (Farina et al. 1997; Zincone 2000), San Francisco (Wong 1998), and Toronto (Hiebert 1990, 1993). However, nearly all of these studies focus on a

---

2 The West Midlands includes inner Birmingham and also the smaller towns of Smethwick, Coventry, Wolverhampton, West Bromwich, and Walsall.

single case.[3] International comparisons are rare; while this may be a weakness in studies of immigrant entrepreneurship in general, it is particularly striking in such a fully globalized sector as garment manufacture. Merely comparing countries will not adequately address this shortcoming, since immigrant economic incorporation is the product of a multitude of factors operating at various levels. Moreover, as Favell (1999) argues with regard to studies that compare policies of integration across countries, many studies lead to repetitive and moribund research and reproduce national stereotypes and assumptions about the nation-state. Favell suggests that the city is a far better unit of analysis. The city "enables both contextual specificity and structural comparisons that allow for the fact that immigrant integration might be influenced simultaneously by local, national, and transnational factors" (see also Light and Rosenstein 1995; Persky and Wiewel 1994; Waldinger 1996a). However, such comparisons are also few.

For the record, immigrants in the rag trade have not been limited to the ranks of entrepreneurs. Quite the contrary; the vast majority joined the workforce as wage laborers doing unskilled and low-skilled work. The focus of this chapter, however, is not immigrant workers. This essay examines the workforce only insofar as it impacts entrepreneurial strategies and opportunities. This is the case when we examine whether entrepreneurs can tap a pool of cheap and flexible labor, how they cope with organized labor, and to what extent this labor pool generates new entrepreneurs. Venturing out of wage labor is an important, gender-specific mobility strategy. Immigrants who enter the labor market as machinists in a sewing shop and seek self-employment will probably set up shop in the garment industry or in an adjacent sector where they can capitalize on the skills and the social network that they acquired in the garment industry (Hiebert 2002; see also Waldinger 1996b).[4]

---

[3] The exceptions are Morokvasic 1988a, 1988b, 1991, and 1993; Morokvasic, Phizacklea, and Rudolph 1986; and Morokvasic, Waldinger, and Phizacklea 1990. Green's excellent book on the garment industry in Paris and New York focuses on labor rather than entrepreneurship as such (1997; see also 1986). Bonacich et al. 1994 covers many countries, but this work is not a comprehensive international comparison.

[4] This rule is not hard and fast, as M. Zhou (1992) demonstrates. Zhou argues that many Chinese immigrants in New York's Chinatown start in the garment industry, only to leave it at the first opportunity. Their flight from the garment industry might be an indication of substandard conditions in the lower end of the sector.

MIXED EMBEDDEDNESS

This chapter is based on the position that entrepreneurship can only be fully understood and explained if one adopts a perspective that is broad enough to capture aspects outside the neoclassical domain of supply and demand (Polanyi 1957). Since Ivan Light published *Ethnic Enterprise in America* in 1972, virtually every student of immigrant entrepreneurship—with the notable exception of economist Timothy Bates (1997)—has avoided the direct use of neoclassical economics. Instead, they focus on structural triggers such as blocked mobility in the labor market (Saxenian 1999) or racist exclusion (Ram 1993), or they zoom in on immigrants' cultural endowment for entrepreneurship (Metcalf, Modood, and Virdee 1996; Werbner 2000), their social embeddedness (Lee 1999; Light 2000; Waldinger 1996b; Yoo 1998; M. Zhou 1992), or combinations of their mobilization of various resources (Light and Gold 2000; Yoon 1997).

In the past, efforts have been made to combine structure- and actor-oriented approaches. *Ethnic Entrepreneurs,* by Waldinger et al. (1990), is probably the best-known example, if only because it is the product of collaboration among prominent international researchers. These authors argue in favor of a more integrative approach that places ethnic entrepreneurial strategies somewhere at the crossroads of group characteristics and the opportunity structure. As such, their interactive model combines ethnocultural and sociocultural factors (agency) with politico-economic factors (structure). According to the authors, the latter entail market conditions (particularly access to ethnic/nonethnic consumer markets) and access to ownership (in the form of business vacancies, competition for vacancies, and government policies). This interactive model represents an important step toward a more comprehensive theoretical approach, even though it is more a classification than an explanatory model. However, it also has been criticized—for its methodology (Light and Rosenstein 1995), lack of attention to gender issues (Collins et al. 1995; Morokvasic 1993), insufficient attention to processes of racialization or the dynamics of class (Collins et al. 1995), the a priori categorization of immigrants as ethnic groups (Collins et al. 1995; Rath 2000), the concomitant assumption that immigrants as ethnic entrepreneurs act differently than mainstream entrepreneurs (Rath and Kloosterman 2000), and the narrow and static way in which it deals with economic and politico-regulatory factors (Bonacich 1993; Rath ed. 2000). In light of the model's integrative pretensions, the latter is particularly striking. The authors conceive market conditions in terms of the ethnicization or de-ethnicization of consumer markets, and they confine politico-regulatory factors to a short list of laws and regulations that specifically apply to immigrants. This is not very sophisticated.

Theoretical development has continued and, oddly enough, led to a convergence of approaches to issues of *social embeddedness*. Many students of immigrant entrepreneurship, especially in the United States, are fervent adherents to a version of economic sociological thought that focuses on the entrepreneurs' social networks and impact on entrepreneurship. Instead of elaborating on the dynamics of agency and structure, they more or less take the political economic structure for granted and confine themselves to refining agency matters. This narrow focus reveals a tendency toward reductionism and is a de facto renouncement of the integrative model.

The *mixed embeddedness* approach is more appropriate for our purpose since it relates social relations and transactions to wider political and economic structures (Kloosterman and Rath 2001, 2003; Rath 2002a; Rath ed. 2000). This sensitizing concept acknowledges the significance of immigrants' concrete embeddedness in social networks, and it conceives that their relations and transactions are embedded in a more abstract way in wider economic and politico-institutional structures.

The first building block refers to entrepreneurs' embeddedness in social networks and their capacity to mobilize these networks for economic purposes. The networks enable entrepreneurs to reduce transaction costs in acquiring knowledge, distributing information, recruiting capital and labor, and so forth, by eliminating formal contracts, offering privileged access to economic resources, and providing reliable expectations as to the consequences of malfeasance. It is likely that most entrepreneurs have a mixed and gendered network comprising co-ethnics, other immigrants, and mainstream people, and that these networks change over time. Social capital is unequally distributed among diverse social groups; is connected to cultural, human, and financial capital; and is the product of the interaction of structural factors such as migration history and processes of social, economic, and political incorporation in the mainstream. The impact of social capital is contingent on the goals being pursued and the political and economic forces at work.

Different markets offer entrepreneurs different opportunities, present different obstacles, demand different skills, require the mobilization of different parts of their social network, and lead to different outcomes in terms of business success or, at a higher level of agglomeration, an ethnic division of labor. The structure and dynamics of markets, including processes of global restructuring, constitute the second building block. Engelen (2001), elaborating upon the work by Max Weber (1968; see also Swedberg 1994, 1998), identifies a number of market dimensions that should help us explain the sorting out of specific groups and individuals. Apart from the degree of social embeddedness and the mode, level, and object of regulation (to be discussed), Engelen distinguishes the objects and subjects of trade, and the structure, level of institutionalization, and locality of the market. These various dimensions basically address the "who, what, how, and where" of economic transactions. Together, they determine the potential competitors within a market and the conditions under which transactions take place. Drawing distinctions between these dimensions helps illustrate that markets are not given; they are products of human action, and their emergence involves economic, social, and political determinants. Some markets have low entry barriers and are quite open to newcomers, while others are less accessible, and this helps explain why starting entrepreneurs with limited resources enter low-barrier markets. The proliferation of immigrant entrepreneurs in the lower tiers of the garment industry has often been approached in this way. However, the ethnic division of labor is not just the result of the specific way in which starters enter the market; entrepreneurs may move around, go up-market, or break into entirely new markets. The odds of this occurring are contingent on the presence or absence of entry barriers to those markets, but also on the growth or shrinkage of the markets in which entrepreneurs operate over time (Kloosterman and Rath 2001).

The dynamics of markets are contingent on processes of regulation or governance. This will be the third building block. Regulation should not be confused with legislation per se, because there are also (financial) incentives and disincentives and various forms of persuasion (Engelen 2001). Nor should regulation be confused with state regulation. In addition to local, national, or international governmental agents, a multitude of agents play a role in regulation processes, including unions, quangos (quasi nongovernmental organizations), nonprofit organizations, voluntary associations, and individuals and their social networks. It should be noted that even in cases where legislation per se seems nonexistent or is conveniently put aside—as might be the case in the informal and criminal economies—individuals' economic transactions are still regulated in one way or another (Epstein 1994). And even in cases where legislation does exist, one must not forget the fundamental difference between rules and the enforcement of rules. It is, moreover, clear that regulation is not just a matter of repression and constraining, but also of enabling. Suppressing illicit practices, such as dodging taxes and labor and immigration laws by prosecuting the perpetrators, is an important manifestation of regulation (repression), but so are decisions to tolerate these practices and not prosecute them. Business support programs also constitute forms of regulation. It is important to understand that regulation does not only occur in advanced welfare states but also in lean welfare states such as the United States. In this country the government supposedly has fewer means to regulate economic life, but economic life in the "land of the free" is severely dogged by litigation. In addition, the federal government regulates markets by its relatively open immigration programs for professionals and businessmen, as the proliferation of immigrant moneymakers in Silicon Valley shows (Saxenian 1999). All across the world, markets are always regulated in one way or another, even if the form and level of regulation may vary.

Let us now undress the garment industry in the seven cities and assess the general and specific configurations of social, economic, and political structures in effect.

SEVEN CITIES

A number of considerations led to the selection of Paris, London, Birmingham, Amsterdam, New York, Miami, and Los Angeles as focal points for this study. These cities represent the immigrant garment industry at different historical stages and different stages in the industry's life cycle. Furthermore, these cities are located in states that represent different regulatory contexts. Besides, the cities, and the countries in which they are located, are in different economic regions. And finally, the development of the garment industry in these cities has been closely connected to the presence of immigrants. Each garment city has a characteristic history, with different groups of immigrants playing different roles in different historical periods. This is important because it puts current experiences in historical perspective and, in so doing, sheds light on explanations that are in vogue today.

In Paris, the immigrant presence in tailoring—particularly Belgian, German, Italian, and Swiss women—dates back to the 1840s (Green 1997). Eastern European Jews began flocking into the Parisian rag trade in the 1880s, and Armenians and Jews from Turkey arrived following the breakup of the Ottoman Empire. In the 1950s and 1960s, with the decolonization of parts of North Africa, a third wave of Jews moved into the garment industry, especially from Tunisia and Morocco, and a new generation of Armenians arrived from Turkey, Lebanon, and Iran. From the early 1980s on, Turkish entrepreneurs began to appear near the Sentier garment district, as did Serbs from Yugoslavia, Kurds from Turkey, and Asian immigrants from Cambodia, Vietnam, Thailand, Hong Kong, and mainland China. The most recent arrivals have been Pakistani, Sri-Lankan, Maurician (mostly of Indian origin), and African (Senegalese and Malian).

The role of immigrants in the London garment industry can be traced to the seventeenth century, when Huguenot exiles set up tailor shops (Panayiotopoulos and Dreef 2002). In the late nineteenth century, London, like Paris, became home for numerous eastern European Jews who opened small garment factories. Greek Cypriots, small pockets of Turkish Cypriots, and Bengali immigrants succeeded these Jewish entrepreneurs, with the Bengalis particularly in the leatherwear sector. This happened despite the central government's attitude in the 1960s and 1970s that textile and garment manufacturing was destined to decline. More recently, ethnic Turks and Kurds from Turkey entered the sector and became associated with Turkish Cypriots.

The situation was somewhat different in the West Midlands, some hundred miles north of London (Ram 1993; Ram, Jerrard, and Husband 2002). In the 1970s, after the decline of the smokestack industries, the West Midlands went into deep economic recession. The local clothing industry did not amount to much until immigrants started to open small garment workshops (see Phizacklea 1990). These immigrants, mostly from India and Pakistan, had been made redundant in the labor market, partly due to racist exclusion, and their only option was self-employment. Their enterprises were born under a lucky star since London garment manufacturers were then seeking cheaper and more flexible modes of production. Farming out to local contractors was precisely what they needed.

Eastern European Jews and Westphalian Catholics gravitated to the Amsterdam textile and garment industries in the nineteenth century (Raes 2000b). A steady influx from Russia and Poland brought a continuous stream of new immigrants, especially young Jewish women, who were employed in needlework. The sector suffered a near fatal blow in World War II when many Jewish entrepreneurs and workers were deported to concentration camps and did not return. In the postwar period the Jewish niche was only partially reestablished, and the local industry declined until being revived by immigrants from Turkey. There were ethnic Turks, Kurds, a few Armenians, and, to a lesser degree, immigrants from Egypt, India, and Pakistan. Since the collapse of the immigrant garment industry in the mid-1990s, no other immigrant group has emerged as their successor.

New York City's dominance over the U.S. garment industry emerged in the nineteenth century, due largely to the role of immigrants (Green 1997; Waldinger 1986; Y. Zhou 2002). Earlier immigrants, particularly Russian and eastern European Jews, laid the basis for the organizational structure of New York City's garment industry today. At the turn of the century, Italians got involved in the sector. Chinese and Dominican groups have succeeded them since the 1960s.

Miami's garment industry developed as a kind of auxiliary branch of New York's (Grenier and Stepick 2002). Manufacturers from New York, primarily Jewish, tried to escape the impact of unionization, and the presence of new Cuban female workers in south Florida in the early 1960s funneled them to Miami. The emergence of Miami's garment industry also provided opportunities for Cuban entrepreneurs who entered the sector as contractors hiring a predominantly Cuban workforce. Over the years this workforce changed as Cuban seamstresses left the sector. Entrepreneurs were reluctant to hire Haitians and African Americans, and by the late 1980s newly arrived Central and South Americans replenished the female labor supply.

In Los Angeles, Asian and Latin American immigrants largely replaced ethnic whites in the garment industry, particularly following the Immigration and Nationality Act of 1965 (Light and Ojeda 2002). As a result of the city's access to immigrant labor, Los Angeles has passed New York as the garment manufacturing capital of the United States. Today Asian (especially Korean), European, and Latin American entrepreneurs hire Mexican and Central American seamstresses (Bonacich and Appelbaum 2000).

It should be noted that Paris, London, the West Midlands, Amsterdam, New York, Miami, and Los Angeles differ sharply in terms of surface area and population—and the size of the local economy in general and the garment industry in particular. The Dutch capital, with approximately 730,000 residents, is the largest city in the Netherlands. But compared to Los Angeles, Amsterdam is an insignificant provincial town. This holds true even if the focus is expanded to include Greater Amsterdam, which has just over a million residents (Gemeente Amsterdam 2000). The five-county Los Angeles region covers an area approximately one and a half times the size of the Netherlands and has almost as many residents (14.5 million in Los Angeles versus the Netherlands' 16 million) (Allen and Turner 1997; Waldinger and Bozorgmehr 1996). A driver leaving Amsterdam would cross the German or Belgian border before someone could drive from one end of Greater Los Angeles to the other. Paris, London, and New York are more compact than Los Angeles but still far larger than Amsterdam or Birmingham. These spatial factors affect the size of the local garment markets, which in turn influences the opportunities for small garment firms. Garment and textile manufacturing in Los Angeles County amounts to US$28 billion, or almost a tenth of the total local economy. At its peak in the early 1990s, Dutch garment manufacturing, including informal production, amounted to roughly $1 billion. To be sure, these differences reflect immense quantitative differences in the opportunity structures.

Despite these differences, it is clear that these cities have long functioned as immigrant hubs. Immigration increased dramatically in the 1950s and 1960s following the breakup of the French, British, and Dutch colonial empires and the influx of guestworkers in Europe, and the 1965 changes in U.S. immigration laws. These processes have altered the ethnic makeup of the urban population, as reflected in the economy generally and in the rag trade in particular. Since the late 1950s and 1960s, when the sector was in decline in most cities due to restructuring, large numbers of immigrants have entered the sector and halted or even reversed the decline. In Paris, London, and New York, the involvement of immigrants distilled down to what Waldinger (1996b) calls "a game of ethnic musical chairs." In other cases, there is little evidence of ethnic succession (cf. Rath 2002b). Still, all the cases demonstrate how the industry has been affected by the inflow of immigrants. At a juncture when de-industrialization is a buzzword, the resilience of the small and medium enterprise (SME) sector in garment manufacturing stands out.

The garment industry tends to be spatially concentrated. Most Amsterdam retailers operate from the World Fashion Center in the western part of the city. This area of tall office buildings confirms in brick the existence of a conglomerate garment industry. It operates in much the same way as do the garment districts of Los Angeles and New York; the London boroughs of Tower Hamlets, Hackney, Islington, Haringey, and Westminster (wholesalers) and the borough of Hackney (manufacturing); and the Sentier neighborhood in Paris. This conglomerate includes designer houses, fashion institutes, fabric and accessory suppliers, manufacturers, contractors, distributors, and marketing firms. There is an extensive web of information and exchange networks central to the industry that helps lower transaction costs. New York's fashion district, in Manhattan between Sixth and Ninth Avenues from 35th to 41st Streets, has become a magnet for garment-related activities. Y. Zhou (2002) argues that this spatial proximity facilitates and encourages a particular division of labor, which gives the New York fashion industry flexibility and efficiency. Zhou also notes that numerous garment factories are moving from Manhattan to Brooklyn. It is not yet clear how this will affect the opportunity structure of the garment contractors.

At the end of the 1990s, the garment industry was still the premier manufacturing sector in New York. In 1998, 132,900 people were employed by fashion-related firms in the five-borough area, from designing to retailing, with most in garment manufacture. Garment and textile manufacturing firms together accounted for almost a third of the city's manufacturing firms. An estimated 30 to 40 percent of the sewing shops had immigrant owners; 30 to 40 percent of these closed or changed their name in the first year. Los Angeles outperformed New York as the garment manufacturing capital of the United States around 1989, mainly as a result of its superior access to (illegal) immigrant labor (Light and Ojeda 2002). In the mid-1990s, when garment industry employment in the United States declined by 17 percent, the number of garment manufacturers and contractors in Los Angeles County increased by 15 percent, expanding the number of jobs by 40 percent to roughly 140,000. Low estimates suggest that the Los Angeles garment sector included 5,070 firms. In London, the garment industry continued to have a significant presence despite the relocation of some garment production offshore or to regions like the West Midlands. In the late 1990s, approximately 2,500 small firms in the London garment industry employed an estimated 30,000 predominantly female workers. In the West Midlands, many small garment factories had emerged since the mid-1970s. Most were Asian-owned, and they mainly operated at the lower end of the market. There were about 500 of these firms in the area. In Amsterdam between 1980 and the early 1990s, numerous mainly Turkish immigrants set up approximately 1,000 small sewing shops, employing roughly 20,000 workers at the peak and contributing to a temporary resurgence of the SME sector in the Dutch garment industry. Paris and Miami experienced similar developments.

The figures are impressive, but their significance is hard to assess. First, the real situation is unclear because there are so many informal workshops and home workers. Informal shops circumvent official legal requirements, resulting in an unknown level of unreporting and unrecording. Second, globalization and other factors put heavy pressure on garment manufacturers in advanced economies, leading to ruthless competition with local and international producers. Under those unfavorable conditions, entrepreneurs are quick to close shop or are forced to do so because of violations of the law. All of this contributes to an extraordinarily high fluctuation rate. The extreme case of Amsterdam shows that it is possible to wipe out a substantial number of contractors within a matter of months. The 1,000 firms in the Lowlands seemed like a goodly number, but in the bubble economy of the rag trade they vanished in no time. This illustrates their vulnerability as well as the arbitrary nature of the figures. Third, the figures are contingent on local conditions. The 500 firms in the West Midlands represent only 20 percent of the total firms in London and less than 10 percent of the total firms in Los Angeles. Still, in the local context of inner Birmingham, Smethwick, Coventry, Wolverhampton, West Bromwich, and Walsall, this figure means a lot, and it is even more significant for the Asian communities that have entered the sector. In short, figures only make sense if they are linked to the specifics of the local situation.

Garment factories are often described as small family businesses or firms critically dependent on family labor, but in practice there are also large businesses with workers from a variety of immigrant groups. There is no typical immigrant garment factory. In some cities, particularly those with long and uninterrupted histories of immigrant involvement in the sector, a pronounced differentiation of immigrant businesses has evolved. A small and marginal garment contractor can become a large manufacturer operating as a micro multinational company and giving orders to newer small contractors. This process sometimes takes more than one generation, as in the case of Greek Cypriots in London or Jewish entrepreneurs in Paris and New York. In other cases, immigrants moved up rapidly, as did Asian entrepreneurs in Los Angeles. In still other cases, this process hardly occurred, because law enforcement agencies put a stop to further development or the market failed to provide sufficient scope for it, as in Amsterdam and the Midlands. A few dozen perceptive Turkish entrepreneurs nevertheless saw their chance and relocated their activities from Amsterdam to Turkey, where they opened large factories.

SOCIAL NETWORKS IN A CHANGING LABOR MARKET

Social networks obviously are important in explaining the formation of immigrant niches, as well as individual entrepreneurs' everyday management, even if they do not always account for how the first immigrants found their way to the garment industry. But networks are not the whole story. The limited skills and low capital required to get into the business and the poor options in the larger labor market account for the continuing influx of immigrants to an industry characterized by cutthroat competition and difficult working conditions.

Immigrants did not initially move to Amsterdam or Birmingham because of the garment industry. Immigrants flocked to these cities for jobs in other industries and, in the Dutch case, because they were recruited to do temporary work. Only when these industries declined did the garment industry emerge as an option. However, not all entrepreneurs took this route, and their entrepreneurship thus illustrates different path dependencies. Apart from a small number who migrated with the explicit purpose of setting up shop in the garment sector, such as the Indian and Pakistani wholesalers in Amsterdam, most immigrant garment entrepreneurs started as wage laborers and became self-employed at a later stage. Newcomers were all too willing to become machinists, cutters, ironers, or general garment workers. Information about job opportunities was widely available and was spread by word of mouth through social networks that extend over long distances and across borders. In Amsterdam, some garment workers from Turkey were explicitly recruited by co-ethnics to perform skilled tasks. Elsewhere, the very existence of clusters of ethnic enterprises fosters new international migration. Once these newcomers have been hired, they often become apprentices. Although some of the workers were tailors at home or had other experience with sewing, sewing *and* contracting are generally learned on the job. After a while, some of these workers leave their jobs to set up their own factories, contributing to the mushrooming, if not supersaturation, of small sewing shops in a hypercompetitive environment.

In a number of cities—notably, New York, Los Angeles, and London—intricate class-based network differentiations can be observed. Y. Zhou (2002) describes how Jewish and Italian immigrants in New

York were able to achieve upward mobility by using their social networks; she argues that this is no longer feasible for newer immigrant groups because the industry has matured. New York's garment industry has evolved into a sophisticated, specialized network characterized by a multi-tier system. The upper tier comprises native-born capitalists, many of them the descendants of Jewish or Italian immigrants. These college-educated manufacturers, jobbers, and retailers are well embedded in the industry. The lower tiers tend to consist of newer immigrants without educational qualifications, English proficiency, or the right social connections. They have been relegated to work as contractors, subcontractors, and small manufacturers of various sorts. The upper tier garners the profits and the prestige of the fashion industry; the lower tiers face fierce competition and low profit levels.

Immigrant groups in the rag trade—Asians in the Midlands, Greek Cypriots in London, Chinese in Paris and New York, Latin Americans in Los Angeles and Miami, and Turks in Paris—are often portrayed as exhibiting high levels of gender segregation. This informs a gender-specific use of social networks as well as a gender-specific division of labor on the shop floor. Most immigrant entrepreneurs are male, and most sewing shop workers are female (except in Amsterdam). Women are employed as machinists or general workers and do unskilled or semiskilled work. Immigrant entrepreneurship researchers commonly explain the role of women in cultural terms: ethnocultural moral codes and practices funnel immigrant women to what seem to be sheltered sectors of the economy, sectors in which these codes and practices are respected. The steady supply of reliable labor, allocated through co-ethnic and familial ties, gives immigrant entrepreneurs a competitive edge.

Phizacklea (1990), however, abandons these culturalist explanations and argues that the position of immigrant women in the rag trade needs to be viewed in a broader context of racism and sexism. Until 1988, racism and sexism were part and parcel of the British immigration legislation that treated women as dependants of men. Most women entered the United Kingdom to join their families or on a voucher sponsored by a relative in business. According to Phizacklea, this legislation helped perpetuate the cultural stereotypes of Asian women as weak and passive. This portrayal lessened their chances in the general employment market and exacerbated their dependency on employment in sewing shops run by family members or co-ethnics. Incidentally, Ram, Jerrard, and Husband (2002) assume that second-generation Asians are more intent on pursuing professional careers than perpetuating the small business tradition of their parents.

Things turned out differently in Amsterdam, where both entrepreneurs and workers were predominantly male. The specific history of illegal migration from Turkey to the Netherlands and the specific features of the Dutch welfare state account for the limited role of Turkish women in Amsterdam. The city's large reserve of undocumented immigrants from Turkey, predominantly relatively young men, was echoed in the workforce in Turkish sewing shops and in the population of Turkish entrepreneurs. In principle, Turkish entrepreneurs could recruit workers, male and female alike, from the ranks of the settled population. However, these legal immigrants were not eager to accept sewing shop jobs. If they were unemployed, the Dutch welfare state provided them with relatively generous benefits, which lessened the need to take up any job. This is an example of how regulation affects the mobilizing power of social networks and the division of labor in the garment industry.

Ethnic or family networks can be instrumental in forging business connections, although the Amsterdam and New York cases show that a strong reliance on these networks can also be detrimental. Developing stable relationships with mainstream retailers appears to be more rewarding. This supports the argument that economic transactions are embedded in social relations, although these relations are not necessarily ethnic or familial. There is strong evidence that ethnic or familial networks serve as an infrastructure to collect capital and recruit, train, and discipline labor. Entrepreneurs' reliance on family or ethnic ties, rather than on formal recruitment processes, obviously affects the workplace regime in various ways. Most authors note that people who are trusted, especially family members, perform key tasks such as bookkeeping, maintaining relations with jobbers, and planning production. This also holds for tasks that require special skills, such as cutting. Allocating these tasks to core, loyal network members, often men, allows a manager a certain degree of control over process. Garment entrepreneurs in London, the West Midlands, and Los Angeles prefer to recruit workers from their networks or their own ethnic group, but this is not always possible in practice; the supply of cheap and flexible co-ethnic labor has contracted as immigration regulations have been tightened and youngsters have come to prefer other jobs. However, the case of Los Angeles also shows that Asian entrepreneurs can continue to rely on immigrant networks as long as Latin American immigrants, legal and illegal, keep flocking to Southern California.

By way of conclusion, it could be argued that an important difference among these cities relates to the link between particular groups' immigration histories and the development of the garment industry. In Paris, London, New York, and Los Angeles, some of the more successful entrepreneurs in the older immigrant groups constituted a strong presence in the sector. They achieved upward social mobility, but because they could no longer rely on co-ethnic and familial social networks, they started recruiting from other groups. In some cases, such as Paris, New York, Los Angeles, Miami, and London to some extent, the entrepreneurs tapped the social networks of newer immigrants, leading to a sharp rise in the numbers of multi-ethnic workshops. This was harder to accomplish in Amsterdam and the Midlands, and entrepreneurs there faced serious survival problems, problems generated primarily, however, by regulatory matters.

MARKET DYNAMICS

Economic restructuring has severely affected the garment industry since World War II. Like many other old manufacturing sectors, the garment industry rationalized production and relocated some part of production to sites outside the traditional economic nodes, particularly to high unemployment areas in the interior and to low-wage countries. This coincided with changing fashion cycles, fragmented consumer tastes, and the breakdown of economies of scale. Until the 1960s, the market was characterized by gradual changes in fashion and was quite predictable, but today collections are changed constantly. Rapid fashion cycles, small and fragmented demands, and short lead times—all factors that do not mesh with economies of scale—have created ample opportunities for small garment factories. These producers supply small batches on short notice, enabling retailers to respond quickly to fashion changes or surges in demand for particular garments. Together, these processes have expanded local subcontracting systems, which involve a multitude of small contractors and home workers. Such putting out systems are not new; as Green (1997) demonstrates, these systems, with their characteristic chains of dependence, were already around in the early days of the industrial era.

The international link is clearly important, albeit in a specific local way. Contractors in the United States do not have to face competition from producers in North Africa, Turkey, or eastern Europe. However, they are operating in a market with contractors in the Mexican *maqui-*

ladoras and offshore contractors in Hong Kong and elsewhere in the Pacific Rim. Globalization—a convenient term to describe the internationalization of economic relations—overstates the case since, in reality, the scale of transactions is far less global. Economic transactions rarely cover the entire globe; they are usually restricted to certain regions, countries, or even districts, depending on regional or local conditions. As for that, Light and Ojeda (2002) argue that the success of the Los Angeles garment industry is contingent on the availability of a cheap and flexible immigrant workforce and on Hollywood's worldwide visibility. Without the prestige that the film industry confers on "California Look" clothing, the Los Angeles garment industry would not have developed as it did, and it would have shrunk significantly with the implementation of the North American Free Trade Agreement (NAFTA). Other cities obviously have no such appeal. In fact, the British Midlands evoke images of dirty smokestacks in leaden skies rather than the glitter of Tinsel Town and the pleasures of sunny California.

The role of manufacturers and retailers is of key importance. Large retailers—Macy's, Gap, Nordstrom, and K-Mart in the United States; Vendex/KBB, C&A, and P&C in the Netherlands; Marks & Spencer and two other leading chains in Britain—account for a substantial share of total garment sales and, with the exception of Gap, which manufactures and produces its own clothing, garment production as well. The fact that these retailers order large quantities of garments from independent manufacturers and contractors enables them to build up considerable corporate power. In this buyers' market, large retailers can play contractors off against each other. In recent decades, large retailers and manufacturers have improved the management of the production and marketing process, and this has affected the opportunity structure of small contractors. Zero stock control, made possible by modern technology, and computerized logistics have increasingly allowed retailers and manufacturers to improve their control over the production process, even if some parts of production take place offshore. In the Amsterdam case, this eventually undermined the market position of most of the Turkish contractors.

Immigrant contractors rarely produce army uniforms or haute couture. Instead, they specialize in lower- to medium-quality, fashionable or medium-fashionable outerwear, especially women's and junior outerwear. In some cases, especially in Los Angeles, they also specialize in sportswear. Los Angeles sells the "California Look." In Amsterdam, before market conditions started deteriorating, garment contractors accepted orders in the less fashionable market segments or engaged in other activities, such as wholesaling or import-export. In London, some of the Greek Cypriot entrepreneurs developed new products or even a new brand, which resulted in a considerable price markup. A more widespread technique, however, was design pinching, using the latest fashion designs without paying for them. These illegal practices are an obvious source of friction, especially if contractors pinch actual samples of a manufacturer's designs. Contractors also engage in "cabbage sales," which are essentially the official or unofficial "allowance" that a contractor squeezes out of the cloth and design provided by the manufacturer. These small batches, sold privately to small retailers or individual customers, constitute a source of extra income. Of course, cabbage sales are only possible if the contractor can do the cutting, turning this task into an important item in the negotiations with the manufacturer. Incidentally, this seems to be more typical in London. In most cases, cutting is part of the service supplied by jobbers.

MODELS OF REGULATION

Regulation influences immigrant entrepreneurs' opportunities through various and complex packages of do's and don'ts, incentives and disincentives, and persuasions. Governmental and nongovernmental regulation alike affects the opportunity structure at various levels.

There are diverse forms of governance at the supranational level. Europe was relatively protectionist with regard to imports in the early 1980s, especially under the second Multifiber Arrangement (MFA). However, the outlook changed in the 1990s, and European countries took steps to liberalize their markets. The European Union played a key role, granting additional import rights to specific nonmember states. Mediterranean and eastern European nonmembers benefited from this policy change to become major competitors of local garment contractors in Britain, France, and the Netherlands. Likewise, NAFTA encouraged garment factories to relocate to Mexico, to the detriment of the U.S. garment industry, although the negative impact was less in Los Angeles. Such supranational arrangements influence the international division of labor and regional economies, and together they help shape the immigrant contractors' opportunity structure.

National and local governments generally influence these entrepreneurs' opportunities more directly. At both levels, the general trend is toward market liberalization. On both sides of the Atlantic—first in the

United States and Britain, and later throughout Europe—governments have cleared the way for free enterprise. Changes in the rules governing the economy—tax reduction and the abolition of business licensing requirements, for example—have stimulated small entrepreneurship. These changes have largely coincided with the reassessments of the welfare state and the role of government in public life. Notwithstanding the similarities, each country—and in the Unites States, each state—dealt with these changed circumstances differently, depending on local political conditions. The various actors involved in political struggles over regulation advocate their own political goals, engage in different political coalitions, and sometimes achieve contradictory outcomes.

A closer review of regulation in our seven cases reveals striking differences that can be reduced to three basic regulatory models. These models differ in terms of the formal controls regarding small immigrant businesses, regulation implementation and enforcement, and the immigrant entrepreneurs' position in the political arena. The first model typifies a situation of ignorance, the second, a situation of active public support, and the third, strict application of nonpermissive regulation. Of course, the local situation is much more complicated than this simple typology suggests. After all, regulation is not static, it is not in the hands of a monolithic entity, and it certainly is not without contradictions. Still, I believe this typology can enhance our understanding of immigrant entrepreneurship in the garment sector.

Ignorance

Los Angeles fits the first model, characterized by substantial ignorance on the part of regulatory agencies, despite the political uproar of the early and mid-1990s. In an effort to improve labor code enforcement, California passed the Montoya Act in 1982, which requires garment contractors to register their factories. Since then, registered firms have been subject to unannounced state inspections, but nonregistration is still widespread, as are labor code violations. In practice, regulation in the California rag trade is rather lax, allowing garment entrepreneurs to violate rules and regulations—more specifically, to hire undocumented workers who then labor under extremely adverse conditions.

Some might argue that this situation reflects a spirit of free enterprise, an understanding of economic citizenship in which tasks and responsibilities are assigned to private individuals rather than to the state, and in which government interference serves only to frustrate economic growth. This argument is simplistic, if only because there *are* formal rules. Nevertheless, arguments of this kind inform a cultural resistance to law enforcement. Violations are overlooked on the assumption that the industry engages in self-regulation. Moreover, jurisdictions are jumbled, and several authorities share responsibility for law enforcement, a situation that enhances an administrative culture of ignorance—or even bribery. In fact, Light and Ojeda (2002) blame corruption in the political system for the blatant nonenforcement of laws. The garment industry, especially its larger firms, constitutes a political lobby that donates funds to California politicians' campaigns. In return, neoliberal politicians, once elected, have reduced law enforcement staffs below the minimum level required for effectiveness. In this light, one might well say that Los Angeles's regulatory model is only ignorant when it comes to the interests of small contractors and workers, since it clearly serves the interests of powerful garment manufacturers.

Neglecting the interests of the weaker actors in the garment sector has provoked an unanticipated outcome. Growing numbers of legal and illegal immigrants who are poorly paid, work under unhealthy conditions, and have no health insurance have turned to the emergency rooms of public hospitals for free medical care, and these costs are being passed on to taxpayers. In effect, tax-supported hospitals subsidize the health care of the garment industry's immigrant workers. There is a similar situation in the educational system. Illegal immigrants send their children to public schools, thereby increasing the costs of the system. This became a public issue in 1994 when California Republicans tried to capitalize on a growing anti-immigrant backlash in the white electorate. Prior efforts by the political left had failed to change the governance of the garment industry, but the right's anger over illegal immigrants using public money reinforced the campaign for stricter regulation. This undermined the prevailing tolerance toward informal practices and pressured employers to pay minimum wage and comply with the labor code and with industrial health and safety legislation. The new law enforcement regime, effective as of 1996, diminished the competitiveness of the garment industry in Los Angeles, but it also suggests that the period of ignorance has come to an end.

In this regard, Los Angeles, New York, and Miami have many features in common. Garment manufacturing was able to thrive in these cities as a result of a favorable immigration regime that allowed a steady influx of new immigrants, in combination with broad tolerance of informal practices. What distinguishes New York, however, is the role of organized labor. Through the unions, garment workers exert a certain political clout. This influences the employers' negotiating position and gives them less scope for the kind of exploitation we find in Los Angeles's outlaw economy. New York does not quite fit the model of ignorance. That being said, it has been reported that much of the immigrant garment sector falls outside union control. The situation in Miami is similar; Miami's garment industry traditionally had been unionized, but economic restructuring undercut unionization.

New York's garment industry, like those in Los Angeles and Miami, has been subject to federal government regulatory efforts. In the mid-1990s, the proliferation of sweatshops evoked growing public criticism, particularly when cases of abuse were disclosed and when Kathie Lee Gifford, a popular television personality, learned that some items in her own line of clothing were being produced under sweatshop conditions in New York's garment district. With public outrage mounting, President Bill Clinton established a presidential task force in 1996 to work toward eliminating sweatshops. The White House Apparel Industry Partnership, comprising companies, trade unions, and human rights and religious groups, formulated a Workplace Code of Conduct—but no new statutory penalties or enforcement efforts. In addition, key labor organizations—including UNITE, the AFL-CIO, and a large union of department store workers—rejected the code as a feeble effort to improve the sector. Y. Zhou (2002) states that the anti-sweatshop campaign did manage to deal with a number of violators, but nonunion sewing shops continue to proliferate, especially in Brooklyn, where many shops moved to escape regulation.

Support

The second regulatory model, illustrated by London, is characterized by strong and active state support for the SME sector in general and the rag trade in particular. Beginning with Margaret Thatcher, the British government has given strong support to small business on the premise that a thriving SME sector would help spread the capitalist ideology to the common people and speed the downfall of the left. Supporting small entrepreneurship was a characteristic Tory policy feature, which, interestingly, has been continued under Tony Blair's Labour government. This does not mean the government abstained from interfering prior to the rise of Thatcherism. On the contrary, during the industrial decline of the 1960s and 1970s, the central government was actively involved in rationalizing the textile and garment industry in the Midlands and North Britain. But as of the 1980s, the central government put more emphasis on developing the SME sector.

The central government's SME support is channeled through soft loans, training schemes, initiatives for inner-city employment, and various kinds of tax cuts. In addition, the government has abolished or relaxed various business regulations. Controls over working conditions, taxes, and social insurance have not been entirely discarded, but the government does not give high priority to controlling and regulating businesses, and it has underfunded the inspectorates. Furthermore, the United Kingdom, like France and the Netherlands, pursues a policy of restricted immigration. However, unlike France and the Netherlands, Britain's immigration policy is generally implemented at the border and only marginally implemented internally. Searching out undocumented aliens can easily equate to hunting "foreign" people, something forbidden under the 1976 Race Relations Act. Only after the mid-1990s, when illegality became a more politicized issue in Britain, did the central government intensify the checks and raids conducted by immigration and internal revenue officers.

These regulatory instances are not meant to suggest that London and Los Angeles are totally different. However, they are differentiated by the kind of regulation implemented by their respective governments. In the early 1980s, local policymakers in Britain considered garment businesses a useful vehicle for promoting objectives ranging from more jobs to racial equality. They engaged in efforts to combat unemployment, protect their constituencies from the economic crisis, counteract racist exclusion, and empower immigrant minorities. The social deprivation that immigrant minorities were suffering was felt to result largely from racism, and the central government was perceived as insufficiently concerned about this serious problem. In response to a series of riots in the early 1980s, particularly the Brixton riots in 1981, a government committee, chaired by the Tory Lord Scarman, recommended promoting entrepreneurship as an antidote to urban racial deprivation. Given the characteristics of the London economy, promoting small entrepreneurship in the rag trade was a logical choice; even in the economic downturn, the rag trade was exhibiting striking vitality because of the demand for higher-value fashion, style, and quality, along with short response times.

The Greater London Council (GLC) and several London boroughs (including Haringey and Hackney) have actively fostered small firms in the garment industry. Not accidentally, all were Labour controlled, reflecting a realignment in local Labour Party politics, with minorities becoming more prominent and winning increased political representation. The GLC and the boroughs implemented various measures aimed at collective services for the sector as a whole, but with special attention devoted to ethnic firms and cooperatives. The measures included decriminalizing homework and easing regulations on building use.

The GLC, which proved to be very controversial, was abolished in 1986; the boroughs ceased their interventions as well. In the mid-1990s, after a decade of nonintervention, attention turned to the rag trade once more, this time in the context of urban renewal. The boroughs of Hackney and Haringey earmarked urban renewal funding for entrepreneurs. In Hackney, a garment-manufacturing zone was developed to promote flexible specialization and to reinforce links between chain stores and local garment factories. These interventions lacked the strong ideological underpinnings that had been typical of the interventions in the early 1980s.

This specific regulatory history is linked to the differentiation of immigrant entrepreneurs. A number of upwardly mobile Greek Cypriots and other immigrant minority entrepreneurs achieved a place in the higher tiers of the industry. These manufacturers were in a stronger economic position, more integrated in the local host society, better embedded in community organizations, and better placed to benefit from state support. The local Labour Party accepted them as ready-made partners, and some became major beneficiaries of local government support. Some of the more successful entrepreneurs also served as political brokers vis-à-vis community representatives and policymakers. Their empowerment was a crucial factor in reshaping relations between garment entrepreneurs and regulatory agencies, and it also informed the regulatory response, be it soft or harsh, promotion or repression.

Notwithstanding Labour Party efforts, the London rag trade retained its sweatshop image. Although some garment entrepreneurs moved up and gained more political power, most stayed on the fringes of the urban economy. This being said, the interventions did save a number of jobs and create several hundred new ones.

A rather different situation in Birmingham and surrounding towns illustrates the role played by local contingencies. Entrepreneurs in the Midlands operate under the same national regulatory framework, but the local situation looks more like Los Angeles. Ram, Jerrard, and Husband (2002) argue that local interventions there have been largely symbolic and have not really affected the position of garment firms. Moreover, the political link between upwardly mobile garment entrepreneurs and major political parties has not been well developed.

Strict Law Enforcement

The third model of regulation is typified by Amsterdam's current strict law enforcement (see Dreef n.d.). Prior to 1989 Amsterdam more appropriately fit the "ignorance" model; the policy shift from the former to the latter is intriguing because it goes against the general tide of regulation in the SME sector. Until recently in the Dutch welfare state, people who wanted to start a business were legally required to have appropriate qualifications and permits and to register. In the 1980s, this system came to be viewed as overly rigid and as an obstacle to full economic development. The government embarked on a fundamental economic reform,[5] and deregulation became the buzzword, much to the business community's satisfaction. The aim was to liberalize the business sector wherever possible and keep regulation to a minimum. The system of rules, qualifications, and permits was cut to the bone. The first effects became apparent in the mid-1990s when the economy experienced record growth, partly due to an unprecedented rise in the number of small businesses.

In the 1980s, when the old regulatory system was still in place, new immigrant garment entrepreneurs typically failed to comply with the rules. Curiously, the state did not take a firm line on these informal activities. Apart from a few officials at the Ministry of Social Affairs and Employment, the government as a whole took little notice, which underscores the importance of distinguishing between rules and their enforcement. Local authorities chose to tolerate the informal practices because of the high unemployment rates among immigrants and the government's inability to provide them with jobs, which, in turn, underlines the importance of distinguishing between various levels of regulation. The authorities welcomed any business that could create jobs and thus contribute to the immigrants' social integration and, perhaps also, to the revival of Amsterdam as an international garment manufacturing center. They were prepared to tolerate informal practices

---

[5] To be sure, the employment and welfare fields have undergone reforms but not to the same extent as the business sector.

temporarily because stricter law enforcement would only frustrate economic progress. Amsterdam and its metropolitan police therefore prioritized hunting down criminals and illegal immigrants who were a nuisance to society, rather than badgering hardworking entrepreneurs.

This tolerance began to give way at the national level around 1990 under a new government whose central policy objectives included welfare reform. The Labour Party, fearing social unrest among its grassroots supporters, negotiated a political alternative: combating illegal residence and the improper use of welfare benefits would reduce public spending and lower the pressure for harsh welfare reforms. The minister of social affairs and employment considered the rag trade an obvious place to put this strategy into practice. In anticipation, the sector was encouraged to self-regulate, and leading business associations introduced several programs for this purpose, though to little avail. In 1994, a package of measures was introduced whose direct consequences included the formation of the Clothing Intervention Team, which paid visits to suspicious Turkish sewing shops and organized frequent raids. Their raids resulted in charges against numerous people for hiring undocumented immigrants, evading taxes, and failing to pay social security premiums. This contributed to the downfall of immigrant contractors, who were already facing increasing international competition.

The trade unions and FENECON (the garment manufacturers association), which had lobbied for strict law enforcement, welcomed the crackdown on the illegal sewing shops. Unlike the situation in London, where raids on undocumented immigrants led to social and political unease in the local community, the events in Amsterdam did not cause a public outcry. The Turkish community did try to mobilize political forces, and a casual organization of Turkish garment entrepreneurs tried to promote the contractors' interests, but they were insufficiently embedded in the local polity to have an impact.

Cities occasionally engage in law enforcement campaigns, though usually not as vigorously as was the case in Amsterdam. In recent years the French government has cracked down on labor and capital practices, especially targeting "creative accounting" and illegal labor. These regulatory changes are often triggered by specific events, and the rag trade seems to abound in them. In Amsterdam in the early 1990s, a plane crashed into a resident tenement, killing many dozens of its undocumented immigrant residents; this incident helped the government gain popular support for its crackdown. In Los Angeles, the anti-sweatshop movement gained momentum in 1996 after a factory raid in El Monte uncovered seventy-two Thai immigrants, mostly women, working as industrial slaves in a guarded compound. Another factor was the Kathie Lee Gifford incident mentioned earlier. Sadly, the role of such coincidences is not new in the rag trade. Concerns about the social conditions of London's poor and a moral panic directed against Jewish immigrants resulted in the United Kingdom's 1905 Aliens Act (Panayiotopoulos and Dreef 2002).

LONG-TERM OUTLOOK

Fluctuating styles, widespread subcontracting, homework, and immigrant labor have been part and parcel of the rag trade ever since it was mechanized and standardized in the late nineteenth century. This suggests that the garment industry, and its tier of immigrant contactors, will continue to exist in advanced economies in one way or another. Despite fears that the SME sector was in jeopardy and that garment manufacturing would relocate to low-wage countries, small businesses in this sector have demonstrated striking resilience.

At the beginning of 2000, the Los Angeles garment industry was still thriving, thanks to two local factors: the powerful image of the "California Look" and the sector's access to illegal immigrant labor. Nevertheless, local manufacturers were fully aware of the processes that had already hurt them. They noted that manufacturing in Los Angeles had been in decline for over three decades, that the garment industry had suffered an outflow of production jobs to Mexico following NAFTA's implementation in 1994, and that stepped-up immigration controls had made them the target of public outrage.

In addition to facing intense international competition, New York's garment industry has been negatively impacted by a number of factors, including slow population growth and the aging of the population. At the same time, deregulation and improved logistics have narrowed the time-space gap between domestic and offshore producers, to the detriment of domestic firms. Moreover, a market shift toward large retailers and the contraction of the local manufacturing sector have pressured New York garment producers to focus on higher-value-added products. They now emphasize more styles, higher quality, and better service. It remains to be seen whether new immigrants can survive in such a demanding environment.

These cases demonstrate that the survival of garment manufacturing in advanced economies cannot be taken for granted, given the political and economic processes that threaten the sector. Interestingly, the cases also demonstrate that the perspective of small immigrant contractors is linked to local market characteristics, be it the appeal of the Californian Look or New York's short lifecycle for quality fashion products. The Midlands and Amsterdam cases, however, suggest that, in some instances, local market characteristics only help accelerate the decline of the contractor sector.

Local market features obviously matter, but so does regulation. For a long time, immigrant contractors survived by capitalizing on their social networks. In doing so, they drew more new immigrants, both legal and illegal and willing to work long hours. In addition to their privileged access to cheap and flexible labor, the fact that these contractors tend to skirt the rules and evade taxes gave them an even greater competitive edge—until law enforcement agencies stopped overlooking these informal practices. Paradoxically, under deregulation, tolerance for such practices is decreasing. In each country under study, there is a perception that thin regulation is a necessary condition for economic growth. There is also, however, growing public awareness that the absence of regulation sometimes leads to excesses and can fuel anti-sweatshop campaigns and crackdowns.

Deregulation of business regimes has not come accompanied by deregulation of immigration regimes. On the contrary, in Europe and the United States, immigration, especially of unskilled immigrants, is tighter now that illegality has become a political issue. There is a decrease in tolerance for undocumented immigrants and an increase in immigration controls, even though controls are usually not as tough as in the Amsterdam case. Irrespective of legitimacy, strict immigration controls have a detrimental effect on any sector that depends on cheap and flexible labor, usually new unskilled immigrants. These controls also undermine the power of network mobilization, especially if the pool of cheap and flexible labor is shrinking. This is particularly apparent in the Midlands and Amsterdam.

To what extent tight immigration controls will remain in force is unclear. In Europe and the United States—public opposition notwithstanding—debates are taking places about relaxing immigration rules. Although immigration is a national policy issue, local authorities sometimes take a position against immigration control in the interests of the local community. This, too, may contribute to the local variations in an otherwise globalized industry.

References

Allen, J.P., and E. Turner. 1997. *The Ethnic Guilt: Population Diversity in Southern California*. Northridge, Calif.: California State University.

Bates, Timothy. 1997. *Race, Self-Employment, and Upward Mobility: An Illusive American Dream*. Baltimore, Md.: Johns Hopkins University Press.

Bonacich, E. 1993. "The Other Side of Ethnic Entrepreneurship: A Dialogue with Waldinger, Aldrich, Ward and Associates," *International Migration Review* 27, no. 3 (Fall): 685–92.

Bonacich, E., and R.P. Appelbaum. 2000. *Behind the Label: Inequality in the Los Angeles Apparel Industry*. Berkeley: University of California Press.

Bonacich, E., L. Cheng, N. Chinchilla, N. Hamilton, and P. Ong. 1994. *Global Production: The Apparel Industry in the Pacific Rim*. Philadelphia, Penn.: Temple University Press.

Bovenkerk, F., R. Miles, and G. Verbunt. 1990. "Racism, Migration and the State in Western Europe: A Case for Comparative Analysis," *International Sociology* 5, no. 4 (December): 475–90.

Collins, J., K. Gibson, C. Alcorso, S. Castles, and D. Tait. 1995. *A Shop Full of Dreams: Ethnic Small Business in Australia*. Sydney: Pluto Press Australia.

Dreef, M.E.P. n.d. "Politiek, Migranten en Informele Economie, Politieke en Bestuurlijke Ontwikkelingen met Betrekking tot de Amsterdamse Naaiateliers 1980–1997." Ph.D. dissertation, University of Amsterdam. Forthcoming.

Engelen, E. 2001. "Breaking In and Breaking Out: A Weberian Approach to Entrepreneurial Opportunities," *Journal of Ethnic and Migration Studies*, special issue on "Immigrant Entrepreneurship," edited by R. Kloosterman and J. Rath, vol. 27, no. 2 (April): 203–23.

Epstein, R.A. 1994. "The Moral and Practical Dilemmas of an Underground Economy," *Yale Law Journal* 103, no. 8: 2157–78.

Farina, P., D. Cologna, A. Lanzani, and L. Breveglieri. 1997. *Cina a Milano. Famiglie, ambienti e lavori della popolazione cinese a Milano*. Milan: Associazione Interessi Metropolitani.

Favell, A. 1999. "Integration Policy and Integration Research in Europe: A Review and Critique." In *Citizenship: Comparisons and Perspectives*, edited by A. Aleinikoff and D. Klusmeyer. Washington, D.C.: The Brookings Institution.

Fröbel, F., J. Heinrichs, and O. Kreye. 1980. *The New International Division of Labour: Structural Unemployment in Industrial Countries and Industrialisation in Developing Countries*. Cambridge: Cambridge University Press.

Gemeente Amsterdam. 2000. *Amsterdam in Cijfers: Jaarboek 2000*. Amsterdam: Bureau O+S.

Green, N.L. 1986. "Immigrant Labor in the Garment Industries of New York and Paris. Variations on a Structure," *Comparative Social Research* 9: 231–43.

———. 1997. *Ready-to-Wear and Ready-to-Work: A Century of Industry and Immigrants in Paris and New York.* Durham, N.C.: Duke University Press.

———. 2002. "Paris: A Historical View." In *Unravelling the Rag Trade: Immigrant Entrepreneurship in Seven World Cities,* edited by J. Rath. Oxford: Berg/University of New York Press.

Grenier, G., and A. Stepick 2002. "Miami: Ethnic Succession and Failed Restructuring." In *Unravelling the Rag Trade: Immigrant Entrepreneurship in Seven World Cities,* edited by J. Rath. Oxford: Berg/University of New York Press.

Hiebert, D. 1990. "Discontinuity and the Emergence of Flexible Production: Garment Production in Toronto, 1901–1931," *Economic Geography* 66, no. 3 (July): 229–53.

———. 1993. "Jewish Immigrants and the Garment Industry of Toronto, 1901–1931: A Study of Ethnic and Class Relations," *Annals of the Association of American Geographers* 83, no. 2: 243–71.

———. 2002. "Economic Associations of Immigrant Self-Employment in Canada," *International Journal of Entrepreneurial Behaviour and Research* 8, nos. 3–4.

Kloosterman, R., and J. Rath. 2001. "Immigrant Entrepreneurs in Advanced Economies: Mixed Embeddedness Further Explored," *Journal of Ethnic and Migration Studies,* special issue on "Immigrant Entrepreneurship," edited by R. Kloosterman and J. Rath, vol. 27, no. 2 (April): 189–202.

———. 2003. *Immigrant Entrepreneurs: Venturing Abroad in the Age of Globalization.* Oxford: University of New York Press.

Lee, J. 1999. "Retail Niche Domination among African American, Jewish and Korean Entrepreneurs: Competition, Coethnic Advantage and Disadvantage," *American Behavioral Scientist* 42, no. 9 (June/July): 1398–1416.

Light, I. 1972. *Ethnic Enterprise in America: Business and Welfare among Chinese, Japanese, and Blacks.* Berkeley: University of California Press.

———. 2000. "Globalisation and Migration Networks." In *Immigrant Businesses: The Economic, Political and Social Environment,* edited by J. Rath. Houndmills: Macmillan Press and St. Martin's Press.

Light, I., and S.J. Gold. 2000. *Ethnic Economies.* San Diego, Calif.: Academic Press.

Light, I., and R.E. Isralowitz, eds. 1997. *Immigrant Entrepreneurs and Immigrant Absorption in the United States and Israel.* Aldershot: Ashgate.

Light, I., and V.D. Ojeda. 2002. "Los Angeles: Wearing out their Welcome." In *Unravelling the Rag Trade: Immigrant Entrepreneurship in Seven World Cities,* edited by J. Rath. Oxford: Berg/University of New York Press.

Light, I., and C. Rosenstein. 1995. *Race, Ethnicity, and Entrepreneurship in Urban America.* New York: Aldine de Gruyter.

Marx, Karl. 1973. *Grundrisse: Foundations of the Political Economy.* Harmondsworth: Penguin.

Metcalf, H., T. Modood, and S. Virdee. 1996. *Asian Self-Employment. The Interaction of Culture and Economics in England*. London: Policy Studies Institute.

Miles, R. 1989. *Racism*. London: Routledge.

Morokvasic, M. 1988a. "Garment Production in a Metropole of Fashion: Small Enterprise, Immigrants and Immigrant Entrepreneurs," *Economic and Industrial Democracy* 9, no. 1 (February): 83–97.

———. 1988b. *Minority and Immigrant Women in Self-Employment and Business in France, Great Britain, Italy, Portugal, and the Federal Republic of Germany*. V/1871/88-Engl. Paris: European Economic Community.

———. 1991. "Roads to Independence: Self-Employed Immigrants and Minority Women in Five European States," *International Migration Review* 29, no. 3 (September): 407–20.

———. 1993. "Immigrants in Garment Production in Paris and Berlin." In *Immigration and Entrepreneurship: Culture, Capital, and Ethnic Networks*, edited by I. Light and P. Bhachu. New Brunswick: Transaction.

Morokvasic, M., A. Phizacklea, and H. Rudolph. 1986. "Small Firms and Minority Groups: Contradictory Trends in the French, German and British Clothing Industries," *International Sociology* 1, no. 4: 397–419.

Morokvasic, M., R. Waldinger, and A. Phizacklea. 1990. "Business on the Ragged Edge: Immigrant and Minority Business in the Garment Industries of Paris, London, and New York." In *Ethnic Entrepreneurs: Immigrant Business in Industrial Societies*, edited by R. Waldinger, H. Aldrich, R. Ward, and Associates. Newbury Park, Calif.: Sage.

Panayiotopoulos, I., and M. Dreef. 2002. "London: Economic Differentiation and Policy-Making." In *Unravelling the Rag Trade: Immigrant Entrepreneurship in Seven World Cities*, edited by J. Rath. Oxford: Berg/University of New York Press.

Persky, J., and W. Wiewel. 1994. "The Growing Localness of the Global City," *Economic Geography* 70: 129–43.

Phizacklea, A. 1990. *Unpacking the Fashion Industry*. London: Routledge and Kegan Paul.

Polanyi, K. 1957. *The Great Transformation*. Boston, Mass.: Beacon.

Raes, S. 2000a. *Migrating Enterprise and Migrant Entrepreneurship: How Fashion and Migration Have Changed the Spatial Organisation of Clothing Supply to Consumers in The Netherlands*. Amsterdam: Het Spinhuis.

———. 2000b. "Regionalization in a Globalizing World: The Emergence of Clothing Sweatshops in the European Union." In *Immigrant Businesses: The Economic, Political and Social Environment*, edited by J. Rath. Houndmills: Macmillan and St. Martin's Press.

Raes, S., J. Rath, M. Dreef, A. Kumcu, F. Reil, and A. Zorlu. 2002. "Amsterdam: Stitched Up." In *Unravelling the Rag Trade: Immigrant Entrepreneurship in Seven World Cities*, edited by J. Rath. Oxford: Berg/University of New York Press.

Ram, M. 1993. *Managing to Survive: Working Lives in Small Firms*. Oxford: Blackwell.

Ram, M., B. Jerrard, and J. Husband. 2002. "The West Midlands: Still Managing to Survive." In *Unravelling the Rag Trade: Immigrant Entrepreneurship in Seven World Cities*, edited by J. Rath. Oxford: Berg/University of New York Press.

Rath, J. 2000. "Immigrant Businesses and Their Embeddedness in the Economic, Politico-Institutional and Social Environment." In *Immigrant Businesses: The Economic, Political and Social Environment*, edited by J. Rath. Houndmills: Macmillan and St. Martin's Press.

———. 2002a. *Unravelling the Rag Trade: Immigrant Entrepreneurship in Seven World Cities*. Oxford: University of New York Press.

———. 2002b. "Do Immigrant Entrepreneurs Play the Game of Ethnic Musical Chairs? A Critique of Waldinger's Model of Immigrant Incorporation." In *West Europe Immigration and Immigrant Policy in the New Century*, edited by A. Messina. Westport, Conn.: Praeger.

Rath, J., ed. 2000a. *Immigrant Businesses: The Economic, Political and Social Environment*. Houndmills: Macmillan and St. Martin's Press.

Rath, J., and R. Kloosterman. 2000. "Outsiders' Business: A Critical Review of Research on Immigrant Entrepreneurship," *International Migration Review* 34, no. 3 (Fall): 657–81.

Rogerson, C.M. 1999. *Johannesburg's Clothing Industry: The Role of African Immigrant Entrepreneurs*. Report for BEES.

———. 2000. "Successful SMEs in South Africa: The Case of Clothing Producers in the Witwatersrand," *Development Southern Africa* 17, no. 5: 687–716.

Saxenian, A. 1999. *Silicon Valley's New Immigrant Entrepreneurs*. San Francisco: Public Policy Institute of California.

Swedberg, R. 1994. "Markets as Social Structures." In *The Handbook of Economic Sociology*, edited by N.J. Smelser and R. Swedberg. Princeton, N.J.: Princeton University Press and Russell Sage Foundation.

———. 1998. *Max Weber and the Idea of Economic Sociology*. Princeton, N.J.: Princeton University Press.

Waldinger, R.D. 1986. *Through the Eye of the Needle: Immigrants and Enterprise in New York's Garment Trades*. New York: New York University Press.

———. 1996a. "From Ellis Island to LAX: Immigrant Prospects in the American City," *International Migration Review* 30, no. 4 (Winter): 1078–86.

———. 1996b. *Still the Promised City? African-Americans and New Immigrants in Postindustrial New York*. Cambridge, Mass.: Harvard University Press.

Waldinger, R., R. Aldrich, R. Ward, and Associates. 1990. *Ethnic Entrepreneurs: Immigrant Business in Industrial Societies*. Newbury Park, Calif.: Sage.

Waldinger, R., and M. Bozorgmehr. 1996. *Ethnic Los Angeles*. New York: Russell Sage Foundation.

Weber, M. 1968. *Economy and Society: An Outline of Interpretative Sociology*. Berkeley: University of California Press.

Werbner, P. 1980. "From Rags to Riches: Manchester Pakistanis in the Textile Trade," *New Community* 8, nos. 1–2 (Spring–Summer): 84–95.

———. 1984. "Business on Trust: Pakistani Entrepreneurship in the Manchester Garment Trade." In *Ethnic Communities in Business: Strategies for Economic Survival*, edited by R. Ward and R. Jenkins. Cambridge: Cambridge University Press.

———. 2000. "What Colour 'Success'? Distorting Value in Studies of Ethnic Entrepreneurship." In *Immigrants, Schooling and Social Mobility: Does Culture Make a Difference?* edited by H. Vermeulen and J. Perlmann. Houndmills: Macmillan and St. Martin's Press.

Wong, B. 1998. *Ethnicity and Entrepreneurship: The New Chinese Immigrants in the San Francisco Bay Area*. Boston, Mass.: Allyn and Bacon.

Yoo, J.K. 1998. *Korean Immigrant Entrepreneurs: Networks and Ethnic Resources*. New York: Garland.

Yoon, I.Y. 1997. *On My Own: Korean Businesses and Race Relations in America*. Chicago: University of Chicago Press.

Zhou, M. 1992. *Chinatown: The Socioeconomic Potential of an Urban Enclave*. Philadelphia, Penn.: Temple University Press.

Zhou, Y. 2002. "New York: Caught under the Fashion Runway." In *Unravelling the Rag Trade: Immigrant Entrepreneurship in Seven World Cities*, edited by J. Rath. Oxford: Berg/University of New York Press.

Zincone, G., ed. 2000. *Primo Rapporto sull'Integrazione degli Immigrati in Italia*. Comissione per le Politiche di Integrazione degli Immigratie. Bologna: Società Editrice il Mulino.

Part III

Governments and Immigrant Incorporation

11

Welfare Reform and Immigrant Participation in Welfare Programs

George J. Borjas

"It's just obvious that you can't have free immigration and a welfare state."
—Milton Friedman

The concern that immigrants may become "public charges" has always been a central component of the debate over immigration policy in the United States. Two related issues have dominated recent discussions over the potential link between immigration and welfare. The first is the perception that there was a rapid rise in the number of immigrants who received public assistance between 1970 and 1990. Although early studies of immigrant participation in welfare programs concluded that immigrant households had a lower probability of receiving public assistance than U.S.-born households, many studies conducted in the 1990s documented that this "stylized fact" was no longer correct—immigrant households had become more likely to receive public assistance than native households.[1] By 1996 Borjas and Hilton (1996) reported that if one included both cash and noncash benefits (such as Medicaid and food stamps) in the definition of welfare, nearly 21 percent of immigrants received some type of assistance, as compared to

[1] The early studies include Blau 1984 and Tienda and Jensen 1986. Borjas and Trejo (1991) provided some of the first evidence that documented the rise in welfare participation rates in the immigrant population.

only 14 percent of natives. The increased enrollment of immigrants in welfare programs spawned a rapidly growing literature that attempts to determine if immigrants "pay their way" in the welfare state. This metric, in turn, has become an important part of any cost-benefit calculation of the economic impact of immigration.[2]

There is also concern over the possibility that the relatively generous welfare programs offered by the United States have become a magnet for immigrants. The magnet hypothesis has several facets. It is possible, for example, that welfare programs attract immigrants who otherwise would not have migrated to the United States, or that the safety net discourages immigrants who "fail" in the United States from returning to their source countries, or that the huge interstate dispersion in welfare benefits affects the residential location choices of immigrants in the United States and places a heavy fiscal burden on relatively generous states. In short, the welfare state creates a magnet that influences the migration decisions of persons in the source countries, potentially changing the composition and geographic location of the immigrant population in the United States in ways that may not be desirable. The potential magnetic effects of welfare raise questions about both the political legitimacy and the economic viability of the welfare state: Who is entitled to the safety net that American taxpayers pay for? And can the United States afford to extend that safety net to the rest of the world? Surprisingly, and despite their potential significance, few studies attempt to determine if such magnetic effects exist or if they are empirically important.[3]

In 1996, Congress responded to these concerns by including key immigrant-related provisions in the Personal Responsibility and Work Opportunity Reconciliation Act (PRWORA). This legislation specified a new set of rules for determining the eligibility of foreign-born persons to receive practically all types of public assistance. In rough terms, PRWORA denies most types of means-tested assistance to noncitizens

---

[2] The recent report of the National Academy of Sciences on the economic impact of immigration (Smith and Edmonston 1997) devotes two chapters to calculating the net fiscal impact. Storesletten 2000 presents a valuable theoretical discussion of this issue.

[3] The exceptions include Borjas (1999a), who examines the geographic distribution of foreign-born welfare recipients in the United States, and Olsen and Reagan (1996), who analyze if welfare participation affects the probability of out-migration for foreign-born persons in the National Longitudinal Surveys of Youth.

who arrived after the legislation was signed, and it limited the eligibility of many noncitizens already living in the United States.

A few studies have already examined the post-1996 trends in welfare use by immigrant households. Fix and Passel (1999) and Borjas (1999b) show that the rate of welfare participation among immigrant households declined sharply—relative to the decline experienced by native households—after the welfare reform legislation was enacted in 1996.[4] The decline is particularly remarkable since most of the provisions for removing immigrants already living in the United States from the welfare rolls were never enforced. Moreover, only a small part of the immigrant population present in the United States in the late 1990s arrived after 1996, making it unlikely that these ineligible new arrivals could have such a dramatic impact on the national trend. The steeper drop in the rate of welfare use experienced by immigrant households led an influential Urban Institute study to conclude that, "because comparatively few legal immigrants were ineligible for public benefits as of December 1997, it appears that the steeper declines in noncitizens' than citizens' use of welfare ... owe more to the 'chilling effect' of welfare reform and other policy changes than they do to actual eligibility changes" (Fix and Passel 1999: 8).

This chapter provides a detailed empirical examination of the impact of PRWORA on welfare participation in immigrant households. The data clearly indicate that the welfare participation rate of immigrants declined relative to that of natives *at the national level*. It turns out, however, that this national trend is *entirely* attributable to the trends in welfare participation in California. Although immigrants living in California experienced a precipitous drop in their welfare participation rate (relative to natives), immigrants living outside California experienced the same decline in participation rates as natives living in those states.

The empirical analysis presented in this chapter shows that the potential impact of welfare reform on immigrants residing outside California was neutralized because both state governments and the immigrants themselves responded to the new political landscape by altering their behavior. In particular, many immigrant-receiving states chose to provide state-funded benefits to their foreign-born populations after 1996. Further, many immigrants quickly learned that they could bypass

---

[4] Espenshade, Baraka, and Huber (1997) present an early assessment of the presumed effects of welfare reform on various socioeconomic outcomes in the immigrant population.

many of the new restrictions on welfare eligibility by becoming naturalized citizens. The very steep decline of immigrant welfare participation in California is harder to understand, but it could be a by-product of the seismic shift that occurred in the mid-1990s in the social contract between California's native population and immigrants when a large majority of California's voters enacted Proposition 187.

HISTORICAL PERSPECTIVE

The limitations on immigrant welfare use included in PRWORA are but the latest in a long line of restrictions, dating back to colonial days, designed to reduce the costs that immigration imposes on resident taxpayers.[5] As early as 1645 and 1655, the Massachusetts colony enacted legislation that prohibited the entry of poor or indigent persons (Albright 1928). In 1691, New York introduced a bonding system designed to discourage the entry of potential public charges: "All persons that shall come to Inhabit within this Province ... and hath not a visible Estate, or hath not a manual occupation shall before he be admitted an Inhabitant give sufficient surety, that he shall not be a burden or charge to the respective places, he shall come to Inhabit" (Hutchinson 1981: 391).

The U.S. Congress first considered the problems arising from the immigration of public charges in 1836, and reconsidered this issue several times between 1840 and 1880 without taking any action.[6] In 1876, however, the Supreme Court unambiguously granted the federal government the sole authority to control immigration, invalidating all the state laws that restricted the entry of poor immigrants. The states most affected by immigration lobbied Congress to grant them relief from the costs imposed by (a nonexistent) federal immigration policy, and Congress responded in 1882 by banning the entry of "any persons unable to take care of himself or herself without becoming a public charge." The wording of this exclusion was changed in 1891 to ban the entry of "persons *likely* to become a public charge" (emphasis added). In 1903 Congress went further and approved the deportation of immigrants who became public charges within two years after arrival in the United States "for causes existing prior to their landing."

---

[5] Edwards (2001) presents a nice discussion of the role that the public charge provision has played in immigration policy throughout U.S. history.

[6] Hutchinson (1981) presents a detailed history of the public charge restrictions in U.S. immigration policy up until 1965.

The current restrictions on public charges have changed little since the beginning of the twentieth century. Section 212(a)(4) of the Immigration and Nationality Act declares that: "Any alien who, in the opinion of the consular officer at the time of application for a visa, or in the opinion of the Attorney General at the time of application for admission or adjustment of status, is likely at any time to become a public charge is inadmissible." The legislation specifies that the factors to be taken into account in determining whether an alien is excludable include age, health, family status, assets, financial status, and education and skills. In addition, Section 237(5) states that: "Any alien who, within five years after the date of entry, has become a public charge from causes not affirmatively shown to have arisen since entry is deportable."

Despite the presence of the public charge provisions in immigration law throughout the twentieth century, the Immigration and Naturalization Service (INS) did not interpret the receipt of public assistance by foreign-born persons in the United States as a potential ground for the deportation of immigrants. In fact, it is extremely rare for an immigrant to be deported on public charge grounds—only thirty-nine immigrants were deported for this reason between 1961 and 1980.[7] In 1999 the INS published a regulation that for the first time outlined the link between the receipt of public assistance and the definition of a public charge.[8] In particular, a public charge is an alien who has become "primarily dependent on the government for subsistence, as demonstrated by either the receipt of public cash assistance for income maintenance, or institutionalization for long-term care at government expense." By definition, the receipt of such noncash benefits as Medicaid and food stamps does not enter into the consideration of whether an immigrant is a public charge. Moreover, even if the immigrant receives cash benefits, immigration law requires that the INS consider other factors—such as age, assets, and skills—in making the public charge determination.[9]

Although the INS did not link the receipt of public assistance and the public charge provision of immigration law between the 1960s and 1990s, it ultimately became apparent that the number of immigrants

---

[7] In contrast, a total of 22,548 immigrants were deported on public charge grounds between 1908 and 1960. See INS 1997: 187.

[8] *Federal Register* 64, no. 101 (May 26, 1999): 28,676–28,688.

[9] The regulation also states that an alien can be deported on public charge grounds only if the alien has failed to comply "with a legally enforceable duty to reimburse the assistance agency for the costs of care."

receiving public assistance was rising rapidly. The U.S. Congress reacted to this trend by making it increasingly difficult for immigrants to qualify for some types of public benefits. Beginning in 1980, immigrants began to be subject to so-called deeming requirements, where the sponsors' income is "deemed" to be part of the immigrant's application for particular types of assistance. This deeming procedure obviously reduces the chances that new immigrants qualify for welfare. The initial deeming rules applied only to SSI (Supplemental Security Income) and lasted only three years, but they were later expanded to AFDC (Aid to Families with Dependent Children) and other programs.

By 1996 Congress tightened the eligibility requirements substantially by including a number of immigrant-related provisions in PRWORA. It has been estimated that almost half of the US$54 billion savings attributed to the welfare reform bill can be traced directly to the restrictions on immigrant use of welfare (Primus 1996–97: 14). In general terms, the legislation, as signed by President Clinton, contained three key provisions:

- Most noncitizens who arrived in the country *before* August 22, 1996, the "pre-enactment" immigrants, were to be kicked off the SSI and food stamp rolls within a year. (This provision of the legislation, however, was never fully enforced.)
- Immigrants who entered the United States *after* August 22, 1996, the "post-enactment" immigrants, are prohibited from receiving most types of public assistance. The ban is lifted when the immigrant becomes an American citizen.
- Post-enactment immigrants are subject to stricter deeming regulations. The eligible income and assets of the immigrant's sponsor will be deemed to be part of the immigrant's application for most types of public assistance, and the deeming period can last up to ten years.[10]

One can loosely interpret the second of these provisions as setting up a five-year "waiting period" before post-enactment immigrants can qualify for public assistance. After five years in the United States, the immigrant can apply for naturalization, and if the application is suc-

---

10 The legislation also tightened the rules for sponsorship. The income of immigrants who reside legally in the United States and who wish to sponsor the entry of family members must exceed 125 percent of the poverty line. The sponsors must also file affidavits of support that are legally binding, making the sponsor financially liable for many of the expenses incurred by the immigrant.

cessful (as it typically is), the ban on immigrant use of welfare is lifted. Partly because of the increasing importance in the distinction between citizens and noncitizens, there was a rapid rise in the number of immigrants who wished to become naturalized in the early 1990s. In 1991 the INS received only 207,000 petitions for naturalization; in 1997 it received 1.4 million (INS 1997: 142).

The restrictions on immigrant use of welfare brought together a number of powerful interest groups after the 1996 presidential election—all of which lobbied hard for their repeal. And in fact many of the immigrant-related provisions of the legislation were never enforced. The balanced budget agreement reached in 1997 between President Clinton and the Republican-controlled Congress repealed the most draconian aspects of the legislation, such as kicking out the pre-enactment immigrants from the SSI and Food Stamp programs. The mandated waiting period for post-enactment immigrants, however, remained on the books. Table 11.1 presents a more detailed summary of the existing restrictions that the welfare reform legislation (and subsequent amendments) impose on immigrant welfare use.

TRENDS IN WELFARE RECIPIENCY: 1994–1998

The Current Population Surveys (CPS) began to collect information on the immigration status of survey participants in 1994. The Annual Demographic Files (also known as the March Supplement) of the CPS provide information on participation in various types of social assistance programs during the calendar year prior to the survey. The CPS data contain relatively large numbers of observations (about 50,000 households per survey), thus permitting a statistically reliable study of socioeconomic outcomes even in relatively small populations.

I used data drawn from the 1995–1999 CPS March Supplements to conduct the empirical analysis reported in this chapter.[11] These surveys

---

[11] I do not use the 1994 Current Population Survey in the analysis because that survey provided limited information on the national origin of immigrants and because there seem to be some problems with the statistics that can be calculated in the foreign-born sample in this survey. In particular, the "official" person weights provided in this survey (as well as in the 1995 CPS) do not yield an accurate enumeration of the immigrant population in the United States. Passel (1996) provides a detailed discussion of this problem and uses a complex algorithm to calculate revised weights for each person in both the 1994 and 1995 surveys. I use the "Passel weights" in all calculations that involve the 1995 survey.

Table 11.1. Alien Eligibility for Means-tested Federal Programs

Category of Alien	Program			
	SSI	Food Stamps	Medicaid	TANF
Immigrant arrived before 8/22/96	Eligible, if receiving SSI on 8/22/96, or subsequently disabled	Eligible, if age 65 or over on 8/22/96, or under age 18, or subsequently disabled	Eligible, for SSI-derivative benefits; otherwise, eligibility is a state option	Eligibility is a state option
Immigrant arrived after 8/22/96	Not eligible	Not eligible	Eligible for emergency services only	Not eligible
Refugees and asylees	Eligible	Eligible	Eligible	Eligible
Non-immigrants and illegal aliens	Not eligible	Not eligible	Eligible for emergency services only	Not eligible

Source: Vialet and Eig 1998: table 1.

Notes: In this table, "immigrant" refers to a foreign-born person who has a permanent residence visa (that is, a "green card"). Non-immigrants include foreign-born persons who are in the United States on a temporary basis, such as foreign students and tourists. The information provided for immigrants who arrived after August 22, 1996, and for refugees and asylees refers to their eligibility status during the first five years after arrival.

provide a history of participation in social assistance programs by both immigrant and native households during the 1994–1998 period. Unless otherwise noted, the household is the unit of analysis. The study is restricted to households that do not reside in group quarters. Initially, a household will be classified as an immigrant household if the household head was born outside the United States and is either an alien or a naturalized citizen. All other households will be classified as native households.

Table 11.2 reports the fraction of immigrant and native households that received particular types of assistance in each year between 1994 and 1998. The first column of the table tracks the trend in a summary measure of welfare participation, indicating if the household received *any* type of assistance (including cash benefits, Medicaid, or food stamps). The data yield a number of interesting results. First, the probability that either immigrant or native households received some type of assistance was roughly constant prior to 1996. About 24 percent of immigrant households received some type of assistance in both 1994 and 1995, as compared to about 16 percent of native households. Second, the recipiency rate of both groups fell immediately after the enactment of PRWORA. By 1997 and 1998, the recipiency rate was around 20 percent for immigrant households and around 14 percent for native households. Third, the post-1996 decline in welfare participation was much steeper in the immigrant population. In fact, one can use the data reported in table 11.2 to calculate the difference-in-differences estimate of the "excess" impact of welfare reform on the propensity that immigrant households receive welfare. The recipiency rate dropped by about 2 percentage points among native households but by 4 percentage points in immigrant households. It seems, therefore, that PRWORA reduced the *relative* immigrant recipiency rate by about 2 percentage points.

The remaining columns of table 11.2 reveal that roughly the same pattern is found for participation rates in specific welfare programs. Immigrant households experienced a steeper decline in the receipt of cash benefits (such as AFDC or SSI), Medicaid, and food stamps.

The national trends summarized in table 11.2 seem to suggest that the welfare reform legislation had a particularly strong impact on the likelihood that immigrant households receive assistance. These trends helped create the current consensus that PRWORA had a "chilling effect" on immigrant participation in welfare programs—either by making some immigrant households ineligible for receiving some types of assistance, or by mistakenly raising concern among eligible immigrant

Table 11.2. National Trends in Welfare Participation Rates (percent of households receiving assistance)

	Program					
	Some Type of Assistance	Some Type of Cash Benefit	AFDC or General Assistance	SSI	Medicaid	Food Stamps
Natives						
1994	15.6	7.9	4.6	4.0	13.5	8.7
1995	15.0	7.6	4.2	4.0	13.2	8.1
1996	15.3	7.5	3.9	4.3	13.5	8.0
1997	14.0	6.6	3.1	4.1	12.5	6.8
1998	13.4	6.0	2.5	3.9	12.1	6.0
Immigrants						
1994	23.4	11.7	7.1	5.7	21.3	12.5
1995	23.8	11.6	6.8	5.8	21.9	11.7
1996	21.9	10.5	5.7	5.6	20.5	10.1
1997	20.2	9.2	4.6	5.3	18.7	9.3
1998	20.0	8.8	3.9	5.4	18.8	7.5

Note: The household receives "some type of assistance" if any household member receives cash benefits, Medicaid, or food stamps.

households that receiving welfare could have adverse repercussions on their immigration status (and perhaps lead to deportation).

However, the national trends over the 1994–1998 period are quite misleading, for they do not reflect *at all* what went on in much of the country during that period. It is well known that immigrants in the United States are not randomly distributed around the country, but are geographically concentrated in a very small number of places. In 1998, for example, 72 percent of immigrants resided in only six states (California, New York, Texas, Florida, Illinois, and New Jersey). The ethnic clustering is even more striking at the level of the metropolitan area. In 1990, 42 percent of immigrants lived in just five metropolitan areas (Los Angeles, New York, Miami, Chicago, and Anaheim), yet only 13 percent of natives lived in those localities.

The demographic importance of California—the state where 29.6 percent of the immigrant households and 9.2 percent of the native households reside—suggests that it might be of interest to examine the trends separately for California and for the other states. Table 11.3 documents these trends for the summary welfare measure that indicates whether the household received some type of assistance; similar trends are obtained for most of the specific programs. The evidence presented in this table is dramatic. The relative decline of immigrant participation in welfare programs at the national level can be attributed *entirely* to what happened to immigrant welfare use in California. The fraction of native households in California that received some type of assistance dropped slightly—by 1.6 percentage points, from 15.2 percent before PRWORA to 13.6 percent afterward. In contrast, the fraction of immigrant households in California that received some type of assistance fell precipitously, from 31.2 percent before PRWORA to 23.2 percent by 1998. Outside California, the welfare participation rate of native-born households declined by about 2.2 percentage points, while the participation rate of immigrant households declined by less than 2 percentage points, from about 20 percent before PRWORA to 18.7 percent by 1998.[12]

---

[12] As noted above, the welfare reform legislation bans immigrants who arrived after August 22, 1996, from receiving most types of public assistance. The strong differences between California and the rest of the country are also evident in the changing welfare use of the most recent cohort that entered the country. In particular, the welfare participation rate of immigrant households that have been in the country for fewer than three years (as of the time of the survey) and that lived in California dropped from 29.9 percent in the pre-PRWORA period to 19.6 percent by 1998. In contrast, the welfare participation rate of the most recent cohort that lived outside California fell only from 19.8 to 17.8 percent.

Table 11.3. Welfare Participation Rates in California and the Rest of the Country (percent of households receiving some type of assistance)

	Natives			Immigrants		
Year	Entire Country	California	Outside California	Entire Country	California	Outside California
1994	15.6	15.2	15.6	23.4	31.2	20.0
1995	15.0	14.5	15.1	23.8	31.1	20.6
1996	15.3	13.6	15.5	21.9	26.3	20.1
1997	14.0	13.5	14.1	20.2	23.7	18.8
1998	13.4	13.6	13.4	20.0	23.2	18.7

Note: The household receives "some type of assistance" if any household member receives cash benefits, Medicaid, or food stamps.

In short, the raw data do not provide any evidence whatsoever that PRWORA had any "chilling effect" on the welfare participation of immigrant households that reside outside California.

To better assess the role played by PRWORA in generating the relative decline in immigrant welfare use, it is instructive to conduct a more detailed analysis of the CPS data, an analysis that takes into account the fact that not all immigrants were equally affected by welfare reform. As noted earlier, the legislation made an important distinction between citizens and noncitizens. Most of the restrictions on welfare use by foreign-born persons are lifted once the immigrant becomes a naturalized citizen. Further, as table 11.1 indicated, refugees and asylees were exempted from almost all of the immigrant restrictions in PRWORA (at least in the first five years after arrival).

Initially, I classify the foreign-born households in the CPS data into citizen and noncitizen status based on the naturalization status of the household head. Table 11.4 reports the relevant trends in the citizen and noncitizen samples. Since most of the restrictions on welfare use targeted noncitizens, it is not surprising that the nationwide decline in welfare use was very steep among noncitizens; their welfare participation rate fell from 29.4 to 22.4 percent. In contrast, the welfare participation rate of citizen households actually *increased* between 1994 and 1998 (from 14.3 to 16.3 percent). Note, however, that California still plays a crucial role in determining the national trend. Much of the decline in welfare participation in noncitizen households occurred in California. In particular, the welfare participation rate of noncitizens fell by about 10 percentage points in California but by only about 4 percentage points in the rest of the country.

Finally, note that the differences between California and the rest of the country remain even when one considers the trend in the population of noncitizen, non-refugee households. Although the CPS data do not report the type of visa used by a particular immigrant to enter the country, one can approximate the refugee population by using information on the national origin of the foreign-born households.[13] I classified all households who originated in the main refugee-sending countries as refugee households, while households originating in all other countries were classified as non-refugee households. The bottom panel

---

[13] The main refugee-sending countries over the 1970–1990 period were: Afghanistan, Bulgaria, Cambodia, Cuba, Czechoslovakia, Ethiopia, Hungary, Laos, Poland, Romania, Thailand, the former U.S.S.R., and Vietnam.

Table 11.4. Welfare Participation Rates in Foreign-born Households, by Citizenship Status (percent of households receiving some type of assistance)

Group/Year	Entire Country	California	Outside California
Citizen head of household			
1994	14.3	18.7	13.0
1995	15.8	19.4	14.7
1996	16.1	17.9	15.4
1997	16.5	18.7	15.8
1998	16.3	18.0	15.7
Noncitizen head of household			
1994	29.4	36.6	25.5
1995	29.3	36.4	25.4
1996	26.6	31.8	24.2
1997	23.2	27.0	21.5
1998	22.9	26.9	21.2
Noncitizen head of household and non-refugee			
1994	27.8	33.7	24.4
1995	26.9	33.1	23.3
1996	25.1	29.8	22.8
1997	21.8	25.1	20.1
1998	21.7	26.5	19.5

Note: The household receives "some type of assistance" if any household member receives cash benefits, Medicaid, or food stamps.

of table 11.4 shows that the participation rate for noncitizen, non-refugee households declined by about 7 percent in California but by only 4 percent in the rest of the country.

The classification of households into citizen and noncitizen status based solely on the naturalization status of the foreign-born household head may be somewhat misleading because some members of the household might qualify for particular types of aid even if the household head does not qualify because he or she is not a citizen. As an example, consider a household headed by someone who entered the United States illegally. Suppose further that this household head has children born in the United States. The illegal alien is ineligible for many types of assistance, but the children of the illegal alien are eligible, for they are American citizens. In other words, the naturalization and nativity status of other household members will help determine the household's eligibility for many programs.

To illustrate the importance of the citizenship composition of the household members, I classified all households into three types: "exclusively citizen households," where everyone is either a native-born person or a naturalized citizen; "mixed households," where there are some citizens and some noncitizens; and "exclusively noncitizen households," where all persons are noncitizens. The first three columns of table 11.5 illustrate the trends in welfare use for these different types of households.[14] The trends at the national level are not surprising. Exclusively noncitizen households experienced a much steeper drop in welfare participation than exclusively citizen households. The welfare participation rate in noncitizen households dropped by about 5 percentage points, from almost 21 percent before PRWORA to 15.4 percent in 1998. In contrast, the participation rate of citizen households dropped by only 2 percentage points, from 15.5 to 13.5 percent.

The data again reveal the importance of California in generating the national trend. The participation rate of citizen households declined by the same amount (about 2 percentage points) both within and outside California. In contrast, the participation rate of noncitizen households declined precipitously in California, from about 28 percent in 1994 to only 14 percent by 1998. Outside California, the participation rate declined only from about 18 to 16 percent. In other words, the presumed chilling effect on noncitizen households at the national level is exclusively a California phenomenon.

The data also indicate that the distinct California and non-California trends cannot be attributed to the differential geographic settlement of refugee households in the United States. Column 4 of table 11.5 shows that the very different trends experienced by noncitizen households in California and in the rest of the country are the same even when we restrict our attention to non-refugee households.

Finally, one could argue that the distinct California trend may reflect the possibility that the California noncitizen population contains a significant overrepresentation of illegal aliens, and particularly of Mexican illegal aliens (INS 1997: 200). The last column of table 11.5 recalculates the trends in the sample of noncitizen, non-refugee households that did not originate in Mexico. It is evident that California's

---

[14] In the pooled 1994–1998 data, 92.0 percent of the households are exclusively citizen, 5.4 percent are mixed, and 2.7 percent are exclusively noncitizen. In contrast, 89.7 percent of the household heads are native-born, 4.4 percent are foreign-born citizens, and 5.9 percent are foreign-born noncitizens.

Table 11.5. Welfare Participation Rates, by Type of Household (percent of households receiving some type of assistance)

	Type of Household				
Sample/Year	All Citizen	Mixed Household	All Noncitizen	All Noncitizen and Non-refugee	All Noncitizen, Non-refugee, and Non-Mexican
Entire country					
1994	15.5	30.4	20.6	16.9	14.2
1995	15.0	29.9	20.9	16.1	14.7
1996	15.2	28.2	17.1	13.9	13.3
1997	14.0	25.6	15.7	12.5	11.5
1998	13.5	25.0	15.4	12.4	11.1
California					
1994	15.2	35.1	27.7	22.0	19.4
1995	14.5	37.8	25.1	19.7	17.8
1996	13.6	32.8	20.1	17.3	17.8
1997	13.5	30.2	17.2	13.7	12.8
1998	13.6	29.8	14.0	12.9	10.5
Outside California					
1994	15.5	27.6	17.7	14.7	12.2
1995	15.0	25.6	19.2	14.6	13.8
1996	15.4	25.9	16.0	12.6	12.0
1997	14.1	23.5	15.2	12.1	11.1
1998	13.4	22.6	15.8	12.2	11.3

Notes: The welfare participation rates give the percent of households that receive some type of assistance, including cash benefits, Medicaid, or food stamps. The types of household classification are defined as follows: an "all citizen household" is one where all members of the household are either native-born or naturalized citizens; a "mixed household" contains both citizens and noncitizens; and a "noncitizen household" is composed exclusively of noncitizens.

precipitous drop in immigrant welfare remains an "outlier" even in this highly restricted sample.

Regression Analysis

It is instructive to formalize and extend some of the descriptive results by estimating a simple regression model. To illustrate the methodology, pool the CPS data available for the calendar years 1994, 1995, 1997, and 1998, and consider the difference-in-differences regression specification:[15]

$$(1)\quad p_i = X_i \beta + \alpha t_i + \gamma_0 MX_i + \gamma_1 (MX_i \times t_i) + \delta_0 NC_i + \delta_1 (NC_i \times t_i) + \varepsilon_i ,$$

where p_i is a dummy variable indicating if household i receives some type of public assistance; X is a vector of socioeconomic characteristics (including age, gender, and educational attainment of the household head, and variables describing the household's composition, such as the number of children and the number of elderly persons); t_i is a dummy variable set to unity if the observation refers to the calendar years 1997 and 1998 (representing the post-PRWORA period); MX_i is a dummy variable indicating if the household is a "mixed" household (containing both citizens and noncitizens); and NC_i is a dummy variable indicating if the household is an exclusively noncitizen household. The coefficients γ_1 and δ_1 give the difference-in-differences estimators of the impact of welfare reform on immigrant participation in welfare programs. For instance, δ_1 measures the pre- and post-PRWORA change in welfare participation in noncitizen households relative to the respective change in citizen households.

Table 11.6 reports the estimated difference-in-differences coefficients. It is evident that the impact of welfare reform on noncitizen households depends entirely on whether or not the sample includes California. The coefficient δ_1 is negative, sizable, and significant in California. Even after controlling for differences in socioeconomic characteristics among the various types of households and for the country of origin of the immigrant household, the participation rate of

---

[15] Note that the regression analysis does not use the data for the 1996 calendar year (that is, the 1997 March CPS). In effect, the data for 1994–1995 represent the pre-PRWORA period, while the data for 1997–1998 represent the post-PRWORA period. For simplicity, all regressions will be estimated using the linear probability model.

Table 11.6. Difference-in-Differences Estimate of the Impact of Welfare Reform on Welfare Participation

	Regression		
Sample/Variable	(1)	(2)	(3)
Entire country: Interaction of post-1996 variable with:			
Mixed household	–.034	–.030	–.032
	(.007)	(.007)	(.007)
All noncitizen household	–.037	–.019	–.016
	(.010)	(.010)	(.010)
California: Interaction of post-1996 variable with:			
Mixed household	–.051	–.040	–.032
	(.015)	(.015)	(.015)
All noncitizen household	–.094	–.059	–.048
	(.023)	(.022)	(.022)
Outside California: Interaction of post-1996 variable with:			
Mixed household	–.021	–.022	–.025
	(.008)	(.008)	(.008)
All noncitizen household	–.014	–.002	–.002
	(.011)	(.011)	(.011)
List of controls:			
Demographic variables	No	Yes	Yes
Country of origin	No	No	Yes

Notes: Standard errors are reported in parentheses. The regressions estimated in the entire country have 207,752 observations; the regressions estimated within California have 17,957 observations; the regressions estimated outside California have 189,795 observations. The "demographic variables" held constant in the regressions reported in columns 2 and 3 include the age, gender, and educational attainment of the household head, the number of persons in the household, the number of children under age eighteen, the number of persons over age sixty-four, and the year of migration (measured by a vector of dummy variables indicating whether the head of the immigrant household arrived after 1994, 1990–1993, 1985–1989, 1980–1984, 1970–1979, or before 1970). The "country of origin" fixed effects represent a vector of 103 dummy variables indicating the country where the head of the immigrant household was born.

noncitizen households in California declined by 4.8 percentage points more than that of citizen households. Outside California, however, the difference-in-differences estimate is numerically and statistically equal to zero, indicating that citizen and noncitizen households experienced the same rate of decline in welfare participation during the 1994–1998 period.

The crucial importance of California in the analysis raises obvious questions about whether welfare reform had *any* chilling effect on welfare participation. And, in particular, what factors explain the "California effect?"

One possibility is that there were specific items in the PRWORA legislation, or in the waivers granted to individual states prior to 1996, that had a particularly adverse effect on the eligibility of immigrant households living in California. No such provisions, however, exist either in the welfare reform legislation or in the state-specific waivers granted before 1996.[16] In other words, there is *no* legislative or regulatory justification that can be used to explain the crucial difference in the trends between California and the rest of the country.

One could also argue that PRWORA might have a more adverse impact on California because of the overrepresentation of illegal aliens in California. This is an incorrect inference, however, for it was illegal for illegal aliens to receive most types of public assistance both before and after 1996. Moreover, as I showed earlier, the California trends are quite similar even when one excludes from the analysis the sample of Mexican immigrants, a population that probably contains a relatively large fraction of illegal aliens.

Finally, the Urban Institute has calculated an index of "welfare generosity" that measures the extent to which particular states offered their state-provided safety nets to the immigrant population after 1996 (Zimmermann and Tumlin 1999: table 18). By this measure, California was one of the most generous states, offering a wide array of benefits to immigrants who would have been kicked off the welfare rolls, as well as to newly arrived immigrants. This fact makes it even more difficult to understand why immigrant welfare use in California dropped so dramatically.

Ultimately, any explanation of the California effect will have to rely on a hypothesis that there were things going on in California—unrelated to the welfare reform legislation—that did not occur in the

---

[16] Schoeni and Blank (2000) analyze how these state waivers affected socioeconomic outcomes in the targeted populations.

rest of the country. One obvious candidate is the enactment of Proposition 187 by California voters in November 1994. This proposition, which denied almost all types of public assistance (including schooling) to *illegal* aliens residing in California, was supported by 59 percent of California voters. Although most of the provisions in the proposition were never enforced, its impact on the political and social climate in California is undeniable. It represented a seismic shift in the relation between the host population (that is, the voters of California) and a particular segment of the immigrant population. Soon after the enactment of Proposition 187, there were numerous newspaper accounts of the chilling effect that the proposition had on aliens applying for particular types of publicly provided benefits (Reyes 1994). Although it is difficult to prove empirically that the social and political forces that culminated in Proposition 187 are an important explanation of the trends documented in this chapter, the possibility that such forces matter should not be easily dismissed.

State-Provided Safety Nets

As noted above, some states chose to offer their safety nets to some of the immigrants adversely affected by PRWORA. For instance, the welfare reform legislation makes most immigrants who entered the United States before August 22, 1996, ineligible for many types of assistance, such as TANF (Temporary Assistance for Needy Families) and Medicaid. The legislation, however, also gives states the option to offer TANF and Medicaid to some of these immigrants, and some states chose to do so. In addition, some states also chose to offer various types of state-funded assistance to immigrants who arrived after August 22, 1996. As we have seen, these immigrants are typically ineligible for most types of federal assistance.

These state activities will further increase dispersion in "welfare opportunities" available to immigrants living in different states. The Urban Institute's index of "welfare generosity" classifies states into four categories according to the availability of the state safety net. The states where such aid was "most available" included California and Illinois; the states where the aid was "somewhat available" included New York and Florida; the states where the aid was "less available" included Arizona and Michigan; and the states where the aid was "least available" included Ohio and Texas. It is worth noting that five of the six states with the largest immigrant populations tended to provide above-average levels of state-funded assistance to immigrants (the exception being Texas).

I use the Urban Institute index to classify states into two types: more generous states (that is, states where aid was most available or somewhat available) and less generous states (that is, states where aid was less available and least available). Table 11.7 shows how the "chilling effect" of welfare reform depends on the actions taken by individual states. For simplicity, I classify households according to the immigration and naturalization status of the household head. The data indicate that the welfare participation rate of noncitizens living in the less generous states dropped by almost 10 percentage points (from 28.4 to 19.4 percent) during the period. In contrast, the participation rate of noncitizens living in the more generous states dropped only by about 5 percentage points (from 29.7 to 24.4 percent). It is worth noting that the participation rates of native or of citizen households do not reveal any such sensitivity to the availability of state-funded assistance.

The effect of the state-funded programs is even stronger when the sample is restricted to the households that live outside California. The welfare participation rate of noncitizen households dropped by 9 percentage points in the less generous states, while the participation rate of noncitizen households dropped by only 1.3 percentage points in the more generous states. Finally, the last row of table 11.7 shows that in the most restricted sample—the non-refugee households that live outside California—the welfare participation rate of these households dropped by almost 10 percentage points if they lived in the less generous states, but it fell by less than 1 percent if they lived in the more generous states. In short, the state-funded programs offered by the more generous states seem to have prevented the chilling effect of federal welfare reform on immigrant welfare participation that would otherwise have occurred.

It is instructive to conduct a more formal analysis of the impact of the state-funded programs to determine if the differences between the more generous and the less generous states can be attributed to differences in characteristics of the populations living in the different states. Consider the linear probability regression model:

$$(2)\quad p_i = X_i \beta + \alpha_0 t_i + \alpha_1 I_i + \alpha_2 G_i + \gamma_0 (I_i \times t_i) + \gamma_1 (I_i \times G_i) + \gamma_2 (G_i \times t_i) + \theta (I_i \times G_i \times t_i) + \varepsilon_i ,$$

Table 11.7. State-funded Assistance and Program Participation (percent of households receiving some type of assistance)

	Households in:					
	Less Generous States			More Generous States		
Sample of Households and Year	Native	Citizen	Noncitizen	Native	Citizen	Noncitizen
Entire sample						
Pre-1996	16.3	15.5	28.4	14.3	14.9	29.7
Post-1996	14.3	14.4	19.4	13.1	17.0	24.4
Non-California households						
Pre-1996	16.3	15.5	28.4	14.2	13.1	23.9
Post-1996	14.3	14.4	19.4	13.0	16.4	22.6
Non-refugee households						
Pre-1996	16.3	16.0	28.8	14.3	14.6	27.0
Post-1996	14.3	14.6	19.1	13.1	15.8	22.8
Non-California and non-refugee households						
Pre-1996	16.3	16.0	28.8	14.2	12.8	21.0
Post-1996	14.3	14.6	19.1	13.1	15.1	20.3

Notes: The welfare participation rates give the percent of households that receive some type of assistance, including cash benefits, Medicaid, or food stamps. The types of household classification are defined according to the immigration and naturalization status of the household head. The more generous states are those states where the state-funded assistance was "most available" or "somewhat available." The less generous states are those states where the assistance was "less available" and "least available." See text for details.

where t_i is again a dummy variable set to unity if the observation refers to the calendar years 1997 and 1998; I_i is a dummy variable set to unity if the head of the household is an immigrant; and G_i is a dummy variable set to one if the state is a "more generous" state, and zero otherwise. The coefficient θ then measures the impact of the state-provided safety net on the *relative* trend in immigrant welfare use. In particular, it measures the extent to which the relative pre- and post-PRWORA change in welfare participation differs between states that were the least generous in extending the safety net to immigrants and states that were the most generous. One would expect that the coefficient θ is positive because the adverse impact of welfare reform on the relative probability that immigrant households receive welfare should be attenuated in those states that were most generous to immigrants.

Finally, note that the regression model in equation (2) reverts to using immigration status—rather than the citizen/noncitizen breakdown—to estimate the impact of the state-funded programs. I do this for two distinct reasons. First, as I showed earlier, the type of breakdown chosen to display the data does not affect most of the key findings presented in this chapter. The differential trends between California and the rest of the country are the same regardless of whether one looks at the difference between immigrants and natives, or at the difference between citizens and noncitizens. More importantly, the analysis of the citizen/noncitizen distinction ignores an important endogenous decision that immigrants can make to bypass many of the restrictions imposed by welfare reform—namely, immigrants can become naturalized citizens. As I noted earlier, there was a substantial increase in citizenship rates *and* the welfare participation rate of households headed by foreign-born citizens rose between 1994 and 1998. As a result, the reduced-form impact of welfare reform is best measured by analyzing the differential trends experienced by native and immigrant households.

Table 11.8 reports the regression coefficient θ from alternative specifications of the regression model in equation (2). As expected, the state-funded programs have a positive impact on the relative rate of change in immigrant welfare participation. The coefficient reported in the first row (for the entire sample) and in the first column (without any controls for socioeconomic differences in the population) is .022, with a standard error of .012. The numerical value of the coefficient implies that the welfare participation rate of immigrant households fell by 2.2 percentage points less in those states that provided generous assistance

Table 11.8. Impact of State-provided Assistance to Immigrants (immigrant households relative to native households)

	Regression Model			
Sample	(1)	(2)	(3)	(4)
Entire sample	.022	.029	.028	.033
	(.012)	(.012)	(.011)	(.011)
Non-California households	.055	.057	.057	.058
	(.012)	(.012)	(.012)	(.012)
Non-refugee households	.030	.034	.034	.038
	(.013)	(.012)	(.012)	(.012)
Non-California and non-refugee households	.060	.062	.061	.063
	(.013)	(.013)	(.013)	(.013)
Controls for:				
Socioeconomic characteristics	No	Yes	Yes	Yes
State-of-residence fixed effects	No	No	Yes	Yes
Country-of-origin fixed effects	No	No	No	Yes

Notes: Standard errors are reported in parentheses. The regressions estimated in the entire country have 207,752 observations; the regressions estimated outside California have 189,795 observations; the regressions estimated in the refugee sample have 204,563 observations; and the regressions estimated in the non-refugee, non-California sample have 187,053 observations. The "demographic variables" held constant in the regressions reported in column 3 include the age, gender, and educational attainment of the household head, the number of persons in the household, the number of children under age 18, the number of persons over age 64, and the year of migration (measured by a vector of dummy variables indicating whether the head of the immigrant household arrived after 1994, 1990–93, 1985–89, 1980–84, 1970–79, or before 1970).

to their immigrant populations than in those states that were less generous. Note, moreover, that this effect actually becomes stronger (both numerically and statistically) if the regression model controls for differences in socioeconomic characteristics, including state of residence and the country of origin of the immigrant household. In the sample of non-refugee households living outside California, and after controlling for all of the socioeconomic background variables, the welfare participation rate of immigrant households fell by 6.3 percentage points more in the less generous states than in the more generous states.

In sum, the fact the some states chose to offer a state-funded safety net to their immigrant populations helped cushion the impact of federal welfare reform. Put differently, PRWORA could indeed have caused a chilling effect outside California, but the actions of individual states, and particularly the states where most immigrants live, prevented much of that chilling effect from occurring.

WELFARE REFORM AND NATURALIZATION

As we have seen, the impact of PRWORA on immigrant participation in welfare programs was attenuated by the responses of individual states to the legislation. There is an additional behavioral response that could further attenuate the impact—the actions of the immigrants themselves. The welfare reform legislation drew an important distinction between citizen and noncitizen status. In rough terms, naturalized citizens are eligible for most programs, while noncitizens are not. This fact obviously raises the incentives for immigrants to become naturalized.[17] I now turn to an investigation of this issue.

It is well known that there was a dramatic increase in naturalization applications in the 1990s. The evidence summarized in the previous section raises two distinct questions about the possible link between naturalization and welfare use in the immigrant population. First, did the immigrants most likely to be affected by the welfare reform legislation experience the highest increases in naturalization rates after 1996? Second, can the relatively steeper drop in welfare receipt experienced

---

[17] Immigrants could also respond by migrating to those states that offered state-provided benefits. This migration response will probably be very weak because most of the immigrants present in the United States in 1996 (with the exception of those who lived in Texas) already lived in states that expanded the safety net available to immigrants.

by California's immigrants be explained in terms of differential trends in naturalization?

Before proceeding to the empirical analysis, it is worth noting that a number of data problems prevent a definitive study of these questions. First, the available data do not allow one to determine if welfare receipt by a particular immigrant was an important factor that determined whether that person chose to become naturalized after 1996. In particular, the CPS does not provide any longitudinal information on whether a foreign-born respondent is a naturalized citizen. The naturalization question is asked only once throughout the sixteen-month rotation period that the person is tracked by the survey. As a result, one cannot analyze—at the micro level—which specific individuals chose to file a naturalization petition after 1996.

Second, it is unlikely that PRWORA was responsible for much of the observed increase in naturalization petitions in the period leading up to 1996. The INS, through the Citizenship USA initiative, took steps to speed up the naturalization of foreign-born persons prior to the 1996 presidential election (Wasem 1998). It is well known that political factors and fraud motivated and marred many of the activities in this program. For instance, nearly 20 percent of the 1.05 million immigrants naturalized in 1996 did not receive the standard FBI fingerprint check for criminal records prior to their naturalization (Branigin 1997; Galvin 1997; Schippers 2000).

Because of the rapid increase in naturalization applications, the INS quickly developed long queues for processing the naturalization petitions. By the end of 1997, more than one million persons awaited a decision on their naturalization application (INS 1997: 134). These queues imply that the available data on naturalization are "truncated" since the available information does not indicate whether the immigrant applied for naturalization, but only whether the immigrant is naturalized.

Trends in Naturalization Rates

I used the 1995–1999 CPS to calculate the naturalization status of foreign-born persons aged eighteen or higher. The analysis is restricted to persons who migrated before 1990 so that the foreign-born persons could, in principle, have become naturalized citizens.

Table 11.9 documents some key trends in naturalization rates between 1994 and 1998. There was a rapid increase in the fraction of the foreign-born population that was naturalized in this period. The naturalization

Table 11.9. Trends in Naturalization Rates (percent of immigrants who are naturalized)

Group/Year	Entire Country	California	Outside California
All foreign-born persons			
1994	40.9	28.5	47.2
1995	43.4	34.4	48.0
1996	47.7	40.6	51.3
1997	51.7	42.0	56.4
1998	53.6	45.2	57.7
Foreign-born persons with twelve or fewer years of schooling			
1994	32.2	17.5	40.7
1995	33.8	21.0	40.8
1996	37.5	24.9	43.7
1997	42.4	30.0	48.7
1998	44.7	33.5	50.6
Foreign-born persons with at least twelve years of schooling			
1994	54.9	50.7	56.7
1995	57.4	56.8	57.7
1996	62.3	63.3	61.8
1997	65.5	61.3	67.4
1998	66.4	64.0	67.6

Note: The naturalization rates are calculated in the sample of foreign-born persons who are at least 18 years old and who migrated to the United States before 1990.

rate rose from 40.9 to 53.6 percent, with about half of the increase occurring *before* the welfare reform legislation was enacted. The timing of the increase in naturalization rates suggests that either the chilling effect of Proposition 187 or the impetus provided by the Citizenship USA initiative is responsible for much of the increase.

As noted above, a simple hypothesis that could potentially explain the steeper drop in welfare participation rates in California is that foreign-born persons in that state did not rush toward naturalization as quickly as foreign-born persons in other states. However, table 11.9 shows that naturalization rates increased *faster* in California than in the rest of the country. The naturalization rate rose from 28.5 to 45.2 percent in California, and from 47.2 to 57.7 percent in the rest of the nation.

Moreover, the naturalization rate in California rose very rapidly among "potential" welfare recipients. Table 11.9 illustrates the trends in naturalization rates by educational attainment, and the data indicate that the naturalization rate of persons with twelve or fewer years of schooling—the pool from which most welfare recipients would be drawn—rose at least as much as the naturalization rates of persons with more education. Therefore, the evidence does not provide support for the conjecture that differences in naturalization behavior between California and the rest of the country can explain the particularly steep decline in welfare recipiency rates observed in California. The trend in California's welfare participation rates remains a puzzle: it cannot be attributed to an endogenous cutback in immigrant benefits by California's state government or to an endogenous response in naturalization behavior by California's immigrants.

Even though the outlying experience of California cannot be attributed to the trends in naturalization rates, it is still possible that the impact of PRWORA on welfare participation among immigrant households was attenuated by the naturalization response of immigrants. Although the CPS does not provide the requisite longitudinal data that would allow one to ascertain if immigrants who were welfare recipients in the pre-PROWRA period were also the ones who were most likely to naturalize in the post-PRWORA period, an alternative strategy for addressing this question can be developed. In particular, it is well known that citizenship rates vary dramatically by country of origin. Table 11.10 illustrates some of those differences, both "before" and "after" the welfare reform legislation. Even though the naturalization rate of immigrants rose dramatically between 1994 and 1998, there was a great deal of diversity in the rates of increase across national origin groups. For instance, the naturalization rate increased from 54.1 to 54.3 percent for Canadian immigrants, from 16.5 to 28.2 percent for Mexican immigrants, and from 65.7 to 81.2 percent for immigrants from the former Soviet Union.[18]

[18] The data reported in table 11.9 contain some puzzling trends. For a small number of national origin groups, the naturalization rate of the immigrants who arrived prior to 1990 actually *declined* during the 1990s. For instance, the naturalization rate of British immigrants fell from 54.7 to 46.3 percent. This result could be due to the measurement error that will inevitably arise when foreign-born persons are asked to report if they are naturalized, or it may reflect the changing age distribution of the immigrant "cohort" over the five-year sample period (as older immigrants exit the sample and immigrants who arrived as young children enter it).

Table 11.10. Naturalization Rates, by National Origin

Country of Origin	Percent of Immigrants Who Are Naturalized 1994–1995	1997–1998	Sample Size in 1997–1998
Cambodia	29.1	57.8	69
Canada	54.1	54.3	460
China	47.6	69.1	401
Colombia	35.5	51.6	417
Cuba	52.5	72.7	947
Dominican Republic	28.8	44.5	595
Ecuador	29.9	38.6	245
El Salvador	18.4	25.4	691
Germany	78.9	75.7	417
Greece	75.2	72.5	184
Guatemala	14.9	21.6	365
Guyana	43.7	63.4	127
Haiti	35.8	43.7	203
Honduras	27.4	33.1	166
India	53.4	59.7	347
Iran	48.9	66.6	179
Ireland	68.2	69.6	121
Italy	72.5	77.5	388
Jamaica	41.5	60.1	222
Japan	47.2	38.0	117
Korea	39.4	55.2	318
Laos	33.2	40.4	108
Mexico	16.5	28.2	5,555
Nicaragua	16.5	36.2	186
Peru	37.1	51.0	178
Philippines	65.4	75.9	761
Poland	65.5	69.7	214
Portugal	59.2	46.8	185
Taiwan	71.8	73.9	177
Thailand	37.5	65.5	48
United Kingdom	54.7	46.3	437
U.S.S.R.	65.7	81.2	226
Vietnam	64.0	73.1	374

Note: The naturalization rates reported in this table are obtained by pooling the 1995–1996 CPS and the 1998–1999 CPS.

Table 11.11. Determinants of Growth in Naturalization Rates

	Regression			
Independent variable	(1)	(2)	(3)	(4)
Fraction of immigrant cohort receiving public assistance in 1994–1995	.178	.291	.236	.204
	(.045)	(.062)	(.065)	(.058)
Mean family income of cohort	—	–.001	–.000	.001
		(.001)	(.001)	(.001)
Mean education of cohort	—	.013	.011	.024
		(.006)	(.006)	(.005)
Mean age of cohort	—	.002	.004	.004
		(.002)	(.003)	(.003)
Fraction of cohort that is male		.095	.065	.124
		(.073)	(.073)	(.065)
Fraction of cohort living in California	—	.023	.023	–.008
		(.040)	(.041)	(.036)
Fraction of households in cohort that have native-born persons	—	—	–.219	–.256
			(.077)	(.068)
Fraction of households with children	—	—	.194	.214
			(.080)	(.071)
Fraction of households with elderly persons	—	—	–.096	.087
			(.103)	(.093)
Fraction of cohort naturalized in 1994–1995	—	—	—	–.442
				(.047)
R-squared	.094	.125	.149	.337

Notes: Standard errors are reported in parentheses. All regressions are weighted by $(N_0^{-1} + N_1^{-1})^{-1}$, where N_0 gives the sample size used in calculating the naturalization rate of the cohort in 1994–1995, and N_1 gives the respective sample size in 1997–1998. The regressions have 325 observations. All regressions include a vector of fixed effects indicating the year of migration of the cohort.

Let $n_{ij}(t_0)$ be the pre-PRWORA (1994–1995) naturalization rate of a group of immigrants born in country i who arrived in the United States at time j; and let $n_{ij}(t_1)$ be the post-PRWORA (1997–1998) naturalization rate of that group. Consider the regression model:

$$(3) \quad n_{ij}(t_1) - n_{ij}(t_0) = X\beta + \alpha\, p_{ij}(t_0) + \varepsilon_{ij},$$

where X is a vector of socioeconomic characteristics; and $p_{ij}(t_0)$ gives the fraction of immigrants in cell (i, j) who received some type of welfare assistance in 1994–1995. The cohorts defined by the index j are the immigrants who arrived between 1985 and 1989, between 1980 and 1984, between 1970 and 1979, and before 1970. The coefficient α would be positive if the immigrant groups most likely to be affected by PRWORA were also the ones most likely to resort to naturalization to "neutralize" the impact of the legislation.

Table 11.11 reports the regression results. The evidence is striking. There is a strong and positive correlation between the fraction of the immigrant group that received welfare before 1996 and the increase in the naturalization rate experienced by the immigrant cohort. Moreover, this correlation is positive and significant regardless of the controls that are included in the regression. The estimate of the coefficient α typically ranges around .2, indicating that a 20 percentage point difference in the pre-1996 welfare participation rates is associated with a 4 percentage point increase in the rate of naturalization during the 1994–1998 period. The regressions reported in the table also indicate that the immigrant groups more likely to have children in the household experienced a faster increase in the naturalization rate, while those groups that are more likely to have native-born persons in the household experienced a slower increase in the naturalization rate. Finally, the last column of the table shows that the coefficient α remains positive and significant even when the regression controls for the initial level of the naturalization rate of the group.

The positive correlation between the immigrant group's pre-PRWORA welfare use and post-PRWORA naturalization rates can be interpreted in two different ways. First, the correlation could be measuring an individual behavioral response. In particular, those immigrants who were most likely to be adversely affected by the welfare reform legislation took a simple (and cheap) action that would neutralize the impact of PRWORA: they filed a naturalization petition and became naturalized citizens. It is also possible, however, that the political activists who ran the Citizenship USA initiative, with its goal of naturalizing one million foreign-born persons in 1996, particularly targeted groups of immigrants, groups that would be the most likely to support the incumbent Democratic administration in the 1996 presidential election. A simple model of statistical discrimination suggests that the welfare participation rate of the ethnic group could serve as a cheap signal to distinguish which groups should be targeted by the initiative. The available data, however, cannot be used to measure the relative importance of these two alternative hypotheses.

POLICY IMPLICATIONS

From a historical perspective, the 1996 welfare reform legislation represents only the latest attempt to minimize the costs imposed by the potential immigration of public charges. The U.S. Congress could just as easily have chosen to achieve many of the same objectives by simply enforcing the public charge provisions of current immigration law—both by denying entry to potential welfare recipients or by deporting immigrants who make extensive use of welfare programs. Instead, the welfare reform legislation hoped to achieve these aims in a more circuitous way. By setting up a five-year waiting period before newly arrived immigrants qualify for many types of assistance, the legislation presumably discourages the immigration of potential public charges. By tightening the eligibility requirements for immigrants already living in the United States, the legislation presumably increases the incentives for some immigrants to return to their home countries.

The empirical analysis presented in this chapter yields four major findings:

- Even though immigrant participation in welfare programs—relative to that of natives—declined at the national level, the national trend can be entirely accounted for by what was happening in the state of California. In particular, the relative participation rate of immigrants dropped precipitously in California but remained roughly constant in the rest of the country.
- Much of the potential impact of PRWORA on welfare use by immigrants residing outside California was undone by the actions of state governments. Some states—and particularly those states where immigrants reside—chose to offer state-provided benefits to the immigrants adversely affected by welfare reform.

- It seems that immigrants quickly learned that the naturalization certificate held the key to many types of public assistance denied to noncitizens. The national origin groups most likely to receive public assistance in the pre-PRWORA period experienced relatively larger increases in naturalization rates after 1996. This endogenous response by immigrants further served to neutralize the potential impact of PRWORA on immigrant welfare use.
- There do not seem to be any *measurable* factors that can explain the precipitous drop in immigrant welfare participation in California. The California experience may indeed reflect a chilling effect, but the chilling effect has nothing to do with welfare reform and may have much to do with the enactment of Proposition 187.

What have we learned from the trends in immigrant welfare participation in the post-PRWORA period? Should the U.S. Congress amend the legislation so as to get more noncitizens on the rolls and remove the burden from the generous states? Or should the restrictions on immigrant welfare use be tightened even further?

The answer to all of these questions depends on the objectives of immigration policy. Since colonial days, immigration policy has been partly motivated by a desire to protect native taxpayers. This policy objective obviously conflicts with a humanitarian desire that would open up economic and social opportunities in the United States—including the opportunities provided by the welfare state—to poor persons from around the world.

Welfare programs in the United States—though not generous by Western European standards—stack up pretty well when compared to the standard of living in most of the world's less developed countries. In 1997 the typical TANF household with two children in California could receive a maximum of $6,780 in cash benefits (U.S. House of Representatives 1998: 416, 985). This household probably qualified for food stamps worth another $3,132 annually. And if this household also participated in the Medicaid program, it received additional benefits valued at over $2,700. At the same time, per capita income in China was $3,600, in Colombia it was $6,600, and in the Philippines it was $3,500.[19]

Such income differences across countries influence a person's decision to move to the United States—*regardless* of whether these differ-

[19] U.S. Central Intelligence Agency 1999. The per capita income data adjust for international differences in purchasing power.

ences arise in the labor market or in the safety net provided by the welfare state. As a result, there are valid reasons to be concerned with the possibility that generous welfare programs might attract a particular type of immigrant. After all, welfare programs will probably attract persons who qualify for subsidies and repel persons who have to pay for them. A strong magnetic effect, combined with an ineffective border control policy, can literally break the bank.

Put bluntly, the immigration of potential public charges can easily fracture the political legitimacy of the social contract that created and sustains the welfare state. No group of native citizens can be reasonably expected to pick up the tab for subsidizing tens of millions of "the huddled masses."

It is inevitable, therefore, that immigration policy impose some restriction on the entry of potential public charges. But how should the restrictions work?

One major problem with PRWORA is its explicit link between the receipt of welfare benefits and the immigrant's naturalization status. It is well known that many immigrants in the United States do not bother to naturalize: only 52.8 percent of the immigrants who entered the country in 1977 had naturalized by 1997 (INS 1997: 140). The welfare reform legislation changed the incentives facing different types of immigrants to become U.S. citizens. Not surprisingly, it seems that the immigrant groups that have relatively high propensities for receiving public assistance also have larger incentives to naturalize in the post-PRWORA era.

One could reasonably argue that such a link between citizenship and welfare is problematic. Many immigrants will choose to become citizens, not because they want to fully participate in the U.S. political system, but because naturalization is the price they have to pay to receive welfare benefits. It obviously does not constitute good social policy to equate a naturalization certificate with a welfare check. In addition, the sample of immigrants who naturalize will be self-selected to include large numbers of persons who qualify to make claims on the welfare state. Combined with the very large size of the current immigrant flow, there is a real possibility that the linkage between naturalization and welfare receipt can significantly alter the nature of the political equilibrium in many localities and states.

In 1996 Congress gave individual states the option to supplement the federal benefits available to immigrants with state-provided benefits. It turned out that almost all of the states with large immigrant populations chose to extend the state-provided safety nets to immigrant households. The political choices made by these states prevented many immigrant households from being removed from the welfare rolls and helped attenuate the impact of welfare reform on immigrant welfare use.

From an economic perspective, the responses made by the states with large immigrant populations seem puzzling. One could reasonably expect that once Congress gave states the opportunity to choose state-specific policies, many of those most affected by immigration would have chosen to discourage welfare use by immigrants residing within their borders—rather than pursue policies that further encouraged welfare use. Why did the race to the bottom not occur? Was it perhaps because the immigrant population in these states is now sufficiently large that elected officials found it essential—from a political perspective—to cater to the needs of this large minority?

The possibility that the immigrants themselves altered the political equilibrium in these states is worrisome, and it raises doubts about the wisdom of granting states the right to enhance the benefits that are available to immigrants. Since 1876, immigration policy has been the sole purview of the federal government. By allowing states to offer more generous safety nets to immigrants than the one provided by the federal government, some states could easily become a magnet for immigration from other countries. A state's actions, though sensible from the narrow perspective of state politicians running for elected office, may not be sensible from a national perspective. After all, the state is responsible for the cost of admitting immigrants only in the very short run. As soon as the immigrants become naturalized citizens, many of the responsibilities shift to the federal government. The state's generosity, therefore, could potentially impose a negative externality on the rest of the country.

Finally, it is worth noting that some of the key immigrant-related provisions in PRWORA—dealing with removing noncitizens who already lived in the United States from the welfare rolls—were revoked soon after they were signed into law. Major social policies seldom unravel in the United States, so that the partial unraveling of this key provision of the welfare reform legislation provides an important lesson. There is little disagreement over the fact that immigrant use of public assistance grew rapidly in the past three decades. So it is hard to argue that the immigrant provisions in the welfare reform bill were based on faulty data or analysis. Congress saw an actual problem—rising welfare use by immigrants—and tried to do something about it.

It seems, however, that the American people do not wish to bear the political, social, and economic costs of removing immigrants *already* in the United States from the welfare rolls. It is naïve, after all, to assume that there are no long-run consequences from denying needy immigrants access to food stamps or medical services. In the end, it is probably easier and cheaper to address the problem raised by the immigration of public charges not by "ending welfare as we know it," but by reforming immigration policy instead.

References

Albright, R.E. 1928. "Colonial Immigration Legislation," *Sociology and Social Research* 12 (May): 443–48.

Blau, Francine D. 1984. "The Use of Transfer Payments by Immigrants," *Industrial and Labor Relations Review* 37 (January): 222–39.

Borjas, George J. 1999a. "Immigration and Welfare Magnets," *Journal of Labor Economics* 17 (October): 607–37.

———. 1999b. "Immigration and the Food Stamp Program." Cambridge, Mass.: Harvard University, June. Mimeo.

Borjas, George J., and Lynette Hilton. 1996. "Immigration and the Welfare State: Immigrant Participation in Means-Tested Entitlement Programs," *Quarterly Journal of Economics* 111 (May): 575–604.

Borjas, George J., and Stephen J. Trejo. 1991. "Immigrant Participation in the Welfare System," *Industrial and Labor Relations Review* 44 (January): 195–211.

Branigin, William. 1997. "INS Says It May Never Find Naturalized Criminals," *Washington Post*, May 1.

Edwards, James R. 2001. "Public Charge Doctrine: A Fundamental Principle of American Immigration Policy," Center for Immigration Studies *Backgrounder*, May.

Espenshade, Thomas J., Jessica L. Baraka, and Gregory A. Huber. 1997. "Implications of the 1996 Welfare and Immigration Reform Acts for U.S. Immigration," *Population and Development Review* 23 (December): 769–801.

Fix, Michael, and Jeffrey S. Passel. 1999. "Trends in Noncitizens' and Citizens' Use of Public Benefits Following Welfare Reform: 1994–97." Washington, D.C.: Urban Institute, March.

Galvin, Kevin. 1997. "Democrats Reaching Out for Immigrant Support," Associated Press Political Service, May 3.

Hutchinson, Edward P. 1981. *Legislative History of American Immigration Policy, 1798–1965*. Philadelphia: University of Pennsylvania Press.

INS (U.S. Immigration and Naturalization Service). 1997. *Statistical Yearbook of the Immigration and Naturalization Service*. Washington, D.C.: U.S. Government Printing Office.

Olsen, Randall J., and Patricia B. Reagan. 1996. "You Can Go Home Again: Evidence from Longitudinal Data." Columbus: Ohio State University, September.

Passel, Jeffrey S. 1996. "Problem with March 1994 and 1995 Weighting." Washington, D.C.: Urban Institute, November 12. Mimeo.

Primus, Wendell. 1996–97. "Immigration Provisions in the New Welfare Law," *Focus* 18 (Fall/Winter): 14–18.

Reyes, David. 1994. "Prop. 187 Ruling Awaited with Confusion and Angst," *Los Angeles Times*, December 31.

Schippers, David P. 2000. "Abusing the INS," *Wall Street Journal*, August 23.

Schoeni, Robert F., and Rebecca Blank. 2000. "What Has Welfare Reform Accomplished? Impacts on Welfare Participation, Employment, Income, Poverty, and Family Structure." NBER Working Paper No. 7627. Cambridge, Mass.: National Bureau of Economic Research, March.

Smith, James P., and Barry Edmonston, eds. 1997. *The New Americans: Economic, Demographic, and Fiscal Effects of Immigration*. Washington, D.C.: National Academy Press.

Storesletten, Kjetil. 2000. "Sustaining Fiscal Policy through Immigration," *Journal of Political Economy* 108 (April): 300–23.

Tienda, Marta, and Leif Jensen. 1986. "Immigration and Public Assistance Participation: Dispelling the Myth of Dependency," *Social Science Research* 15 (December): 372–400.

U.S. Central Intelligence Agency. 1999. *Handbook of Economic Statistics*. Washington, D.C.: CIA.

U.S. House of Representatives. 1998. *Background Material and Data on Programs within the Jurisdiction of the Committee on Ways and Means*. Washington, D.C.: The Committee.

Vialet, Joyce C., and Larry M. Eig. 1998. "Alien Eligibility for Public Assistance," Congressional Research Service, Report No. 96-617, November 6.

Wasem, Ruth Ellen. 1998. "Naturalization Trends, Issues, and Legislation," Congressional Research Service, Report No. 98-190. Washington, D.C.: CRS, June 24.

Zimmermann, Wendy, and Karen C. Tumlin. 1999. "Patchwork Policies: State Assistance for Immigrants under Welfare Reform." Occasional Paper No. 24. Washington, D.C.: Urban Institute, May.

12

Human Capital and Earnings of Female Immigrants to Australia, Canada, and the United States

HEATHER ANTECOL, DEBORAH A. COBB-CLARK, AND STEPHEN J. TREJO

The international migration of women is an important demographic phenomenon worldwide. For example, the United Nations reports that of the 77 million people who were enumerated in various national censuses between 1970 and 1986 as living outside their country of birth, 48 percent were women (United Nations 1995). While immigration streams in many corners of the world (most notably Africa and parts of Asia) are male dominated, in the major immigrant-receiving nations such as Australia, Canada, and the United States, women have figured prominently in the immigration flow for many decades. Female immigrants to the United States have actually outnumbered their male counterparts in every period since 1930 (Houstoun, Kramer, and Barrett 1984; United Nations 1995: table 2),[1] and since 1960 in Australia and Canada the proportion of all immigrants who are women has exceeded 45 percent (Madden and Young 1993; United Nations 1995: table 2). Despite the fact that, worldwide, immigrants are as likely to be women as men, much of the immigration literature has tended to focus exclusively on men.[2]

---

[1] The single exception appears to be 1980–1984, although the sex composition of immigrants for fiscal year 1980–1981 cannot be determined (United Nations 1995).

[2] There are exceptions. For example, Reitz (1998) uses 1980 census data for the United States and 1981 census data for Australia and Canada to examine the role that human

Our objective is to contribute to an emerging literature on the experiences of female immigrants by comparing the observable skills—language fluency, education, and income—of female immigrants to Australia, Canada, and the United States. While we (Antecol, Cobb-Clark, and Trejo 2003) and others (Duleep and Regets 1992; Borjas 1993) have examined these issues for men, little is known about how the skills of female immigrants vary across destination countries.[3]

This exercise is important for a number of reasons. First, much of the current debate about legal immigration centers on how best to craft the policies used to select immigrants. In general, there has been a movement toward skill-based selection criteria. In the United States, for example, concerns about declining skill level among the immigrant population (Borjas 1995) have prompted calls for an increased emphasis on skills in the immigrant selection process. In light of this debate, it is important to understand how immigration policy influences immigrant skill levels. Second, there appear to be substantial differences in the extent to which policy is used to select immigrant men and women for their labor market skills. There are important gender differences in the distribution of immigrants across visa categories. In addition, women disproportionately migrate as dependents of principal applicants and as such are not subject to any specific selection criteria. Thus it is important to consider women explicitly.

A comparative analysis of Australia, Canada, and the United States provides a productive way of addressing these issues. While these nations' economies are similar in many fundamental respects and the countries share a common history as major immigrant-receiving countries,[4] their labor market policies and institutions differ markedly. Most importantly, while U.S. immigration policy is primarily one of family reunification, Australia and Canada have made a number of attempts to screen workers on the basis of special skills or high education levels (Boyd 1976;

---

capital factors (such as education) and labor market institutions (such as unionization) play in generating cross-national differences in entry-level earnings of both male and female immigrants in the urban labor force. Further, Reitz et. al. (1999) conduct a similar analysis for Canada and Germany using the first wave of the 1984 German Socio-Economic Panel and the 1986 Canadian census.

[3] There is a growing literature that examines the labor market assimilation of female immigrants; see, for example, Funkhouser and Trejo 1998; Schoeni 1998.

[4] During the period 1975–1980, for example, nearly two-thirds of all immigrants chose one of these three countries as their destination (Borjas 1991). More recently, other countries have emerged as important immigrant destinations, but Australia, Canada, and the United States remain dominant receiving countries.

Price 1979; Green and Green 1995). This institutional variation provides a means of assessing the effects of policy on the skills of immigrants.

Our results indicate that, overall, women immigrating to Australia and Canada are more skilled than women immigrating to the United States. They are more likely to be fluent in the destination country language, have higher levels of education (relative to native-born women), and have higher incomes (relative to native-born women) than their U.S. counterparts. To a large degree, however, the skill deficit of U.S. female immigrants is driven by the relatively high proportion of them who hail from Central and South America. Consistent with previous findings for men (Duleep and Regets 1992; Borjas 1993; Antecol, Cobb-Clark, and Trejo 2003), the observable skills of foreign-born women in Australia, Canada, and the United States look quite similar once we consider only those immigrants originating outside of Latin America.

In the following section we provide institutional detail about the immigration programs of Australia, Canada, and the United States and consider how these programs are expected to influence the skills of female immigrants. An overview of each of our data sources and estimation samples is provided in the next section. In later sections of the chapter we assess how language fluency, educational attainment, and income of female immigrants vary across destination countries.

IMMIGRATION POLICY AND THE SKILLS OF FEMALE IMMIGRANTS

In Australia and Canada, "independent" migrants without immediate relatives are selected on the basis of a "points test" that takes into account factors such as the applicant's age, education, language ability, and occupation.[5] Immigrants are also selected because they have special talents or because they meet certain investment requirements and intend to establish a business in the destination country. Immigrants entering Australia or Canada through any of these avenues are typically categorized as "skilled" immigrants because their human capital and potential labor market success play a key role in their admission. In contrast, "family" immigrants consist of those applicants admitted solely on the basis of having an immediate relative in the destination country, and "refugees" are admitted on humanitarian grounds.

---

[5] Some applicants with relatives in the destination country are also evaluated by a points test, with the number of points required for admission lowered when the family relationship is sufficiently close.

In the United States, immediate family members of U.S. citizens are "numerically unlimited" and can enter without counting against the overall cap set for annual immigrant admissions. "Numerically limited" family immigrants include more distant relatives of U.S. citizens and the immediate relatives of U.S. permanent residents. In 1990 these individuals entered the United States under one of four family-related preference categories (first, second, fourth, or fifth). U.S. immigrants entering under the third or sixth preference categories are considered to be "skilled" because their occupation or labor market skills played a role in their admission.[6]

Skills play a much larger role in immigrant selection in Australia and Canada than in the United States (Boyd 1976; Price 1979; Green and Green 1995).[7] Around 1990, half of Australian immigrants and almost 40 percent of Canadian immigrants were admitted because of their labor market skills, whereas less than 10 percent of U.S. immigrants gained entry in this way.[8] Conversely, two-thirds of U.S. immigrants were admitted on the basis of their family relationships, as compared with only a quarter of Australian immigrants and 37 percent of Canadian immigrants.[9] The relative importance of skilled versus family migration varies somewhat across regions of origin; but for all source regions, the share of skilled immigrants is much higher and the share of family immigrants is much lower in Australia and Canada than in the United States. Furthermore, although the share of immigrants admitted under a point system has varied over time (particularly for Canada), since at least the early 1970s the percentage of immigrants admitted on the basis of labor market criteria has been much

---

[6] Rather than ranking family- and skill-based immigrants under a single preference system, the 1990 Immigration Act established a three-track preference system for family-sponsored, employment-based, and diversity immigrants (Vialet and Eig 1990). Our data predate this change in policy, however.

[7] For detailed discussions of immigration policy in these three countries, see Boyd 1976; Briggs 1984; Chiswick 1987; Borjas 1988; Vialet 1989; Cobb-Clark 1990; Reimers and Troper 1992; Green 1995; Green and Green 1995; Lack and Templeton 1995; Reitz 1998.

[8] The "skilled" category includes the immediate family members who accompany those admitted on the basis of their labor market skills. Therefore, these figures overstate the number of immigrants granted entry because of their own skills rather than family relationships, but adjusting for this feature of the reported data would not alter the conclusion that the skilled category constitutes a much larger share of immigrant admissions in Australia and Canada than in the United States. In addition, these figures pertain only to legal admissions. The sizable flow of undocumented migrants entering the United States outside formal channels implies that the share of all U.S. migrants admitted because of their skills is even lower than the reported figures suggest.

[9] The cited figures are from Antecol, Cobb-Clark, and Trejo 2003. See that work for details and further discussion.

higher in Australia and Canada than in the United States (Wright and Maxim 1993; Reitz 1998).

There are, however, important gender differences in the visa categories through which immigrants gain admission. In fiscal year 1990–1991, for example, men immigrating to Australia were about equally likely to have entered in a skilled migration category as in a family migration category, whereas female immigrants were much more likely to have entered in a family category (Madden and Young 1993; United Nations 1995). A similar pattern holds in Canada and the United States: compared to male immigrants, women are underrepresented in skilled migration categories and overrepresented in family migration categories (Houstoun, Kramer, and Barrett 1984; United Nations 1995). In general, women are much more likely than men to gain immigrant status through their family ties to other immigrants or to receiving-country citizens and residents.[10]

How might these differences in immigration policy influence the skill content of immigrant flows to the three destination countries? On the one hand, the Australian and Canadian practice of admitting a large fraction of immigrants through a point system that screens for labor market skills suggests that these countries should receive a more skilled immigrant flow than the United States. On the other hand, the theory of selective migration (Borjas 1991) predicts that the generous redistribution systems and relatively egalitarian wage structures in Australia and Canada work in the opposite direction by attracting less skilled immigrants residing in the bottom half of the income distribution.[11] Because of these conflicting forces, it is not immediately obvious how differences in immigration policies and institutional frameworks across these countries will affect the skill selectivity of immigrant flows.

To a large extent, however, the immigration point systems employed in Australia and Canada select immigrants based on easily observed characteristics such as age, education, language, and occupation. In terms of these characteristics, immigrants to Australia and Canada should be more productive than those migrating to the United States. Our tests of this hypothesis will reveal how successful immigration point systems are, in

---

[10] Houstoun, Kramer, and Barrett (1984) conclude that more than 90 percent of the overall sex differential in immigrant admissions to the United States can be accounted for by the preponderance of women among immediate family members.

[11] For many reasons (stronger labor unions, higher minimum wages, national health insurance, more generous unemployment insurance and welfare systems), workers in the lower end of the income distribution are generally better off in Australia and Canada than in the United States, especially relative to the average worker in each country (Card and Freeman 1993; Gregory and Daly 1994).

practice, at selecting immigrants with favorable skill measures, and how much this screening process raises the labor market productivity of immigrant workers.[12]

Interestingly, the opposite pattern should emerge if we first control for the characteristics that immigrant point systems screen on. In particular, among immigrants with similar observable skill measures, the most productive should locate in the United States, where there is less social insurance against poor labor market outcomes but a greater individual return to favorable outcomes. Our tests of this hypothesis will indicate to what extent immigrant location choices based on difficult-to-observe attributes, such as ability and ambition, are able to undo the selectivity intended by point systems. Alternatively, a finding that Australian and Canadian immigrants are superior to U.S. immigrants in terms of unobservable as well as observable determinants of earnings would suggest that the "personal assessment" portion of a point system successfully screens for some of the difficult-to-observe attributes related to labor market productivity.

Finally, recall that, in all three countries, men are much more likely than women to gain admission on the basis of immigration criteria related to labor market considerations rather than family relationships. For this reason we might expect that the stronger emphasis on skill-based admissions in Australia and Canada compared to the United States would have a larger impact on cross-country differences in the skill content of male rather than female immigration flows.

THE DATA

Individual-level data from the 1991 Australian and Canadian censuses and the 1990 U.S. census are used throughout the analysis. These censuses provide comparable data on demographic characteristics, labor force be-

[12] For several reasons it is not a foregone conclusion that the Australian and Canadian systems lead to an immigrant flow that is highly selective in terms of characteristics associated with labor market success. First, both systems admit many immigrants who are not screened by a points test, including applicants with immediate family who are citizens of the destination country, refugees, and the family members who accompany those admitted by a points test. Second, both systems award a significant number of points based on a "personal assessment" of the applicant by the immigration official conducting the face-to-face interview. Finally, Reitz (1998) argues that the Australian and Canadian points tests can be passed by applicants with quite modest skill levels, and therefore these tests may provide only very weak filters for immigrant labor market skills.

havior, country of birth, and year of arrival for immigrants,[13] in each of the three countries.[14] The large samples available in census data are ideal for our purposes because immigrants constitute a small fraction of the total population, and it will be important to disaggregate the immigrant population according to variables such as year of arrival and country of origin.

Our analysis is restricted to women between the ages of twenty-five and fifty-nine who are not institutional residents. This allows us to concentrate on women who have completed their formal schooling and who are in prime working ages. To control for cross-country differences in social or economic conditions or in the manner in which the census data were collected, outcomes for immigrants will be compared to outcomes for otherwise similar native-born women. To increase comparability of the native samples and improve their usefulness as a comparison group, nonwhites are excluded from the native (but not the immigrant) samples.[15] Finally, residents of the Atlantic Provinces and the Territories are excluded from the Canadian samples because for these individuals the information about country of birth and year of immigration is not reported in sufficient detail.

These restrictions produce final samples of immigrant women totaling 10,948 for Australia, 39,016 for Canada, and 309,903 for the United States. Table 12.1 displays the region-of-birth distribution of those female immigrants arriving in the ten years prior to the census. In some cases the proportion of the total immigrant flow arriving from a particular region of birth is similar across destination countries. For example, despite considerable variation in the geographic distance between source and destination countries, women from the Philippines make up about 7 percent of the female immigrant flow into all three countries. In other cases, however, destination countries receive

---

[13] We use the term "immigrant" here as synonymous with foreign-born individuals, in contrast to the official terminology of the U.S. Immigration and Naturalization Service, in which immigrants are legal permanent residents, and other foreigners—tourists, business travelers, and recent refugee arrivals—are "nonimmigrant aliens." The census data analyzed here cannot make such distinctions among foreign-born individuals.

[14] The Australian data constitute a 1 percent sample of the population, while the Canadian data form a 3 percent sample and the U.S. data represent a 5 percent sample. Thus the U.S. sample is much larger than the other two. To lighten the computational burden, we employ a 0.1 percent (or 1 in a 1,000) sample of U.S. natives, but we use the full 5 percent sample of U.S. immigrants, and we use the full samples of natives and immigrants available in the Australian and Canadian data. The Australian and Canadian census data are self-weighting, whereas the 1990 U.S. census provides sampling weights that we use in all of the calculations reported in the chapter.

[15] In particular, we exclude blacks, Asians, Hispanics, and aboriginals from the native sample for each destination country.

Table 12.1. Region of Birth Distributions of Post-1980/81 Female Immigrant Arrivals, by Destination Country

Region of Birth	Destination Country		
	Australia	Canada	United States
United Kingdom	18.3	5.3	2.0
Europe[1]	12.5	19.3	8.9
Middle East	4.7	6.5	3.2
Africa	3.6	5.4	2.3
China	4.2	5.9	3.7
Hong Kong	3.2	8.3	0.7
Philippines	7.6	7.1	6.9
Southern Asia	4.8	8.7	3.9
Other Asia	19.9	11.8	16.4
Central/South America	2.5	16.1	45.6
United States	2.0	4.5	NA
Other North America	1.0	NA	1.7
Oceania/Antarctica	15.7	NA	0.6
Other	NA	1.1	4.0
All regions	100.0%	100.0%	100.0%
Sample size	3,329	10,677	109,994

[1] Europe is defined to include the former USSR.

Note: Data are from the 1991 Australian and Canadian censuses and the 1990 U.S. census. The samples include foreign-born women ages 25 to 59 who immigrated during 1981–1991 in the Australian and Canadian data or during 1980–1990 in the U.S. data. Entries of "NA" indicate regions of birth that cannot be defined for a particular destination country. Columns may not sum to 100 percent because of rounding error. Sampling weights were used in the U.S. calculations.

dramatically different shares of female immigrants from particular source regions. Most importantly, close to half of the women immigrating to the United States after 1980 hail from Central or South America (including Mexico and the Caribbean), whereas the same is true of only 16 percent of Canadian immigrants and less than 3 percent of Australian immigrants. In Australia and Canada, a quarter or more of recent female immigrants originated in either the United Kingdom or Europe, compared to the corresponding figure of only 11 percent in the United States. Another difference is that Asians make up a somewhat larger share of the immigrant flow to Australia (40 percent) and Canada (42 percent) than to the United States (32 percent). Lastly, note that Australia receives a sizable number of immigrants from New Zealand.

Although in general these patterns for female immigrants closely resemble those observed for men, the Philippines is an important exception (Antecol, Cobb-Clark, and Trejo 2003). While only 2.4 percent of recent male immigrants enumerated in the Australian census were born in the Philippines, this was true of 7.6 percent of female immigrants. Similar disparities show up in the Filipino shares of male (4.0 and 4.1 percent) and female (7.1 and 6.9 percent) immigrants in Canada and the United States, respectively. These differences imply that Filipino migration to the three destination countries is heavily female. In Australia, fully 76 percent of Filipino immigrants arriving after 1980 are women, and the analogous figures are 65 percent for Canada and 61 percent for the United States.[16]

FLUENCY IN THE DESTINATION COUNTRY LANGUAGE

Measures of English language ability are very similar in the Australian and U.S. censuses. In each case, respondents were first asked whether they speak a language other than English at home. Individuals responding affirmatively were then asked whether they spoke English "very well," "well," "not well," or "not at all." In the Australian and U.S. data, individuals are defined as "fluent in the destination country language" if they speak English at home or if they report speaking English "very well" or "well." Unfortunately, the language questions in the Canadian census are not directly comparable with the Australian and U.S. questions. When using the Canadian data, individuals are defined as fluent in the destination country language if they report being able to conduct a conversation in either English or French.[17]

Given these definitions, table 12.2 reports for each destination country the percentage of immigrant women who are fluent in the native language, by five-year arrival cohorts.[18] In all three destination countries,

16 Overall, among post-1980 arrivals, women constituted 50 percent of the immigrant population in Australia, 51 percent in Canada, and 48 percent in the United States.

17 In their study of immigrants to Canada and the United States, Duleep and Regets (1992) use these same definitions in an attempt to create roughly comparable measures of language fluency from the 1981 Canadian census and the 1980 U.S. census.

18 The intervals listed in table 12.2 (and in subsequent tables) for the immigrant arrival cohorts are those that pertain to the Australian and Canadian data; the slightly different immigrant cohorts that pertain to the U.S. data are as follows: pre-1970, 1970–74,

Table 12.2. Percent of Female Immigrants Fluent in Destination Country Language, by Arrival Cohort and Destination Country

	Destination Country		
Immigrant Cohort	Australia	Canada	United States
Pre-1971 arrivals	92.5	97.5	89.3
	(0.4)	(0.1)	(0.1)
	[5,291]	[17,177]	[111,652]
1971–1975 arrivals	90.7	95.9	77.3
	(0.8)	(0.2)	(0.2)
	[1,320]	[6,427]	[41,656]
1976–1980 arrivals	87.8	94.9	72.1
	(1.0)	(0.3)	(0.2)
	[1021]	[4,722]	[46,600]
1981–1985 arrivals	83.5	92.6	64.0
	(1.1)	(0.4)	(0.2)
	[1,212]	[3,903]	[54,748]
1986–1991 arrivals	79.1	86.2	56.2
	(0.9)	(0.4)	(0.2)
	[2,104]	[6,787]	[55,247]

Note: Standard errors are in parentheses, and sample sizes are in brackets. Data are from the 1991 Australian and Canadian censuses and the 1990 U.S. census. The samples include foreign-born women ages 25 to 59. In the Australian and U.S. data, immigrants are designated as "fluent in the destination country language" if they speak only English or report speaking English "very well" or "well." In the Canadian data, the corresponding measure of fluency identifies immigrants who can conduct a conversation in either English or French. The intervals listed above for the immigrant arrival cohorts are those defined in the Australian and Canadian data; the slightly different immigrant cohorts defined in the U.S. data are as follows: pre-1970, 1970–1974, 1975–1979, 1980–1984, and 1985–1990. Sampling weights were used in the U.S. calculations.

1975–79, 1980–84, and 1985–90. For ease of exposition, henceforth we will refer to particular immigrant cohorts using the year intervals that pertain to the Australian and Canadian data, with the implied understanding that in the U.S. data the actual cohort intervals begin and end one year earlier.

immigrant fluency rates rise monotonically with the length of time since arrival. This pattern is largely due to the fact that immigrants who do not speak the destination country language when they arrive tend to acquire fluency over time as they adapt to their new home. We must caution, however, that differences between immigrant arrival cohorts observed at a single point in time may reflect permanent differences between these cohorts as well as the changes that occur for a given cohort as it spends more time in the destination country.[19]

For every arrival cohort, fluency rates are lower for U.S. immigrants than for Australian and Canadian immigrants, and the gap is particularly large for cohorts arriving after 1970. For example, among the most recent immigrants (those arriving within five years of the census), only 56 percent of U.S. immigrants are fluent, as compared to 79 percent of Australian immigrants and 86 percent of Canadian immigrants. This gap does not disappear with time. Even among immigrants who have spent between fifteen and twenty years in the destination country (1971–1975 arrivals), the fluency rate of U.S. immigrants (77 percent) is well below that of Australian immigrants (91 percent) and Canadian immigrants (96 percent).[20]

Does the fluency deficit of U.S. immigrants arise because the Australian and Canadian point systems are successful at screening the language ability of applicants? Previous results for men (Duleep and Regets 1992; Borjas 1993; Antecol, Cobb-Clark, and Trejo 2003) suggest that, to a large extent, differences in immigrant skills across destination countries are driven by the national origin mix of the immigrant flow. To explore whether a similar pattern holds for women, table 12.3 reports fluency rates separately by immigrant region of birth. In this table, we limit the sample to female immigrants who have been in the destination country for ten years or less.[21] The comparison between Australia and the United States is particularly informative given the similarities in how fluency is

[19] By tracking cohorts of U.S. immigrants between the 1980 and 1990 censuses, Carliner (1995, 1996) and Funkhouser (1996) show that English proficiency does indeed improve markedly with duration of U.S. residence and that this improvement plays an important role in immigrant wage growth.

[20] Note that the relative fluency of Canadian immigrants is probably overstated because of the particular wording of the language questions asked in the Canadian census. The U.S. and Australian language measures are much more comparable.

[21] In table 12.3, we also exclude immigrants from the four source regions listed in table 12.1 that cannot be defined for all three destination countries. The excluded regions are the following: United States, Other North America, Oceania/Antarctica, and Other.

Table 12.3. Percent of Post-1980/81 Female Immigrant Arrivals Fluent in Destination Country Language, by Birthplace and Destination Country

Region of Birth	Destination Country: Australia	Canada	United States
United Kingdom	99.5	100.0	99.6
	(0.3)	(.)	(0.1)
Europe	72.7	88.7	76.2
	(2.2)	(0.7)	(0.5)
Middle East	59.2	89.3	75.3
	(3.9)	(1.2)	(0.8)
Africa	97.5	95.6	89.7
	(1.4)	(0.9)	(0.7)
China	41.4	55.6	43.4
	(4.2)	(2.0)	(0.8)
Hong Kong	81.0	92.5	74.2
	(3.8)	(0.9)	(1.6)
Philippines	98.0	99.5	94.1
	(0.8)	(0.3)	(0.3)
Southern Asia	95.0	85.6	83.0
	(1.7)	(1.2)	(0.6)
Other Asia	56.9	78.7	54.0
	(1.9)	(1.2)	(0.4)
Central/South America	46.3	92.1	46.6
	(5.5)	(0.7)	(0.2)
All regions listed above	76.8	87.9	59.0
	(0.7)	(0.3)	(0.2)
All regions, excluding Central/South America	77.8	87.0	70.8
	(0.7)	(0.3)	(0.2)

Note: Standard errors are in parentheses. Data are from the 1991 Australian and Canadian censuses and the 1990 U.S. census. The samples include foreign-born women ages 25 to 59 who immigrated during 1981–1991 in the Australian and Canadian data or during 1980–1990 in the U.S. data. In the Australian and U.S. data, immigrants are designated as "fluent in the destination country language" if they speak only English or report speaking English "very well" or "well." In the Canadian data, the corresponding measure of fluency identifies immigrants who can conduct a conversation in either English or French. Sampling weights were used in the U.S. calculations.

measured in these censuses. Immigrant women from a given source country generally report similar levels of English language ability in Australia and the United States. Even so, the overall fluency rate for U.S. immigrants (59 percent) falls well short of the Australian rate (77 percent). This fluency deficit of female immigrants in the United States is due in large part to the sizable share of Latin Americans in the U.S. immigration flow. Once Latin American immigrants are excluded, 71 percent of female immigrants in the United States report being fluent in English, as compared to 78 percent of immigrant women in Australia.

Even among women originating outside of Latin America, however, English fluency is lower for U.S. immigrants than for Australian immigrants. In particular, immigrants from Asian countries tend to speak English at higher rates in Australia than in the United States. After excluding Latin American immigrants, the remaining fluency gap of 7 percentage points for foreign-born women in the United States relative to their Australian counterparts is larger than the corresponding gap of less than 3 percentage points observed for men (Antecol, Cobb-Clark, and Trejo 2003). Therefore, although a large portion of the overall fluency gap of U.S. immigrants is attributable to national origin, this factor is somewhat less important for women than for men.

EDUCATION

We turn now to education. Table 12.4 reports the results of least squares regressions in which the dependent variable is years of schooling and the independent variables include dummies identifying arrival cohorts.[22] Natives as well as immigrants are included in the analysis. Model 1 (see column 1) includes only the arrival cohort dummies, and as a result the intercepts represent the average education level of natives in each destination country while the coefficients on the arrival cohort dummies reflect the education differentials between immigrants in each arrival cohort and natives. U.S. native-born women have the highest mean education level (13.2 years), followed by Canadian-born women (12.6), and Australian-born women (11.3).[23] Female immigrants in the United States have between one and two fewer years of education than do native-born U.S. women. Female immigrants in Canada also have less education than their native-born counterparts, although the gap is much smaller in magnitude

[22] Robust standard errors are reported throughout the chapter.

[23] This pattern of education differences for the native-born in each of the three countries is similar to what Evans, Kelley, and Wanner (1998) and Reitz (1998) report.

Table 12.4. Determinants of Years of Education for Female Immigrants, by Destination Country

	Destination Country					
	Australia		Canada		United States	
Regressor	(1)	(2)	(1)	(2)	(1)	(2)
Intercept (natives)	11.32	11.51	12.57	13.25	13.15	13.38
	(0.02)	(0.03)	(0.01)	(0.01)	(0.01)	(0.02)
Immigrant cohort						
Pre-1971 arrivals	–0.12	0.01	–0.73	–0.20	–1.15	–0.98
	(0.04)	(0.04)	(0.03)	(0.03)	(0.02)	(0.02)
1971–1975 arrivals	0.31	0.35	–0.21	–0.17	–1.93	–1.98
	(0.07)	(0.07)	(0.05)	(0.04)	(0.03)	(0.03)
1976–1980 arrivals	0.71	0.67	–0.10	–0.19	–2.04	–2.16
	(0.08)	(0.08)	(0.05)	(0.05)	(0.03)	(0.03)
1981–1985 arrivals	0.86	0.80	–0.11	–0.27	–2.09	–2.22
	(0.07)	(0.07)	(0.06)	(0.05)	(0.02)	(0.02)
1986–1991 arrivals	1.34	1.25	–0.03	–0.25	–1.58	–1.71
	(0.06)	(0.06)	(0.04)	(0.04)	(0.02)	(0.02)
Age group						
30–34		0.09		–0.20		0.04
		(0.04)		(0.02)		(0.03)
35–39		–0.03		–0.25		0.10
		(0.04)		(0.02)		(0.04)
40–44		–0.26		–0.55		0.04
		(0.04)		(0.02)		(0.04)
45–49		–0.47		–1.12		–0.39
		(0.05)		(0.02)		(0.04)
50–54		–0.71		–1.85		–0.88
		(0.05)		(0.03)		(0.04)
55–59		–0.86		–2.53		–1.22
		(0.06)		(0.03)		(0.04)

Note: The dependent variable is years of schooling. The coefficients were estimated by least squares; robust standard errors are shown in parentheses. Data are from the 1991 Australian and Canadian censuses and the 1990 U.S. census. The samples include women ages 25 to 59, with nonwhites excluded from the native but not the foreign-born samples. The sample sizes for these regressions are 31,291 for Australia, 181,277 for Canada, and 354,426 for the United States. The intervals listed above for the immigrant arrival cohorts are those defined in the Australian and Canadian data; the slightly different immigrant cohorts defined in the U.S. data are as follows: pre-1970, 1970–1974, 1975–1979, 1980–1984, and 1985–1990. The reference group for the age dummies is 25- to 29-year-olds. Sampling weights were used in the U.S. calculations.

and the difference is not always statistically significant. Women migrating to Australia, however, are relatively more educated than Australian-born women.

Model 2 (see column 2) includes dummy variables identifying five-year age groups. In these regressions, the intercepts now represent the average education level of 25- to 29-year-old natives (the omitted age group), the arrival cohort coefficients measure immigrant-native differentials after conditioning on age, and the coefficients on the age dummies reflect education differentials between each age group and 25- to 29-year-olds. Controlling for age, which captures the secular rise in schooling levels that took place over this period, has little effect on the estimated immigrant-native schooling differentials or on the conclusion that the United States and Canada have been less successful than Australia in attracting female immigrants with more education than native-born women.

Interestingly, the relative education disadvantage of immigrant women in the United States and the relative education advantage of immigrant women in Australia are similar to what we found previously for men (Antecol, Cobb-Clark, and Trejo 2003). Among U.S. men, immigrants average one to two fewer years of schooling than natives, just as reported here for women. Among Australian men, immigrants possess more schooling than natives, which is what we find for women. In Canada, however, immigrant-native comparisons differ by gender. Compared to their native-born counterparts, foreign-born Canadian men have more education, whereas foreign-born Canadian women tend to have less. Given the similarities in the schooling levels of native-born men and women in Canada, these patterns suggest that Canada's attempts to encourage the immigration of highly educated individuals have been more successful among men then women. This result is not surprising because women often immigrate to Canada as dependent family members for whom no selection criteria apply.

The educational attainment of women arriving after 1980–1981 is presented in table 12.5 by region of birth. Average years of schooling for women in each destination country are reported in the first three columns. Within most regions of origin, the average education of female immigrants to the United States is generally as high or higher than that of female immigrants to Australia and Canada. Overall, however, foreign-born women in the United States have substantially less schooling (gaps of 1.2 to 1.4 years) than foreign-born women in the other two destination countries. As was the case with language fluency, the explanation for this pattern is the large share of female immigrants from Latin America in the U.S. immigration flow. Women migrating to the United States from Central and South America average less than 10 years of schooling, which is very low when

Table 12.5. Average and Relative Education of Post-1980/81 Female Immigrant Arrivals, by Birthplace and Destination Country

	Average Years of Schooling			Schooling Relative to Natives		
Region of Birth	Australia	Canada	United States	Australia	Canada	United States
United Kingdom	11.95	13.59	13.69	0.63	1.03	0.54
	(0.10)	(0.08)	(0.05)	(0.10)	(0.08)	(0.05)
Europe	12.65	12.89	13.22	1.34	0.33	0.07
	(0.13)	(0.08)	(0.04)	(0.13)	(0.08)	(0.04)
Middle East	12.72	12.61	12.67	1.41	0.05	-0.48
	(0.22)	(0.14)	(0.07)	(0.22)	(0.14)	(0.07)
Africa	12.63	12.89	13.50	1.31	0.33	0.35
	(0.21)	(0.13)	(0.07)	(0.21)	(0.13)	(0.07)
China	12.81	11.04	11.70	1.50	-1.52	-1.45
	(0.20)	(0.17)	(0.08)	(0.20)	(0.17)	(0.08)
Hong Kong	13.24	13.28	12.86	1.93	0.72	-0.29
	(0.18)	(0.08)	(0.13)	(0.18)	(0.08)	(0.13)
Philippines	13.35	13.80	14.04	2.03	1.24	0.90
	(0.15)	(0.10)	(0.04)	(0.15)	(0.10)	(0.04)
Southern Asia	13.44	11.97	14.17	2.12	-0.59	1.03
	(0.21)	(0.13)	(0.07)	(0.21)	(0.13)	(0.07)
Other Asia	12.71	10.94	11.75	1.39	-1.62	-1.40
	(0.08)	(0.12)	(0.04)	(0.08)	(0.12)	(0.04)
Central/South America	13.10	12.01	9.67	1.78	-0.55	-3.48
	(0.23)	(0.08)	(0.02)	(0.23)	(0.08)	(0.02)
All regions listed above	12.63	12.42	11.27	1.32	-0.14	-1.88
	(0.05)	(0.03)	(0.01)	(0.05)	(0.03)	(0.01)
All regions, excluding	12.62	12.50	12.79	1.31	-0.06	-0.36
Central/South America	(0.05)	(0.04)	(0.02)	(0.05)	(0.04)	(0.02)

Note: Robust standard errors are in parentheses. Data are from the 1991 Australian and Canadian censuses and the 1990 U.S. census. The samples include women ages 25 to 59, with nonwhites excluded from the native but not the foreign-born samples. The foreign-born samples are limited to women who immigrated during 1981–1991 in the Australian and Canadian data or during 1980–1990 in the U.S. data. Sampling weights were used in the U.S. calculations.

compared to the corresponding average for either U.S. native-born women or for Central and South American women who immigrate to Australia or Canada. Excluding Latin American immigrants from the calculations causes the mean education level of U.S. immigrants to jump from 11.3 years to 12.8 years. After making this exclusion, female immigrants to the United States have slightly more education than women migrating to Australia and Canada.

These kinds of international comparisons of education levels might be distorted by differences across countries in educational practices and in the census questions used to elicit information about educational attainment. Within a destination country, however, we would expect such factors to affect the measured education level of immigrants and natives in the same way. Therefore, we also examine a relative education measure (see the last three columns of table 12.5), which is defined as the difference in average years of schooling between a particular immigrant group and natives in the same destination country. When we consider only recent female immigrants who are not from Latin America (the bottom row of table 12.5), we find that Australian immigrants average 1.3 years more schooling than do native-born Australian women, Canadian immigrants have essentially the same education level as native-born Canadian women, and American immigrants have about a third of a year less schooling than native-born women in the United States. By this relative education measure, then, excluding immigrants from Central and South America dramatically shrinks—but does not completely eliminate—the educational disadvantage of foreign-born U.S. women compared to their counterparts in Australia and Canada. Regardless of whether immigrant education is measured in absolute terms or relative to natives, however, the overall educational gap between U.S. female immigrants and immigrant women in the other two destination countries arises in large part because the United States receives a sizable flow of comparatively uneducated immigrants from Latin America.

INCOME

We turn now to a consideration of personal income. An analysis of personal income—holding constant observable productivity-related characteristics—sheds light on how country-specific immigration policies influence the unobserved skills of immigrants. Ideally, we would prefer to analyze earnings rather than income, but unfortunately the Australian

Table 12.6. The Effect of Immigrant Cohort on Female Immigrant Income, by Destination Country

	Destination Country					
	Australia		Canada		United States	
Regressor	(1)	(2)	(1)	(2)	(1)	(2)
Immigrant cohort						
Pre-1971 arrivals	–.027	.004	.122	.068	.064	.169
	(.024)	(.025)	(.016)	(.016)	(.014)	(.017)
1971–1975 arrivals	.021	.031	.047	.008	–.036	.153
	(.029)	(.029)	(.018)	(.018)	(.015)	(.020)
1976–1980 arrivals	.002	.016	–.004	–.036	–.109	.105
	(.033)	(.034)	(.020)	(.019)	(.015)	(.020)
1981–1985 arrivals	–.055	–.035	–.113	–.127	–.236	–.001
	(.027)	(.028)	(.020)	(.020)	(.015)	(.020)
1986–1991 arrivals	–.074	–.057	–.342	–.352	–.413	–.197
	(.026)	(.026)	(.019)	(.019)	(.016)	(.021)
R^2	.321	.373	.137	.186	.278	.328
Sample size	20,612	18,396	139,342	139,333	240,423	240,423
Control variables						
Age dummies	Yes	Yes	Yes	Yes	Yes	Yes
Education	No	Yes	No	Yes	No	Yes
Fluency dummies	No	Yes	No	Yes	No	Yes

Note: The dependent variable is the natural logarithm of weekly personal income. The coefficients were estimated by least squares, and robust standard errors are shown in parentheses. Data are from the 1991 Australian and Canadian censuses and the 1990 U.S. census. The samples include women ages 25 to 59, with nonwhites excluded from the native but not the foreign-born samples. Only employed women are included in the samples. The income and employment measures in the Australian data refer to the usual week and the census survey week, respectively, whereas in the Canadian and U.S. data these measures refer to the calendar year preceding the census. In addition to the control variables listed above, all regressions include indicators for geographic location and hours worked during the census survey week. The coefficients of the controls for geographic location, weekly hours of work, and fluency are restricted to be the same for immigrants and natives, whereas the coefficients of the age and education variables are allowed to vary by nativity. The intervals listed above for the immigrant arrival cohorts are those defined in the Australian and Canadian data; the slightly different immigrant cohorts defined in the U.S. data are as follows: pre-1970, 1970–1974, 1975–1979, 1980–1984, and 1985–1990. The immigrant cohort coefficients reported in this table have been normalized to represent immigrant-native income differentials for women who are aged 25 to 29 (in both specifications) and who have 12 years of education (in specification (2)). Sampling weights were used in the U.S. calculations.

data do not distinguish earnings from other income sources.[24] To increase the correspondence between income and earnings, in this section we will restrict our estimation samples to employed women.[25] The income and employment measures in the Australian data refer to the usual week and the census survey week, respectively, whereas in the Canadian and U.S. data these measures refer to the calendar year preceding the census. We have converted the Canadian and U.S. income measures to a weekly basis so as to match the Australian data.[26]

For these samples of employed immigrant and native-born women, tables 12.6 and 12.7 present ordinary least squares (OLS) estimates of the determinants of weekly income.[27] Two specifications are reported for each destination country. In model 1, the independent variables include immigrant arrival cohort dummies, age dummies, controls for geographic location, and indicators for hours worked during the census survey week. The coefficients of the geographic location and weekly hours of work variables are restricted to be the same for immigrants and natives, whereas the coefficients of the age dummies are allowed to vary by nativity. Model 2 also includes a measure of years of schooling—which is allowed to vary by nativity—and indicators for fluency in the language of the destination country.

The estimated cohort effects from these regressions are presented in table 12.6, and table 12.7 reports the coefficients of the age, education, and language fluency variables. In model 1 the cohort coefficients have been

---

[24] Earnings information is available in the Canadian and U.S. censuses, however, and for these two countries we have replicated the analyses reported below using earnings rather than income as the dependent variable. The income and earnings regressions produce similar results.

In the Canadian sample, we exclude immigrants who arrived during the census year (1991), because income data are not available for these recent arrivals.

[25] Restricting the sample to employed women raises the potential for selection bias, as employment rates are likely to be correlated with labor market opportunities. Under certain circumstances, statistical techniques can be used to adjust for this bias (Heckman 1980), but the data that we analyze here do not provide the information necessary to make credible adjustments of this type.

[26] Another difference between the income measures available for each country is that the Australian census reports income in fourteen intervals, whereas the Canadian and U.S. censuses provide continuous measures of income. For Australia, we use the midpoints of the reported income intervals to construct the income variable employed in our regressions. For Canada and the United States, the results reported here employ a continuous income variable, but we obtain similar results when we instead group these data into intervals and assign midpoints so as to mimic the Australian data.

[27] The dependent variable in these regressions is the natural logarithm of weekly personal income.

Table 12.7. The Effect of Age, Education, and Language Fluency on Female Immigrant Income, by Destination Country

	Destination Country					
	Australia		Canada		United States	
Regressor	(1)	(2)	(1)	(2)	(1)	(2)
Age group						
30–34	.056	.051	.103	.092	.091	.091
	(.016)	(.016)	(.008)	(.008)	(.018)	(.017)
35–39	.044	.051	.149	.143	.138	.131
	(.016)	(.016)	(.009)	(.009)	(.018)	(.017)
40–44	.009	.049	.208	.228	.163	.160
	(.016)	(.016)	(.009)	(.009)	(.018)	(.017)
45–49	–.010	.044	.188	.247	.167	.196
	(.018)	(.018)	(.010)	(.010)	(.019)	(.018)
50–54	–.008	.067	.141	.244	.137	.207
	(.020)	(.021)	(.011)	(.011)	(.021)	(.021)
55–59	–.056	.052	.145	.288	.175	.263
	(.028)	(.030)	(.013)	(.013)	(.023)	(.023)
Immigrant × age group						
30–34	–.035	–.006	–.123	.042	–.025	–.011
	(.031)	(.032)	(.020)	(.020)	(.019)	(.019)
35–39	–.014	.001	–.131	.024	–.044	–.006
	(.031)	(.031)	(.020)	(.020)	(.019)	(.019)
40–44	–.033	–.024	–.167	–.031	–.074	–.022
	(.031)	(.031)	(.020)	(.020)	(.020)	(.019)
45–49	–.025	–.005	–.153	–.034	–.092	–.037
	(.033)	(.035)	(.021)	(.021)	(.021)	(.020)
50–54	–.076	–.071	–.140	–.022	–.084	–.043
	(.038)	(.040)	(.023)	(.023)	(.023)	(.022)
55–59	.028	–.011	–.160	–.052	–.140	–.084
	(.050)	(.054)	(.025)	(.025)	(.025)	(.025)

Table 12.7 continued

Education	.066	.093	.104
	(.002)	(.001)	(.002)
Immigrant × education	–.012	–.038	–.047
	(.004)	(.001)	(.003)
Ability to speak English (or French in Canada):			
Well or Very well	–.107	–.073	–.035
	(.015)	(.011)	(.018)
Not at all or Not well	–.326	–.041	–.182
	(.039)	(.030)	(.023)

Note: These coefficients are from the same income regressions as table 12.6; see the note to that table for more information. Robust standard errors are shown in parentheses. The reference group for the age dummies is 25- to 29-year-olds. The reference group for the fluency dummies is women who speak only English in the Australian and U.S. data, and women who speak only English and/or French in the Canadian data.

normalized to represent immigrant-native income differentials for women who are aged twenty-five to twenty-nine, whereas in model 2 the cohort coefficients represent the same differentials for women aged twenty-five to twenty-nine with twelve years of education.[28] To facilitate interpretation, the immigrant-native income differentials implied by these regressions are also depicted in figure 12.1. Model 1 is shown in the top panel, and model 2 is shown in the bottom panel of the figure.[29] Each line in the figure corresponds to a different destination country, and immigrant arrival cohorts are distinguished by years since arrival, which is measured along the horizontal axis.

These graphs are only intended to illustrate the income differences between immigrants of various arrival cohorts and natives at a given point in time. The plots are not meant to portray the life-cycle trajectories of immigrants as they gain experience in the destination country labor market, because analyses of immigrant outcomes using a single cross-section of data cannot distinguish assimilation and cohort effects.

When we do not control for education and language ability (the top panel of figure 12.1), the income gap between female immigrants and their native-born counterparts is largest in the United States and smallest in Australia, with Canada falling in between but not too different from the United States. Once we condition on education and language fluency (the bottom panel of figure 12.1), however, this gap shrinks dramatically in the United States. Now the relative income disadvantage of female immigrants to the United States is smaller than that of women migrating to Australia or Canada, except for the most recent arrival cohort of Australian immigrants. These comparisons suggest that the smaller income deficits (relative to natives) initially observed for immigrant women in Australia

---

[28] Note that the interactions between nativity and age in these regressions imply that the immigrant-native income gaps presented in table 12.7 for ages twenty-five to twenty-nine will differ at older ages.

[29] To control for age differences, both across countries and between immigrants and natives within a country, these calculations assign the same age distribution to all groups. In particular, we use the age distribution observed for our sample of U.S. immigrants: 18.0 percent are in the 25–29 age range, 18.9 percent are 30 to 34, 17.4 percent are 35 to 39, 16.1 percent are 40 to 44, 12.5 percent are 45 to 49, 10.0 percent are 50 to 54, and 7.1 percent are 55 to 59. Because the immigrant-native income differentials estimated for each country are allowed to vary by age group, the overall differentials shown in figure 12.1 depend on the particular age distribution used. However, similar patterns emerge from using the age distributions observed for any of the immigrant or native samples in our three destination countries. Note that the calculations displayed in the bottom panel of figure 12.1 pertain to individuals with twelve years of education.

Figure 12.1
Predicted Immigrant-Native Income Differentials

A. Without Controls for Education and Fluency

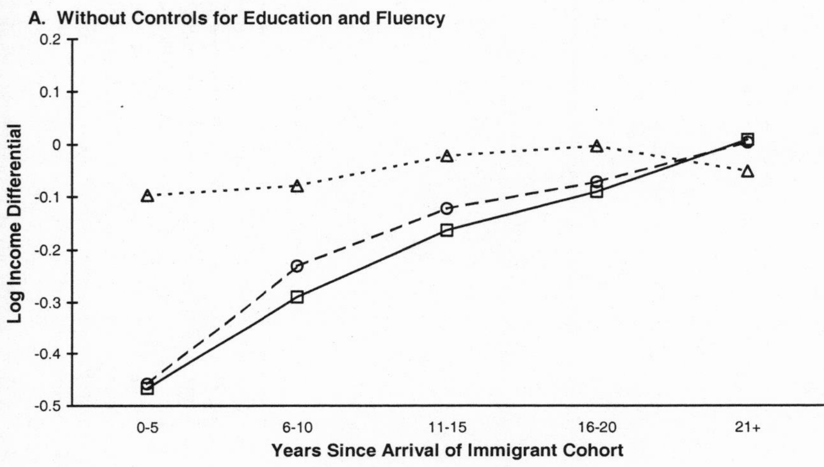

B. With Controls for Education and Fluency

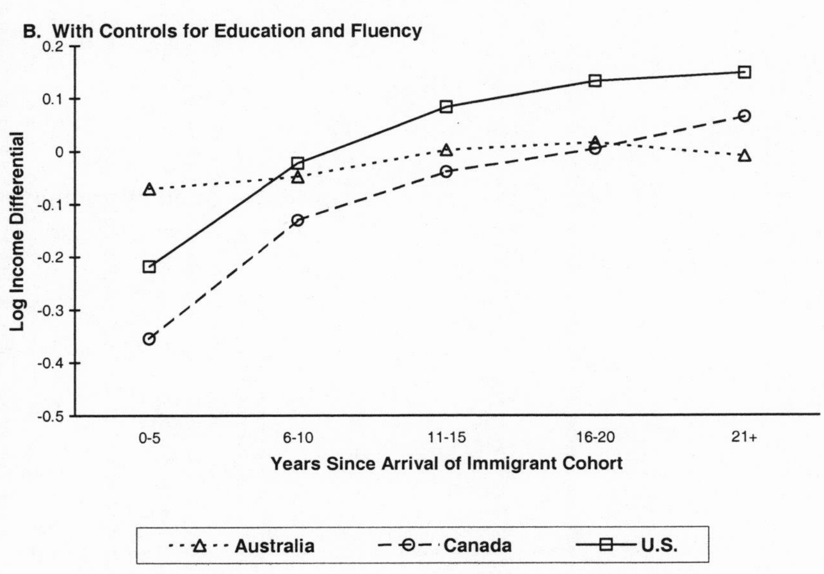

Australia — Canada — U.S.

Table 12.8. The Effect of Immigrant Cohort on Female Immigrant Income, Excluding Immigrants from Central/South America, by Destination Country

	Destination Country					
	Australia		Canada		United States	
Regressor	(1)	(2)	(1)	(2)	(1)	(2)
Immigrant cohort						
Pre-1971 arrivals	–.026	.008	.115	.071	.123	.178
	(.024)	(.025)	(.017)	(.017)	(.015)	(.017)
1971–1975 arrivals	.027	.036	.052	.024	.091	.177
	(.029)	(.029)	(.020)	(.019)	(.017)	(.021)
1976–1980 arrivals	.000	.015	.007	-.017	.028	.131
	(.033)	(.034)	(.021)	(.021)	(.016)	(.022)
1981–1985 arrivals	–.054	–.033	–.101	–.109	–.090	.026
	(.027)	(.028)	(.022)	(.022)	(.016)	(.023)
1986–1991 arrivals	–.069	–.053	–.338	–.341	–.293	–.191
	(.026)	(.027)	(.021)	(.021)	(.017)	(.024)
R^2	.321	.373	.137	.187	.282	.330
Sample size	20,512	18,319	135,370	135,361	154,769	154,769
Control variables						
Age dummies	Yes	Yes	Yes	Yes	Yes	Yes
Education	No	Yes	No	Yes	No	Yes
Fluency dummies	No	Yes	No	Yes	No	Yes

Note: The dependent variable is the natural logarithm of weekly personal income. The coefficients were estimated by least squares, and robust standard errors are shown in parentheses. Data are from the 1991 Australian and Canadian censuses and the 1990 U.S. census. The samples include women ages 25 to 59, with nonwhites excluded from the native but not the foreign-born samples. Only employed women are included in the samples. These particular regressions exclude immigrants born in Central and South America. The income and employment measures in the Australian data refer to the usual week and the census survey week, respectively, whereas in the Canadian and U.S. data these measures refer to the calendar year preceding the census. In addition to the control variables listed above, all regressions include indicators for geographic location and hours worked during the census survey week. The coefficients of the controls for geographic location, weekly hours of work, and fluency are restricted to be the same for immigrants and natives, whereas the coefficients of the age and education variables are allowed to vary by nativity. The intervals listed above for the immigrant arrival cohorts are those defined in the Australian and Canadian data; the slightly different immigrant cohorts defined in the U.S. data are as follows: pre-1970, 1970–1974, 1975–1979, 1980–1984, and 1985–1990. The immigrant cohort coefficients reported in this table have been normalized to represent immigrant-native income differentials for women who are aged 25 to 29 (in both specifications) and who have 12 years of education (in specification (2)). Sampling weights were used in the U.S. calculations.

and Canada are largely explained by their higher levels of education and language ability. Once we control for these observable skill measures, the relative incomes of female immigrants in the United States are higher than those of Canadian immigrants from all arrival cohorts, and they are higher than those of Australian immigrants from all cohorts but the most recent.

In Australia, immigrant-native income differences are relatively small to begin with, do not change much after controlling for education and fluency, and vary little by immigrant year of arrival. In addition, table 12.7 indicates that although the economic return to a year of schooling for native-born women is much higher in the United States (10.4 percent) and Canada (9.3 percent) than in Australia (6.6 percent), the return to education for immigrant women is similar in all three countries (ranging from 5.4 percent in Australia to 5.7 percent in the United States). Therefore, in terms of both the intercept and the return to education, the wage structure is much more similar for immigrant and native-born women in Australia than in Canada or the United States. Previously we found this same pattern for men (Antecol, Cobb-Clark, and Trejo 2003).

Tables 12.8 and 12.9, along with figure 12.2, replicate the preceding analysis of immigrant-native income differentials, but now excluding women born in Central and South America. This exclusion has little effect on the immigrant income gaps estimated for Australia or Canada, which is not surprising because Latin American immigrants constitute a small share of the overall immigration flow into these countries. In the United States, however, excluding women born in Central and South America serves to substantially reduce the immigrant income disadvantage (compare the top panels of figures 12.1 and 12.2). In fact, the impact of excluding Latin American immigrants on immigrant-native income differentials in the United States is similar to the impact of controlling for English fluency and education (compare the bottom panel of figure 12.1 with the top panel of figure 12.2), a finding that reflects the very low levels of fluency and schooling possessed by U.S. immigrants from Latin America (as we documented earlier in tables 12.3 and 12.5). The income analyses display the same general pattern that we have already seen for language fluency and education: unskilled immigration from Latin America accounts for a large portion of the overall gap in human capital between U.S. female immigrants and women migrating to Australia and Canada. Once again, these results for women mirror our previous findings for men (Antecol, Cobb-Clark, and Trejo 2003).

Even after excluding women from Latin America, however, the incomes of U.S. immigrants improve relative to Australian and Canadian immigrants once controls are added for fluency and schooling (compare

Table 12.9. The Effect of Age, Education, and Language Fluency on Female Immigrant Income, Excluding Immigrants from Central/South America, by Destination Country

	Destination Country					
	Australia		Canada		United States	
Regressor	(1)	(2)	(1)	(2)	(1)	(2)
Age group						
30–34	.057	.051	.099	.093	.091	.091
	(.016)	(.016)	(.008)	(.008)	(.018)	(.017)
35–39	.044	.051	.144	.143	.137	.131
	(.016)	(.016)	(.009)	(.009)	(.018)	(.017)
40–44	.009	.050	.204	.228	.162	.159
	(.016)	(.016)	(.009)	(.009)	(.018)	(.017)
45–49	–.009	.045	.184	.247	.167	.195
	(.018)	(.018)	(.010)	(.010)	(.019)	(.018)
50–54	–.008	.068	.137	.244	.137	.206
	(.020)	(.021)	(.011)	(.011)	(.021)	(.021)
55–59	–.056	.053	.141	.290	.175	.263
	(.028)	(.030)	(.013)	(.013)	(.023)	(.023)
Immigrant × age group						
30–34	–.038	–.012	–.118	.041	–.016	–.010
	(.031)	(.032)	(.021)	(.022)	(.020)	(.020)
35–39	–.016	–.005	–.136	.015	–.049	–.019
	(.031)	(.031)	(.021)	(.021)	(.020)	(.020)
40–44	–.034	–.026	–.158	–.028	–.087	–.040
	(.031)	(.031)	(.021)	(.021)	(.021)	(.020)
45–49	–.023	–.007	–.143	–.029	–.092	–.048
	(.033)	(.035)	(.022)	(.022)	(.022)	(.021)
50–54	–.078	–.074	–.137	–.020	–.097	–.058
	(.038)	(.040)	(.025)	(.024)	(.024)	(.024)
55–59	.028	–.013	–.160	-.054	–.155	–.096
	(.049)	(.054)	(.027)	(.027)	(.026)	(.026)

Table 12.9 continued

Education	.066	.093	.103
	(.002)	(.001)	(.002)
Immigrant × education	–.012	–.038	–.044
	(.004)	(.002)	(.003)
Ability to Speak English (or French in Canada)			
Well or Very well	–.107	–.078	–.015
	(.016)	(.012)	(.022)
Not at all or Not well	–.327	–.042	–.118
	(.041)	(.031)	(.038)

Note: These coefficients are from the same income regressions reported in table 12.8; see the note to that table for more information. Robust standard errors are shown in parentheses. The reference group for the age dummies is 25- to 29-year-olds. The reference group for the fluency dummies is women who speak only English in the Australian and U.S. data, and women who speak only English and/or French in the Canadian data.

Figure 12.2
Predicted Immigrant-Native Income Differentials Excluding Latin American Immigrants

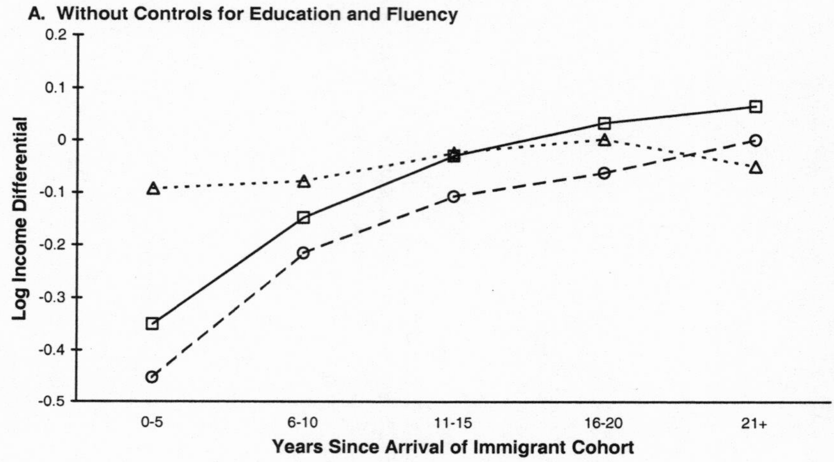

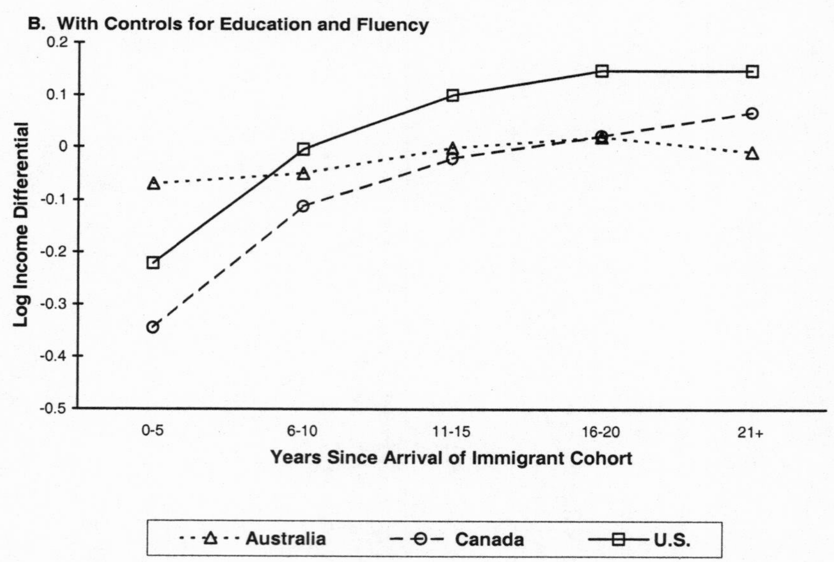

the top and bottom panels of figure 12.2). Because the immigration point systems in Australia and Canada explicitly screen for language ability and education, this finding provides some evidence that female immigrants to the United States are more favorably selected in terms of "unobservable" characteristics that may escape the filter of a point system. Such a pattern is consistent with the prediction of selective migration models (Borjas 1991) that the less compressed income distribution in the United States (compared to Australia and Canada) should attract the most productive immigrant workers, particularly with respect to those attributes (such as ability and ambition) that immigration officials would have difficulty discerning prior to admission.

CONCLUSION

On average, women who immigrate to Australia and Canada have larger endowments of productivity-related skills than do women who immigrate to the United States. In particular, they are more likely to be fluent in the destination country language, possess more education (relative to native-born women), and have higher income (relative to native-born women) than their U.S. counterparts.

To a great extent, however, this skill disadvantage of U.S. foreign-born women arises because the United States receives a much larger share of unskilled immigrants from Latin America than do the other two countries. When we exclude women born in Central and South America, the fluency gap for U.S. immigrants is substantially reduced, and educational attainment (in absolute terms) for female immigrants is now higher in the United States than in Australia or Canada. Even when adopting a relative measure of education that compares immigrants with natives in the same destination country, the relative schooling gap of U.S. immigrants shrinks dramatically (but does not disappear entirely) once Latin American immigrants are excluded. Given these findings—and the importance of language ability and education in the earnings determination process—it is not surprising that national origin differences can account for all of the income disadvantage (relative to natives) of U.S. female immigrants compared to their Canadian counterparts, and most of the disadvantage compared to Australian immigrants. Even after excluding women originating in Central and South America, however, the incomes of U.S. immigrants improve relative to Australian and Canadian immigrants once controls are added for fluency and schooling. This result suggests that female immigrants to the United States may be more favorably selected in terms of difficult-to-observe characteristics that escape the filter of an immigration point system.

These patterns in the labor market skills of foreign-born women in Australia, Canada, and the United States are very similar to what we found previously for men (Antecol, Cobb-Clark, and Trejo 2003), and we think our earlier interpretation of the male results applies here as well. In particular, we do not believe that our cross-country comparisons provide much support for the proposition that the skills of U.S. immigrants would improve if the United States were to adopt an immigration point system similar to those used in Australia and Canada. For one thing, the skill disadvantage of U.S. immigrants is largely driven by the substantial inflows from Central and South America, and we strongly suspect that the Australian and Canadian point systems are not the primary reason that these countries receive few Latin American immigrants relative to the United States. The fact that the United States shares a wide border and a long history with Mexico undoubtedly contributes to the large presence of Latin American immigrants in the United States. Moreover, Australia and Canada never received many immigrants from Latin America, even before immigration point systems were introduced in Australia in the 1970s and in Canada in the late 1960s (see Reitz 1998: table 1.1). Another reason to doubt the efficacy of a point system in the United States is that much of U.S. immigration from Latin America is undocumented (Warren and Passel 1987; Woodrow and Passel 1990) and subject to limited official control (Bean et al. 1990; Donato, Durand, and Massey 1992; Kossoudji 1992). Therefore, a point system that screens legal immigrants for skills may do little to raise the skills or restrict the entry of Latin American immigrants to the United States, because these immigrants seem to find it relatively easy to enter outside of the official admissions system.

Finally, in all three countries, men are much more likely than women to gain admission on the basis of immigration criteria related to labor market considerations rather than family relationships. For this reason, we might expect that the stronger emphasis on skill-based admissions in Australia and Canada compared to the United States would have a larger impact on cross-country differences in the skill content of male rather than female immigration flows. Therefore, our findings of similar patterns for men and women and of the key role played by national origin both suggest that factors other than immigration policy per se are important contributors to the observed skill differences between immigrants to these three destination countries.

References

Antecol, Heather, Deborah A. Cobb-Clark, and Stephen J. Trejo. 2003. "Immigration Policy and the Skills of Immigrants to Australia, Canada, and the United States," *Journal of Human Resources* 38, no. 1 (Winter): 192–218.

Bean, Frank D., Thomas J. Espenshade, Michael J. White, and Robert F. Dymowski. 1990. "Post-IRCA Changes in the Volume and Composition of Undocumented Migration to the United States: An Assessment Based on Apprehensions Data." In *Undocumented Migration to the United States: IRCA and the Experience of the 1980s*, edited by Frank D. Bean, Barry Edmonston, and Jeffrey S. Passel. Washington, D.C.: Urban Institute Press.

Borjas, George. J. 1988. *International Differences in the Labor Market Performance of Immigrants*. Kalamazoo, Mich.: W.E. Upjohn Institute for Employment Research.

———. 1991. "Immigration and Self-Selection." In *Immigration, Trade, and the Labor Market*, edited by John M. Abowd and Richard B. Freeman. Chicago: University of Chicago Press.

———. 1993. "Immigration Policy, National Origin, and Immigrant Skills: A Comparison of Canada and the United States." In *Small Differences That Matter: Labor Markets and Income Maintenance in Canada and the United States*, edited by David Card and Richard B. Freeman. Chicago: University of Chicago Press.

———. 1995. "Assimilation and Changes in Cohort Quality Revisited: What Happened to Immigrant Earnings in the 1980s?" *Journal of Labor Economics* 13, no. 2 (April): 201–45.

Boyd, Monica. 1976. "Immigration Policies and Trends: A Comparison of Canada and the United States," *Demography* 18, no. 1: 83–104.

Briggs, Vernon. M., Jr. 1984. *Immigration Policy and the American Labor Force*. Baltimore, Md.: Johns Hopkins University Press.

Card, David, and Richard B. Freeman, eds. 1993. *Small Differences That Matter: Labor Markets and Income Maintenance in Canada and the United States*. Chicago: University of Chicago Press.

Carliner, Geoffrey. 1995. "The Language Ability of U.S. Immigrants: Assimilation and Cohort Effects." Working Paper 5222. Cambridge, Mass.: National Bureau of Economic Research.

———. 1996. "The Wages and Language Skills of U.S. Immigrants." Working Paper 5763. Cambridge, Mass.: National Bureau of Economic Research.

Chiswick, Barry R. 1987. "Immigration Policy, Source Countries, and Immigrant Skills: Australia, Canada, and the United States." In *The Economics of Immigration*. Canberra: Australian Government Publishing Service.

Cobb-Clark, Deborah A. 1990. "Immigrant Selectivity: The Roles of Household Structure and U.S. Immigration Policy." Ph.D. dissertation, University of Michigan.

Donato, Katharine M., Jorge Durand, and Douglas S. Massey. 1992. "Stemming the Tide? Assessing the Deterrent Effects of the Immigration Reform and Control Act," *Demography* 29, no. 2: 139–57.

Duleep, Harriet Orcutt, and Mark C. Regets. 1992. "Some Evidence on the Effects of Admissions Criteria on Immigrant Assimilation." In *Immigration, Language and Ethnic Issues: Canada and the United States*, edited by Barry R. Chiswick. Washington, D.C.: American Enterprise Institute.

Evans, M.D.R., Jonathan Kelley, and Richard A. Wanner. 1998. "The Consequences of Divorce for Children's Education: Australia, Canada, and the U.S.A., 1940–1990." Canberra: Australian National University. Manuscript.

Funkhouser, Edward. 1996. "How Much of Immigrant Wage Assimilation Is Related to English Language Acquisition?" Santa Barbara: University of California, Santa Barbara. Manuscript.

Funkhouser, Edward, and Stephen J. Trejo. 1998. "Labor Market Outcomes and Female Immigrants in the United States." In *The Immigration Debate: Studies on Economic, Demographic, and Fiscal Effects of Immigration*, edited by James P. Smith and Barry Edmonston. Washington, D.C.: National Academy Press.

Green, Alan. G. 1995. "A Comparison of Canadian and U.S. Immigration Policy in the Twentieth Century." In *Diminishing Returns: The Economics of Canada's Recent Immigration Policy*, edited by Don J. DeVoretz. Toronto: C.D. Howe Institute/Laurier Institution.

Green, Alan G., and David A. Green. 1995. "Canadian Immigration Policy: The Effectiveness of the Point System and Other Instruments," *Canadian Journal of Economics* 28, no. 4b: 1006–41.

Gregory, Robert G., and Anne E. Daly. 1994. "Welfare and Economic Progress of Indigenous Men of Australia and the U.S., 1980–1990." Canberra: Australian National University. Mimeo.

Heckman, James J. 1980. "Sample Selection Bias as a Specification Error." In *Female Labor Supply: Theory and Estimation*, edited by J.P. Smith. Princeton, N.J.: Princeton University Press.

Houstoun, Marion F., Roger G. Kramer, and Joan Mackin Barrett. 1984. "Female Predominance in Immigration in the United States since 1930: A First Look," *International Migration Review* 38, no. 4: 908–63.

Kossoudji, Sherrie A. 1992. "Playing Cat and Mouse at the U.S.-Mexican Border," *Demography* 29, no. 2: 159–80.

Lack, John, and Jacqueline Templeton. 1995. *Bold Experiment: A Documentary History of Australian Immigration since 1945*. Melbourne: Oxford University Press.

Madden, Ros, and Susan Young. 1993. *Women and Men Immigrating to Australia: Their Characteristics and Immigration Decisions*. Bureau of Immigration Research. Canberra: Australian Government Publishing Service.

Price, Charles. 1979. "Australia." In *The Politics of Migration Policies*, edited by Daniel Kubat. New York: Center for Migration Studies.

Reimers, David M., and Harold Troper. 1992. "Canadian and American Immigration Policy since 1945." In *Immigration, Language and Ethnic Issues: Canada and the United States*, edited by Barry R. Chiswick. Washington, D.C.: American Enterprise Institute.

Reitz, Jeffrey G. 1998. *Warmth of the Welcome: The Social Causes of Economic Success for Immigrants in Different Nations and Cities*. Boulder, Colo.: Westview.

Reitz, Jeffrey G., Joachim R. Frick, Tony Calabrese, and Gert C. Wagner. 1999. "The Institutional Framework of Ethnic Employment Disadvantage: A Comparison of Germany and Canada," *Journal of Ethnic and Migration Studies* 25, no. 3: 397–443.

Schoeni, Robert F. 1998. "Labor Market Assimilation of Immigrant Women," *Industrial and Labor Relations Review* 51, no. 3: 483–504.

United Nations, Department for Economic and Social Information and Policy Analysis, Population Division. 1995. *International Migration Policies and the Status of Female Migrants*. New York: United Nations.

Vialet, Joyce C. 1989. *Immigration: Numerical Limits and the Preference System*. Washington, D.C.: Congressional Research Service, Library of Congress.

Vialet, Joyce C., and Larry M. Eig. 1990. *Immigration Act of 1990 (P.L. 101-649)*. Washington, D.C.: Congressional Research Service, Library of Congress.

Warren, Robert, and Jeffrey S. Passel. 1987. "A Count of the Uncountable: Estimates of Undocumented Aliens Counted in the 1980 United States Census," *Demography* 24, no. 3: 375–93.

Woodrow, Karen A., and Jeffrey S. Passel. 1990. "Post-IRCA Undocumented Immigration to the United States: An Assessment Based on the June 1988 CPS." In *Undocumented Migration to the United States: IRCA and the Experience of the 1980s*, edited by Frank D. Bean, Barry Edmonston, and Jeffrey S. Passel. Washington, D.C.: Urban Institute Press.

Wright, Robert E., and Paul S. Maxim. 1993. "Immigration Policy and Immigrant Quality: Empirical Evidence from Canada," *Journal of Population Economics* 6, no. 4: 337–52.

13

Institutions, Ethnic Leaders, and the Political Incorporation of Immigrants: A Comparison of Canada and the United States

IRENE BLOEMRAAD

Immigrants' political activities have long been viewed with suspicion in receiving countries; their foreignness raises questions of loyalty and suitability. Immigrants often are perceived as too radical or too conservative, too unversed in democracy to participate, or so well versed in the political game that they manipulate outcomes. It is consequently not surprising that at a time when rights are increasingly decoupled from citizenship and citizenship restrictions on employment and licensing requirements gradually disappear (Soysal 1994; Plascencia, Freeman, and Setzler 1999), political rights such as voting and running for office have remained, for the most part, tied to citizenship (Brubaker 1989; Layton-Henry 1990; Schuck 1998). Some localities in the United States allow noncitizens to vote (Harper-Ho 2000), but most suggestions for fostering immigrant political participation reaffirm the

This chapter benefited from comments from Andy Andrews, Bayliss Camp, Marshall Ganz, Jennifer Hochschild, Ziad Munson, and Karthick Ramakrishnan. Financial support from the National Science Foundation (SES 00-00310), the Canadian Social Science and Humanities Research Council, the Social Science Research Council, the Weatherhead Center for International Affairs, and the Hauser Center for Non-Profit Organizations is gratefully acknowledged.

link between citizenship and politics. For example, calls to recognize dual citizenship maintain the relationship between citizenship status and political involvement, even as they relax the boundaries of national and political belonging (Jones-Correa 1998).

Given the importance of legal citizenship, recent data that show a decrease in immigrant naturalization elicit concern from many quarters (Pan 2000; Camarota 2001). In 1970, 63.6 percent of immigrants in the United States were naturalized, but by 1997 only 35.1 percent had acquired U.S. citizenship (Schmidley and Gibson 1999). The steep decline is in part a statistical artifact: citizenship levels are calculated by dividing the total number of foreign-born by the number of naturalized individuals, so during periods of rapid immigration—such as in the post-1965 period—the denominator grows much more quickly than the numerator.[1] Nonetheless, Schmidley and Gibson (1999) estimate that changes in migrant cohorts account for only a third of the citizenship decline, implying that recent immigrants are less likely to naturalize or will wait longer to do so than those who came earlier. Some analysts consider this trend a troubling indication that "recent immigrants may not be developing a strong attachment to the United States.... [A] very large percentage of established immigrants have chosen not to participate fully in the civic life of their new country" (Camarota 2001: 10).

It is an open question, however, whether immigrants choose to stay out of U.S. political and civic life or whether the United States has failed to invite them in. Naturalization is one facet of a broader process of political incorporation by which immigrants progressively become part of mainstream political debates, practices, and decision making.[2] In North America, most explanations of immigrants' naturalization and political participation focuses on immigrants' attributes, examining socioeconomic and demographic variation among individuals or characteristics common to certain immigrant groups (Frideres et al. 1987; Liang 1994; Ramakrishnan and Espenshade 2001; Uhlaner, Cain, and Kiewiet 1989). Few scholars ask whether host societies exert a similar

---

[1] Immigrants are required by law to wait five years before applying for citizenship, and most wait years longer.

[2] The end point of this process is difficult to identify, but incorporation is generally achieved when immigrants' participation is comparable to patterns among the native-born, though different individuals and groups might privilege certain forms of participation over others.

influence on citizenship and participation, despite a recognition that an immigrant's home country can affect political incorporation (Jasso and Rosenzweig 1986; Portes and Mozo 1985; Yang 1994). The lack of attention stems partly from a methodological bias: North American scholars tend to study immigrant political incorporation in a single receiving country, making it difficult to identify the ways in which contexts of reception influence integration.

Despite the predominant focus on immigrants' attributes, there are a number of reasons why we might expect the institutions of the host society to affect political integration. Previous research highlights the impact of perceived discrimination on naturalization and voting (Portes and Curtis 1987; Uhlaner 1996) and the relationship between local or state political institutions and immigrant political incorporation (Jones-Correa 1998, 2002). A more developed European literature suggests that a country's political opportunity structure influences immigrant naturalization (Brubaker 1992; Clarke, van Dam, and Gooster 1998; de Rham 1990), organizing strategies (Soysal 1994), and the discourses migrants use to make claims (Koopmans and Statham 1999). Here I suggest that if we compare immigrants' political incorporation in the United States to that of a similar country of reception—Canada—we can better identify the institutional factors that shape incorporation. Such an analysis might also tell us something about American political institutions more generally since declining levels of naturalization appear to parallel a more general decline in civic engagement and political participation among the American population (Putnam 2000).

This chapter consequently has two goals. First, I offer a framework to examine and understand immigrant political incorporation in traditional countries of immigration. Such a framework employs comparative methods to isolate institutional effects and emphasizes four analytically distinct features of participatory citizenship: naturalization (legal citizenship), organizational capacity, leadership, and claims-making. Second, I develop a U.S.-Canada comparison focused on Portuguese immigrants to demonstrate the applicability of an institutional approach in the area of leadership. I suggest that political institutions exert a selection effect on potential immigrant community leaders before and after migration. These selection processes reinforce prevailing political discourses and shape the way ordinary immigrants become engaged in the civic and political life of their new country.

TOWARD A FRAMEWORK FOR STUDYING IMMIGRANT POLITICAL INCORPORATION

An Institutional Approach

It is clearly plausible that host societies or contexts of reception matter in integration processes. To analyze such effects, I propose a framework built on theories of institutionalism and analytical concepts from the study of social movements. An institutional framework directs attention to the ways in which a state channels resources, legitimacy, access, and taken-for-granted understandings of politics in such a way as to significantly impact the path immigrants take to political involvement and their perceptions of the relative benefits or value of doing so. The social movement literature underscores the importance of material and symbolic resources, organizational capacity, leadership, framing, and political opportunity structures.

Institutionalism arose out of a movement to "bring the state back in": scholars of politics were urged to consider how states exert an independent and significant effect on political processes and societal actors (Evans, Rueschemeyer, and Skocpol 1985; March and Olsen 1984). This "state-centric" approach quickly evolved to a more general institutional framework encompassing similar movements in fields such as economics and organizational behavior (DiMaggio and Powell 1991; Clemens and Cook 1999). Institutional frameworks consequently consider how objective constraints, such as legal structures, and more subjective higher order effects, such as cognitive maps and cultural norms, regularize the actions and understandings of actors without recourse to coercive force.

Given that immigrant political incorporation directly implicates the state—as a target of collective mobilization and the source of public policy—I pay particular attention to the role of state institutions in shaping the integration experience. Influence can be material, funneling monies or expertise to certain groups rather than to others, or symbolic, legitimizing certain discourses over alternative understandings. Such actions affect the interests of immigrant actors and organizations, and they can shape self-understandings and identities. State action also interacts with and influences other actors in the polity, such as political parties, philanthropic foundations, or mainstream interest groups.

Insights from the study of social movements add an important dynamic element to an institutional theory of immigrant political incorporation. Various formulations of (neo)institutional theorizing have been criticized for eliminating the role of agency or concentrating too much on continuity and constraint (Hirsch 1997; Powell 1991: 194–200; Thelen and Steinmo 1992: 14–15). These criticisms have some foundation, but an institutional framework can incorporate change. Although institutions appear to exert an independent effect "outside" the individual, individuals and collective bodies need to reproduce the institutional structure through their actions (Giddens 1984; Sewell 1992). Change is possible when there is disruption to this process of structuration (Clemens and Cook 1999; Jepperson 1991; Pierson 1993). Disruption can occur through the reallocation of resources (McCarthy and Zald 1977, 2002), judicious use of organizations (Clemens 1997; Staggenborg 1991), strategic leadership (Ganz 2000), and innovative (re)framing of problems and solutions (Snow et al. 1986; Snow and Benford 1992; Benford and Snow 2000). In particular, leadership, organizations, and legitimate public discourses (a type of framing activity) are critical to immigrant incorporation.

Leaders facilitate political and civic participation by representing and mobilizing the immigrant group. They also facilitate political claims-making since "the state and polity's authorities cannot deal with abstractions, but have recourse to privileged actors or individuals, namely to ethnic leaders and elites" (Martiniello 1993: 241).[3] The famed urban political machines of the nineteenth and early twentieth centuries encouraged certain local ethnic leaders to mobilize immigrant compatriots, but by the end of the twentieth century, even this partial mobilization is rare (DeSipio 2001; Erie 1988; Jones-Correa 1998). Rosenstone and Hansen (1993) find that citizens tune out, and feel detached from, the political process when elites stop engaging in personal appeals. Understanding the development of leadership in the immigrant community consequently plays an important role in explaining political incorporation.

Changes in elite mobilization styles parallel changes in the way people engage in collective politics. Immigrants in particular benefit from political mobilization around group membership. New to a country, often speaking a different language, immigrants come together in religious congregations, ethnic business associations, social clubs, and

[3] Given its importance, the dearth of contemporary scholarship on ethnic leadership is surprising. Yet Higham's comment almost twenty-five years ago that the subject is neglected due to a "general distrust of elites and [scholars'] desire to look at history from the bottom up" continues to hold true (1978: 1).

cultural organizations. In the past, politicians often sought out such groups as an easy and efficient channel through which to reach large numbers of potential voters (Parenti 1967). However, the dawn of the twenty-first century finds an organizational landscape dominated by professional interest and advocacy groups such as the American Association of Retired People, the Sierra Club, and the National Council of La Raza (Minkoff 1994; Walker 1991). These Washington-based advocacy groups usually employ professional paid staff, while membership, if any, often rests on annual dues rather than regular participation. Although the presence of these groups appears to have widened the range of issues considered in political circles, the new advocacy industry can exclude many ordinary people (Skocpol 1999). Success requires unique skills associated with higher education, excellent command of the English language, and familiarity with American political structures. For those who lack these skills—particularly immigrant communities—arenas of participation can narrow substantially. Immigrant political incorporation might well suffer from this change as television ads and professional advocacy politics replace traditional forms of political mobilization.

Finally, political activity involves claims-making and the framing of both problems and solutions to coincide with citizens' and policymakers' understandings of the world around them. Collective action frames can define the social world as unjust (punctuation), assign blame and propose a line of action to remedy that injustice (attribution), and provide a lens for individuals to interpret the "world out there" according to a certain schemata (articulation) (Snow and Benford 1992: 137–38). Competing groups can engage in "framing contests" to capture the hearts and minds of voters and politicians (Zald 1996). Since such frames have to resonate with at least some prior understandings of the world, we can ask what impact societal and government-promoted discourses around immigration, race, and social justice have on immigrants' political claims. More generally, does the political or civic culture of a receiving society matter for immigrant incorporation? Almond and Verba (1963) argued that nations have particular civic cultures that promote or depress political participation. Immigrants bring certain civic traditions from their host country when they migrate, but they also must adapt to the particular political culture of the receiving society. Claims made in one context might not resonate as well as those espoused in a different society.

The Power of Comparison: The Canadian Case

In order to evaluate whether institutional configurations influence immigrant political incorporation, we need a cross-national comparative methodology. Comparing the United States and Canada provides an ideal research design since both are "classic countries of immigration" (Brubaker 1989). The resulting "most similar" comparison better enables us to pin down the mechanisms by which small institutional differences become magnified into large behavioral differences. Some contrast the United States with western European countries such as France, Germany, and Great Britain, but fundamental differences in attitude and policy differentiate the two continents (Joppke 1999). Instead, Canada, like the United States, accepts large numbers of permanent immigrants each year, embraces an expansive citizenship regime, and possesses a relatively open political system capable of accepting newcomers. In addition, Canada shares with the United States past policies of Asian exclusion, Japanese internment, and, up until the mid-1960s, an immigration system that favored white Europeans, although Canada largely lacks a history of slavery.

At an institutional level, Canada exhibits some significant differences, providing needed variation in the independent variable. Perhaps most important, Canada administers a relatively developed immigrant settlement policy, providing federal funding for such programs as English language training and job placement assistance to new arrivals. This interest in settlement dates from 1950 with the establishment of the Department of Citizenship and Immigration. Funding was initially limited but underwent rapid expansion in the late 1960s following a philosophical shift in political circles.[4] Henceforth the state would not only oversee immigration flows but also become an active player in the integration process (Lanphier and Lukomskyj 1994). By the early 1970s it was estimated that about half of all newly arriving immigrant workers visited one of 360 Canada Manpower Centres for job counseling and training (Hawkins 1988: 339).[5] Most money went to programs

[4] Despite limited funding, the department was able to field "liaison" officers in key reception areas, oversee a relatively large language training program with some citizenship classes, and offer small grants to nonprofit voluntary organizations working with immigrants and ethnic minorities (Hawkins 1988).

[5] The Department of Citizenship and Immigration was split in 1966. Responsibility for social, cultural, and political integration fell to the Citizenship Branch, now housed in the Secretary of State, while economic integration became the purview

aimed at working-age males—it was felt that successful integration began with reliable employment for the family breadwinner—but grants were also dispersed to voluntary agencies for language training, citizenship classes, and welcome services.[6] Provinces receiving especially large numbers of immigrants, such as Ontario, followed suit with provincial settlement programs. Although lack of coordination plagues newcomer settlement, one level of government will often supplement or add to services offered by another (Lanphier and Lukomskyj 1994).

The growth and expansion of immigrant settlement services parallel the rise of official multiculturalism in Canada, a normative ideology with programmatic backing. When it was first announced in 1971, multiculturalism policy committed the government to supporting ethnic organizations, helping to eliminate cultural barriers to participation in Canadian society, promoting dialogue between cultural groups, and assisting immigrants to learn one of Canada's two official languages. As the prime minister of the day explained, government intervention was needed because "We are free to be ourselves. But this cannot be left to chance. It must be fostered and pursued actively" (House of Commons 1971: 8547). Multiculturalism monies financed local ethnic associations, promoted immigrant cultural activities, and supported programs where the children of immigrants could learn their parents' language.[7] When the face of immigration to Canada began changing, multiculturalism's focus shifted from cultural retention to attacking barriers of racism and discrimination in the 1980s and 1990s (Fleras and Elliott 1992; Canada 1984).

Canadian settlement and multiculturalism programs have their limits, but they represent much more than what is offered by the U.S. federal government. While the Immigration and Nationality Act appears to allow some programmatic intervention, especially around citizen-

---

of the Department of Manpower and Immigration (later the Department of Employment and Immigration).

[6] By the early 1990s, funding for newcomer language programs became more equitable as eligibility criteria moved away from the male breadwinner model (Boyd, DeVries, and Simkin 1994).

[7] The prime minister assigned primary responsibility for multiculturalism to the Citizenship Branch of the Secretary of State with initial funding of $5 million in 1972 (Hawkins 1991: 219–21). The fortunes of multiculturalism rose in the 1980s—over fiscal year 1987–88 the multiculturalism program distributed more than $20 million in grants—but fell again in the 1990s (Pal 1993: 200; Fleras and Elliott 1992; Abu-Laban 1994). For example, in the 1990s, funding for heritage language classes was passed on to local school boards and lower levels of governments.

ship promotion, in practice the U.S. Immigration and Naturalization Service (INS) has not engaged in such activities (North 1985, 1987). Indeed, under terms set by Congress, the INS does not have legal authority as a grant-making agency.[8] Instead, the location of the INS in the Department of Justice focuses the agency's priorities around enforcement and administration.[9] A former INS commissioner notes that "the dominant culture of the agency ... [is] rooted in a view of immigration as a source of security and law enforcement vulnerability more than of continuing nation building" (Meissner 2001: 2). During the 1910s and 1920s, a widespread "Americanization" movement, involving private voluntary organizations, local school boards, and governments, encouraged immigrants to assimilate to American life. By the 1950s, however, very few organizations or programs directed at settlement remained, a function of reduced immigration and bureaucratic reorganization.[10] Today federal intervention is limited to offering support to those legally designated as refugees. Other newcomers are expected to integrate using their own resources or with help from the ethnic community.[11]

We find some suggestion that institutional differences contribute to immigrant political incorporation when we compare naturalization statistics in the United States and Canada. Whereas levels of citizenship have steadily declined over the postwar period in the United States, immigrants in Canada naturalize at higher rates today than those who came thirty years earlier. Figure 13.1 tracks the percentage of immigrants twenty-one years or older who report that they are a naturalized

---

[8] Interviews with INS officials, November 6, 2001, and May 2, 2002. The INS's lack of grant-making authority stands in stark contrast to the Department of Health and Human Services, within which is housed the Office for Refugee Resettlement (ORR). ORR is mandated to grant public funds to public and private organizations providing social services to refugees.

[9] The INS ceased to exist on March 1, 2003, as its functions were absorbed by the new Department of Homeland Security.

[10] Prior to the outbreak of war in Europe, the INS was in the Department of Labor, but under the president's 1940 Reorganization Plan (Number V) the agency was transferred to Justice, reflecting increased security concerns. Intervention along a model of "Americanization" also lost favor with the growth of the civil rights movement in the 1960s.

[11] We can ask whether other U.S. programs might fulfill a settlement function. Space limitations prevent a thorough discussion, but programs aimed at racial minorities can serve as a resource for 1.5 and second-generation immigrants. However, because these programs were not usually created with immigrants in mind, they do not serve exactly the same function as in Canada.

Figure 13.1. Naturalization of Adult Immigrants (21 years or older) in the United States and Canada over the Twentieth Century

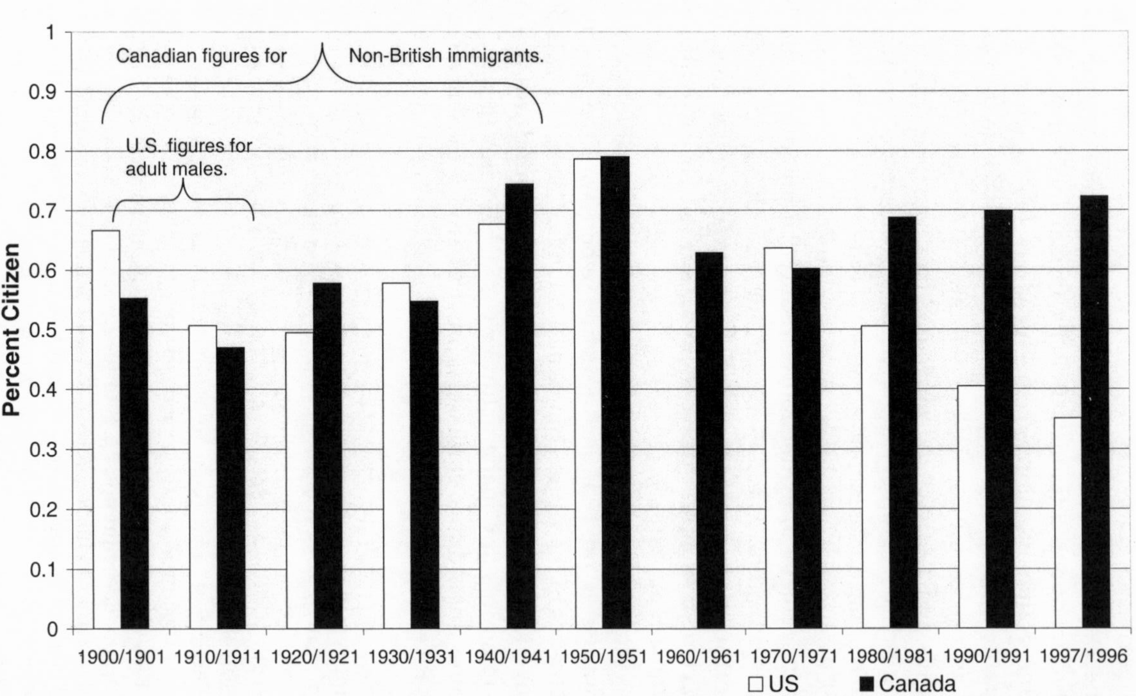

citizen on the national census.[12] Naturalization levels rose and fell in tandem over the first half of the century, peaking in 1950–51 when 79 percent of the adult immigrant population in both countries reported naturalized citizenship. No comparison is possible in 1960 because the U.S. census did not ask a citizenship question that year, but in 1970–71, the first census after Canada and the United States ended racially based immigration restrictions, citizenship levels were again roughly equal.[13] However, the pattern of historic similarity ends abruptly after 1970. U.S. citizenship levels have plummeted from 64 percent in 1970 to 35 percent in 1997, while Canadian citizenship levels have risen slightly, from 60 percent in 1961 to 72 percent in 1996.

The acquisition of legal citizenship is an imperfect indicator of civic engagement and political participation: many activities do not require citizenship, while motivations other than political involvement can lead to naturalization. Nevertheless, certain core political acts, such as voting and running for office, are restricted to citizens. Despite claims that we are heading into a postnational age where legal citizenship loses its importance (Soysal 1994; Jacobson 1996), opinion polls reveal that even among immigrant groups with low levels of naturalization, the vast majority want to acquire citizenship (de la Garza et al. 1992).[14] This desire for citizenship makes the recent declines in U.S. naturalization all the more puzzling.

Of course, migration streams to the United States and Canada have some important differences. The United States, for example, attracts

---

[12] The immigrant population is defined as all those born outside of the country. For those censuses where it is possible, this excludes those who received U.S. or Canadian citizenship via their parents at birth. The U.S. figures include only adult males in 1900 and 1910 since census enumerators did not collect citizenship information on women. In the Canadian case, the data from 1901 to 1941 refer to non-British immigrants. Prior to 1947, Canadian nationals were legally defined as British subjects. Immigrants from Britain or other areas of the Commonwealth therefore already possessed the citizenship status of Canadians when they immigrated (Angus 1937; Kaplan 1993).

[13] The significant drop in Canadian naturalization in 1961 largely stems from massive post–World War II migration. In the 1950s, over 1.5 million newcomers arrived in a country with a population of only 14 million at the start of the decade. The pool of foreign-born consequently increased much more quickly than the number that naturalized since immigrants had to wait five years before applying for Canadian citizenship.

[14] Mexican immigrants have extremely low levels of naturalization. Yet when asked in the National Latino Survey, only 14 percent claimed to have no interest in becoming a U.S. citizen.

Figure 13.2. Percent of Adult Immigrants Naturalized, by Country of Birth, with 11-15 Years Residence in 1990/91

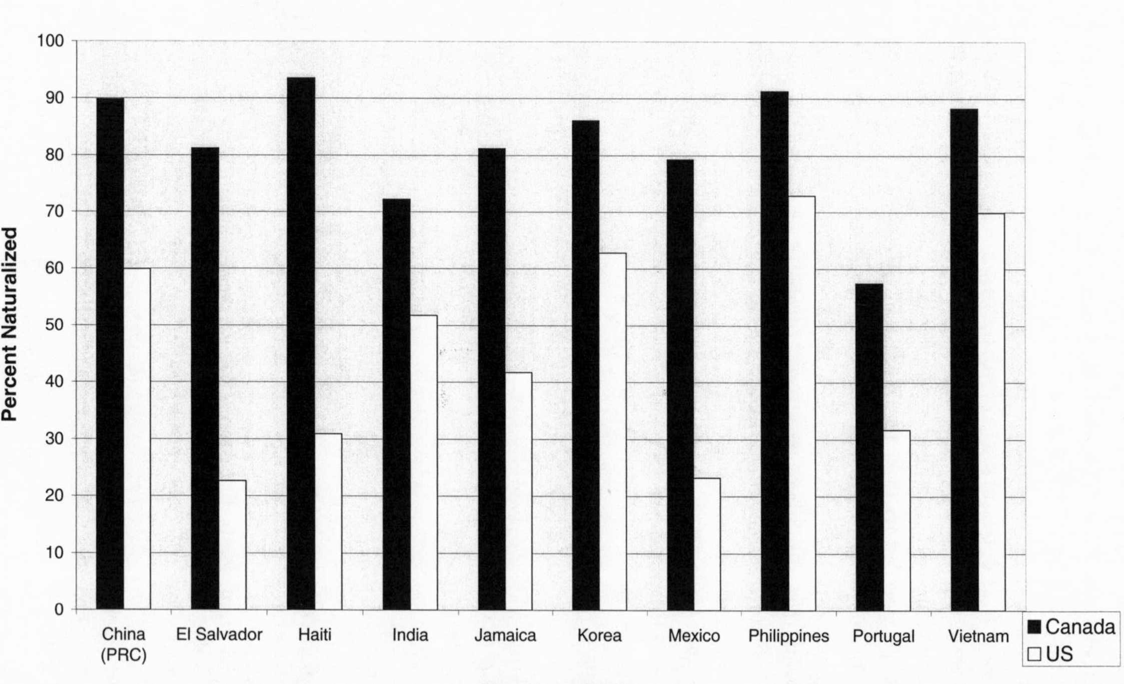

large percentages of immigrants from Mexico and Latin America. Canada receives few immigrants from these areas, but instead draws heavily from Asia, both the Indian subcontinent and East Asia. Since we know that immigrant groups differ significantly in their propensity to naturalize (Portes and Mozo 1985; Liang 1994), selection effects might produce striking aggregate differences. Yet even when we control for country of birth, a North American naturalization gap persists, as can be seen in figure 13.2. Comparing only established immigrants—those who have been in North America for eleven to fifteen years—we find that citizenship levels are much higher in Canada than in the United States across a variety of migrant groups. Elsewhere I demonstrate that the U.S.-Canada citizenship gap remains robust even after taking into account citizenship regulations, the relative advantages and disadvantages of citizenship in the two countries, and the individual attributes of newcomers (Bloemraad 2002). The timing of the divergence is telling: as Canadian government intervention in immigrant settlement accelerates and promotion of multiculturalism picks up steam, the historic similarity ends.

THE PORTUGUESE CASE STUDY: DATA AND METHODOLOGY

While Canada and the United States may be grouped together as traditional countries of immigration, differences in migration streams complicate the comparison. Ideally, we would need to study one immigrant group whose members are randomly sent to Canada or the United States, thereby controlling for extraneous variability not linked to the characteristics of the host society. While such random assignment is clearly impractical if not unethical, the case of Portuguese migration approaches such laboratory conditions. Portuguese migration to North America is extremely similar. Indeed, Almeida (2000) claims that Portuguese immigrants share so many sociocultural features that the two North American populations are largely interchangeable. In my own interviews, many respondents told of a sibling, cousin, or friend who lives on the other side of the border. We have, in effect, a quasi-natural experiment: if individuals who come to North America with similar cultural, socioeconomic, and political backgrounds differ in their political incorporation, we can conclude that such differences probably stem from the institutional structures of the receiving society and not the characteristics of the immigrants. In fact, we find that political incorporation appears to be moving more quickly in Ontario than in Massachusetts.

Census estimates put the number of Portuguese immigrants at 155,770 in Canada (2001) and 203,119 in the United States (2000). In both countries, approximately 60 to 70 percent hail from the Azores, another 20 to 30 percent from mainland Portugal, and smaller groups from Madeira or Portugal's former African colonies (Anderson 1983; Ito-Alder 1980; Teixeira and Lavigne 1992). Here I concentrate on the substantial post–World War II flow of Portuguese to Massachusetts and Ontario, the bulk of whom arrived in the late 1960s and early 1970s. In 2000 the Portuguese represented approximately 9 percent of all foreign-born residents in Massachusetts, the largest immigrant group in the state, while in Ontario they accounted for a bit under 4 percent of all immigrants in 2001, the eighth largest immigrant group in the province.[15]

Interregional differences exist between Portuguese immigrants—Azoreans and mainlanders continue to express stereotypes of each other—but the overall picture is of broad similarities. Portuguese immigration is largely ethnically homogeneous, and almost all are Roman Catholic.[16] Before moving to North America, the majority of Portuguese engaged in subsistence farming, fishing, or manual labor. Many have low levels of education because free schooling only extended to grade four. Nonetheless, Portuguese workforce participation rates in North America resemble those of the native-born. Many Portuguese are employed in manual and semiskilled jobs, such as cleaning, factory work, and construction. Importantly, the majority of Portuguese immigrants lived part of their lives under the dictatorship, a time when citizens had few political rights and the secret police repressed political

---

[15] The United States has a longer history of Portuguese migration. Starting in the nineteenth century with the whale boats, and continuing with the pull of New England factories and California agriculture, substantial numbers of Portuguese moved to the United States between 1880 and 1920. As with most other groups, immigration quotas in the 1920s reduced Portuguese migration to a trickle. It only regained steam in the 1950s after a series of natural disasters in the Azores led New England senators, including John F. Kennedy, to convince Congress to admit a special quota of Portuguese immigrants (Pap 1981). A few years earlier, Canadian immigrant officials had begun recruiting Portuguese laborers to work on Canadian farms, mines, and railroads (Marques and Marujo 1993).

[16] In the past, when Cape Verde was still a Portuguese colony, Americans in New England would occasionally call all Portuguese "black Portugee" (Pap 1981), expanding the southern one-drop rule to a whole immigrant population. I do not include those born in Cape Verde in my study.

dissent. Portugal's fascist history is often advanced as the reason that Portuguese immigrants are politically "invisible" in North America.

The bulk of my data comes from qualitative interviews I conducted with first- and second-generation Portuguese living in the greater Boston and Toronto areas. Everyone interviewed had at some time lived and/or worked in the "traditional" areas of Portuguese settlement: East Cambridge and Somerville in the Boston metropolitan area, or west of Kensington Market in downtown Toronto. Interviews were split into two roughly equal sets. First I sought out "ordinary" Portuguese immigrants. I used referrals from a variety of sources to select people with varying backgrounds, migration histories, and sociodemographic characteristics that I felt would be theoretically and substantively important to political incorporation.[17] For the second set of interviews, I spoke with Portuguese community leaders. These people either were involved in an organization that served the Portuguese community or were identified by others as spokespersons or advocates. In total, I interviewed twenty-nine members of the Portuguese community in Boston and thirty-three in Toronto, and I conducted an additional twenty interviews with government officials and non-Portuguese active in immigrant settlement.[18] The interview data are supplemented by documentary evidence from various organizations serving the Portuguese in the United States and Canada.

INSTITUTIONAL EFFECTS ON THE DEVELOPMENT OF COMMUNITY LEADERSHIP

The complex interaction between a host society's institutions and political incorporation can be seen when we examine leadership development and advocacy in the Toronto and Boston-area Portuguese communities. In the following section I consider how institutional con-

[17] I purposely did not use organizational referrals or extended snowball sampling for this group because I did not want a sample biased by prior civic engagement or political activity.

[18] The interviews were conducted between July 1997 and January 2001. I followed a semi-structured interview schedule that asked questions about the individual's migration history, experiences living in Portugal and North America, citizenship and political participation, organizational involvement, and general feelings about the United States or Canada. Most interviews lasted ninety minutes, though in a few memorable cases we talked over five hours. The majority of the interviews were conducted in English, taped, and transcribed. When a respondent preferred to speak in Portuguese, I used a co-ethnic interpreter.

figurations can act as ideological screens to channel immigrants to one country or another, and how government intervention favors certain types of leadership formation. In particular, an impression of Canada as a more social democratic country led certain future leaders of the Toronto Portuguese community to migrate to Canada, producing a strong culture of social justice advocacy among a vocal minority. Advocacy around social justice is also fueled by government intervention in the area of immigrant settlement. Material and symbolic support from the state has created a bigger, more robust employment sector dedicated to immigrant services in Toronto than in Cambridge/Somerville. Career ladders in this "newcomer settlement industry" promote the use of an advocacy model directed to equity concerns by first- and second-generation Portuguese-Canadian leaders. Institutional configurations consequently influence who becomes a leader and the discourse a community leader employs.

Pre-Migration Selection and Ideological Congruence

Two processes filter the type of immigrants a country receives: immigration policy screens would-be migrants according to a state's priorities, and immigrants select a destination according to their preferences and networks.[19] The impact of immigration policy has received particular attention by researchers studying immigrants' economic success. Canada administers a mixed immigration system that accords entry based on skills and resources, family ties, or the need for asylum. The United States also grants permanent residency along these three lines, but the relative proportions are quite different. Most legal immigrants to the United States acquire their status through family ties: a relative who already lives in the United States sponsors their application to migrate. In contrast, a significant proportion of immigrants to Canada are admitted under the "point system," which selects people according to job skills, language ability, age, and other personal characteristics.[20]

---

[19] Of course, the two processes are not necessarily independent of one another. For example, perceptions about a country's immigration policy can influence individuals' interest in migrating, and the types of migrants a country accepts influences the networks others can use to migrate.

[20] In the 1990s the mix tended toward roughly 50 percent independent immigrants (including dependents of the principal applicant), 30 to 40 percent family reunification, and about 10 to 20 percent refugees and special admissions. (Special admissions include humanitarian cases not falling under the refugee category, home caregiver admissions, and other specialized programs.) Under the current U.S.

Scholars such as George Borjas (1999) contend that a point system screens out individuals with low human capital, resulting in better integration outcomes for immigrants and the host society. Others claim that the impact of the point system is exaggerated since Canada's "skill" selection seeks to fill employment shortages—thereby including people with experience as cooks or welders—and, in any case, the United States consistently attracts better-educated immigrants from most sending countries (Reitz 1998).[21]

Whatever its impact on economic incorporation, the influence of selection mechanism on *political* incorporation is rarely discussed.[22] I find that although a certain selection mechanism influences community leadership in the Toronto area, selection is based on political ideologies, not human capital attributes. While more people in Canada reported migrating as an independent immigrant or as the family member of an independent immigrant than in Boston, many of these independent immigrants do not possess the human capital skills commonly associated with the Canadian point system. In the early postwar period, officials were told to search for applicants with "roughened and hardened" hands since the Canadian economy needed agricultural and manual laborers (Marques and Marujo 1993). I found few notable differences in the socioeconomic backgrounds of Portuguese immigrants in Toronto and Boston.

While the vast majority of immigrants in both countries told me that they and their families left Portugal for economic reasons, searching for a better life in North America, a few individuals in Toronto explicitly labeled themselves as political migrants. They pointed to ideological "fit" as one reason they chose Canada over the United States. No one I met in the United States explained his or her migration in political

---

preference system, only about 20 percent of numerically limited visas are given based on employment (Usdansky and Espenshade 2001). This percentage has remained relatively constant since 1965 and drops even lower if we consider all immigrant admissions.

[21] Exceptions include Mexico and some other Latin American countries.

[22] Camarota raises the possibility of such a link when he suggests that the relative decline in immigrants' educational attainment compared to the American native-born might account for contemporary immigrants' increased poverty, lower rates of homeownership, and decreased propensity to naturalize. There might also be an indirect effect between education and political participation, mediated by homeownership, because homeowners "are more likely to take an active interest in the long-term condition of their neighborhood, the quality of the local schools, and their community in general" (Camarota 2001: 8).

terms.[23] According to Martin Seymour Lipset (1990), desires for ideological congruence should attract more conservative immigrants to Canada. Lipset believes that the American Revolution created two distinct political cultures on the North American continent: a culture of individualism, universalism, and distrust of the state promoted by revolutionary radicals in the United States, and a statist, group-oriented political culture in Canada that tends to defer to authority, established by the Loyalists who fled north. Lipset argues that initial differences in political culture were reinforced by migrant selection mechanisms: radical democrats would choose republican America, while conservative migrants were attracted to monarchical Canada (1990: 183). Yet whatever its historical accuracy, this prediction does not ring true for contemporary Portuguese migration.[24] Community advocates in Toronto are, in general, more to the left than the community as a whole, and they are more actively engaged in social justice issues than their compatriots in the Boston area.[25]

There are two types of "political" immigrants: a few ethnic Portuguese who lived most of their lives in Portugal's African colonies and then left after the colonies gained independence, and a group from mainland Portugal who were involved in the Communist Party and its efforts to overthrow the Salazar/Caetano dictatorship. Of the latter, some individuals embraced the Communist Party and its ideology. Others, probably the majority, were less enamored, but since there was no other viable opposition, they joined in events or participated in networks organized by the Communists. U.S. society and government were perceived as strongly anti-Communist in the Cold War period, so that, as one community leader remarked, if you tried to engage in left-wing political behavior in the United States, "you get the CIA or the FBI after you in a second." Canada, in contrast, was seen as a more

---

[23] A number of immigrants left Portugal for either the United States or Canada to avoid being drafted in the colonial wars of the 1960s and early 1970s. Avoiding the draft was not seen as a political statement but rather as an act of self-preservation.

[24] I am not entirely convinced that Lipset's observation is historically accurate either, but it is worth further investigation. Others critique the type of values that Lipset assigns to those living on either side of the 49th parallel (Arnold and Tigert 1974; Baer, Grabb, and Johnston 1990a, 1990b).

[25] While I find no evidence that more conservative migrants prefer Canada, preference for social democracy does promote government intervention and a more "statist" approach to politics.

welcoming country, influencing these individuals' migration decisions.[26]

These individuals not only brought a left-wing ideology to Canada, but they also continued their left-leaning political involvement. Some became active in the labor movement. Others helped establish the Portuguese Canadian Democratic Association, created in 1959 "to form a front against the Fascist regime in Portugal" (Marques and Medeiros 1984). Prior to the Portuguese revolution, the Association would invite Central Committee members of the Portuguese Communist Party to speak.[27] In contrast, no one with whom I spoke in Massachusetts can remember any antifascist club in the Boston area. There are some reports that in the early postwar period a few individuals wrote to Portuguese-language newspapers advocating a republican government along U.S. lines, but any incipient attempts to organize such opposition quickly fizzled into neutrality or apathy toward the regime at home (Pap 1981; Rogers 1974).

Jose Manuel is one of these self-identified political migrants. When I asked why he left Portugal, he explained, "I left for political reasons, period. I was in the first year of [university] when I was arrested for the first time by the political police. I was not affiliated with any movement or any party. I was against fascism." He was released and continued to live in Portugal, but when he felt conditions had become intolerable, he followed a friend's advice and entered Canada on a tourist visa. His vague positive impression of Canada was confirmed in those early days and he decided to stay, regularizing his situation. In Toronto he occasionally attends meetings of the Portuguese Canadian Democratic Association, and he has been active trying to bridge what he considers the substantial gap between ordinary Portuguese immigrants and the Canadian political system.

Valadao also considers himself a political migrant, although he entered Canada legally as an independent immigrant. Valadao partici-

---

[26] Although Canada does not necessarily have a history of welcoming left-leaning immigrants with open arms (Whitaker 1987; Kelley and Trebilcock 1998), this perception has some basis in reality in the post–World War II era. In the United States, an individual must formally declare past Communist affiliation on the naturalization application. Past membership in the Communist Party constitutes grounds upon which the INS can refuse to grant U.S. citizenship. There is no similar question on Canadian citizenship forms.

[27] The Association was home to many leftist Portuguese immigrants. Today it is active in intellectual circles, occasionally bringing in a writer, politician, or artist from Portugal.

pated in a number of organizations opposed to the dictatorship in the 1960s, drawing the attention of the secret police. When he found his chances for professional advancement blocked, he went into exile. After careful research, he chose Canada as a potential country of settlement. Initially he had hoped to return to Portugal once the dictatorship fell, but with the passage of time he decided to stay. His decision has probably been to the benefit of the Portuguese-Canadian community: Valadao has held leadership positions in a number of community organizations and is widely respected.

The presence of these political migrants also influenced a number of young Portuguese immigrants going to school in Toronto. Nelson came to Canada as a fifteen-year-old in 1968 to avoid being drafted into the Portuguese army. He entered on a tourist visa and then had family sponsor his request for permanent status. Soon Nelson was attending a Canadian high school and participating in his local church youth group. He vividly remembers what he terms his first political awakening. He innocently asked whether the church youth group couldn't imitate the one found in Portugal:

> It was a crossbreed of the Scouts. They did a lot of camping, knot-tying, and singing the praises of government. I only realized they were a fascist organization when I arrived in Canada, because one of the guys once had a Scouts group, and I suggested, "Why not a *mocidade portuguesa* chapter?" And he was one of those who had been politically involved in Portugal with the Communist Party. He told me, "My God, can't you see that's a fascist organization, the way they salute with their fists clenched, and their arms outstretched?" And the "S" on the buckles was like a square "S" for Salazar, for a semi-swastika.
>
> And only at age fifteen did I come to realize—and I had to come to Canada to realize it—that I had lived the first fifteen years of my life in a fascist government. I had never come to that conclusion on my own.

This experience led Nelson to reevaluate his beliefs and become more interested in Canadian politics, especially the left-leaning New Democratic Party (NDP).[28] Initially the party's ideology attracted him

---

[28] Until recently, Ontario—and especially Toronto—was characterized by a three-party system: the New Democratic Party to the left, the Liberals in the center, and

as an antidote to fascism, then later as a party opposed to any system of privilege. "I knew by then that the NDP was my party because it was then that I had decided to turn against the system, because I saw the system in Portugal.... So by now, any party that was against the system was my party." Almost thirty years later, he remains a committed party member and is active in the labor movement.

The Formation of Leaders in the Newcomer Settlement Industry

Perceptions of a host society's political culture made it more likely that left-leaning individuals would go to Canada, and they, in turn, influenced some young Portuguese to adopt similar beliefs, although along lines congruent with the Canadian political system. However, ideological selection processes are not sufficient to explain the overrepresentation of left-wing community leaders in Toronto compared to the more conventional political ideologies found among Boston-area activists. A number of Toronto community leaders are Canada-born and make no mention of formative experiences such as the one that Nelson recounted. Furthermore, we can imagine that young immigrants in Boston could be as ideologically open to a variety of beliefs as their compatriots north of the 49th parallel. Rather, I argue, a discourse of social justice can be reinforced or develop independently through exposure to the host society's institutions. Particularly important in this regard are the state-assisted "newcomer settlement industry" and the political party system.

The newcomer settlement industry includes all entities, programs, and employed positions catering to the specific needs of migrant newcomers. It can include nonprofit voluntary associations and social service agencies, public hospitals, and government departments, as well as for-profit private businesses.[29] Many of the community activists I interviewed regularly moved between public, for-profit, and nonprofit employment. What unites these different jobs and organizations is a shared concern with helping immigrants and their families adjust to life in a new country. This industry lies in a larger societal sector com-

---

the Progressive Conservatives on the right. Recently a new party of the right, the Alliance, has been making limited gains at the federal level in Ontario.

[29] Although the term "industry" might project a negative connotation when used to include nonprofit organizations, it best describes the constellation of interdependent organizations and services available to immigrants, even when a group's "product" might be a monthly Friday evening dance for members of a social club.

prised of entities not directly implicated in service provision but which have influence through vertical and horizontal ties, such as through funding relationships and regulatory supervision (Scott and Meyer 1991).

In Canada, because of the state's material assistance to immigrant-serving organizations and its symbolic support of newcomer settlement, we find a greater number and diversity of organizations dedicated to immigrants. Such organizations provide career ladders and training opportunities for those interested in community leadership, and it encourages those without predispositions to advocacy to become community spokespeople. In the United States, where the state favors more distant, neutral relations with immigrants, ethnic organizations, and community advocates, we find fewer sustained leadership opportunities and more episodic advocacy.

Recruiting Leaders: Advocacy Jobs

One does not need to be working in newcomer settlement in order to be engaged in the community. The Toquevillean image of the United States suggests that active citizens should contribute to their community within the broader category of citizen rather than employee. Indeed, in both Toronto and Cambridge/Somerville, individuals with no paid position in the settlement industry provide an active voice and hours of volunteer time to promote community interests. At a leadership level, however, these people are often the exception. Most of those who do not work in the newcomer settlement sector have little time to devote to community activism (many work two jobs or regular overtime), and they have little chance to learn the skills needed to be a community leader, such as running meetings, writing grant proposals, and speaking to the media. The majority of those extremely active in the Portuguese community combine their volunteer work with professional or job-related tasks.

Some people are interested in taking a leadership role from a young age, and they seek out appropriate opportunities for their interests. The newcomer settlement industry provided such an opportunity for Dan, the Canadian-born son of immigrant parents. Dan is the executive director of a large nonprofit organization serving Portuguese in downtown Toronto. He has been a vocal community advocate, particularly around issues of domestic violence and family counseling. Dan recalls that as a teenager, he already had an interest in social services and community work:

> I remember going through high school and being encouraged to become an accountant or a lawyer. The guidance counselor had me pegged for one or the other ... [but] I always wanted to go the social services route. I always wanted to listen to people and to help people as best I could.... I've always wanted to do that with the Portuguese community, because I saw the need here as being the greatest, and it's my roots. It's always been the community I wanted to work with.

After completing a university degree, Dan found that the newcomer settlement industry provided him with an outlet to combine his dual interests: "I've dedicated some of the best years of my working life to this particular community.... All of my jobs over the last sixteen years have been because of the Portuguese-speaking connection." Those positions included working as a coordinator of interpretation services, as a paralegal specializing in immigration matters, and as a staff member at various nonprofit organizations.

It is perhaps not surprising that someone like Dan would eventually assume a position of leadership. However, many paths to community leadership evolve over time and begin with the need for a job, not out of a strong internal conviction. For example, shortly after graduating from university, Celia found a government job that required language skills and focused on immigrant outreach. Celia was an immigrant, having moved to Canada at age eight, but:

> I wasn't interacting with the Portuguese community all that much.... It wasn't until I worked [for the government] that my interaction became one of people calling and saying, "Do you know where we can get grants?" and "Do you know who I can call to get this information or that information?" Once a member of your community is perceived to have some knowledge or some power, you automatically get those calls and invitations to go to events and so on—even though I wasn't in a powerful position.

It was during Celia's first job in the newcomer settlement industry that she began to see her work as important. "Those were very positive experiences.... [The job] gave me an opportunity to make [government] a little more accessible to ethnic groups who hadn't had the opportunity to step in there and get a feel of how the government works." Such experiences convinced Celia to stay in immigrant advocacy; she later worked for a nonprofit community agency and then in another public-sector job, gaining confidence in her ability to help people and advocate on their behalf. Over the last fifteen years, she has been involved in many community projects and in bringing more Portuguese into politics by, for example, encouraging naturalization in the community.

Agostinho provides a more extreme example of this dynamic of community elites becoming community advocates through experience in the settlement industry. Agostinho came to Canada as a professional and initially wanted little to do with the Portuguese community. He perceived that a gulf separated his socioeconomic background and geographic origins in Africa from the majority of Portuguese, who hail from the Azores and possess limited education. He initially sought work in his field, but employers were reluctant to accept his foreign credentials or they required "Canadian experience." Eventually Agostinho found a job in the immigrant settlement industry:

> I still have fifty-two letters of "Don't call us, we'll call you." Eventually I decided, given my knowledge of English and Portuguese, to do something else. I put my name down at a few translation agencies and approached the Immigration Department to see if they were in need of interpreters.... That's how I started, doing some translations.

This work quickly got Agostinho more involved in community activism. Today he runs his own business providing consultation services to immigrant compatriots.

Fewer people in Massachusetts tell stories like those of Dan, Celia, and Agostinho. Some of them develop careers in newcomer settlement, but it is harder because of the limited government support, along with a discourse of ethnicity centered on race rather than language or national origin. Rosana made such a career late in life, although she migrated to the United States as a child and has a long history of providing informal settlement assistance. Like many immigrant youngsters, she helped her family deal with their new environment; as she puts it, "I became everybody's caretaker." Rosana picked up English relatively quickly from school and the neighborhood, so she was called on to phone the utility company if there was a problem with a bill or to translate letters sent to her parents. "I became an advocate at the age of nine." She was not, however, immediately able to channel her experience into a career. After attending secretarial college, she worked as an administrative assistant in the health care sector, where she was again called on informally to act as an interpreter for patients who had trouble conversing with the medical staff. Another ten years passed before Rosana became a caseworker for newcomers at a large nonprofit organization. Today she works for a different nonprofit, advocating on behalf of immigrant rights.

Although some immigrants find a career in immigrant settlement, this is much harder to achieve in Massachusetts than in Ontario. Because of the smaller and less diverse immigrant settlement industry in the United States, there are fewer immigration-related employment opportunities for community leaders, and individuals tend to take jobs unrelated to immigrant settlement. For example, Victor now works as a public servant dealing with immigrant and refugee issues, but he previously sold insurance, worked as a teacher, and owned a small company. People like Victor tend to see their civic engagement either as an extension of their work or as purely voluntary, and they do not link it to a broader political agenda. They are no less dedicated than immigrants in Toronto, but they are more likely to center their activism on short-term projects. A set of short-term projects can bring important benefits to a community, but sustained leadership often requires a particular advocacy framework.

Developing an Advocacy Framework

The Canadian government's larger presence in immigrant integration not only provides jobs, but it also indirectly helps fuel an advocacy framework. Pal (1993), for example, documents how programs and funding from multiculturalism established a network of advocacy organizations (see also Biles 1999). Such groups and immigrant service organizations facilitate the development of an advocacy framework by providing long-term employment around the same constituency and toward the same broad integration goals. To some extent, a larger settlement industry encourages more people to become community advocates because an individual's employment is tied to the community. Those who are being paid to do settlement work have a strong economic interest in showing government and other potential funders that their services are needed. More subtly, however, working with other immigrants often provides a better understanding of the barriers compatriots face in making their homes in a new country. Such cross-class interactions are especially important for ethnic elite, who often possess superior language skills and higher education, and therefore encounter fewer integration problems.

Continuous employment in the immigrant settlement industry allowed Dan to sustain and deepen his interest in helping the Portuguese community. Like many others, Dan has had occasional doubts: "At times I've wondered whether I should have just strayed a little bit wider in my career path. I might be earning a little bit more ... and perhaps achieving a little more respect." However, his daily contact with immigrants reaffirms his belief that his work is important and worth fighting for:

> I helped establish this agency because I felt the need for this type of service for the Portuguese-speaking community.... It's one thing to say that these people should learn English, but what if they don't? What are you going to do? Every service that we offer works toward giving empowerment, toward the ultimate goal of being self-sufficient. But you've got to start where people are; otherwise you're marginalizing. That was an argument we'd been making for so, so long.... It's a struggle.

Such beliefs led Dan to advocacy work, pressuring government to funnel more resources to the community. The agency that Dan helped establish and which he runs receives 70 percent of its funding from provincial and municipal governments and 30 percent from sources such as the United Way. Obtaining government funding required intensive lobbying by a broad coalition of Portuguese community leaders, including representatives of the church, businesspeople, and social service workers.

In contrast to Dan, whose politics are left of center, Agostinho espouses right-leaning views and is a member of Canada's Progressive Conservative Party. Yet when asked why he remains active in his community despite his initial reluctance, his response highlights a similar dedication to community service:

> It's the nature of my business.... If I had found a job with [a large corporation], I might have gone in a different direction. But my occupation brought me into very close dealings with the community.... You live in a community, you have to be

> part of the community. And in whatever small way you can, you have to do something.

Had it not been for the employment opportunities available in immigrant settlement and Agostinho's exposure to his compatriots' integration problems, it is likely that he would have directed his energies elsewhere. Instead, he has been active in various Portuguese civic associations and has acted as an informal liaison between the Portuguese community and government.

THE PARTY SYSTEM: FINDING A PLACE

The normative thrust of official multiculturalism also pushes other political actors, such as political parties, to develop structures that promote ethno-racial involvement, although perhaps at a relatively low level (see Stasiulis and Abu-Laban 1991). Involvement in a political party often reinforces an individual's commitment to ethnic diversity and, on the left, social justice. I found that Portuguese leaders in Toronto were more likely than their Boston-area compatriots to be actively involved in electoral politics related to immigrant integration, further fueling a strong advocacy framework.

Such reinforcement is especially pronounced among those who work in the newcomer settlement industry, where individuals often learn a specific advocacy language. For example, Rosemary, who works with the public school board in Toronto, devotes many volunteer hours to promoting Portuguese parents' participation in school decision making. She is also a member of the New Democratic Party. I asked her whether her activism relates to her political involvement:

> Well, they overlap, certainly. They're not separate. I know that the way I work—you call it a vocation, which it is—fits in the NDP philosophy. Education for all. Taking care of the disadvantaged. Equity. Antiracism education. All those things, they are the philosophy of the NDP. So yes, they go hand in hand.

Individuals like Rosemary do not promote their political party during their community work, but they do share a discourse centered on equity and social justice that animates many of their activities.

Community leaders in Massachusetts rarely link their community activism to clear political ideologies or sustained party involvement.

Tony, for instance, votes Democrat and has occasionally assisted with local candidates' campaigns. The political concerns he identifies, however, do not parallel the standard platform of the Democratic Party. When I asked him what he felt was the key issue facing the Portuguese community, he answered:

> Family, because I believe that it is in the house that everything starts. If the family is good, then we get a great foundation, and we can get these people to develop in this country, in the American sense of the word, and be more involved in politics and so forth....
>
> [Portuguese immigrants] come to America, and they think the government is going to take care of them.... There are a lot of services here that help those who don't have a job, who have problems financially. And then they feel, "Hey, this is good." And this is a setback; I'm against this kind of service. I'm not saying that I'm a Republican, but people should be forced to go ahead and succeed.

Tony's political activities have not been linked to party politics. He became very involved in a campaign to have a Portuguese language station added to the basic cable television package, and he did some outreach around health education with a local nonprofit organization. Today he runs his own construction company. Like many Portuguese in the Boston area, Tony's activism is issue by issue, rather than part of a larger political agenda.

Indeed, most Boston-area community leaders rarely combine community-based work, whether volunteer or remunerated, with their mainstream political participation. Armando, for example, is active in state and federal politics and widely recognized for his leadership in the community, helping to organize the annual Day of Portugal parade and raising money for the Portuguese church. Armando is a senior manager in a private company employing many Portuguese immigrants, and, like Agostinho in Toronto, Armando explains that both business interests and personal commitment fuel his civic engagement:

> I want to give back to the community what they gave to me. I keep saying that part of my success—having a tie around my neck, driving my nice car, having a nice house—was a mutual thing. Me helping them, and at the same time I was helping myself too.

Armando noted that by assisting many recently arrived immigrants in getting a job with his employer, he helped the company—and his career—since these people are a hardworking and relatively cheap source of labor.

When it comes to U.S. politics, however, his participation mostly takes the form of donations and acting as a liaison between U.S. politicians and elites from Portugal, not between the U.S. political system and members of the Portuguese-American community. This is not to say that he is unconcerned about the lack of Portuguese political participation: "That's something we need to develop even more," he laments. "It's very unfortunate." One problem that he notes is the lack of a coordinating organization to assist Portuguese-American candidates in local and state elections, but this is not something that he has tried to organize. To a large extent, his reticence reflects his impression of American politics:

> In political life today, if you have the money, you are elected. If you don't have the money, good-bye. Unfortunately, that's the reality. If you make a study of the past five or ten years, which candidates were reelected? Go see the fund-raising. You'll see which folks win.

Armando's sizable income allows him to make regular donations to political parties and candidates, but few Portuguese share his economic success. Armando's community participation is personal while his political activities are "at a different level."

More generally, political involvement in Ontario is facilitated by the relatively lower costs of participating and the greater importance of the party in contemporary Canadian politics. Relative to the United States, Canada's robust party system provides an easier path to political engagement for community leaders with political aspirations, and this increases the political visibility of the Portuguese population among mainstream actors and institutions.

In Massachusetts, largely a Democratic state, competition for office often occurs between members of the same party, rather than between two parties with clear differences in platform. Potential candidates must raise significant amounts of money to win the primary election, and then even more to run in the general election. Significant startup costs dissuade many immigrants from competing for office, particularly when this barrier is added to their newcomer status. As one Portuguese immigrant who has run for office explained, "For those not born here, the odds, are greater.... I didn't have the school buddies, the friends from elementary school that would be natural supporters." Support from the ethnic community can partially compensate for the lack of long-standing roots in an area, but ethnic-specific voting rarely suffices in either a primary or a general election.

Stiff internal competition for party nominations can exist in Ontario as in Boston, but nominations take place within riding associations rather than through a primary, and this reduces costs.[30] Ethnic ties, though not sufficient to win a general election, can serve an important role in the nomination process. If a potential candidate can convince fellow ethnics to become party members and attend the riding nomination meeting, these supporters can swing the nomination.[31]

The stronger Canadian party system and tighter campaign finance laws make nominees' personal financial resources somewhat less important in Ontario than in Massachusetts. When I asked one politically active Portuguese immigrant in Toronto how difficult it had been to raise money for a failed election bid, the individual dismissed the question with a shrug, "I didn't really raise funds.... If you establish your networks right away, it's okay." In contrast, an informant in Massachusetts described a quite different situation: "It's very difficult to raise money. You have to start with your own natural constituency. But it's easier to organize a function to collect money for the parish—even one in the Azores—than to support a politician." Since candidates have to raise their own money for primaries, they have less party loyalty:

> The party really doesn't have the clout and the kind of influence because it doesn't support [candidates] as it should. Therefore, the representatives don't have that much loyalty

---

[30] In the United States, individuals who register to vote will be asked for a party affiliation. They can then vote in their respective primary in their district. In Canada, voter lists do not contain party information; those interested in joining a party do so on their own initiative and pay a small fee. Party members may vote in riding association elections to determine the party's candidate for that riding (district). Given the greater effort associated with party affiliation in Canada, the internal electoral pool is much smaller, and running a nomination campaign is less costly.

[31] This strategy—creating "instant" party members who support a compatriot's bid for nomination—generated significant press attention in the 1980s and early 1990s. It had long been used by party insiders, but as immigrants took advantage of such tactics their activities became redefined as an "ethnic" issue of political abuse rather than a weakness in the parties' regulations (Stasiulis and Abu-Laban 1991).

> to the party. That's why you see Democrats voting every which way. The representatives are much more independent.

In Toronto, stronger party ties also draw in volunteers to work on a campaign. Longtime Liberal, NDP, or Progressive Conservative supporters might assist the nominated candidate even if they do not know the individual personally. In contrast, would-be politicians in Massachusetts must work hard to build up their own personal corps of volunteers.

INSTITUTIONAL REPERCUSSIONS: LINKING LEADERS AND COMMUNITY MEMBERS

A larger immigrant settlement industry thus allows more people to combine advocacy with employment, and a more robust party system provides easier paths to electoral involvement for interested individuals. One might well wonder whether such institutional effects have a substantive impact on ordinary immigrants. I suggest that they do. Community advocates who espouse social justice frameworks and who have links to political parties facilitate political participation among ordinary immigrants. A discourse of social justice allows some Portuguese to overcome hesitancy with political participation. Combined with a more open party system, this generates greater electoral success among Portuguese-Canadian candidates in Toronto than in Boston, providing a relatively stronger voice for the community in formal political institutions.

Ordinary Immigrants and Social Justice

Numerous studies shows that political participation correlates strongly with individuals' education level and their sense of political efficacy (Miller and Shanks 1996; Verba, Schlozman, and Brady 1995; Rosenstone and Hansen 1993). Consequently, it is not surprising that many Portuguese immigrants fail to become involved in their host country's political system. Many have only an elementary education, and the majority were socialized during the dictatorship when, as one man explained, politics was the "realm of witches." Maria, for example, grew up in the Azores during the 1950s; she had to leave school after only four years to help with housework and the family farm. She moved to Cambridge in 1966 with her husband and two children and became a citizen five years later. Yet when I interviewed her in 1997, she had never voted: "I'm afraid to vote for the wrong person. I am not confident in myself.... I always feel that I am going to make a mistake." For Maria, citizenship remains a legal status, not a participatory act, and many Portuguese immigrants share her fear and hesitation.

Despite such sentiments, relatively more Portuguese immigrants in Ontario view citizenship as an invitation—or obligation—to participate politically. Community leaders' activism, when combined with a message of social justice, can provide a mechanism through which some Portuguese immigrants translate their economic experiences and frustrations into political participation. In Massachusetts such a transfer is more difficult. Even for the majority of Portuguese-Canadians who do not see themselves as supporters of the political left, the left's discourse provides a language for making legitimate claims against the political system. In the United States, claims-making by minority groups tends to be legitimated through the language of race, a usage that does not serve a community like the Portuguese that has consciously defined itself as white.[32]

Tilla's experiences exemplify how institutions and discourses interact to promote political engagement among ordinary immigrants. Tilla, who has only a primary education, took a factory job immediately after arriving in Canada from the Azores as a teenager in the early 1960s. Later, like many other Portuguese women in Toronto, she worked as a cleaner. She recalls her Portuguese male supervisor: "He's an evil man.... He's give to us too much work. Like slavery, it's like slavery there, and not many jobs at that time." When she told another cleaner that their working conditions would improve if they formed a union, she was fired for being a troublemaker.

Losing her job spurred Tilla to contact the NDP. Her local politician was not Portuguese, but he worked closely with a Portuguese lawyer. With the help of these two men, Tilla sued her former employer and won damages. This incident led to her further involvement in helping to organize cleaners in downtown office towers. Talking about her activities, Tilla explains:

> The opposition [in the Ontario legislature] was quite good at that time because they fight for the working-class people. You had a little protection because of the opposition, the left.

---

32 Due to a lack of space, I do not deal with the impact of race-based political claims here.

> So then they pay me [damages], then I start to be involved ... with Sandy. She's the one who works with working-class cleaners to fight for the woman's rights, the union's rights.... And me and Sandy and the other Portuguese woman ... we go to the doors, to the woman's work [in downtown] to see if we can do something to put [in] the union.

Tilla's activism was not only connected to a political party; it was also tied to a local immigrant settlement organization, St. Christopher House. St. Christopher House provided the group with meeting facilities and also paid Tilla and the other two women a small wage.

Similar support is hard to find in Massachusetts, even though it is one of the most staunchly Democratic U.S. states. Manuela, who lives in Cambridge and who worked as a cleaner after she moved to the United States with her husband and daughter in 1968, talked about socioeconomic injustices, though in her case the target was high rents:

> The rents can't be paid.... The poor don't have the means. They are immigrants, they buy little. How are they going to pay $700 in rent, $300 for the home?... If you don't or can't work, you can't live. But [the government] doesn't know how it is.... You can't say, "Sir, send people that care about the immigrants, because they are the people who can't speak up." There is nowhere to complain, and we can't complain.

Unlike Tilla, Manuela cannot identify people or organizations to help her protest exorbitant rents. After a "Jewish man" came to her door, Manuela attended a meeting at City Hall to voice disapproval over the end of rent control in Cambridge, but her participation was a one-time event. There was no follow-up by a political party and little involvement by Portuguese organizations in her area. So, unlike Tilla's case, Manuela's participation did not develop into further activism.

Electoral Outcomes

These differences may explain why Portuguese-Canadians have enjoyed more electoral success than Portuguese in Cambridge or Somerville. Most Portuguese in Ontario support the Liberals, Canada's centrist political party. Loyalty is often tied to a person—in this case, former prime minister Pierre Elliot Trudeau—rather than a platform or ideology. For those worried about voting for the "wrong" side, the

Liberals also offer the Goldilocks advantage: neither too far to the right nor too far to the left. In Massachusetts, Portuguese-Americans tend to support the Democratic Party. Given their immigrant background and socioeconomic status, their choice is not surprising. However, as in Toronto, their loyalties tend to be personal. Many see themselves as Kennedy Democrats, placing their faith in the Kennedy clan rather than in any particular party platform.[33]

Given that community leaders in Toronto are more radical than the average community member, we would expect them to have less electoral success than compatriots in the Cambridge/Somerville area. Yet the opposite is true: six Portuguese-Canadians have been elected to municipal school boards, two have served as city councilors, and one has been elected to provincial office. Of these individuals, one is a Progressive Conservative, four are members of the NDP, and the rest are Liberals.[34] In contrast, no Portuguese-American from Cambridge or Somerville has been elected to city, state, or federal government in the past twenty-five years, and only one Portuguese-American has been elected to the school board.[35]

The difference is all the more surprising when we consider that the Portuguese constitute similar proportions of the population in Toronto, Somerville, and Cambridge. In 1996, those of Portuguese ethnicity made up 3.3 percent of the population in metropolitan Toronto, while they constituted 3.1 percent of the population in Cambridge and a much higher 7.5 percent of the population in Somerville, according to the 2000 census. In the early 1990s, Portuguese representation at the local level in metropolitan Toronto was approximately equal to the proportion of Portuguese ethnics in the population (Siemiatycki and Isin 1997). In the Boston area, the Portuguese are unrepresented, with no one from this ethnic group sitting on a city council.[36]

---

[33] It appears that more California Portuguese support the Republican Party than do those in Massachusetts.

[34] School board and city elections are nonpartisan. I determine party affiliation based on interview data and self-identification by candidates during election campaigns.

[35] Nearly all of the few Portuguese-origin individuals serving at the state level come from the New Bedford/Fall River area in southeastern Massachusetts, a region estimated to be 30 to 60 percent Portuguese. No one of Portuguese origin has been elected to federal politics from Massachusetts in the post–World War II period.

[36] In 1994 there were 106 council seats available to candidates in the Toronto metropolitan area across a two-tier system of government comprising city councils and a larger metro council. Three of these seats were held by Portuguese-origin indi-

CONCLUSION

More Portuguese immigrants living in Toronto have become citizens of their new home than is the case for Portuguese immigrants in the Boston area. A larger proportion of the Toronto immigrants appear to be politically active, and a greater number have succeeded in winning elected office. I began this chapter with the observation that naturalization levels in the United States have been falling steadily since the 1970s, prompting some to worry about the quality of the immigrants admitted and to bemoan their apparent lack of interest in becoming active members of the polity. Such concerns are not new; they echo long-standing concern about the suitability of immigrant newcomers as future citizens and voters. Taking an institutional approach to immigrant political incorporation—and thus considering seriously the impact that host societies have on migrants' integration experiences—forces a reevaluation of such issues. When we consider how political cultures and government intervention affect immigrants' ability to organize, develop leadership, and make claims in the political space, we find that the "problem" of newcomers' political incorporation may not lie with the immigrants we receive, but rather with the reception we give them.

References

Abu-Laban, Yasmeen. 1994. "The Politics of Race and Ethnicity: Multiculturalism as a Contested Arena." In *Canadian Politics*, edited by J.P. Bickerton and A.G. Gagnon. 2d ed. Peterborough, Ont.: Broadview.

Almeida, Onésimo T. 2000. "Value Conflicts and Cultural Adjustments in North America." In *The Portuguese in Canada: From the Sea to the City*, edited by C. Teixeira and V. da Rosa. Toronto: University of Toronto Press.

Almond, Gabriel A., and Sidney Verba. 1963. *The Civic Culture: Political Attitudes and Democracy in Five Nations*. Princeton, N.J.: Princeton University Press.

Anderson, Grace M. 1983. "Azoreans in Anglophone Canada," *Canadian Ethnic Studies* 15, no. 1: 73–82.

Angus, H.F. 1937. "Canadian Immigration: The Law and Its Administration." In *The Legal Status of Aliens in Pacific Countries*, edited by N. MacKenzie. London: Oxford University Press.

---

viduals, at a time when the Portuguese constituted 3 percent of the metro area. In 1997, metro Toronto was amalgamated into one "megacity" with 56 council seats and a mayor. Only one Portuguese-origin politician managed to hang on to office.

Arnold, Stephen J., and Douglas J. Tigert. 1974. "Canadians and Americans: A Comparative Analysis," *International Journal of Comparative Sociology* 15, nos. 1–2: 68–83.

Baer, Douglas, Edward Grabb, and William Johnston. 1990a. "Reassessing Differences in Canadian and American Values." In *Images of Canada: The Sociological Tradition*, edited by J. Curtis and L. Tepperman. Scarborough, Ont.: Prentice Hall Canada.

———. 1990b. "The Values of Canadians and Americans: A Critical Analysis and Reassessment," *Social Forces* 68, no. 3: 693–713.

Benford, Robert D., and David A. Snow. 2000. "Framing Processes and Social Movements: An Overview and Assessment," *Annual Review of Sociology* 26: 611–39.

Biles, John. 1997. "It Is All a Matter of Priority: Multiculturalism under Mulroney (1984–1988)." M.A. research essay, Carleton University.

Bloemraad, Irene. 2002. "The North American Naturalization Gap: An Institutional Approach to Citizenship Acquisition in the United States and Canada," *International Migration Review* 36, no. 1: 193–228.

Borjas, George J. 1999. *Heaven's Door: Immigration Policy and the American Economy*. Princeton, N.J.: Princeton University Press.

Boyd, Monica, John DeVries, and Keith Simkin. 1994. "Language, Economic Status and Integration." In *Immigration and Refugee Policy: Australia and Canada Compared*, edited by H. Adelman, A. Borowski, M. Burstein, and L. Foster. Toronto: University of Toronto Press.

Brubaker, William Rogers. 1992. *Citizenship and Nationhood in France and Germany*. Cambridge, Mass.: Harvard University Press.

Brubaker, William Rogers, ed. 1989. *Immigration and the Politics of Citizenship in Europe and North America*. Lanham, Md.: University Press of America.

Camarota, Steven A. 2001. *The Slowing Progress of Immigrants: An Examination of Income, Home Ownership, and Citizenship, 1970–2000*. Brief in *Backgrounder* series. Washington, D.C.: Center for Immigration Studies.

Canada. 1984. *Equality Now! Report of the Special Committee on Visible Minorities in Canadian Society*. Ottawa: House of Commons.

Clarke, James, Elsbeth van Dam, and Liz Gooster. 1998. "New Europeans: Naturalization and Citizenship in Europe," *Citizenship Studies* 2, no. 1: 43–67.

Clemens, Elisabeth S. 1997. *The People's Lobby: Organizational Innovation and the Rise of Interest Group Politics in the United States, 1890–1925*. Chicago: University of Chicago Press.

Clemens, Elisabeth S., and James M. Cook. 1999. "Politics and Institutionalism: Explaining Durability and Change," *Annual Review of Sociology* 25: 441–66.

de la Garza, Rodolfo, Angelo Falcón, F. Chris García, and John A. García. 1992. *Latino Voices: Mexican, Puerto Rican and Cuban Perspectives on American Politics*. Boulder, Colo.: Westview.

de Rham, Gérard. 1990. "Naturalisation: The Politics of Citizenship Acquisition." In *The Political Rights of Migrant Workers in Western Europe*, edited by Zig Layton-Henry. London: Sage.

DeSipio, Louis. 2001. "Building America, One Person at a Time: Naturalization and the Political Behavior of the Naturalized in Contemporary American Politics." In *E Pluribus Unum? Contemporary and Historical Perspectives on Immigrant Political Incorporation*, edited by G. Gerstle and J. Mollenkopf. New York: Russell Sage Foundation.

DiMaggio, Paul J., and Walter W. Powell. 1991. "The Iron Cage Revisited: Institutional Isomorphism and Collective Rationality in Organizational Fields." In *The New Institutionalism in Organizational Analysis*, edited by W.W. Powell and P.J. DiMaggio. Chicago: University of Chicago Press.

Erie, Steven P. 1988. *Rainbow's End: Irish-Americans and the Dilemmas of Urban Machine Politics, 1840–1985*. Berkeley: University of California Press.

Evans, Peter B., D. Rueschemeyer, and Theda Skocpol, eds. 1985. *Bringing the State Back In*. New York: Cambridge University Press.

Fleras, Augie, and Jean Leonard Elliott. 1992. *Multiculturalism in Canada: The Challenge of Diversity*. Scarborough, Ont.: Nelson.

Frideres, J.S., S. Goldenburg, J. Disanto, and J. Horna. 1987. "Becoming Canadian: Citizen Acquisition and National Identity," *Canadian Review of Studies in Nationalism* 14, no. 1: 105–21.

Ganz, Marshall. 2000. "Resources and Resourcefulness: Strategic Capacity in the Unionization of California Agriculture: 1959–1966," *American Journal of Sociology* 105, no. 4: 1003–62.

Giddens, Anthony. 1984. *The Constitution of Society: Outline of the Theory of Structuration*. Berkeley: University of California Press.

Harper-Ho, Virginia. 2000. "Noncitizen Voting Rights: The History, the Law and Current Prospects for Change," *Law and Inequality Journal* 18: 271–322.

Hawkins, Freda. 1988. *Canada and Immigration: Public Policy and Public Concern*. 2d ed. Montreal: McGill-Queen's University Press.

———. 1991. *Critical Years in Immigration: Canada and Australia Compared*. 2d ed. Montreal: McGill-Queen's University Press.

Higham, John. 1978. "Introduction: The Forms of Ethnic Leadership." In *Ethnic Leadership in America*, edited by J. Higham. Baltimore, Md.: Johns Hopkins University Press.

Hirsch, Paul M. 1997. "Sociology without Social Structure: Neoinstitutional Theory Meets Brave New World," *American Journal of Sociology* 102, no. 6: 1702–23.

House of Commons. 1971. *Debates* 8545. [Ottawa].

Ito-Alder, James P. 1980 [1972, 1978]. *The Portuguese in Cambridge and Somerville*. Combined ed. Cambridge, Mass.: Cambridge Department of Community Development.

Jacobson, David. 1996. *Rights across Borders: Immigration and the Decline of Citizenship*. Baltimore, Md.: Johns Hopkins University Press.

Jasso, Guillermina, and Mark R. Rosenzweig. 1986. "Family Reunification and the Immigrant Multiplier: U.S. Immigration Law, Origin-Country Conditions, and the Reproduction of Immigrants," *Demography* 23, no. 3: 291–311.

Jepperson, Ronald L. 1991. "Institutions, Institutional Effects, and Institutionalism." In *The New Institutionalism in Organizational Analysis*, edited by W.W. Powell and P.J. DiMaggio. Chicago: University of Chicago Press.

Jones-Correa, Michael. 1998. *Between Two Nations: The Political Predicament of Latinos in New York City*. Ithaca, N.Y.: Cornell University Press.

———. 2002. "Institutional and Contextual Factors in Immigrant Naturalization and Voting," *Citizenship Studies*.

Joppke, Christian. 1999. *Immigration and the Nation-State: The United States, Germany, and Great Britain*. Oxford: Oxford University Press.

Kaplan, William. 1993. "Who Belongs? Changing Concepts of Citizenship and Nationality." In *Belonging: The Meaning and Future of Canadian Citizenship*, edited by W. Kaplan. Montreal: McGill-Queen's University Press.

Kelley, Ninette, and Michael Trebilcock. 1998. *The Making of the Mosaic: A History of Canadian Immigration Policy*. Toronto: University of Toronto Press.

Koopmans, Ruud, and Paul Statham. 1999. "Challenging the Liberal Nation-State? Postnationalism, Multiculturalism, and the Collective Claims Making of Migrants and Ethnic Minorities in Britain and Germany," *American Journal of Sociology* 105, no. 3: 652–96.

Lanphier, Michael, and Oleh Lukomskyj. 1994. "Settlement Policy in Australia and Canada." In *Immigration and Refugee Policy: Australia and Canada Compared*, edited by H. Adelman, A. Borowski, M. Burstein, and L. Foster. Toronto: University of Toronto Press.

Layton-Henry, Zig. 1990. "The Challenge of Political Rights." In *The Political Rights of Migrant Workers in Western Europe*, edited by Zig Layton-Henry. London: Sage.

Liang, Zai. 1994. "Social Contact, Social Capital, and the Naturalization Process: Evidence from Six Immigrant Groups," *Social Science Research* 23: 407–37.

Lipset, Seymour Martin. 1990. *Continental Divide: The Values and Institutions of the United States and Canada*. New York: Routledge.

March, James G., and Johan P. Olsen. 1984. "The New Institutionalism: Organizational Factors in Political Life," *American Political Science Review* 78, no. 3: 734–49.

Marques, Domingos, and Manuela Marujo. 1993. *With Hardened Hands: A Pictorial History of Portuguese Immigrants to Canada in the 1950s*. Etobicoke, Ont.: New Leaf.

Marques, Domingos, and Joao Medeiros. 1984. "Portuguese Immigrants in Toronto," *Polyphony*, Summer, pp. 154–58.

Martiniello, Marco. 1993. "Ethnic Leadership, Ethnic Communities' Political Powerlessness and the State in Belgium," *Ethnic and Racial Studies* 16, no. 2: 236–55.

McCarthy, John D., and Mayer N. Zald. 1977. "Resource Mobilization and Social Movements: A Partial Theory," *American Journal of Sociology* 82, no. 6: 1212–41.

———. 2002. "The Enduring Vitality of the Resource Mobilization Theory of Social Movements." In *Handbook of Sociological Theory*, edited by J.H. Turner. New York: Kluwer/Plenum.

Meissner, Doris. 2001. *After the Attacks: Protecting Border and Liberties*. Policy Brief No. 8. Washington, D.C.: Carnegie Endowment for International Peace.

Miller, Warren E., and J. Merrill Shanks. 1996. *The New American Voter*. Cambridge, Mass.: Harvard University Press.

Minkoff, Debra C. 1994. "From Service Provision to Institutional Advocacy: The Shifting Legitimacy of Organizational Forms," *Social Forces* 72, no. 4: 943–69.

North, David S. 1985. *The Long Grey Welcome: A Study of the American Naturalization Process*. Washington, D.C.: National Association of Latino Elected and Appointed Officials Education Fund.

———. 1987. "The Long Grey Welcome: A Study of the American Naturalization Program," *International Migration Review* 21, no. 2: 311–26.

Pal, Leslie. 1993. *Interests of State: The Politics of Language, Multiculturalism, and Feminism in Canada*. Montreal: McGill-Queen's University Press.

Pan, Philip A. 2000. "Naturalization: An Unnatural Process for Many Latinos," *Washington Post*, July 4.

Pap, Leo. 1981. *The Portuguese-Americans*. Boston, Mass.: Twayne.

Parenti, Michael. 1967. "Ethnic Politics and the Persistence of Ethnic Identification," *American Political Science Review* 61, no. 3: 717–26.

Pierson, Paul. 1993. "When Effect Becomes Cause: Policy Feedback and Political Change," *World Politics* 45, no. 4: 595–628.

Plascencia, Luis F.B., Gary P. Freeman, and Mark Setzler. 1999. *Restricting Immigrant Access to Employment: An Examination of Regulations of Five States*. Austin, Tex.: Tomás Rivera Policy Institute.

Portes, Alejandro, and John W. Curtis. 1987. "Changing Flags: Naturalization and Its Determinants among Mexican Immigrants," *International Migration Review* 21, no. 2: 352–71.

Portes, Alejandro, and Rafael Mozo. 1985. "The Political Adaptation Process of Cubans and Other Ethnic Minorities in the United States: A Preliminary Analysis," *International Migration Review* 19, no. 1: 35–63.

Powell, Walter W. 1991. "Expanding the Scope of Institutional Analysis." In *The New Institutionalism in Organizational Analysis*, edited by W.W. Powell and P.J. DiMaggio. Chicago: University of Chicago Press.

Putnam, Robert D. 2000. *Bowling Alone: The Collapse and Revival of American Community*. New York: Simon and Schuster.

Ramakrishnan, S. Karthick, and Thomas J. Espenshade. 2001. "Immigrant Incorporation and Political Participation in the United States," *International Migration Review* 35, no. 3: 870–907.

Reitz, Jeffrey G. 1998. *Warmth of the Welcome: The Social Causes of Economic Success for Immigrants in Different Nations and Cities*. Boulder, Colo.: Westview.

Rogers, Francis M. 1974. *Americans of Portuguese Descent: A Lesson in Differentiation*. Beverly Hills, Calif.: Sage.

Rosenstone, Steven J., and John Mark Hansen. 1993. *Mobilization, Participation, and Democracy in America*. New York: Macmillan.

Schmidley, A. Dianne, and Campbell Gibson. 1999. *Profile of the Foreign-Born Population in the United States: 1997*. U.S. Census Bureau Current Population Reports, Series P23-195. Washington, D.C.: U.S. Government Printing Office.

Schuck, Peter H. 1998. *Citizens, Strangers, and In-Betweens: Essays on Immigration and Citizenship*. Boulder, Colo.: Westview.

Scott, W. Richard, and John W. Meyer. 1991. "The Organization of Societal Sectors: Propositions and Early Evidence." In *The New Institutionalism in Organizational Analysis*, edited by W.W. Powell and P.J. DiMaggio. Chicago: University of Chicago Press.

Sewell, William H., Jr. 1992. "A Theory of Structure: Duality, Agency, and Transformation," *American Journal of Sociology* 98, no. 1: 1–29.

Siemiatycki, Meyer, and Engin Isin. 1997. "Immigration, Diversity and Urban Citizenship in Toronto," *Canadian Journal of Regional Sciences* 20, nos. 1–2: 73–102.

Skocpol, Theda. 1999. "Advocates without Members: The Recent Transformation of American Civic Life." In *Civic Engagement in American Democracy*, edited by T. Skocpol and M.P. Fiorina. Washington, D.C.: Brookings Institution Press.

Snow, David A., and Robert D. Benford. 1992. "Master Frames and Cycles of Protest." In *Frontiers in Social Movement Theory*, edited by A.D. Morris and C.M. Mueller. New Haven, Conn.: Yale University Press.

Snow, David A., E.B. Rochford, S.K. Worden, and Robert D. Benford. 1986. "Frame Alignment Processes, Micromobilization, and Movement Participation," *American Sociological Review* 51: 464–81.

Soysal, Yasemin Nuhoglu. 1994. *Limits of Citizenship: Migrants and Postnational Membership in Europe*. Chicago: University of Chicago Press.

Staggenborg, Suzanne. 1991. *The Pro-Choice Movement: Organization and Activism in the Abortion Conflict*. New York: Oxford University Press.

Stasiulis, Daiva K., and Yasmeen Abu-Laban. 1991. "The House the Parties Built: (Re)Constructing Ethnic Representation in Canadian Politics." In *Ethno-Cultural Groups and Visible Minorities in Canadian Politics: The Question of Access*, edited by K. Megyery. Research Studies, Royal Commission on Electoral Reform and Party Financing, vol. 7. Toronto: Dundurn.

Teixeira, Carlos, and Gilles Lavigne. 1992. *The Portuguese in Canada: A Bibliography*. Toronto: Institute for Social Research, York University.

Thelen, Kathleen, and Sven Steinmo. 1992. "Historic Institutionalism in Comparative Politics." In *Structuring Politics: Historical Institutionalism in Comparative Analysis*, edited by S. Steinmo, K. Thelen, and F. Longstreth. New York: Cambridge University Press.

Uhlaner, Carole J. 1996. "Latinos and Ethnic Politics in California: Participation and Preference." In *Latino Politics in California*, edited by Aníbal Yáñez-Chávez. La Jolla: Center for U.S.-Mexican Studies, University of California, San Diego.

Uhlaner, Carole J., Bruce E. Cain, and D. Roderick Kiewiet. 1989. "Political Participation of Ethnic Minorities in the 1980s," *Political Behavior* 11, no. 3: 195–231.

Usdansky, Margaret L., and Thomas J. Espenshade. 2001. "The Evolution of U.S. Policy toward Employment-Based Immigrants and Temporary Workers: The H-1B Debate in Historical Perspective." In *The International Migration of the Highly Skilled: Demand, Supply, and Development Consequences in Sending and Receiving Countries*, edited by Wayne A. Cornelius, Thomas J. Espenshade, and Idean Salehyan. La Jolla: Center for Comparative Immigration Studies, University of California, San Diego.

Verba, Sidney, Kay Lehman Schlozman, and Henry E. Brady. 1995. *Voice and Equality: Civic Voluntarism in American Politics*. Cambridge, Mass.: Harvard University Press.

Walker, Jack L., Jr. 1991. *Mobilizing Interest Groups in America: Patrons, Professions, and Social Movements*. Ann Arbor: University of Michigan Press.

Whitaker, Reg. 1987. *Double Standard: The Secret History of Canadian Immigration*. Toronto: Lester and Orpen Dennys.

Yang, Philip Q. 1994. "Explaining Immigrant Naturalization," *International Migration Review* 28, no. 3: 449–77.

Zald, Mayer N. 1996. "Culture, Ideology and Strategic Framing." In *Comparative Perspectives on Social Movements: Political Opportunities, Mobilizing Structures, and Cultural Framings*, edited by D. McAdam, J.D. McCarthy, and M.N. Zald. New York: Cambridge University Press.

14

Immigration and Housing Shortage in Los Angeles, 1970–2000

IVAN LIGHT

The theory of cumulative causation proclaims that migrations produce the conditions of their own continuation chiefly by the expansion and maturation of migrants' boundary-spanning social networks. As Massey (1988: 396) put it, once under way, migrations levitate above the terrain whence they originally emerged, and then self-propagate. In addition to this basic formulation, the theory of cumulative causation can be expanded to include migration-expanding changes in the economy of destinations, such as the formation of immigrant economies and ethnic economies (Light, Bhachu, and Karageorgis 1993). These economies offer employment to immigrants above and beyond what the mainstream labor market offers them, thus partially compensating any saturation of immigrants' employment opportunities that arises in the mainstream labor market (Light and Bernard 1999). For both these reasons, once well under way, migrations build momentum that is increasingly difficult to stop and that supersedes whatever initiating conditions may have first liberated the migratory process.

On the other hand, migrations usually end well short of the theoretically limiting moment when—everyone in the country of origin having already emigrated—depopulation of the destination brings the migration to an end. Evidently, then, cumulatively caused, self-propelling migration encounters or provokes resistance in settlement areas. If no resistance materialized, migrations once begun would always end with depopulation of sending regions. However engendered, this resistance to migration first brakes, then slows, and finally stops the migration juggernaut short of depopulation. From a scientific viewpoint, the elucidation and explication of resistance to immigration is just as important as is the explanation and elucidation of cumulative causation itself, the other side of this coin.

Real economic resistance arises when migrants cannot find jobs or housing because markets are saturated. Of course, full market saturation is just the theoretically limiting economic condition; it *never* materializes in reality. Nonetheless, the concept is useful because, as conditions move toward saturation and housing and jobs become scarcer, immigrants experience greater difficulties finding jobs and housing. Search times increase, and satisfaction with the results of searches diminishes. These enhanced difficulties brake the self-propelled migration process or deflect it to other destinations. However, thanks importantly to research by Waldinger (1996), Ellis and Wright (1999), and others, we have become skeptical of the real potential of economic saturation to slow, much less to halt, cumulatively caused migration.[1] First, migrants deploy efficient social networks that enable them to outcompete native workers in the search for increasingly scarce housing and employment. Second, unacculturated migrants from poor countries require a material standard of living much lower than do native-born Americans. Therefore, scarce housing and scarce jobs affect them less than nonmigrants. At least until they acculturate, immigrants enjoy a competitive economic advantage for these reasons.

Political resistance arises when states curtail immigration at the borders, and possibly even repatriate immigrants already arrived. In this sense, the United States' Immigration Act of 1924, which terminated the mass migration from Europe, was the culminating political statement of an anti-immigrant social movement that had begun with the anti-Chinese movement of the 1870s. Political resistance to immigration can solidify behind any popular complaint, specious or real, but this chapter attends to a *municipality's* political resistance to immigrants' housing needs. When municipal opposition curtails local responsiveness to immigrants' housing needs, many immigrants cannot find housing. Lack of housing then deflects cumulatively caused immigration to other destinations. When immigrants cannot find housing because none exists, they confront an economic constraint. When im-

---

[1] For additional discussion of this point, see Light, Kim, and Hum 2000.

migrants cannot find housing because local housing codes prevent them from obtaining access, then they confront a political constraint. Even in a laissez-faire housing market like the United States, housing competition can become openly political (Cuomo 1974).[2]

HOUSING RESEARCH

Immigration research has amply attended to housing issues, but usually in the context of segregation studies or of suburbanization studies rather than of process studies. Segregation studies ask how restricted immigrants are to residential communities of co-ethnics (Ellen 2000; Clark 1996; Massey and Denton 1993; Massey 1985). Findings of high residential clustering among immigrants, identified as residential segregation, are deemed "social exclusion." And social exclusion is generally deemed contrary to enlightened social policy (Buck and Harloe 1998). Meliorist in orientation, segregation studies thus focus upon undesirable housing conditions in cities, helping to arouse public awareness and even to induce relief efforts.

Sharing an interest in social exclusion as an unwanted state of affairs, suburbanization studies have addressed the causes and the extent to which immigrants now settle in suburbs rather than in central cities (Galster 1999; Fong and Gulia 2000). Frey (1994) found that an egress of whites from immigrant-reception regions opens residential opportunities for immigrants and ethnic minorities in regional suburbs. The trend toward minority suburbanization that Frey first identified is real. In 1990, 43 percent of recent immigrants resided in suburbs rather than in central cities. Reviewing the evidence, Alba et al. (1999: 458) conclude that, "Recent immigrants seem much more inclined to settle outside of urban enclaves than were immigrants of previous eras." Initially researchers thought that suburbanization of immigrants only affected affluent and educated East Asian and Middle Eastern immigrants, not working-class immigrants. However, Fong and Shibuya (2000) showed that the suburbanization of minorities often includes working-class renters, not just middle-class homeowners. In their opinion, the key issue is home ownership rather than suburbanization. Central-city homeowners have much higher incomes than do suburban renters.[3]

---

[2] Laissez-faire or not, zoning laws are conventional in U.S. cities. Of major U.S. cities, only Houston lacks zoning laws (see Feagin 1988: 156).

[3] "Central city home owners in general have higher socioeconomic status and acculturation levels than suburban renters. For example, the median household income

Process studies address the processes by which migrations begin, crest, disperse, and end. Viewed from the perspective of cumulative causation—the key immigration process—housing market research must ask whether, to what extent, and how local housing conditions affect the flow or destination of immigrants. For example, in European welfare states, when immigrants occupy public housing in short supply, they trigger resentments among nonimmigrants, who claim to believe, often without substance, that their own housing chances were thereby diminished. Given the welfare state's investment in housing in European societies—a policy that does not characterize the United States—native/immigrant political conflict can affect the volume or destination of international migration to Europe. Conditions are different in the United States, where open political conflict over housing does not now pit immigrants against natives.[4] That is, immigrants are not openly battling nonimmigrants for housing, *nor* are nonimmigrants organizing politically to redress housing deprivations immigrants have imposed upon them, *nor* is open political conflict over housing redirecting or reducing immigration to the United States. As a result, with the exception of William Frey, researchers have ignored immigrant/native housing competition as a source of internal migration. Even studies of immigrants' dispersion from port-of-entry cities like Los Angeles ignored the possibility that housing shortages in port-of-entry cities deflect immigrants' internal migration to new regions and new cities outside Southern California (Johnson, Johnson-Webb, and Farrell 1999) and from suburban to peripheral areas within Southern California (S. Gold 2001).

Starting from a processual vantage point, this chapter reaches a different conclusion. Beneath the surface, it is argued, immigrant/nonimmigrant political conflict over housing supply is already serious in Los Angeles, and by extension in other immigrant-reception cities of the United States, where housing shortages have been intensifying for two decades (Mutchler and Krivo 1989).[5] Intergroup conflict is not an open and conscious political conflict between natives and immigrants,

of Mexican homeowners living in the central city is $41,700 as compared with $27,900 for Mexican suburban renters" (Fong and Shibuya 2000: 145).

4 No conflict, but Frey (1995: 354) does find evidence of native/immigrant *competition* for housing in California.

5 "We can see the same effect in the retreat of many real estate developers from the low and medium income housing market who are attraced to the rapidly expanding housing demand by the new highly paid professionals and the possibility for vast overpricing of this housing supply" (Sassen 2000: 6).

but it could become one. In the United States, the characteristically decentralized political structure of metropolitan areas conceals immigrant/native housing conflict that is manifest in European welfare states. As a result, even the parties to conflicts over housing do not realize they are in a conflict.

HOUSING LOS ANGELES

Since approximately 1970, the Los Angeles metropolitan area has been the United States' largest center of immigrant reception (Sabagh and Bozorgmehr 1996). It is also well known, and abundantly documented, that Los Angeles has not always been a center of immigrant absorption, as have New York City, Boston, Chicago, Detroit, and Philadelphia. On the contrary, Los Angeles was a center of anti-Chinese sentiment during the agitation that led finally to the Chinese Exclusion Act of 1882. With Asians legally excluded, only small Chinese and Japanese communities continued to exist in Los Angeles after 1900. Seeking population, Los Angeles's growth machine solicited the internal migration of native-born Midwestern and Southwestern whites, whose descendants still formed the majority of Los Angeles's white population in 1970 (Dawes et al. 2000: 73).[6] Los Angeles attracted few European immigrants (Laslett 1996). As a result, with Asians excluded from the United States, the County of Los Angeles historically had a lower share of immigrants in its population than did the United States as a whole.

The founders of Los Angeles had a distinctive vision of the region's urbanism, which they successfully projected to the internal migrants they recruited from Iowa, Oklahoma, and Texas (Hise 1997; Pincetl 1999). This vision stressed a unique urban morphology thought to harmonize with the region's mild climate and to exploit the technological possibilities of twentieth-century transportation (Soja and Scott 1996). Unlike the crowded, tenement-ridden cities of the Northeast, which were the negative pole against which the city's boosters were reacting, Los Angeles offered low-density, decentralized urbanism in which residents occupied single-family bungalows on large tracts. In the initial phase, 1880–1920, the suburbanization of Los Angeles depended upon the world's most extensive streetcar system, the Pacific Electric Railroad (Light 1984: 210). After 1920, as automotive transportation became an alternative, Los Angeles's growth machine switched

---

[6] On the concept of growth machine, see Molotch 1976, 1988.

its transportation allegiance, encouraging and promoting highway construction and private passenger automobiles rather than streetcars (Bottles 1988: 22–52).[7] In the 1950s and 1960s, suburbanization and highway construction proceeded at a frantic pace, and public transportation disintegrated. The last Pacific Electric car ran in 1964. The upshot was a metropolitan region whose urban core was suburban in character when compared to Northeastern cities, and whose suburbs were numerous and bucolic. Detractors ridiculed Los Angeles as suburbs in search of a city. However, the Los Angeles region's experiment in decentralized and low-density urbanization became the model around which American civilization organized the entire twentieth century.[8]

By 1970, when the current mass immigration of Latinos began, the urban morphology of Los Angeles was already firmly in place. The City of Los Angeles stands at the center of the County of Los Angeles (Light 1988). The metropolitan suburbs are the County of Los Angeles outside the city. Table 14.1 shows the population of the City of Los Angeles and its metropolitan region in 1980, 1990, and 2000. In city and suburbs, the population of non-Hispanic whites declined between 1980 and 2000, largely as a result of emigration (Sabagh and Bozorgmehr 1996). The population of non-Hispanic blacks remained stable but shifted slightly to the suburbs. As a result of immigration, the population of Asians in the region increased threefold, more than that of any other group, and shifted strongly toward the suburbs. The suburban shift of the Asian population reflects the high socioeconomic origins of Asian immigrants. Thanks to immigration, the population of Hispanics doubled in both city and suburbs. In both the City of Los Angeles and its suburbs, Hispanics had become the largest single group in 2000. Between 1980 and 2000, more Hispanics lived in the suburbs of Los Angeles than lived in the City of Los Angeles.

The City of Los Angeles represents the urban core of Los Angeles County. About 30 percent of the county's population of 9,519,338 still lives in the city. Surrounding the city are eighty-eight incorporated municipalities of various sizes.[9] These satellite cities are the nearest suburbs of Los Angeles and also the most urbanized suburbs. Of the 4,243,000 Hispanics who resided in Los Angeles County in 2000, only

[7] For a discussion of the Los Angeles growth machine, see Light 2002.

[8] For a critical history of suburbanization in the United States, see Gottdiener 1985: 241–50.

[9] The largest satellite is Long Beach, whose population is 461,552; the smallest is Vernon, population 91.

46 percent resided in the City of Los Angeles. By contrast, 1,232,000 Asians lived in the County of Los Angeles in 2000, but 61 percent of these were suburban.

Table 14.1. Population of the City of Los Angeles and Metropolitan Suburbs by Ethno-Racial Category, 1980–2000 (1000s)

	1980	1990	2000	Index[a]
City of Los Angeles				
Non-Hispanic white	1,767	1,645	1,367	70.1
Non-Hispanic black	561	542	534	91.9
Hispanic	892	1,544	1,958	205.0
Asian	223	415	486	206.8
Total	3,491	4,145	4,409	116.9
Suburbs				
Non-Hispanic white	2,183	1,973	1,593	79.7
Non-Hispanic black	364	391	417	120.8
Hispanic	1,173	1,801	2,285	206.0
Asian	212	540	746	374.8
Total	3,980	4,710	5,110	138.2
Metropolitan area	7,471	8,854	9,519	127.4

Source: U.S. Census, available at http://mumford1.dyndns.org/cen2000.

[a] Index = 2000/1980 x 100.

Note: The table excludes minor ethnic categories, so numbers do not sum to the total shown.

The City of Los Angeles and each of its eighty-eight satellite cities have housing codes that define what kinds of housing are legally permissible within the respective city. The framers of these codes intended to protect the low-density, automobile-dependent lifestyle that had attracted native-born white citizens to Los Angeles. City councils framed these housing restrictions with the knowledge and approval of those voters. Municipal housing codes discouraged multifamily, high-rise housing and public transportation in favor of the preferred housing form, a one- or two-story single-family home and garage on a large owner-occupied lot.[10] Restrictions on residential density were a favorite legal device for guaranteeing that housing would conform to the pre-

[10] The average single-family home in Los Angeles County occupied 0.2 acre in 2001.

ferred suburban style. Cities set maximum residential densities too low to accommodate multifamily, high-rise housing. By requiring new houses to have wide setbacks from the street, large lots, and attached garage space, city councils built automobile dependency into their municipal housing codes.

Given that this legal structure was firmly in place when the new immigration began in 1970, its designers had no conscious anti-immigrant, much less anti-Latino, motives. City councils merely intended to safeguard the suburban way of life and to protect the property investment this lifestyle required. However, after thirty years of low-income Mexican and Central American migration to Los Angeles, it has become apparent that Los Angeles County's decentralized legal structure protects a suburban standard of living incompatible with the housing needs of Latinos, who now represent the largest population group in the county. Low-wage Latino immigrants need low-cost rental housing, not home ownership on big lots (Krivo 1995; Allen and Turner 1997: 93; Keil 1998: 121; Wedner 2001a, 2001b, 2001c). Figure 14.1 shows that Hispanics in Los Angeles County reside in cities that offer abundant rental housing, whereas Asians, a much more affluent category, live in cities that stress home ownership.

Because single-family homes are too expensive for low-income people, Hispanics must locate in cities that offer the most rental housing. Residential clustering of low-wage immigrants increases rates of overcrowding and overpayment.[11] Moreover, low-wage immigrants require low-cost public transportation. Immigrant households cannot afford private passenger automobiles. However, existing housing and building regulations inhibit the ability of Los Angeles County's many cities to permit high-rise, multifamily housing construction in their jurisdictions. The existing housing code, a legacy of the previous white population, now inhibits construction of the extensive multifamily housing that immigrants need.

RELIEVING LOS ANGELES COUNTY'S HOUSING SHORTAGE

Los Angeles County has experienced a shortage of affordable housing for a generation, but the shortage has appreciably worsened since the end of the last recession (M. Gold 2001). In 1999, 40 percent of the re-

---

[11] Overpayment is defined by the Southern California Association of Governments (SCAG) as paying more than one-third of household income in rent.

gion's households spent 30 percent or more of their income on housing (Strickland 1999). True, San Francisco also suffers a shortage of affordable housing, but the causes of the housing shortage are different in the two cities. In San Francisco, new-economy wealth caused gentrification of inner-city neighborhoods, to the disadvantage of the city's middle and working classes, who were forced out of their homes by rising rents. However, in Los Angeles County, despite a net loss of approximately one-fourth of the non-Hispanic white population, the thirty-year influx of low-income Latino immigrants has driven rents beyond the level that poor people can pay (García and Clarke 2001: 3). Rents are higher for everyone, not just immigrants, and elderly whites are also forced out of their homes as a result (Stewart 2001a).

Explaining the affordability crisis, Fulton (1997) and Purcell (2000) stress the slow-growth political ideology that has taken control of city councils everywhere in the Los Angeles metropolitan region.[12] Fulton even proclaimed (prematurely) the "death of the growth machine" in Los Angeles (Light 2002).[13] There is, nonetheless, little doubt that slow-growth political movements in the Los Angeles metropolitan region have captured most city halls in Los Angeles, Ventura, and Orange counties.[14] Los Angeles voters (60 percent of whom are white) often oppose growth in the name of environmental protection. These voters' slow-growth ideology has reduced the incentives for city councils to open their low-density cities to high-density housing for the benefit of Latino immigrants. Although open and frank anti-immigrant ideology still plays only a negligible role in slow-growth ideology in Los Angeles County, slow growth's political success objectively reduces the housing access of Latino immigrants.[15]

---

12 "The problems created by runaway development are eroding the California dream and threatening the state's economic vitality" (*Los Angeles Times* editorial, August 4, 1988). On slow-growth movements in Los Angeles suburbs, see Horton 1995: 88–92.

13 "For our city and our region to grow and prosper," said the mayor of Los Angeles, the city requires affordable housing. The mayor's statement suggests that he still adheres to the ideology of growth (M. Gold 2001).

14 Nevertheless, the growth machine is still in power in outlying Riverside and San Bernardino counties (S. Gold 2001).

15 In 1998, Sierra Club members voted against adding an anti-immigration plank to its slow-growth program, but the vote was close.

Figure 14.1. Housing Characteristics of Hispanics and Asians in Los Angeles County, Part 1

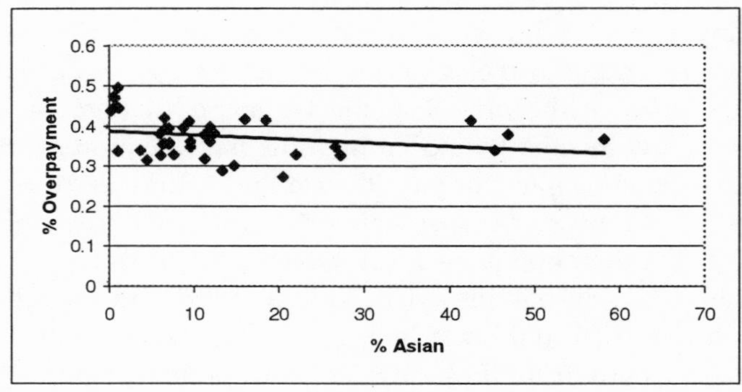

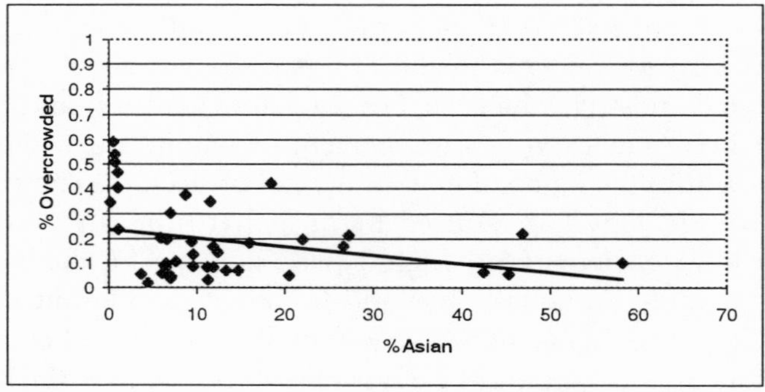

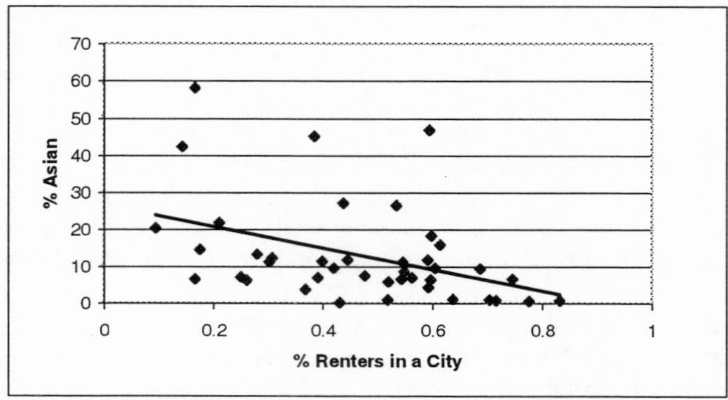

Source: www.scag.ca.gov.

Figure 14.1. Housing Characteristics of Hispanics and Asians in Los Angeles County, Part 2

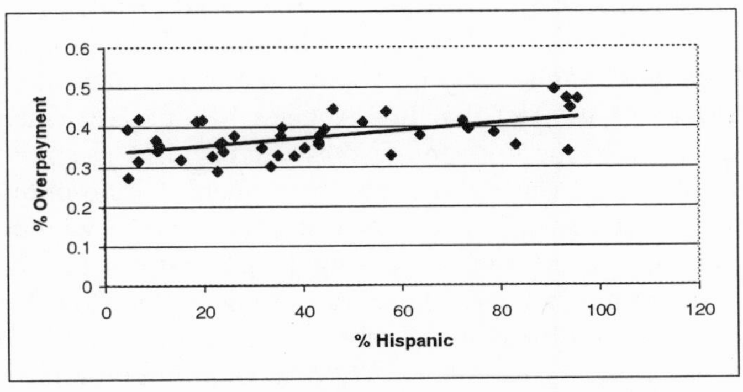

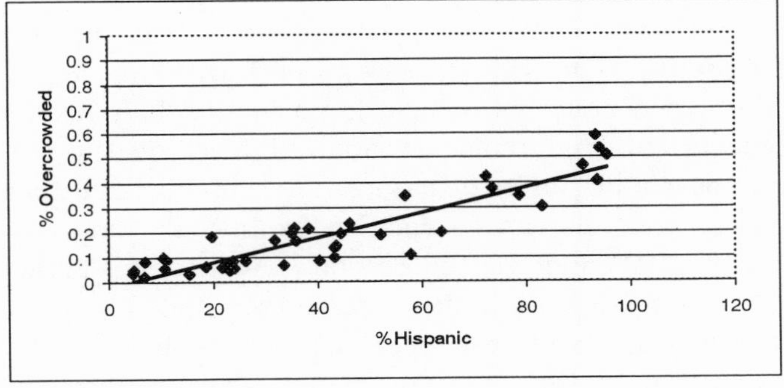

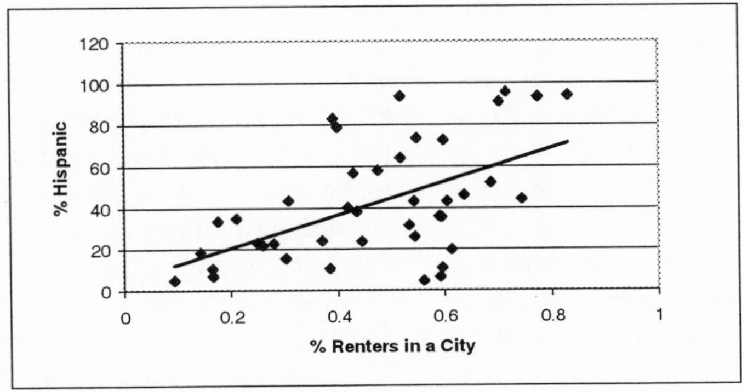

Source: www.scag.ca.gov.

Dear (2001) blames Los Angeles's shortage of affordable housing on the depletion of available land, as decades of sprawl collide with natural limits—ocean, mountains, water supply, and deserts—to habitation. Noting that "sprawl hit the wall," Dear concludes that natural limits have foreclosed the possibility of "sprawl as usual," with natural obstacles causing the current shortage of affordable housing in a direct sense. On the other hand, every metropolitan area has natural limits to its expansion, and the fact that Los Angeles has already reached its limits owes much to the unrelenting pressure of thirty years of immigration. If, in a counterfactual thought experiment, Latino immigrants were abruptly withdrawn from Los Angeles, Los Angeles would not be facing a shortage of affordable housing or the natural barriers that complicate the resolution of the housing shortage. In effect, the natural barriers that constrain the housing access of current Latino immigrants were reached precisely because of thirty years of immigration.

Given the restricted housing supply caused by the combination of natural obstacles and slow-growth city councils, housing prices and rents have risen on par with increased demand.[16] Housing becomes unaffordable when households have to pay more than 50 percent of their income in rent. High rents particularly impact low-income Latino immigrant households for two reasons. First, low-income housing is generally less profitable to construct, so Latinos can only move into vacated housing (Wedner 2001c). Second, low-income Latino households have to compete with higher-income households in the housing market. Latino households can only acquire housing if they pay a higher proportion of their income in rent than do higher-income households. Thus, by raising the price of rental housing, the housing market is sending a signal to low-income immigrants: "go elsewhere." Immigrant/nonimmigrant economic competition for housing need not become openly political before the market's control measures begin. The housing market's price signal may reduce the flow of poor Latino immigrants into Los Angeles, causing the self-propelled migration from Mexico and Central America to seek new settlement areas where housing is affordable (Hernández-León and Zúñiga 2002). If none can be found, cumulatively caused migration implodes. In other words, Los Angeles County's high housing prices are a *spontaneous mechanism for immigration restriction* which, arising in response to cumulatively caused migration, tends to deflect, brake, or even halt migration.

---

[16] The median price of a single-family home in Los Angeles County was $231,000 in 2001, compared to a national average of $142,000.

REGIONAL HOUSING NEEDS ASSESSMENT

The Los Angeles housing market is just a messenger of the housing shortage, of course, not its cause. Exacerbating the shortage are municipal housing codes that constrain and restrict the ability of the county's eighty-eight cities to convert existing single-family, low-density housing into multiple-family, high-density housing. Absent these legal constraints, the housing market could gradually convert Los Angeles County from a suburban, automobile-dependent, low-density region to the medium-density region of apartment houses and public transit that it must become if it is to serve its new Latino majority.[17] To be sure, metropolitan governments are under conflicting pressures in this regard. On the one hand, operating through the Department of Housing and Urban Development, the federal government employs legal pressure and financial incentives to compel local governments to tolerate low-cost housing in their jurisdictions. Moreover, the State of California also seeks to compel local governments to comply with open housing laws that are intended to make more low-cost housing available. This pressure from state and federal government is intense, but it comes from outside the cities for which the low-income housing is proposed. And when federal and state housing goals are applied to a specific locality, local voters reject them.

Evidence for these conclusions comes from the Regional Housing Needs Assessment, compiled by the Southern California Association of Governments (SCAG). SCAG is an umbrella association of independent local governments that makes available to member governments its research on housing conditions in the region and its suggestions on how to comply with federal and state housing laws.[18] SCAG's Web site provides access to local governments' strategies for dealing with the housing shortage. According to SCAG's Regional Needs Housing Assessment, Los Angeles's already severe housing shortage will grow worse unless remedied because, "The SCAG region will grow by more than 6 million people between 1997 and 2020." Latino immigrants will

---

[17] Indeed, this transition is slowly under way despite resistance (see Stewart 2001b). The rate of home ownership in Los Angeles declined from 40.9 percent in 1970 to 38.6 percent in 2000.

[18] "The existing need assessment simply examines key variables from the most recent Census to measure ways in which the housing is not meeting the needs of current residents. These variables include the number of low-income households paying more than 30 percent of their income for housing, as well as severe overcrowding." See SCAG's Web site: http://www.scag.ca.gov.

account for most of this growth. Advising member governments on how to react to the existing housing shortage, SCAG notes that, "[local] political support for housing is critical to the adoption and implementation of local housing programs. The voices in favor of housing, especially affordable housing, are frequently quiet and few, and finding support for local efforts to address housing needs can be difficult." In other words, SCAG anticipates local voter resistance and hostility to the measures SCAG proposes for local governments.

Under the circumstances, SCAG recommends a multiplicity of procedural reforms that will permit construction of multifamily housing in cities whose housing codes do not currently authorize such housing. All of these procedural reforms are legal changes. One is *rezoning*.[19] "Recognizing that administrative delay adds to developmental costs, jurisdictions have reviewed and streamlined their land use and development procedures. The intent is to simplify and coordinate the means of obtaining rezonings, use permits, subdivisions, approval of design and engineering plans, and building permits." Another SCAG suggestion is that local governments waive fees for publicly desired projects that will augment the housing supply within their borders. Here SCAG recognizes that existing zoning laws stand in the way of increasing the housing supply within member cities.

SCAG also recommends that local governments *lower existing development standards* to permit more housing construction. Noting that "Site planning and building design innovations can cut the costs of housing construction," SCAG recommends that communities modify "their requirements on setbacks, street widths, and building materials, or use performance-based standards in place of restrictive building and planning standards." By lowering development standards, local communities can reduce building costs, thus permitting "more affordable housing to be built." SCAG also recommends changes in site design to allow for higher densities or fewer parking design requirements, because these changes "can significantly reduce construction costs," thus permitting lower housing costs. Of course, after implementing all of these legal changes, the resulting urban environment would consist of multifamily housing that abuts sidewalks, fronts onto narrower and more congested streets, and utilizes cheaper housing materials in construction, reducing the quality of the housing environment in member cities.

Legal zoning densities pose a problem to construction of low-income housing everywhere in Los Angeles County. SCAG advises

[19] On zoning enforcement in suburbs, see Baumgartner 1988: 18, 80–89.

member cities, which are required to build more low-income housing, to raise "general plan and zoning densities to allow for higher residential development. This is the most basic technique for increasing the supply of housing." Lest there be any misunderstanding, SCAG adds that the goal of higher density zoning is "to increase the amount of housing that can be built on any given site." The benefit of this legal change would be to increase "the overall potential supply of housing" in member cities.[20]

This benefit would accrue to those who do not already have affordable housing, rather than to those who already live in the area's suburban one-family homes. Homeowners are mostly native-born whites. To sweeten the pie for area governments who need to construct affordable housing that would primarily benefit the area's immigrant Latinos, SCAG notes that local cities that rezone can obtain a "density bonus" above what is normally permitted on a site when they provide "some below market rate housing units." The bonus is usually a percentage of the density allowable under existing zoning regulations. "California law [Government Code Section 65915] requires local governments to grant a 25 percent density bonus ... to a developer in exchange for an agreement that the extra units be affordable." Moreover, cities can grant bonuses "in excess of those called for by state law to encourage affordable housing or other residential development to meet a community's special housing needs." The density bonuses are intended to provide member cities with incentives for complying with state directives that they are perceived to have a motive to resist.

SCAG also counsels its member cities that *vacant land* can be made available for affordable housing. Much vacant land has been "set aside for commercial, office, and industrial use" rather than for residential use. If existing set-asides could be voided, reserved land would become available for low-cost housing. Unfortunately, SCAG observes, "neighbors [predominantly native-born whites] sometimes resist nearby and infill development."[21] Clearly, suburban white homeowners do not perceive the infilling of vacant land with low-density housing for immigrant Latinos to be in their self-interest.

---

20 "Higher densities can improve the affordability of housing because per unit land costs are lower and construction can be performed more efficiently" (SCAG).

21 "Politically, changing the general plan and rezoning surplus industrial and/or commercial land can be an effective way to make a significant amount of land available for housing" (SCAG).

Mixed use development is another strategy that SCAG recommends to its member cities as a means to obtain space for affordable housing in their jurisdiction. Mixed use development of land or structures combines residential uses with one or more nonresidential uses, such as office, retail, public, entertainment, or even manufacturing use. Mixed uses are currently illegal in most cities, so legal changes would be necessary to implement this strategy. Unfortunately, according to SCAG, it is difficult to win political support for mixed use development in member cities. "Mixing uses often requires changes to the zoning ordinance or planned unit development regulations. To encourage housing, a community can allow residential uses in commercial areas and other non-residential zones."

Infill development occurs on sites that have been bypassed by previous development. SCAG suggests that member governments consider making infill land available for low-income housing developments. Unfortunately, SCAG acknowledges, "Proposed infill development can cause controversy in the neighborhood due to the threatened loss of local open space, change in community appearance, and increased traffic that may result." Under the circumstances, SCAG concludes, local governments cannot expect successful outcomes of infill schemes unless they "anticipate, plan for, and resolve conflicts between builders and local interest groups."

Self-help housing means structures that low-income people construct for themselves. Major cities in Mexico are ringed by shantytowns whose inhabitants have used available materials to construct their own shelters. Although shantytowns are illegal in Los Angeles County, SCAG does recommend that member cities permit potential homeowners to contribute their own labor to the construction or renovation of their homes, thus lowering their housing costs. This plan requires legal changes in most communities, where electricians, plumbers, carpenters, and the like must be certified and paid area-standard wages. SCAG asks its member governments to relax "city design standards" in the interest of promoting self-help housing, anticipating that member cities will tolerate the reduced quality of housing that results.

Many suburban cities in Los Angeles County exclude *factory-built homes* by law. The reasons are familiar. In the public vernacular, "trailer trash" lowers residential quality. Yet SCAG notes that factory-built housing is "the least expensive to construct." This is its sovereign virtue. A more favorable attitude to factory-built housing would reduce the average housing cost in member cities, and SCAG advises its member governments to combat "citizen resistance due to negative, often inaccurate perceptions" of manufactured housing's appearance. Manufactured housing can be rendered more attractive if local governments revise their "design review process to encourage compatible design" with existing site-built homes.

Shared living provides another way to lower housing costs. "Shared living has various names: communal living, home sharing, and group living. It occurs when people reside together for social contact, mutual support, and assistance, and/or to reduce housing expenses." For instance, four immigrant families can occupy a four-bedroom house, one family to a bedroom, and share the rent. Alternatively, one immigrant family can rent rooms to lodgers, providing food and laundry service as well as shelter. Boardinghouses were essential support institutions for the European migrants who came to the United States a century ago (Bodnar 1985: 82–83). However, shared living arrangements violate the housing code in many Los Angeles suburbs. Even where shared living is legal, neighbors disapprove. Accordingly, SCAG advises local governments to promote shared living to relieve the housing shortage while addressing "the misconceptions or lack of knowledge" that cause neighborhoods to reject shared living.

"A *second unit* is an additional self-contained living unit, either attached to or detached from the primary residential unit on a single lot." Second units have cooking, eating, sleeping, and sanitation facilities. California law permits second units, but it establishes minimum standards for their development. For example, a second unit must have a flushing toilet and electric wiring that meets code requirements. Unable to ban second units, many Los Angeles County cities regulate the number of second units allowed. Additionally, municipalities regulate their location, size, parking requirements, and architectural compatibility, rendering second units expensive to construct—and expensive to rent. SCAG concedes that second units are not popular: "Opposition ... generally comes from neighborhood concern over parking and traffic impacts." To promote second unit construction, SCAG encourages member governments to "legalize existing second units and bring them up to construction codes." As matters stand, thousands of immigrant Latinos live illegally in unconverted garages because local governments cannot—or do not wish to—enforce second unit regulations.[22]

---

[22] Unemployed homeowners sometimes move into their own garages as well, using the rent collected on the main house to maintain them.

In the 1920s the Chicago School referred to *single-room-occupancy hotels* (SROs) as "flophouses." SCAG acknowledges that single-room-occupancy hotels "are one of the most traditional forms of affordable private housing for single and elderly low-income people and for new arrivals to an area." Rooms in SRO hotels are tiny; they contain a sink and closet, and have access to a shared bathroom and shared kitchen. Cities in Los Angeles County have enacted laws to exclude SRO hotels on the grounds that they attract vagrants and diminish residential quality, yet there is strong market demand for this housing type. According to SCAG, member cities should amend zoning and building codes that exclude SRO hotels.

The homeless represent a housing constituency that local cities find difficult to serve. According to SCAG, "Long-standing zoning practices, restrictive building codes, and demanding requirements for provision of parking spaces have all stymied construction of new housing for the homeless." If these legal obstacles can be reduced or eliminated, member cities can provide more housing for the homeless in their own jurisdictions. Unfortunately, SCAG confesses, "neighborhood activists rarely, if ever, welcome the homeless into their immediate communities."

Finally, SCAG identifies NIMBYism as a "major obstacle hindering the provision of affordable housing" in Los Angeles County.[23] NIMBYism is flourishing in all of Los Angeles County's cities, with locally resident NIMBYs actively working to prohibit or retard the construction of low-cost housing in their neighborhood.[24] Wherever city councils propose to waive, modify, or discard legal impediments to low-cost housing, NIMBYs arise to challenge them, using the ballot box to sanction city council members who fail to stand with them against state and federal housing policy. Absent the NIMBYs, it would be fairly easy to overturn local ordinances that obstruct affordable housing. NIMBYism is a key political weapon in preserving the housing status quo in Los Angeles.

To assist the legal departments of its member cities, SCAG has listed fifteen recent decisions in which courts ruled on affordable housing or group housing issues, the latter chiefly involving disabled persons. Of the fifteen, ten favored the expansion of affordable housing or group

---

[23] NIMBYism is an acronym for "Not In My Backyard." NIMBYism is the doctrine that urban growth should occur somewhere else, just not here.

[24] Although the terminology is recent, NIMBYism has a long history in U.S. cities (see Light 1977).

home facilities in cities around the United States. The case law will empower member cities' legal departments when they engage in comparable litigation. In a representative Los Angeles case,[25] the court ruled that city council members enjoy absolute personal immunity from prosecution when they vote against opening access to local housing to the disabled. SCAG also provided representative analyses for housing discrimination cases involving small, medium, and large cities, explaining what actions jurisdictions can undertake to "eliminate impediments." Suggested measures include introducing local legislation declaring it illegal to refuse to rent based on a household's source of income, enacting local ordinances requiring that large developers "set aside" a proportion of affordable units in order to obtain approval from the municipality, and holding "neighborhood forums" to convince "local White residents" they have nothing to fear from racial changes.

DISCUSSION

The SCAG archives depict a regional housing conflict that pits the interests of homeowners against those of immigrant Latinos and their allies—the disabled, blacks, and the elderly. Local governments, meanwhile, are under pressure from the federal government and the state to expand affordable housing at the same time that they are facing pressure from local activists to retain municipal building and housing codes that *prohibit* what the state and federal governments wish to accomplish. Herein lies a social conflict between low-income immigrants and natives. True, this conflict does not involve open hostilities between immigrants and natives, and it joins certain native-born persons (disabled, elderly, and blacks) with low-income immigrants. The public discourse about Southern California's housing shortage contains no significant anti-immigrant or anti-Latino themes. In fact, a Latino candidate nearly won the mayoralty in 2000.

Nonetheless, native-born homeowners have housing and community interests that differ from those of low-income immigrants. Within Los Angeles County, each metropolitan city's reform plans represent a separate jurisdiction in which a local NIMBY movement has opposed housing reform. Indeed, by the time that Latino renters actually establish themselves in a city, their allies in City Hall have already succeeded in gaining authorization for low-income housing. In effect, the

[25] San Pedro Hotel Co., Inc. vs. City of Los Angeles.

immigrants arrive after the battle has been won, and hence the parties to the political conflict never become aware that they are in conflict with one another.

The well-being of Latino immigrants already in Los Angeles County requires that existing housing codes be reformed to permit low-cost multifamily housing. However, suburban homeowners have no interest in tolerating the requisite changes in housing in their locality. In all candor, what economic or social advantage do homeowners gain by authorizing self-built housing, low-cost apartments, SRO hotels, or boardinghouses in their locality? Existing homeowners have a financial and personal stake in maintaining the residential quality in their city. They do not act with the goal of deflecting immigration, but this is the outcome of their self-interested NIMBYism.

To the extent that activist homeowners block or retard housing reform, they derail the cumulatively caused migration that has brought millions of Latinos to Southern California—and that would bring many more in the future if affordable housing were available. With the exception of San Francisco, all U.S. cities in the West and Southwest offer housing that is more affordable than housing in Los Angeles, providing a powerful incentive for immigrants to leave Los Angeles County if they can. Indeed, the internal migration of immigrant Latinos to secondary settlements may reflect the pressure of housing costs (Johnson, Johnson-Webb, and Farrell 1999).

As high housing costs deflect Latino migrants to other regions, the same housing battle gradually heats up in those locales. Extrapolating over decades, we can envision a country in which all reception cities have housing codes that prohibit affordable housing, thus shutting down the cumulatively caused migration from Mexico and Central America. This is a quasi-Darwinian process in which affected cities and regions attract immigrants, but then increasing housing competition encourages immigrants to seek alternative destinations until the point is reached when no more alternative destinations exist, the cumulatively caused migration network implodes, and the migration process stops.

By implication, the same quasi-Darwinian process helps to explain how *social exclusion* results from immigrant influx into metropolitan regions. Cities that compete for rich people also compete to exclude poor people (Molotch 1972: 216–17). Within any metropolitan region, poor immigrants cluster in cities that authorize low-cost housing. In immigrant-friendly cities like El Monte and Montebello in suburban Los Angeles County, housing and building codes authorize the low-cost, multifamily housing that poor immigrants require. However, within the same metropolitan region, cities like San Marino and Palos Verdes Estates—whose housing and building codes prohibit low-cost, multifamily housing—effectively exclude poor immigrants from their jurisdiction.[26] Social exclusion then characterizes residential housing in the whole metropolitan region because immigrants crowd into the cities that make low-cost housing available to them. Poor immigrants cannot reside in places where laws prohibit low-cost housing. Social exclusion of low-income immigrants is the natural and spontaneous result of multiple housing markets attached to suburban cities, even though the constellation of local political forces is different in each of them.

References

Alba, Richard D., John R. Logan, Brian J. Stults, Gilbert Marzan, and Wenquan Zhang. 1999. "Immigrant Groups in the Suburbs: A Reexamination of Suburbanization and Spatial Assimilation," *American Sociological Review* 64: 446–60.

Allen, James P., and Eugene Turner. 1997. *The Ethnic Quilt: Population Diversity in Southern California*. Northridge: California State University.

Baumgartner, M.P. 1988. *The Moral Order of a Suburb*. New York: Oxford University Press.

Bodnar, John. 1985. *The Transplanted*. Bloomington: Indiana University Press.

Bottles, Scott. 1988. *Los Angeles and the Automobile*. Berkeley: University of California Press.

Buck, Nick, and Michael Harloe. 1998. "Social Exclusion in London." Paper presented at the World Congress of Sociology, Montreal, July 26.

Clark, William A.V. 1996. "Residential Patterns: Avoidance, Assimilation, and Succession." In *Ethnic Los Angeles*, edited by Roger Waldinger and Mehdi Bozorgmehr. New York: Russell Sage Foundation.

Cuomo, Mario. 1974. *Forest Hills Diary: The Crisis of Low-Income Housing*. New York: Random House.

Dawes, Amy, Michael Diehl, Carla Lazzareschi, and Stacey R. Strickler. 2000. *Imagining Los Angeles*. Los Angeles: Los Angeles Times.

Dear, Michael. 2001. *Sprawl Hits the Wall: Confronting the Realities of Metropolitan Los Angeles*. Los Angeles: Southern California Studies Center, University of Southern California.

Ellen, Ingrid Gould. 2000. "A New White Flight? The Dynamics of Neighborhood Change in the 1980s." In *Immigration Research for a New Century*, ed-

[26] San Marino and Palos Verdes Estates house many rich immigrants, who often own lavish homes; but they house few poor immigrant renters.

ited by Nancy Foner, Rubén G. Rumbaut, and Steven J. Gold. New York: Russell Sage Foundation.

Ellis, Mark, and Richard Wright. 1999. "The Industrial Division of Labor among Immigrants and Internal Migrants to the Los Angeles Economy," *International Migration Review* 33: 26–54.

Feagin, Joe. 1988. *Free Enterprise City*. New Brunswick, N.J.: Rutgers University.

Fong, Eric, and Milena Gulia. 2000. "Neighborhood Change within the Canadian Ethnic Mosaic, 1986–1991," *Population Research and Policy Review* 19: 155–77.

Fong, Eric, and Kumiko Shibuya. 2000. "Suburbanization and Home Ownership: The Spatial Assimilation Process in U.S. Metropolitan Areas," *Sociological Perspectives* 43: 137–57.

Frey, William. 1994. "Minority Suburbanization and Continuing White Flight in U.S. Metropolitan Areas: Assessing the Evidence from the 1990 Census," *Research in Community Sociology* 4: 15–42.

———. 1995. "Immigration and Internal Migration Flight: A California Case Study," *Population and Environment* 16: 353–75.

Fulton, William. 1997. *The Reluctant Metropolis: The Politics of Urban Growth in Los Angeles*. Pt. Arena, Calif.: Solano.

Galster, George. 1999. "Neighborhood Opportunity Structures of Immigrant Populations," *Housing Policy Debate* 10: 395–442.

Garcia, Norma Edith, and Patrick Clarke. 2001. *Housing in Southern California: A Decade in Review*. Los Angeles: Southern California Association of Governments.

Gold, Matea. 2001. "Fannie Mae Allots $50 Billion to Ease Area's Housing Crunch," *Los Angeles Times*, November 10.

Gold, Scott. 2001. "Paying the Price of Growth in Inland Empire," *Los Angeles Times*, November 25.

Gottdiener, M. 1985. *The Social Production of Urban Space*. Austin: University of Texas Press.

Hernández-León, Rubén, and Víctor Zúñiga. 2002. "Mexican Immigrant Communities in the South and Social Capital: The Case of Dalton, Georgia." Working Paper No. 64. La Jolla: Center for Comparative Immigration Studies, University of California, San Diego.

Hise, Greg. 1997. *Magnetic Los Angeles: Planning the Twentieth Century Metropolis*. Baltimore, Md.: Johns Hopkins University Press.

Horton, John. 1995. *The Politics of Diversity*. Philadelphia, Penn.: Temple University Press.

Johnson, James H., Karen D. Johnson-Webb, and Walter C. Farrell. 1999. "Newly Emerging Hispanic Communities in the United States: A Spatial Analysis of Settlement Patterns, In-migration Fields, and Social Receptivity." In *Immigration and Opportunity*, edited by Frank D. Bean and Stephanie Bell-Rose. New York: Russell Sage Foundation.

Keil, Roger. 1998. *Los Angeles: Globalization, Urbanization, and Social Struggles*. Chichester, Eng.: John Wiley.

Krivo, Lauren J. 1995. "Immigrant Characteristics and Hispanic-Anglo Housing Inequality," *Demography* 32: 599–615.

Laslett, John. 1996. "Historical Perspectives: Immigration and the Rise of a Distinctive Urban Region, 1900–1970." In *Ethnic Los Angeles*, edited by Roger Waldinger and Mehdi Bozorgmehr. New York: Russell Sage Foundation.

Light, Ivan. 1977. "The Ethnic Vice Industry, 1880–1944," *American Sociological Review* 42: 464–70.

———. 1984. *Cities in World Perspective*. New York: Macmillan.

———. 1988. "Los Angeles." In *The Metropolis Era: Mega-Cities*, edited by Mattei Dogan and John D. Kasarda. Newbury Park, Calif.: Sage.

———. 2002. "Immigrant Place Entrepreneurs in Los Angeles, 1970–1999," *International Journal of Urban and Regional Research* 26: 215–28.

Light, Ivan, Richard B. Bernard, and Rebecca Kim. 1999. "Immigrant Incorporation in the Garment Industry of Los Angeles," *International Migration Review* 33: 5–25.

Light, Ivan, Parminder Bhachu, and Stavros Karageorgis. 1993. "Migration Networks and Immigrant Entrepreneurship." In *Immigration and Entrepreneurship*, edited by Ivan Light and Parminder Bhachu. New Brunswick, N.J.: Transaction.

Light, Ivan, Rebecca Kim, and Connie Hum. 2000. "Globalization, Vacancy Chains, or Migration Networks? Immigrant Employment and Income in Greater Los Angeles, 1970–1990." In *The Ends of Globalization*, edited by Don Kalb, Marco van der Land, Richard Staring, Bart van Steenbergen, and Nico Wilterdink. Boulder, Colo.: Rowman and Littlefield.

Massey, Douglas S. 1985. "Ethnic Residential Segregation: A Theoretical Synthesis and Empirical Review," *Sociology and Social Research* 69: 315–50.

———. 1988. "Economic Development and International Migration in Comparative Perspective," *Population and Development Review* 14: 383–413.

Massey, Douglas S., and Nancy A. Denton. 1993. *American Apartheid*. Cambridge, Mass.: Harvard University Press.

Molotch, Harvey. 1972. *Managed Integration*. Berkeley: University of California Press.

———. 1976. "The City as a Growth Machine," *American Journal of Sociology* 82: 309–30.

———. 1988. "Strategies and Constraints of Growth Elites." In *Business Elites and Urban Development*, edited by Scott Cummings. Albany: State University of New York Press.

Mutchler, Jan E., and Lauren J. Krivo. 1989. "Availability and Affordability: Adaptation to a Housing Squeeze," *Social Forces* 68: 241–61.

Pincetl, Stephanie S. 1999. *Transforming California*. Baltimore, Md.: Johns Hopkins University Press.

Purcell, Mark. 2000. "The Decline of the Political Consensus for Urban Growth: Evidence from Los Angeles," *Journal of Urban Affairs* 22: 85–100.

Sabagh, Georges, and Mehdi Bozorgmehr. 1996. "Population Change: Immigration and Ethnic Transformation." In *Ethnic Los Angeles,* edited by Roger Waldinger and Mehdi Bozorgmehr. New York: Russell Sage Foundation.

Sassen, Saskia. 2000. *Cities in a World Economy.* 2d ed. Thousand Oaks, Calif.: Pine Forge Press.

Soja, Edward W., and Allen J. Scott. 1996. "Introduction to Los Angeles: City and Region." In *The City: Los Angeles and Urban Theory at the End of the Twentieth Century.* Berkeley: University of California Press.

Stewart, Jocelyn Y. 2001a. "Being Forced Out by Low Incomes, Rising Rents," *Los Angeles Times,* September 29.

———. 2001b. "L.A. Becoming a City of Renters," *Los Angeles Times,* November 29.

Strickland, Daryl. 1999. "Rising Rents Squeeze Area's Working Poor," *Los Angeles Times,* September 10.

Waldinger, Roger. 1996. *Still the Promised City?* Cambridge, Mass.: Harvard University Press.

Wedner, Diane. 2001a. "Fewer New Homes Go on the Block Even as Demand Swells," *Los Angeles Times,* May 21.

———. 2001b. "Education, Employment Gains Help More Latinos Become Homeowners," *Los Angeles Times,* August 27.

———. 2001c. "Incentives Proposed to Build Affordable Housing," *Los Angeles Times,* October 16.

Part IV

International Boundaries and Globalization

15

Transnational Communities: A New Form of Social Relations under Conditions of Globalization?

STEPHEN CASTLES

Social science has its intellectual fashions, and migration studies is no exception. In the early postwar period, many analysts focused on immigrant *assimilation* and then shifted to the softer notion of *integration*. By the 1980s, *multiculturalism* was the buzzword. A public backlash against this approach in the 1990s led to a new emphasis on *citizenship* and intergroup relations in the *city*. The buzzword of the first decade of the twenty-first century is undoubtedly *transnationalism*. A confusing plethora of books, papers, and conferences on the theme makes it hard to judge whether we are dealing with an important new development in migrant consciousness and behavior, or with old wine in new bottles.

Some scholars argue that increasing numbers of migrants perceive themselves as members of transnational communities based on common identity with co-ethnics in the ancestral homeland and other migration destinations. Transnational community belonging thus replaces nation-state belonging as the main source of loyalty and solidarity,

---

This chapter is based on a paper given at the Fifth International Metropolis Conference, Vancouver, November 2000. The author thanks Ellie Vasta, of the Institute of Social and Cultural Anthropology, University of Oxford, for comments on an earlier draft. I also thank the participants in the discussion of the paper at the Vancouver conference.

which in turn can cause a loss of social cohesion in the country of residence. Such trends may be condemned as a threat to the democratic nation-state—summed up in the polemical notion of "nations of tribes"—or celebrated as harbingers of a more rational and peaceful post-national order. However, there are also scholars of transnational communities who argue that they may constitute a new form of immigrant adaptation, which may in the long run lead to more successful forms of assimilation into receiving societies. A third group argues that there is nothing new about transnational communities and that they have existed since time immemorial in the form of *diasporas*.

These are far from being mere scholastic debates. They have considerable practical importance because virtually all Western nations have experienced large-scale immigration in the last half-century and have found that immigrants do not simply assimilate into the existing society and culture. Increasing mobility and cultural diversity pose difficult questions with regard to policies on immigration and citizenship. The proliferation of dual citizenship and multiple citizenship is particularly significant since it conjures up fears of "divided loyalties"—the nemesis of nationalism. As South-South migration increases—for instance to the fast-growing East Asian economies—similar issues are becoming crucial there too. Such debates gained added impetus after the events of September 11, 2001, which put the spotlight on the Al-Qaeda terrorist network, apparently held together by bonds of transnational religious and ethnic affinity. Migration and security have become a key theme, and the perceived growth of separatist communities within Western countries is seen a major threat (Weiner and Russell 2001).

In my view, the notion of transnational communities *is* useful in helping us to understand contemporary patterns of international migration and settlement. However, it is important to ground transnational theory in a broader analysis of historical changes and contemporary macro-social trends. It is also important not to use the notion of transnational communities in an inflationary manner, but rather to define and limit it to allow its use in empirical research. In this chapter I will put forward seven propositions that may assist in the discussion.

1. **Transnational communities have deep historical roots**, especially in the diaspora phenomenon, but they are currently proliferating due to social and technological changes associated with globalization.

Transnational communities are not new, even if the term is. The diaspora concept goes back to ancient times and was used for peoples displaced or dispersed by force (such as the Jews and African slaves in the New World). It was also applied to certain trading groups such as Greeks in Western Asia and Africa or the Arab traders who brought Islam to Southeast Asia, as well as to labor migrants (Indians in the British Empire, Italians since the 1860s) (Cohen 1997). There is no clear demarcation between the notions of transnational community and diaspora: certain authors use them as synonyms, others to refer to different types of group. For instance, some reserve diaspora for forcibly dispersed groups or "nations without states," and use transnational communities to refer to economic migrants who maintain strong homeland links (Van Hear 1998). For historical reasons, diaspora has strong emotional connotations, while the term transnational community is more neutral—and therefore preferable for social scientific use.

Moreover, the migrants of the nineteenth and early twentieth centuries did not cut off all links to their homelands, even in classical immigration countries like the United States, Canada, and Australia. Personal, cultural, economic, and political relationships were maintained, and return migration and circulatory migration were not uncommon. The well-known "chain migration" phenomenon is one aspect of such relationships (Price 1963: 108–10). However, such linkages were restricted by the high costs and difficulties of transport and communication. After 1945, as technology improved, *migrant networks* became increasingly important, as was recognized in migration theory from the 1980s (Boyd 1989; Fawcett 1989). Research on Mexican migrants in the 1970s showed that 90 percent of those surveyed had obtained legal residence in the United States through family and employer connections (Portes and Bach 1985). Today many authors emphasize the role of information and "cultural capital" (knowledge of other countries, and capabilities for organizing travel, finding work, and adapting to a new environment) in starting and sustaining migratory movements. Informal networks include personal relationships, family and household patterns, friendship and community ties, and mutual help in economic and social matters. Such links provide vital resources for individuals and groups, and may be referred to as "social capital" (Bourdieu and Wacquant 1992: 119).

The factor that justifies the emergence of a new field of study is the rapid proliferation of transnational communities under conditions of globalization. As Vertovec points out:

> Transnationalism (as long-distance networks) certainly preceded "the nation." Yet today these systems of ties, interactions, exchanges and mobility function intensively and in real time while being spread throughout the world. New technologies, especially involving telecommunications, serve to connect such networks with increasing speed and efficiency (Vertovec 1999: 447).

The proliferation of transnational communities in recent years can perhaps best be understood as part of the process of global integration and time-space compression currently gaining momentum. This is partly a technological issue: improved transport and accessible real-time electronic communication are the material basis of globalization. But above all, it is a social and cultural issue: globalization is closely linked to changes in social structures and relationships, and to shifts in cultural values concerned with place, mobility, and belonging. This is likely to have important consequences, which we are only just beginning to understand (Bauman 1998; Castells 1996; Held et al. 1999).

A problem of much of the discussion is that changing forms of migrant consciousness and behavior are viewed against the backdrop of relatively static notions of society. Analyses are often implicitly based on the traditional model of the independent nation-state as a privileged location for political identity, economic affairs, social relations, and culture. Unquestioned sovereignty within internationally recognized boundaries made each country an autonomous unit. Each nation-state was meant to have a unique and homogenous people, based on common cultural characteristics and shared heritage. In this "world of nation-states," immigration was the exception, and immigrants could only become part of the nation through a process of adaptation and assimilation (Castles and Davidson 2000).

This model, the ideal of nationalism, was rarely achieved in practice since the overwhelming majority of nation-states have always included diverse ethnic groups. But major shifts in the last half-century have made even the myth unsustainable. In the mobile world of the twenty-first century, all societies experience increasing flows across their borders—flows of capital, commodities, cultural products, and people. Major aspects of sovereignty have moved to supranational or subnational levels. Peoples have become more connected across boundaries, and populations have become increasingly diverse. This has negative aspects—such as erosion of local cultures—but also positive aspects like increased personal choice and growing emphasis on human rights.

Obviously, migration is a major factor in such changes, but even countries with little migration are changing rapidly due to the material and virtual flows that constitute globalization.

Social theories based on the nation-state model cannot fully explain current developments nor provide adequate solutions. Globalization means a change in the spatial organization of the world from "a space of places" to a "space of flows," as Castells put it (1996: chap. 6). Or, as Faist argues, we are witnessing a shift from nation-states as "containers" for politics and culture to new forms of "transnational social space," in which culture and politics are based on groups and networks that transcend national boundaries (Faist 2000). In this emerging reorganization of space, prior modes of migrant adaptation may no longer function for significant groups.

2. **The majority of migrants do not form transnational communities.** It is vital to have clear definitions of transnational communities and related concepts, and to analyze the conditions under which migrants do or do not become members of transnational communities.

Groups whose consciousness and regular activities transcend national borders constitute transnational communities. However, it is important not to overstate the case by treating all or most migrants as transnationals or "transmigrants"—a tendency often found in postmodern theories, which celebrate "nomadism" and "hybridity." Clear definitions are a precondition for empirical study.

Transnational communities may be defined as groups based in two or more countries that engage in recurrent, enduring, and significant cross-border activities, which may be economic, political, social, or cultural. The notion of a transnational community puts the emphasis on human agency: such groups are the result of cross-border activities that link individuals, families, and local groups. Under conditions of globalization, previous face-to-face communities based on kinship, neighborhoods, or workplaces may be extended into far-flung virtual communities that communicate at a distance. Transnational communities do not necessarily refer to migrants since cross-border groups with common business, cultural, sporting, or political interests might well consider themselves a community. However, for discussions of social relations and citizenship, groups arising from migrations are the most significant type. Portes and his collaborators emphasize the significance of transnational business communities, but they also note the importance of political and cultural communities. Portes makes the useful distinction between *transnationalism from above*—activities "conducted by powerful institutional actors, such as multinational corporations and states"—and *transnationalism from below*—activities "that are the result of grass-roots initiatives by immigrants and their home country counterparts" (Portes, Guarnizo, and Landolt 1999: 221).

Types of transnational community include:

- Transnational business communities, based on the use of cross-border ethnic connections as a resource to run businesses of many different types and sizes. The small ethnic business that trades in homeland products and services in the ethnic neighborhood—and sends back host country goods and possibly capital—is an example of transnationalism from below (Marques, Santos, and Araújo 2001). The multinational corporation that creates its own transnational corporate culture and abandons the base country or "headquarters" mentality (Ohmae 1991) is a form of transnationalism from above.
- Transnational political communities, involving the use of solidarity with co-ethnics in two or more countries, usually to bring about change in the homeland, though sometimes also to improve the situation of the group in settlement countries. Transnational political diasporas are often the result of forced exoduses from the homeland. This often leads to multiple migrations and a strong consciousness of being a refugee or exile (Van Hear 1998). An example of a refugee diaspora that now often functions as a political, business, and cultural community is the Vietnamese who left their country in the 1970s and 1980s.
- Transnational cultural communities seeking to maintain the homeland heritage and language among settler group. They also often seek recognition from homeland authorities that the diaspora is part of the nation. Demands for voting rights while abroad or for dual citizenship are typical. In such cases there is no clear distinction between the cultural and the political community.
- Transnational social communities. These exist in situations in which migration becomes part of normal life for people from a certain place—for instance, where there is regular cross-border migration from a village or town of origin to a specific destination. Sometimes migration becomes a normal part of life for substantial elements of a whole society, so that the transnational social com-

munity includes most or all of a nation (either as migrants, their relatives, or people whose lives are influenced in some way by the process). This was true of Italy between the 1860s and the 1960s, and it applies to the Philippines today.

Glick Schiller has suggested the term *transmigrants* for "people who live their lives across borders, developing social, familial, political, economic and religious networks that incorporate them into two or more states" (Glick Schiller 1999: 203). Transmigrant can be used to identify someone whose existence is shaped in important ways through participation in a transnational community based on migration.

However, inflationary use of the terms "transnational community" and "transmigrant" should be avoided. Temporary labor migrants who work abroad for a few years, send back remittances, communicate with their family at home, and visit them occasionally are not necessarily transmigrants. If the central focus of their life is in the homeland and they intend to return there, then they lack transnational consciousness. Similarly, permanent migrants who leave their country of origin forever and simply retain loose contact with their homeland are not transmigrants because their life focus is in the country of settlement. The key defining features are that *transnational activities are a central part of an individual's life and that two or more societies form a continual frame of reference for them.* This transnational focus can also be at the collective level. Individuals can be seen as members of a transnational community if the transnational activities of their social group form the main context of their lives, even if they themselves are not directly involved in the transnational activities. Key research questions are therefore to work out which migrant groups become transmigrants, and to establish what conditions bring about or hinder this outcome. Many research projects on this theme are currently under way. The recent Transnational Communities Programme at Oxford University (funded by the British Economic and Social Research Council) provides a wealth of empirical detail (see www.transcomm.ox.ac.uk).

3. **Earlier modes of immigrant incorporation are still powerful**, and it is important to examine the relationship between these modes and transnational communities.

Each immigration country has its own way of regulating the situation of newcomers, but—as I have argued elsewhere (Castles 1995;

Castles and Miller 1998: 244–50)—it is possible to summarize three main approaches to the incorporation of immigrants into society.[1]

Assimilation means encouraging immigrants to learn the national language and take on the social and cultural practices of the receiving community. Immigrants are expected to give up their own homeland cultures and to become indistinguishable from the rest of the population, at least by the second generation. This approach has been used in "classical immigration countries" like the United States, Canada, and Australia, where it has been coupled with easy access to citizenship. Assimilationist practices have also been used in somewhat different contexts in some European immigration countries. Many sociologists (especially in the United States) have viewed assimilation as an inevitable and necessary process (Alba and Nee 1997; Gordon 1964; Portes, Guarnizo, and Landolt 1999).

Differential exclusion is the model associated with "guestworker systems" in European countries such as Germany up to the 1970s and with recruitment of "overseas contract workers" in Gulf oil countries and Asian tiger economies today. In this model, immigrants are integrated temporarily into certain societal subsystems such as the labor market and limited welfare entitlements, but they are excluded from others such as political participation and national culture. The migrant workers are discouraged from bringing in family members, and they are not supposed to settle permanently. Citizenship is not an option.

However, both these approaches share an important common principle: that immigration should not bring about major changes in the receiving society. A belief in the *controllability of ethnic difference* could be sustained in the past, but it began to be questioned from the 1970s onward in Western immigration countries. In the "guestworker" countries, temporary migrants were turning into settlers. Democratic states found themselves incapable of deporting large numbers of unwanted workers. Nor could immigrants be completely denied social rights since this would lead to serious conflicts and divisions. The result was family reunion, community formation, and the emergence of new eth-

[1] Such typologies have been criticized as being simplistic in that they focus on certain dimensions but neglect others, or that they ignore specific national patterns. For instance, both Dutch and British approaches to pluralism do not readily fit these models, nor do the approaches followed in southern European countries as spontaneous inflows of migrant workers developed from the 1980s. Some authors have suggested typologies that emphasize differing aspects (for an overview, see Entzinger 2000). However, in my view, the typology used here remains a useful conceptual aid to analysis.

nic minorities. In both types of immigration country, the expectation of long-term cultural assimilation proved illusory, with ethnic communities maintaining their languages and cultures into the second and third generations. Immigrants began to establish cultural associations, places of worship, and ethnic businesses.

The introduction of policies of multiculturalism (under a variety of labels) seemed the best solution. *Multiculturalism* means abandoning the myth of homogenous and monocultural nation-states. It means recognizing rights to cultural maintenance and community formation, and linking these to social equality and protection from discrimination. Yet multiculturalism can still be seen as a way of controlling difference within the nation-state framework because it does not question the territorial principle. It implicitly assumes that migration will lead to permanent settlement and to the birth of second and subsequent generations who are both citizens and nationals. Thus multiculturalism maintains the idea of a primary belonging to one society and a loyalty to just one nation-state.

Most migration and settlement experiences still fit into one of these three models—and sometimes into a mixture of them. The majority of migrants want either to stay temporarily in a destination country or to settle permanently and give up their former affiliation. This does not necessarily mean giving up linguistic and cultural identity, and multiculturalism accepts this. But increasingly, significant groups do not fit any of these patterns. Transnational communities have much in common with the diverse ethnic communities recognized by multiculturalism with regard to cultural maintenance and community formation. But they differ in an important way: because they maintain strong cross-border affiliations, possibly over generations, their primary loyalty is not to one nation-state or one territory. This is why they present a challenge to nation-states and appear so threatening to nationalists.

4. **Transnational identities are complex and contradictory**. They can take a variety of forms, which may either complement existing modes of immigrant incorporation or work against them.

An obvious consequence of the rise of transnationalism could be the end of the nationalist dream of the homogenous nation, as Cohen points out:

> What 19th century nationalists wanted was a "space" for each "race", a terrritorialising of each social identity. What

> they got instead is a chain of cosmopolitan cities and an increasing proliferation of sub-national and transnational identities that cannot easily be contained in the nation-state system (Cohen 1997: 175).

Since more and more countries are experiencing migration, the implication is that the old nation-state project of ethnic homogenization has little chance any more. That fact in itself should lead to a fundamental rethinking of some basic tenets on national identity and political culture. Patriotism based on emotional identification with national symbols may be declining in power as a means for mobilizing multicultural or transnational populations.

If the primary loyalty of transnational communities is not to one nation-state or territory, to what does it relate? Here we come to an inherent tension in transnational theory. Transmigrants are sometimes portrayed as *cosmopolitans* capable of crossing cultural boundaries and building multiple or hybrid identities. But other theorists argue that transnational consciousness is based overwhelmingly on *common ethnicity*: transmigrants feel solidarity with co-ethnics in their homeland and elsewhere. In this approach, transnationalism appears as a revalorization of exclusionary ethnic identity, and transnational communities take on the form of exile diasporas, determined to establish their own nation-states—a sort of "transnational nationalism," as Ang (2000) puts it.

Again, we lack the empirical evidence for clear statements. There probably are highly cosmopolitan groups who feel at home everywhere; global business and professional elites might correspond with this image. There are also "nations without states"—generally groups based on forced dispersal—who mobilize politically to create or transform their homelands. But most members of transnational communities fall between these extremes and probably have contradictory and fluctuating identities. A long tradition of oral history and migrant literature has shown how migrants have to negotiate their way between complicated choices of return, assimilation, and community formation. These are not exclusive options, and individuals and groups find creative ways of simultaneously adapting to and changing their social environments. The human agency they develop applies not only to overt political or social action but also to strategies for everyday life.

The same applies to members of transnational communities. Individuals and groups constantly negotiate choices with regard to their participation in host societies, their relationships with their homelands, and their links to co-ethnics (Kastoryano 1996). Their life strategies bring together elements of existence in both national and transnational social space. There may be no exclusive loyalty to a specific territory, but transmigrants need political stability, economic prosperity, and social well-being in their place of residence, just like most other people. Successful transnational strategies are likely to involve adaptation to multiple social settings as well as cross-cultural competence. In a mobile world of culturally open societies, such capabilities should not be seen as threatening; on the contrary, they should be seen as highly desirable. The notion of primary loyalty to one place is therefore misleading: this icon of old-style nationalism is of declining importance for migrants in a mobile world.

5. **Global cities have become the sites of encounter for transnational communities**. However, this should not be misunderstood as a form of re-territorialization of identity.

The ambiguous character of transnational communities and the ambivalence of their consciousness and identity are particularly evident when linked to discourses on global cities. The idea of studying the impact of migration on cities rather than on society as a whole has been given considerable emphasis by the development of the Metropolis Program. This program was started by North American scholars in the mid-1990s with Canadian government support, and it has become one of the largest international networks linking researchers, policymakers, and civil society organizations. It was designed to move away from the normative assumptions of multicultural models, and instead to focus on concrete experiences and policy implications of living together in increasingly diverse cities. It is also a result of a growing understanding of the key role of major cities in the development of new global forms of production and distribution (Sassen 1991). As the boundaries of the nation-state become blurred and porous, there is a temptation to put increasing emphasis on subnational belonging—that is, to re-territorialize identity at the level of the city. Local social and political relations are seen as crucial, and local citizenship can be perceived as a substitute for diminishing chances for political influence at the national and supranational levels.

This focus on the city can be linked to an attempt to redefine transnational consciousness. The old diaspora, seen as "long-distance nationalism" in "transnational virtual space," can be replaced by "local transnationalism," understood as the hybridization of cosmopolitan transnational communities sharing local territorial space (Ang 2000). Put more simply, the idea is to counter fears of separatist nationalist diasporas by emphasizing the ways in which ethnic minorities undergo cultural and social change through living together in multi-ethnic neighborhoods. Hybridity rather than nationalism in global cities is an appealing perspective, but again, it is far from clear that this is the most frequent outcome. Two problems must be noted.

The first is that cultural diversity in global cities does not in any way indicate equality or harmony between ethnic groups. Processes of differentiation based on class, race, gender, and legal status lead to complex hierarchies of privilege in global cities. Certain groups—both local and immigrant—have the chance for mobility into positions of high income, status, and power, while others have to do the "3D-jobs" ("dirty, difficult, and dangerous") or are excluded altogether from the labor market. Portes and others have used the notion of "segmented assimilation" to indicate that assimilation has always meant incorporation into a specific segment of society. Selectivity on the basis of economic and social factors, as well as stereotypes and discriminatory practices, has caused certain groups to experience "upward assimilation" and others, "downward assimilation" (Portes, Guarnizo, and Landolt 1999; Zhou 1997). In the United States this might mean assimilation into the white population for privileged groups (such as Europeans or Asians with high human capital) as against assimilation into the black underclass (for Mexican and Central American laborers and low-skilled Asian migrants).

The second problem is that a focus on the city as the key site for intergroup relations can lead to misconceptions regarding its relative autonomy. The city is no more self-sufficient or closed off than the nation-state. Rather, it should be understood as a node where various types of global networks intersect (Castells 1996: chap. 6). The transnational communities can be seen as one form of such networks. Thus members of transnational communities are likely to have both transnational ethnic consciousness and local hybrid consciousness—in varying measures and at different times.

6. **The effects of transnational communities on social relations and citizenship can vary** considerably according to the social and political context. Attitudes and policies in both migrant-sending and migrant-receiving countries play an important part.

Individuals and groups develop transnational linkages because these provide the best ways of dealing with the social situations and opportunity structures they encounter. The states and civil societies of both sending and receiving countries do much to shape these contextual factors.

The governments of *emigration countries* often try to bind their expatriates to the homeland because this can bring economic, political, or cultural benefits. There is a long history of such efforts. For instance, the overseas Chinese have played an important role in political change at home, and both nationalist and communist Chinese governments have sought to control and mobilize the diaspora (Sinn 1998). The Philippines government has special laws and programs to maintain links with nationals abroad—even when these individuals take the citizenship of another state (Aguilar 1999). The Mexican government's recent introduction of dual citizenship was designed to retain the affiliation of the millions of citizens who have taken up residence and citizenship in the United States. Such measures are likely to strengthen transnationalism on the part of migrants.

Immigration countries also influence transnational community formation in various ways, both negative and positive. Practices of exclusion or discrimination against immigrants can prevent integration and encourage a homeland orientation. In such cases, enclave communities with their own economic, cultural, and political infrastructures may emerge. Where immigrants experience marginalization or racism, their best chance of success lies in mobilizing community solidarity and transnational links—a sort of "reactive ethnicity." Interestingly, Portes (1999) argues that transnational activities can in the long run empower low-status immigrants and help them secure better living standards and education for their children—leading to a better chance of assimilation in the future.

More positive attitudes on the part of immigration countries can also encourage transnational communities. Policies that accept linguistic and cultural maintenance are conducive to transnational linkages. On the other hand, antidiscrimination policies make it easier for immigrants to succeed in mainstream society. Since these are both aspects of multicultural policy, it seems that multiculturalism does not automatically encourage transnationalism, but perhaps it gives immigrants more choice on the degree to which they want to carry out cross-border activities.

It seems that both discrimination and multiculturalism can lead to transnational communities—but of different types. Discrimination leads to separatism and *closed-off communities*, which are relatively isolated in their country of residence and compensate through transnational linkages. This may have negative effects on social cohesion and citizenship. Multiculturalism leads to *cosmopolitan communities*, which negotiate both local and cross-border linkages, bringing benefits in terms of cultural openness and economic opportunities. This type of transnational community is not likely to undermine social cohesion and citizenship, but it may bring about transformations in their character.

7. **The growth of transnational communities makes it necessary to transform institutional frameworks** to correspond with new forms of social identity. In particular, the model of singular and exclusive nation-state citizenship needs to be revised.

Nation-state citizenship was the adequate form for a world of relatively autonomous nation-states. Such citizenship was meant to be singular and exclusive, and naturalization was seen as an exceptional and irreversible act that implied loss of the original citizenship. But this model is no longer appropriate for a world in which *flows* are replacing *places* as the key loci of economic and social organization. If people move frequently between different countries and maintain important affiliations in each of them, citizenship needs to be adapted to the new realities.

In fact, this is already happening. Over the last thirty years virtually all Western countries have changed their citizenship rules in response to immigration and settlement. In many cases this has meant a shift away from *jus sanguinis* (citizenship through descent), which tends to exclude immigrants and their descendants, and toward more inclusive forms of citizenship based on *jus soli* (citizenship through birth in the territory) and *jus domicilii* (citizenship on the basis of residence) (Aleinikoff and Klusmeyer 2000; Castles and Davidson 2000: chap. 4). The new German citizenship law of 1999 replaced a long tradition of citizenship through descent with much greater openness to acquisition of citizenship by former foreign workers and their descendants. It is a significant milestone because it represents an important move toward the *jus soli* principle. However, such changes are still not on the agenda in more recent Asian immigration countries like Malaysia and Japan, where policymakers are still determined to prevent settlement and ethnic community formation.

Dual (or multiple) citizenship is a key issue for migrants because it is the best way of recognizing multiple affiliations and identities. In recent years many countries have changed their laws to recognize dual citizenship (Vertovec 1999). Emigration countries do so as a way of binding emigrants to the home country, because this brings benefits in the forms of remittances, technology transfer, political allegiance, and cultural maintenance. Immigration countries do so as a way of improving the social integration of minorities and preventing the linking of ethnicity with social disadvantage, which is at the root of ethnic conflicts and racism. This is why even former "guestworker" importing countries have now changed their laws. Again, there is an empirical deficit. Nobody seems to know how many dual citizens there are, nor what proportion of the population they compose. In Germany—which still officially rejects dual citizenship—there are thought to be up to two million dual citizens. In Australia there may be three to five million—up to a quarter of the population (Zappalá and Castles 2000: 56). Overall, dual citizens are a small minority but a fast growing one, with great potential significance.

The growth of transnational communities may in the long run lead to a rethinking of the very content of citizenship. Differentiated forms of state membership may be needed to recognize the different types of relationships transmigrants have with different states—such as political rights in one place, economic rights in another, and cultural rights in a third (Bauböck 1994; Bauböck and Rundell 1998). In practice this already happens when immigration states create forms of "quasi-citizenship" or "denizenship" (Hammar 1990) by granting rights with regard to residency, employment, or welfare to specific groups of immigrants. But such practices have developed in a piecemeal way, without much consideration of their long-term consequences for citizenship.

These debates raise very difficult questions about the future of democracy under conditions of globalization. Democratic government in modern polities focuses primarily on the nation-state. Yet more and more of the decisions that affect our lives are made at the supranational level. Global and regional governance is rapidly gaining in significance, yet transnational democratic institutions hardly exist—with a few limited exceptions such as the European Union. In the future, then, we need to think about transnational forms of democratic participation—not just for members of transnational communities but for all citizens affected by the rapid shift in the location of political power. This goes beyond the scope of this chapter, but it does help us to realize that transnational developments not only affect people who clearly belong to transnational communities; they affect all of us.

References

Aguilar, F.V.J. 1999. "The Triumph of Instrumental Citizenship? Migrations, Identities and the Nation-State in Southeast Asia," *Asian Studies Review* 23, no. 3: 307–36.

Alba, Richard, and Victor Nee. 1997. "Rethinking Assimilation Theory for a New Era of Immigration," *International Migration Review* 31: 826–74.

Aleinikoff, T.A., and D. Klusmeyer, eds. 2000. *From Migrant to Citizens: Membership in a Changing World*. Washington D.C.: Carnegie Endowment for International Peace.

Ang, I. 2000. "Beyond Transnational Nationalism: Questioning Chinese Diasporas in the Global City." Presented at the conference "Transnational Communities in the Asia-Pacific Region," Singapore.

Bauböck, R. 1994. *Transnational Citizenship: Membership and Rights in International Migration*. Aldershot: Edward Elgar.

Bauböck, R., and J. Rundell, eds. 1998. *Blurred Boundaries: Migration, Ethnicity, Citizenship*. Aldershot: Ashgate.

Bauman, Z. 1998. *Globalization: The Human Consequences*. Cambridge: Polity.

Bourdieu, P., and L. Wacquant. 1992. *An Invitation to Reflexive Sociology*. Chicago: University of Chicago Press.

Boyd, M. 1989. "Family and Personal Networks in Migration," *International Migration Review* 23, no. 3: 638–70.

Castells, M. 1996. *The Rise of the Network Society*. Oxford: Blackwells.

Castles, Stephen. 1995. "How Nation-States Respond to Immigration and Ethnic Diversity," *New Community* 21, no. 3: 293–308.

Castles, Stephen, and A. Davidson. 2000. *Citizenship and Migration: Globalisation and the Politics of Belonging*. London: Macmillan.

Castles, Stephen, and Mark J. Miller. 1998. *The Age of Migration: International Population Movements in the Modern World*. London: Macmillan/Guilford.

Cohen, R. 1997. *Global Diasporas: An Introduction*. London: UCL Press.

Entzinger, H. 2000. "The Dynamics of Integration Policies: A Multidimensional Model." In *Challenging Immigration and Ethnic Relations Politics,* edited by R. Koopmans and P. Statham. Oxford: Oxford University Press.

Faist, T. 2000. "Transnationalization in International Migration: Implications for the Study of Citizenship and Culture," *Ethnic and Racial Studies* 23, no. 2.

Fawcett, J.T. 1989. "Networks, Linkages and Migration Systems," *International Migration Review* 23, no. 3: 671–80.

Glick Schiller, N. 1999. "Citizens in Transnational Nation-States: The Asian Experience." In *Globalisation and the Asia-Pacific: Contested Territories*, edited by K. Olds, P. Dicken, P.F. Kelly, L. Kong, and H.W-C. Yeung. London: Routledge.

Gordon, Milton. 1964. *Assimilation in American Life: The Role of Race, Religion and National Origins*. New York: Oxford University Press.

Hammar, T. 1990. *Democracy and the Nation-State: Aliens, Denizens and Citizens in a World of International Migration*. Aldershot: Avebury.

Held, D., A. McGrew, D. Goldblatt, and J. Perraton. 1999. *Global Transformations: Politics, Economics and Culture*. Cambridge: Polity.

Kastoryano, R. 1996. *La France, l'Allemagne et leurs immigrés: négocier l'identité*. Paris: Armand Colin.

Marques, M.M., R. Santos, and F. Araújo. 2001. "Ariadne's Thread: Cape Verdean Women in Transnational Webs," *Global Networks* 1, no. 3: 283–306.

Ohmae, K. 1991. *The Borderless World*. New York: Harper Collins.

Portes, Alejandro. 1999. "Conclusion: Towards a New World—The Origins and Effects of Transnational Activities," *Ethnic and Racial Studies* 22, no. 2: 463–77.

Portes, Alejandro, and Robert L. Bach. 1985. *Latin Journey: Cuban and Mexican Immigrants in the United States*. Berkeley: University of California Press.

Portes, Alejandro, Luis E. Guarnizo, and P. Landolt. 1999. "The Study of Transnationalism: Pitfalls and Promise of an Emergent Research Field," *Ethnic and Racial Studies* 22, no. 2: 217–37.

Price, C. 1963. *Southern Europeans in Australia*. Melbourne: Oxford University Press.

Sassen, Saskia. 1991. *The Global City: New York, London, Tokyo*. Princeton, N.J.: Princeton University Press.

Sinn, E., ed. 1998. *The Last Half Century of Chinese Overseas*. Hong Kong: Hong Kong University Press.

Van Hear, N. 1998. *New Diasporas: The Mass Exodus, Dispersal and Regrouping of Migrant Communities*. London: UCL Press.

Vertovec, S. 1999. "Conceiving and Researching Transnationalism," *Ethnic and Racial Studies* 22, no. 2: 445–62.

Weiner, M., and S.S. Russell, eds. 2001. *Demography and National Security*. New York: Berghahn.

Zappalá, G., and Stephen Castles. 2000. "Citizenship and Immigration in Australia." In *From Migrants to Citizens: Membership in a Changing World*, edited by T.A. Aleinikoff and D. Klusmeyer. Washington, D.C.: Carnegie Endowment for International Peace.

Zhou, M. 1997. "Segmented Assimilation: Issues, Controversies, and Recent Research on the New Second Generation," *International Migration Review* 31, no. 4: 975–1008.

16

Mexican Workers and U.S. Agriculture: The Revolving Door

PHILIP MARTIN

The agricultural industry is frequently misunderstood. Farming is often considered a crown jewel of the U.S. economy, reflecting the fact that relatively low expenditures on food mean that consumers have more money to buy other goods. The United States has about two million farms, defined as places that normally sell US$1,000 or more of farm goods in one year. Farmers had cash receipts from sales of food and fiber of $223 billion in 2000, and about 25 percent of U.S. farm production was exported, continuing a consistent U.S. agricultural trade surplus.[1]

This picture of an efficient agricultural sector in which family farmers provide a living link to the founding fathers is clouded by the fact that most U.S. farms lose money farming, and that government payments typically account for between 25 and 50 percent of net farm income.[2] The value of U.S. farmland and buildings was $1.1 trillion in 2000, and these assets generated a net cash income that year of $56

---

1 In 2000, farm exports were $51 billion and imports were $39 billion, for a $12 billion trade surplus.

2 Not all farmers receive government payments; in 1999 about 42 percent of U.S. farms received an average of $16,800 in government payments. Farms not receiving government payments had average gross cash incomes of $44,200, probably not generating enough net cash income to support a family.

billion, of which $22 billion, or 39 percent, was direct government payments to farmers.

There are many ways to analyze farm structure. Traditionally, farms were grouped by their annual farm sales. The 1997 Census of Agriculture, for example, found 1.9 million U.S. farms that sold commodities worth $197 billion. When the number of farms is compared to their share of total farm sales, the result is an X-shaped distribution, in which the 51 percent of small farms that had sales of less than $10,000 (and on average lost money farming) accounted for 1 percent of total farm sales, while the 26,000 largest farms that each had $1 million or more in sales accounted for 42 percent of total farm sales (see table 16.1). If farmers are asked their main occupation, two-thirds of U.S. "farmers" say they are something other than farmers—most are retired or are primarily nonfarm workers who operate a farm part time.

Table 16.1. U.S. Farm Structure, 1997

Farm Sales	Farms (%)	Sales (%)
Under $10,000	51	1
$10,000–$25,000	13	2
$25,000–$50,000	9	3
$50,000–$100,000	8	6
$100,000–$250,000	10	15
$250,000–$500,000	5	15
$500,000–$1,000,000	2	15
$1,000,000 or more	1	42

Source: Census Bureau 1999: table 1105.

Note: There were a total of 1.9 million farms and $197 billion in sales in 1997.

Although these data make it clear that it is hard to generalize about "the average farmer," most farmers display two characteristics that affect the immigration and integration of farmworkers. First, the 1997 Census of Agriculture reported that 98 percent of U.S. farmers were white and only 1.5 percent (28,000) were Hispanic, while Hispanics are about 90 percent of farmworkers. Thus U.S. agriculture is distinguished by a striking ethnic difference between employers and workers. Second, farmers are much older than farmworkers. The average age of farmers in 1997 was fifty-four, and 48 percent were fifty-five or older.

The average age of hired crop workers was thirty-one in 1997–98, and 67 percent were under thirty-five (U.S. Department of Labor 2000: 9).

There are three other background facts about agriculture and farming that affect immigration and integration policies:

- Agriculture was the largest U.S. industry until early in the twentieth century, and its status as an economic success story gives farmers advocating favorable labor and immigration policies a powerful position at the political bargaining table.
- Agriculture is an industry in which the number of employers—about 650,000 in the 1997 Census of Agriculture—is high relative to the number of employees, about 2.5 million. This makes farm employers more important in employer organizations than farmworkers are in employee organizations.
- Agriculture is a widely dispersed industry experienced in obtaining government assistance in areas ranging from subsidized inputs, such as water, to special marketing and export promotion programs. Agriculture's political influence is noticeable in the U.S. Congress, where it tends to have more support in the Senate than in the House of Representatives.

The subsector of U.S. agriculture that is most closely associated with immigration is so-called FVH agriculture (fruits, vegetables, and horticultural products). In 1997 this sector comprised 208,000 U.S. farms: 86,000 produced fruits and nuts, 54,000 produced vegetables and melons, and 68,000 produced horticultural specialties such as flowers and nursery products. Not all of these farms reported hiring labor in 1997, but among those that did, the distribution of expenses for hired farm labor is very similar to the distribution of farm production. That is, the largest farms account for most of the hired labor expenses (see table 16.2). The Census of Agriculture does not provide data to calculate the exact shares of hired labor expenses by farm size, but if each farm assigned to a hired labor expense class had average wages at the midpoint of the class, and if the remaining hired labor expenses were paid by the largest farm employers, the result is as follows: the largest 1,800 fruit and nut farms accounted for 87 percent of hired labor expenses in 1997. This suggests that farm labor is even more concentrated than farm employment.

FVH farms that hire most seasonal farmworkers would be considered large U.S. employers by any definition. An example is the Zaninovich

Table 16.2. Hired Farm Labor Expenses, 1997

Income from Fruits and Nuts Production	Farms	Average[1]	Expenses[1]	Per Farms	Per Expenses
< $5,000 in 1997	19,666	2,500	22,166	48%	1%
$5,000–$25,000	10,026	12,500	22,526	24	1
$25,000–$100,000	7,246	62,500	69,746	18	3
$100,000–$250,000	2,368	175,000	177,368	6	8
> $250,000	1,809	2,000,000	2,001,809	4	87
Estimated total	41,115		2,293,615		
Census total	41,115		2,331,413		

Source: Department of Agriculture 1997: table 51, p. 144.

[1] Average is an estimate of average hired labor expenses for each farm in this group.

table grape farm in California's San Joaquin Valley, an operation that hires 1,000 farmworkers to produce 5 million 21-pound boxes of table grapes annually. At an average of $10 a box, this farm generates sales of some $50 million a year. The grape pickers work 500 to 1,000 hours and earn between $6 and $8 an hour, giving them annual grape-picking earnings of $3,000 to $8,000. When the federal government makes immigration and labor law exceptions for family farmers, most of the benefits of the exceptions go to the largest farms that hire the most workers.

SEASONALITY, WAGES, AND GUESTWORKERS

The demand for hired workers in agriculture is seasonal—more workers are needed during some months of the year than others. The classic response to seasonality was diversified family farming, which is why most U.S. farms were (and are) crop and livestock enterprises in which all members of (typically large) families worked during times of peak seasonal labor needs, and went to school, tended livestock, and so on in the off-season. There were two other U.S. responses to seasonality: slavery/sharecropping in the South, and migrant and seasonal workers in the West. Slavery was an economically viable way to produce crops like tobacco and cotton, which need large quantities of labor for long periods, and migrancy was rational for large and specialized farms that needed large numbers of workers for short periods.

The migrant farm labor system depended on an army of workers willing to accommodate themselves to seasonality. Such workers were often hard to find in a society offering upward mobility. In the western states, seasonal workers were usually newcomers who could not find other jobs in the area. The key economic development in the rise of the migrant farm labor system was the completion of the transcontinental railroad in 1869, which lowered transportation costs and encouraged the switch from dryland grain production and cattle grazing to labor-intensive fruit crops, which could be dried or canned and transported to customers in the eastern parts of the country. At the time of the railroad's completion, the West was dominated by a small number of very large farms of a size suitable for dryland agriculture. It was anticipated that the number of farms and their size would change in the 1870s and 1880s because of the following: (1) it was assumed that only family farms could supply the seasonal labor needed for labor-intensive fruit farms; and (2) the Chinese Exclusion Act of 1882 was expected to end the supply of workers who had no other U.S. job options and thus were willing to work as migrant and seasonal farm labor.

Both of these assumptions proved false. Large farms were able to switch to labor-intensive fruit production by relying on waves of newcomers who had few other job options; the Chinese were followed by Japanese immigrants, Indians and Pakistanis, Mexicans, Dust Bowl migrants, and then Mexicans again. These waves of immigrant farmworkers—willing to work at relatively low wages whenever they were needed—held down farm production costs and raised the price of California farmland. In effect, the low wages paid to farmworkers were capitalized into higher land prices. Landowners whose wealth was increased by low farm wages strongly resisted any changes to immigration and labor policy that might raise wages and reduce land prices.

The United States came closest to changing the structure of western agriculture in the late 1930s, but the country opted instead for a guestworker program that became the basis for today's Mexico-U.S. migration. John Steinbeck's description of the life of Dust Bowl migrants in California in the 1930s (*Grapes of Wrath*, published in 1940) reportedly prompted President Franklin Roosevelt to say that "something must be done and done soon" about farm labor in California. A subcommittee of the U.S. Senate's Education and Labor Committee, chaired by Robert LaFollette, Jr. (R-WI), held hearings on the conditions of farmworkers and recommended an end to "agricultural exceptionalism," the tendency to exclude agriculture from labor law protections and obligations.

However, the outbreak of World War II interrupted any farm labor reforms and, in fact, allowed farmers to press for the importation of Mexican workers under a series of guestworker programs. Farm labor reformers opposed the importation of Mexican workers, but the farmers' pleas for labor to produce "food to win the war"[3]—in combination with foreign policy interests that wanted a guestworker program to enlist Mexico's support in the war effort—led to the Bracero program, an exception in immigration law for "native-born residents of North America, South America, and Central America, and the islands adjacent thereto, desiring to perform agricultural labor in the United States." Under various programs over the next twenty-two years, some

---

[3] In one carefully phrased summary of the need for additional labor in 1942, the Congressional Research Service (1980: 16) noted, "Many of the reports of [labor] shortages in specific areas were based, not so much on the inadequacy of a supply sufficient to maintain full production, as on inability to continue the peacetime methods of employment, with underemployment, and low wages."

4.6 million Mexicans were admitted temporarily to do farmwork, many of them returning year after year. In total, somewhere between one and two million Mexicans gained U.S. work experience as a result of their participation in the Bracero program.

As with most guestworker programs, the major effects of the Bracero program became apparent only over time. Three effects stand out:

First, legal Braceros were accompanied by illegal migrants and by a rise in legal immigration (see table 16.3). During the twenty-two years of Bracero programs, there were 4.6 million Bracero admissions and 5.3 million apprehensions (both data series count events, not individuals). Legal Mexican immigration rose from between 6,000 and 7,000 a year in the mid-1940s to 55,000 a year in the early 1960s.

Second, the availability of Braceros permitted the U.S. Southwest to become the country's garden. Although California fruit and vegetable production rose sharply in the 1950s, average farmworker earnings rose much more slowly than did factory wages: farmworkers' wages rose from $0.85 an hour in 1950 to $1.20 an hour in 1960; factory workers' wages rose from $1.60 to $2.60 over the same period; that is, during the 1950s, farm wages fell from 53 percent to 46 percent of factory wages.

Third, Braceros in the fields and a booming nonfarm economy changed the Mexican American population in the Southwest from a predominantly rural to a mostly urban population, reinforcing the truism that economic mobility required geographic mobility.

The Bracero program ended in 1964, ushering in a "golden age" that lasted until about 1980. During this golden age, farmworker earnings rose faster than construction workers' earnings, and there was a widespread expectation that the farm labor market would evolve like that in construction—that is, into a heavily unionized industry in which the union organized the seasonal labor market by operating hiring halls to deploy seasonal workers to farms as needed. César Chávez and the United Farm Workers (UFW) seemed to prove true this theory of inevitable and desired labor market evolution when in 1966 the UFW won a 40 percent wage increase (from at least $1.25 to $1.75 an hour) for many table grape pickers. However, this golden age for farmworkers began to fade in the early 1980s as a result of leadership fumbles within the UFW, a switch from Democratic to Republican governors in California (and concurrent changes in appointments to the board that administered the state farm labor relations law), rising illegal immigration, and a changing structure of agriculture as large growers realized they could hire farmworkers via intermediaries.

Table 16.3. Mexican Braceros, Apprehensions, and Immigrants: 1942–1964

	Bracero Admissions	Apprehensions	Mexican Immigrants
1943	52,098	11,175	4,172
1944	62,170	31,174	6,598
1945	49,454	69,164	6,702
1946	32,043	99,591	7,146
1947	19,632	193,657	7,558
1948	35,345	192,779	8,384
1949	107,000	288,253	8,803
1950	67,500	468,339	6,744
1951	192,000	509,040	6,153
1952	197,100	528,815	9,079
1953	201,380	885,587	17,183
1954	309,033	1,089,583	30,645
1955	398,650	254,096	43,702
1956	445,197	87,696	61,320
1957	436,049	59,918	49,321
1958	432,857	53,474	26,721
1959	437,643	45,336	22,909
1960	315,846	70,684	32,708
1961	291,420	88,823	41,476
1962	194,978	92,758	55,805
1963	186,865	88,712	55,986
1964	177,736	86,597	34,448
Total	4,646,199	5,307,035	545,941

Sources: Congressional Research Service 1980: 36–37. Total illegal Mexicans located and those in agriculture are from House of Representatives 1963: 47.

The major issue that would affect farmworker immigration and integration in the early 1980s was that of illegal immigration. The unauthorized share of the farm workforce was estimated to be about 25 percent in California (it was much lower elsewhere in the United States), but farmers opposed the "Grand Bargain"—employer sanctions to stop illegal immigration combined with amnesty for unauthorized foreigners—that was recommended by the Select Commission on Immigration and Refugee Policy in 1981. Fearing a shrinking pool of unauthorized farmworkers, farmers demonstrated that they could block this Grand Bargain in Congress unless they were assured a replacement supply of legal guestworkers.

Farmers persuaded Congress to approve guestworker programs in the House of Representatives (in 1984) and the Senate (in 1985), over the bitter objections of Representative Ron Mazzoli (D-KY) and Senator Alan Simpson (R-WY). These guestworker programs for agriculture would have allowed U.S. farmers to obtain legal guestworkers without U.S. Department of Labor (DOL) certification of a farmer's need for guestworkers on a job-by-job basis. The certification process allowed the DOL to control the border gate, permitted the government to require farmers to provide housing for guestworkers, and enabled the government to oblige farmers to hire U.S. workers, including union supporters.

IRCA: SAWS AND RAWS

The compromise that enabled passage of the Immigration Reform and Control Act of 1986 (IRCA) was reached in private negotiations in the summer of that year. The compromise contained two major elements: an easy legalization program for currently illegal workers (the Special Agricultural Worker, or SAW, program) and two guestworker programs through which farmers could obtain additional workers in the event of labor shortages. The latter provision included an H-2A certification program, under which farmers had to provide housing and demonstrate to the DOL's satisfaction that they had tried and failed to find U.S. workers, and a noncertification Replenishment Agricultural Worker (RAW) program that would allow foreign farmworkers to circulate within agricultural regions in the United States.[4]

A major goal of the SAW and RAW programs was to give agriculture a legal workforce, the theory being that legal workers would be more likely to join unions and press for wage increases at the bargaining table. The assumption was that, with stepped-up border control efforts and employer sanctions "closing the door" to unauthorized workers, U.S. farmers would have no choice but to raise wages and improve conditions if they wanted to retain legal workers.

IRCA's legalization programs, which legalized 2.7 million foreigners, were considered very successful, but border controls and employer sanctions failed to stop illegal immigration, largely because of inadequate enforcement at the workplace and the proliferation of false

[4] There were no farm labor shortages in the late 1980s and early 1990s, so this program never went into effect, and detailed regulations were not developed.

documents that illegal immigrants presented to would-be employers. The major legalization surprise was in the SAW program, which allowed unauthorized foreigners to become legal immigrants if they could prove that they had worked at least ninety days in agriculture in 1985–1986. There was no official estimate of the number of qualifying unauthorized farmworkers, but Congress and the U.S. Immigration and Naturalization Service (INS) accepted a U.S. Department of Agriculture estimate of 350,000 unauthorized farmworkers and made this number the maximum number of Group 1 SAWs who could obtain immigrant status.[5]

Even though it was widely asserted that only 15 to 20 percent of the undocumented workers in the United States in the mid-1980s were employed in agriculture, 1.3 million aliens applied for SAW status, or nearly three-fourths the number who applied for the general legalization program (1.8 million). These SAW applicants were mostly young Mexican men; their median age was twenty-four, and 82 percent were male (see table 16.4). In surveys, SAWs had an average education of five years and earned between $30 and $35 daily for 100 days of farmwork in 1985–1986, or between $3,000 and $3,500 a year.

Table 16.4. IRCA Legalization Applicants

Characteristic	LAW[1]	SAW[2]
Median age at entry	23	24
Applicants age 15 to 44 (%)	80	93
Male (%)	57	82
Married (%)	41	42
From Mexico (%)	70	82
Applied in California (%)	54	52
Total applicants	1,759,705	1,272,143

Source: INS 1991: 70–74.

Note: About 80,000 farmworkers received legal immigrant status under the pre-1982 legalization program.

[1] Persons filing I-687 legalization applications.

[2] Persons filing I-700 legalization applications.

[5] Group I SAWs did at least ninety days of SAS (seasonal agricultural services) work in each of the years ending, respectively, May 1, 1984, 1985, and 1986. Group II SAWs, by contrast, did ninety days of SAS work only in the year ending May 1, 1986. Over 90 percent of all SAW applicants were in the Group II category.

The SAW program was a turning point for immigration and integration in U.S. agriculture for two major reasons. First, the program was riddled with fraud. The estimate of 350,000 unauthorized farmworkers was probably closer to the true number of qualifying individuals than the 1.3 million applications or 1.2 million foreigners who became legal immigrants through the SAW program. Most SAW applicants submitted a letter with their application for legalization, often signed by a farm labor contractor, asserting that "Juan González picked tomatoes for me for ninety-two days in Salinas in 1986." Such a letter was sufficient to obtain an immigration visa, so that the SAW program taught a generation of farmworkers to use false documents to obtain immigration benefits.

Second, the SAW program had massive impacts in rural Mexico. There were only about six million adult men in rural Mexico in the mid-1980s, and the SAW program enabled about one million of them to become legal U.S. immigrants. Their family members were not legalized, however, because it was widely asserted that Mexican farmworkers simply wanted to cross the border legally; they did not want to move to the United States with their families. This stay-in-Mexico assumption proved false, as a combination of nonfarm job opportunities in the United States and changes in rural Mexico encouraged many SAWs to settle in the United States with their families.

THE QUEST FOR SEASONAL WORKERS

History is repeating itself in agriculture. Since 1986, labor-intensive agricultural production has expanded, especially in remote areas where there is little infrastructure for migrant workers, such as southwestern Florida (oranges) and central Washington (apples). Most of the SAWs, who were in their twenties in the late 1980s, have since moved out of farmwork, and the farm workforce is now about 55 percent unauthorized (see table 16.5). IRCA demonstrated that giving legal status to 1.2 million unauthorized "farmworkers" improved conditions and opportunities for many individuals, but it did not improve farmworker wages and working conditions relative to the nonfarm labor market.

IRCA created a Commission on Agricultural Workers (CAW) to review the effects of legalization and enforcement on the farm labor market. This commission, dominated by growers, listed three major findings in its 1992 report.

Table 16.5. SAWs and Unauthorized Crop Workers as Shares of the Farm Workforce, 1989–1998

	SAWs	Unauthorized Migrants
1989	37%	8%
1990	30	17
1991	27	19
1992	23	33
1993	12	44
1994	20	38
1995	19	40
1996	16	50
1997	17	51
1998	15	52

Source: Department of Labor, NAWS, various years.

First, virtually all SAW-eligible undocumented workers gained legal status, but so many other unauthorized individuals did so as well that the SAW program was "one of the most extensive immigration frauds ever perpetrated against the U.S. government." Second, CAW attributed the declining farm wages and working conditions observed in the early 1990s to a continued influx of illegal workers, and it called for stepped-up enforcement of U.S. immigration and labor laws. And third, the commission noted the widespread poverty of farmworkers and recommended more social services for farmworkers and their children, along with better enforcement of labor laws. But the commission divided on the question of ending agricultural exceptionalism; a majority of commissioners supported ending the patchwork quilt of immigration and labor exceptions for agriculture.

Farmers were disappointed that CAW did not recommend a continuation of the RAW program or a new guestworker program. However, there were few labor shortages in the early 1990s that could have justified such a program.

Beginning in 1995, western farm employers pressed for an alternative to the H-2A guestworker program that would impose fewer requirements on farmers. Farmers argued in congressional hearings that the H-2A program was "broken," as evidenced by the declining number of U.S. farm jobs certified by the DOL as needing to be filled with H-2A foreign workers. The low point was reached in 1995, the year after the Florida sugarcane harvest was mechanized (see table 16.6).

Table 16.6. H-2A Certifications, 1985–1999

	Workers			
Fiscal Year	Certified	Sugarcane	Tobacco	Sheep
1985	20,682	10,017	831	1,433
1986	21,161	10,052	594	1,043
1987	24,532	10,616	1,333	1,639
1988	23,745	10,751	2,795	1,655
1989	26,607	10,610	3,752	1,581
1990	25,412	9,550	4,666	1,677
1991	25,702	7,978	2,257	1,557
1992	18,939	4,271	3,080	1,522
1993	17,000	2,319	3,570	1,111
1994	15,811	1,419	3,720	1,305
1995	15,117		4,116	1,350
1996	19,103		9,756	1,366
1997	23,562		14,483	1,667
1998	34,898		16,984	1,961
1999	41,827			
2000	44,017			

Sources: Department of Labor, various years. H-2A Report, Annual, U.S. Department of Labor, Division of Foreign Labor Certifications

Notes: The sugarcane harvest was mechanized after 1995. The 1996 and 1997 tobacco certifications include some vegetable workers.

Farmers wanted a noncertification alternative to the H-2A program. Their cause was helped by sporadic enforcement efforts which made more credible the growers' argument (advanced via their Washington lobbyists) that a Republican-controlled Congress would be sympathetic to a new guestworker program. In 1997 a bill was introduced to create a 24-month pilot program, administered by the U.S. Department of Agriculture, for 25,000 temporary foreign agricultural workers a year. Employers could gain access to these workers by attesting that they had satisfied recruitment and wage obligations in a process similar to that used to admit H-1B workers. However, this push for a new guestworker program stalled when the General Accounting Office released a report in December 1997 that concluded that there was "no national agricultural labor shortage at this time" and that "a sudden, widespread farm labor shortage requiring the importation of large numbers of foreign workers is unlikely to occur in the near future."

Nevertheless, in July 1998 the Senate approved the Agricultural Job Opportunity Benefits and Security Act of 1998 (AgJOBS) on a 68–31 vote.[6] AgJOBS created a new guestworker program and got around the certification-attestation issue by ordering the creation of registries in each state that would register legally authorized farmworkers who were available to be deployed to fill seasonal farms jobs. Farmers would apply to the registry for workers, and the registry would refer the number of workers requested or certify that the farmer needed foreign workers. For example, if a farmer requested one hundred workers and only sixty were on the registry, the farmer would be certified to employ forty foreigners.

Under AgJOBS, as many foreign workers as needed to fill farmer request–registry gaps could enter the United States for up to ten months a year. If too many stayed longer than ten months, up to 20 percent of their earnings could be withheld, to be returned to the worker in Mexico when he surrendered his "counterfeit proof" identification card. AgJOBS eliminated the requirement that farm employers provide free housing to legal guestworkers; instead, farm employers had the option of providing a "housing allowance."

There was widespread opposition to AgJOBS. A majority of House members signed a letter asserting that AgJOBS "will only further burden our communities without providing a long-term solution to the labor needs of the agricultural industry." President Clinton threatened to veto the appropriations bill if it included AgJOBS, and so the program was removed. However, in 1999 some "immigration advocates" joined farm employers in advocating a new guestworker program. Farmers hired Rick Schwartz, founder of the National Immigration Forum, to find a compromise guestworker program. And Demetrios Papademetriou, of the Carnegie Endowment for International Peace and the Migration Policy Institute, recommended a guestworker program with most of the features that farmers desired, including a registry, a farmworker trust fund to encourage returns, and housing vouchers; the only pro-worker recommendation was for improved enforcement of labor laws in agriculture. Most farmworker advocates remained adamantly opposed to a new guestworker program, and their opposition, combined with the absence of farm labor shortages, prevented enactment of any new program in 1999 and 2000.

---

6 AgJOBS was attached to the Commerce-Justice-State Department appropriations bill.

The momentum for a new guestworker program continued to build as officials on both sides of the border expressed support for such a program. In October 1999 a new version of AgJOBS was introduced; S1814 was AgJOBS with an earned legalization program, and S1815 was an earned legalization program only. Earned legalization meant that unauthorized workers who could prove they did at least 150 days or 880 hours of farmwork in the twelve months ending October 27, 1999, could apply for new temporary resident status. In order to maintain this temporary resident status—and eventually convert it to an immigrant status—the temporary resident would have had to do at least 180 days of farmwork each year for five years and to have left the United States each year for at least 65 days. After receiving immigrant status, the immigrant worker could apply for immigration visas for his family.

If labor shortages developed, additional foreign workers would have been admitted under a revised H-2A program which would have eliminated most worker protections, including the requirement that farmers attempt to recruit U.S. workers under guidelines set by the DOL, that farmers guarantee work for at least three-fourths of the time they say they will need workers, and that farmers continue to hire U.S. workers who seek jobs until the work is at least 50 percent completed.

There were congressional hearings on a new guestworker program in 2000, but Representative Cal Dooley (D-CA) proved correct when he predicted in June 2000 that a new guestworker program for agriculture would be too controversial to win approval in an election year. During the congressional hearings, growers testified that there were no farm labor shortages—only shortages of "legally authorized" farmworkers. Farmers said they only became aware of the large numbers of unauthorized workers when they received letters from the Social Security Administration informing them of "mismatches" between their employees' names and the Social Security numbers they had provided; between 20 and 50 percent of their workers were potential mismatches.

In fall 2000, there was a renewed push for a new guestworker program. To head off this initiative, Secretary of Labor Alexis Herman sent a letter to congressional leaders, stating, "The President has been and remains opposed to establishing a new agricultural guestworker program.... If [AgJOBS] were presented to the President, I would recommend that he veto it." After the November 2000 elections, there was yet another push, and some worker advocates—noting that President Bush and Mexico's President Vicente Fox both favored a new guestworker program—thought they could get a better deal for farmworkers under President Clinton than Bush. They came close to agreement in the so-called December 2000 Compromise, which would have admitted additional guestworkers for agriculture under the current H-2A program, but it also would have frozen the adverse effect wage rate (AEWR)[7] for two or three years; given H-2A workers 25 percent of the Section 8 housing allowance for a region instead of free housing if the state governor certified there was sufficient housing available;[8] and granted temporary resident status to unauthorized farmworkers who did at least a hundred days of farmwork in the preceding eighteen months. If a probationary immigrant did at least 360 days of farmwork in the next six years, including 275 days in the first three years, he could obtain immigrant status.

Senator Phil Gramm (R-TX) blocked enactment of the December 2000 Compromise and called instead for a guestworker program that would not lead to the settlement of Mexican workers in the United States. Gramm's proposal marks one end of a spectrum with three major options: guestworkers only, legalization only, and guestworkers and legalization combined. Gramm's proposal would permit unauthorized Mexicans already in the United States to obtain seasonal or year-round work permits. Seasonal guestworkers could return to the United States indefinitely, while year-round workers could work in the United States for three consecutive years and then have to remain in Mexico for at least one year before returning. Gramm's proposal would give unauthorized workers and their U.S. employers six months to register for the new program, and then enforcement of employer sanctions laws would be stepped up and penalties for employing unauthorized workers would increase. The 15.3 percent of wages that employers and workers paid for Social Security would be diverted to a fund to provide emergency medical care for guestworkers, with the balance placed in individual IRA-type funds that Mexican workers would receive when they return to Mexico and give up their work permits.

The other extreme, legalization only, is favored by the AFL-CIO and most immigrant advocates. The AFL-CIO called for a general legaliza-

[7] The adverse effect wage rate is the average hourly earnings of crop and livestock workers as measured in a USDA survey of farm employers the preceding year.

[8] Section 8 fair market rents in California farming areas range from $400 a month for a one-bedroom unit in the cheapest areas to $600 or more for a two-bedroom unit, suggesting that farmers would provide $100 to $150 a month as a housing allowance.

tion program for unauthorized foreigners in the United States but no new guestworker program. Union representatives met with Representative Luis V. Gutiérrez (D-IL) who, on February 7, 2001, introduced HR 500, the U.S. Employee, Family Unity and Legalization Act, which would grant temporary legal status to persons in the United States prior to February 6, 2000, and immediate immigrant status to persons in the United States before February 6, 1996. The legalization date would then roll forward one year in each of the next five years, eventually encompassing all of those now in the country illegally.

The third option was the December 2000 Compromise, supported by Senator Bob Graham (D-FL), Representative Howard Berman (D-CA), and Senator Gordon Smith (R-OR), as well as the United Farm Workers and the National Council of Agricultural Employers. The Compromise includes the AgJOBS legalization program, but it maintains most of the worker protections under the current H-2A program. The Compromise would do the following:

- Grant temporary resident alien status to unauthorized farmworkers who could prove that they did at least a hundred days of farmwork during one of the two seasons prior to the law's passage.[9] Temporary resident aliens could enter and exit the United States and work in most U.S. jobs, but they could not receive welfare benefits. After satisfying a three-part farmwork test, temporary resident aliens (and their families) could become immigrants in five to six years.[10]
- Admit additional farmworkers under a revised version of the H-2A program, whose major features include attestation replacing certification (government-supervised recruitment), freezing the adverse

[9] Unauthorized workers would apply to the INS directly or via "qualified designated entities." After receiving temporary resident alien status, the worker's family illegally in the United States could not be deported if located by the INS, but family members also would not receive work authorization. Family members could become legal immigrants along with the farmworker head of household without regard to per-country waiting lists or queues.

[10] Temporary resident aliens could become immigrants if they: (1) did at least 360 days in agriculture within about 5.5 years, (2) did at least 240 of those farm workdays during the first three years of the program, and (3) did at least 75 days of farmwork per year in each of at least three years. The temporary alien workers could also do nonfarm work, but it would not count toward immigrant status. Farm employers would be required to provide both temporary resident aliens and the INS with employee work histories.

effect wage rate at 2000 levels for at least three years,[11] and allowing farmers in states in which governors certify that there is sufficient housing to provide nonlocal U.S. and H-2A workers with a housing allowance instead of free housing.[12] Most H-2A requirements do not apply if the employer has a collective bargaining agreement with a union.

Regardless of which approach or combination of approaches is enacted, there is little prospect that immigrant farmworkers will be integrated into agriculture, replacing farmers who retire. Instead, agriculture appears likely to remain a port of entry for immigrants with little education. Most will remain seasonal workers for ten to twenty years, and then they and their children will seek nonfarm jobs. Most new farmworkers are drawn from the ranks of the rural poor abroad. If the U.S. mobility escalator works as well in the twenty-first century as it did in the twentieth, immigrant farmworkers and their children will enjoy upward mobility when they leave the rural and agricultural areas that drew them into the United States. If the mobility escalator does not work as well and farmworkers remain in rural and agricultural areas, the United States may, through immigration, convert rural Mexican poverty into rural American poverty (Martin 1999; Taylor, Martin, and Fix 1997).

CONCLUSION

Rural and agricultural areas have emerged as important ports of entry to the United States, especially for immigrants from rural and agricultural areas abroad, and rural Mexicans often begin their American journey in the fields and in farm-related industries such as meat and poultry processing. For much of the twentieth century, rural America was associated with poverty.[13] However, rural poverty was sharply

---

[11] Under the current and compromise H-2A programs, farmers who want to employ H-2A workers must pay the higher of three wage rates: the federal or state minimum wage, the local prevailing wage for the particular job, or the adverse effect wage rate. AEWRs in 2000 were between $6.50 and $7.00 an hour.

[12] If the governor of the state certifies that there is adequate housing available for U.S. and H-2A farmworkers in the area, employers may provide a housing allowance of at least 25 percent of the fair market rental for HUD Section 8 housing, assuming two bedrooms and two workers per bedroom.

[13] Michael Harrington's *The Other America*, which describes rural poverty, is often credited with launching the U.S. War on Poverty.

reduced in the 1960s, largely due to rural-urban migration; an average of one million farm residents left the farm each year during the 1960s.

Mechanization and the consolidation of farming into fewer and larger units were expected to make the farm labor market much like other U.S. labor markets that hire largely unskilled workers. Analysts predicted a significant role for unions and collective bargaining in a mechanized production system in which workers would spend a career. For a time in the 1970s it appeared that agriculture was indeed coming to resemble other U.S. labor markets, with ports of entry, job ladders, and assertions that there was a need for brains, not brawn.

During the 1980s and 1990s, the farm labor market reversed direction, reverting to the more familiar revolving door with layers of intermediaries between farmworkers and farm operators. There were many reasons for this reversal—ending an era of personnel managers, written employment applications, and collective bargaining—but two reasons stand out: (1) changes in the food system that push profits forward toward food retailers and direct risk and pressure to reduce costs back toward farmers, and (2) increased illegal immigration from Mexico.

As companies such as United Brands and Dole sold their own farming operations and began to buy produce from farmers to supply to food retailers, unions lost the ability to bargain with companies accustomed to collective bargaining. Instead, the unions often found themselves dealing with operators who leased land and used labor contractors and other intermediaries to obtain seasonal workers as needed. Farm operators were able to play these intermediaries against each other, especially after their ranks were swelled by the SAW program. The result was that "direct hire" farmworker employment in California fell, and indirect employment through intermediaries, many of whom hired unauthorized workers, rose.

Farm leaders dealing with labor supply issues began to see labor availability much like water availability. Most fruit and vegetable farms are irrigated, and there are two major options for assuring sufficient water. The first is to work collectively to "develop" the water supply—to ensure that dams are built to store water and that canals can deliver water where needed so that all farmers have sufficient water. If water is plentiful and sufficiently cheap, sloped fields can simply be flooded until the excess drains off. The second option is to minimize the amount of water needed by installing drip irrigation systems. This involves laying plastic pipes throughout fields to deliver water and fertilizer to each plant. Far less water is needed, but installing a drip irrigation system requires a significant up-front investment.

During the 1970s, rising farm wages and benefits encouraged a "drip-type" approach to farm labor. Many large farmers hired personnel managers, and others formed labor co-ops in which hiring and deployment were handled by professionals. One result was the settlement of farmworkers with their families in agricultural communities. However, these settled workers aged out of seasonal farmwork, which was not mechanized in the 1980s, to be replaced in the fields by young and often unauthorized workers.

If the status quo continues, rural America's likely future may already be visible in the agricultural areas of California. In the three leading farm counties of the United States—Fresno, Tulare, and Kern, with combined farm sales of $9 billion in 1999—socioeconomic indicators suggest that between 30 and 40 percent of residents have incomes below the poverty line, 15 to 25 percent receive welfare assistance, and 10 to 20 percent are unemployed (Taylor and Martin 2000).

These data suggest that first-generation immigrants pick fruits and vegetables seasonally as needed for about ten years. However, when they age out of the seasonal farm workforce, they have few skills that might enable them to climb the farm or nonfarm job ladders. If they remain in the area, they tend to be poor and often jobless. Their U.S.-educated children tend to reject seasonal farm jobs; and if they remain in the area, they are often poor and on welfare. Thus the guestworker choices made in 2001 will shape immigration and integration policy, as well as the socioeconomic fabric of rural and urban America, for decades to come.

References

Census Bureau. 1999. *Statistical Abstract of the United States*. Washington, D.C.: U.S. Department of Commerce, Economics and Statistics Administration, U.S. Census Bureau.

Congressional Research Service. 1980. "Temporary Worker Programs: Background and Issues." Prepared for the Senate Committee on the Judiciary. February.

Department of Agriculture, National Agricultural Statistics Service. 1997. *Census of Agriculture 1997*. Washington, D.C.: U.S. Government Printing Office.

Department of Labor. 2000. *Findings from the National Agricultural Workers Survey (NAWS) 1997–1998*. Washington, D.C.: U.S. Department of Labor, Office of the Assistant Secretary for Policy, Office of Program Economics.

———. Various years. National Agricultural Workers Survey (NAWS). U.S. Department of Labor, Office of Program Economics.

———. Various years. H-2A Report. U.S. Department of Labor, Division of Foreign Labor Certifications.

Harrington, Michael. 1968 [c1962]. *The Other America*. New York: Macmillan.

House of Representatives, Committee on Agriculture. 1963. Extend the Mexican Farm Labor Program: Hearing before the Subcommittee on Equipment, Supplies, and Manpower. Eighty-eighth Congress, 1st session. Washington, D.C.: U.S. Government Printing Office.

INS (U.S. Immigration and Naturalization Service). 1991. *1991 Statistical Yearbook of the Immigration and Naturalization Service*. Washington, D.C.: U.S. Department of Justice, Immigration and Naturalization Service.

Martin, Philip L. 1999. "Emigration Dynamics in Mexico: The Case of Agriculture." In *Mexico, Central America and the Caribbean*, edited by Reginald Appleyard. *Emigration Dynamics in Developing Countries*, vol. 3. Brookfield, Vt.: Ashgate. At http://www.ashgate.com.

Taylor, J. Edward, and Philip L. Martin. 2000. "California's New Rural Poverty," *California Agriculture* 54, no. 1: 26–32. At http://danr.ucop.edu/calag.

Taylor, J. Edward, Philip Martin, and Michael Fix. 1997. *Poverty amid Prosperity: Immigration and the Changing Face of Rural California*. Washington, D.C.: Urban Institute Press. At http://www.urban.org.

17

Triangular Human Capital Flows: Empirical Evidence from Hong Kong and Canada

DON J. DEVORETZ, JOHN MA, AND KENNY ZHANG

A literature emerged in the early 2000s that argued that the "brain drain" was being replaced by a "brain exchange" (DeVoretz and Ma n.d.; Anderson and Konrad 2001a, 2001b). This brain exchange implied that highly skilled immigrants were now often highly skilled temporary movers with a strategic plan. In the first instance these immigrants choose to acquire their education at home (often in a less developed country) or, perhaps more likely, move to a developed country that supplies subsidized education (Zhang 2001). After spending time in the developed country to gain education or job experience, they make a second locational choice: to remain, to return home, or to move on to a third country. Unlike the traditional neoclassical migration model, which argued that a highly skilled immigrant only returned home if he/she were disappointed, this new literature argued that the temporary movement of the highly skilled was part of an investment process that improved the immigrant's lifetime income.[1] Borjas and Bratsberg (1996) first formally challenged the neoclassical failure hypothesis by presenting a model that allowed temporary highly skilled immigrants to accumulate human capital in the destination country and then return home with this capital in order to improve their earnings. DeVoretz

[1] In fact, history has shown that 30 percent or more of North American immigrants returned in the twentieth century.

and Iturralde (2000a, 2000b) extended this argument by adding life-cycle features of the household (marital status, age, and dependents) to the simple earnings argument to predict whether highly skilled immigrants would stay or leave after they had obtained their education abroad. Finally, DeVoretz and Ma (2002) brought these various arguments together and added the role of the state to model and predict the complex movement patterns, or brain exchange, for a representative highly skilled immigrant household. The purpose of this chapter is to add empirical content to the DeVoretz-Ma model by adding stylized facts and testing the prediction of the triangular movement model for one important case—namely, the movement between Hong Kong–Canada and the rest of the world (ROW).

The organization of the chapter is as follows. We first outline the reasons why the triangular flow phenomenon is of interest and, in particular, the importance of the Hong Kong–Canada–ROW example. Next we briefly outline the model and its major hypotheses. Then, with the aid of the 2000 Hong Kong census, we document the triangular nature of Hong Kong's recent immigration-emigration patterns for the highly skilled. Finally, we present some econometric evidence to support the DeVoretz-Ma model.

The DeVoretz-Ma model argues that human capital transfers are part of a general global system that transfers human capital from sending countries such as India-China (including Hong Kong) to entrepôt countries (Canada and Europe), and then on to the rest of the world (United States).[2] In particular, immigrants enter an entrepôt country because it supplies subsidized human capital and other free public goods. DeVoretz and Ma further argue that Canada is an excellent entrepôt example, given its unique immigration and integration policies and its strategic geographical location.[3] In turn, these immigrants, after a period of stay in the entrepôt country, make a decision to either return to their source country or stay in their original entrepôt destina-

---

[2] An entrepôt country is one in which traditionally exported goods are held in storage to be re-exported at a later date. Thus Singapore and Hong Kong were traditional entrepôt centers. In this context, an entrepôt country is an immigrant-receiving country that provides human capital to the immigrant before she/he emigrates.

[3] McInnis (2001) argues persuasively that Canada's emigration experience in the last half of the nineteenth century can be partially characterized by this entrepôt model for its nineteenth-century semiskilled and skilled labor movement from Canada to the United States. Dales (1964) also presented a similar model for early-twentieth-century flows from Canada and the United Kingdom to the United States.

tion country or move to a third destination (ROW).[4] Major issues arise in the Canadian or entrepôt context from this complex trilateral movement of the highly skilled. For example, is Canada or any entrepôt country simply participating in a zero (or negative) sum game? In other words, do the immigrant arrivals to Canada just offset (or not) the loss of highly skilled Canadian émigrés to the United States and the ROW?[5] Do the highly skilled immigrants that remain in Canada have an inferior (superior) skill set when compared to those immigrants who return or move on to the rest of the world?[6] Furthermore, what are the roles, respectively, of the entrepôt labor market and its immigration (emigration) policies in sorting the immigrants into non-movers or movers after they arrive in the entrepôt country?[7]

Implications of this triangular human capital transfer on the sending region (Hong Kong) can also be profound. For example, how long will it take before a reverse flow occurs from the entrepôt country to the original source country? Moreover, what fraction of the original leavers will return home and why? Finally, as noted above, are these returnees the most or the least able of the highly skilled?

TRIANGULAR HUMAN CAPITAL TRANSFER

In order to draw explicit hypotheses from this stylized view of the world, we present figure 17.1, which schematically reproduces the potential movement pattern outlined above. In this figure, we argue that there initially exists a prototypical sending region (Hong Kong) and three possible receiving regions: an entrepôt destination (Canada), the United States, and, after a period abroad, the home or sending region.

---

4 Canada is one example of an entrepôt country. Others include Israel, Ireland, Germany, the United Kingdom, and perhaps the entire European Union.

5 Israel could be another zero-sum case. Here Russian émigrés may be replacing Sabra (native-born) Israelis who have left for the rest of the world.

6 This model is capable of predicting the skill level of the movers and stayers if we visualize the state as a tax agent who provides services to its immigrant clients. Borrowing on the work of Epstein, Hillman, and Ursprung (1999), if the Emperor (or state) redistributes benefits away from the highly skilled and the lobbying costs are too high to recover these lost benefits, then the highly skilled will leave. DeVoretz and Iturralde 2000a, with its stayer model, empirically tests and confirms the existence of sorting in the Canadian context circa 1992–1996.

7 ROW countries are characterized by a lack of agents. Since these states provide no services, their tax rates are low, and those emigrants who expect an extremely high income will leave the entrepôt country for the ROW. This argument is embedded in Borjas and Bratsberg's model (1996) and simply extended here.

Figure 17.1. Triangular Human Capital Transfers

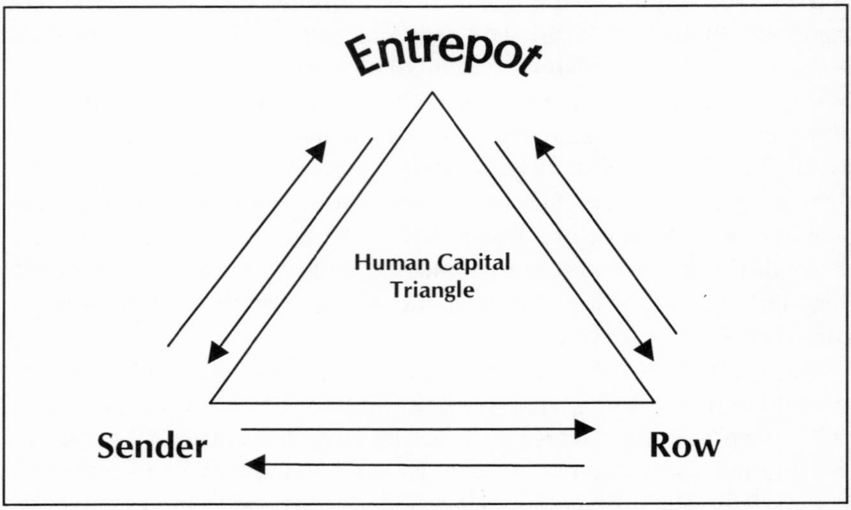

Furthermore, we note that three movement options exist for each emigrant after the initial move to the entrepôt country while in residence in the entrepôt country.[8] These options include staying permanently in the new entrepôt country (Canada), returning to the origin country (Hong Kong), or moving on to a third country (ROW). Permutations of this three-stage movement become complex when multiple moves are considered.[9] However, first we must recognize that the vast majority of highly trained people do not emigrate from the original sending region. Thus a fundamental question arises: how does the sorting mechanism, which allocates non-movers and leavers within the sending country, work? To answer these questions we formulate a three-stage model. In the first stage we model who stays in the origin country and why. Zhang (2001) argues that students leave the origin

[8] This model contains two periods since agents in the entrepôt destination country must equip the immigrant arrivals with human capital and offer a public good that will influence the immigrant's decision to stay or move on in the second period.

[9] For example, the initial movement from the sending country to the entrepôt country can next result in an onward move to the rest of the world, followed by a final move back to the original sending country. This example essentially describes some recent Hong Kong émigrés to Canada, who originally came from Mainland China (the PRC) and, after their stay in Canada, returned to Hong Kong as Canadian citizens. They now are easily able to enter China, their original sending country, as Canadian citizens resident in Hong Kong.

country to train in an entrepôt destination in order to maximize their returns for an educational investment. DeVoretz and Iturralde (2000a) postulate that demographic arguments after arrival in the entrepôt country and the provision of public goods condition the probability that a highly skilled worker will stay in a developed country. For example, university education, health care, and subsidized day care are all conferred on the immigrant household in an entrepôt country when the highly skilled head is middle-aged with children. These transfers will reduce the probability of movement.

Finally, the decision to stay or move is determined by several agents introduced in our model. These agents include: the role of the Emperor (state) in the country of origin and two immigrant settlement agents in the entrepôt country.[10] In short, we assert that each agent, in either the sending or entrepôt country, dispenses gifts or services on a stayer or a potential mover that influence their decision to stay, move on, or return to the original sending country given their stage in the life cycle. We outline below the various agents' roles in both the sending and entrepôt countries.

Emperor and Emigrants

Epstein, Hillman, and Ursprung (1999) note that the role of the Emperor—typically in the origin country—is to raise taxes, which in turn allows him to dispense favors to cliques within his society. These favored cliques in turn must lobby the Emperor to ensure that they continue to receive these gifts and pay the minimum taxes for these benefits. Under these conditions of uncertainty, if the Emperor introduces a mobility option, the highly skilled will leave if the Emperor's reward to the prospective émigré is less than his/her time cost of lobbying and taxes paid.[11]

But the role of the Emperor in conditioning mobility does not stop here, after the skilled subject has decided to emigrate or stay. The Emperor can control the exit conditions of his subjects and their subse-

[10] Epstein, Hillman, and Ursprung (1999) also argue that, in the context of a poor sending country, the probability of moving is a function of the state's (or Emperor's) willingness to confer benefits on or tax the highly skilled.

[11] This leads, of course, to the question of why the Emperor would ever permit the highly skilled to leave. We return to that question later; we simply note here that the omnipotent Emperor would only confer mobility rights to the resident highly skilled population if there exists a high enough probability of return migration by a sufficient number of the best of the highly skilled émigrés.

quent return conditions after their stay in the entrepôt country. In sum, the Emperor's actions can condition who initially stays at home, who leaves the Kingdom, and who returns to the Kingdom after leaving.

Agents in the Entrepôt Country

After the immigrants enter the entrepôt country, two types of agents—private and public—appear in two subperiods. The private or volunteer settlement agent offers the recent arrival specific human capital in the first period, while a government agent offers a public good with positive externalities in the second period.

Period 1: Settlement Worker

After arrival, the recent immigrant is offered subsidized general human capital training (language, knowledge of labor market channels, cultural conventions) and specific human capital (programming skills, retraining for certification, access to modern technology) by a settlement worker. The agent's goal in this case is to increase the probability of staying for the recent immigrant at the end of the first period.[12] As Borjas and Bratsberg (1996) have shown, acquisition of different types of specific human capital can increase the probability that a portion of the highly skilled immigrant arrivals will leave (or stay in) the entrepôt country. Thus this settlement worker's activity can perversely affect the staying probability and, in addition, may produce distributional consequences on the quality of those who stay and those who leave. In sum, the settlement worker's activities in period 1 can increase (decrease) the probability of staying (leaving) for the best (or weakest) immigrant arrivals. Moreover, only one outcome in three (at the end of period 1)—namely, staying—is the preferred goal of the settlement agent.[13]

---

[12] The settlement worker by definition provides human capital to increase the productivity of all immigrant arrivals in the entrepôt society and reduce the risk of return migration. Settlement workers may also have altruistic motives, namely, to ease the immigrant's integration into society. However, in entrepôt countries such as Australia, Canada, Germany, and especially Israel, government subsidies to private altruistic agencies are predicated on increasing the staying probability of the recent arrival and increasing the immigrant's contribution to society. To this extent this governmental motive is not altruistic.

[13] The other two outcomes are inferior for the settlement worker, but not necessarily so for the potential émigré. In addition, the model predicts that only those types of human capital acquisition that enhance the rate of return in the entrepôt country relative to the ROW or sending region will enhance the probability of staying in the entrepôt country. In the Canadian context, human capital acquisition to be

Period 2: Public Agent

If the immigrant chooses to stay for a second period in the entrepôt country, a public agent appears and confers on the immigrant a public good that offers free rider benefits—namely, citizenship. If the immigrant remains in the entrepôt country in period 2 and ascends to citizenship, then the immigrant's job market widens and the mobility costs of moving to the rest of the world fall.[14] For example, a Hong Kong immigrant to Canada who eventually acquires Canadian citizenship is then free to work in the United States or move on to a third country.

At this point in period 2 the Emperor in the original sending country can reappear and raise the costs of the entrepôt immigrant's departure to the rest of the world in period 2, and influence the potential émigré's probability of returning home.[15] The Emperor, of course, can induce return migration and deflect a potential move to the ROW by acting in a positive fashion and conferring a unique set of benefits on the potential émigré after he/she acquires citizenship in the entrepôt country and returns home. For example, Lam (2000) points out that there is a recent shortage of highly skilled workers in Hong Kong, and the government proposes favorable policies to induce well-trained former emigrants to return. Also, Ma (2000) suggests that the return of emigrants in the face of financial crisis can be partly explained by the resulting ongoing economic restructuring, which speeds up the opening of new sectors and hence attracts previous emigrants who have acquired relevant human capital from developed countries. Thus it is all a matter of which policy, punitive or benign, appears to be the most

---

exploited in the Canadian economy is the central investment provided by the agent in period 1. Examples of the agents' activities include: access to labor market information, validation of certificates, recognition of professional credentials, and language training (English and French).

[14] The mobility costs for Chinese immigrants living in Canada without Canadian citizenship are the waiting and legal costs to obtain a permanent visa (E type) for the United States. These are considerable costs since the waiting period may be indefinite. However, with Canadian citizenship, a NAFTA visa can be obtained immediately. Furthermore, there is no queue for the NAFTA visa, and thus the probability of entry is certain if limited side conditions are met.

[15] If the Emperor cashes in the bond that is held at home, or more punitively revokes the emigrant's citizenship in the home country upon citizenship acquisition in the entrepôt country, the probability of leaving for the rest of the world is reduced. A variation of this behavior arises when the entrepôt or receiving country confers citizenship on the immigrant and requires that he/she renounce home country citizenship. Germany and the United States currently do this; Canada does not.

efficient mechanism a priori to the Emperor to induce return migration of the very highly skilled from the entrepôt country.

In sum, the model at this stage can predict the probability of staying in the entrepôt country—Canada—after Canadian agents provide human capital and a public good in periods 1 and 2. Now any outcome in period 2 in the entrepôt destination is possible, with either highly skilled or less skilled people staying or the best of the highly skilled returning home or moving on to the rest of the world as a consequence of these entrepôt agents' actions. What ultimately determines whether immigrants stay in the entrepôt destination or move on is the rate of return of their acquired capital in Canada, the ROW, or home.

Period 3: Rest of the World and Beyond

A subset of the immigrants who leave the entrepôt country at the end of period 2 after gaining entrepôt citizenship do not return home. Rather, they opt to move on to the rest of the world or, more likely, to the United States. The choice to move on to the United States depends on the risk aversion of the mover and the visa available to him or her. Details of the underlying theory behind this third choice are complex and not germane to our case study of Canada–Hong Kong (they appear in DeVoretz and Ma n.d.). Some summary observations can still be made about the decision to leave the entrepôt country for the ROW.

In the case where the potential pool of émigrés from the entrepôt destination to the ROW is risk neutral, both the number and quality of leavers can now be determined. At the first stage of residence in the entrepôt country, the highly skilled immigrant will only leave for the ROW if his or her reservation wage in the entrepôt country is at least matched by the expected income gain earned by moving to the ROW.[16] The stylized facts reported by DeVoretz and Iturralde (2000a) indicate that the actual population at risk of moving will be relatively young, small in size relative to the immigrant cohort in the entrepôt country, and have an extensive prior mobility experience.[17]

Based upon the above stylized triangular human capital transfer model, a number of hypotheses appear to forecast who is more likely to stay or leave Hong Kong, why they leave for an entrepôt destination, and their motivation to return to Hong Kong:

---

[16] As DeVoretz and Iturralde (2000a) have shown, this is a small percentage of the stock of potential movers—approximately 5 to 20 percent.

[17] These conditions either increased the probable income gain from a move or lowered the mobility costs of movement.

- Hypothesis 1: People leave Hong Kong to acquire human capital. In other words, the non-mover in Hong Kong will have less human capital than the leaver—the returnee and the Hong Kong–born stayer in the entrepôt destination.
- Hypothesis 2: The motivation to return to Hong Kong is to earn a greater rate of return on acquired human capital in Hong Kong than can be obtained in the entrepôt destination.
- Hypothesis 3: In order to maximize their lifetime return to acquired human capital, the higher the human capital level and the younger the age, the more likely a person will return.

The choice of Hong Kong as the first test case for this triangular model is easy to rationalize. Hong Kong's recent political history, limited access to higher education, and structural changes in its economy all point to push and pull forces that have first propelled and then attracted back its skilled population. A brief history follows. Large-scale movement of Hong Kong immigrants to Canada[18] predated the 1997 transition to a special administrative region. After 1997 the movement of Hong Kong émigrés to Canada stopped, leaving a large stock of Hong Kong residents in Canada who were now eligible to attain Canadian citizenship. Next, Hong Kong's tertiary educational system has been limited, which has sent students abroad or enticed parents to move to Canada (and the United States) to access education for their children. Finally, Hong Kong has transformed its economic structure from a trading and manufacturing base to a financial and high-technology center, which has increased the demand for skilled workers abroad.

TESTING THE HONG KONG, CANADA, AND "ROW" CASE

Given these stylized facts, which describe a very robust immigration and emigration history, this section employs census data to confirm the model's predictions about the human capital and demographic profiles of Hong Kong mover-leaver populations. Then we compare the earnings across non-movers, returnees, and stayers in the destination country to see if the model's predictions are confirmed.

---

[18] A total of 342,456 immigrants arrived in Canada from Hong Kong in the 1985–2000 period; 90 percent of them (305,599) arrived before 1997 (CIC, various years).

Data and Some Definitions

Data utilized in this chapter were obtained from special runs of the 2001 Hong Kong census (Department of Census and Statistics, Hong Kong Special Administrative Region, PRC), unless otherwise specified. We had access to the complete census, which included 6,423,591 cases in total.[19] The data set contained information on person's place of birth, place of residence five years previous (1996), and place of residence at the time of the census (2001). Therefore, in this chapter, non-movers, migrants, and stayers are defined by their answers to Hong Kong census questions. For the Canadian portion of the essay, the 1996 census public use microdata file is used for comparisons to the Hong Kong census. Given these data sets, we define four distinct groups:

- Non-movers: people who were born in Hong Kong and did not migrate from Hong Kong; that is, people whose place of residence was the same at all three points in time.
- Returnees: people who were born in Hong Kong, Macao, or Mainland China and out-migrated before 1996 but returned to Hong Kong between 1996 and 2001; that is, people whose place of birth was either Hong Kong, Macao, or Mainland China and place of residence in 2001 was Hong Kong, but whose place of residence in 1996 was none of the above three regions.
- Migrants: people who migrated to Hong Kong either before 1996 or between 1996 and 2001; that is, people whose place of birth was not Hong Kong, but whose place of residence in 1996 and/or 2001 was Hong Kong.
- Canadian immigrant stayers: people who were born in Hong Kong and were resident in Canada in 1996.

These definitions are summarized in table 17.1. Definitions of the remaining variables are taken directly from the Hong Kong 2001 census coding classification, which is available upon request.

In order to answer the questions regarding who returns and why, we compare the socioeconomic characteristics of non-movers to returnees, other migrants, and immigrant stayers in Canada, with the Hong Kong non-movers as the reference group. This decomposition will allow us to better understand differences in both human capital and

[19] This is derived from the long census form samples, which consist of one-seventh of the total population in Hong Kong.

earnings profiles between the mover (including returnee and stayer at destination) and non-mover groups. Because our model argues that returnees are a special case of movers, we will also draw comparisons between different movers (returnees and other migrants). In particular, we will distinguish between migrants from Mainland China and from other more developed or less developed countries to complete the picture of movement into Hong Kong. Finally, given the theory presented in this chapter, we will look at returnees in a more in-depth manner by comparing Hong Kong returnees from Canada and immigrant stayers in Canada, as well as comparing returnees from Canada with those returned from the United States and other countries. Tables 17.2 and 17.3 report the characteristics of non-movers, returnees, and other migrants circa 2001.

Table 17.1. Definitions of Mobility Status

	At Birth	1996	2001
Non-mover	1	1	1
Returnee	1	0	1
Migrant (previous)	0	1	1
Migrant (recent)	0	0	1
Stayer in Canada	1	0	NA

Note: 1 = Yes (at the time when the place of residence was Hong Kong, Macao, and Mainland China). 0 = No.
NA = Not available.

Human Capital Characteristics

We first report the human capital characteristics for each defined mover or stayer group. These human capital characteristics refer to educational attainment and occupational skill levels, as well as other demographic indicators. The inclusion of demographic indicators, such as age and gender, will help us to demonstrate the life-cycle nature of capturing the rewards from human capital accumulation and migration as predicted by our model.

As shown in tables 17.2 and 17.3, 92 percent of the total population in Hong Kong consists of non-movers, while returnees and outside migrants compose 1.3, 4.0, 2.0, and 0.9 percent, respectively, of the Hong Kong population. This conforms to the model's proposition that

Table 17.2. Attributes of Non-movers and Returnees in Hong Kong

					Migrants from:		
	Total	All	Non-movers	Returnees	Mainland	LDCs[1]	MDCs[2]
		6,423,591 (100.0%)	5,898,35 (91.8%)	85,793 (1.3%)	254,620 (4.0%)	129,189 (2.0%)	55,638 (0.9%)
Age							
0–19	1,279,908	19.9	19.5	9.6	41	3.9	20.5
20–29	994,949	15.5	14.5	37.8	12	52.4	20.9
30–39	1,265,627	19.7	19.1	23.3	22.5	32.9	36.3
40–49	1,206,450	18.8	19.3	14.4	13.5	8.6	14.4
50–59	676,287	10.5	11	7.3	5.6	1.8	5.4
60 +	1,000,370	15.6	16.6	7.5	5.5	0.5	2.6
Sex							
Female	3,287,782	51.2	49.7	49.9	64.9	92.5	54.6
Male	3,135,809	48.8	50.3	50.1	35.1	7.5	45.4
Relation to head of household							
Head	2,096,185	32.6	34.1	34	12.3	4.7	36.6
Spouse	1,346,710	21	21	17.2	29.2	4.7	21.3
Children	2,354,072	36.6	36.9	37.8	50.3	3.5	24.2
Maid	180,164	2.8	1.1	0.1	0.1	83.5	12.5
Other	446,460	7.0	6.9	10.9	8.1	3.6	5.4
Education							
Primary school or less	2,234,765	34.8	35	10.7	52	16	18.3
Secondary school, diploma	3,480,396	54.1	54.9	36.5	43.2	66.8	31.2
Local university degree	401,373	6.3	6.5	14.7	1.5	0.4	4.7
Overseas degree	307,057	4.7	3.7	38.1	3.3	16.8	45.7

Occupation (income > 0)							
Low skill	179,737	68.4	67.9	26.7	85.9	96.9	31.5
Assistant professional	349,606	15.3	15.9	30.8	5.5	0.9	15.7
Professional	2,220,192	5.5	5.4	21.1	1.7	0.8	18
Managerial	498,542	10.8	10.8	21.3	6.9	1.4	34.8
Total	3,248,077	100	100	100	100	100	100
Income from main employment (income > 0)							
0–5,999	622,594	19.1	15.8	5.3	42.7	92.4	24.1
6,000–9,999	793,042	24.4	25.4	11.8	35.8	2.7	4.5
10,000–14,999	742,635	22.9	24.1	24.4	10.5	1.9	7.7
15,000–19,999	370,862	11.4	12	15.9	3.8	0.7	6.8
20,000--29,999	362,154	11.1	11.7	16.5	3.7	0.7	11.5
> = 30,000	356,790	11	10.9	26.2	3.6	1.6	45.4
Total	3,248,077	100	100	100	100	100	100
Median income (HK$/month)		10,000.00	10,500.00	16,520.38	6,000.00	3,671.00	25,000.00
Mean income (HK$/month)		15,812.00	15,972.00	25,543.01	9,084.50	5,227.70	39,310.00
Gini coefficient[3]		27.21	26.62	11.96	23.23	46.47	4.48

Source: 2001 census data, Department of Census and Statistics, Hong Kong SAR, PRC.

[1] LDC = less developed country.

[2] MDC = more developed country.

[3] Authors' calculation.

Table 17.3. Attributes of Returnees to Hong Kong and Stayers in Canada: Hong Kong–Born

	Returnee to Hong Kong from:					Hong Kong–born Stayer in Canada*	
	All		Canada	United States	Other		
Total	85,793	100.0%	33,676 (39.3%)	17,778 (20.7%)	34,339 (40.0%)	6,955	100.0
Age							
0–19	8,236	9.6	9.4	4.4	11.1	1,506	21.7
2–29	32,430	37.8	37.5	39.4	37.6	1,272	18.3
3–39	19,990	23.3	21.5	26.1	23.8	1,745	25.1
4–49	12,354	14.4	14.9	14.4	14.1	1,630	23.4
5–59	6,263	7.3	8.5	8	6.3	413	5.9
60+	6,434	7.5	8.1	7.7	7.1	389	5.6
Sex							
Female	42,811	49.9	53.0	48.0	49.0	3,519	50.6
Male	42,982	50.1	47.0	52.0	51.0	3,436	49.4
Relation to head of household							
Head	29,170	34.0	33.5	35.9	33.9	1,966	28.3
Spouse	14,756	17.2	18.2	18.0	16.3	1,634	23.5
Children	32,430	37.8	38.2	37.1	37.7	2,741	39.4
Maid	86	0.1	0.0	0.0	0.1	NA	NA
Other	9,351	10.9	10.1	9.1	12.0	614	8.8
Education							
Primary school or less	9,180	10.7	9.2	6.4	13.1	392	6.4
Secondary school, diploma	31,314	36.5	40.3	23.6	37.5	4,201	68.2
Local university degree	12,612	14.7	15.3	15.8	13.9	1,571	25.5
Overseas degree	3,2687	38.1	35.2	54.2	35.5		

Occupation (income > 0)							
Low skill	13,509	26.7	25.8	16.9	30.2	1,068	27.7
Assistant professional	15,584	30.8	33.7	29.8	29.2	951	24.7
Professional	10,726	21.2	16.9	28.4	21.9	1,038	26.9
Managerial	10,777	21.3	23.6	25.0	18.7	796	20.7
Total	50,596	100	100	100	100	3,853	100.0
Earnings (income > 0)							
1–5,999	2,682	5.3	5.1	4.4	5.6	2,382	45.7
6,000–9,999	5,970	11.8	10.0	8.3	14.1	739	14.2
10,000–14,999	1,2345	24.4	26.7	17.6	24.7	753	14.5
15,000–19,999	7,994	15.8	17.0	17.6	14.7	552	10.6
20,000–29,999	8,348	16.5	18.3	17.5	14.8	525	10.1
> = 30,000	13,256	26.2	22.8	34.6	26.0	256	4.9
Total	50,596	100.0	100.0	100.0	100.0	5,207	100.0
Median (HK$/month)		16,520.38	16,500.00	20,000.00	15,500.00		7,091.03
Mean (HK$/month)		25,543.01	23,314.00	33,682.00	24,657.00		10,234.78
Gini coefficient[2]		11.96	13.21	5.55	1.55		34.38

Source: 2001 census data, Department of Census and Statistics, Hong Kong SAR, PRC.

[1] 1996 Canadian census public use individual microdata files, CHASS, University of Toronto, at http://datacentre.chass.sutoronto.ca/census/mainmicro.html. For earnings, sample selected: age 15 and over; income > 0; adjusted to 2000 real Canadian dollar value; exchange rate as of December 31, 2000, at Can$1 = HK$5.20777.

[2] Authors' calculation.

moving is costly, and hence most people stay. Among all returnees, 39 percent and 21 percent, respectively, are returnees from Canada and the United States, while 40 percent have returned from other countries.

The education metric reveals marked variations across the mover and non-mover groups. Non-movers are concentrated at low levels of education, with 90 percent possessing less than a postsecondary degree (see figure 17.2). All leaver groups, including returnees and immigrant stayers in Canada, show a significantly higher level of educational attainment, again as our model would predict. On average, 53 percent of returnees possess a postsecondary degree, mainly obtained from overseas schools. Returnees from the United States have the highest level of educational attainment; 70 percent of this group had a postsecondary degree. However, only about 50 percent of returnees from Canada and elsewhere possess a postsecondary degree. An even lower level of postsecondary degree attainment (26 percent) was found among Hong Kong–born immigrant stayers in Canada.

Migrants from Mainland China (PRC) have the lowest education level, and there is a twofold explanation for this phenomenon. First, PRC migrants to Hong Kong came under the family unification category and hence required no educational background to enter. Also, because many entrants from the PRC are children of Hong Kong residents and are still of school age, the educational attainment measure in the census is not particularly revealing. In contrast to PRC migrants, migrants from less developed countries (LDCs) and more developed countries (MDCs) have obtained higher levels of education; this is especially evident for the MDC group. Given that migrants from MDC areas to Hong Kong are labor-market oriented, their educational background corresponds to their need to secure a job in Hong Kong.

In addition to these educational characteristics, the distribution of occupational skills again reveals significant human capital differences across the defined mover groups (see figure 17.3). The non-movers and migrants to Hong Kong from Mainland China and from the LDCs are predominantly in the lowest job skill category. Returnees are mainly in entry-level skilled occupations (31 percent) or professional and managerial occupations (42 percent). In fact, compared to non-movers, Hong Kong returnees are four times more likely to report professional jobs and twice as likely to be managers. Again, this supports the sorting hypothesis of our theory.

Returnees from Canada are more heavily concentrated in entry-level professions (34 percent) or higher-level professional or managerial

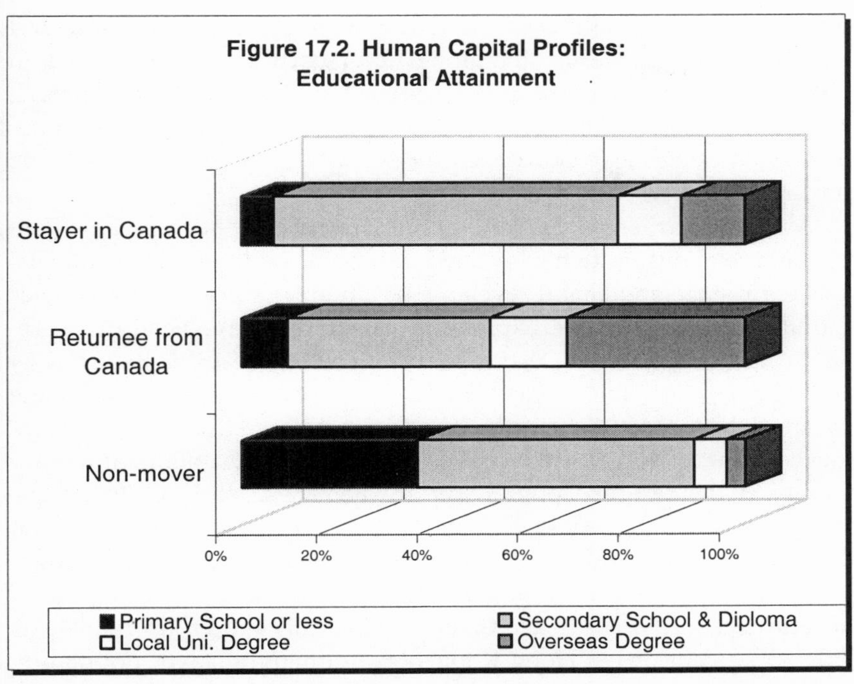

Figure 17.2. Human Capital Profiles: Educational Attainment

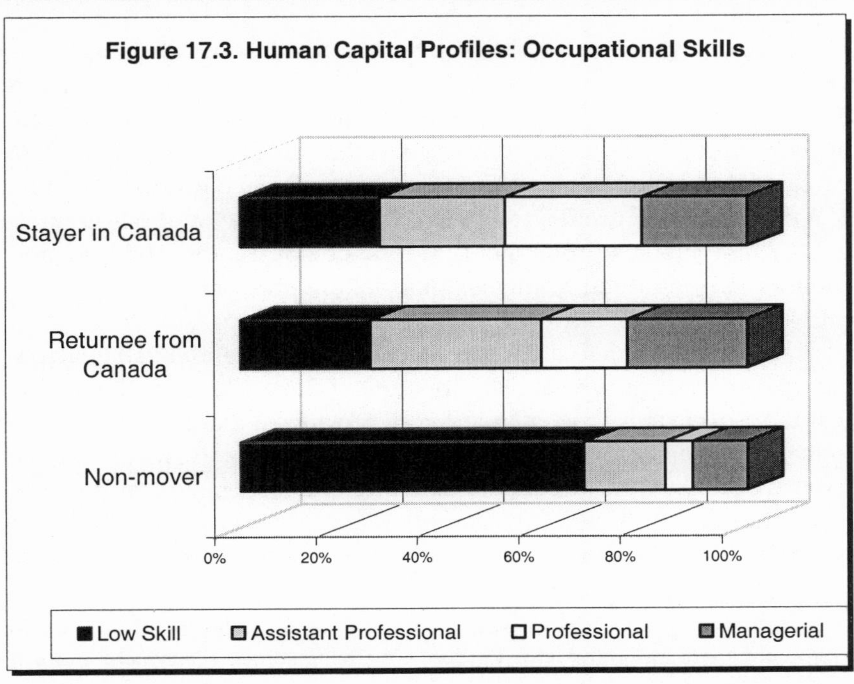

Figure 17.3. Human Capital Profiles: Occupational Skills

jobs (40 percent) than those who returned from the United States and other countries. If we use the Hong Kong–born immigrant stayers in Canada as a reference group with respect to the Canadian returnees, we find that they are more evenly distributed among the four occupational skill categories than are returnees. Again, this corresponds to the sorting prediction of our model.

As noted earlier, other demographic measures—such as age, gender, and relationship to the head of household—will reflect the movers' (stayers') stage in the life cycle. The model predicts that returnees should be young and, perhaps, still dependents of the head of household if they have recently acquired foreign human capital. Figures 17.4 and 17.5 confirm the model's prediction since the non-movers' age pyramid has a standard population structure, while returnees are much younger than the non-mover population. The dominant age intervals in the returnee population are the 20–29 and 30–39 groups, which represent the most economically active group in the population.[20] More specifically, returnees from Canada are much younger than Hong Kong–born immigrant stayers in Canada, with 59 percent of returnees in the 20–39 age bracket, while this age group represents only 43 percent of the Hong Kong–born immigrant-stayer population in Canada.

Migrants from countries other than Mainland China also produce a very young population pyramid, with the age shares for the 20–29 and 30–39 intervals comprising 71 percent. Moreover, the dependency rate of these immigrants is even lower than that of returnees, at about 16 percent. However, Mainland China migrants reveal a different picture. The dominant age groups from the PRC are the 0–19 and 30–39 intervals. These movers from the PRC are obviously the children and spouses of Hong Kong residents, thus yielding the highest dependency rate—87 percent—of any of our defined mover groups.

Apart from this age diversity, the variation in gender ratios across various migrant groups is also apparent. Tables 17.2 and 17.3 reveal that the percentages of women and men are almost identical in the non-mover, returnee, and Hong Kong–born stayer groups. However, female movers dominate the three remaining migrant groups, with an extreme concentration (92.5 percent) among migrants from less developed countries. Thus the Hong Kong experience indicates that acquisition of

---

[20] These findings are in sharp contrast to evidence for Australia and Canada, where returnees are found in the retired group, not among students (Newbold and Bell 2001: 1168).

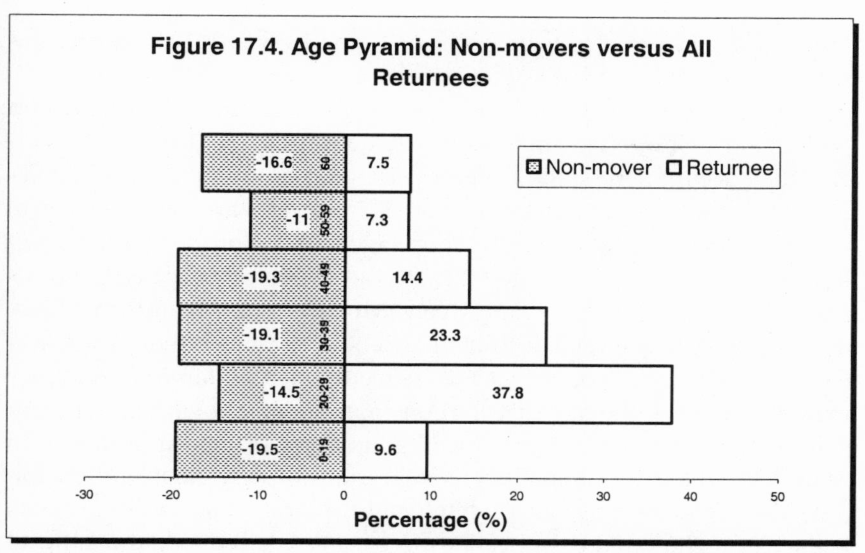

Figure 17.4. Age Pyramid: Non-movers versus All Returnees
Non-mover
Returnee
60
50-59
40-49
30-39
20-29
0-19
-16.6
7.5
-11
7.3
-19.3
14.4
-19.1
23.3
-14.5
37.8
-19.5
9.6
-30
-20
-10
0
10
20
30
40
50
Percentage (%)

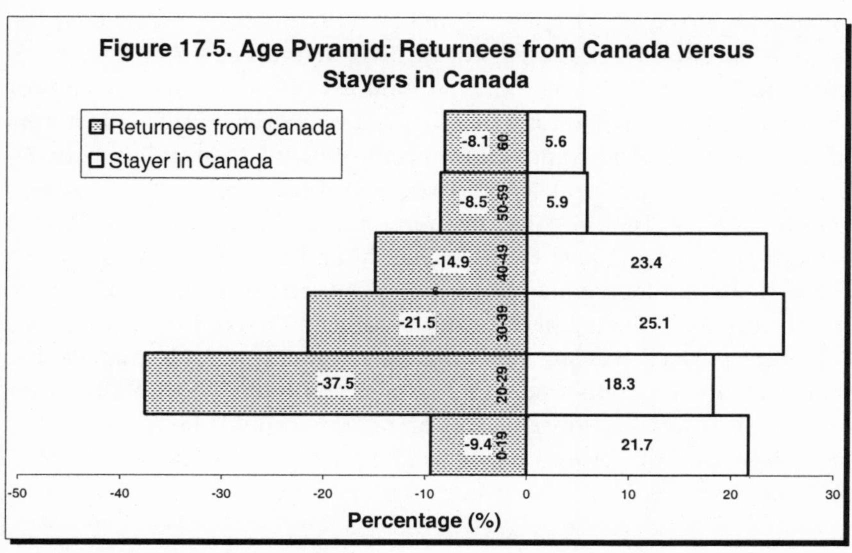

Figure 17.5. Age Pyramid: Returnees from Canada versus Stayers in Canada
Returnees from Canada
Stayer in Canada
60
50-59
40-49
30-39
20-29
0-19
-8.1
5.6
-8.5
5.9
-14.9
23.4
-21.5
25.1
-37.5
18.3
-9.4
21.7
-50
-40
-30
-20
-10
0
10
20
30
Percentage (%)

human capital upon arrival leads to a gender-neutral flow, but unskilled labor does not. This again confirms our mover-stayer model.

The "relationship to head of household" measure, in conjunction with age distribution, completes the demographic picture of the diversity that occurs across the non-mover, returnee, migrant, and stayer groups. First, similar to the non-movers, returnees are concentrated in either the "head of household" group (aged 30–39) or the "young adult in the household" group (aged 20–29); the shares for these two groups are 34.0 and 37.8 percent, respectively. Migrants from Mainland China, as noted earlier, are related to the household head as either "children" (50.3 percent) or "spouse" (29.2 percent). These familial relations match, of course, the age distributions mentioned above. The relationships reflect the family reunification pattern of immigration from Mainland China to Hong Kong, while the returnees' distribution follows the predictions of our model. Finally, a large majority of migrants from LDCs cite "maid" or "domestic worker" as their relationship to the household head. This designation accounts for 83.5 percent of the total migrants from LDCs residing in Hong Kong.

Comparing Hong Kong returnees from Canada to Hong Kong–born immigrant stayers in Canada reveals more "heads of household" (34 versus 28 percent) and fewer "spouses" (18 versus 23 percent) in the returnee group. These data indicate that a returnee from Canada is more likely to be a household head who may have left spouse and/or children in Canada. We can cite two arguments inherent in our model to rationalize this outcome. First, returnees want their children to receive a Canadian education, and spouses must remain in Canada to care for the children. Second, the spouse and children may remain in Canada to hedge against changing social and economic conditions in Hong Kong that may make a return move necessary in the future.

In sum, the reported demographics allow us to confirm Hypothesis 1: Hong Kong returnees in general have a higher level of human capital than Canadian stayers and Hong Kong non-movers, with the latter group obtaining the lowest level of human capital. Hypothesis 3 is confirmed as well, because returnees to Hong Kong are better educated and younger than Hong Kong–born stayers in Canada.

Earnings Profiles

The differences in human capital characteristics discussed above will ultimately affect the respective groups' earnings profiles. In fact, tables

17.2 and 17.3 report substantial earnings differences for the non-mover, returnee, and other migrant groups (see also figures 17.6 and 17.7). The highest earners are migrants from more developed countries (a mean monthly income of HK$39,310), followed by returnees (HK$25,543). Migrants from less developed countries (HK$5,227) and Mainland China (HK$9,085) earn the lowest mean monthly incomes. A non-mover's mean income (HK$15,972) falls very close to the average (HK$15,812). In other words, on average, returnees in Hong Kong earn 60 percent more than non-movers, and migrants from more developed countries earn 2.5 times the earnings of non-movers, as our model predicted. However, migrants from Mainland China earn 43 percent less than the non-movers, and the earnings of those coming from less developed countries are only 33 percent of the earnings of the non-movers.

Among all returnees, those who returned from the United States earned more than all other groups, and Canadian returnees earned the lowest income among the three groups. Returnees from Canada to Hong Kong earn about 30 percent less than returnees from the United States and 5 percent less than returnees from elsewhere. Although returnees from Canada in Hong Kong earn less than other returnees, they still earn much more than Hong Kong–born stayers in Canada. This again supports the sorting argument of our model. As shown in table 17.3, the mean monthly earnings of Canadian returnees to Hong Kong are 2.3 times those of Hong Kong–born stayers in Canada.

Not only do income levels vary across groups, but there is also an uneven distribution of income within each group. Our calculated Gini coefficient[21] reveals that the lower the group income level, the greater the income inequity within the group. For example, the Gini coefficient is only 4.5 for the highest income group—migrants from MDCs—but it rises as high as 46.5 for the lowest income group—migrants from LDCs. The returnees also have a very low Gini coefficient—12.0, or half that of the non-movers. This finding counters the model's prediction that risk takers or persons who would tolerate a more unequal income distribution would return.

In sum, our data partially confirm Hypothesis 2—namely, that returnees to Hong Kong earn more than Hong Kong–born stayers in

[21] The Gini coefficient measures income inequality in a society. The Gini coefficient lies between 0 and 100, where 0 means perfect equality (everyone has the same income) and 100 means perfect inequality (one person has all the income; everyone else earns nothing).

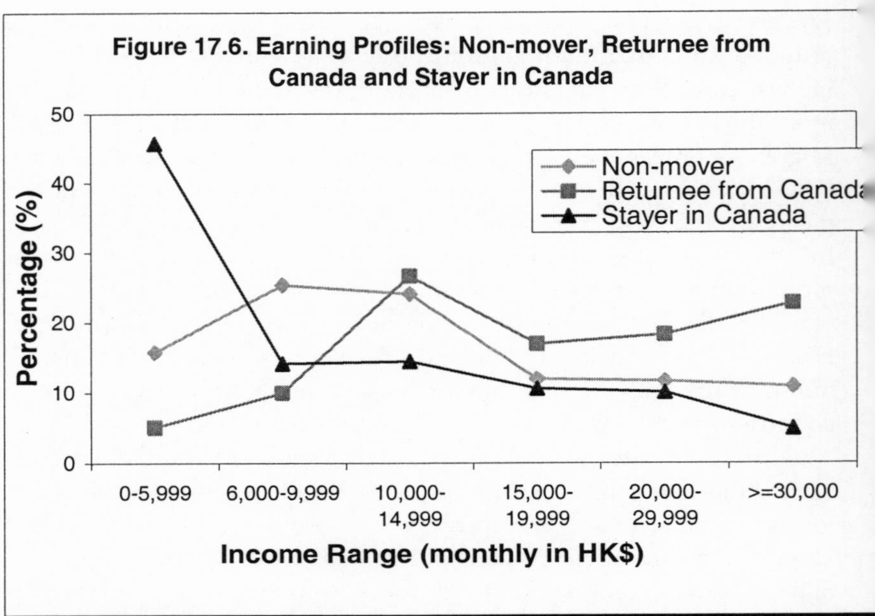
Figure 17.6. Earning Profiles: Non-mover, Returnee from Canada and Stayer in Canada
Percentage (%)
50
40
30
20
10
0
Non-mover
Returnee from Canada
Stayer in Canada
0-5,999
6,000-9,999
10,000-14,999
15,000-19,999
20,000-29,999
>=30,000
Income Range (monthly in HK$)

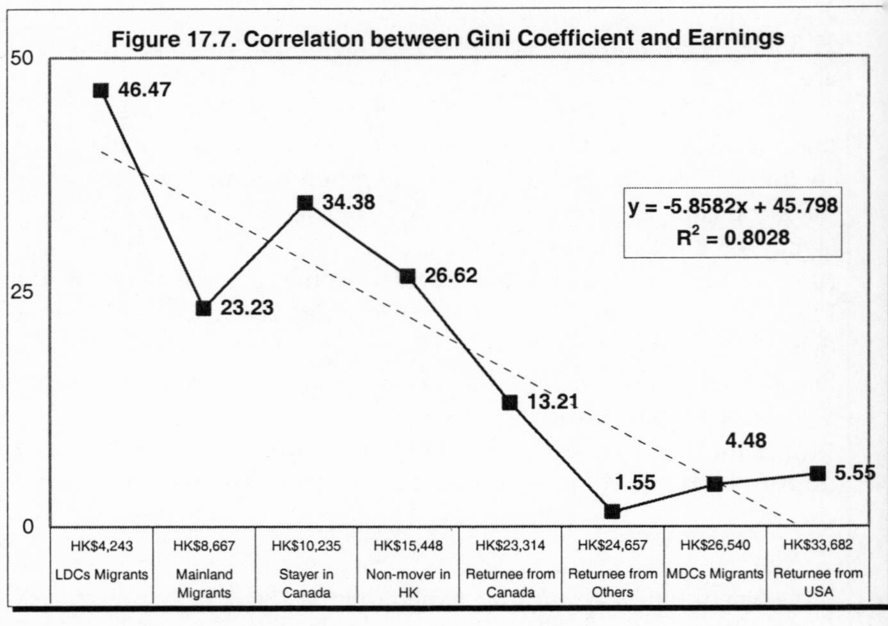
Figure 17.7. Correlation between Gini Coefficient and Earnings
50
25
0
46.47
23.23
34.38
26.62
13.21
1.55
4.48
5.55
y = -5.8582x + 45.798
R² = 0.8028
HK$4,243 LDCs Migrants
HK$8,667 Mainland Migrants
HK$10,235 Stayer in Canada
HK$15,448 Non-mover in HK
HK$23,314 Returnee from Canada
HK$24,657 Returnee from Others
HK$26,540 MDCs Migrants
HK$33,682 Returnee from USA

Canada and non-movers in Hong Kong. However, our risk-taking hypothesis is not supported for returnees.

CONCLUSION

We can conclude that returnees to Hong Kong are more likely to be young, to be recent graduates of overseas institutions, and to be at the beginning of their careers. There is no significant gender difference among returnees, and most returnees are children of Hong Kong citizens. More than half of all returnees have a postsecondary degree, with the majority of these degrees obtained overseas, and the returnees are just entering skilled jobs. Most importantly, returnees' earnings are higher than all other resident groups in Hong Kong, except immigrants from developed countries. Also, the low Gini coefficient for returnees indicates less income inequality than that reported for other groups.

By comparing the non-mover, returnee, and stayer groups, we also find that returnees to Hong Kong have acquired more human capital than both Canadian stayers and Hong Kong non-movers; the latter have the least human capital. In addition, returnees to Hong Kong are better educated and younger than Hong Kong–born stayers in Canada, and they earn more. These findings confirm the three central hypotheses of the triangular human capital transfer model.

Apart from these general observations, a particular set of conclusions arises in our entrepôt Canadian context. First, Hong Kong returnees from Canada are young adults in the most economically active age group, while the Hong Kong–born stayers in Canada fall predominantly into the (pre)school and older (40+) age groups. Second, "household head" Hong Kong returnees from Canada are more mobile, and these individuals' spouses and children are more likely to be stayers in Canada. Third, Canadian returnees to Hong Kong earn a great deal more than their stayer counterparts.

References

Anderson, F., and K. Konrad. 2001a. "Globalization and Human Capital Formation." IZA Discussion Paper No. 245. Bonn: Institute for the Study of Labor.

———. 2001b. "Human Capital Investment and Globalization in Extortionary States." IZA Discussion Paper No. 239. Bonn: Institute for the Study of Labor.

Borjas, George, and B. Bratsberg. 1996. "Who Leaves? The Outmigration of the Foreign-born," *Review of Economics and Statistics* 78: 165–76.

CIC (Citizenship and Immigration Canada). Various years. *Facts and Figures: Immigration Overview.*

Dales, J. 1964. "The Cost of Protectionism with High International Mobility of Factors," *Canadian Journal of Economics and Political Science* 30: 512–25.

DeVoretz, Don, and Chona Iturralde. 2000a. "Probability of Staying in Canada." RIIM Working Paper 00-06. Vancouver: RIIM.

———. 2000b. "Why Do the Highly Skilled Stay in Canada?" *Policy Options,* March, pp. 59–63.

DeVoretz, Don, and Z. Ma. 2002. "Triangular Human Capital Flows between Sending, Entrepôt, and Rest-of-the-World Regions," *Canadian Population Studies* 29, no. 1: 53–69.

Epstein, G.S., A.L. Hillman, and D.H. Ursprung. 1999. "The King Never Emigrates," *Review of Development Economics* 3: 107–21.

Lam, Kit-Chun. 2000. "Shortage of Highly Skilled Workers in Hong Kong and Policy Responses," *Journal of International Migration and Integration* 1, no. 4 (Fall): 405–26.

Ma, Z., 2000. "Immigration Transition in Hong Kong in the 1990s." Proceedings of the International Workshop on International Migration and Human Resources Development in the APEC Member Economies, January 20–21, Chiba, Japan. APEC #00-HR-04.2: 215-35.

McInnis, M. 2001. "The Anglo-Canadian Hemorrhage: The Great Canadian Emigration from Canada, 1861–1901." Paper presented at the meetings of the Canadian Historical Association, Laval University, May.

Newbold, K.B., and M. Bell. 2001. "Return and Onwards Migration in Canada and Australia: Evidence from Fixed Interval Data," *International Migration Review* 35, no. 4 (Winter): 1157–84.

Zhang, K. 2001. "Human Capital Investment and Flows: A Multiperiod Model for China." Paper prepared for the International Metropolis Conference, Rotterdam, The Netherlands, November.

Part V

Host Societies in the Old and New Immigration

18

Institutional Change and Immigrant Assimilation in the United States

VICTOR NEE

The experience of contemporary immigrants and their children is shaped by institutions. Defined as the web of formal and informal rules governing social relationships, institutions provide the context of legitimate social action within which actors pursue interests. Formal rules are the laws and regulations produced and enforced by the state. Monitoring and enforcement of these rules encompass one of the most powerful mechanisms by which any complex society reproduces, organizes, and regulates itself. The role of formal rules in molding the underlying constitution of society is especially pronounced in highly legalized and bureaucratized postindustrial societies. Informal rules include customs, conventions, and social norms produced and enforced within close-knit groups. They uphold the other institutional arrangements of civil society—associations, churches, clubs, social networks, families. It is difficult to imagine self-organized social life in the absence of informal rules; without them, every social transaction would need to be negotiated anew.

In multicultural societies like the United States, institutions enable members of diverse ethnic and racial groups to conduct workaday communal life with a degree of civility and without a need to resort to violence to resolve differences. Legislative and judicial institutions elaborate and refine the foundational rules specifying the civil rights of citizens and aliens, providing a conduit for nonviolent contestation and reformulation. Regulatory institutions monitor and enforce rules of equality of rights, albeit imperfectly, but in a manner that allows predictable transactions to take place between individuals of different ethnic groups with at least a modicum of fair play. Market institutions conform to the underlying rules of cooperation and competition in a manner that makes it possible for diverse groups to transact in an economy where ethnic boundaries are made porous by routine market exchanges. Educational institutions admit and instruct youth regardless of whether they are children of old-stock families or of recent immigrants. Social institutions embedded in communities and networks of kin, friends, and acquaintances organize civil life from the vantage point of welfare-maximizing norms, which favor exclusive rights for members over inclusiveness. But they operate under the shadow of the law, and the appearance of legitimacy gained through conformity with the laws of a diverse society enhances their claim on resources.

In this chapter, I elaborate why institutions matter in understanding the assimilation of immigrants and their children in a multicultural society. Although I focus on the United States, the arguments pertain equally well to other advanced postindustrial societies. I discuss three core *institutional mechanisms* of postindustrial economies that combine and interact to support and reproduce a stable institutional framework for contemporary immigration. Specifically, I focus on the role of the state in monitoring and enforcement of formal rules, the role of labor markets in the economic assimilation of immigrants, and the importance of classificatory schemas embedded in institutional processes.

I argue that institutional change dismantling the formal rules of racial separatism after World War II and especially during the civil rights era of the 1960s shaped a new institutional environment for immigrant minorities, one that for the first time extended the principle of formal equality of rights to immigrants not of European ancestry. This sea change in the legal system governing immigration opened the way for the assimilation of immigrant minorities in a way that formerly was not possible. I briefly highlight the substantive differences between the contemporary period and the American past to explain why in the post–civil rights era the possibility for assimilation for immigrant minorities and their children has become greater than in any previous period (see also Alba and Nee 2003). I argue that institutional change has opened up predictable chances for success by dismantling the legal structures of racial separatism, making mainstream institutions and opportunities more accessible for racial minorities.

Today, informal racism is not sufficiently powerful as a social force to create insurmountable barriers to social mobility for immigrants in postindustrial societies, either in higher education or in labor markets. The concept of *unequal or divergent outcomes* better fits the assimilation experience of contemporary immigrants and their children. Many in the second generation experience upward, horizontal, and downward social mobility relative to the educational and occupational attainments of their immigrant parents, but such unequal or divergent outcomes are a characteristic feature of advanced capitalist economies, for both the foreign and native-born populations.

INSTITUTIONAL MECHANISMS SHAPING ASSIMILATION

Early in the twentieth century at the Sorbonne, Emile Durkheim established sociology as a discipline devoted to the social scientific study of institutions. Institutions, he argued, existed as social facts not reducible to psychological or economic processes. Sociology would study the manner in which social institutions shaped all dimensions of human activity, from religious practices to economic action. This "social mold" approach to the study of institutions has had an enduring influence on the development of modern sociology.

Within the social sciences, there has been a marked resurgence in theoretical and empirical interest in institutions. The rise of new institutional economics has revitalized economic analysis of institutions and institutional change (Williamson 1975; North 1990). In contrast to the new institutional economics, sociologists tend to view institutions in realist terms, not as disembodied rules but as social structures involving actors in ongoing social relationships (Nee and Swedberg n.d.). Institutional arrangements provide a framework and conduit for the pursuit of tangible interests.

Two institutional pillars of modern capitalism are the centralized state—especially its legal and regulatory systems—and the market as an institution of exchange. These two institutions are interconnected with all the other key institutions of modern capitalism and play a crucial role in determining the structure of property rights, the openness of labor markets, and incentives for entrepreneurship. Thus, to understand the institutional framework shaping the experiences of contemporary immigrants and their children requires attention to the legal and economic institutions of modern capitalism.

The Rule of Law

A defining feature of modern American capitalism is the evolution of a national institutional environment characterized by homogeneity rather than by regional variability. The uniformity in the formal rules of the federal government has meant that mainstream firms and organizations have little incentive to move to new locations within the United States to get out from under federal rules. Firms move to capture marginal gains stemming from variations in state and local tax laws and labor conditions. Likewise, firms move to tax havens in the Caribbean Basin. But within the United States, whether a firm is located in the South or Northeast, its institutional environment with respect to federal rules remains constant. Because larger firms are more readily monitored by government, the homogeneity in institutional environment is especially applicable with respect to the behavior of mainstream firms. For example, corporate America routinely screens for undocumented workers by requesting documentation of legal status at the point of recruitment, a practice followed more stringently in the post–September 11 climate of heightened security. By contrast, small businesses and households are difficult to monitor; the high costs of enforcement at this level make inspections less frequent. This is why undocumented workers tend to be employed by very small firms, often operated by immigrant entrepreneurs in ethnic economies, or as domestic servants in households.

In the post–civil rights era, mainstream corporations and public organizations generally have shown a good-faith effort to observe guidelines of Title VII of the Civil Rights Act of 1964, which outlaws racial discrimination. Personnel departments of mainstream firms and organizations monitor compliance to the formal rules of Title VII, even if this amounts to symbolic conformity through offering diversity and multicultural training workshops. Many mainstream corporations and public organizations take into account the increased costs of discrimination that the civil rights–era changes brought about, and they institutionalize within the firm the substantive meaning of equality of rights (Dobbin and Sutton 1998). These firms are concerned not merely with the risk of expensive class action suits if their firms fail to conform—something that Texaco and Coca-Cola recently experienced—but with the potential damage to a firm's reputation and brand name. To be labeled a racist business in a multicultural society carries substantial costs for any firm.

As the American workforce has become more heterogeneous, firms have an even stronger incentive to foster workplace norms that promote an atmosphere of racial tolerance and fair play, thereby avoiding the higher transaction costs stemming from ethnic conflict and tension. This ethos is especially manifest in high-technology firms and the like that depend on a high level of cooperation among workers as a basis for productivity gains and competitive advantage. For example, Microsoft maintains a "zero tolerance" policy regarding racism, not simply to avoid costly litigation but because 24 percent of its workforce is nonwhite. Many of Microsoft's leading engineers and staff come from immigrant backgrounds.

Although originally intended to lower entry barriers for racial minorities and women in mainstream firms and public organizations, Title VII and other legislative initiatives of the civil rights era have benefited legal immigrants (Nee and Alba n.d.). Moreover, affirmative action programs have benefited immigrants from the Caribbean Basin, Latin America, and Africa, along with their children, even though these groups did not suffer from the United States' cultural legacy of slavery and past discrimination (Skrentny 1996). It is difficult to build a class action case charging racial discrimination per se when a firm can document fair employment policies implemented in recruiting and promoting nonwhite immigrants. Waters's (2000) study of Caribbean blacks documents that employers prefer immigrant workers over African Americans not only because immigrant workers are perceived to be a more diligent and pliant workforce, but also because employers hold negative stereotypes of black Americans. Prejudice against African Americans remains deeply rooted in American culture, as Waters vividly demonstrates through interviews with white managers. But this prejudice does not seem to extend to immigrants who have similarly dark complexions. For example, South Asian immigrants are not residentially segregated, they are commonly employed as professionals in mainstream firms, and their children secure comparable levels of educational attainment as their immigrant parents.

In sum, civil rights–era legislative changes profoundly altered the institutional environment of immigration. Not only have these changes opened the door for legal immigration to nontraditional sources of migrants, such as Asia, but the extension of formal rules of equality to nonwhites has lowered barriers to entry into mainstream institutions and organizations for immigrants and their children. This has enabled immigrants with forms of capital useful in a high-technology society to experience rapid economic assimilation, more so than in any previous period in American history (Alba and Nee 2003).

Labor Markets as Economic Institutions of Assimilation

It would be very costly for a modern capitalist economy to maintain an apartheid system, especially in a society as ethnically and racially diverse as the United States. Such a system would require separate rules and their enforcement for whites and nonwhites. It would result in massive inefficiencies in the allocation of human capital to the extent that talented nonwhites were barred from positions in which their abilities could be most productively utilized. Similarly, it would result in incompetence being structured into managerial and professional positions by limiting recruitment to preferred ethnic groups. Apart from the obvious moral and political objections, the outcome of a segregationist institutional order in a multicultural postindustrial economy would lead to such an enormous increase in transaction costs—the costs stemming from social relationships (and conflict)—that it would greatly reduce the United States' competitiveness in the world economy.

Adam Smith and Karl Marx both emphasized the free mobility of labor as a requirement for the development of capitalism as an economic order. Max Weber picked up this theme, arguing that the market operates as an integrative mechanism under capitalism because the dynamics of market exchange work to break down segmented boundaries. Weber hypothesized that buyers and sellers seeking to optimize the gains from trade tend to widen the circles of interaction (Weber 1978).

In their study of the labor market experiences of Asian immigrant workers in Los Angeles, Nee, Sanders, and Sernau (1994) examine Weber's insight by means of event history analysis of job histories. These authors found that recent Asian immigrants tend to change jobs frequently as they seek better conditions of employment and pay. Although many begin as low-wage workers in the immigrant ethnic economy, the trajectory of job changes confirms that the social boundaries between the ethnic and mainstream labor markets are very porous, allowing immigrant workers to move freely in and out of the ethnic economy as they seek to optimize on their stock of human-cultural capital. Moreover, interviews show that immigrant workers prefer jobs in mainstream firms, which offer them a more regulated work environment and hence better conditions of employment.

Although immigrant workers testify that they fear exploitation by co-ethnic bosses, many nonetheless remain in the immigrant economy, in part because they lack the cultural competence to gain employment outside the immigrant enclave. Overall, the immigrant labor market studies conducted by Nee and his colleagues confirm that the economic assimilation of immigrants in labor markets turns on the *forms of capital* they possess (see Nee and Sanders 2001). Immigrants with a low stock of human-cultural capital marketable in the mainstream economy find employment as low-wage workers or immigrant entrepreneurs in the immigrant enclave, whereas immigrant professionals from English-speaking countries like the Philippines or those educated in U.S. universities generally find employment in mainstream occupations and firms.

During the sustained economic expansion of the 1990s, the U.S. economy generated 23.7 million new wage and salaried jobs, which lowered the country's unemployment rate from 6.8 to 4.0 percent even as the labor force expanded by 17.5 million. In their analysis of the 2000 U.S. census, Sum, Fogg, and Harrington (2002) show that the decade witnessed the greatest volume of immigration in the history of the United States, with 13.65 million net new immigrants arriving to find employment and residence.[1] These authors document that the impact of the 1990s arrivals on labor markets was far more significant than initially realized. Immigrants arriving over the course of the decade represented 41 percent of the population growth experienced during the 1990s, and they accounted for a remarkable 50 percent of overall growth in the civilian labor force. These immigrants tended to be young and disproportionately male; 83 percent were of working age, compared to 76 percent for the native-born population. Despite their recent arrival and the high costs associated with immigration, these new immigrants' labor force participation rate was remarkably similar to that of the native-born population (see table 18.1). For both groups, the labor force participation rate was 67.3 percent. The unemployment rate was somewhat lower for native-born workers than for the recent arrivals. However, the employment-to-population ratio for the two groups was essentially the same.

---

[1] By contrast, during the high tide of mass immigration from Europe, 3.3 million entered the United States in the 1890–1900 period and 5.6 million between 1900 and 1910.

Table 18.1. U.S. Civilian Labor Force Participation Rates, Unemployment Rates, and Employment/Population Ratios of the Working-age Population by Nativity, 2000–2001

	All	Native-born	Foreign-born	New Immigrant
Civilian labor force participation rate	67.2%	67.3%	66.6%	67.6%
Unemployment rate	4.4	4.4	4.9	5.8
Employment/ population ratio	64.2	64.3	63.4	63.7

Sources: U.S. Bureau of Labor Statistics, *Employment and Earnings*, January 2002; 2001 monthly Current Population Surveys (CPS), public use files, tabulations by Sum, Fogg, and Harrington 2002.

The description of labor force participation in Sum, Fogg, and Harrington 2002 shows that new immigrants to the United States were regionally concentrated in the West and Northeast. New immigrants contributed 72 percent of the growth in the civilian labor force in the West and a surprising 100 percent in the Northeast, where, absent the new immigration, the labor force would have declined by 1.3 million workers.

As in earlier post-1965 immigration, the human capital stock of new immigrants was bimodal, with a third having less than a high school education. However, these immigrants maintained a higher labor force participation rate than the native-born with a comparable education level. As was true in previous decades, nearly a third of immigrants arriving during the 1990s came with four years or more of university education. Overall, the data point to multiple immigration streams, some composed of traditional labor migrants with low human-cultural capital stocks and others comprising skilled technical workers and highly educated professionals with university and postgraduate degrees.

Testifying to the openness of U.S. labor markets, immigrants arriving in the 1990s quickly dispersed into all sectors of the economy. However, sectors that require English language competency and other forms of cultural capital useful in a high-technology society, such as professional services and public administration, have lower immigrant representation (table 18.2).

Table 18.2. Distribution of Native-born, All Foreign-born, and Recent Immigrant Workers in the United States, by Major Industrial Sector, 2000–2001 Averages

Industrial Sector	Native-born Workers	Foreign-born Workers	New Foreign Immigrants
Agriculture, forestry, fishing, mining	2.8%	3.9%	4.6%
Construction	6.8	8.3	10.0
Manufacturing	13.9	17.5	17.4
Durable goods	8.6	10.0	9.7
Nondurable goods	5.3	7.5	7.7
Wholesale trade	3.9	3.7	3.4
Retail trade	16.6	18.0	20.6
Finance, insurance, real estate	6.7	5.1	3.6
Business/repair services	6.9	8.8	10.4
Personal services	4.9	8.0	8.5
Professional services	25.3	18.0	15.9
Public administration	4.8	2.0	1.0

Sources: Monthly CPS surveys, 2000 to 2001, public use files, tabulations by Sum, Fogg, and Harrington 2002.

Given the high proportion of labor migrants with low educational attainment, it is not surprising that immigrants are more heavily concentrated in jobs that the native-born do not want, including jobs in agriculture and other low-skill, low-wage sectors of the economy. Nevertheless, the overall impression suggests a pattern of convergence in the distribution of native-born and foreign-born across industrial sectors. With the exception of jobs in public administration, the difference narrows between immigrants arriving prior to 1990 and the native-born by comparison with newly arrived immigrants. These patterns are consistent with the accounts of economic assimilation for immigrants based on 1980 and 1990 census data (Chiswick 1977, 1979; Chiswick and Sullivan 1995).

As for the specific occupational distribution, newly arrived immigrants are heavily represented in manual and service occupations and in agriculture (see table 18.3). Thirty-four percent found jobs as assemblers, fabricators, machine operators, low-skilled laborers, and service workers. However, 28 percent of the new immigrants found jobs in manufacturing, and 29 percent found work in professional occupations as engineers, physical scientists, computer scientists, and in higher education.

Table 18.3. Distribution of Native-born, All Foreign-born, and Recent Immigrant Workers in the United States, by Major Occupational Group, 2000–2001 Averages

Occupational Group	Native-born Workers	Foreign-born Workers	New Foreign Immigrants
Professional	16.1%	13.5%	13.3%
Managerial/administrative/executive	15.5	10.1	7.0
Technical	3.3	2.9	2.7
High-level sales	7.2	4.9	3.2
Low-level sales	5.2	4.7	5.3
Administrative support	14.5	9.1	7.1
Services	12.8	19.4	22.4
Farm/forestry/fishing	2.3	4.0	5.0
Skilled blue collar	10.7	12.7	12.8
Assemblers/fabricators/operators	8.8	12.8	13.4
Laborers/helpers/cleaners	3.7	5.9	7.9

Sources: Monthly CPS surveys, 2000 to 2001, public files, tabulations by authors.

In sum, this study provides yet another confirmation of the hypothesis that labor markets in modern capitalist economies operate as an integrative mechanism in an institutional environment that has extended formal equality of rights to racial minorities. Early analyses of the 2000 census and Current Population Surveys (CPS) data for 1999 and 2000 confirm descriptively that recent immigrants assimilate rapidly into U.S. labor markets to acquire salaried and wage employment in all sectors of the economy. Overall, in examining the current sectoral and occupational distribution of new and old immigrants, the broad dispersion conforms more to the Weberian interpretation of the market mechanism than to the segmented labor force imagery advanced by neo-Marxist scholars (Gordon 1964; Gordon, Reich, and Edwards 1982). There is little support in the 1999 and 2000 CPS data for the segmented labor market theorists' view that there is a "fundamental dichotomy between the jobs of migrants and the jobs of natives" (Piore 1979: 35). There is little evidence to support the view of segmented assimilation, at least in the labor market experiences of recent immigrants.

INSTITUTIONS CLASSIFY PEOPLE INTO CATEGORIES AND GROUPS

As Mary Douglas (1986) has argued, institutional structures perform a categorizing role by means of cognitive mechanisms that sort and match people according to classificatory schemas. In postindustrial societies, classificatory schemas embedded in regulatory and normative structures have a profound influence on how powerful agents deal with people. Classificatory systems embedded in formal rules backed by state agencies specify differential treatment for individuals and regulate boundaries between groups, as in the specification of the hierarchy of rights that distinguish different categories of aliens—documented and undocumented—from citizens. Accordingly, registered aliens are entitled by the rules of permanent residence to seek employment in mainstream firms and to apply for citizenship through naturalization procedures. Undocumented aliens risk deportation and are restricted from access to those same workaday rights.

Classificatory schemas, moreover, can create new group identities and ethnic boundaries. In the case of the United States, an example is the Census Bureau's invention of the "Asian American" and "Hispanic" categories, which include diverse ethnic groups that in the past maintained discrete ethnic boundaries and identities. Similarly, social science ideas can form the basis of classificatory schemes that frame the action of agencies of the welfare state, as in the concept of the "underclass." Social scientists may unintentionally reify a classificatory label that reinforces negative stereotypes of poor nonwhite people.

Because underclass is associated with pathological social behavior born of concentrated poverty in inner cities, the underclass category tends to sharpen the perception of difference between whites and blacks. Traits associated with the concept of underclass—disinterest in schooling, high dropout rates, violent crime, drugs, chronic unemployment, loitering, out-of-wedlock pregnancy, oppositional culture of hostility toward authority, and welfare dependence—contrast sharply with culturally legitimated traits associated with the white middle class. The concept of underclass is associated with negative stereotypes of *the other* in direct opposition to the cultural orientation of mainstream society.

African Americans and Latinos in the northeastern United States are an overwhelmingly urban population residing in central cities. As Jencks (1993) has documented, most adult blacks in central cities have jobs, are married, and have middle-class aspirations for themselves and their children. They view themselves as the working poor, but now they are at risk of being classified as belonging to the underclass. To the extent that underclass becomes an institutionalized label for poor racial minorities who live in central cities, institutional mechanisms theorized by Douglas (1986) will tend to reinforce social boundaries, in effect segregating a population of minorities that is substantially larger in size than the numbers that authentically conform to the traits attributed to the underclass. There is an inherent danger here. As Jencks (1993) has forcefully argued, social scientists need to be attentive to a very serious potential problem: concepts that are advanced in the form of hypotheses must not be treated as objective accounts of reality unless and until they are confirmed through repeated and rigorous empirical tests.

CONCLUSION

The institutional changes that since World War II have dismantled formal racism have profoundly altered the assimilation experiences of immigrant minorities and their descendants. To be sure, informal racism is still practiced by informal networks, and it can effectively exclude racial minorities from opportunity structures in the mainstream economy.[2] But the legal system matters. The legislation outlawing racial discrimination has increased in nontrivial ways the cost of discrimination (Nee and Alba n.d.). Moreover, because the law fundamentally is expressed through normative ideas, legal change alters ideology as well. Today, few whites openly state racist views without some form of public censure. Even within the private domain, racist remarks are often checked by informal sanctions between friends and acquaintances.

[2] Research by Granovetter (1973) and others has shown that many good jobs are allocated through networks.

The institutional changes have hastened assimilation processes compared to those of the pre–World War II period (Alba and Nee 2003), increasing racial minorities' chances for success and increasing their access to mainstream institutions and opportunities. Although informal racism has not disappeared, it is not sufficiently powerful to raise insurmountable barriers to social mobility, either in higher education or in labor markets.

Current assimilation patterns seem not to fit the model of segmented assimilation, with its intellectual lineage emphasizing impermeable social boundaries. Rather, the assimilation experiences of contemporary immigrants and their children seem to accord with the concept of unequal outcome. Many migrants are experiencing social mobility—upward, horizontal, and downward—but such divergent outcomes are a characteristic feature of advanced capitalist economies, for both the foreign and the native-born populations.

References

Alba, Richard, and Victor Nee. 2003. *Remaking the American Mainstream: Assimilation and Contemporary Immigration.* Cambridge, Mass.: Harvard University Press.

Chiswick, Barry R. 1977. "Sons of Immigrants: Are They at an Earnings Disadvantage?" *American Economic Review* 67: 376–80.

———. 1979. "The Economic Progress of Immigrants: Some Apparently Universal Patterns." In *Contemporary Economic Problems,* edited by William Fellner. Washington, D.C.: American Enterprise Institute.

Chiswick, Barry R., and Teresa Sullivan. 1995. "The New Immigrants." In *State of the Union: America in the 1990s,* edited by Reynolds Farley. New York: Russell Sage Foundation.

Dobbin, Frank, and Frank R. Sutton. 1998. "The Strength of a Weak State: The Rights Revolution and the Rise of Human Resources Management Division," *American Journal of Sociology* 104: 441–76.

Douglas, Mary. 1986. *How Institutions Think.* Syracuse, N.Y.: University of Syracuse Press.

Gordon, David. 1964. *Theories of Poverty and Underemployment: Orthodox, Radical and Dual Labor Market Perspectives.* Lexington, Mass.: Lexington.

Gordon, David, Michael Reich, and Richard Edwards. 1982. *Segmented Work: Divided Workers.* Cambridge: Cambridge University Press.

Granovetter, Mark. 1974. *Getting a Job: A Study of Contacts and Careers.* Cambridge, Mass.: Harvard University Press.

Jencks, Christopher. 1993. *Rethinking Social Policy: Race, Poverty, and the Underclass.* New York: Perennial.

Nee, Victor, and Richard Alba. n.d. "A Theory of Assimilation." In *Reinventing the Melting Pot*, edited by Tamar Jacoby. New York: The Free Press. In press.

Nee, Victor, and Jimy Sanders. 2001. "Understanding the Diversity of Immigrant Incorporation: A Forms of Capital Model," *Ethnic and Racial Studies*.

Nee, Victor, Jimy Sanders, and Scott Sernau. 1994. "Job Transitions in an Immigrant Metropolis: Ethnic Boundaries and the Mixed Economy," *American Sociological Review* 59: 849–72.

Nee, Victor, and Richard Swedberg, eds. n.d. *The Economic Sociology of Capitalism*. Princeton, N.J.: Princeton University Press. In press.

North, Douglass C. 1990. *Institutions, Institutional Change and Economic Performance*. Cambridge: Cambridge University Press.

Piore, Michael J. 1979. *Birds of Passage: Migrant Labor and Industrial Societies*. Cambridge: Cambridge University Press.

Skrentny, John David. 1996. *The Ironies of Affirmative Action: Politics, Culture and Justice in America*. Chicago: University of Chicago Press.

Sum, Andrew, Neeta Fogg, and Paul Harrington. 2002. "Immigrant Workers and the Great American Job Machine: The Contributions of New Foreign Immigration to National and Regional Labor Force Growth in the 1990s." Boston, Mass.: Center for Labor Market Studies, Northeastern University. Manuscript.

Waters, Mary C. 2000. *Black Identities: West Indian Dreams and American Realities*. Cambridge, Mass.: Harvard University Press.

Weber, Max. 1978 [1922]. *Economy and Society*. Berkeley: University of California Press.

Williamson, Oliver. 1975. *Markets and Hierarchies: Analysis and Antitrust Implications*. New York: The Free Press.

19

To Farms or Cities: A Historical Tension between Canada and Its Immigrants

HAROLD TROPER

In 2000 the government of Canada published an introductory primer on the history of Canadian immigration. The volume, *Forging our Legacy*, is a celebratory received history of Canada's immigration past that somehow even manages to wrap a silver lining around hateful episodes of racism and anti-Semitism. Treating history as if it were something of a ethical lesson, the volume maintains that Canada and Canadians, as if guided by a moral compass of collective memory, have learned from these dark chapters in their national past and are the better for it. And what is better in this case? Better is knowing that if Canada has not always been the most welcoming of societies, Canadians can still feel justly proud that in the end, as *Forging our Legacy* states, they "opened the country's door to successive waves of immigrants, each with a contribution to make" (Knowles 2000: 95).

Open doors in return for contributions. Homes and opportunities for services rendered. Here is immigration presented as a mutually advantageous contract between immigrants and the native-born, balanced beneficence. Immigrants make contributions; Canada offers homes and opportunities. If execution was sometimes a little uneven, overall immigration is judged a good deal for all involved. And, in truth, countless immigrants benefited from their immigration as much as Canada did. But, equally true, improving the lot of immigrants was not the primary intent of immigration policy. Immigration policy, including that during the decades of mass migration that straddled the turn of the century, had far more to do with what was thought best for Canada than it did with what was best for immigrants. Whatever the individual agenda of immigrants, the degree of welcome that immigrants received during much of the previous century was in direct proportion to their willingness to confine their contribution within a narrowly defined geographic and economic corridor. Indeed, what distinguishes Canadian immigration during the first half of the twentieth century—and makes it so different from that of the United States—is the extent to which Canadian immigration and settlement policy and practice were predicated on government streaming of non-English-speaking immigrants, *foreigners,* as they were commonly called, onto the vast interior hinterland, where government assumed they and their Canadian-born children and children's children would remain employed in farming and extractive labor. As a result, until after World War II, there was little or no positive room in the Canadian imagination for urban-bound immigrants. The immigration of *foreigners* was palatable so long as they demonstrated a willingness to stay on the farm, out of sight, out of mind, and, most certainly, out of cities.

How different this is from today. Barely one generation after the end of World War II, immigration is a singularly salient fact of Canadian urban life. According to the 1996 census, while just over 17 percent of all Canadians were born outside of Canada, approximately 90 percent of all the foreign-born live in Canada's fifteen largest urban centers. Toronto affords a clear example of the citified nature of Canada's current immigration experience. Just before the outbreak of World War II, Toronto was a city of about 650,000 persons, the vast majority of whom traced their roots back to Britain. The dominant community imagination was so overwhelmingly Anglo-centric that Toronto was commonly described as the "Ulster of the North," a municipal bulwark of Anglo-Protestant values and traditions. If this was a point of municipal pride, it was not to everyone's taste. As late as 1940, visiting English author Wyndham Lewis dismissed Toronto as "a mournful Scottish version of an American city," and Canada for that matter as "a sanctimonious icebox."

Whatever the prevailing urban tone, there was also an "otherness" to the city as well, a small community of mostly working-class Jews, alongside a sprinkling of immigrant Italian laborers and other southern and eastern Europeans and their children. Together, all these immigrant communities constituted only about 9 percent of the city's population. But forget about any celebration of the mosaic. This was not an era of multicultural appreciation. These immigrants and their children were in the city but not of it. Widely seen as outsiders, *foreigners* were kept at arm's length from the mainstream social and political life of the community, even as every effort was made to hurry their children down the road to assimilation. And what was assimilation? In the Canadian urban context, that was hard to define (Harney 1985: 2–3; Harney and Troper 1975). In *Under the Ribs of Death*, John Marlyn's classic tale of an immigrant child growing up in pre–World War II Winnipeg, the hero, wanting only to peel away his immigrant skin so he might fit in, attempts to explain to his Old World father that to become a real Canadian one must become "English."

> "The English," he whispered. "Pa, the only people who count are the English. Their fathers get all the best jobs. They're the ones nobody ever calls foreigners. Nobody ever makes fun of their homes or calls them "bologny-eaters" or laughs at the way they dress or talk. Nobody." He concluded bitterly, "because when you're English it's the same as bein' Canadian" (Marlyn 1964: 24).

How different things are today. Toronto in the immediate post-millennium is a sprawling metropolitan region of approximately 4,500,000 people. And the "Ulster of the North" is long gone. The once parochial Presbyterian town, where the Sunday blue laws, draconian liquor legislation, and the Orange Order held sway, now has a Roman Catholic plurality and trades on its cultural diversity as a selling point for tourists. And Toronto is Canada's major immigrant-receiving center. As many as three-quarters of all Toronto household heads were either born outside of Canada or have at least one parent who was. This is comparable to New York during the height of the immigration influx at the turn of the century (Ward 1971: 51–53).

And Toronto is also a poli-ethnic city. In 2000 the newly structured metropolitan government adopted as its motto, "Diversity Our Strength." Strength, perhaps. Diversity, most surely. Unlike cities like Los Angeles or Miami, no one or two immigrant groups stands as the dominant other. Included among the city's overlapping series of ethnic and immigrant communities are an estimated 450,000 Chinese, 400,000 Italians, and 250,000 Afro-Canadians, the largest component of which are of Caribbean background, although a separate and distinct infusion of Somalis, Ethiopians, and other Africans is currently taking place. There are upwards of 200,000 Jews and large and growing populations from the Indian subcontinent, Southeast Asia, Greece, Portugal, Poland, Russia, from across Hispanic America, and from the former Yugoslavia. More than one hundred different languages are spoken in this city (CIC 1999).

As a consequence of immigration, by the end of this decade it is estimated that the majority of those living in what was until recently an almost totally white Toronto will be people of non-European origin. This is impacting institutional life at all levels. For the past five years, for example, the majority of first-year students entering the University of Toronto, the national flagship university, were not white—all this in a Canada which, compared to the United States, has no appreciable history of involuntary migration by black slaves and no land border with the developing world. And this ethnic and racial diversity shows no sign of lessening. Compared with the Toronto of tomorrow, the Toronto of today may be recalled as a city of relative cultural homogeneity (Siemiatycki and Isin 1997; Orenstein 2000).

If Toronto can lay claim to being the most ethnically and racially diverse city in Canada, it is only by degree. Other Canadian cities are also characterized by a pluralism of origins that gives credence to the often overtaxed rhetoric of multiculturalism. What is more, the unprecedented population mix represented in today's Canadian urban complex—a mix that varies from city to city—is continually reshaping municipal politics, residential housing patterns, social service delivery, even the structure of class and the urban streetscape.

As noted, what makes this urban reality all the more remarkable is the degree to which earlier Canadian immigration policy deliberately and systematically designed to stream immigrants away from cities. Believing that Canada's economic future lay in the export potential of Canada's vast storehouse of extractive wealth, including agriculture, and carefully nurturing domestic industry growth sheltered behind tariff walls, Canadian immigration advocates rejected what they saw as the more laissez-faire American-style immigration policy. Instead, for much of Canadian history, officials favored a very much more closely managed and streamed immigration. Through the nineteenth and into the twentieth century, this translated into both aggressive government-funded recruitment of European agricultural settlers, people the government expected would take up farming in Canada, and more active engagement in the settlement process than was true of the American immigration experiment (Gates 1934).

Understanding themselves in competition for immigrants with other receiving countries—Australia, Argentina, and especially the United States—during much of the nineteenth century, Canadian immigration officials were often sparing with the truth as they actively hustled would-be settlers. With exaggerated claims of vast fertile lands available at low cost, abundant crops, and ready markets ringing in their ears, hundreds of thousands arrived in Canada ready to turn soil into gold. Too often, dirt stayed dirt. With the Canadian prairies still cut off from eastern Canada by the then impregnable Canadian shield, many settlers quickly discovered that the better agricultural lands near markets were expensive or already taken. Immigrants who did manage to farm often found themselves battered by an unforgiving Canadian climate, unstable prices for farm commodities, and marginal or cut-over timber lands unyielding to the plow. Despite their toil and sacrifice, it was only a matter of time before many found their resources drained and hopes dashed. Conditions were so difficult that tens of thousands of immigrants and Canadian-born alike, unable to find alternative employment in Canadian cities, turned their backs on Canada and moved to urban factory jobs or new lands in the United States. In fact, in the decades between Canadian Confederation in 1867 and the turn of the century, more people left Canada than entered (Bumsted 1992: 341, 347; Kelley and Trebilcock 1998: 61–110). So pronounced was the outflow of population to the United States that one wag claimed Canada's story was foretold in the books of the Bible: "It begins in Lamentations and ends in Exodus" (Hamilton 1952: 69).

This changed with the turn of the century. The completion of the first Canadian transcontinental railway in 1885, the Canadian Pacific, built with borrowed capital and cheap imported labor, opened the vast interior Canadian prairie northwest to agricultural settlement and resource exploitation. And the timing was auspicious. Only a few years later, a seemingly insatiable world market for Canadian raw materials and agricultural products, grains, lumber, and metals coincided with major population upheavals in central, southern, and eastern Europe. Millions were cutting loose to seek homes in the New World. While the lion's share of those who crossed the Atlantic settled in the United States, the outflow of population from Europe also produced a major wave of Canada-bound immigration, immigration that the government—working in league with the Canadian Pacific Railway, agricultural land marketing companies, and labor-intensive extractive industries—did all it could to transplant onto the vast agricultural hinterland of western Canada or into bush-based employment (Avery 1995).

The name most associated with this peak period of Canadian immigration is Clifford Sifton, Canada's aggressive minister of the interior. Sifton revitalized Canada's immigration recruitment program. Priority remained fixed on encouraging the immigration of experienced farmers. But this was not his only criterion. "Racial" or national origin was also a consideration. Unabashedly colonial, the government of the day defined those from outside the British Isles as *foreign;* and, unabashedly North American, the government also excluded white, American settlers (thousands of whom looked north to the lands of western Canada as their last best west) from the *foreign* category. In this pro-British and pro-American bias, Sifton and the Canadian government were no more racist in their thinking than the culture of their times. Canadian immigration policy, nonetheless, was as racially selective as it was economically self-serving. The question was how to balance the two, how to juggle economic necessity with racial selectivity.

With a demand for agricultural labor and workers for newly expanding extractive industry far outstripping the supply of the "preferred types" of immigrants willing to commit to Canada, Sifton authorized recruitment of other European agricultural settlers, albeit in a descending order of ethnic or racial preference. British and white American agriculturalists were obviously still ranked as the most desirable. They were closely followed by northern and western Europeans (Troper 1972a). Then came eastern European agriculturalists, Sifton's much-praised "peasants in sheep skinned coats." Lower still on the preferential ladder came those who, in both the public's and the government's mind, were less assimilable and less suitable to agriculture but amenable to supervised labor, southern Europeans. Bottoming out the racial sweepstakes came Asians, blacks, Gypsies, and eastern European Jews—all groups that were regarded as racially problematic, resistant to assimilation, or indisposed to farming and immigrant-intensive lumbering or mining.

Some of these less favored groups proved easier to exclude than others. Tough anti-Asian immigration regulations increasingly prevented all but a small number of Asians from entering Canada. Immigration regulations were also read so as to restrict the entry of blacks, including American blacks, into Canada (Munro 1971; Troper 1972b). Fear and prejudice against Gypsies was the legacy of all Western thought, and their immigration was discouraged. Controlling the admission of eastern European Jews, the most urban-inclined of all immigrant groups, proved somewhat more problematic. While immigration officials did not implement regulatory barriers specific to Jewish immigration, at least not until after World War I, Jews, like Gypsies, were informally excluded from the government's active recruitment program.

Overall, the government's program for recruiting farm- and extractive industry–bound immigration can be judged a success at least as measured in numbers. Between the turn of the century and World War I, Canada soaked up immigrants. While immigration into Canada never reached the absolute number that entered the United States in this era, the ratio of immigrants to the Canadian-born population was much higher. In 1896, the year Sifton took command of Canadian immigration, only 17,000 immigrants entered Canada. In 1913, a year before the outbreak of World War I halted immigration from Europe, Canada took in more than 400,000 immigrants. So massive was this immigration that in the first decade of the century Canada's population shot up by 40 percent. Most non-English-speaking settlers were ushered into geo-economic niches reserved for them in prairie agriculture and on the rugged mining and lumbering frontier (Kelley and Trebilcock 1998: 111–13).

If European immigration fueled economic expansion, it also became a source of some anxiety. For many English-speaking Canadians, the continuing influx of strange peoples speaking strange languages—people so recently subject to foreign kings, czars, and kaisers, and who prayed to alien gods—raised questions about whether these *foreigners* could ever be assimilated into Canadian society. French-Canadian leaders, on the other hand, fretted that these *foreigners* would indeed assimilate—into English-speaking society, further tipping the national political and demographic balance in favor of *les anglais.* Nevertheless, so long as immigrants continued to play the subservient economic and social role reserved for them, so long as the larger community remained sold on the economic value of immigration, and so long as *foreigners* remained tucked away on the agricultural and resource extractive hinterland, then anti-immigrant sentiment stayed more or less in check.

It did not stay in check for long. No laws compelled immigrants to live their lives to suit immigration policy planners or gatekeepers. As a result, while many immigrants remained committed to farming or stayed employed in lumbering or mining, others did not. Thousands who found the going rough spilled off farms and out of the bush. They flowed from farm to city, from agricultural labor into a factory wage economy. In defiance of immigration policy, some never even made it to the farm gate but instead headed straight from port of entry into the urban marketplace in search of jobs. Thus, despite government priority given to keeping immigrants out of cities, and in obvious violation of expressed policy intent, almost half of all immigrants who came to Canada in the years after the turn of the century eventually ended up in cities.

Why did this happen? Was not the policy assumption that immigrants would remain tucked away in rural Canada? Was not streaming immigration the policy assumption underpinning Canada's welcome to so many *foreigners?* Yes, but immigration policy fell victim to its own success. Even if many immigrant farmers suffered economic setbacks and many immigrant laborers reached out for something better, the wealth and energy that flowed from western economic activity, from agricultural expansion and exploitation of the mining and lumbering frontier, proved a tonic for urban growth. It stimulated urban industrial expansion and development of the urban infrastructure. This translated into jobs in the urban labor market, jobs for immigrants. Before long, immigrants escaping or avoiding the land were drawn into urban wage labor—paving streets, laying trolley tracks, laboring in the expanding textile factories, tunneling the sewer systems, or working as household domestics.[1]

But this was not the way it was supposed to be, and many worried about the consequences. Indeed, the more Canadian cities became home to cheap immigrant labor, the more urban immigration became a source of sharp public debate. In a series of press articles, Mackenzie King weighed the impact of immigrant enclaves on Toronto. "Does their presence here portend an evil for this city such as [those] which have come upon the United States," he asked, "or, is the class of foreigners in this city here cast in a better mould and are they likely to prove at once good citizens and a strength to the community?" (*Daily Mail and Empire*, September 25, 1897).

For some, the answer was self-evident. Immigrants piling up in Canadian cities were trespassing in an Anglo-Canadian urban domain. They did not belong. Their presence violated a covenant the government had made with mainstream Canadians that Canadian cities

---

[1] A classic novel of urban immigrant labor of the day is Michael Ondaatji's *In the Skin of a Lion*, about Macedonian laborers in urban Canada in the 1920s.

would not be centers of major immigrant population. Yet here they were. And these *foreigners* in the city were seen by many as a threat to community health, a threat to urban social stability, and incompatible with a desire to maintain Canadian cities as the high ground of a British–North American way of life. Looking south across the border, guardians of the Canadian city gate borrowed American anti-immigrant arguments to warn against the dangers of unchecked urban immigration, an immigration, they charged, that threatened to bring municipal blight, political corruption, and miscegenationist race suicide. And what of violence? Immigrants, some argued, were given to violence among themselves. What would it take to provoke them to violence against their Canadian-born betters?

> An Italian and a Pole seldom see eye to eye when they happen to be sufficiently interested in each other to try it; and both exhibit little reluctance to filling up the chasm of conversation with a knife or pistol. The Swede prefers his fists, the Italian a knife, the Pole and Russian a revolver, and the Hungarian uses anything from a rock to his teeth (Amy 1913: 219).

The signs of urban decay, some insisted, were easy to find. Were not these *foreigners* in Canadian cities in defiance of Canadian immigration policy? Did not these *foreigners*, largely Catholics and Jews, cleave to Old World ways and one another, rather than showing any inclination to assimilate? In 1919 a prestigious Canadian medical journal reflected growing unease when it warned, "Canada has been the dumping ground for thousands of undesirable immigrants—from the slums of the British cities, from Austria, Poland and other eastern European countries. She is also the victim of colonies of sects who refuse to become assimilated—to become Canadian. This must stop. Our asylums and jails are overfull of degenerates, criminals and mental defectives" (*Canadian Journal of Medicine and Surgery* 1919: 278–279; see also Godler 1977).

Of course, there were those who countered that immigrant labor was required in cities to do the work that the native-born rejected, and that, with time and a spirit of openness, the redemptive power of assimilation would turn them into us. But these arguments were only convincing so long as immigrants in the city played their assigned economic role. It was one thing if immigrants were content to spend their days in sweat labor. It was another to find *foreigners* daring to compete and compete successfully with skilled native-born artisans and small businessmen. And what about the children of immigrants, untutored in Canadian ways, who still excelled in the public educational system and were pressing for access to universities, to professions, and to the political arena? No. If these *foreigners* in the city did not respect boundaries, did not know their place—and at best their place was at the margins of urban society—perhaps immigrant groups that tended to gravitate toward cities in Canada should be denied entry to Canada.

In the aftermath of World War I, the clamor for wholesale immigration restriction grew so loud the government could not ignore it without paying a price in electoral support. For its part, the government was also increasingly convinced of the need for immigration restriction. After years of encouraging settlement of the Canadian west, better prairie agricultural land was reaching its carrying capacity. Less and less agricultural immigrant labor was going to be needed in the future. A slowdown in immigration made sense. Accordingly, during the early 1920s Canada moved quickly to restrict immigration. In the process it closed the immigration door first and hardest against those groups that had proven themselves most likely to settle in cities.

The method used to restrict unwanted European immigration was as artfully simple as it was administratively transparent. Unlike the U.S. Congress, which in 1924 responded to growing nativist and restrictionist sentiment by passing quota legislation that effectively closed the United States to the European world, the Canadian Parliament passed no new legislation. Rather, the cabinet approved draconian changes to immigration regulations that accomplished much the same end. Under the new regulations, all European applicants were divided into three classes—a preferred class, a non-preferred class, and a permit class. The preferred class was made up of northern and western Europeans. Their immigration was allowed to continue unfettered so long as individual applicants met standard health and other regulatory provisions of the existing legislation. The non-preferred class was set up as a concession to influential Canadian railway interests and land companies still hoping to sell off their remaining agricultural real estate, no matter how marginal the quality. This concession allowed for limited immigration of central and eastern Europeans, so long as they were committed to buying farmland, could prove to authorities that they had the independent means to do so, and would guarantee never to become a public charge.

The permit class was something else again. It was composed of those who in the past had shown little or no inclination to farm—southern Europeans and all Jews irrespective of country of origin (except those from Britain or the United States). Under the new regulations, these immigrant categories were flatly denied entry to Canada except for those very few individuals who could somehow acquire an immigration permit issued not by immigration authorities but by a specific order of cabinet and at the discretion of cabinet. For those in the permit class, permission to enter Canada was now shifted from routine administrative process to the murky world of political patronage. The only crack in this wall of exclusion was an exemption allowing for reunification of Canadian residents with a narrowly defined category of first-degree family members abroad. Otherwise, Canada's doors were now closed to most eastern Europeans and to virtually all southern Europeans and Jews (Troper 1987).

Following the market bust of 1929, with mass unemployment in urban Canada and a collapse in farm income, any residual sympathy for admitting immigrants evaporated. The immigration door was further sealed. Immigration officials who had once beat the bushes for immigrants now stood guard against any breach in the Canadian wall of restriction. So difficult was it to enter Canada during the 1930s and 1940s that Canada had arguably the worst record of all possible western receiving states in the admission of refugees from Nazi Germany (Abella and Troper 1982). In the anti-immigration climate of the day, even *foreigners* already in Canada were not safe. Former immigrants made destitute by the Great Depression were warned against registering for welfare assistance lest they and their families be subject to deportation for becoming a public charge. The pointed stick of urban racism never dug deeper than it did with the mass internment of Japanese Canadians during World War II and, often forgotten, the short-lived program of "voluntary repatriation" of Japanese Canadians back to Japan at the war's end (Drystek 1982; Sunahara 1981).

But World War II and its aftermath also proved a critical watershed in the history of both Canadian immigration and Canadian cities. While many government policy planners at first feared that a postwar downturn in public spending would propel Canada back into the job-hungry economic depression of the 1930s, the exact opposite took place. After a shaky start, Canada's much expanded wartime industrial capacity was quickly retooled to meet pent-up demand for peacetime consumer goods and services preciously beyond the reach of many

Canadians, not just since the beginning of the war but since the beginning of the depression that preceded it. What is more, exploding domestic consumer demand was matched by huge and expanding export markets for Canadian goods and raw materials spurred by the American Marshall Plan's determination to kick start the reconstruction of western Europe. Rather than a shortage of jobs in Canada, within a year or so after the war's end there was a severe shortage of labor, especially in the industrial and service sectors.

An informal coalition of labor-intensive industry bullish on the economy, along with older if politically unsure eastern European ethnic groups pressing for admission to Canada of kith and kin, began lobbying to have Canada's immigration door reopened. The government was at first hesitant if not distrustful. How strong was domestic economic growth? Would foreign markets hold up? How well would the larger Canadian public respond to any reopening of *foreign* immigration? The government might have preferred a go-it-slow policy, but this was not to be. With industrial spokesmen warning that labor shortages would stall growth, the Canadian government was forced, however reluctantly at first, back into the immigrant importation business.

Fearing a negative public response to any sudden influx of previously unwelcome immigrant categories, Canadian authorities at first prioritized the arrival of all but British and western Europeans. Prime Minister Mackenzie King was only reflecting the national mood when he observed that "the people of Canada do not wish to make a fundamental alteration in the character of their population through mass immigration." Ethnic selectivity in admitting immigrants from Europe, he stated, would remain in place. "Canada is perfectly within her rights in selecting the persons whom we regard as desirable to our future. It is not a 'fundamental human right' of any alien to enter Canada. It is a privilege. It is a matter of domestic policy" (House of Commons 1947).

Privileged or not, those determined to retain Canada's racial wall of immigration restriction were increasingly outflanked. Labor-intensive industry demanded far more labor than British or western European sources could supply, and the government confronted withering pressure to deliver. Before long the immigration door was reopened to eastern and, soon thereafter, southern European immigrants. The door was also reopened to Jews. But as government expanded the circle of ethnic acceptability, it was not about to forgo a hands-on role in streaming immigrants to areas of high labor need. And the high-need areas were no longer predominantly in agriculture. In a reversal of the former policy of promoting farm-bound immigration, an overwhelming number of postwar immigrants were systematically channeled into industrial, service, skilled labor, and even professional employment, largely in the urban context. With government blessing, Canadian cities were becoming immigrant cities.

What of the bedrock vitriolic and politically acidic xenophobia that had so colored Canadian urban thinking only a few years earlier? What about the long-standing certitude, bordering on sacred trust, that Canada's cities should remain bulwarks of British civility in North America? Put simply, the past was jettisoned, abandoned in the headlong rush to accommodate the new urban-bound immigration tide.

Much was written in the decades after World War II about the process of accommodating the inflow of postwar immigration into Canada, including discussion of immigration policy management, immigrant reception and settlement issues, housing, jobs, education, provision of social services, factors in community formation, and intergroup relations.[2] One area not nearly so well explored, but one that is central to the success of the urban settlement and integration process, involves the extension of human rights legislation and the revamping of citizenship regulations.[3] Not only do these bear directly on the life chances of individual immigrants and ethnic groups in Canadian society, but in many ways the campaign for rights protection, especially human rights legislation, can be seen as the political coming of age of ethnic communities and their leadership.

This is not to argue that the enshrining of human rights in Canada was a dependant consequence of urban-bound immigration or ethnic activism. It was not. But it is to argue that the poli-ethnic postwar infusion of new immigrants into the Canadian urban context, an infusion shaped by economic necessity and overseen by government, added an ethnic dimension to the campaign on behalf of human rights legislation. What is more, immigrants of the previous generation, those who came to Canada after the turn of the century, and their children supplied much of the organizational leadership and lobbying muscle to the human rights struggle. The result proved something of a social and legal revolution. In less than one generation a new Canadian urban mind-set shifted the law from defense of Anglo-privilege and Anglo-

---

[2] See, for example, Carbide 1957; Richmond 1967; Hawkins 1972; Green 1976; Allyn 1977; Callback 1974.

[3] Two exceptions are Backhouse 1999 and Walker 1997.

conformity to a public embrace of human rights and a celebration of the mosaic.

Let us take an admittedly cursory look at this revolution by focusing on three interlocking public policy areas of debate that cover a period of three decades. The first involves a redefinition of the legal framework for what it meant to be Canadian; the second swirls around the campaign, inclusive of ethnic communities, for passage of legally binding human rights legislation; and the third explores a uniquely Canadian formulation of the ethnic and racial mosaic as a positive Canadian value. Each of these areas of public policy debate affected or was affected by the postwar influx of immigrants into the urban complex.

The first policy debate was about Canadian citizenship itself. Little remembered today is the fact that until 1947 there was legally no such thing as Canadian citizenship. Grounded in an already antiquated notion that Canada and those who lived in Canada were the North American extension of the British imperial destiny, until 1947 those who lived in Canada were designated British subjects resident of Canada, not Canadians citizens. The person most remembered in the citizenship debate is Paul Martin. Toward the end of the war, this Liberal backbencher was appointed secretary of state. He claimed to have previously toyed with the notion of replacing the British designation with a separate and distinct Canadian citizenship, but, as he recounted in his memoirs, his commitment to press the idea on cabinet and Parliament came during a 1945 official visit to then just liberated Europe. While in France, he asked to visit the Canadian military cemetery at Dieppe. As Martin recalled, he walked amid the rows of graves, some still fresh with wooden markers, and was deeply moved by the incredible variety of family names found among the Canadian fallen—names that spoke to the pluralism of origins even then making up Canadian society. "Of whatever origin, these men were Canadians." They had fought and died for Canada. They deserved to be remembered as Canadians. In their memory, Martin claimed, he championed legislation to create a separate and distinct Canadian citizenship (Martin 1983: 437–54; Brown 1996).

Without negating Martin's account of events or his major contribution to the passage of citizenship legislation, it has to be acknowledged that the government had other pressing reasons for proclaiming Canadian citizenship. It hoped that a distinct homemade Canadian citizenship—separate from the designation of Britain subject, with all its association to a crumbling empire—would among other things enhance Canada's profile as an independent voice in the community of nations and benefit Canada's bilateral and trade relations with the developing world.

Still more important, the government intended that a separate and distinct Canadian citizenship would further its domestic national unity agenda. By proclaiming Canadian citizenship, the government was stating that all Canadians—native-born and immigrant, French- and English-speaking—need not share a common heritage in order to share a common destiny as Canadians.

In 1947, Canadian citizenship became the right of all those born in Canada or formerly naturalized as British subjects in Canada. It was also made accessible to the new generation of largely urban bound immigrants, not just to regularize their legal status but, more importantly, in order to instill in them a sense of belonging, of membership in the national community. How much sweeter that belonging must have felt to the previous generation of urban immigrants and their children, so recently treated as interlopers, marginalized if not unwelcome in the cities where they struggled to put down roots. And they did not regard the granting of citizenship as an act of state largesse, a gift bestowed from above. No; it was not a gift. It had been paid for at a high price. During the recent war, these former immigrants and their children sacrificed for the common cause. Not only did they enlist in the Canadian military in disproportionate numbers, but many also applied their skills and entrepreneurial acumen, once unvalued, to furthering the war effort. In the postwar period they were no longer ready to accept second-class status. Canada was their home. They had helped build it and had defended it; they felt a proprietary right to share in its life. Canadian citizenship, proclaimed on January 1, 1947, was hailed as a major step toward achieving that goal.[4]

Whether the government intended or not, Canadian citizenship turned out to be far more than a simple affirmation of national unity, a symbolic statement of belonging. For many newly minted Canadians, citizenship carried with it an implicit promise of equality of access and participation in Canadian society—irrespective of whether Canadian or

---

[4] This short discussion on the proclamation of Canadian citizenship and how it related to public and government acceptance of urban-bound immigration does not pretend to deal with larger issues of identity and citizen participation, which are so much a part of current debate on immigration and citizenship. A useful introduction to these issues can be found in Bloeraad 2000.

foreign-born—of whatever heritage, religion, national origin, and irrespective of any historical claim that a group might make to being more Canadian than any other. If it would take time for the legal reality to match the promise, the proclamation of an inclusive Canadian citizenship became a prerequisite foundation on which to build an aggressive campaign for human rights.

From our vantage point today, it is easily forgotten that, following World War II, discrimination in housing, employment, education, and access to public facilities was both common and tolerated in law. By the late 1940s and early 1950s, however, an urban-based coalition—including organized labor, liberal churches, progressive political voices, academics, educators, and older urban-based ethnic communities—was pressing demands for a comprehensive and enforceable package of human rights legislation. The coalition could take heart from widespread revulsion at the racial excesses of Nazism, wide rejection of scientific racism, of social Darwinist and eugenic thinking of the past, and the continued withering away of an Anglo-centrism rendered anachronistic by the withering of the British imperial dream. Moreover, to the south there was the example offered by similar human rights campaigns in the United States. Adding fuel to the Canadian human rights fire was growing public acceptance of urban-bound immigration and an increased understanding that smoothing the way for immigrant integration into the larger civil society would require a legal affirmation of human rights.

Nevertheless, human rights activists did not have it all their own way. There was still deep-seated resistance to change, resistance to government interjection in what some proclaimed was their private domain. Just as Mackenzie King warned that immigrants should not be allowed to undermine the existing social order, there were those who warned that any legally entrenched human rights code would do just that. What human rights activists labeled as discrimination and prejudice, the opposition defended as freedom of choice, freedom of association, and the right to the enjoyment of one's private property and the control of one's own business. Turning one of the human rights activists' arguments on its head, opponents protested that human rights legislation would spell the end of traditional values and the right that Canadians had fought a war to protect. As human rights activists pressed government for legislated remedies to human rights abuses, naysayers just as passionately cautioned against the dangers of government encroachment in the private sphere.

To win political support for their cause, the human rights advocates required both capitalization and leadership. Both were brought to the human rights table by a rights coalition shaped in large part by prewar immigrants, now urban ethnic communities. In Ontario, Canada's most populous province and also the country's postwar economic and population powerhouse, the small but organized Jewish community in Toronto played a low-key but pivotal role in the human rights campaign. Ironically, those characteristics that had previously marked Jews as a potential threat to the larger community values—their overwhelming urbanness, their commitment to community (read clannishness), their degree of organizational completeness, and their readiness to embrace education as a tool in upward mobility and competitive engagement in business or professional markets—equipped the organized Jewish community to assume a leadership role in the human rights coalition. As a result of hard-won Jewish entry into previously restricted professional, commercial, and educational activity, by the early 1950s an increasingly English-speaking Jewish polity could tap the expertise of well-placed lawyers, academics, labor leaders, media personalities, and newly affluent businessmen. And for Jews, as with other ethnic and immigrant communities, the issue of human rights legislation was not simply one of abstract values or national image. Still feeling the sting of legally sanctioned racism, and so recently the target for Canadian immigration restriction, now urban ethnic communities regarded the human rights struggle as crucial to ensuring and legitimizing their place in Canadian society.[5]

With an infusion of funds and an increasingly well organized political and media lobbying effort, the Canadian human rights coalition gradually carried the day. In the first decade after the war, Canadian provinces, with Saskatchewan leading the way, enacted fair employment and accommodation legislation barring discrimination on account of race, religion, or country of origin. In the international arena, Canada signed the Universal Declaration of Human Rights, adding momentum to the human rights agenda. Ontario, home to the largest percentage of new immigrants, passed its first fair employment and fair accommodation legislation in 1954. Courts, responding to legisla-

[5] Patrias and Frager 2001; Lambertson 2001; Tulchinsky 1998: 269–76; Mar 2002. The high-profile Jewish community role in human rights lobbying is not peculiar to Canada. Although the legal and political context was different, the Jewish community was equally active in U.S. human rights campaigning. See Svonkin 1997.

tion and the spirit of the day, began using their powers to extend the reach of human rights legislation (Walker 1997).

This rolling acceptance of both a singular Canadian citizenship and the legal guarantees of human rights for all Canadians mirrored the larger turnaround in postwar urban Canadian thinking with regard to the legitimate place of immigrants and ethnic communities. They were no longer in the cities by sufferance. They were there by right, and now by right of law. This new thinking even affected language. By the early 1960s, immigrants were no longer *"foreigners."* Increasingly, they were "New Canadians."

It was also only a matter of time before domestic human rights successes spilled over into Canadian immigration policy and administration. Beginning in the mid-1950s and through the next decade, ethnic and racial immigration barriers, which still closed off Canada to most immigration by non-Europeans, were chipped away. The last racially discriminatory provision in the immigration legislation—a sop to British Columbia restricting Asian family reunification—was finally expunged from immigration regulations in 1967, Canada's Centennial Year. Four years later, in 1971, for the first time in Canadian history the majority of all immigrants entering Canada in any one year were of non-European origin. Since then, non-European immigrants have remained in the majority, becoming a Canadian immigration fact of life and remaking the racial face of major Canadian cities (Kelley and Trebilcock 1998: 350–51).

The year 1971 also brought with it a focus on the third area of public policy debate. That year the federal government articulated its policy of multiculturalism. The political inspiration and purpose of official multiculturalism were widely argued at the time, and much of the criticism of the policy reflected distrust of government motives. Some dismissed official multiculturalism as a calculated political trade-off. The federal Liberals were accused of delivering up multiculturalism to ethnic leaders in return for ethnic support of then beleaguered federal bilingualism. Others, especially in Quebec, scoffed that multiculturalism was a cynical federal ploy designed to delegitimate Quebec's national aspirations by arguing that French Canadian nationalism was but one of many parochial expressions of ethnic revivalism then stirring in Canada. Still others, including sociologist John Porter, suggested that multiculturalism was anti-progressive by diverting the energy of ethnic leaders away from mainstream engagement into parochial, ethnic-based activity. In so doing, he warned, it served to perpetuate the dominance of the existing Anglo-Canadian social and business power elite. Rulers would rule while ethnics danced in church basements. Still others charged that multiculturalism was just federal pork-barrel politics in folk costume, another chance for politicians to buy voters with their own money.[6]

Oddly, what all these accusations had in common was their acceptance of a mid-1960s notion that a "third force" was abroad in the land—a collective of increasingly urban, middle-class, and politically restive ethnic groups—who were challenging the traditional French/English duality that had so long dominated Canadian political and cultural life. Certainly the Royal Commission on Bilingualism and Biculturalism, set up in the early 1960s to examine the state of English/French relations, was besieged by ethnic spokespersons purportedly speaking for this "third force" and demanding government recognition of cultural "rights" in Canada for others besides French and English charter groups.

While the existence of a "third force" as a united ethnic political voice would ultimately prove more imagined than real, there can be little doubt that both the Royal Commission and the government of the day recognized that the traditional model of Canadian cultural politics, constructed along the fault line of English/French relations, was no longer viable in a changed Canada. The Commission advised the government accordingly (Royal Commission 1970). The government, with wide public support, responded in 1971 by proclaiming its policy of multiculturalism. Whatever else the federal multiculturalism policy did, it articulated a new, urban-based, and pluralistic Canadian vision. As first outlined, the federal multiculturalism policy statement eschewed formal recognition of any overriding or primary national cultural tradition. In so doing, it affirmed bilingualism, and English and French as the two official national languages, but it rejected biculturalism—a notion of Canada as a product of the nation-building efforts of two charter groups—British and French—who retain a proprietary right to determine the boundaries of Canadian identity and a custodial prerogative to preserve the primacy of their respective cultural heritages. Instead, multiculturalism promised respect for diversity, and pluralism as the true and only basis of Canadian identity, while at the

6 For different views on the origins of the 1971 federal multicultural policy and response to it, see Burnet 1976, 1979; Troper 1978; Porter 1972; Lupul 1983; Breton 1979.

same time pledging to remove all remaining barriers to full and equal participation in Canadian society.

Again, it might be interesting in another context to speculate as to whether multiculturalism was good policy—or, for that matter, how and whether it worked at all. But what is important for us today is that in proclaiming its multiculturalism policy, the Canadian government, picking its way through a minefield of cultural identity issues, was acknowledging that no overriding national cultural consensus had taken root through more than one hundred years of national development. Rather than see this as a vice, the policy statement argued that this lack of a singular agreed cultural consensus was a national virtue. In fact, it was a core feature of Canadian identity. As the policy statement asserted, "there is no official culture, nor does any ethnic group take precedence over any other. No citizen or group of citizens is other than Canadian, and all should be treated fairly." Accordingly, the government declared that the binding force in the Canadian social compact henceforth would be understood as grounded in mutual respect rooted in cultural diversity, the same cultural diversity that, as a result of postwar immigration, was increasingly the lived reality of the Canadian street (*Encyclopedia of Canada's Peoples* 1999).

In the late 1990s, multiculturalism would again become a source of sharp public debate.[7] But at the time the policy was first proclaimed, multiculturalism struck a responsive cord, especially in urban Canada. Whatever else multiculturalism did or did not do, it symbolically rounded the circle begun with the enactment of a separate and distinct Canadian citizenship. If multiculturalism was not the Magna Carta for group rights that some hoped for and others feared, it did reassure Canadians of all backgrounds that a personal and individual cultural affinity was not antithetical with the common good. Not only was encouraging urban immigration a federal priority, but the resulting pluralism of origins was seen as a public good, a characteristic underscoring Canadian uniqueness.

In retrospect, it is easy to be cynical about official multiculturalism and the failure of government to deliver on a promise of a truly inclusive Canadian social context. And it is also easy to find gaps in the net of Canadian human rights protections and to agree that, although racism is no longer sanctioned in law, it is too often quietly sanctioned in community practice. And nobody can deny that the lot of current immigrants in urban Canada is anything close to problem free. Not by a

---

[7] See Bassoondath 1994; Bibby 1990; Davetian 1994; Abu-Laban and Stasiulis 1992.

long shot. But it is true that the Canadian urban experience is now an immigrant and ethnic experience; and equally important, it is accepted as such by both government and the larger civil society. Contrast this with a generation ago, when the very idea of sanctioned urban-bound immigration—let alone immigration of non-Europeans—would have been dismissed as a nightmare vision. Any government advocating it would have been squashed by the weight of voter rage. But the postwar injection of immigrants in the urban context—not in opposition to, but as part of, a government-managed labor strategy—shaped and was shaped by the package of human rights advances that now defines modern Canada. This is a hard-won legacy of urban-bound Canadian immigration.

References

Abella, Irving, and Harold Troper. 1982. *None Is Too Many: Canada and the Jews of Europe, 1933–1948.* Toronto: Lester, Orpen and Dennys.

Abu-Laban, Yasmun, and Daiva Stasiulis. 1992. "Ethnic Pluralism under Siege: Popular and Partisan Opposition to Multiculturalism," *Canadian Public Policy* 18: 365–86.

Allyn, Nathaniel Constantine. 1977. *European Immigration into Canada, 1946–1951.* Toronto: McClelland and Stewart.

Amy, W. Lacy. 1913. "The Life of the Bohunk," *Canadian Magazine,* January.

Avery, Donald H. 1995. *Reluctant Host: Canada's Response to Immigrant Workers, 1896–1994.* Toronto: McClelland and Stewart.

Backhouse, Constance. 1999. *Colour-Coded: A Legal History of Racism in Canada.* Toronto: Osgood Society/University of Toronto Press.

Bassoondath, Neil. 1994. *Selling Illusions: The Cult of Multiculturalism.* Toronto: Penguin.

Bibby, Reginald. 1990. *Mosaic Madness: The Poverty and Potential of Life in Canada.* Toronto: Stoddart.

Bloeraad, Irene. 2000. "Citizenship and Immigration: A Current Review," *Journal of International Migration and Integration* 1: 9–37.

Breton, Raymond. 1979. "From a Different Perspective: French Canada and the Issue of Immigration and Multiculturalism," *TESL Talk* 10, no. 3: 45–56.

Brown, Robert Craig. 1996. "Full Partnership in the Fortunes and Future of the Nation." In *Ethnicity and Citizenship: The Canadian Case,* edited by Jean Laponce and William Safran. London: Frank Cass.

Bumsted, J.M. 1992. *The Peoples of Canada: A Post-Confederation History.* Toronto: Oxford.

Burnet, Jean. 1976. "Ethnicity: Canadian Experience and Policy," *Sociological Focus* 9: 199–207.

———. 1979. "Myths and Multiculturalism," *Canadian Journal of Education* 4: 43–98.

Callback, Warren. 1974. *The Effect of Immigration on Population*. Ottawa: Manpower and Immigration.

Canadian Journal of Medicine and Surgery. 1919. " Diseased Immigrants."

Carbide, David. 1957. *Canadian Immigration Policy: A Critique*. Toronto: University of Toronto Press.

CIC (Citizenship and Immigration Canada). 1999. *Facts and Figures 1998: Immigration Overview*. Ottawa: Public Works.

Davetian, Benet. 1994. "Out of the Melting Pot and into the Fire: An Essay on Neil Bassoondath's Book on Multiculturalism," *Canadian Ethnic Studies* 26: 135–40.

Drystek, Henry F. 1982. "The Simplest and Cheapest Mode of Dealing with Them: Deportation from Canada before World War II," *Social History* 15: 407–43.

Encyclopedia of Canada's Peoples. 1999 "Multiculturalism," pp. 997–1006. Toronto: University of Toronto Press.

Gates, Paul W. 1934. "Official Encouragement of Immigration by the Provinces of Canada," *Canadian Historical Review* 15: 24–38.

Godler, Zlata. 1977. "Doctors and the New Immigrants," *Canadian Ethnic Studies* 9: 6–17.

Green, Alan. 1976. *Immigration and the Postwar Canadian Economy*. Toronto: Macmillan.

Hamilton, Robert M., ed. 1952. *Canadian Quotations and Phrases, Literary and Historical*. Toronto: McClelland and Stewart.

Harney, Robert F. 1985. "Ethnicity and Neighbourhoods." In *Gathering Place: Peoples and Neighbourhoods of Toronto, 1834–1945*, edited by Robert F. Harney. Toronto: MHSO.

Harney, Robert F., and Harold Troper. 1975. *Immigrants: A Portrait of the Urban Experience*. Toronto: Van Nostrand Reinhold.

Hawkins, Freda. 1972. *Canada and Immigration: Public Policy and Public Concern*. Montreal: McGill-Queen's University Press.

House of Commons. 1947. *House of Commons Debates*, May 1, 2644-47.

Kelley, Ninette, and Michael Trebilcock. 1998. *The Making of the Mosaic: A History of Canadian Immigration Policy*. Toronto: University of Toronto Press.

Knowles, Valerie. 2000. *Forging Our Legacy: Canadian Citizenship and Immigration, 1900–1977*. Ottawa: Public Works.

Lambertson, Ross. 2001. "'The Dresden Story': Racism, Human Rights, and the Jewish Labour Committee of Canada," *Labour* 47: 43–82.

Lupul, Manoly. 1983. "Multiculturalism and Canada's White Ethnics," *Canadian Ethnic Studies*, pp. 99–107.

Mar, Lisa Rose. 2002. "From Diaspora to North American Civil Rights: Chinese Canadian Ideas, Identities and Brokers in Vancouver, British Columbia, 1924 to 1960." Ph.D. dissertation, University of Toronto.

Marlyn, John. 1964. *Under the Ribs of Death*. Toronto: New Canadian Library.

Martin, Paul. 1983. *A Very Public Life: Far From Home*. Ottawa: Deneau.

Munro, J.A. 1971. "British Columbia and the Chinese Evil: Canada's First Anti-Asiatic Immigration Law," *Journal of Canadian Studies* 6: 42–51.

Orenstein, Michael. 2000. *Ethno-racial Inequality in the City of Toronto: An Analysis of the 1996 Census*. Toronto: Access and Equality Centre.

Patrias, Camela, and Ruth A. Frager. 2001. "'This Is Our Country, These Are Our Rights': Minorities and the Origins of Ontario's Human Rights Campaigns," *Canadian Historical Review* 82: 17–35.

Porter, John. 1972. "Dilemmas and Contradictions of a Multi-ethnic Society," *Transactions of the Royal Society of Canada*, pp. 193–205.

Richmond, Anthony. 1967. *Post-War Immigrants in Canada*. Toronto: University of Toronto Press.

Royal Commission on Bilingualism and Biculturalism. 1970. *Royal Commission on Bilingualism and Biculturalism Book IV: The Cultural Contribution of the Other Ethnic Groups*. Ottawa: Information Canada.

Siemiatycki, Mayer, and Engin Isin. 1997. "Immigration, Ethno-racial Diversity and Urban Citizenship in Toronto," *Canadian Historical Review* 15: 73–102.

Sunahara, Ann M. 1981. *The Politics of Racism: The Uprooting of Japanese Canadians during the Second World War*. Toronto: Lorimer.

Svonkin, Stuart. 1997. *Jews against Prejudice: American Jews and the Fight for Civil Liberties*. New York: Columbia University Press.

Troper, Harold. 1972a. *Only Farmers Need Apply*. Toronto: Griffin House.

———. 1972b. "The Creek-Negroes of Oklahoma and Canadian Immigration, 1909–1911," *Canadian Historical Review* 48: 255–81.

———. 1978. "Nationalism and the History of Curriculum in Canada," *History Teacher* 12: 11–27.

———. 1987. "Jews and Canadian Immigration Policy, 1900–1950." In *The Jews of North America*, edited by Moses Rischin. Detroit, Mich.: Wayne State University Press.

Tulchinsky, Gerald. 1998. *Branching Out: The Transformation of the Canadian Jewish Community*. Toronto: Stoddart.

Walker, James. 1997. *"Race," Rights and the Law in the Supreme Court of Canada: Historical Case Studies*. Toronto: Osgood Hall and Wilfred Laurier University Press.

Ward, David. 1971. *Cities and Immigrants: A Geography of Change in Nineteenth Century America*. New York: Oxford.

Index